# Community Care Practice and the Law

# Community Care Practice and the Law
# Third Edition

*Michael Mandelstam*

Jessica Kingsley Publishers
London and Philadelphia

First edition published in 1995
Second edition published in 1999

This edition published in 2005
by Jessica Kingsley Publishers
116 Pentonville Road
London N1 9JB, UK
and
400 Market Street, Suite 400
Philadelphia, PA 19106, USA

*www.jkp.com*

**Library of Congress Cataloging in Publication Data**
Mandelstam, Michael, 1956-
  Community care practice and the law / Michael Mandelstam.-- 3rd ed.
    p. cm.
  Includes bibliographical references and index.
  ISBN 1-84310-233-1 (pbk.)
    1. Public welfare--Law and legislation--Great Britain. 2. Social service--Great Britain. 3. Community health services--Law and legislation--Great Britain. I. Title.
  KD3299.M26 2005
  344.4103'16--dc22

                                                              2004024472


**British Library Cataloguing in Publication Data**
A CIP catalogue record for this book is available from the British Library


ISBN-13: 978 1 84310 233 5
ISBN-10: 1 84310 233 1


Printed and Bound in Great Britain by
Athenaeum Press, Gateshead, Tyne and Wear

# CONTENTS

# Acknowledgements

Community care law and practice have continued to become increasingly wide in scope, complicated and contentious. I am greatly indebted to the many people with whom I continually discuss matters and try to understand what is going on. In particular I should like to thank Simon Bull and Pauline Thompson for constantly putting me right. Maura McCallion very kindly assisted me with Northern Ireland references. Of course any errors are my own. Huge thanks as ever to Jessica Kingsley and her staff for all that patience, encouragement and sheer hard work.

# Note

I have tried to ensure that the information is correct or at least represents a reasonable interpretation. However, a book such as this is likely to contain some errors, although I obviously hope that these are both minor and minimum in quantity. The reader should bear in mind that the law changes constantly and that advice may need to be sought on individual disputes that inevitably possess their own set of circumstances. The time of writing is December 2004. In case of query the author can be contacted by e-mail at michael.mandelstam@btinternet.com.

PART I

# Introduction, Overview, Underlying Mechanisms, Legal Principles and Good Administration, Remedies

CHAPTER 1

# Introduction

## 1.1 HOW TO USE THE BOOK

The book is designed for use in different ways and at different levels. For the reader wishing for a brief overview of the legal framework and a view of the mechanisms underlying community care, Chapters 2 and 3 will serve. The rest of the book comes in more detail:

- **Chapter 4** picks out key legal principles applied by the law courts and axioms applied by the local ombudsmen. These are the tools that the courts and ombudsmen apply to analyse and unpick community care decision making; and **Chapter 5** outlines a range of remedies and how they work.

- **Part II** of the book then deals with specific elements of community care in relation to local social services authorities, including assessment, care planning, service provision, direct payments, carers and charging for services. These lie at the heart of community care.

- **Part III** covers provision of home adaptations by local housing (and social services) authorities and of health services by the NHS. Although not legally defined as community care services, such services are clearly essential to community care in its wider everyday meaning. Matters such as discharge from hospital, continuing NHS health care, and community health services have a direct impact on local authorities' provision of community care.

- **Part IV** covers a number of issues that have become increasingly prominent in community care over the past few years: adult protection, decision-making capacity, information sharing, human rights and disability discrimination. These are areas of law and practice that are all in a state of flux for one reason or another, but all of which affect community care decision making.

- **Part V** covers health and safety at work, negligence and the regulation of care providers. Health and safety at work and negligence are included, in particular because they continue to give rise to anxiety and to misunderstanding amongst staff concerning the assessment of risk and potential liability for accident.

The detail in the book is not included for the sake of it; it reflects the very issues that local authority managers, staff and service users come up against on a daily basis.

The large volume of legislation and guidance is selectively quoted or paraphrased at key points. Much of the legislation and relevant guidance is accessible on the internet through, for example, the Department of Health website (www.dh.gov.uk: for policy and guidance), the HMSO website (www.hmso.gov.uk: for legislation), as well as the websites of other government departments.

The book gives considerable prominence to judicial case law and ombudsman investigations. The reason for this is twofold. First, community care is ultimately about everyday practice and how it affects individual service users. The extensive legislation and large volume of Department of Health guidance tend not to indicate how the law works in practice and affects individual service users. They represent only policy and aspiration. It is the legal case law and ombudsman investigations that illuminate matters better, providing an insight into what the community care legislation and guidance mean in practice.

Second, in any case, some practitioners and managers have neither the time nor inclination to read through the legislation and guidance, and may query anyway its connection with everyday practice. However, they might much more readily identify with case law – and even a reading of the case examples alone will give an indication as to how community care law works in practice.

### 1.2 WHOM THE BOOK IS FOR

The book has been written for (a) the staff and managers of local social services (and housing) authorities, NHS primary care trusts, NHS trusts and health authorities; (b) voluntary and advice-giving organisations; (c) advocates and advocacy organisations; (d) interested users of services and their informal carers; (e) other care providers; (f) lawyers; (g) academic staff and their students.

### 1.3 FUNCTION OF THE BOOK

The book brings together a wide range of information and analysis relating to community care practice and law. By including many practical examples and using non-legal language, the book attempts to bridge the gap between law and practice. Community care practice is – or at least should be – based on legislation, the decisions of the law courts and Department of Health guidance. It is important for all concerned to be aware of these sources. Neither service providers nor service users can understand how the system works without being aware of relevant powers, duties, rights and remedies.

Few disputes reach the stage of formal legal proceedings, and few even get as far as social services complaints procedures or the local ombudsmen. Therefore, although the book aims to assist people involved in formal disputes, its predominant aim is to give useful information about legislation and guidance as a way of avoiding, not just solving, disputes. For example, the well-informed statutory service manager is less likely to try to implement a legally dubious policy; likewise the front-line practitioner will be more confident about decisions he or she makes. Conversely, well-informed service users (or their representatives) are more likely to be able to challenge successfully at the outset, and perhaps informally, particular decisions or policies.

## 1.4 SCOPE OF THE BOOK

The book principally covers relevant social, health and housing services for various groups of vulnerable people including some elderly people, younger adults with disabilities (physical, sensory or learning), people with mental health needs, people with drug or alcohol problems, carers, and services for children in need and their families.

The 'community care services' defined in legislation are provided by local social services authorities. However, in the sense that community care is about caring for people in their own homes or in institutional accommodation, health and housing services are very much part of the picture. There are also practical reasons why all concerned need to know about the range of responsibilities across social, health and housing sectors. For example, a statutory authority might be planning services and demarcation of responsibilities between it and another authority (e.g. between social services and the NHS). It is clearly important that both authorities are aware not only of their own legal powers and duties, but also those of the other authority. Conversely, for service users and their representatives or advisers, it is important to know the duties and responsibilities of different authorities; if one does not deliver a service, another might.

However, when decisions are made and services provided, those decisions have to be consistent also with a range of other law relating to, for example, decision-making capacity, information sharing, human rights, disability discrimination, health and safety at work legislation, common law duty of care, and regulatory legislation. In addition, adult protection policies, procedure and practices need to be applied with an awareness of other legislation relevant to that area of work, including criminal justice legislation, civil torts, environmental health legislation, etc.

Thus the scope of the book is wide. However, much has not been included and some topics have inevitably been covered in greater depth than others. In particular the detail of legislation and guidance relating to general organisational and planning matters has been left out, where in the author's view it less directly applies to the lawfulness of, or good administration in, everyday decision making in respect of individual service users.

## 1.4.1 APPLICABILITY ACROSS THE UNITED KINGDOM

For reasons of space and also readability, this book applies in detail essentially to England only insofar as community care legislation is concerned.

Each chapter contains a note at the end of the 'key points' section, outlining very broadly the equivalent provisions in the rest of the United Kingdom. These notes should be taken as rough pointers only. In summary:

- **Wales**. As far as Wales is concerned, the primary community care legislation (comprising Acts of Parliament) is the same as for England; secondary legislation (regulations) may differ. For instance, at the time of writing, the Community Care (Delayed Discharges) Act 2003 applies to both England and Wales; but regulations actually implementing it have only been passed in England.

   Welsh Assembly guidance and directions are not referred to in the main text of the book (although examples are given in some of the introductory notes to each chapter). The references to guidance and directions in the book are thus to the English versions; and although many of them will have a Welsh equivalent, this will not always be the case; and even where there is an equivalent, the content and detail sometimes differs.

- **Scotland**. Scotland has different community care legislation and guidance. Some of this is very similar to that of England (e.g. the Chronically Sick and Disabled Persons Act 1970). Some is very different; for instance the Community Care and Health (Scotland) Act 2002 which introduced free personal care to Scotland; this does not exist in England. Likewise the Adults with Incapacity (Scotland) Act 2000 is peculiar to Scotland.

   Examples of Scottish legislation and guidance are given in some of the introductory notes to each chapter.

- **Northern Ireland**. Northern Ireland has different community care legislation and guidance, although much of it is very similar in effect to the equivalent English and Welsh provisions. Unlike in the rest of the United Kingdom, health and social services are combined in Northern Ireland in the form of health and social services boards and health and social services trusts.

   Examples of Northern Ireland legislation and guidance are given in some of the introductory notes to each chapter.

The courts in judicial review, and the ombudsmen in their investigations, take the same approach throughout the United Kingdom. Thus the illustration in the case law contained in this book, of how they apply legal principles and axioms of good administration respectively, is of general applicability not just in England and Wales, but also in Scotland and Northern Ireland. Where an English (or Welsh) review decision concerns legislation that is identical or very similar in effect to legislation in Scotland or Northern Ireland, then that decision will normally be of direct relevance in those two countries.

- **United Kingdom-wide applicability**. The case of *R v Gloucestershire CC, ex p Barry* (withdrawal of home care services) concerns s.2 of the Chronically Sick and Disabled Persons Act 1970, which applies in Scotland (by virtue of the Chronically Sick and Disabled Persons (Scotland) Act 1972) and has a direct equivalent in the Chronically

Sick and Disabled Persons (Northern Ireland) Act 1978. As a House of Lords case, it is binding across the United Kingdom. Had the case reached only the English High Court or Court of Appeal, then its effect elsewhere in the United Kingdom would have been only 'persuasive' rather than binding in nature.

- **Limited applicability.** The case of *Robertson v Fife Council* (about care home placements), another House of Lords case, is of limited (or at least uncertain) relevance to the rest of the United Kingdom, since it hinges in part on peculiarly Scottish legislation (particularly ss.12A and 13A of the Social Work (Scotland) Act 1968).

- **Limited applicability.** In Northern Ireland, the courts have held that a key element of the decision of *R v Sefton MBC, ex p Help the Aged* (duty to fund care home placements) does not apply in Northern Ireland, because s.21 of the National Assistance Act 1948 has no direct equivalent in the Health and Personal Social Services (Northern Ireland) Order 1972 (*Re Margaret Hanna*).

Nevertheless, in the field of community care, the vast majority of cases have involved English local authorities; the cases reported, concerning Welsh and Scottish local authorities, and health and social services trusts in Northern Ireland, number but a handful.

Fundamental duties relating to healthcare provision are the same in England and Wales, and very similar in Scotland and Northern Ireland (though under different legislation). In terms of local authority housing functions relating to the provision of home adaptations, disabled facilities grants are provided under the same legislation (though with variation contained in regulations) in England and Wales, and under different legislation (containing some variation) in Northern Ireland. In Scotland, a different system of home improvement grants operates.

In addition, human rights, disability discrimination, data protection, health and safety work legislation – and the common law of negligence – effectively apply across the United Kingdom. For instance, the Health and Safety at Work Act 1974 applies directly to England, Scotland and Wales; and the Health and Safety at Work (Northern Ireland) Order 1978 applies the same provisions to Northern Ireland. The law of negligence is effectively the same in Scotland, although there it is part of the law of delict; in the rest of the United Kingdom it is part of the law of tort.

In the case of decision-making capacity, there is a divergence; Scotland has stolen a march on the rest of the United Kingdom by being the first to implement new legislation relating to decision-making capacity (the Adults with Incapacity (Scotland) Act 2000).

In summary, the book is in general highly applicable to Wales, lacking only some of the more minor divergences in, and references to, regulations and guidance. It also contains many pointers to community care in Scotland and Northern Ireland.

## 1.5 CHANGES FROM THE SECOND EDITION

The book has been substantially reworked from the second edition. It contains a large number of new legal cases and ombudsman investigations. These have been embedded in the text of this new edition rather than collected in a separate digest at the back of the book in order to make them more accessible. In addition, new legislation and guidance include:

- direct payments legislation (Health and Social Care Act 2001)
- carers' legislation (Carers and Direct Payments Act 2000; Carers (Equal Opportunities) Act 2004)
- hospital discharge legislation (Community Care (Delayed Discharges) Act 2003)
- joint working legislation (Health Act 1999)
- human rights legislation (Human Rights Act 1998)
- immigration legislation (Immigration and Asylum Act 1999; Nationality, Immigration and Asylum Act 2002)
- 'fair access to care' guidance (LAC(2002)13)
- fairer charging guidance (LAC(2001)32)
- 'free nursing care' guidance (HSC(2001)17; HSC (2003)6)
- continuing NHS health care guidance (HSC 2001/5)
- decision-making capacity legislation (Mental Incapacity Bill 2004)
- adult protection guidance (DH 2000).

CHAPTER 2

# Overview

**KEY POINTS**

Community care is about services and assistance for vulnerable groups in society, such as some elderly people, people with disabilities (physical, sensory or learning), people with mental health problems, people with problems arising from the use of drugs or alcohol, and asylum seekers. Primary responsibility for community care rests with local social services authorities. In addition, however, there is a range of other law (including housing and health service legislation) that affects, directly and indirectly, how local authorities carry out their community care functions.

The relevant law is considerable in quantity, thus making an overview all the more essential. Furthermore, local authorities appear sometimes to forget that their policies, procedures, criteria of eligibility and everyday practice should be based on, and consistent with, legislation and accompanying guidance. Local authorities themselves are 'creatures of statute', that is bodies existing by virtue of legislation. Likewise, community care functions can only be lawfully performed with reference to powers and duties conferred by the relevant legislation. Therefore, for local authorities to apply local policies that are formulated without reference to the legislation is illogical and in that sense absurd. It also leads inevitably to local authorities running a significant risk of acting unlawfully.

This chapter provides first of all a general outline of the legal framework (together with its implications) relevant to community care decision-making as covered in this book. Second, the chapter sets out, in bare form but broken down into categories, a list of

the relevant legislation (Acts of Parliament) and other law, in order to give the reader a
birds' eye view of this extensive legal landscape.

**Note: Wales, Scotland and Northern Ireland**. This chapter applies to England and almost wholly to
Wales. As far as Scotland and Northern Ireland are concerned, some of the chapter is applicable directly
(where the legislation is the same), some indirectly (where similar principles are contained in different legislation), and some not at all. Specific pointers as to applicability to Wales, Scotland and Northern Ireland are
given not in this chapter, but in notes at the beginning of most of the chapters in this book.

## 2.1 OUTLINE AND IMPLICATIONS OF THE LEGAL FRAMEWORK
The following represents an outline of the legal framework and some of its practical
implications.

- **Fair decision making (Chapters 4 and 5)**. When local authorities take decisions
  about people's community care needs and about providing services, they have an
  obligation to do so fairly in a legal and administrative sense. The courts apply
  principles of fairness in judicial review cases, whilst the ombudsmen do the same in
  their investigations. It is surprising how little acquainted some local authorities
  appear to be with these principles, and therefore how potentially vulnerable their
  decision making is to adverse analysis by the courts and the ombudsmen.
- **Assessment (Chapter 6)**. The community care system revolves around assessment
  under s.47 of the NHS and Community Care Act 1990. Such assessment is to
  determine people's needs for community care services. These services are not
  contained in the 1990 Act but are scattered across five other pieces of legislation
  stretching back over fifty years as far as the National Assistance Act 1948.
  Assessment is meant to be 'needs' rather than 'service' led. This means in principle
  that service provision should be moulded to people's needs, rather than people's
  assessed needs fitted into whatever services happen to be available.
- **Threshold of eligibility (Chapter 6)**. Local authorities do not necessarily have a
  duty to meet all the needs that they have identified. This is because each local
  authority can, quite lawfully, set a 'threshold of eligibility'. Any needs that are
  assessed to come beneath this threshold do not have to be met and are sometimes
  labelled 'unmet needs'. In contrast, needs coming above the threshold must generally
  be met, irrespective of a lack of resources within the relevant local authority budget.
  However, the local authority is permitted to offer the cheapest option to meet such
  needs, so long as that option is consistent with fully meeting the assessed needs under
  both community care legislation and under any other relevant legislation such as the
  Human Rights Act 1998.
- **Setting the threshold of eligibility in line with available resources (Chapter
  6)**. The duty to meet a person's 'eligible' needs, even if the local authority is short of
  resources, prevents arbitrary refusal or withdrawal of some services. Nevertheless, any
  duty to make provision is diluted overall by the fact that a local authority can, from
  time to time, rework (by formally raising or lowering) the threshold of eligibility in
  the light of new policies and reduced resources. Raising the threshold allows the
  authority not only to assess new applicants for services more restrictively – but also
  to reassess existing users of services and accordingly to remove or reduce services

even if a person's needs or situation have not changed. This illustrates how local authorities have considerable legal and practical leeway in which to tailor services to available resources, and so to allow just enough people to qualify for services within budget.

- **Mismatch between threshold of eligibility and resources (Chapter 6)**. Part of the ability to set a reasonable threshold of eligibility depends on local authorities being well informed about needs among the local population. Yet it seems that some authorities do not have good quality information of this type. In addition, a rational setting of the threshold requires political honesty, which is not easily come by in every local authority. In other words, there is sometimes a political incentive for an authority to set a low threshold (and thus demonstrate how generous and 'caring' the authority is). However, without a correspondingly generous allocation of resources, a mismatch will arise between the duty to meet people's assessed, eligible needs and the financial ability to meet those needs.

  Once such a mismatch arises, local authorities are then sometimes tempted to cut services in an arbitrary and unlawful manner. For instance, some might unofficially and almost 'secretly' reset the previously agreed and publicised threshold of eligibility in order to relieve the pressure on an inadequate budget. Others might – irrespective of a person's assessed, eligible needs – begin to apply blanket policies in terms of what services they will provide, or of imposing rigid cost ceilings on care provision for individual service users. Such shortcuts risk findings of unlawfulness by the law courts or of maladministration by the local government ombudsmen.

- **Care plans (Chapter 7)**. Following a decision about what services will be provided, various guidance (but not legislation) states that a care plan should be drawn up containing details about objectives, services, agencies to be involved, costs, needs which cannot be met, date of first review, and so on. The form and complexity of a care plan will vary greatly depending on the level and types of service involved. The law courts have held that either a failure to follow, or at least to have proper regard to, this guidance about care plans, can amount to unlawfulness. In addition, the courts have accepted that a care plan is likely to be evidence of what a local authority has accepted as its duty to meet a person's assessed needs. Thus significant non-adherence by the local authority to a care plan is likely to indicate breach of its duty to meet a person's assessed, eligible, needs.

- **Residential and nursing home accommodation (Chapter 8)**. Local authorities have in some circumstances a duty to make arrangements under the National Assistance Act 1948 for the provision of residential accommodation (often in care homes) for people who because of age, illness, disability or other circumstances are in need of care and attention not otherwise available to them. When local authorities have found themselves short of money in relation to this duty, disputes have predictably arisen about when it arises and its extent – for instance, in relation to vulnerable older people in the north west of England or destitute asylum seekers in the south east.

- **Charges for residential and nursing home care (Chapter 9)**. When local authorities place people in care homes, they have a duty to assess them financially and charge (or not charge) according to the result of a legally prescribed means test. Depending on what sort of needs people have, and thus what sort of home they need to go to, local authorities set a 'usual cost level' which represents a maximum amount they are generally prepared to pay in relation to different levels of need. Some local authorities have attempted to find loopholes in the rules so as either to evade or at least to defer their obligations.

- **Non-residential community care services (Chapter 10)**. Community care services are defined by legislation to include a range of non-residential services (such as personal care, day services, equipment and adaptations to people's homes). Such services are provided under a range of legislation for groups of people such as those with disabilities (physical, sensory or learning), elderly people, people with a mental disorder, people with drugs or alcohol problems, and people who are ill. Central to community care non-residential services is s.2 of the Chronically Sick and Disabled Persons Act 1970.

- **Charges for non-residential community care services (Chapter 11)**. For non-residential services, local authorities can charge if they wish (although they do not have to) but only if the charge is a reasonable one. This is under the Health and Social Services and Social Security Adjudications Act 1983.

  However, if the local authority is satisfied, following representations from the person being charged, that it is not 'reasonably practicable' for him or her to pay it, then it must reduce the charge to a level at which it will be reasonably practicable for the person to pay it. Central government has issued guidance with the purpose of achieving a generally more consistent approach to charging by local authorities, but it is by no means clear that such consistency has yet been achieved. The guidance sets out a number of 'rules'. One of these is that if people's disability benefits are taken account of as income, then there should be an assessment of their 'disability-related expenditure' (i.e. special or extra costs/outgoings stemming from their disability).

  If people do not pay the assessed charges, it is thought that local authorities cannot legally withdraw services – at least those that they have a duty (as opposed to a power) to provide. But authorities do have the power to recover money owed as a debt. One significant continuing trend has been the shift in definition of certain services to 'social' rather than 'health' in nature. For example, services such as bathing or respite care, previously provided free of charge by the NHS, might now be provided by local social services authorities for a charge.

- **Direct Payments (Chapter 12)**. If certain conditions are met, local authorities have a duty under the Health and Social Care Act 2001 to make direct payments to people who have been assessed as having eligible needs. This means that instead of the local authority arranging the required services, it gives people a reasonable sum of money to enable them to purchase services or equipment themselves.

- **Carers (Chapter 12)**. In certain circumstances, local authorities have a duty to assess, or at least to have regard to the ability of informal carers to provide, or to continue to provide, a substantial amount of care on a regular basis. This is under the Carers (Recognition and Services) Act 1995, the Carers and Disabled Children Act 2000, and the Carers (Equal Opportunities) Act 2004 (expected to come into force during 2005). In addition to this duty to assess, local authorities also have a power, under the 2000 Act, to provide services for carers.

The purpose of the legislation covering carers relates not only to their welfare, but also to a saving of costs. This is because informal caring is widespread and is of similarly high financial value – compared to what it would cost local authorities to provide the same amount of care. In practice, the extent and thoroughness with which the needs of carers are taken into account by local authorities seems variable.

- **Asylum seekers and immigration control (Chapter 13)**. A prominent part of community care provision since 1996 has been, at least in some local authorities, the provision of residential accommodation and related services for asylum seekers and other people subject to immigration control. The law and rules concerning such persons' eligibility for community care services – or for assistance from the National Asylum Support Service – have been subject to continual legal challenge, change and confusion. The rules are labyrinthine.

- **Ordinary residence (Chapter 14)**. Sometimes the existence of a duty on a local authority to provide community care services depends on whether a person is 'ordinarily resident' within the area of the authority, or indeed on whether he or she is without ordinary residence altogether and is instead of 'no settled residence'. In the case of homeless people, or of people seeking residential or non-residential services in an area to which they have recently moved, the question of ordinary residence can sometimes cause delay in provision, or non-provision, of services. This is despite the fact that guidance from the Department of Health emphasises that disputes between local authorities should not result in assessment and service provision being delayed.

- **Housing and home adaptations (Chapter 15)**. Common sense would suggest that, since the preferred aim of community care is to enable people to remain in their own homes, housing services would be particularly important. However, they are not for the most part defined legally as community care services.

  It is beyond the scope of this book to examine housing law in detail. However, home adaptations are mentioned in community care policy guidance as one of the key elements in enabling people to remain in their own homes. Such adaptations are available by means of disabled facilities grants provided by local housing authorities under the Housing Grants, Construction and Regeneration Act 1996. Although there are examples of good practice, the local ombudsmen have consistently found, over many years, maladministration in the provision of adaptations, as well as general chaos caused by an apparent lack of resources allocated to provision.

  In addition, a degree of uncertainty attaches to the interplay between the duty of local housing authorities to provide home adaptations under the 1996 Act, and the duty of local social services authorities to assist with adaptations under the Chronically Sick and Disabled Persons Act 1970.

- **NHS provision (Chapter 16)**. The NHS has a general duty to provide services. This includes the provision of medical and nursing services as well as the prevention of illness, care of people who are ill, and after-care for people who have been ill. The duty is a general one only (towards the local population, but not towards individuals) and extends only to providing services 'necessary to meet all reasonable requirements'. The effect is that the duty is far from absolute and confers a wide discretion on the NHS, involving local decisions about the setting of priorities and the allocation of resources.

The law courts have generally denied relief to people complaining about the rationing or withholding of health services, and have declined to exercise the much closer scrutiny that they have brought to bear in other welfare fields such as housing, education and community care. The wide discretion enjoyed by the NHS has been checked occasionally by the health service ombudsman and by Department of Health guidance, of which blatant disregard might attract the censure of the courts. In addition, the NHS sometimes loses cases because of inadequate consultation about changes to services. It has also been successfully challenged for imposing blanket policies on services, and thus unlawfully fettering its discretion. Nevertheless, by and large, the NHS would appear to have more to fear from public outcry than from serious legal challenge.

- **NHS charges for services (Chapter 16)**. The NHS does not have the same wide powers and duties as local social services authorities to make charges. Certain items are charged for if specified in legislation – for example, equipment and drugs prescribed by general practitioners, as well as certain items supplied in hospitals, such as wigs, surgical brassieres, and spinal supports. But everything else, both services and equipment, which is not so specified, must be provided free of charge. Legally, this would seem to be straightforward. However, in practice, it appears that the NHS continues in some instances to make legally dubious charges, mainly because of confusion or ignorance about what the legislation actually permits.

- **NHS continuing care (Chapter 16)**. People's entitlement to what has become known as NHS continuing health care has become a significant issue because of consistent and trenchant criticism by the health service ombudsman. She has exposed the fact that the Department of Health's policy about eligibility for such care has been anything but clear and fair; and that many people have consequently been charged large sums of money for care (particularly in nursing homes), which they should not have had to pay. Instead the NHS should have funded the care, free of charge to the patient. As a result, significant reimbursement of moneys by the NHS took place during 2004; and central government at last indicated in December 2004 that it would issue new guidance, in order to clarify the rules. (A further confusion in some parts of the NHS has been an inability to clearly distinguish NHS continuing health care from NHS responsibility for paying for the registered nursing care element of care provided in care homes).

- **Discharge from hospital (Chapter 16)**. Hospital discharge involves decisions about where, how, and with whom a person is going to live. Of particular importance is whether suitable and effective arrangements have been made and whether people's needs and wishes have been taken into account.

People's needs when leaving hospital can be complicated, requiring consideration of many factors including physical ability, mental ability and attitude, social and environmental factors and financial situation. There are sometimes many arrangements to make and a number of variable factors to consider. This makes the discharge process unpredictable and yet one more uncertainty in community care.

Central government has attempted to concentrate minds locally by implementing the Community Care (Delayed Discharges) Act 2003 which imposes financial penalties on local social services authorities, if they are responsible for delays in people's discharge from hospital.

- **Adult protection (Chapter 17)**. Guidance from central government charges local social services authorities with taking the lead in 'adult protection'; that is the protection of adults from various forms of abuse including physical, sexual and financial. Legislation relevant to adult protection includes not just community care legislation, but also a range of other law concerning, for example, mental health, environmental health, criminal matters, decision-making capacity and undue influence.
- **Decision-making capacity (Chapter 18)**. The law relating to the decision-making capacity of adults in relation to health and welfare matters has become an increasingly prominent issue. It is subject to various uncertainties and has been developed by the law courts in the absence of Parliament's passing of pertinent legislation. However, the Mental Capacity Bill 2004 is intended to introduce greater clarity and formality.
- **Information sharing (Chapter 19)**. Issues about information sharing and confidentiality, in relation to health and social care generally and adult protection in particular, arise under the Data Protection Act 1998, Human Rights Act 1998 and the common law of confidentiality.
- **Human rights and disability discrimination (Chapters 20 and 21)**. In addition to complying with community care legislation, local authorities and the NHS must also take decisions that are consistent with the Human Rights Act 1998 (and therefore European Convention on Human Rights) and the Disability Discrimination Act 1995.
- **Health and safety at work legislation (Chapter 22)**. Community care decisions should be consistent with health and safety at work legislation, such as the Health and Safety at Work Act 1974 and the Manual Handling Operations Regulations 1992. The courts have on occasion analysed in detail the juxtaposition of community care, human rights and health and safety at work legislation.
- **Negligence (Chapter 23)**. Sometimes service users allege they have suffered harm as a consequence of a local social services authority's actions and sue for damages under the common law of negligence.
- **Regulation of care provision (Chapter 24)**. Registration and inspection of care providers (both the independent sector and local authorities) comes under the Care Standards Act 2000 and are the responsibility of the Commission for Social Care Inspection and of the Health Commission.

## 2.2. LIST OF LEGISLATION RELEVANT TO COMMUNITY CARE

The following is a list of legislation (Acts of Parliament) and other law, providing a bird's eye view of the extensive legal landscape within which community care decision-making lies.

### 2.2.1 GENERAL (PART I)

**Local Authority Social Services Act 1970, s.7: acting under Department of Health guidance.** Duty to act under the general guidance of the Secretary of State (see 4.1.6).

**Judicial review by the law courts.** Decision making by public bodies such as local authorities and the NHS: reasonableness, rationality, taking account of relevant factors, legitimate expectations, not fettering discretion (not applying blanket policies). These are common law principles (i.e. not to be found in legislation), which are applied by the law courts (see 4.2).

**Local Government Act 1974: local ombudsman.** Investigations into maladministration causing injustice in local authorities (see 4.3.1 and 5.9).

**Health Service Commissioners Act 1993: health service ombudsman.** Investigations into maladministration and breach of duties in the NHS (see 4.3.2 and 5.11).

**Local Authority Social Services Act 1970, s.7: statutory social services complaints procedures.** Informal, formal and review panels stages (see 5.5).

**Health and Social Care (Community Health and Standards) Act 2003.** Introduces new complaints procedure systems for local social services authorities and the NHS.

### 2.2.2 SOCIAL SERVICES ASSESSMENT AND PROVISION OF SERVICES (PART II)

**NHS and Community Care Act 1990, s.47: community care assessment.** Duty to assess and to decide about service provision (see 6.1). Guidance on: 'fair access to care' and eligibility criteria (LAC(2002)13), 'single assessment' (LAC(2002)1), on community care generally (DH 1990; SSI/SWSG 1991) – all covering care plans and reviews, amongst other things (see 6.11 and Chapter 6 generally).

**Disabled Persons (Services, Consultation and Representation) Act 1986, ss.4, 5: assessment.** Duty to assess disabled person on request (s.4), and to assess in relation to disabled people leaving education (s.5) (see 6.2).

**National Assistance Act 1948, ss.21–6: residential accommodation.** Care home placements, etc. (see Chapter 8).

**National Assistance Act 1948, s.22: charges for residential accommodation.** Statutory, detailed test of resources in respect of care home placements (see Chapter 9).

**National Assistance Act 1948, s.29: range of non-residential welfare services for disabled people.** Social work services, advice and support, etc. (see 10.1).

**Chronically Sick and Disabled Persons Act 1970, s.2: range of non-residential welfare services for disabled people.** Practical assistance, recreation activities, travel, adaptations and additional facilities, holidays, etc. (see 10.2).

**Health Services and Public Health Act 1968, s.45: range of non-residential services for older people.** Practical assistance, visiting, support, adaptations and additional facilities, etc. (see 10.3).

**NHS Act 1977, schedule 8: range of non-residential services in respect of illness.** Range of services for preventing illness, caring for people who are ill, or aftercare (see 10.4).

**NHS Act 1977, schedule 8: home help and laundry facilities** (see 10.4).

**Mental Health Act 1983, s.117: mental health aftercare services** (see 10.5).

**Health and Social Services and Social Security Adjudications Act 1983, s.17: charges for non-residential services.** Guidance on 'fairer charging' (LAC(2001)32; DH 2003j) (see Chapter 11).

**Health and Social Care Act 2001, s.57: direct payments** (see 12.1).

**Disabled Persons (Services, Consultation and Representation) Act 1986, s.8: having regard to the carer.** Duty to have regard to the carer's ability to care (see 12.4).

**Carers (Recognition and Services) Act 1995: carers' assessment** (see 12.4).

**Carers and Disabled Children Act 2000: carers' assessment and services** (see 12.4).

**Carers (Equal Opportunities) Act 2004: carers' assessment and services** (see 12.4).

**Children Act 1989, s.17 and schedule 2: assessment of children in need.** Assessment of children in need, and service provision for those children and their families (see 12.5).

**National Assistance Act 1948, s.21(1A): prohibition on social services assisting destitute people subject to immigration control** (see Chapter 13).

**Nationality Immigration and Asylum Act 2002, schedule 3: prohibition on social services assisting some people subject to immigration** (see Chapter 13).

**Asylum and Immigration (Treatment of Claimants) Act 2004** (see Chapter 13).

## 2.2.3 HOUSING, HOME ADAPTATIONS AND THE NHS (PART III)

**Housing Grants, Construction and Regeneration Act 1996: home adaptations for disabled occupants.** System of mandatory disabled facilities grants operated by local housing authorities (see 15.4).

**NHS Act 1977: provision of health services.** General duty to provide on the NHS to provide range of health care services. Guidance on NHS continuing health care (HSC 2001/15), on 'free nursing care' (HSC 2001/17; HSC 2003/6), on the Care Programme Approach (HC(90)23; DH 1999b). National service frameworks on older people (DH 2001c) and mental health (DH 1999a). Single assessment process guidance (HSC(2002)1) and intermediate care guidance (HSC 2001/1) (see 16.1–16.18).

**Community Care (Delayed Discharges) Act 2003.** System of local authority reimbursement payments, made to the NHS, in case of local authority failure to enable hospital discharge from acute beds in limited period of time (see 16.10).

**Health Act 1999, s.31: joint working between the NHS and local authorities** (see 16.19).

## 2.2.4 ADULT PROTECTION, DECISION-MAKING CAPACITY, INFORMATION SHARING, HUMAN RIGHTS, DISABILITY DISCRIMINATION (PART IV)

*No Secrets* **guidance (DH 2000): adult protection.** Guidance on adult protection policy and practice (see 17.1).

**Care Standards Act 2000: protection of vulnerable adults (POVA) list** (see 17.3).

**Police Act 1997: criminal record certificate system.** Criminal Records Bureau: standard and enhanced criminal records certificates (see 17.3).

**National Assistance Act 1948, s.47: removal by local authorities of people from their homes** (see 17.5).

**National Assistance Act 1948, s.48: protection of people's property by local authority** (see 17.5).

**Mental Health Act 1983: interventions relevant to adult protection.** Including guardianship (see 17.5).

**Environmental Protection Act 1990: environmental health interventions** (see 17.5).

**Public Health Act 1936: environmental health interventions** (see 17.5).

**Criminal Justice Act 2003: multi-agency public protection arrangements (MAPPA).** Arrangements for serious offenders (see 17.7).

**Assault and battery (criminal law), trespass to the person (civil tort)** (see 17.8).

**Sexual Offences Act 2003: offences relating to people with a mental disorder and to carer workers** (see 17.8).

**Youth Justice and Criminal Evidence Act 1999: special measure in respect of giving evidence for vulnerable witnesses.** Guidance on 'achieving best evidence' from Home Office (2002a) (see 17.9).

**Protection from Harassment Act 1997: offence of harassment and restraint orders** (see 17.10).

**Family Law Act 1996: non-molestation and occupation orders** (see 17.11–17.12).

**Setting aside transactions (e.g. gifts, wills): lack of capacity** (see 17.15).

**Setting aside transactions (e.g. gifts, wills): undue influence** (see 17.15).

**Theft Act 1968: theft** (see 17.15).

**Care Standards Act 2000: abuse.** Obligations on care providers (under regulations) in relation to safeguarding service users from abuse (see 17.17).

**Common law: necessity and best interests.** Acting out of necessity and in the best interests of a person lacking the capacity to take a decision for himself or herself (see Chapter 18).

**Inherent jurisdiction of courts to determine a person's best interests** (see 18.8).

**Enduring Powers of Attorney Act 1985.** Enduring power of attorney in respect of a person's affairs, when he or she loses capacity (see 18.3).

**Mental Health Act 1983 (part 7): Court of Protection.** Court of Protection involvement where a person cannot manage his or her affairs: appointment of receiver (see 18.3).

**Mental Capacity Bill 2004: proposed changes in law in respect of decision-making capacity.** Including lasting powers of attorney, deputies appointed by the Court of Protection, rules on advance statements about health care treatment (see Chapter 18).

**Data Protection Act 1998: personal data.** Access to personal information, disclosure with or without consent etc. (see Chapter 19).

**Human Rights Act 1998 and European Convention on Human Rights.** Various rights including right to life, not being subject to inhuman or degrading treatment, not being arbitrarily deprived of liberty, right to respect for privacy, home and family life, not being discriminated against (see Chapter 20).

**Disability Discrimination Act 1995: goods and services, premises.** Various obligations on local authorities and the NHS in respect of the provision of goods and services, and the disposal and management of premises (see Chapter 21).

## 2.2.5 HEALTH AND SAFETY AT WORK, NEGLIGENCE, REGULATION OF CARE PROVIDERS (PART V)

**Health and Safety at Work Act 1974, ss.2 and 3: duties of employer toward both employees and any non-employees affected by the undertaking.** Duties subject to reasonable practicability (see Chapter 22).

**Management of Health and Safety at Work Regulations 1999: risk assessment, cooperation and coordination etc.** (see 22.2).

**Manual Handling Operations Regulations 1992: management of risk.** Manual handling risk to be managed by avoidance or reduction, so far as is reasonably practicable (see 22.2).

**Common law of negligence.** Duty of care, carelessness, causation of harm (see Chapter 23).

**Care Standards Act 2000: registration and inspection of care providers** (see Chapter 24).

CHAPTER 3

# Underlying mechanisms

**KEY POINTS**

This chapter identifies underlying mechanisms in community care. These include the very considerable uncertainties present, the tension between people's needs and resources and the way in which legislation, guidance, the law courts and the ombudsmen all function.

In particular the chapter highlights how both central government and local government exploit such uncertainties when under pressure of finance and resources; and that this is made possible on account of the many 'escape routes' built into community care. However, this can be at the cost of a lack of transparency about community care, and of a significant gap between aspiration and presentation on the one hand, and everyday practice on the other.

**Note: Wales, Scotland and Northern Ireland.** This chapter has been written particularly with England in mind; and there are some significant differences in community care elsewhere in the United Kingdom. For example, in contrast to England, Scotland has introduced free personal care for older people, in line with the recommendations of the Royal Commission on Long Term Care. However, overall, the underlying mechanisms of community care, as identified in this chapter, are, in the author's view, applicable throughout the United Kingdom.

## 3.1 UNCERTAINTIES IN COMMUNITY CARE

Community care is about services and assistance for (including gaining or maintaining independence) vulnerable groups in society, such as some elderly people, people with disabilities (physical, sensory or learning), people with mental health problems, and people with problems arising from the use of drugs or alcohol. Services are of many sorts, including residential or nursing home accommodation, practical assistance in the home, personal assistance, home help, respite care (breaks for people being cared for, or for their carers), holidays, daily living equipment, home adaptations, meals-on-wheels, day centres, recreational activities and so on. This is not to mention the equally wide range of NHS or housing services.

Even central government conceded in a White Paper the importance of services of this nature: '...social services are for all of us... Any decent society must make provision for those who need support and are unable to look after themselves' (Secretary of State for Health 1998, p.4).

Notwithstanding the importance of such services, community care is rife with legal and practical uncertainties. Indeed, these uncertainties are so prevalent as to be an integral and essential part of the system. Perversely, it could even be argued that it is certainties, rather than uncertainties, which are chimerical and anomalous in this context. The same government White Paper made no bones about this:

> Up to now, neither users, carers, the public, nor social services staff and managers have had a clear idea which services are or should be provided, or what standards can reasonably be expected. There is no definition of what users can expect, nor any yard-stick for judging how effective or successful social services are. Individuals do not know what services are available, in what circumstances they might get them, or whether they will have to pay. This lack of clarity of objectives and standards means that on the one hand social services cannot be easily held to account, and on the other hand they can get blamed for anything that goes wrong. (Secretary of State for Health 1998, p.6)

However, as this chapter argues, there is some indication that the situation described in the White Paper actually suits central government. A lack of clarity veils problems that are difficult for central government to solve and have large resource implications. At the same time, the blaming of local authorities for defects in central government policy is politically tempting. Indeed, the uncertainties identified in 1998 are flourishing in 2004.

It is plain that these uncertainties multiply in number and degree when resources are short or local authorities come under pressure for other reasons (such as poor practice or financial inefficiency). Their practical function is to give the system some flexibility or 'give', and to allow authorities to regulate it according to their resources and priorities. These uncertainties can be thought of as, for example, safety valves, escape routes, discretionary elements, or variables with unpredictable values – and as thus constituting a mechanism that allows authorities to ration services. When triggered, they in turn allow the proliferation of problems, existence of which in the past has been conceded by central government. They include a lack of protection for vulnerable people, poor coordination between services, a lack of clarity about what services are available, and inconsistency in provision both between local authorities and within a single authority (Secretary of State for Health 1998, pp.5–7).

The uncertainties and potential safety valves exploited by local authorities are all too evident throughout most of this book. In other words, authorities variously try to limit or escape potential obligations, for instance, in relation to:

- 'screening people out' when they are referred for assessment
- waiting times for assessment
- setting and varying thresholds of eligibility
- not carrying out full assessments
- placing cost ceilings on care packages
- simply not providing services that have been assessed as needed
- waiting times for service provision
- cost shunting between different statutory bodies
- not monitoring and reviewing people's care packages adequately to ensure needs are being met
- reassessing people in order to reduce provision.

Some of these escape routes can be adopted lawfully, others cannot. For instance, up to a point it is lawful for a local authority formally to set a relatively high threshold of eligibility on the basis of limited resources. But it is not lawful, having set that threshold formally, for it to be then varied informally, arbitrarily and often covertly – depending on the state of local social services team budgets. The more adept and better organised local authorities tend to utilise the escape routes that are likely to be lawful; the less adept err toward routes that are unlawful, sometimes blatantly so.

The uncertainties creep out of the community care framework at all points, legal, quasi-legal and practical. The framework can be seen to consist of at least the following:

- **Acts of Parliament**. Primary legislation conferring duties and powers on local authorities.
- **Regulations**. Secondary legislation, made under the primary legislation.

- **Directions**. Directions and powers made under the authority of legislation, creating duties and powers, but not in themselves legislation.
- **Guidance** issued by the Department of Health. It is not law, but is legally relevant to greater or lesser extent, depending on whether it is of a stronger or weaker type.
- **Local policies, etc**. Local authority policies, procedures and practice.
- **Judicial review**. Public law supervision by the law courts.
- **Ombudsmen**. Local government (and health service) ombudsman investigations.

All of these generally form a rich medium within which, when necessary, uncertainties flourish. Uncertainties are normally highlighted in proportion to the financial pressures on local authorities (see 3.4); and the safety valves and escape routes are made all the easier to utilise by the lack of precision and transparency (see 3.5) that arguably pervades community care policy, legislation and guidance.

### 3.1.1 RIGHTS AND OBLIGATIONS

It is at the points of uncertainty, referred to above, that significant decisions are made and actions taken. It is at these points too that disputes arise between service providers and users of services; for example, when a person's view of 'need' does not correspond with that of a local authority. A consequence of the 'give' in the system at these points is that local authorities have very considerable discretion to regulate the provision and level of services – and to resolve the tension between people's needs and available resources.

The existence of this tension has increasingly led local authorities, users of services, voluntary organisations and lawyers to attempt to identify the extent of the existence of legal rights and corresponding obligations in community care. The answer has turned out to be that users of services have perhaps surprisingly few absolute legal rights or entitlements – although there are a few significant ones. This is seen not only in the often vague and qualified language of legislation and guidance, but also in some of the limitations of the various remedies open to people in case of dispute (since a right only exists insofar as, when necessary, it is practically enforceable).

### 3.1.2 CLEAR LEGAL ANSWERS?

Even the law courts, in principle trying to establish certainty, might in practice fail to do so. Their decisions are made on a piecemeal basis, are dependent on which disputes happen to reach them in the first place, are neither predictable nor consistent, and sometimes raise more questions than they answer.

Furthermore, the tempting belief that law can be learned like multiplication tables and so yield certain answers is false. Such a belief depends on the assumption that there are always right answers that exist in some objective form, waiting only to be uncovered by the correct judicial utterance. This notion was famously dismissed by a leading judge, Lord Reid, as a discredited fairy tale (Lee 1988, p.3). This lack of pre-ordained answers was exposed in the context of community care by the case of *R v Gloucestershire CC, ex p Barry*. It concerned the removal of services from elderly disabled people, and whether disabled people's needs could be measured taking into account the resources of a local authority:

**High Court**. Two judges in the High Court decided the main issue one way.

**Court of Appeal**. Three judges in the Court of Appeal reached a 2–1 split decision that which overruled the High Court.

**House of Lords**. The Court of Appeal was then in turn overruled by the House of Lords, with five law lords arriving at a split 3–2 decision (R v Gloucestershire CC, ex p Barry).

**Subsequent judicial reflections**. The House of Lords seemed to betray, in the later case of R v East Sussex CC, ex p Tandy (an education case), some apparent regrets about the Gloucestershire decision, though without questioning its basic correctness. The Court of Appeal, in a subsequent community care case about residential care, followed the Gloucestershire case only with reluctance and some qualification (R v Sefton MBC, ex p Help the Aged).

The *Gloucestershire* case also shows that the uncertainties in community care do not simply affect the odd aggrieved individual. The case was brought originally by four individuals, but in fact stemmed from a reduction in care services to as many as 1500 people. Similarly, the case of *R v Sefton MBC, ex p Help the Aged* about funding for residential care concerned a policy applied by the local authority to more than just the two people referred to in that case – and was symptomatic also of what was going on in other authorities. The local ombudsmen, too, sometimes investigate policies that clearly affect many people within a local authority, for example in respect of long waits for home adaptations or the improper introduction of a system of charges for non-residential services. In other words, the uncertainties affecting community care are far from peripheral.

### 3.1.3 OBSCURING THE PURPOSE OF COMMUNITY CARE

It follows too, from the uncertainties inherent in the system, that the very aim of community care is sometimes obscured. On its face, community care is about assisting people with social care needs, and enabling them to remain living at home, as independently as possible for as long as possible, apparently on the assumption that this is what most people want. If this is its purpose – and a reading of both early (DH 1990) and later (LAC(2002)13) guidance might suggest that this is a reasonable interpretation – then community care should be straightforward, at least in principle. However, this is by no means the case; instead a system has developed that is generally characterised by extraordinary contortion and complexity.

This apparently straightforward aim of community care seems at times to have evaporated and been replaced by constant anxiety about resources, cost shunting between statutory services, ever stricter eligibility criteria, waiting times for services, and attempts by local authorities to evade or continually to reinterpret legal duties. Local authority staff and managers seem, in many areas at least, to be as concerned about how to say no to meeting people's needs as to say yes.

## 3.2 COMMUNITY CARE LEGISLATION: FRAGMENTATION

In the light of scarce resources, intense scrutiny has taken place of community care legis-lation in the search for rights and obligations. Irregular in look even at a distance, it is no surprise that on closer inspection legislation reveals considerable ambiguity, lack of cohe-sion and sometimes flaws and contradictions.

However, even if the legislation were to be clearer and more cohesive, it would inevi-tably still develop cracks if placed under undue pressure and scrutiny. Therefore, a tenable view is that the shortcomings of community care legislation have been exaggerated be-cause of the strain exerted on it by, ultimately, the consequences of government policy, aided and abetted by local authorities who have hastened to exploit uncertainties.

Community care legislation as a whole is not easily understood, spread as it is across a number of different Acts of Parliament that have continued to proliferate (see 2.2). For in-stance, s.47 of the NHS and Community Care Act 1990, for the main part, only puts in place a framework for assessment; it is not an Act which introduced a whole new and inte-grated system of services. To find the real 'community care services' other than assess-ment, one has to look back to a range of pre-existing pieces of legislation stretching back several decades to 1948. In addition, there are at least four separate pieces of legislation now covering assessment and services for carers, and a separate Act dealing with direct payments (see summary in Chapter 2).

Thus community care legislation is highly fragmented as well as extensive; in addi-tion some of the individual pieces of legislation have themselves been significantly amended. Sometimes this not only perplexes local authority staff and managers, but also lawyers. In one case, the judge concluded by lamenting the fact that during the hearing he had been supplied by the lawyers with defective copies of s.29 of the National Assistance Act 1948 and of s.1 of the Community Care (Direct Payments) Act 1996 (now super-seded). He had been shown the originals, yet both had been amended. Worse, the same had happened to him in a previous case (*R(AandB) v East Sussex CC(no.1)*).

Once different pieces of social services legislation have been identified and their con-tent understood, their compatibility with one another – or indeed with NHS or housing legislation – is not always evident. For instance, the relationship between the Chronically Sick and Disabled Persons Act 1970 and the rest of the community care legislation is one of some uncertainty. Similarly vague is the dividing line between provision of community care services under social services legislation, and of health services under the NHS Act 1977.

The disparate nature of the community care statutes has predictably led to calls for new, integrated legislation. These calls have not so far been heeded by central govern-ment. Nevertheless, as already mentioned, the shortcomings of existing legislation have only been exposed so glaringly because of the close attention it has received in the light of a series of judicial review cases brought over the last few years. These disputes for the most part arise when local authorities, pleading lack of resources, withdraw or withhold services from people who need them.

Thus, legislative reform might be a necessary element in producing an effective system of community care, but scarcely a sufficient one, since the issue of resources must also be dealt with. For instance, s.2 of the Chronically Sick and Disabled Persons Act 1970 survived for about 25 years with relatively little exposure in the law courts and for that reason might have been supposed to be relatively clear in its meaning. However, the case of *R v Gloucestershire CC, ex p Barry*, brought only because of resource problems in a harsh financial climate, suddenly made the 1970 Act look distinctly equivocal.

Finally, individual pieces of legislation sometimes give little away. Reading the words does not reveal much about everyday practice. For instance, s.47 of the NHS and Community Care Act 1990, which forms the gateway of assessment through which people must pass to obtain any community care services at all, is notable for its brevity. It places a duty on local authorities to assess people who appear to be in need of community care services and then to decide whether services are called for. Yet the Act is perfectly silent about what the terms assessment, need, appearance or called for mean or might look like in practice.

### 3.2.1 ADDITIONAL LEGISLATION

Local social services authority obligations do not stop with the community care legislation. In addition, community care decision making has to be consistent with a range of other legislation, including, for example, that relating to human rights, disability discrimination, health and safety at work, common law duty of care, information sharing. In addition, 'joint working' means that, more than ever, social services staff need to understand, at least up to a point, NHS and housing legislation. Some staff will need to know about the Mental Health Act 1983 and also some criminal justice legislation. Adult protection work increasingly requires at least a rough grasp of various other areas of law that might be relevant to interventions in abusive situations.

### 3.2.2 PERFORMANCE INDICATORS

As if the legislative burden, both direct and indirect, were not enough, central government has added pressure by the imposition of a performance assessment framework in the form of performance indicators. These are used to measure a local authority's performance, and ultimately its 'star' rating. There are various indicators relating to, for instance, number (or percentage) of (DH 2004d):

- households receiving intensive home care (over 10 hours a week)
- people receiving direct payments
- people receiving a statement of their needs
- carer assessments
- people receiving reviews

- equipment and minor adaptations delivered within seven working days from the decision to supply
- older clients whose assessment commenced in two days of first contact and were completed within four weeks from that point of first contact.

There are some 50 such indicators applied to social services adult and children's services. Such is the political pressure to perform well against indicators that some local authorities seem more concerned about returning impressive statistics than about complying with substantive community care law. With equanimity some local authority managers sometimes preside over policies that are clearly unlawful and potentially deprive people of services they are entitled to and yet complain when statistical returns against a particular indicator do not represent the desired result.

In turn, this can lead to strategies devoted to manipulating statistical returns; it would not be surprising if, on a significant scale, local authority statistics were suspect, just as NHS returns on waiting lists have been found to be (e.g. Audit Commission 2003). For instance, manipulation of social services indicators might involve the following types of practice:

**Ten-hour care packages**. A team manager might tell staff routinely to make up packages of care of seven to nine hours to ten hours, even though the ten hours have not been assessed as required (the intensive home care indicator refers to ten hours).

**Deleting unwanted figures**. Less subtle is a direction from a senior manager simply to delete figures from collated statistics that do not conform to the particular indicator.

**Undermining the performance indicator**. In respect of the equipment indicator, some local authorities have considered the idea of stating that the 'decision to supply' is only made when the equipment has been delivered and is demonstrated; because up to demonstration a final decision has not been made. Thus what in effect might be, for instance, a six-week wait would be recorded as a wait of 24 hours or less.

**Waiting for assessment**. Concerning the assessment indicators, local authorities wrestle with how to redefine assessment; one strategy employed is to argue that assessment is complete even when all that has been determined (within four weeks) is that further specialist assessment is required (which might take many months or even longer to complete). Local authorities attempt to justify this on the basis that the specialist assessment – such as that performed by occupational therapists – is not the same as community care assessment. This is sleight of hand and no consolation for the service user.

Nevertheless, successful manipulation of statistics (for which both central and local government arguably have an incentive) is one thing, but acting lawfully and without maladministration quite another. Thus in one case, a first level assessment was achieved reasonably quickly. However, the woman then had to wait nearly 18 months for the full assessment; the local ombudsman found maladministration. This length of wait meant that the inadequacies of the first level assessment were not remedied so as to prevent significant harm (*Ealing LBC 1999*).

Whether or not manipulation occurs on a significant scale, it is by no means certain that indicators achieve an improvement in service. The newspapers might report that social workers would have to 'reach for the stars' when the star ratings were introduced for social services (*The Times,* 30 May 2002). However, the Chief Inspector of the Social Services Inspectorate reportedly stated that local authorities should not 'slavishly' pursue indicators – because they didn't reflect what was actually happening to people in practice (*Community Care,* 24–30 October 2002). Indeed, the following comment about the NHS and other public services (such as local authorities) is of similar import:

**Clatter of bedpans in the House of Commons.** 'More accountability is the last thing the NHS needs just now. It needs less. It needs a minister who is brave enough to call off his rottweilers, his auditors, his league tables, his commissioners. It needs doctors and nurses ready to answer to their patients for the money they spend not to Whitehall and Gordon Brown. Like the rest of the public services, it needs professionals ready to profess their craft, not count government beans.' This was to avoid the realisation of Aneurin Bevan's 'longing for the clatter of every bedpan to echo through the House of Commons' (Jenkins 2002).

Likewise concern has been expressed about the burden imposed on care providers generally by the national minimum standards published under the Care Standards Act 2000 (see Chapter 24). Central government's Better Regulation Task Force has observed that these standards have resulted in a 'bureaucratic paper chase' concentrating on compliance rather than in understanding and meeting individual needs. Thus, a care home resident might be denied the choice of having a hot bath because of standards specifying a maximum temperature of 43 degrees; or small charities might withdraw small scale services (for instance involving helping people out of chairs, going to the bathroom or toenail cutting) because they have been obliged to register as care providers (BRTF 2004, pp.13–14).

## 3.2.3 BEST VALUE

The performance assessment framework within which the performance indicators sit is part of a wider 'best value' regime to which local authorities are subject (DH 2003k, p.8), under s.3 of the Local Government Act 1999. The Act describes best value as being about the securing of a continuous improvement in the way in which functions are exercised, having regard to a combination of economy, efficiency and effectiveness. However, best value in practice might add to the pressures; the suspicion is that instead of being used to promote genuine cost-effectiveness, it is sometimes misused in order to promote other government policies or simply cost cutting for its own sake.

**Transferring care homes at all costs?** A report into the transfer of council care homes to the independent sector in Birmingham argues compellingly that it was not true 'best value' (in terms of cost-effectiveness, including quality) that was driving the closures – but instead a pre-determined cost-cutting exercise. Rather the transfers were determined by a central government policy that favoured using independent sector care providers, and which could scarcely be resisted because of the associated rules on borrowing money (in this case for upgrading the homes) that placed particular restrictions on the local authority. This had the consequence that 'one of the largest municipal councils in Europe had become a mere agent of a government policy which demands savings even at the expense of the all too modest needs of the vulnerable elderly' (McFadyean and Rowland 2002, p.33).

The courts would not interfere with the transfer process described in the above report (*R(Hands) v Birmingham CC*). Nevertheless, on other occasions both they and the ombudsmen have intervened, pointing out in effect that best value may be *how* functions are performed, but not about *whether* they are performed. One such example concerned a decision to close a care home that had not been taken properly; the judge stated that best value could not interfere with the local authority's duty to assess people's needs (*R(Bodimeade) v Camden LBC*).

In another case, the local ombudsman found that the council's strict best value policy of only purchasing domiciliary care services from a small number of providers meant that it had fettered its discretion and lost sight of its duty to meet the person's need (*Cambridgeshire CC 2002*). The ombudsman has also pointed out the shortsightedness of blind adherence to a best value type of policy in another case. This policy was not to pay more than a certain hourly rate for domiciliary care, which resulted in failure to meet the needs of an elderly vulnerable couple (who died shortly afterward). However, it was also perverse because the cost of the alternative (respite care) was likely to outweigh (by far) the cost of the domiciliary care, even had the latter been provided at a more expensive rate than usual (*Essex CC 2001*).

Nevertheless, the introduction by central government of a 'mixed economy of care' (in the name of cost-effectiveness) and its concerted efforts to reduce the 'unit' costs of community care have resulted in both contradictions and also a diminution in people's legal rights. Thus, on the one hand, central government fills its guidance and 'national minimum' care standards with immense amounts of verbiage relating to good practice – which often of course involves adequate, reasonably trained staff. Yet, the 'best value' side of community care, together with the local council tax 'capping' impressed by central government, may militate against high standards of care. Care homes and care agencies sometimes struggle to hire, train and retain good quality staff, or indeed sometimes an adequate number of staff at all (Robinson 2004, p.2). The result can be to the great detriment of service users – and potential breach of all manner of legal obligations – as revealed by a disturbing Panorama programme on domiciliary care agencies under contract to local authorities (*A Carer's Story*, broadcast Sunday 16 November 2003 at 10.15pm).

The diminution in people's potential legal rights arises because the courts have held that independent care providers are not to be classed as public bodies; in which case judicial review and human rights legal cases cannot lie directly against such care providers (e.g. *R(Heather) v Leonard Cheshire Homes*; see 4.2.7). Indeed, one judge remarked that he sympathised with residents of a care home, and that his inability to assist them judicially demonstrated 'an inadequacy of response' to their plight, now that 'Parliament has permitted public law obligations to be discharged by entering into private law arrangements' (*R v Servite Houses, ex p Goldsmith*).

In addition, further obstacles lie in wait for service users who wish to complain against the local authority, using the social services complaints procedure. This is because local authorities would expect a complaint about a service to lie first against the care provider, through use of that provider's complaints procedure; if the complaint is unresolved, then it could be taken against the local authority. Nevertheless, it is by no means certain that preventing direct access to the social services complaints procedure would always be lawful; and in any case, it will mean delay before the local authority becomes aware of, and can deal with, the complaint. For instance, essentially for this reason, in one case a complaint raised with the care provider in 1998 did not ultimately come to the attention of the local authority until 2001 (*Cambridgeshire CC 2004*).

Such outcomes, in terms of dilution of potential rights, are something of an irony, since central government of different hues has for well over a decade held itself out as the champion of the individual 'consumer' of public health and welfare services.

## 3.3 COMMUNITY CARE GUIDANCE

Guidance issued by the Department of Health and other government departments to supplement legislation represents substantial uncertainty because of its indeterminate legal status and effect. Quantity, incorrectness, impenetrability, jargon and repetitiveness all add to the problems it generates.

Community care is littered with guidance: the Department of Health website is awash with it; local authority staff and managers spend vast amounts of time and money trying to understand and implement the numerous policies contained in it; and community care legal case law is strewn with references to it.

The dichotomy between legislation and guidance is longstanding, and there are various well-rehearsed arguments for and against the greater use of guidance in the implementation of policy (e.g. Baldwin 1995; Ganz 1987). For instance, guidance can be written in ordinary and helpful language, be produced and disseminated more quickly than legislation, and tends to give the relevant public bodies (e.g. local authorities) flexibility in how to implement policy.

On the other hand, it is not placed before and considered by Parliament as is legislation. This means that important policy matters which seriously affect people can bypass Parliamentary scrutiny altogether. Guidance might simply be badly written, and even if the language is clear, the obligations (if any) created might be indistinct.

The general drawbacks and uncertainties of government guidance are nothing new. Some 50 years ago, a court characterised it as 'four times cursed': (a) it did not go through Parliament; (b) it was unpublished and inaccessible by those affected; (c) it was a jumble of legal, administrative or directive provisions; (d) it was not expressed in precise legal language. This was in contrast to legislation which was 'twice blessed' when it passed through both Houses of Parliament (*Patchett v Leathem*).

Sometimes, guidance simply does not resolve the issues. For instance, a glance back to the debates in 1989 and 1990 on the NHS and Community Care Bill reveals that some of the proposed amendments, so dismissively rejected by government at the time, were about matters that have continued to be troublesome and have precisely not been solved by guidance. These include hospital discharge procedures, care plans, giving of reasons for decisions, advocacy, incontinence services, assessment of carers, direct payments, and so on. Indeed, some of these issues have belatedly triggered legislation: for example, the Carers (Recognition and Services) Act 1995; Carers and Disabled Children Act 2000; Carers (Equal Opportunities) Act 2004; Health and Social Care Act 2001 (covering direct payments); the Community Care (Delayed Discharges) Act 2003.

Thus the very bareness of s.47 of the NHS and Community Care Act 1990 governing community care assessment was deliberate. During the Parliamentary passage of the Bill, the government repeatedly opposed amendments that would have given it rather more substance – on the grounds that such legislative detail would have placed local authorities in a bureaucratic straitjacket. Far better express what was wanted in guidance, and leave local authorities all the more freedom to get on with it.

The following quotes from Parliament, concerning community care legislation, provide a strong flavour of the arguments for and against the use of guidance (the fourth example being a reminder that it is not just guidance that might be ineffective, but legislation too):

**Forgetting guidance in the hurly burly and rush**. 'We feel that it is important to have such a provision written into the [NHS and Community Care] Bill. I say that because when a Bill becomes an Act of Parliament people look upon it as legislation and they forget everything else. They forget about White Papers and Green Papers and also, with the hurly-burly and the rush which ensue, they forget about the circulars issued by the department' (Baroness Masham: House of Lords Debates, 24/4/1990, col.551).

**Ineffectiveness of guidance on incontinence services**. 'The Minister referred to government health notice 88/26… That circular is what the Government recommend. It is from that circular that the wording of the amendment [duty to provide a district-wide continence service] comes. It is what the Government want, but the Minister went on to say that district health authorities should be left to decide on their own priorities. The situation has continued to deteriorate since the health notice went out. That shows how ineffective notices without legislation can be… There is therefore a need for an amendment such as this so that provision is guaranteed under legislation' (Baroness Masham: House of Lords Debates, 7/6/1990, col.1589).

**A couple of 'silly circulars' and inaction**. 'Apart from a couple of silly circulars they have sent to local authorities, the Government's excuse for inaction is that they do not wish to dictate to local authorities. They say that they respect local autonomy' (Jack Ashley: House of Commons Debates, 9/4/1973, col.1024).

**It is 'all in circulars'**. Lord Mottistone demanded of Baroness Blatch: 'Is she telling us that effectively – and until we see it we cannot believe it – regulations and guidance will replace this part of the Bill? Does she not agree with me that it is very important to have in major legislation underpinning matter from which circulars can be developed rather than circulars, even if they are already in existence? Circulars can be changed at the drop of a hat because they do not even have to come before Parliament. The whole burden of my noble friend's remarks, as I saw it, was: "Oh yes, it is all in circulars." Does she not agree that that is a very inadequate reply? It is terrible that, after seeing my noble friend, this very important matter is being left to circulars, whether or not they are issued. I just do not like this.'

In reply: 'My Lords…my noble friend has in a sense contradicted himself in his last remarks in that he has pointed to a matter which is enshrined in legislation and then said that that was not effective – that is section 117 of the Mental Health Act' (House of Lords Debates, 14/6/1990, col.492).

## 3.4 ALLOCATION OF SCARCE RESOURCES: RATIONING

As already noted, it is a lack of resources that so often activates the points of uncertainty within community care. Allocation of resources (priority setting, rationing or whatever name is chosen) is highly sensitive, not new, but increasingly highlighted by community care policy, guidance and the decisions of the law courts. The allocation of scarce resources is a thankless task whether planned and executed by central or local government – or even, at the other extreme, not planned at all but allowed to develop in haphazard fashion or by lottery. It not only involves 'tragic choices' but can also too easily bring opprobrium on rationing agents (e.g. central or local government), whatever strategy or lack of strategy is adopted (Calabresi and Bobbit 1978).

Scarce resources invite harsh decisions as well as the apportioning of blame when things go wrong or expectations are not met. For example, users of services might blame 'front-line' professionals (such as social workers or occupational therapists), and the latter in turn their managers; those managers might in turn reproach their senior managers, who point the finger at the relevant local authority committee; it might in turn blame central government – and so on. Perhaps the recrimination comes full circle if a government, keen to reduce public spending, is voted in by electors apparently shy of paying tax, yet wishing to enjoy high quality services: a case of 'won't pay must pay' (*Economist* 1998). The matter then boils down to three main options: insurance, taxation or liquidation of personal assets (Grimley Evans 1995).

In April 1993, financial responsibility for funding residential care and nursing home care was shifted from central government to local authorities. This meant that what previously had been an open-ended, demand-led, central government budget would now be subject to finite resources at local level. This looked to be highly convenient for central government; not only could local authorities introduce systems of rationing, thus controlling expenditure, but it would also be those authorities, rather than central government, that would reap any adverse criticism. In addition there was an essentially covert reduction in the number of NHS beds available for people with continuing health care needs.

All this would predictably lead to problems and to legal cases (and ombudsman investigations) – whether about residential care (e.g. *R v Sefton MBC, ex p Help the Aged*), non-residential services (*R v Gloucestershire CC, ex p Barry*) or continuing health care (as evidenced by highly critical reports by the health service ombudsman spanning a decade).

### 3.4.1 ROYAL COMMISSION ON PAYING FOR CARE

The diminishing of NHS continuing care, replaced by means-tested care in residential and nursing homes, has led to accusations that central government has abandoned the 'cradle-to-grave' philosophy of the welfare state and broken its promises to people who believed they would be cared for at no cost – with a policy which is unfair and favours the spendthrift over the thrifty (House of Commons Health Committee 1996, p.xxiv). People might feel cheated because they had been led to believe – whilst paying National Insurance contributions, and 'scrimping and saving' all their lives – that the state would care for them in their time of need, that they and their spouses would not be reduced to penury, and that their inheritance would be safeguarded for their children (Salvage 1995, p.3).

A Royal Commission on Long Term Care for the Elderly sat during 1998 with a brief to report on the future funding of long-term care for elderly people, both in their own homes and other settings. In the event, central government has failed to implement the Commission's central proposal that personal care be provided free of charge (Royal Commission on Long Term Care 1999). Instead, central government in England has gone only so far as to introduce a limited system of 'free nursing care' for people in certain care homes. (By comparison, free personal care in addition to free nursing care was introduced for older people in Scotland: Community Care and Health (Scotland) Act 2002.) This restrictive and cost-capped system of nursing care funding, linked with the Department of Health's apparent connivance at running down continuing NHS health care, makes it arguable that central government has in fact been rowing in quite the opposite direction to that indicated by the Royal Commission.

### 3.4.2 WHEN LOCAL BUDGETS RUN OUT

When resources are not forthcoming because of the financial policies of the moment (local or central government driven), the potential effect on clear statutory duties laid down by Parliament is highly corrosive. The courts have accepted that resources cannot be conjured up out of thin air (e.g. *R v Islington LBC, ex p Rixon*), but decided also that financial cuts must stop somewhere if legal duties are not to become meaningless (*R v East Sussex CC, ex p Tandy*). In this last case, the House of Lords stated that when there is an absolute statutory duty imposed on an authority to do something, it must find the resources, even if it has to raid other budgets. It is not sufficient to claim that one budget in particular has been exhausted and that therefore the statutory duty cannot be performed. This statement confirmed what had been established previously; namely that once an eligible community care need had been assessed, there is an absolute duty to meet it one way or another (*R v Gloucestershire CC, ex p Barry*).

Despite this clear statement, it appears that in practice many social services managers will pay very much more attention to limiting expenditure than to the statements made in the *Tandy* and *Gloucestershire* cases. This is understandable, given the pressures that are sometimes placed on such managers to remain within budget, come what may.

Whatever the uncertainties about the issue of resources, one thing at least is clear; many of the community care judicial review cases heard to date have focused on an apparent lack of resources to meet people's community care needs. This was predictable. Some ten years ago, the Griffiths report (1988, pp.iii, ix) on community care emphatically denied that it represented a cost-cutting exercise, although it did concede that many local authorities felt that 'the Israelites faced with the requirement to make bricks without straw had a comparatively routine and possible task'. It also stated, perhaps naively, that what could not 'be acceptable is to allow ambitious policies to be embarked upon without the appropriate funds'. In retrospect, this last was a telling comment.

The ensuing White Paper spoke of better use of taxpayer's money, but arguably did not confront sufficiently forcibly or transparently the inevitable conflict which would follow between people's needs and available resources (Secretaries of State 1989, p.5). Subsequent policy guidance (DH 1990) and practice guidance (SSI/SWSG 1991) tended to camouflage, in verbiage relating to good practice, the issue of resources.

The disparity between the stated policy of central government and the policy actually pursued was highlighted in 1997 by one of the members (Lord Lloyd) of the House of Lords in *R v Gloucestershire CC, ex p Barry*. He confirmed the soundness of the warning (about appropriate funding) given in the Griffiths report nearly ten years before, when he stated that central government had indeed departed from its 'fine words' in its 1989 White Paper and simply failed to supply the resources required.

## 3.5 TRANSPARENCY OF LEGISLATION AND POLICY

Given the (perhaps inevitable) mismatch in the community care system between aspiration and policy on the one hand, and on the other, resources (money, staff, time, expertise), local authorities need to be able to escape what they would regard as otherwise ruinous expenditure. Such escape comes in the form of exploiting the uncertainties built into the system. However, it would not be politically advantageous to trumpet such uncertainties, so central (and sometimes local) government would often appear to place their faith in a lack of transparency.

### 3.5.1 ASPIRATION, POLICY AND PRACTICE

Policy guidance states that the preferable option for each individual is to provide care in people's own homes where this 'would provide a better quality of life' than would entry into a residential or nursing home, and wherever it is 'feasible and sensible'. Certainly, it also refers to resource issues, such as the need for 'cost-effective' services and for difficult decisions sometimes having to be made (DH 1990, para 3.25). However, this language does not on its face appear to sanction the common practice over the past decade of imposing stringent ceilings on the weekly cost of domiciliary care packages for older people (above which they have to enter residential or nursing home care) – or of making wholesale reductions in the availability of home help services. Thus, although resources are referred to, the policy guidance as a whole does not portray community care as an exercise in limiting expenditure on groups of vulnerable people.

Similarly, when other guidance (e.g. SSI/SWSG 1991, p.54) refers to priorities, it does so in an orderly and rational way, suggestive of an outcome where people who really 'need' help will get it quickly, others will get it in good time, and that everything will work out in the end. Yet the financial pressures on community care from the very start meant that the measured language of guidance was always at risk of fraying on contact with reality. All this is a salutary reminder that community care guidance from central government must generally be examined carefully for its true implications.

The point about transparency is not about whether the real, as opposed to the superficial, community care policy has been sensible or defensible, politically or morally, but about the lack of hard-nosed public explanation. To the extent that there has been such a lack of explanation, then both care professionals and the general public are ill-informed. This in turn means that at one general level it becomes difficult to hold a well-informed debate about community care because nobody is quite sure what is, or is meant to be, going on. At another level, it means that people either have false expectations, or simply don't know what to expect at all. An example of this general unawareness is sometimes illustrated by outrage expressed in the media:

**Local outrage.** The *Basingstoke and North Hampshire Gazette* (24 July 1998) contained a feature of several pages on community care. About withdrawal of home help services from a number of disabled people, the article referred to people's age, wheelchairs, polio, blindness, six heart attacks, dignity and anger – and to the response of the chairman of the social services committee that 'no one is going to die from cuts in cleaning'.

This sort of newsworthy article and the indignation it stirs up might suggest that the scale of rationing implicit in government policy has outstripped the general public's awareness. Otherwise it would presumably be barely worth reporting. Occasionally, such stories make the national news, especially when centurions, in age, are concerned.

**National outrage.** On 9 July 2003, the *Daily Telegraph* carried a large headline: 'Woman, 102, dies after eviction from care home'; the care home had evicted her 17 days previously, after the care home had claimed that the local authority was not prepared to pay an adequate fee (a claim denied by the local authority).

Other such headlines are aimed at central government; this occurred on a significant scale in 2002 when Rose Cottle protested at the proposed closure of her care home, after the owners agreed to sell it to Bryant Homes for redevelopment as flats. The owners claimed they had lost £3 million in ten years because of lack of public funding for care home residents. The headlines fell over themselves: 'When Rose saw red' in *Disability Now* (June 2002), 'Rose, 102, storms Downing Street in fight to save her care home' in the *Evening Standard* (18 March 2002), 'Downing Street protest by care home woman, 102' in *The Times* (19 March 2002), 'A retiring champion' also in *The Times* (23 March 2002).

Notwithstanding such flourishes in the national press, central government remained, in substance, unmoved by such stories; care home closures, sometimes to the great distress of residents and their relatives, have continued apace.

The 1998 government White Paper, *Modernising Social Services* (Secretary of State for Health 1998), severely criticised the way in which community care is working. Like its predecessor dealing with community care nearly ten years before, *Community Care in the Next Decade and Beyond* (Secretaries of State 1989), it contained many high-sounding aspirations. The real question is whether, almost seven years on, the words of the 1998 White Paper have turned out to be as hollow as those of the 1989 White Paper.

In 1997, Lord Lloyd's comments in the *Gloucestershire* case about the 1989 White Paper was reference to a lack of transparency in central government policy:

**Fine words and noble aspiration.** The local authority was in an 'impossible position; truly impossible, because even if the Council wished to raise the money themselves to meet the need by increasing council tax, they would be unable to do so by reason of the government-imposed rate capping'. Furthermore, it was the government's departure from its 'fine words' in the community care White Paper that had brought about the situation. The 'passing of the 1970 Act was a noble aspiration. Having willed the end, Parliament must be asked to provide the means' (*R v Gloucestershire CC, ex p Barry*).

Whether there is now a greater alignment between aspiration, policy and practice can in part be answered by considering some of the responses of the Department of Health since the 1998 White Paper.

### 3.5.2 LACK OF TRANSPARENCY: SPECIFIC EXAMPLES

The White Paper identified a need for consistency and fairness in terms of assessment, eligibility, service provision and charging. It undertook to produce guidance on fair access to care (Secretary of State for Health 1998, para 2.36). At first blush, central government would appear to have made a genuine attempt to remedy these defects. One key part of this attempt is in the form of eligibility criteria and 'fair access to care':

**Lack of transparency: fair access to care guidance.** In 2002, the Department of Health issued guidance entitled 'fair access to care' (LAC(2002)13). Many local authority professionals assumed from the title and the foregoing White Paper that this guidance would be aiming at greater consistency and equity across community care generally – and that it was making good on the White Paper's promise. However, this was perhaps an optimistic view.

In fact, the guidance contains an arguably misleading title, allows for substantial inconsistencies between local authorities, took five years to implement, fails to explain how the guidance links to the legislation it is meant to be based on – and has been judicially regarded as less than clear (*R(Heffernan) v Sheffield CC*). Furthermore, in essence, many of its key points derive either from judgments of the law courts (which it fails to explain), or merely repeat in varied wording what had already been stated in Department of Health guidance of a decade before.

In other words, the guidance is arguably simply more of the same of what had already gone before and had led to the very consistencies the White Paper had identified.

Whatever the reason for this state of affairs, central government has a strong incentive not to impose a uniform system of eligibility for community care services, despite what it stated in the White Paper. To do so would be to begin to remove the uncertainties on which the system so heavily relies.

Similarly guidance (LAC(2001)32 and DH 2003j), issued on charging for non-residential services, has done little to remedy the very inconsistencies across local authorities that the White Paper identified (Thompson and Mathew 2004); it precisely allows, and arguably encourages, them. A further substantial example of what is arguably a lack of transparency on a large scale is the matter of 'continuing NHS health care' (see 16.7).

**Lack of transparency: continuing NHS health care.** Over at least the last 15 years, the NHS has been shedding long-stay, 'continuing health care' beds. This has been done without new legislation being passed to this effect, and with no formal policy being debated in Parliament. Essentially it has been covert and by stealth. Because of sustained criticism from the health service ombudsman, as well as from the Court of Appeal, the Department of Health has twice been forced, against its better judgement, to issue guidance.

Both sets of guidance were criticised by the ombudsman (and one set by the law courts), the most recent (and current guidance) severely so. One of the strongest criticisms is that central government has produced guidance that is barely comprehensible and has in effect deliberately presided over a policy of inaction and uncertainty.

In response, central government has refused to acknowledge that its most recent guidance is flawed. Instead it issued directions in 2004 concerning the duty to assess people's continuing care needs against this guidance. But central government can scarcely claim that these directions go to the heart of matter. Stipulating that assessments take place, but against guidance that has been condemned as virtually meaningless, is arguably peripheral to the real issue and represents form without substance. It should also be noted that in this case the lack of transparency penalises extremely vulnerable and unwell people – in terms of stress, distress, financial consequences (they may have to sell the house to pay for care) – as well as their informal carers.

As both evidence, and consequence, of the problem, the health service ombudsman reported that during 2003–2004, she received some 4000 complaints about continuing NHS health care (HSO 2004b, para 5).

A government minister inadvertently highlighted the real problem concerning continuing NHS health care. Interviewed as part of a highly disturbing programme into the plight of certain people with advanced dementia who had been denied NHS continuing health care, he stated that it was a question of money. This was something 'we' all had to decide; namely whether care for such vulnerable people should be free of charge or not (Stephen Ladyman speaking on *Panorama*, shown on BBC1, 18 July 2004). However, the problem is that central government has precisely failed to hold this debate, presumably aware of the unpopularity that its policy would incur if explained to an unsuspecting public.

Another apparent example of lack of transparency on the part of central government arose concerning continence supplies in nursing homes:

**Lack of transparency: continence supplies in nursing homes.** During April 2001, considerable Parliamentary pressure had been applied (especially by Baroness Masham) for the Health and Social

Care Bill to be amended, so as explicitly to set out a duty on the NHS to provide people in nursing homes with continence supplies free of charge. The government refused to do this; however, on 3 May a government minister stated that it agreed with the principle that continence pads and other equipment should be available on that basis. However, a legislative amendment would not be required; instead a direction (see 16.5) would be issued to the NHS (Lord Hunt, House of Lords Debates, 3/5/2001, col.848). No such formal direction was ever issued; instead, guidance only was issued on free nursing care, containing reference to continence supplies. Indeed, in 2004, another government minister referred to it as guidance, not as a direction (Dr Stephen Ladyman, House of Commons Written Answers, 19/4/2004, col.262). Yet Baroness Masham has herself in the past pointed out how guidance is routinely ignored by the NHS (see 3.3); and central government knows this only too well: guidance is third down the 'pecking order' after legislation and formal directions.

## 3.6 LOCAL AUTHORITY POLICIES, PROCEDURES AND PRACTICE

If central government policy and legislation lacks transparency, sometimes grossly mismatches aspiration with what can realistically be achieved, and therefore opens the door to uncertainty – local authorities are not slow to enter through that door. This is unsurprising because it is local authorities that are at the sharp end of political aspiration, the actual meeting of people's needs and lack of resources.

### 3.6.1 LOCAL AUTHORITY ADHERENCE TO THE LAW

It would be tempting to accede to the following propositions: (a) that local authority members and officers are as a matter of course always and fully aware of their legal obligations; (b) that when local authority members and officers are aware of the law, then they always adhere to it. Unfortunately, neither of these propositions appears to be correct.

The first is undermined by the observation of the local ombudsman that a frequent cause of maladministration is that officers are not aware of their legal obligations (CLAE 1993, p.5).

The second proposition assumes that if local authorities and their staff were conversant with the law, then they would adhere to it. This proposition fails on a number of counts. Knowledge of the law might be located only in selective parts of a local authority (e.g. the legal department) without reaching key managers and staff. In addition, knowledge of the legislation, national guidance or latest ruling in the courts is one thing, but converting it into local procedures, policies and guidelines is quite another; neatly delineated legal principle is not always easily superimposed on the rough edges of everyday practice.

**Misinterpreting national guidance at local level.** One local authority tampered with the indicators of risk set out in a risk assessment framework in Department of Health guidance on 'fair access to care' (LAC(2002)13). This was unlawful (R(Heffernan) v Sheffield CC).

It appears that sometimes senior officers and councillors do know very well what the law is but consciously choose to breach it, taking a calculated risk that financially it is probably cheaper to breach the law and run the (hopefully small) risk of a legal challenge than to adhere to it.

Even if the law does find its way successfully into policies and procedures, these might (a) not be known to staff; (b) not be followed by staff; (c) might be informally varied by staff; or (d) simply become out of date. The courts and local government ombudsmen have repeatedly identified such shortcomings.

### 3.6.2 LOCAL AUTHORITIES TAKING LEGAL SHORT CUTS

Whether or not they are acquainted with the relevant law, hard-pressed local authorities sometimes search creatively for escape routes to relieve financial and resource pressures. Most coveted are the escape routes that will be lawful and effectively exploit loopholes in the legislation and guidance. In their absence, those routes that at least have a degree of ambiguity as to their lawfulness will be the next most favoured.

Last, least subtle but by no means least used are those routes that are almost certainly unlawful, whether or not staff or managers are aware of this. For instance, it is not unknown for councillors formally to consult on, set and then apply a threshold of eligibility for services for the financial year, only for an individual team manager two months later, 'secretly' and almost certainly unlawfully, to instruct her staff to operate a higher threshold, because her particular budget is running down too quickly.

Certain legislation will afford far more lawful escape routes than others. For instance, legislation containing general target duties such as the NHS Act 1977 barely imposes concrete obligations on the NHS (see 4.1). Thus, the NHS can avoid providing most services with relative impunity and quite lawfully. In contrast, specific enforceable legislation, such as the Chronically Sick and Disabled Persons Act 1970, provides fewer and narrower lawful opportunities for evasion of potential responsibility. In which case some local authorities regularly resort to legally dubious avenues of escape.

## 3.7 JUDICIAL REVIEW AND THE LOCAL OMBUDSMEN

If the legislation is labyrinthine, and guidance intangible in meaning, understanding community care law has been complicated further by a stream of judicial review decisions in the law courts. Thus, anyone wishing to understand community care law must not only grapple with the legislation and guidance, but try to make sense of these legal cases. The courts apply a number of common law principles in judicial review, as a test of whether a public body is acting fairly in terms of how it has reached a decision.

Since April 1993, there has been a steady flow of judicial review cases concerning community care. This is particularly notable since, as explained above, all the legislation covering community care services had long been in place before 1993, but had provoked relatively few legal challenges (but see *Wyatt v Hillingdon LBC, R v Ealing LBC, ex p Leaman*, and *R v Department of Health and Social Security, ex p Bruce* – all concerning the Chronically Sick and Disabled Persons Act 1970). There are no doubt a number of reasons for this change of pattern:

- A shortage of resources inevitably invites dispute.
- Central government, with general initiatives such as the Citizen's Charter (Prime Minister 1991), and with local authority statutory complaints procedures in particular, encouraged people to complain about services. Although the complaints procedures are in part intended to keep people away from the law courts, it is inevitable that the more people are encouraged to complain, so the greater the proportion that might spill its grievances over into legal action.
- Judicial review has itself been a developing area of the law, with the courts constantly trying to strike a balance between protecting individuals from the unfair exercise of power by public bodies and letting public bodies get on with a difficult job, judicially unhindered.

The complexity of the legislation, the morass of guidance and the contradictory elements of community care policy were always likely to provoke judicial intervention. Given the instability and uncertainty of community care policy and legislation from the outset, the uncertainties were never going to be merely peripheral; it was eminently foreseeable both to onlookers and to civil servants within the Department of Health that the courts would have to try to work out the legal and practical implications of the new system.

The degree to which the courts have brought certainty – from the point of view of service users – to community care law is questionable. Some questions they answer clearly, some not; whilst some are never considered at all if they never happen to get to court. Even when particular questions are answered, with uncertainty replaced with certainty and perhaps an escape route (from potential legal obligations) closed off, local authorities will immediately seek out further uncertainties and alternative escape routes.

Nevertheless, what the courts have certainly done is to throw light on the uncertainties; and they have also brought to bear a number of common law principles that are designed to bring at least a degree of fairness to decision making by local authorities. A footnote to the flurry of legal activity in community care is that nearly 20 years ago the sponsor of the Chronically Sick and Disabled Persons Act 1970 had this to say during a debate about an ultimately unsuccessful amendment to the Act (which would have allowed resort to a county court to enforce service provision):

**Light industry for lawyers.** 'As I have said on many occasions, my own concern over the years has been to argue not for litigation but for full implementation of the Act. I have never seen the judge as some kind of ayatollah of the disabled. Nor, in promoting the Act [CSDPA 1970], did I ever wish to create a new light industry for lawyers. What clause I of the Bill will do is to bring the law into line with what was always thought to be the effect of section 2 of the parent Act. I believe it will be helpful, but we should not expect too much from legal intervention' (Alfred Morris: House of Commons Debates, 2/2/1979, col.1922).

These words were prophetic: nearly 20 years later, their speaker was moved to write an article in *The Times* newspaper, heavily criticising the House of Lords for its decision in the case of *R v Gloucestershire CC, ex p Barry* (Morris 1997).

## 3.8 GOOD ADMINISTRATION: LOCAL GOVERNMENT OMBUDSMEN

The extraction of legal principle in judicial review cases sometimes entails obscuring untidy realities, in order to identify a point of law. In comparison, the local government and health service ombudsmen consider not only legal principles, but also the everyday, down-to-earth events and facts of a dispute. In this way, on balance, they provide a more detailed and richer, if less boldly delineated, picture of community care than that achieved by the courts.

The ombudsmen investigate maladministration and injustice perpetrated by local authorities. Their findings do not constitute part of 'the law', and their recommendations, though usually followed, are not legally binding. However, they usefully apply axioms of good administration (see 4.3.1), which if adhered to by local authorities arguably greatly improve decision making. They also expose the sometimes chaotic nature of policies, procedures and practices that underline community care decision making, and which add a layer of uncertainty to the outcome of any one individual case.

Ombudsman investigations therefore reflect the fact that local authority staff and service users find themselves in the grip of unlike influences: on the one hand, complex legislation and abstract legal principle, on the other humdrum daily administrative activity. Like the courts, within the overall context of an uncertain system, the local ombudsmen attempt to impart a reasonable standard of fairness in decision making.

## 3.9 GOOD PRACTICE AND THE LAW

As noted immediately above, a glance through the local ombudsmen's axioms of good administration (CLAE 1993) quickly reveals their consonance with what both professionals and users of services are likely to equate with 'good practice' (for the axioms, see 4.3.1). In addition, a number of the principles or interpretations enunciated by the law courts in judicial review cases also equate with good practice. For instance:

**Dignity, integrity, etc.** When assessing two women with learning and physical disabilities and how they would be physically transferred daily within and without the home, the local authority had to take account of their wishes, feelings, reluctance, fear, refusal, dignity, integrity and quality of life (R(AandB) v East Sussex County Council (no.2)).

**Flexibility.** Rigid policies should be avoided and exceptional needs looked out for (R v Ealing LBC, ex p Leaman; R v North Yorkshire CC, ex p Hargreaves (no.2); British Oxygen v Board of Trade).

**Low threshold for assessment.** 'Screening' procedures should not be restrictive (R v Bristol CC, ex p Penfold).

**Assessment valuable in its own right.** Assessment is useful and a potential entitlement in its own right (R v Bristol CC, ex p Penfold).

**Waiting times.** People should not be kept waiting interminably for a decision about services (R v Sutton LBC, ex p Tucker).

**Preferences.** People's preferences should be considered (R v North Yorkshire CC, ex p Hargreaves).

**Recreational needs**. People's needs should be viewed broadly including social, recreational and leisure needs (*R v Haringey LBC, ex p Norton*).

**Individual assessment**. People's needs should be assessed and reassessed individually and attentively (*R v Gloucestershire CC, ex p Mahfood* and *R v Gloucestershire CC, ex p RADAR*).

**Distinguish need from services**. Assessment should distinguish needs from services (*R v Lancashire CC, ex p RADAR*).

**Accurate letters**. Accurate letters should be written (*R v Bristol CC, ex p Bailey*).

**Explanations for decisions**. Decisions should be explicable in terms of reasoning rather than unsupported assertions (*R v Ealing LBC, ex p C*).

There is an undercurrent, too, of good professional practice running through the legislation itself, particularly as it is interpreted and explained by community care guidance issued by the Department of Health. For instance, this is in terms of full and proper assessment, considering people's needs in the round, assessing risks to independence, taking an approach in terms of a social model of disability, considering carefully the role and needs of informal carers (e.g. LAC(92)13; SSI/SWSG 1991a).

The application of such principles and rules, all consistent with professional good practice, can make a real difference as to whether any one individual service user receives a service – or at least to the fairness of the decision as to whether or not services are to be provided. Yet it is surprising how often local authority officers are unaware of the good administration axioms of the ombudsman, of the principles applied in judicial review cases, or of what exactly the relevant guidance states.

Too often, in both local authorities and the NHS, it is possible to come across statements of professionally (and 'politically') correct principle, made by managers and staff who are at the same time applying inequitable, restrictive and sometimes unlawful policies and practices. Thus, it has been pointed out that in relation to political correctness, words should not be mistaken for deeds (Philpot 1999, p.11). For instance, the General Social Care Council's code of practice for social workers states that they must:

- treat each person as an individual
- respect and promote individual views and wishes of users and carers
- support people's rights to control their own lives
- respect and maintain dignity and privacy
- promote equal opportunities, and respect diversity (GSCC 2002).

The Council's code of practice for employers states, amongst other things, that the employer must have written policies and procedures in place to enable social workers to adhere to their code of practice (GSCC 2002a).

It will be noted that some of these principles are similar to those applied by the law courts; and such principles are frequently subscribed to by staff, managers and local authorities as a whole. However, sometimes they seem to be treated as rather abstract statements of grand intent, rather than working tools that can be used in everyday practice to ask awkward, but ultimately constructive, questions of the local policy and budget. To take but three of the principles so often not realised:

**Equal opportunities**. Older people continue, on the basis of age, to suffer from restrictive assessment and cost ceilings that are not applied to other groups of people (e.g. Clark, Gough and Macfarlane 2004, p.56).

**Treatment of person as individual**. Local authorities continue to be riddled with rigid, restrictive policies that are inconsistent with the assessment and meeting of people's individual needs.

**Control over own life**. In respect of people controlling their own lives, local authorities have been busily closing down care homes, on the basis of assessments by social workers, against the wishes, and to the great distress of, residents. This, even if 94 per cent of the residents in the council homes, faced with transfer to the independent sector, are in opposition (McFadyean and Rowland 2002, p.20).

Despite the presence of 'good practice' elements in community care legislation and guidance, the financial and other pressures on local authorities and their staff make them difficult to adhere to. Whilst such guidance can have the effect of promoting good practice and motivating staff, it also makes all the more stark the gap between aspiration and practice – when staff are unable to follow the good practice elements of guidance, owing to the restrictive nature of the policies and procedures they are having to follow.

This can result all too easily in good practice being undermined. For example, a Chief Inspector of the Social Services Inspectorate explained that personal family experience had opened her eyes to the weaknesses of the health and social care system more effectively than years of experience as a social worker (Ivory 1998). There are, no doubt, countless service users and their relatives who could have told her the same thing. This is a simple reminder that the needs of people (patients, clients, users of services – however called) easily become sidelined in the community care system.

### 3.9.1 GOOD PRACTICE AND LEGAL FAIRNESS IN DECISION MAKING

Organisational pressures can sometimes cause even experienced and senior social workers and other care professionals to lose sight of the good practice, which they would as individuals pride themselves upon. The late Sir Douglas Black, president of the Royal College of Physicians and author in 1980 of *Inequalities in Health: The Black Report*, was reported as making a telling comment when alluding to organisational aberration: 'People banded together are capable of follies and excesses beyond what the same people, acting as individuals, would perpetrate on other individuals. Such activities may be termed corporate tyranny' (quoted in Richmond 2002).

Such a comment is not necessarily to overstate the case. For instance, when a local authority failed to meet the needs of a disabled child in foster care, apparently concealing or altering the evidence as to her situation and needs, the judge did not question the good faith of any of the local authority staff involved. However, he referred to the 'demon' that had entered into and 'infected' the local authority's decision making for a period of two years (*CD (A Child) v Anglesey CC*).

Another community care case is suggestive of how badly wrong, for whatever reasons, community care decision making can go. It illustrates predetermined decision making, misrepresentations, non-adherence to local good practice guidelines, breach of human rights, apparent suppression or deliberate ignoring of the main community care assessment, and potential risk to a 95-year-old woman's well-being and indeed life:

**Manifestly flawed and defective decision making in the case of a frail 95-year-old woman.** A local authority decided that a 95-year-old woman could not continue to live in the care home in which she had lived for many years. Instead she would have to move to a nursing home. Her daughter vigorously opposed the decision. The Court of Appeal ruled that the decision was manifestly flawed. A catalogue of serious criticism of the local authority underlay this judgment.

*Misplaced reliance on local continuing care panel.* Reliance was placed by the local authority on the recommendations of the local continuing care panel, without ensuring that it had taken account of all relevant factors (which it had not). This meant the local authority was not reaching a lawful community care decision.

*Not considering all relevant factors.* The local authority had reached a decision without taking account of the most impressive and comprehensive assessment of the woman's needs, carried out by one of its own social work team managers, who knew the woman best. Instead the authority had relied on the panel's recommendations, which in turn rested on the reports of health professionals who assessed the woman in hospital. Furthermore a doctor, who had endorsed these reports, had not seen the woman. Thus, the decision was taken without a full and up-to-date community care assessment.

*Misrepresenting the daughter's position.* A letter written by one of the local authority managers to the doctor involved had misrepresented the dispute. It portrayed the daughter as a lone voice without any professional support; when in fact the team manager's assessment concurred with the daughter that her mother was 'residential care fit'.

*Predetermined decision.* The court concluded that the decision taken by the local authority was predetermined; those responsible had approached it with 'entirely' closed minds.

*Local policy on 'partnership' with service users.* The local policy stated that decisions should be made in full partnership with service users and their carers. The team manager's assessment had taken this approach, but was ignored. In addition, the daughter was prevented from attending the panel meeting on the grounds that only clinical matters were being discussed. The court pointed out that this was less than transparent and logical; social work managers were present who could scarcely be called clinicians, and in fact there had been a reference to resources contained in the report submitted to the panel. This was in terms of the additional costs involved if the woman stayed in her present care home. The court pointed out that this was scarcely a clinical issue and so was an irrelevant consideration for the panel.

Furthermore, the panel failed to keep a written record of its meetings; this was unacceptable and extraordinary. In turn therefore the local authority had not put forward a reasoned, balanced and transparent decision.

*Human rights.* The court also found that article 8 of the European Convention on Human Rights had been breached. This was because the court could not accept that the decision-making process safeguarded the woman's physical and psychological integrity. Interference by the local authority had to be proportionate in terms of weighing up the doctor's and panel's recommendations in the wider context of the woman's needs and rights. The local authority had not done this. And it was not an academic matter since it was not in dispute that a change to a strange environment for such a frail person 'could have serious if not fatal consequences'.

The court ordered the local authority to take the decision again. The court could not determine the outcome; but it hoped that what was left of the woman's life could be lived out with maximum dignity and the minimum of psychological harm (R(Goldsmith) v Wandsworth LBC).

Doubtless, the professionals in this case all acted in good faith in the light of various pressures; but from the point of view of service users and their carers it makes sorry reading. The criticism of the court comes close to a full-scale demolition of the local authority's decision-making process; it referred to 'seriously defective' decision making throughout. The case appears to serve as something of an object lesson in fairness and in the importance of guarding against 'shortcuts' in decision making at the expense of extremely vulnerable people.

However, to conclude on a more heartening note, the court in the *Goldsmith* case recognised the importance of a good quality professional assessment and documentation. This was the 40-page report by a social work team manager, which had concluded, like the daughter, that the woman was 'residential care fit'. Although it had apparently been ignored in the local authority's decision-making process, nevertheless it was in the end the effort that the team manager had put into the report that served the woman and her daughter so well. Its very quality meant that the court viewed it as 'critical' to the decision-making process. Thus, those social care professionals who are wont to feel that their efforts are sometimes in vain in the pressured world of community care should take heart from this aspect of the case.

# Legal principles and good administration

## KEY POINTS

A number of legal principles are fundamental to an understanding of how the law underpins community care. These in turn relate to the various legal and other remedies that may be available to service users, which are covered in Chapter 5.

This chapter explains in outline how community care practice is governed and affected by legislation, central government guidance, judicial review in the law courts and investigations by the ombudsmen. Legislation is the logical starting point, because without it local authorities would neither exist (e.g. Local Government Act 1972) nor know what their functions were (e.g. NHS and Community Care Act 1990). Without knowing the latter, local authorities could barely act because, broadly speaking, a public body only acts lawfully if it acts within the relevant legislation.

Law is not located solely in legislation but in the decisions of the law courts as well. Apart from interpreting the meaning of legislation, the courts bring to bear a number of common law principles when they judicially review the decision of public bodies such as local authorities and the NHS. These principles broadly translate into what can be termed 'fairness' in decision making and generally complement professional good practice. For instance, local authorities should take account of all relevant matters before reaching a decision; and should not impose rigid policies that in practice exclude the possibility of exceptions in the light of particular individual needs and circumstances.

For local authority and NHS staff, such principles are particularly important because they concern the manner in which staff and managers take decisions when they assess service users and decide whether to provide services. Whether they are saying 'yes' or 'no' to people, most staff and managers would wish to feel that they were doing so fairly. Acquaintance with these principles is likely to result in a better quality of decision making and at the same time reduce the likelihood of successful litigation against the local authority.

Likewise, the axioms of good administration as applied by the local government ombudsmen (and the health service ombudsman) are very much about fairness in decision making. They offer valuable lessons.

**Note: Wales, Scotland and Northern Ireland**. This chapter applies in principle across the United Kingdom. However, there are some distinctions. Wales has its own local government ombudsman (the Commission for Local Administration in Wales) and own health service ombudsman (Health Service Commissioner, since November 2003). The same person currently fulfils both functions, with a view to legislation being passed to create, as in Scotland, a single public services ombudsman.

In Scotland, the Public Sector Ombudsman carries out the equivalent function of the local government ombudsman and health service ombudsman – under the Scottish Public Services Ombudsman Act 2002.

The Northern Ireland Ombudsman carries out the equivalent functions of health service ombudsman and local government ombudsman under the Ombudsman (Northern Ireland) Order 1996 and the Commissioner for Complaints (Northern Ireland) Order 1996.

In Northern Ireland, primary legislation sometimes comes in the form of an Order rather than an Act, and secondary legislation in the form of statutory rules rather than statutory instruments.

## 4.1 LEGISLATION (AND GUIDANCE): DUTIES AND POWERS

The logical starting point is legislation, since local authorities and their staff are creatures of statute; they exist only by virtue of legislation. Thus, in a straightforward sense, if decisions, policies and criteria are inconsistent with legislation, then the local authority will go wrong in law. Legislation confers functions on public bodies such as local authorities, the NHS and central government departments. These functions basically comprise duties and powers.

### 4.1.1 GENERAL DUTIES

Some duties are regarded as general or 'target' in nature. They are typically expressed as being toward the local population rather than each individual person. As such they are difficult to enforce. Typical general duties are to be found in ss.1 and 3 of the NHS Act 1977 (health services: see *R v Inner London Education Authority, ex p Ali*), s.29 of the National Assistance Act 1948 (welfare services for disabled people: *R v Islington LBC, ex p Rixon*) or s.17 of the Children Act 1989 (services for children in need: *R(G) v Barnet LBC*).

### 4.1.2 SPECIFIC DUTIES

Other duties are regarded as specific duties towards individual people. As such, once any relevant conditions have been met, they can in principle be enforced by individuals. They are sometimes referred to as absolute duties, although the term 'absolute' is to some extent misleading. Such duties are often subject to certain (sometimes stringent) conditions being met; also, a failure to meet the duty will sometimes be excused if reasonable or best endeavours have been made (e.g. *R(W) v Doncaster MBC*). Nonetheless, they are very much stronger than target or general duties.

A stronger duty of this type has been identified by the courts, for instance in s.2 of the Chronically Sick and Disabled Persons Act 1970 (CSDPA: welfare services for disabled people), s.21 of the National Assistance Act 1948 (residential accommodation) and s.117 of the Mental Health Act 1983 (mental health aftercare).

**Individual enforceable duty.** When a local authority proposed to remove or reduce services from up to 1500 people, the courts examined s.2 of the CSDPA 1970. The House of Lords concluded that in setting criteria of eligibility, the local authority could have regard to resources. However, once any individual person had been assessed as eligible for services, then lack of resources would be no defence for not performing the duty (*R v Gloucestershire CC, ex p Barry*).

An indicator of such a specific duty typically comes in the form of a reference to 'any person'; for instance, s.2 of the 1970 Act carries this reference; whereas s.17 of the Children Act 1989, a target duty only, refers to a duty to children in need generally, not to any specific child. However, this is not a wholly reliable indicator; s.21 of the 1948 Act has been held to give rise to just such an individual duty (*R v Sefton MBC, ex p Help the Aged; R v Kensington and Chelsea RBC, ex p Kujtim*), but does not carry the reference to 'any person', referring instead only to 'persons' generally.

### 4.1.3 POWERS

Powers constitute what may but does not have to be done. An example of a power is contained in s.45 of the Health Services and Public Health Act 1968 (provision of services for older, non-disabled people).

### 4.1.4 DIRECTIONS

Legislation sometimes gives central government the power to pass directions under it. Although not strictly legislation and not subject to Parliamentary approval, directions create legal duties; they tell the local authority (or NHS) what it must do. For instance, directions have been passed in relation to residential accommodation (National Assistance Act 1948, s.21), welfare services for disabled people (National Assistance Act 1948, s.29), and services in relation mental disorder (NHS Act 1977, schedule 8).

Directions normally bear a clear label. However, in one case concerning the NHS, the courts stated that although the word 'direct' is not necessarily required in order for a direction to be made, clarity is desirable (*R v Secretary of State for Health, ex p Manchester Local Committee*).

### 4.1.5 APPROVALS
Legislation sometimes gives central government the power to pass approvals under it. Although not strictly legislation, approvals give local authorities legal powers. For instance, approvals have been passed in relation to residential accommodation (National Assistance Act 1948, s.21), welfare services for disabled people (National Assistance Act 1948, s.29), services in relation to illness (NHS Act 1977, schedule 8) and welfare services for older people (Health Services and Public Health Act 1968, s.45).

### 4.1.6 GUIDANCE FROM CENTRAL GOVERNMENT
Beyond legislation, by way of supplement, lies the copious quantity of guidance issued by the Department of Health to local authorities and to the NHS. As far as local social services authorities are concerned, there are two types of guidance, stronger and weaker. Stronger guidance, sometimes referred to as statutory or policy guidance, is identifiable because it states that it is made under s.7 of the Local Authority Social Services Act 1970. This places a duty on local authorities, in the exercise of their social services functions, to act under the general guidance of the Secretary of State. Such guidance must normally be followed by local authorities; deviation would be permissible only for good reason, and even then without substantial departure from the guidance (*Robertson v Fife Council*). In which case, a failure to follow it can amount to a breach of statutory duty (*R v North Yorkshire CC, ex p Hargreaves*: local authority failing to take account of the preferences of a service user).

Even the weaker type of guidance, sometimes referred to as practice guidance and not made under s.7 of the 1970 Act, should still be had regard to by local authorities; and a failure substantially to adhere to it without good reasons could be unlawful (*R v Islington LBC, ex p Rixon*).

For the NHS, there is no formal distinction between stronger (statutory) and weaker guidance. But even for the NHS, a failure to take proper account of guidance can also result in unlawfulness. This is so, even if the guidance does not bear a 'badge of mandatory requirement' denoted by words such as 'shall', rather than just 'ask' or 'suggest' (*R v North Derbyshire Health Authority, ex p Fisher*).

### 4.1.6.1 Judicial approach to guidance

If central government had originally hoped to use guidance as a non-statutory veil – in which to swathe community care and so conceal its problems, and behind which the law courts would not venture – then it must be disappointed. Faced with the sparse nature of s.47 of the NHS and Community Care Act 1990, the courts have shown themselves willing to scrutinise and use guidance, in order to understand the implications of the legislation. They have also been prepared to identify its shortcomings, both general and specific. This means, as the following examples show, that it is by no means always clear how – or sometimes even whether – to follow guidance, since it is not always necessarily comprehensible or correct.

On the one hand, the courts might place considerable weight on adhering to guidance; when a local authority failed to adhere to community care police guidance (DH 1990) and practice guidance (SSI/SWSG 1991) in respect of care plans, it was found to have acted unlawfully (*R v Islington LBC, ex p Rixon*). More recently, when a local authority tampered with the wording of policy guidance on eligibility criteria, the court found it had done so unlawfully (*R(Heffernan) v Sheffield CC*). Alternatively, the courts sometimes dismiss guidance with varying degrees of severity.

**Judicial approach to Department of Health guidance.** In a case about home care services for disabled people, one of the law lords merely stated of the relevant guidance that he did not regard it as 'proper material for the construction of the critical provision' but still found it satisfactory that his view, arrived at independently of the guidance, nevertheless was consistent with it (*R v Gloucestershire CC, ex p Barry*).

In another, given the complexity of the legislation, the judge expressed his respect and sympathy to the authors of practice guidance (SSI/SWSG 1991) but gently questioned its coherence and logic (*R v Gloucestershire CC, ex p RADAR*). In a third, the House of Lords went further, again according its respect to the Department of Health, but concluding that the guidance in issue was simply wrong (*R v Wandsworth LBC, ex p Beckwith*); the government department had in effect misunderstood its own legislation. In a fourth, the courts referred to aspects of the Department of Health's 1995 guidance on continuing care as 'elusive' and unclear (*R v North and East Devon HA, ex p Coughlan*); likewise guidance on 'fair access to care' on eligibility criteria was not as clear as it might have been (*R(Heffernan) v Sheffield CC*).

## 4.2 LAW COURTS AND JUDICIAL REVIEW

Law is also located in the decisions of the law courts. In particular, judicial review cases are of fundamental importance in understanding the meaning and effect of community care legislation. The common law principles applied by the courts in judicial review test, overall, the fairness of decisions taken by public bodies. Some of these principles are summarised, non-exhaustively, below. It should also be noted that these principles tend to run into one another and are arguably used by the courts with a degree of imprecision and flexibility. (For procedural aspects of judicial review, see 5.13.)

## 4.2.1 JUDICIAL REVIEW: SUPERVISORY, 'HANDS-OFF' APPROACH

Judicial review is sometimes referred to as a supervisory jurisdiction applying to public bodies. In other words, the courts ensure that public bodies stay within reasonable bounds when they take decisions.

The courts recognise that local authorities and the NHS have a difficult job to do and give them considerable leeway to get on with it. That is, they generally afford such public bodies a fairly wide area of discretion, with which the courts will not interfere. However, if public bodies stray outside this area of discretion, the courts will strike down decisions as unlawful.

It is important to remember that judicial review is, in principle at least, about ensuring that local authorities have acted within the law, rather than about the merits of decisions. If a local authority has made an unlawful decision, the court usually orders it to go away and retake it – this time in a lawful manner – rather than tell the authority exactly what the outcome of the decision should be.

Indeed, the authority might still reach the same conclusion as it did before, but this time around it will do so on the 'right' grounds (see the court's comments in *R v North Yorkshire CC, ex p Hargreaves (no.2)* about holidays for disabled people).

On the other hand, the implications of an adverse ruling might sometimes give a local authority little room for manoeuvre; and in some circumstances the court will directly order provision of a service. This occurred, for instance, in three cases concerned with the provision of ordinary residential accommodation (i.e. ordinary housing) by local social services authorities under s.21 of the National Assistance Act 1948 (*R v Wigan MBC, ex p Tammadge, R v Islington LBC, ex p Batantu* and *R(Bernard) v Enfield LBC*).

The courts do not wish usually to step into the shoes of professionals – such as social workers or occupational therapists – and question the merits of decisions. However, they might do so on occasion (see discussion on proportionality at 4.2.3.1). There is thus room for professionals to make poor decisions without triggering judicial intervention; in other words, a 'bad' decision is not necessarily an unlawful one.

**Doubtful decision but not unlawful.** A man with multiple sclerosis, receiving a 24-hour-a-day package of care, had his needs reassessed by the local authority. The upshot was that his care package was reduced to five hours. The judge had grave misgivings as to whether the five hours could meet the man's needs, but felt unable to interfere since the decision did not constitute irrationality (*R v Haringey LBC, ex p Norton*: although the reassessment was in fact found to be unlawful on other grounds).

## 4.2.2 FETTERING OF DISCRETION: RIGID POLICIES

The courts generally react against the application of a rigid policy, such that exceptions cannot be taken account of. This is an important principle for both local authorities and service users to remember. The courts (and the ombudsmen) are likely to look to see whether the authority has a genuine mechanism for considering whether to make exceptions.

**Rigid policies and fettering of discretion.** A local authority's policy on holidays meant that it would never, as a matter of policy, render full assistance – whatever the person's needs. The court held that this policy fettered its discretion (*R v North Yorkshire CC, ex p Hargreaves no.2*).

For the local ombudsman, the imposition by a local authority of a ceiling on home care packages for older persons constituted maladministration, because it had fettered its discretion; the mechanism the council had for considering exceptions was ineffective because it never made exceptions (*Liverpool CC 1998b*).

Rigidly imposing a policy preventing council tenants' transferring home if in rent arrears resulted in a fettering of discretion and an 'appalling catalogue of neglect' by the local authority which was both welfare authority and landlord. This was because the policy was imposed on a family with a severely disabled son with exceptional needs; the local ombudsman recommended £20,000 compensation (*Bristol CC 1998*).

Although judicial review cases are more difficult to win against the NHS, nevertheless even it should avoid fettering its discretion. It was found by the Court of Appeal to be doing so when a health authority effectively operated a blanket prohibition on gender reassignment surgery (*R v North West Lancashire Health Authority, ex p G,A,D*).

A reassurance to penurious local authorities is that the principle that they should not fetter their discretion will, by its very nature not open 'floodgates', because it is precisely about making exceptions. On the other hand, because of the widespread nature of rigid policies in community care, it is a principle that can often be employed to challenge local authority decisions and to invalidate them.

Thus, the principle of not fettering discretion should not be treated lightly. Furthermore, not only have the courts held that it applies to the application of policies where a statutory duty exists, but also even where only a statutory power exists (*British Oxygen v Board of Trade*). For instance, in one case, a policy never to award discretionary housing grants would have amounted to a fettering of discretion, if this had indeed been the policy (*R v Bristol CC, ex p Bailey*).

## 4.2.3 TAKING ACCOUNT OF RELEVANT FACTORS AND UNREASONABLENESS

In the context, for example, of community care assessment, the courts have on a number of occasions scrutinised the decision-making process in order to ensure that all relevant factors have been taken account of.

Relevant factors identified as part of a lawful assessment have included, for instance, psychological issues (*R v Avon CC, ex p M*), cultural and language issues (*R(Khana) v Southwark LBC*), medical factors (*R v Birmingham CC, ex p Killigrew*), people's preferences (*R v North Yorkshire CC, ex p Hargreaves*), a background of domestic violence (*R v Oxfordshire CC, ex p Khan*), and health and safety of staff (*R v Cornwall CC, ex p Goldsack; R(AandB) v East Sussex CC (no.2)*).

### 4.2.3.1 Relevant factors: giving them weight

Traditionally, the courts have often looked only to see that all the relevant factors were taken account of, and not expressed a view about how much weight should have been placed on any particular factor. They would normally have only interfered if, despite all relevant factors being taken account of (and irrelevant factors having been disregarded), the decision was so unreasonable that no reasonable authority could possibly have come to it (*Associated Provincial Picture Houses v Wednesbury Corporation*). Another way of putting such unreasonableness has been to describe it as irrational (*Council of Civil Service Unions v Minister of State for the Civil Service*) or a taking leave of senses (*R v Secretary of State for the Environment, ex p Nottinghamshire CC*).

However, on occasion, especially where human rights are concerned, the courts may employ what they refer to as heightened scrutiny or greater interference (*R(Daly) v Secretary of State for the Home Department*); in which case they may come much closer to considering the merits of a decision, in terms of considering the weighting given to particular factors and whether a correct balance between competing factors has been struck (*R(A&B) v East Sussex CC (no.2)*: dispute about the manual handling and human rights of two people with profound and physical disabilities). When the courts interfere in this way, they sometimes explain it in terms of a principle known as proportionality. This is used to question whether the decision maker has maintained a sense of proportion and balance when weighing up competing factors.

## 4.2.4 ILLEGALITY: BREACH OF DUTY AND BLATANT CONTRAVENTION OF LEGISLATION

Sometimes local authorities explicitly breach duties that are clearly set out in legislation. For example, a failure as a matter of policy to consider whether to provide for a person's social, recreational and leisure needs undermined the direct reference to such matters in s.2 of the Chronically Sick and Disabled Persons Act 1970 (*R v North Yorkshire CC, ex p Hargreaves*). Likewise, under the same Act, the failure to consider assistance with holidays, which had not been arranged by the local authority, was unlawful. This was because the 1970 Act explicitly refers to holidays 'otherwise arranged' (*R v Ealing LBC, ex p Leaman*).

## 4.2.5 LEGITIMATE EXPECTATIONS

The courts sometimes consider whether people's legitimate expectations have been properly observed and respected. Such expectations relate sometimes to a right to be consulted before a service is changed or withdrawn; and sometimes to a right actually to receive, or to continue to receive, a service. The courts might consider that the demands of fairness are higher when an authority intends to remove an existing benefit, rather than in the case of a 'bare application for a future benefit' (*R v Devon CC, ex p Baker*).

**Breaking an explicit promise of a home for life.** A health authority made an explicit oral promise to a group of severely disabled people that if they moved into a specialist NHS unit it would be a home for life for them. Some years later it proposed to close the unit. The Court of Appeal found that the breach of this explicit promise was not justified by some overriding public interest; that it constituted an abuse of power by a public body; and that it was a breach of article 8 of the European Convention on Human Rights (*R v North and East Devon HA, ex p Coughlan*).

The consultation in issue might sometimes be with a voluntary organisation rather than individual service users. Thus, when a local authority decided to withdraw funding from such an organisation, without informing it about the criteria (based on 'fair access to care guidance': see 6.11) that it was using to take the decision, the court found the decision to be unfair and unlawful (*R(Capenhurst) v Leicester CC*).

## 4.2.6 GIVING REASONS

For the most part in community care legislation, there is no explicit duty to give reasons; and where there is no statutory obligation, a common law duty cannot be assumed in every context (*R v Secretary of State for the Home Department, ex p Doody*). However, the courts may still effectively demand reasons if only as evidence that a local authority has reached a lawful decision concerning a person's needs and how they might be met. If, as already pointed out above, the courts are often exploring not what the final decision has been, but how it has been reached, they will often expect to find an explanation. An absence of such explanation may raise the suspicion of unlawfulness (see 6.13).

Indeed, in judicial review, the courts are generally more interested in how a decision has been reached, rather than in what that decision is. A simple analogy would be with the school teacher of mathematics who points out that most marks will be scored for showing the 'working out', rather than for the precise answer itself. An absence of reasoning begins to equate to an absence of working out. For instance, the Court of Appeal seriously criticised a local authority because 'judicial review is about process; and in my judgement the process here has been manifestly defective'. This was where the decision to place a woman in a nursing home had been taken without considering critically important factors or providing proper reasons (*R(Goldsmith) v Wandsworth LBC*: see 3.9.1 for details).

## 4.2.7 PUBLIC BODIES

Judicial review applies only to what the courts deem to be public bodies. In the context of care home closures, they have ruled that independent care home providers are not subject to judicial review. It therefore follows that a local authority is not subject to judicial review on account of a care home's actions over which the local authority has no control (*R v Servite Houses, ex p Goldsmith; R(Heather) v Leonard Cheshire Foundation*).

Nevertheless in one of the home closure cases, the court did consider, hypothetically, what the position would be in the case of domiciliary care providers. It noted that s.30 of the National Assistance Act 1948, which gives local authorities the power to contract with independent domiciliary care providers, refers to such providers as 'agents'. This might have suggested that judicial review would lie against the local authority for the actions of its agent (*R v Servite Houses, ex p Goldsmith*).

## 4.3 OMBUDSMEN: PRINCIPLES OF GOOD ADMINISTRATION

The local government ombudsmen and the health service ombudsman are independent, created by Act of Parliament (Local Government Act 1974 and Health Service Commissioners Act 1993). Both types of ombudsman look for maladministration causing injustice; the health service ombudsman in addition can explicitly look for breach of duty or failure in service. The health service ombudsman is permitted to question clinical judgements of staff; the local government ombudsmen are barred from questioning professional judgements directly.

The scope of ombudsman investigations covers the legal principles applied by the courts in judicial review cases, but also other practical matters that tend to be administrative rather than legal in nature. This greater scope is significant, because people might in practice suffer just as much detriment through poor administrative practice (e.g. lost letter, poor communication, lack of information) as through an explicit breach of legal duty.

The ombudsmen therefore operate far more freely than the courts and investigate in detail many different types of act and decision, exploring both high (legal or quasi-legal issues) and low ('nitty gritty' everyday matters). Procedural issues concerning the ombudsmen are covered in Chapter 5.

### 4.3.1 LOCAL GOVERNMENT OMBUDSMEN

The local government ombudsmen (there are three in England) investigate maladministration causing injustice (Local Government Act 1974). Findings of maladministration might relate, for instance, to breach of duty, fettering of discretion (blanket policies), poor screening of referrals, failure to prioritise referrals, double-queuing on waiting lists, excessive waiting times for assessment or service provision, unjustified queue jumping, lack of communication and information giving in respect of service users, lack of communication between different departments in the same local authority, lack of communication between different local authorities, withholding information about legal entitlement, absence of policy, and failure of staff to follow a policy (or even to know about it).

Maladministration may or may not also potentially constitute unlawfulness (it is not for the ombudsman to state definitively), depending on its particular form and the context. But for service users, administrative failings can be just as detrimental as unlawful actions. Thus the following 42 axioms of good administration published by the local government ombudsmen are a useful guide to what decision making in community care should look like (CLAE 1993):

| | |
|---|---|
| **1 (law)** | Understand what the law requires the council to do and fulfil those requirements. |
| **2 (law)** | Ensure that all staff working in any particular area of activity understand and fulfil the legal requirements relevant to that area of activity. |

| | |
|---|---|
| **3 (policies)** | Formulate policies which set out the general approach for each area of activity and the criteria which are used in decision making. |
| **4 (criteria)** | Ensure that criteria are clear and relevant, and can be applied objectively so that decisions are not made on an inconsistent, ad hoc or subjective basis. |
| **5 (communication)** | Communicate relevant policies and rules to customers. |
| **6 (policies)** | Ensure that all staff understand council policies relevant to their area of work. |
| **7 (policies)** | Ensure that the council does what its own policy or established practice requires. |
| **8 (exceptions)** | Consider any special circumstances of each case as well as the council's policy so as to determine whether there are exceptional reasons which justify a decision more favourable to the individual customer than what the policy would normally provide. |
| **9 (consistency)** | Ensure that decisions are not taken which are inconsistent with established policies of the council or other relevant plans or guidelines unless there are adequate and relevant grounds for doing so. |
| **10 (guidance)** | Have regard to relevant codes of practice and government circulars; and follow the advice contained within them unless there are justifiable reasons not to do so. |
| **11 (relevance)** | Ensure that irrelevant considerations are not taken into account in making a decision. |
| **12 (relevance)** | Ensure that adequate consideration is given to all relevant and material factors in making a decision. |
| **13 (views)** | Give proper consideration to the views of relevant parties in making a decision. |
| **14 (purpose)** | Use the powers of the council for their proper purpose and not in order to achieve some other purpose. |
| **15 (hastiness)** | Ensure that decisions are not made or action taken prematurely. |
| **16 (reasons)** | Give reasons for an adverse decision and record them in writing for the customer concerned. |
| **17 (time)** | Ensure that any necessary decisions or actions are taken as circumstances require and within a reasonable time. |
| **18 (delegation)** | If a decision is being taken under delegated powers, ensure that there is proper and sufficient authority for this to be done and that use of delegated powers is appropriate to the circumstances. |

| | |
|---|---|
| **19 (investigation)** | Carry out a sufficient investigation so as to establish all the relevant and material facts. |
| **20 (advice)** | Seek appropriate specialist advice as necessary. |
| **21 (consultation)** | Consult any individuals or organisations who might reasonably consider that they would be adversely and significantly affected by a proposed action. |
| **22 (errors)** | Detect major errors which materially affect an issue under consideration. |
| **23 (options)** | Give adequate consideration to the reasonable courses of action which are open to the council in any particular circumstance. |
| **24 (reports)** | Ensure that a committee is provided with a report when circumstances require and that the report is materially accurate and covers all the relevant points. |
| **25 (correctness)** | Ensure that the correct action is taken both to implement decisions when they are made and generally in the conduct of the council's business. |
| **26 (systems)** | Have adequate systems and written procedures for staff to follow in dealing with particular areas of activity. |
| **27 (liaison)** | Have a system for ensuring proper liaison and cooperation between different departments, different sections of a department or different areas in the authority. |
| **28 (records)** | Compile and maintain adequate records. |
| **29 (monitoring)** | Monitor progress and carry out regular appraisals of how an issue or problem is being dealt with. |
| **30 (problems)** | Seek to resolve difficulties or disagreements by negotiations in the first instance but take formal action when it is clear that informal attempts at resolution are not working. |
| **31 (misleading)** | Avoid making misleading or inaccurate statements to customers. |
| **32 (responsibility)** | Formulate undertakings with care and discharge any responsibilities towards customers which arise from them. |
| **33 (enquiries)** | Reply to letters and enquiries and do so courteously and within a reasonable period; and have a system for ensuring that appropriate action is taken on every occasion. |
| **34 (information)** | Keep customers regularly informed about the progress of matters which are of concern to them. |
| **35 (information)** | Provide adequate and accurate information, explanation and advice to customers on issues of concern to them. |

| 36 (fairness) | Ensure that the body taking a decision on a formal appeal from a dissatisfied customer does not include any person previously concerned with the case or who has a personal or otherwise significant interest in the outcome. |
| 37 (discrimination) | Avoid unfair discrimination against particular individuals, groups or sections of society. |
| 38 (balance) | Maintain a proper balance between any adverse effects which a decision may have on the rights or interests of individuals and the purpose which the council is pursuing. |
| 39 (dispute) | Where an individual is adversely affected by a decision, or the decision is otherwise one which the individual potentially might wish to challenge, inform him or her of any right of appeal or avenues for pursuing a complaint. |
| 40 (interests) | Ensure that members and officers are fully aware of the requirements for declaring an interest where appropriate and the reasons for doing so. |
| 41 (complaints) | Have a simple, well-publicised complaints system and operate it effectively. |
| 42 (remedies) | Take remedial action when faults are identified, both to provide redress for the individuals concerned and to prevent recurrence of the problem in the future. |

## 4.3.2 HEALTH SERVICE OMBUDSMAN

The health service ombudsman investigates complaints about injustice or hardship sustained as a result of a failure in a service, failure to provide a service for which there is a duty to provide, or maladministration. Since April 1996, the health service ombudsman has also been able to question the merits of professional decision making by NHS staff (Health Service Commissioners Act 1993).

Procedural matters concerning the health service ombudsman are covered in Chapter 5. Otherwise, reference to health service ombudsman investigations is made particularly in Chapter 16 – including those that have so effectively exposed the serious shortcomings in both government policy on, and in the delivery of, continuing NHS health care services.

### 4.3.2.1 Maladministration

Maladministration has been described by the health service ombudsman's office as covering, non-exhaustively (HSC 1996a, p.13):

- bias, neglect, inattention, delay, incompetence, ineptitude, perversity, turpitude, arbitrariness
- rudeness, unwillingness to treat the complainant as a person with rights; refusal to answer reasonable questions; neglecting to inform a complainant on request of his or her rights or entitlement; knowingly giving advice which is misleading or inadequate

- ignoring valid advice or overruling considerations which would produce an uncomfortable result for the over-ruler; offering no redress or manifestly disproportionate redress; showing bias whether because of colour, sex or any other grounds; omission to notify those who thereby lose a right of appeal; refusal to inform adequately of the right of appeal
- faulty procedures; failure by management to monitor compliance with adequate procedures; cavalier disregard of guidance which is intended to be followed in the interest of equitable treatment of those who use a service; partiality; and failure to mitigate the effects of rigid adherence to the letter of the law where that produces manifestly inequitable treatment.

Thus, in common with the local government ombudsman, the health service ombudsman is able to investigate a much wider range of issues than the law courts.

CHAPTER 5

# Remedies

## KEY POINTS

This chapter covers what are often called remedies – in other words, courses of action that people can follow when trying to pursue and resolve disputes. These range from the informal at one extreme to, at the other, judicial review proceedings as well as actions for negligence – that might sometimes be argued up the judicial ladder to the House of Lords and beyond to the European Court of Human Rights (e.g. *Z v United Kingdom*: a negligence case involving social services and children; *Pretty v United Kingdom*: a case about the lawfulness of assisted suicide).

The question of remedy is significant, because apparent obligations in legislation and guidance in themselves arguably mean little, if it is unclear when, if at all, they are enforceable. The following sections briefly summarise these remedies, and include some observations on their relative advantages and disadvantages.

Note: **Wales, Scotland, Northern Ireland**. This chapter applies generally to Wales. (The Health and Social Care (Community Health and Standards) Act 2003 applies in principle to Wales in respect of new social services and complaints procedures, although when regulations will be passed bringing them into force is a matter for the National Assembly for Wales.)

The chapter applies in broad principle to Scotland, but with some particular differences. For instance, the social services complaints procedure comes under s.5B of the Social Work (Scotland) Act 1968 (and guidance: SWSG 5/96); the Secretary of State can issue directions to local authorities under s.5 of the 1968 Act; and order an inquiry into a local authority under s.6A of the 1968 Act. And in Scotland, 'leave' or permission to bring a judicial review case is not required. The law of negligence comes under the Scottish law of delict (as opposed to the law of tort elsewhere in the United Kingdom).

The chapter applies in broad principle also to Northern Ireland, but again with some specific distinctions. For example, social services complaints procedures come under the Social Services Complaints Procedures Directions (Northern Ireland) 1996 and the Miscellaneous Complaints Procedures (Northern Ireland) 1996 (and guidance: DHSS 1991a). Default powers of intervention, to be exercised by the Northern Ireland Department of Health, Social Services and Public Safety (DHSSPS), come under a.53 of the Health and Personal Social Services (Northern Ireland) Order 1972.

The functions of the ombudsmen in Wales, Scotland and Northern Ireland have already been outlined in the equivalent note to Chapter 4.

## 5.1 INFORMAL REMEDIES

Informal channels for seeking a remedy – for instance, provision or restoration of a service – might include gently querying the actions and decisions of local authority staff without pursuing a formal 'complaint'. Some disputes might be defused earlier still, because well-informed service users or their advisers nip in the bud potentially dubious decisions. For instance, local authority staff can sometimes be quite disconcerted when a service user or a representative 'waves' legislation or guidance from the Department of Health in front of them and points out that they are following an ostensibly unlawful policy. Alternatively, well-informed staff and managers might know that they are on firm legal ground and demonstrate this from the outset; in which case a challenge might simply not be worth making.

Resolving disputes informally is often the preferable option; generally speaking neither service user nor authority wishes to incur the time, trouble, stress and expense of engaging in a formal dispute. The possible souring of future relations between authority and user might also be a significant consideration in practice.

## 5.2 COUNCILLORS, MPS, NEWSPAPERS

Complaining to a local councillor or MP or contacting the local newspaper or radio will in some circumstances be effective. For instance, MPs and local councillors might take up the cases of constituents not on compelling legal grounds but simply for benevolent, compassionate or local political reasons.

The importance and potential effectiveness of utilising all available channels, legal or otherwise, to challenge decisions felt to be unfair or clearly detrimental is demonstrated by the following example. There is of course no guarantee at all that concerted opposition to decisions taken by central government, local authorities or the NHS will succeed (indeed it often fails), but at least the chances of success are increased in proportion to the strength and breadth of that opposition. The following example serves perhaps to illustrate this.

**Threatened closure, and reprieve for, community hospital**. In late October 2004, an NHS (acute hospital) Trust announced that it might have to close down rapidly a community hospital some years in advance of its planned closure (by which time a new health centre would have been built). This was because it had commissioned a fire report from an independent company, the findings of which might, it stated, force imminent closure. The hospital provides inpatient services (68 beds, including rehabilitation but generally not long-stay beds) and outpatient services (e.g a falls prevention clinic) for elderly people. The announcement caused considerable distress to both patients and staff.

*Safety or financial and strategic reasons?* The Trust argued that its sole concern was safety in relation to the fire risk; the local community believed the reason to be strategic and financial. This belief was fuelled by the proposed speed of events – and the apparent undue emphasis by the Trust on closure even before the final fire report had been delivered and before the Fire Service had been finally consulted as to its recommendations (in the light of the new fire report). It seemed also to the local community that both the estimated costs of works related to the fire risk, and extreme anxiety about legal liability, were either being exaggerated or were at the very least premature. The local community was also fully aware that both the NHS Trust and the local NHS primary care trust (which was also involved) were both in significant financial deficit.

*True cost of works*. By the end of November, when the decision was due to be taken by the Trust Board, the Trust was referring to resources and letting it be known that it would cost millions of pounds to make the hospital safe and involve severe disruption. It was also suggesting that its own

Trust Board would be currently liable to manslaughter charges. In fact, once the Fire Service had been consulted in late November, it became clear that the rolling programme of works required would cost no more than some £250,000-£300,000, in order to keep the hospital open for the next three years until the arrival of the new health centre.

At the end of November, the decision was deferred for a fortnight; within a further fortnight, the Trust stated that the community hospital would remain open after all (for a general chronology, see *Suffolk Free Press*, 16 December 2004).

The labyrinthine nature of NHS decision making in such cases (which in this instance appeared to involve not just the NHS Trust but also, in the background, the local NHS primary care trust and the strategic health authority) often makes it difficult to say with certainty what is going on 'behind the scenes'. It may also be that in such circumstances poor communication fuels local hostility and at least a degree of misunderstanding.

However, what seems not to be in doubt in such cases is that the speed with which opposition is formed, together with its breadth and determination, will play a full part in making sure that such proposals and decisions come under close scrutiny. In this particular instance, it was such scrutiny that resulted in the health and safety risk and related expenditure (the ostensible reasons given for closure) being put in a fuller and proper perspective.

Such episodes reveal the importance of a local community 'pulling together'. Almost certainly this contributed decisively in this instance to an apparently significant reversal of approach by the Trust (and behind the scenes, by the strategic health authority and NHS primary care trust). The various ingredients in the local community's opposition included, or involved, staff at the hospital, general medical practitioners, the general public, a public meeting, petition to the Prime Minister, legal threat of a judicial review, a Parliamentary question, mayors, councillors (town, district, county), members of Parliament, trade unions etc. Of key importance also was the interest and coverage of the local newspapers, as well as local BBC radio and television. The newspaper headlines (they are samples only: there were many more), listed chronologically below, reveal the breadth of opposition and a flavour of events:

**Possible closure: 'Hospital in fire threat'.** The NHS Trust announces possible, imminent closure of the hospital in the light of an independent fire report it has commissioned (*Suffolk Free Press*, 28 October 2004).

**Hospital staff: `Hands off our hospital'.** Staff react immediately and defiantly to the announcement of possible closure. Elderly, disabled, sick and vulnerable patients in the hospital are reported to be distressed and 'in tears' (*Suffolk Free Press*, 4 November 2004).

**Local newspaper launches campaign.** The *East Anglian Daily Times* launches a 'hands off our hospital' campaign following the announcement on 27th October that the hospital might have to close (*East Anglian Daily Times*, 9 November 2004).

**Mayors: 'Leaders oppose closure: Sudbury Mayor fears serious implications for health care'.** Two local mayors voice their opposition (*East Anglian Daily Times*, 9 November 2004).

**Hospital employees: 'Staff hit out over threat to hospital'**. Staff at the hospital speak out publicly about their concerns (*East Anglian Daily Times*, 10 November 2004).

**General public: 'Hospital closure would be a true horror story'**. The local newspapers are deluged with well-reasoned letters of concern (e.g. *East Anglian Daily Times*, 11 November 2004, letters page, Andy Janes).

**Parish councillors: 'Fire risk could be part of a hidden agenda'**. A parish councillor voices concern that the Trust may be playing the 'health and safety card' to cloak a hidden agenda (*East Anglian Daily Times*, 11 November 2004, letters page, Frances Jackson).

**Town Council public meeting: 'Come and face us'**. The Town Council calls a public meeting and challenges the NHS Trust, the NHS primary care trust and the strategic health authority to attend (*Suffolk Free Press*, 11 November 2004).

**Peer: '...backs campaign to save hospital'**. A local life peer (and lawyer) demands proper consultation at the very least and that otherwise the town 'should rise up' (*East Anglian Daily Times*, 15 November 2004).

**General practitioners: 'Doctors in fight to save hospital: Walnuttree closure would be huge blow to people'**. General practitioners express their opposition to closure (*East Anglian Daily Times*, 16 November 2004).

**Trade unions: 'Union calls for fire report's public viewing: challenge over hospital's risk truth'**. The trade union Unison demands disclosure of the fire report the NHS Trust has commissioned (*East Anglian Daily Times*, 17 November 2004). Its claim, that the works required to manage the risk would probably be only some £250,000 over three years, turns out to be correct (see below).

**NHS labyrinth: '10-week deadline to reduce £23 million deficit'**. It becomes clear that the hospital closure proposed by the NHS Trust is entangled in a much wider picture involving also the local NHS primary care trust and the strategic health authority – and a crisis in NHS finance right across Suffolk (*East Anglian Daily Times*, 18 November 2004).

**Member of Parliament: 'Hospital should be kept open'**. The MP for South Suffolk supports opposition to closure (*Sudbury Mercury*, 19 November 2004).

**Legal challenge by hospital patients: 'Close the hospital and we'll take you to court'**. A leading law firm is instructed by hospital patients to launch judicial review proceedings against the NHS Trust in case of a decision to close the hospital. This is on the grounds that the Trust would be in breach of its duties to consult under ss.7 and 11 of the Health and Social Care Act 2001 (see 16.5.8), and that the fire risk was not such as to warrant sudden closure (*East Anglian Daily Times*, 23 November 2004).

**Prime Minister: 'Protestors take Walnuttree fight to No. 10'**. A 10,000 signature petition (gathered in a matter of some two weeks) is delivered to Downing Street by coach (*Suffolk Free Press*, 25 November 2004).

**Public meeting: 'Hundreds at crisis meeting'**. The town's largest public meeting for many years runs for over three hours, during which time representatives from the NHS Trust, the NHS primary care trust and the strategic health authority are bombarded with questions (*Suffolk Free Press*, 25 November 2004).

**Health and safety fears fuelled: 'Death trap'**. The Trust's director of facilities states that expenditure of £2 million would be required to make the hospital safe and that, even at present, the Trust Board would be prosecuted for manslaughter were a fire and loss of life to occur (*Sudbury Mercury*, 26

November 2004). (This was arguably a rash thing to say; hitherto the Trust had apparently always complied with Fire Service recommendations and thus behaved reasonably. Reasonableness precludes findings of manslaughter. This statement to the Press was therefore suggestive, to the local community, of an 'overplaying' of the health and safety argument.)

**County councillor: 'Council: fire report wrong'; 'Work on threatened hospital 'overstated'.** A senior county councillor (and prospective Parliamentary candidate) raises concerns that the fire report commissioned by the NHS Trust had overplayed the amount of work required to bring the hospital up to standard, and that it had cited unrealistic figures (£3 million). Having herself spoken to the Fire Service, she claims that the work could be carried out at a much lower cost (*Sudbury Mercury*, 3 December 2004; *East Anglian Daily Times*, 29 November 2004).

**Member of Parliament: 'Walnuttree Hospital saga in absurd twist'.** Having begun to empty beds even before any decision to close had formally been taken, the Trust suddenly refills them with new admissions – because the main acute hospital is on 'red alert' due to a shortage of beds. This is despite the Trust having stated the previous week that the hospital was so dangerous that the Trust Board would be prosecuted for manslaughter (see above). The MP for West Suffolk describes the whole situation as 'absurd' (*East Anglian Daily Times*, 30 November 2004).

**Parliamentary question: 'Walnuttree Hospital (risk assessments)'.** A local MP asks the Secretary of State for Health about the most recent fire risk assessments (Tim Yeo: *House of Commons Written Answers*, 6/12/2004, c.362W).

**'Back from the brink'; 'Saved: Walnuttree Hospital will stay open after campaign victory'.** A 'dramatic twist' is reported as the NHS Trust states that it is, after all, prepared to spend some £300,000 in keeping the hospital open for the next three years until the new health centre is ready (*Suffolk Free Press*, 16 December 2004; *East Anglian Daily Times*, 11 December 2004).

**County councillor: 'MP's inquiry demand'.** A senior county councillor (and prospective Parliamentary candidate) expresses grave concern about how the NHS Trust handled the whole affair, including poor communication with staff, an unbalanced approach to the presentation of facts concerning the fire risk, unbalanced information presented to the Trust Board, and an inadequate explanation given to the Board about the law relating to manslaughter and health and safety (*Sudbury Mercury*, 31 December 2004).

## 5.3 LOCAL AUTHORITY MONITORING OFFICERS

Local authority monitoring officers (each authority is obliged to have one) have a duty to report on actual or potential contraventions by the local authority of legislation or codes of practice made under legislation, and on any actual or possible maladministration or injustice caused by the authority. Any proposal, act, omission or actual contravention might be by the authority, any committee, subcommittee or officer of the authority, or by any joint committee, on which the authority is represented (Local Government and Housing Act 1989, s.5).

## 5.4 DISTRICT AUDITORS

Indirect redress might be had by complaining to the district auditor, who might be concerned at unlawful or wasteful expenditure.

**Day services, complaint to district auditor.** The mother of an autistic man complained to the local government ombudsman and the district auditor that the council was paying an independent provider for a level of day services which, she claimed, her son was not receiving. The complaint led to the council stating that it would investigate and attempt to recover some money from the provider (*Liverpool CC 1998a*).

## 5.5 LOCAL AUTHORITY SOCIAL SERVICES COMPLAINTS PROCEDURE

A new social services complaints procedure is due to be implemented in 2005 under the Health and Social Care (Community Health and Standards) Act 2003 (s.114). However, at the time of writing (December 2004), the soon to be 'old' system is still operational; furthermore, the many ombudsman investigations into its operation offer insight into characteristics common to both existing old and proposed new system, and into some of the pitfalls which the new system is, it is hoped, designed to avoid. Therefore, references to the existing system have been left within the text below.

As far as the new procedure is concerned, the 2003 Act gives the Secretary of State the power to make regulations concerning the handling of complaints by the local authority, by the Commission for Social Care Inspection, an independent panel or by anybody else. Regulations may also be made concerning referral of complaints to the local government ombudsman.

In summary, two consultation documents (CSCI 2004a and DH 2004g) cover the proposals thus:

- **Complainants**: a complaint may be made by any person to whom the local authority has a power or duty to provide services, whose need (or possible need) has come to authority's attention – or the complaint may be made by a representative.
- **Time limits**: a complaint should be made within 12 months; after that the local authority need not consider it although it has a discretion to do so.
- **Advocacy**: the local authority will need to consider advocacy where appropriate.
- **Local authority investigation**: local social services authorities will investigate complaints in the first place.
- **Local resolution and formal investigation**: local (i.e. informal) resolution is limited to ten days; after that time the complaint moves to a formal investigation stage; normally this investigation should be completed and a response made within 25 days of the complaint being made, although this can be extended in some circumstances.
- **Review function of Commission for Social Care Inspection**: a second stage review function will be carried out not by local authorities as at present, but by a Complaints Review Service (CRS) operated by the Commission for Social Care Inspection (CSCI):
  - The CRS will decide whether to take no further action, refer back to the relevant local authority, or itself to conduct a review.
  - A CRS review may take the form of an independent complaints panel, an investigation by the CRS or a referral to the local government ombudsman.

- ◦ The independent complaints panels will operate to national standards.
- ◦ Timescales will be set out in regulations.

**Note**. At present, complaints procedures for children come under ss.24 and 26 of the Children Act 1989. However, like adult complaints procedures, these are due to be overhauled; these sections of the 1989 Act have been amended by the Adoption and Children Act 2002. In addition, the Health and Social (Community Health and Standards) Act 2003 gives powers to the Commission for Social Care Inspection parallel with those it will have for adults. The changes have been outlined in a consultation document (DES 2004).

## 5.5.1 GENERAL POINTS ABOUT THE EXISTING COMPLAINTS SYSTEM

The local authority social services complaints procedure is probably – in principle at least – suitable for most grievances. Given the statutory time limits applying to formal complaints, the procedure is not meant to be protracted. There is an appeal procedure involving review panels, which have wide powers to examine not only whether an authority has adhered to policy and procedure, but also the factual decisions that it reached. As such the existence of a statutory complaints procedure in community care appears useful. However, there are some provisos:

- The local ombudsmen have repeatedly found that complaints procedures are in practice too often ineffective and long winded.
- The law courts have pointed out that the complaints procedure is unsuitable for resolving matters of law.
- If over 50 per cent of complaints concern the rationing of resources (Simons 1995, p.40), then arguably the complaints procedure will be impotent in effecting remedies. This will be especially the case if local authorities are utilising lawful loopholes, rather than taking unlawful shortcuts, in order to limit expenditure.
- It is therefore something of an irony that significant political energy and resources are put into complaints procedures, in order to field a potentially large volume of complaints that arguably the complaints procedure is not equipped to resolve. In which case, the complaints procedure runs the risk – up to a point – of being an irrelevant diversion. Clearly, people would rather have good services than a good complaints system.
- Overworked staff can easily become demoralised if they are subject to a continual barrage of complaints; half a day spent recording a complaint made by a relative that morning means they are not seeing other service users. It is at least questionable where the balance of the greater public good lies – in terms of how much time should be spent on complaints by scarce professional staff such as social workers and therapists, when they could be assessing and providing services for other people.
- Another potential weakness in the system is that (a) the independent person required to sit on a review panel can be outvoted by other (council) officers on the panel; and (b) local authorities are not obliged to follow a panel's recommendations (though they should have good reasons for not doing so).
- Lastly, and more simply perhaps, a drawback of reliance on complaints procedures to ensure a good quality of decision making is simply that (a) many service users do not want to be in the spotlight or upset those providing services; and (b) it is stressful,

exhausting and demanding to complain, unless the complainant is a 'persevering, single-handed warrior, who thrives on skirmishes with public authorities'. These are not the characteristics of vulnerable, 'inarticulate and meek' people, in the words of one social services officer (Coombs 1998, p.48).

## 5.5.2 SUMMARY OF EXISTING SOCIAL SERVICES COMPLAINTS PROCEDURE

Local authorities have a duty to establish, operate and publicise complaints procedures in relation to social services functions under the Local Authority Social Services Act 1970 (s.7B), regulations (SI 1990/2244) and directions (DH 1990a). A person (or a representative) can complain only if the person is a 'qualifying' individual – that is, the local authority must, or could, provide (or secure the provision of) services for the person. The local authority must also be aware of the person's need, or possible need, for services (s.7B). The complaints procedure consists of three main stages: informal, formal and review.

## 5.5.3 INFORMAL AND FORMAL STAGES (EXISTING PROCEDURE)

Local authorities must try to solve the matter informally. If this is not possible, they must send or give the person an explanation of the procedure and ask the person to submit formally the complaint in writing. The local authority must then respond to the complaint within 28 days or alternatively explain why this is not possible – and then, in any case, respond within three months (DH 1990a).

Guidance states that the person can request to go directly to the formal stage, by missing out the informal (DH 1990, para 6.30; SSI 1991, para 4.9). The time limits apply only to formal complaints; thus there is scope for delay until a complaint is acknowledged to be formal.

**Stalling a complaint at the informal stage.** When a response took 219 days, instead of 28 days, the local ombudsman identified the fact that an understandable wish to solve a complaint informally does not mean that the informal stage should go on longer than necessary; otherwise complaints can simply stall altogether (*Sheffield CC 2002*).

The local authority must send its decision in writing to the complainant, normally (if different) the person on whose behalf the complaint has been made, and anybody else it thinks has sufficient interest (DH 1990a). An obligation to give reasons is not explicitly required, although the ombudsman – and possibly the courts – might insist that reasons be given, even if only to make the decision comprehensible and to give the complainant material on which to judge whether to challenge the decision.

Councils often set up an (independent) investigation at the formal stage, a matter that has been commented on by the local ombudsman on a number of occasions:

**Independence of complaints procedure investigations.** Investigations should not only be independent but also seen to be so; for instance in one case the ombudsman had no reason to doubt the 'integrity and professionalism' of the investigating officer; but to the complainants, the officer, who worked within the same directorate of the council involved in the complaint, did not appear to be independent – whilst the ombudsman, too, stated that in fact she may not have been independent (*Manchester CC 1996b*).

In another case (involving a complaint under a non-statutory complaints procedure), the council asked an officer to carry out an initial investigation into the actions of another officer – despite the fact that the two officers were in conflict. As the ombudsman put it, this beggared belief. A highly critical report emerged without the second officer having had the opportunity to put her point of view. Nothing was then done about the complaint until the two officers had left the council; this was 'shocking' to the ombudsman (*Durham CC 1998*).

If an investigation is to be effective, the officer responsible should fully understand her role and have been given guidance and support (*Salford CC 1996*).

## 5.5.4 REVIEW PANELS (EXISTING PROCEDURE)

If the complainant is not satisfied and he or she writes to this effect within 28 days, then the local authority has to appoint a review panel (which must contain an independent person). The panel must meet within 28 days, and then within 24 hours send its written recommendations to the local authority, the complainant, the person on whose behalf the complaint has been made (if appropriate) and anybody else the local authority thinks has sufficient interest. The local authority must then decide what it is going to do and write to the same people as above within 28 days and likewise give reasons. The panel must also make a written record of the reasons for its recommendations (DH 1990a).

**Failure of panel and local authority to give reasons.** A failure of either the panel or the local authority to give reasons meant that the applicant was denied what she was entitled to; the court made a declaration that they should have been supplied (in *R v Cornwall CC, ex p Goldsack*).

Guidance stresses the need for informality at the panel hearing and states that if a complainant is accompanied by a person (who might also speak for the complainant at the meeting), then the person should not be a barrister or a solicitor acting in a professional capacity. The complainant or accompanying person should be given the opportunity to make an oral submission before the authority (DH 1990, chapter 6, annex A). Nevertheless, the courts might in some circumstances state that sometimes professional representation is permissible if, for example, legal complexity is involved or the local authority is legally represented (Gordon and Mackintosh 1996, p.72) – despite what the guidance says.

Conversely, it will scarcely seem fair to complainants if the authority deploys a member of its legal department in the proceedings. Indeed, the local ombudsman included in a finding of maladministration the observation that he found it 'hard to see how a solicitor employed by the Council could be seen as an "unbiased observer" and consider[ed] the way in which he joined at the outset in the in camera deliberations of the Panel to be unwise at the very least' (*Cleveland CC 1993*).

## 5.5.5 SCOPE OF REVIEW PANELS (EXISTING PROCEDURE)

There is sometimes uncertainty about the legitimate scope of the review panel's deliberations. Some panels do consider the actual merits of decisions, while others concentrate only on whether procedures have been followed. An example of the broader approach was reported in one legal case, when the complaints review panel found that the social services department had discharged its functions properly in relation to the complainant's application for services – but went on nevertheless to recommend that the department consider providing precisely those services it had hitherto denied (*R v Wigan MBC, ex p Tammadge*).

Arguably a policy that excludes consideration by review panels of considering the merits of the decision would be an unlawful restriction of a statutory framework that says nothing about not questioning the merits of a decision. The courts frequently refer to the suitability of the complaints procedure, rather than of the courts for investigating disputed facts as opposed to legal issues (e.g. *R v Plymouth CC, ex p Cowl*). In turn, the investigation of facts might then lead to a question of the merits of a decision.

## 5.5.6 REVIEW PANEL MEMBERSHIP (EXISTING PROCEDURE)

The fact that, apart from the independent member of a panel, the other two members of the panel are likely to be from the local authority sometimes gives rise to the claim that the review panel system is unfair, since the latter can dominate, and indeed, overrule the independent person.

However, the courts have held that the social services complaints procedure does not breach article 6 of the European Convention on Human Rights relating to a fair hearing. This is because the fairness of the local authority's reaction to review panel recommendations is subject to judicial review; and taken together, the complaints procedure coupled with the fallback of judicial review comply with the demands of fairness under a.6 (*R(Beeson) v Dorset CC*, Court of Appeal).

## 5.5.7 REVIEW PANEL PROCEDURES (EXISTING PROCEDURE)

The local ombudsman has investigated review panel matters on a number of occasions. Apparently conscious decisions not to offer the option of a review panel are maladministration (*Manchester CC 1996b*), or even gross maladministration, in the judgement of the local ombudsman:

**Gross maladministration and refusal to convene review panel.** Two complaints were made by the father concerning assessment and provision for his son on leaving school; his son had mild learning disabilities, a stress-related condition and was later diagnosed as schizophrenic. The first complaint in September 1995 was about the level of care, the second in October about the care provided in a mental health hostel. The father contacted the local ombudsman in January 1996, who in turn wrote to the council. The director of social services then wrote to the father outlining the services being provided but not referring to the second complaint or to the right to a complaints review panel. The local ombudsman asked the council to respond again and to deal with these matters; the council sent a second letter that covered some of the issues concerning the mental health hostel, but still failed to mention the review panel. The ombudsman asked the council to convene a review panel, pointing out that it appeared to be in breach of its duty.

The father received a letter in February asking him to contact the complaints section. He did so by telephone, saying that he would like his solicitor present at the panel hearing; this conversation was never formally recorded. In March, he received another letter, asking him for a response to the February letter and saying that if no reply was forthcoming by the end of March, it would be assumed that he did not wish to pursue the complaint. The father never received a letter explaining why his complaints could not be dealt with in 28 days and indicating how long they would take; and a review panel was never convened.

The ombudsman found 'gross maladministration' in the handling of the complaint. The time taken was 'entirely unacceptable' (by July 1996, nothing had been resolved). The council should not have been chasing up letters it had already received a response to. It was only because of the ombudsman's involvement that the father was ever informed about his right to have a review panel convened. Furthermore, although the council pointed out, rightly, that a request for a review panel is required in writing, it was 'disingenuous of the council to imply blame on the complainants when it failed to fulfil undertakings to put matters in writing and failed to respond to correspondence' (*Liverpool CC 1997a*).

Basic fairness might be lacking and mean the local ombudsman will find maladministration:

**Procedures at the panel hearing.** Not to give advance notice that it would not allow a hearing impaired complainant to make a tape recording of the panel proceedings was maladministration; as was asking the same complainant to consider at the panel hearing a chronology that he had not been given in advance (*Southwark 2001*).

### 5.5.8 OUTCOME OF REVIEW PANEL RECOMMENDATIONS (EXISTING PROCEDURE)

Even in case of unanimity within the review panel, the directions (DH 1990a) do not oblige local authorities to follow panel recommendations and in practice they sometimes decline.

The courts have with varying force suggested that local authorities should follow the recommendations. In *R v Avon CC, ex p M*, the judge stated that it was unlawful to disregard the review panel's findings without a good reason, given the weight and 'one way' nature of the evidence that had informed the panel's decision. In *R v Islington LBC, ex p Rixon*, the court stated that the greater the departure from the review panel's recommendations, the greater the need for 'cogent articulated reasons'.

Slightly milder was the statement of the court in *R v North Yorkshire CC, ex p Hargreaves* that there was no general rule that local authorities must follow the recommendations of a review panel – but that in some circumstances it might be unlawful not to do so without a good reason.

The local ombudsman has found maladministration where the local authority failed to produce, as requested by the review panel, a detailed report within a year (*Hounslow LBC 1995*). If the complaint is about a decision taken by the director of social services, the ombudsman has stated that the recommendations of the review panel should be referred to someone else, such as the chief executive of the authority or the social services committee (*Carmarthenshire CC 1999*).

There have been many other local ombudsman investigations relating to a review panel's recommendations or to the local authority's response to those recommendations – in terms of compliance, non-compliance or clarity of response. For example:

**Inadequate review panel outcomes.** A review panel's findings might be flawed on their face and lead to findings of maladministration by the local ombudsman – for instance, because of deficient evidence considered by the panel or apparent misinterpretation of a coroner's report (*Cleveland CC 1993*). Or a panel might fail to evaluate a claim for compensation and to make adequate recommendations back to the council despite being ideally placed to do so (*Warwickshire CC 1997*).

**Local authority responses to review panel.** It was not maladministration when the local authority refused to follow a panel's recommendation about arranging a residential placement for a man with learning disabilities. This was because no assessment of the man's needs had been carried out, although this failure to assess was itself maladministration in its own right (*Kent CC 1998*).

When a local authority was prepared to follow its review panel's recommendations for compensation after poor advice about state benefits had been given, the local ombudsman nevertheless criticised the panel for taking into account an immaterial factor when coming to its decision about the level of compensation. The panel had been prepared to recommend only £750 instead of the £5000 the woman had lost, on the grounds that it should not reimburse money that it was not responsible for issuing; the ombudsman held that this was an irrelevant consideration (*East Sussex CC 1995a*).

When a panel recommended in December 1996 that the local authority carry out an urgent assessment of a woman with learning disabilities, it took seven months for the authority to allocate the task, a further seven months to gather the relevant information, and a further three months to complete the reassessment. It was not sent to the woman's parents for a further two months. Services were not in place until December 1998. This was a year longer than it should have taken. The local ombudsman found maladministration and recommended compensation, including the cost of two hours of day care per week for 50 weeks (*Oxfordshire CC 1999*).

In any event the local authority's response to a complaint and what it proposed to do should be clear. Thus the local ombudsman criticised the fact that the complaints officer first wrote to the complainants stating that the reviewer's conclusions had been accepted; but then a second letter from the chief executive expressed disagreement with some of those conclusions (*Bury MBC 2004*).

## 5.5.9 PUBLICITY (EXISTING PROCEDURE)

Local authorities have a duty to publicise their complaints procedure in a way 'they consider appropriate'. The basic duty, but not the way in which it is carried out, is stipulated in legislation (LASSA 1970, s.7B); policy guidance provides further detail (DH 1990, para 6.26).

## 5.5.10 SOCIAL SERVICES COMPLAINTS AND LOCAL OMBUDSMAN INVESTIGATIONS (EXISTING PROCEDURE)

The local government ombudsmen have frequently made adverse findings in relation to the operation of local social services complaints procedures. For instance, the following cases relate to systemic and general failures, the recording of complaints, delay, and focusing on the substance of complaints.

**Systemic failure in the complaints procedure.** In one particular case, the local ombudsman identified a 'catalogue of maladministration' and went on to draw some particular conclusions.

There was a failure to (a) clarify who was to deal with the complaint; (b) make adequate cover arrangements for the absence of the complaints manager from work for more than a few days; (c) inform the complainant in writing of how long the complaint would take (i.e. by telling him about both the council's and statutory timescales); (d) comply with council policy by producing a report within 14 days; (e) comply with statutory timescales by not responding within 28 calendar days; (f) appoint an independent investigator without unreasonable delay; (g) appoint an investigator who could start work promptly (there was instead a further delay of a month); (h) brief the investigator about his role and task; (i) apply council policy to the investigator of requiring a report within 14 days; (j) monitor the investigation and ensure timescales were met; (k) provide promptly a written response to the complaint once the investigation report had been received.

In the following case the local ombudsman identified an unrealistic and aimless approach to complaints and a clear gap between policy and practice:

**Worrying attitude to complaints.** The ombudsman identified a worrying attitude to complaints that undermined the assertion by the director of social services that every investigation was approached from the premise that the 28-day timescale would be met. He also stated that measures should be required to ensure that adequate staff would be available for complaints handling; investigators were promptly appointed who could start their work within the timescales; and that staff required for interview should offer interviews within a few days (except in case of holiday or sick leave). The ombudsman was 'appalled' that the council recorded no data that would inform it as to whether it was meeting complaints timescales (*Nottinghamshire CC 1998*).

Confusion, lack of clarity, poor investigation and information, inadequate recording and breached timescales might all lead to findings of maladministration by the local ombudsman:

**General failure to treat complaint properly.** Serious concerns (and maladministration) arose when there was confusion about which stage of the complaints procedure was being followed; the complaint was being handled informally but the complainant had wanted it formally dealt with; there was no thorough investigation; 'presenting problems' were focused on to the exclusion of underlying issues; relevant case records were not examined and key people not interviewed; timescales were not adhered to and the complainant not informed about progress; and a letter sent at the end of investigation neither enclosed the relevant report nor indicated the next step of the procedure (*Newham LBC 1996*).

**Failure properly to record complaint.** The local ombudsman found maladministration when an authority could not produce documentary evidence that a complaint had been thoroughly investigated and had failed to send 'a full, written response' following the investigation. This finding was made despite the 'enormous staffing problems' (caused by an industrial dispute) in the local authority's neighbourhood office at the time (*Islington LBC 1994*).

A wide gap between aspiration and practice may be all too evident:

**Delays in handling complaints.** One local ombudsman investigation found admirable aims in one complaints procedure – but serious flaws in practice. The maladministration was based on a number of criticisms. The complaints coordinator apparently made no real attempt to analyse the contents of a letter of complaint. The council did not respond to the complaint within 28 days as the law demanded – nor did it explain in writing to the complainant why it could not respond in that time. No 'substantive reply' to the complaint had been forthcoming from the council after 16 months. Delay is compounded if, despite a special request for the complaint to be handled quickly, the complainant dies before the outcome is known (*Salford CC 1996*).

In one case, the response to a person's complaint took 219 instead of 28 days; and the ombudsman doubted whether it was realistic of the council not to appoint special complaints investigators but instead to use social services managers – who might not be able to take on the complaints task because of pressure of other work (*Sheffield CC 2002*).

The local ombudsman reminds local authorities that they must try to retain a focus on the substance of complaints, even if they are brought by service users regarded by staff as 'difficult' or unreasonable:

**Focusing on the substance of the complaint.** The local ombudsman has pointed out that the purpose of a complaint is 'first and foremost' to scrutinise a local authority's actions; therefore the focus of an investigation on the complainant's own background and history was maladministration (*Cornwall CC 1996*).

In another case, there was a question of whether the staff involved had sufficient training to 'distance themselves from the personal, and to identify the very real, issues' with which the complainant was concerned (*Haringey LBC 1993*).

The local ombudsman sometimes criticises responses to complaints, for instance in terms of gathering facts and evidence, recording meetings, acknowledging fault, conveying decisions, making written responses and taking an objective approach that enables staff to deal with difficult complainants (see e.g. *Islington LBC 1994, Liverpool CC 1997b*).

Similarly, sending responses which do not address what a complainant has written, and inappropriately concluding that the complainant was satisfied, are maladministration; and councils should beware not to filter out complaints informally, thus preventing them from proceeding (*Liverpool CC 1998a, Manchester CC 1993*).

A council should not mistake a second complaint about how the original complaint has been handled for an appeal against the outcome of the original complaint (*Sandwell MBC 1995*).

It might be maladministration to refuse to carry out particular home adaptations, simply because the applicant involved is complaining and threatening litigation in relation to other adaptations already installed. (But on the other hand, delay caused by the person's unreasonable demands on the council, the personalising of the dispute and failure to take up the council's offer of using an independent advocate was not the fault of the council (*Waltham Forest LBC 1993*).)

## 5.6 SECRETARY OF STATE'S DEFAULT POWERS

If a local authority fails, unreasonably, to carry out any of its social services duties, the Secretary of State can declare that the local authority is 'in default', and direct it to perform its duty. In the case of social services, the default would not be declared if the authority had a 'reasonable excuse' for not complying with its duty. Such a direction can be enforced by the High Court (Local Authority Social Services Act 1970, s.7D).

In some circumstances, the courts use the existence of the powers to argue that Parliament did not intend that people should resort to the courts for a remedy to their grievances. However, the usefulness to service users of this judicial approach is in some doubt, given that the default powers have apparently never been used. Even so, the Department of Health does apparently make preliminary enquiries with a view potentially to using the powers; and these enquiries can be presumed, at least sometimes, to exert pressure on local authorities and to effect informal solutions.

Nevertheless, it seems clear that the obligation to use the powers is one that may be extremely difficult to enforce, as the following legal case suggests:

**Use of the default powers.** A challenge was made against a local authority for breach of its duty in providing practical assistance in the home under s.2 of the Chronically Sick and Disabled Persons Act – and against the Secretary of State for failing to exercise his default powers (then contained in s.36 of the National Assistance Act 1948) against the local authority.

The judge dismissed the case, setting out the difficult hurdles to be surmounted. First, the Secretary of State was not to be regarded as a factual review body. Second, his power to intervene would only arise in the same situation in which the court's power to do so arose. For this to occur, the applicant would first have to establish (a) the specific need; (b) the specific arrangements required to meet it; (c) that an express request had been made to the local authority to meet the need; and (d) that the authority had clearly failed to satisfy the request. Third, the applicant would have then to show – 'and no doubt it would be yet more difficult' – that 'the refusal to meet the identified need or contended for need was irrational...that no local authority, properly discharging their duty and having regard to the facts before them, would have declined that request' (R v Department of Health and Social Security, ex p Bruce).

Although the new default powers in the 1970 Act differ from the old (in the 1948 Act), the judicial statement in the *Bruce* case is probably still a relevant guide. Nevertheless, in a more recent case involving the present default powers, the courts held that the default powers would be more appropriate where there were disputed facts:

**Default powers.** In a case concerning provision of residential accommodation for asylum seekers under s.21 of the National Assistance Act 1948, the court found that it would be more convenient, expeditious and effective to use the default powers rather than judicial review, especially since in its view the real dispute was apparently about facts (whether or not there was available accommodation in London) rather than law (R v Westminster CC, ex p P).

Thus, there appears to be a possible discrepancy in the judicial approach taken in these two cases; the first (*Bruce*) stating that the default powers were not applicable to a factual dispute; the second (*Westminster*) seeming to suggest that they were. Equally, the courts sometimes explain why judicial review is more appropriate than the default powers – for instance, when the issue is one of law in a developing field (R v Devon CC, ex p Baker).

## 5.6.1 SLOW RESPONSE TO REFERRALS

Whatever the proper application of the default powers, the Department of Health has anyway moved slowly in the past in considering whether to use them. The Parliamentary ombudsman has been duly critical:

**Delay in a decision about exercising the default powers (1).** The British Deaf Association (BDA) complained of unreasonable delay in the response of the Department of Health and Social Security (DHSS, as it was then) to a claim that a borough council was in breach of its duty to supply a Vistel (deaf communicating terminal) telephone aid under the Chronically Sick and Disabled Persons Act 1970.

The dispute was about whether the council was using blanket criteria precluding the supply of a telephone aid for any disabled person who did not meet the criteria for telephone provision.

Overall, the BDA had to wait over three years before the Department gave its decision. This was 'appalling delay for which they merit the strongest criticism'. The ombudsman felt bound to say that 'the Department's papers in the case suggested prolonged periods not so much of deliberation as of inattention'.

The ombudsman accepted the apologies of the Department and assurances about the future handling of such applications as an appropriate response by the Department to his investigation and findings (PCA C.656/87).

**Delay in decision about exercising the default powers (2).** In another Parliamentary ombudsman investigation, concerning the provision of holidays by a local authority under the Chronically Sick and Disabled Persons Act 1970, the DHSS (as it was then) was again faulted. It took over a year to respond to the Royal Association for Disability and Rehabilitation's application that the default powers be used. In particular, it took over a month even to contact the local authority concerned, and took several months to consider the reply and to prepare a response.

The Department considered that the duties imposed in relation to the default powers were cumbersome and time-consuming; and that local authorities were likely to be helpful in such cases if they were given time to change – rather than if the Department adopted a confrontational approach. However, the ombudsman pointed out that whilst it was not for him to determine the Department's priorities or how it should use its limited staffing resources, nevertheless he was surprised at the delay, in the light of a Ministerial assurance in the House of Commons that the investigation would be handled rapidly.

Thus the Department's standard of service fell short of what the complainant was entitled to expect; there was no absolute failure to act, but 'their action was slow'. However, even had progress been quicker, the outcome for the complainant was unlikely to have been markedly different: the local authority had now recognised its potential obligation to assist disabled people with holidays (PCA C.799/81).

## 5.7 SECRETARY OF STATE'S GENERAL AND SPECIFIC DIRECTIONS

The Secretary of State has the power to make both specific and general directions for local authorities under s.7A of the Local Authority Social Services Act 1970. They can be made in respect of a particular authority, a particular class of authority or authorities generally. The following local ombudsman investigation identified that the Department of Health was somewhat perplexed about how, or whether, to use the power:

**Using specific directions.** In a local ombudsman investigation concerning a dispute between two local authorities about where a person was ordinarily resident, the Secretary of State was asked not only to resolve the dispute under s.32(3) of the National Assistance Act 1948, but also to make a specific direction as to which authority should provide a service.

The Department of Health appeared to be somewhat surprised by the request for a specific direction; it had never previously been asked for one and had no established procedure. In the event, it first of all appeared to do nothing; when it did reply after a further request, it stated that it would be improper for the Secretary of State to direct that a council arrange a service that it considered inappropriate. This was because (a) there was no evidence that the judgement of either of the two local authorities involved was unreasonable, and (b) it was natural and proper that professional judgement should differ (Redbridge LBC 1998).

## 5.8 SECRETARY OF STATE'S INQUIRIES

The Secretary of State has the power to institute inquiries in relation to the social services functions of a local authority under s.7C of the Local Authority Social Services Act 1970.

## 5.9 LOCAL GOVERNMENT OMBUDSMEN

The local government ombudsmen investigate maladministration in local authorities and can recommend remedies, including financial compensation, where people have suffered injustice (Local Government Act 1974, s.26). There are three local ombudsmen in England.

The ombudsmen can investigate in response not just to the complaint in respect of an individual person (alive or deceased), but also of an appropriate organisation (s.27): for example, a local advice agency might make representations on behalf of a number of people affected by a common problem. They can also call for and examine information about other service users in a similar situation to that of the complainant (ss.28–29).

They will normally investigate only once the local authority complaints procedure has been exhausted (Local Government Act 1974, s.26). However, clearly where that procedure itself is operating unsatisfactorily, the ombudsmen might take up complaints before such exhaustion. The complaint will then not only focus on the original issue but the failure of the complaints procedure as well. Indeed, not only have the local ombudsmen been critical in a number of investigations of local authority complaints procedures, but they have also published their own guidance on devising complaints systems in local authorities (CLAE 1992). There is normally a 12-month limit (i.e. from the time the complainant first knew of the matter complained of) on the bringing of the complaint to the ombudsman, but this can be waived if the ombudsman thinks it reasonable (Local Government Act 1974, s.26).

The local ombudsmen are also precluded from investigating where an alternative remedy exists (e.g. a judicial review case), unless they are satisfied that it would not be reasonable to expect the complainant to utilise the alternative remedy. This exclusionary principle was confirmed in one case when judicial review proceedings were brought in a special education case. They were resolved in the applicant's favour by a consent order. A complaint was then made to the ombudsman with a view to obtaining financial compensation, which is not available in judicial review proceedings. The courts held that the ombudsman was justified in refusing to entertain a complaint relating to that delay (*R v Commissioner for Local Administration, ex p PH*). The ombudsmen are also precluded from challenging decisions taken without maladministration (Local Government Act 1974, s.34); for instance, professional judgements or the merits of decisions.

For reasons of time, effort and potential expense, service users are probably well-advised to use, where possible, the local ombudsman rather than the courts. The principles applied by the local ombudsmen are set out in Chapter 4.

## 5.9.1 LOCAL OMBUDSMEN RECOMMENDATIONS AND ENFORCEMENT

Local authorities are empowered, though not obliged, to follow ombudsman recommendations (including payment of compensation), although they are under a duty at least to consider them (Local Government Act 1974, s.31). Legislation now makes absolutely clear that, in the light of maladministration that has adversely affected a person, the local authority has the power to make a payment to, or provide some other benefit for, the person (Local Government Act 2000, s.92).

If a council refuses to follow the ombudsman's recommendations, even after a second report, it can be forced to publish an agreed statement in a local newspaper at its own expense (s.31). Avoidance of this bad publicity is an additional incentive for local authorities to comply with ombudsman recommendations. Over a period of 10 years from 1994 to 2004, the ombudsmen report that out of 2145 reports in which maladministration and injustice were found, only 38 cases (less than 2%) resulted in unsatisfactory outcomes in terms of non-compliance (CLAE 2004, p.30).

## 5.9.2 LOCAL OMBUDSMEN REMEDIES

When maladministration has caused injustice, the ombudsmen can recommend any lawful remedy, including financial compensation (Local Government Act 1974, s.31). Recommendations typically include providing the disputed service for the complainant, providing an apology, and rewriting and implementing new policies and procedures to avoid the same thing happening to other service users. If concerned about an issue of wider importance, the ombudsmen sometimes write to the Department of Health or other government department.

Financial compensation recommended by the ombudsman, though often involving only smaller amounts, ranging from £500 to £5000 can be considerably larger as the following examples illustrate:

**Financial compensation awarded by the local ombudsmen.** In two investigations concerning assessment and provision of a residential placement for a person with learning disabilities (*Kent CC 1998*), and rehousing of a family with a severely disabled son (*Bristol CC 1998*), sums respectively of £15,000 and £20,000 were recommended. In another investigation, extreme stress, caused by a rigid ceiling imposed by the council on the cost of home care packages and suffered by the daughter of a woman with severe disabilities and high needs, warranted £10,000 in compensation (*Liverpool CC 1998b*).

When a local authority failed for ten years to make arrangements to enable a person with learning disabilities to leave hospital and live in the community, the ombudsman recommended payment of £20,000 (*Wakefield MDC 2003*). Leaving a man with learning disabilities without an appropriate residential placement for some two years merited £30,000 by way of remedy (*East Sussex CC 2003*). And when a father of a woman with learning disabilities wrongly had to organise and pay for his daughter's care for some two years, an £80,000 remedy was recommended (*Hertfordshire CC 2003*). Considerably more financial redress was recommended when a local authority had wrongly charged one service user £60,000 for aftercare services; this was the amount that the council should repay (*Wiltshire CC 1999*).

Unlike the Commissioner for Complaints in Northern Ireland (acting under the Ombudsman (Northern Ireland) Order 1996 and the Commissioner for Complaints (Northern Ireland) Order 1996), the local government ombudsmen in England do not have a power to seek enforcement of their recommendations through the law courts.

## 5.10 NHS COMPLAINTS PROCEDURE

A new NHS complaints procedure was implemented in July 2004 by regulations (SI 2004/1768) made under the Health and Social Care (Community Health and Standards) Act 2003 (s.113). In summary, the new procedure provides for:

- designation by each NHS body of a complaints manager
- complaints by patients or their representative
- oral or written complaints
- a six-month time limit for making a complaint, although the complaints manager can choose to disregard this limitation if there is good reason for the delay
- written acknowledgement of the complaint within two days of receipt
- duty of investigation by the complaints manager
- arranging of conciliation, mediation or other assistance for resolving the complaint if the complainant is agreeable to this
- written response to the complaint
- onward referral of the complaint to the Healthcare Commission (i.e. the Commission for Healthcare, Audit and Inspection) if the complainant is not satisfied with the result of an investigation
- the Healthcare Commission to, amongst other things, take no further action, make recommendations to the body complained against, investigate the complaint further (and it may appoint a panel made up of three independent lay people), refer the complaint to a health regulatory body or refer the complaint to the health service ombudsman
- a complaints procedure operated by independent providers providing NHS services, run as if the regulations applied to them (SI 2004/1768).

## 5.11 HEALTH SERVICE OMBUDSMAN

The health service ombudsman investigates injustice or hardship caused to a patient through failure in service, failure to provide a service which there is a duty to provide, or maladministration (Health Service Commissioners Act 1993). This gives the ombudsman broad powers of investigation. The ombudsman sometimes exposes important legal and policy issues: for example, the provision of continuing NHS health care.

Normally, although he can decide otherwise, the ombudsman cannot investigate incidents which happened more than a year ago, or complaints for which there are alternative remedies. The principles applied by the health service ombudsman are set out in Chapter 4.

## 5.11.1 HEALTH SERVICE OMBUDSMAN CLINICAL JUDGEMENTS

The health service ombudsman has been able since April 1996 to investigate clinical, as well as administrative, aspects of decisions – and also complaints against GPs, dentists, pharmacists or opticians providing NHS services. Special assessors are used by the ombudsman to investigate clinical matters, who will use the civil law test of the 'balance of probabilities' in reaching conclusions about causation. The ombudsman has noted that (a) many complaints that appear to be related to clinical matters are in fact about administrative lapses such as breakdown in communications or failure to follow proper procedure; but (b) where clinical judgement is in question, the test for maladministration is not appropriate (HSC 1996c, pp.3, 10).

## 5.11.2 HEALTH SERVICE OMBUDSMAN REMEDIES

Legislation does not lay down formal remedies, although the health service ombudsman can make recommendations. The ombudsman will send a report of the findings to the complainant and the NHS. If the complaint, or at least part of it, is upheld the ombudsman seeks a remedy – this could include getting a decision changed, or a repayment of unnecessary costs incurred by patients or their families. Otherwise, the ombudsman does not recommend financial damages. The ombudsman might also recommend that changes be made to procedures so that the same problem does not recur for other people (HSC 1996c, p.7).

## 5.12 NHS DEFAULT POWERS

Under s.85 of the NHS Act 1977, the Secretary of State can declare NHS bodies to be in default of their duty. This would be where 'they have failed to carry out any functions conferred or imposed on them by or under this Act, or have in carrying out those functions failed to comply with any regulations or directions relating to those functions'. It seems unclear whether any such default order has ever been issued.

## 5.13 JUDICIAL REVIEW

Judicial review in the law courts is what is known as a 'public law' remedy and is used to challenge the decisions and actions of public bodies. It is generally not used to obtain damages, but instead the law courts 'supervise' the decision making, actions and omissions of public bodies. This is to ensure that they are acting according to legislation and to common law principles that define fairness and good administration (in a legal sense) by public bodies. Since 1993, judicial review has been used extensively to challenge local authority decision making in the field of community care. The principles applied in such cases are covered in Chapter 4.

Human rights challenges are sometimes brought as part of a judicial review case (see Chapter 20) and may involve the award of damages, unlike most ordinary judicial review cases (see e.g. *R(Bernard) v Enfield LBC*: damages awarded for failure, akin to maladministtration, of the local social services authority to find suitable accommodation for a disabled woman and her family).

### 5.13.1 PERMISSION FOR JUDICIAL REVIEW

Unlike other types of legal action (such as negligence actions), permission from a High Court judge is first required to bring a judicial review case. Permission will be generally granted if the judge is satisfied that there is an arguable case (SI 1998/3132, r.54).

### 5.13.2 TIME LIMITS FOR JUDICIAL REVIEW

An application for judicial review must be brought promptly and in any event within three months from the date when the grounds of action arose; the court can extend this time limit if there are good reasons why the case has been brought later (SI 1998/3132, r.54). However, even within the three-month limit, it is open to a court to deny permission on grounds that the application has not been made promptly.

Because of this time limit and the possible requirement that alternative remedies (such as the complaints procedure) be used first, an application for judicial review could be made but then adjourned until the outcome of a complaint brought under the local authority's complaints procedure is known. If this were not done, then it might be too late to make the application.

### 5.13.3 LENGTH OF JUDICIAL REVIEW PROCESS

Judicial review cases can take a considerable time (months or over a year) to come to court. However, urgency can be pleaded, in which case it might not take more than a few weeks. Similarly, an appeal might be heard quickly in certain circumstances, as occurred in *R v Cambridge HA, ex p B* (about urgent leukaemia treatment for child) when the High Court and Court of Appeal sat on the same day.

If a case is going to take a long time to come to court, an interim injunction ('interim relief') is sometimes possible. This might be in a sufficiently serious case where the court could order that services be provided until the dispute is finally heard and resolved (see e.g. *R v Staffordshire CC, ex p Farley* involving withdrawal of night sitter services). This might be one argument for using the judicial review system directly in some circumstances, rather than going through the complaints procedure, which can in practice, despite the statutory time limits, be drawn out.

### 5.13.4 STANDING AND STATUS OF APPLICANT

The applicant must have a 'sufficient interest' in the case (Supreme Court Act 1981, s.31). This is known as having sufficient standing. For example, service users themselves or carers affected by a decision clearly have such an interest. Sometimes established advisory organisations, representing particular groups of people, will also be recognised by courts (see e.g. *R v Sefton MBC, ex p Help the Aged; R v Gloucestershire CC, ex p RADAR; R v Newham*

*LBC, ex p Medical Foundation for the Care of Victims of Torture*). In such cases, voluntary organisations may play a useful role in highlighting matters of public interest.

## 5.13.5 JUDICIAL REVIEW OR ALTERNATIVE REMEDIES

If the courts believe that there are appropriate 'alternative remedies' then they might insist that those remedies be used first, before judicial review can be applied for. The obvious alternative remedies in the community care field are the social services complaints procedure, and the powers of the Secretary of State to declare authorities in default of their duties. However, there are sometimes reasons why the courts might not insist on these two remedies.

### 5.13.5.1 Judicial review as appropriate remedy

As far as the community care complaints procedure goes, service users could argue that a hearing before a panel of non-lawyers without legal representation is inadequate to deal with questions of law. For instance, in a case concerning delay in providing community care services, the court ruled that it would not have been 'convenient, expeditious or effective' for the applicant to argue points of law before a non-qualified body, namely the complaints review panel (*R v Sutton LBC, ex p Tucker*). Likewise, where the complaints procedure could consider only procedural matters, but not substantially deal with the issue in question – because no investigating officer could substitute his decision for that of the NHS trust involved – the court accepted that judicial review was appropriate; the complaints procedure would not be an effective mechanism (*R(Rodriguez-Bannister) v Somerset Partnership NHS and Social Care Trust*).

Indeed, where there is a question of law in a developing field, the courts will state that it is for them, and not for the local authority or Secretary of State, to decide it (*R v Devon CC, ex p Baker* about residential home closure).

### 5.13.5.2 Judicial review not appropriate remedy

If, in the view of the courts, questions of law are absent, then the complaints procedure might be more appropriate (*R v Lambeth LBC, ex p A* about rehousing for child and family; and *R v Birmingham CC, ex p A* about delay in providing a placement for a child). The courts might view the complaints procedure as more effective and quicker than judicial review, and able to get to the heart of the matter and the facts (*R v Kingston upon Thames, ex p T*: a child care case).

In an asylum seeker case concerning place and choice of accommodation, the default powers of the Secretary of State were regarded as more appropriate than judicial review (*R v Westminster CC, ex p P*). Moreover, some of the community care disputes that have reached the law courts have involved complex problems, which might simply not be amenable to judicial resolution, since they are 'beyond the competence of courts of law' (*R v Islington LBC, ex p Rixon*).

**Heavy obligation to avoid litigation.** In one case, the Court of Appeal was critical of the fact that a dispute – concerning a care home closure and the adequacy of the assessments of the residents concerned – had resulted in so much litigation. Instead the complaints procedure should have been used; indeed the court declined to decide the matter. The lawyers were under a 'heavy obligation' to resort to litigation only if it was really unavoidable (*R(Cowl) v Plymouth CC*).

**Using the courts as a last resort.** When a care home was being converted into supported housing, the court stated that the dispute about what was in a care plan was a matter for the complaints procedure; and failure to follow the Secretary of State's guidance should first of all involve reference to the Secretary of State. The courts should be used as a last resort (*R(Lloyd) v Barking and Dagenham LBC, CA*).

Sometimes the courts might explicitly criticise the lawyers in the case, suggesting that there might have been no need for the case to be brought:

**Fallacious ground for bringing litigation.** The court stated that the case had been argued eloquently but on the fallacious contention that promises of a home for life had been made to the residents of NHS premises for mentally disordered people; and that this contention had proceeded more on the legal construction of the lawyer involved than on an evidential foundation (*R v Brent, Kensington and Chelsea and Westminster NHS Trust, ex p C*).

## 5.13.6 JUDICIAL REVIEW REMEDIES AVAILABLE

The court has discretion, not an explicit obligation, to award a remedy in judicial review (Supreme Court Act 1981, s.31). A court can grant a (Supreme Court Act 1981, ss.29–33; SI 1998/3132, r.54):

- **quashing order**: overturning a decision and ordering the authority to take the decision again (formerly known as certiorari)
- **mandatory order**: obliging an authority to take a positive action (formerly known as mandamus)
- **injunction**: similar to a mandatory order but in an interim form until the full hearing and resolution of the dispute – and obliging an authority to do or not to do something (e.g. not withdrawing services)
- **prohibiting order**: forbidding an authority from doing something inconsistent with its legal powers (formerly known as prohibition)
- **declaration**: that makes a statement about rights, remedies and the general legal position of the parties (formerly known as declaration). It is effective in that public bodies would act in accordance with a declaration.

However, the discretion to grant a remedy means that the court does not have to award one at all, even if the claimant has 'won' the judicial review case in principle. For example, a judge found himself unable to do more than suggest a declaration that the local authority was 'quite wrong' when he found that it had not acted in accordance with the law (the CSDPA 1970) in refusing (nearly two years previously) to consider assisting a person with a holiday (*R v Ealing LBC, ex p Leaman*). It was too late to do anything else.

## 5.13.7 PRACTICAL EFFECTS OF JUDICIAL REVIEW

First, when cases go to a full hearing (see below), the decisions of the courts set precedents for the future and have ramifications far beyond the particular applicant or applicants in the case. However, precedents can be sidestepped by, for instance, 'distinguishing' a later from a previously decided case, and so avoiding the precedent set by the earlier case. This seemed to occur in *R v East Sussex CC, ex p Tandy* (about resources in education decisions) in which the House of Lords 'explained away', without overruling, their earlier decision in *R v Gloucestershire CC, ex p Barry* (about resources in community care), in order to come to a different conclusion in the later case.

Second, even the threat of judicial review might be effective in resolving a dispute. For instance, if leave (permission) to proceed to a full hearing is given by a judge, then the authority against whom the case is being brought will be aware that the case is an arguable one and might be tempted to settle the dispute before it goes further. Authorities might wish to avoid (a) adverse publicity; (b) high legal costs; and (c) the danger of losing the case and the setting of an unwanted, expensive precedent (which might apply to many other service users in a similar position to the applicant).

## 5.14 NEGLIGENCE, BREACH OF STATUTORY DUTY/CONTRACT

Civil actions for negligence, breach of statutory duty or breach of contract are known as *private law* actions, compared to judicial review, which is a *public law* remedy.

The common law of negligence is well established in the health care field in relation to clinical decisions, but is perhaps less straightforward in the social care field (see Chapter 23). Most private law claims for breach of statutory duty are generally unlikely to succeed in either the health or social care fields.

In addition, a third possible private law remedy, namely an action for breach of contract, appears generally not to be available to individual users of social services or the NHS (except in the case of private patients). The reason for this is that, because the provision of such services is governed by statute, legally enforceable contracts between statutory agencies and service users are precluded (see 7.2.1). Nevertheless, the law of contract is of very considerable importance as between local authorities or the NHS and independent care providers (see 7.2.2).

## 5.14.1 NEGLIGENCE/BREACH OF DUTY ACTIONS COMPARED TO JUDICIAL REVIEW

The existence of private law remedies is, or would be, significant (if they were more commonly available), because there are a number of differences between private and public law procedures.

First, the claimant does not, at the outset, have to gain the permission of a judge to pursue a private law case. Second, the court can in private law actually make a final decision about the matter in dispute, whereas judicial review often involves authorities themselves retaking a decision about services. Third, when a claimant wins a case, the judge in private law cases must normally grant a remedy of some sort; whereas in public law cases, the judge does not have to do this. Furthermore, a remedy in private law, but not usually in public law, can be in the form of financial compensation (damages).

Lastly, in private law involving claims for negligence or breach of statutory duty, the claimant must have suffered some sort of harm: physical, psychological (in some circumstances only), property or financial (in limited circumstances only). For instance, if there is no harm, then a negligence case cannot succeed. However, in judicial review, such harm does not have to be shown – although the applicant still has to show that he, she or it (in the case of an organisation) has sufficient interest in the case.

## 5.14.2 BREACH OF STATUTORY DUTY

An action for breach of statutory duty in private law (as opposed to judicial review in public law) requires identification of definite, potentially enforceable, individual rights. Such rights are difficult to identify in welfare legislation for a number of reasons – and private law actions in this field (compared, for example, to the health and safety at work field where they are well established) do not seem to be generally viable.

At one time, the courts distinguished decisions about whether an obligation was owed to a person from the actual carrying out of the duty. Failure to take the first type of decision properly could not result in private law actions for breach of duty; however, failure to discharge the latter 'executive' type of obligation could (*Cocks v Thanet DC*).

However, the courts have since further refined the test for liability and imposed additional obstacles; identification of such executive obligations will not be enough. For instance, the claimant must also show (a) that the legislation was designed to protect a specific class of people and also to confer a right to sue for damages; (b) clear statutory language to this effect; and (c) that there were no alternative remedies such as an appeal to the Secretary of State (see e.g. *O'Rourke v Camden LBC*).

The difficulties posed by this test can be seen in cases concerning the neglect of children and the failure of the local authority to act (*X v Bedfordshire CC*), failure to provide housing (*O'Rourke v Camden LBC*), failure to provide adequate home help (*Wyatt v Hillingdon LBC*), and failure to provide aftercare for a mentally disordered patient (*Clunis v Camden and Islington HA*). In the light of these cases, the speculation of the judge in *R v Bexley LBC, ex p B* that damages might be possible for breach of the duty to arrange services under the Chronically Sick and Disabled Persons Act 1970 is of probably little significance.

Even so, there have been some cases in which the courts do seem to have entertained the possibility of damages for a breach of statutory duty. For example, the Court of Appeal has ruled that non-payment of a mandatory housing repair grant could give rise to private law rights – which could allow for a private law action to recover, as an ordinary debt, the amount of the unpaid grant (*Dennis Rye Pension Fund v Sheffield City Council*).

# PART II

# Community care legislation and guidance

CHAPTER 6

# Assessment

## KEY POINTS

This chapter considers the main elements of referral, assessment, and decisions about services. This involves questions of access to the assessment process, how referrals are 'screened' by local authorities, the making of priorities in terms of how quickly the assessment will be performed, the depth and scope of assessment, eligibility for services, and waiting times for services. It is at such pivotal points in the assessment process that local authorities are routinely forced to explore and exploit the uncertainties (see Chapter 3) inherent in the community care system. They do this in order to limit expenditure and to find escape routes from their potential obligations imposed by law and by the aspiration of central government policy and guidance.

### ACCESS TO ASSESSMENT

The NHS and Community Care Act 1990 makes assessment a duty and a service in its own right. Assessment itself is pivotal to the provision of community care services, including both residential and non-residential care services (see Chapters 9 and 11), and so access to it is crucial. A number of considerations control who will be assessed, when they will be assessed and what sort of assessment they will get.

The legislation states that a local authority has first to decide whether a person appears to be in possible need of community care services; if the answer is affirmative, there is a duty to assess, if negative, there is none. Having carried out the assessment, the local authority has a duty to decide whether the person's needs call for services.

If, during the assessment, it appears to the authority that the person is disabled then the authority must specifically decide about what services are required under s.2 of the Chronically Sick and Disabled Persons Act 1970.

### SCREENING AND ACCESS TO ASSESSMENT

In order to determine who is eligible for an assessment, how quickly they should be assessed and what type of assessment they will get, local authorities normally operate screening procedures. Such screening is not legally prescribed, but in practice it acts as a powerful filter. This is particularly so because (within fairly wide limits) local authorities often apply their own operational definitions of terms such as 'need', 'priorities', 'levels' of assessment, 'urgency' – and so on. Thus, although only a 'pre-assessment' stage, screening can determine what happens to people, and is a tool used by authorities to regulate their responses to the demands made on them. Screening is a somewhat shadowy area of activity and can give rise to some of the uncertainties identified in Chapter 3 of this book and consequently to disputes.

Nevertheless, the courts resolved one such dispute by stating that local authorities should set a low threshold for access to assessment, that in any case they could not take account of resources when setting that threshold – and that it was irrelevant that a person was unlikely to qualify for services, since assessment was of benefit in its own right (*R v Bristol CC, ex p Penfold*).

The case also illustrated the fine line – and the significant legal implications falling either side of it – dividing what local authorities call screening and what they refer to as 'simple' or 'initial' assessment. The local ombudsmen too have emphasised the importance of adequate information gathering by authorities at the screening stage, since otherwise they are simply not in a position to make competent judgements about need and priority for assessment.

Furthermore, some local authorities appear to forget that because of the continued freestanding nature of s.4 of the Disabled Persons (Services, Consultation and Representation) Act 1986, they have a duty anyway, on the request of a disabled person or carer, to make a decision about services under the Chronically Sick and Disabled Persons Act 1970; in other words, they cannot refuse disabled people an assessment.

WAITING TIMES FOR ASSESSMENT
Alternative to denying people assessment, local authorities sometimes make them wait a long time. Inevitably the question arises as to the point at which the slow carrying out of a duty amounts to not carrying it out at all and to unlawfulness. Absent timescales set out in legislation, both law courts and ombudsmen state that local authorities must carry out their duties within a reasonable time; and what is reasonable will depend on all the circumstances of the case (although the courts might anyway be reluctant to intervene if a dispute about delay involves a consideration of facts only, rather than points of law). This approach has both advantages and disadvantages; it allows for considerable flexibility in reacting to individual needs, but at the same time deprives all concerned of an easy rule of thumb.

ASSESSMENT OF NEED
The concept of 'need' goes to the heart of community care assessment. If a person is not acknowledged by a local authority to have a need that calls for or necessitates provision,

then he or she will not get any services. Local authorities are obliged to follow central government guidance on 'fair access to care' in terms of how they assess people's needs.

The law courts have confirmed that when local authorities set policy and criteria of eligibility, they can take account of the resources they have available when deciding what need is and whether it is necessary to meet it. On this basis they can also formally alter policies and criteria from time to time. Consequently, people's assessed needs and the services they receive can fluctuate not just according to their own changing conditions and circumstances, but also as a result of the changing financial situation and policies of local authorities. This can lead over time in any one local authority to the application of more stringent tests of eligibility for both existing users and potential new users of services.

Eligibility criteria and thresholds of eligibility can cause confusion. If they are not set realistically in relation to allocated resources, they might allow too many people to qualify for services and strain budgets to breaking point. Local authorities then attempt to execute shortcuts that run the risk of being unlawful.

## NEED, PREFERENCE AND UNMET NEED

When assessing people's needs and deciding about services, a local authority is likely to distinguish 'preferences', 'desires' or 'wants' from needs. A further division is then likely between those needs which the authority agrees it will meet, and those which it will not ('unmet need'). A theme that has emerged from some of the judicial review cases in the law courts is the importance for both local authorities and service users about how need is identified and recorded in the assessment. Both financial and legal implications flow from the level of generality or specificity with which a person's need is expressed. For instance, need specified at a general level might leave open a number of options for service provision, some of which might be considerably cheaper and any one of which will meet identified need. The courts have confirmed that local authorities can take account of resources when deciding which option to choose.

Note: Wales, Scotland and Northern Ireland. This chapter applies fairly closely to Wales, although there are caveats. For instance, although the primary legislation (e.g. the NHS and Community Care Act 1990) applies to Wales, the National Assembly for Wales often publishes its own directions and guidance. The Assembly has a discretion whether (or when) to publish equivalent guidance to that existing in England; and, at the time of writing, it has not passed directions on community care assessment in Wales. Also, the content might differ. For example, Welsh guidance, setting out the rules concerning the application of eligibility criteria and 'fair access to care' (NAFWC 9/02), looks at first blush to be identical to the English guidance (see 6.11). But on closer inspection it is not.

In Scotland, the legislation governing community care assessment is similar (but not identical) to that in England, although it is contained in different legislation: s.12A of the Social Work (Scotland) Act 1968. However, Scottish guidance generally differs; for instance, the Scottish Executive has not published guidance equivalent to that covering 'fair access to care' and eligibility criteria in England and Wales. On the other hand, occasionally the guidance is one and the same; for instance, the 1991 guidance entitled *Care Management and Assessment: Practitioners' Guide* (SSI/SWSG 1991) was published jointly by the Department of

Health and the Scottish Office (as it was then). The Scottish Office also published its own policy guidance at the outset of community care on assessment and care management (SWSG 11/1991).

In Northern Ireland, in contrast to the rest of the United Kingdom, there is no specific duty of assessment contained in the relevant legislation (the Health and Personal Social Services (Northern Ireland) Order 1972), although guidance on community care assessment was published in 1991 entitled *Care Management: Guidance on Assessment and the Provision of Community Care* (DHSS 1991).

Nevertheless, there is still a duty to make a decision, on request by a disabled person or informal carer, about the person's needs for services under s.2 of the Chronically Sick and Disabled Persons (Northern Ireland) Act 1978 (see Disabled Persons (Northern Ireland) Act 1989, s.4).

## 6.1 OVERALL DUTY OF ASSESSMENT: NHS AND COMMUNITY CARE ACT 1990

Overall, local authority social services departments assess people aged 18 years or over under s.47 of the NHS and Community Care Act 1990. In order to gain services set out in other legislation, people need to 'get through' this assessment process, which therefore serves as a gateway. In summary, section 47 of the 1990 Act is as follows:

- **Main duty of assessment**. If it appears to a local authority that a person, for whom it may provide or arrange for the provision of community care services a service, may be in need of any such services, then:
  - it must carry out an assessment of his or her needs for those services
  - having regard to the results of that assessment, the authority must decide whether his or her needs call for the provision by the local authority of any such services (s.47(1)).
- **Disabled people**. If during the assessment it appears that the person is disabled, then:
  - the local authority must take a decision as to whether he or she requires the services mentioned in s.4 of the Disabled Persons (Services, Consultation and Representation) Act 1986 (in effect services under s.2 of the Chronically Sick and Disabled Persons Act 1970)
  - the authority must inform the person about what it is doing and of his or her rights under the 1986 Act (s.47(2)).
- **Assistance from the NHS or housing authority**. If, during the assessment, it appears to the local authority that the person may need health services under the NHS Act 1977 from a health authority or NHS primary care trust (PCT) or from a housing authority (that is not the social services authority carrying out the assessment), then:
  - the local authority must invite the PCT, health authority or housing authority to invite them to assist in the assessment, to such extent as is reasonable in the circumstances
  - in making its decision as to what services the person needs, the local authority must take into account any services likely to be made available by the PCT, health authority or housing authority (s.47(3)).
- **Urgency**. Nothing prevents a local authority from temporarily providing or arranging for the provision of community care services for any person, without

carrying out a prior assessment, if the authority is of the opinion that the person requires those services as a matter of urgency; in which case, the local authority must carry out an assessment as soon as practicable (s.47(5,6)).

## 6.1.1 TRIGGERING OF DUTY OF ASSESSMENT

The duty to assess is triggered if it appears to the local authority that a person for whom it may provide community care services may be in need of such services. If so, it must then carry out an assessment of the person's needs for such services (NHS and Community Care Act 1990, s.47). The duty is not absolute, but has been held by the courts to be a strong one. They have stated that the duty is set at a low threshold; furthermore the state of the local authority's resources is not relevant:

**Assessment of person reporting anxiety and depression.** A 52-year-old woman suffered from anxiety and depression. She was unintentionally homeless, but had rejected an offer of accommodation under the Housing Act 1996, and sought an assessment and provision of accommodation from social services. Social services refused to assess, partly on the basis that it would be futile and a poor use of resources to do so, where there was no hope of meeting the need.

   The court rejected this approach, stating that resources were irrelevant to the duty to assess, that the threshold for entitlement to assessment was very low, and that in any case assessment served a useful purpose even if services did not follow (*R v Bristol CC, ex p Penfold*).

The courts have also held that the duty to assess arises even if a local authority knows that it would only ever have a power rather than a duty to provide services for the person – and that those services were anyway not physically available within the area of the local authority.

**Assessment of a person not ordinarily resident.** A seriously disabled man suffering from viral brain damage and epilepsy was resident at the British Home and Hospital for Incurables. His mother, through solicitors, requested that a local authority assess his needs, because she felt he needed different types and levels of care than he was receiving at the hospital. The local authority argued that he was not ordinarily resident in its area, that therefore it had only a power to provide services under s.29 of the National Assistance Act 1948, and that anyway the services in question were not physically available in its area. Thus, it had no duty to assess.

   The court rejected the authority's argument, pointing out that the duty of assessment hinged not on a factual capacity to provide services but on a legal capacity (*R v Berkshire CC, ex p Parker*).

Despite legal cases such as the above, local authorities appear still to fall into the trap of not assessing people's potential needs, on the ground that they will probably not be eligible for services. Typically, such a refusal concerns cleaning and shopping needs, as picked up by the local government ombudsman in the following case:

**Failure to assess for cleaning and shopping needs.** A woman suffered from severe health problems: sarcoidosis, extensive fibrosis of the lungs, chronic obstructive airways disease, atrial fibrillation, epilepsy and a learning disability and a heart problem. The slightest exertion made her breathless. Twice she and her husband requested assistance with cleaning and shopping, but the council did not assess her needs. Instead it had a policy of not providing cleaning and shopping services; it referred her to an independent company. In effect, the woman and her husband had been screened out.

The local ombudsman found maladministration, since the council had failed to carry out an assessment, and it could not lawfully delegate its duty to assess to an independent provider. Furthermore, the ombudsman noted that Department of Health guidance reinforces the legal position that the duty of assessment depends on potential need, and not on the service requested (*Salford CC 2003*).

Sometimes local authorities apparently fail altogether to carry out assessments and formulate care plans as in the following local ombudsman investigation:

**Informality with man with mild learning disabilities.** A man with mild learning disabilities got 'lost in the system' because of the informal way his long-term social worker had managed his case, without a formal recorded assessment. For a lengthy period he became nobody's responsibility, his mother's efforts gained no response, and he was not even told when the social worker left the council. This was maladministration. His circumstances deteriorated in relation to his drug-taking 'friends' and his ability to clean his flat and prevent damage. He then abandoned his tenancy (previously the social worker had helped prevent him being evicted) (*Derbyshire CC 2001*).

There needs also to be clarity about who is formally responsible for carrying out the assessment and taking the final decision. In the following case, the court could only conclude that the local authority had not legally taken an assessment decision:

**Who is making the decision?** A health authority occupational therapist (OT) recommended that an elderly couple should have installed either a vertical lift or a stairlift to give them ingress and egress from their first floor council flat. The recommendation was also backed by an 'advocacy officer' of the council. The recommended home adaptations were eventually refused by the housing department of the council on grounds of cost. The applicants claimed that having assessed the need, the council was obliged to meet it.

The judge decided that, in fact, the council had failed to carry out an assessment under s.47 of the NHS and Community Care Act 1990 and s.2 of the Chronically Sick and Disabled Persons Act. Confusingly for the service users, the statements of the advocacy officer, the care plan she had drawn up and the recommendation of the occupational therapist did not carry sufficient weight, since the provision of services was 'the concern of the council itself or of any committee or officer to whom a specific power is delegated'. The OT and the advocate were not authorised to carry out assessment and to decide about service provision. Thus, the judge found not that the authority was in breach of its statutory duty to provide the stairlift, but that it had been profiting from its failure to carry out the assessment (*R v Kirklees MBC, ex p Daykin*).

Or, if there is an assessment, it is not a full one:

**Lack of full assessment.** Over a period of six years, the local authority failed properly to assess the needs of a girl/woman who had multiple and profound mental and physical disabilities. However, it had assessed a need for weekend respite care to be provided at a care home; but when the charity that provided this care was forced to close the home on Sundays, the local authority stated that it could not be held responsible for this effective withdrawal of service. It did not respond with a formal reassessment that would have had to conclude that either there was no longer a need, or that it was in breach of its duty. Instead it simply denied its commitment to the family. The local ombudsman found maladministration (*North Yorkshire CC 2002*).

In another case, the Court of Appeal found a local authority's decision manifestly flawed; it had simply acted on the defective recommendations of a local continuing care panel, the function of which was anyway advisory only. The local authority should have cured the defects by itself taking a fully informed decision (*R(Goldsmith) v Wandsworth LBC*).

## 6.1.2 DIRECTIONS AND GUIDANCE ON ASSESSMENT

The 1990 Act gives the Secretary of State the power to issue directions about how assessments should be carried out (NHS and Community Care Act 1990, s.47). The Department of Health has issued directions (DH 2004f):

- When assessing a person under s.47, a local authority must consult the person being assessed, consider whether the person has any carers, and – if the local authority thinks it appropriate – consult those carers.
- The local authority must take all reasonable steps to reach agreement with the person and – if the local authority thinks it appropriate – with any carer, concerning any community care services it is considering providing.
- The local authority must provide information to the person and – if it thinks appropriate – to any carer, about the amount of any charge payable for the services.

These directions link directly to the plentiful guidance issued about involving service users (see 6.8) and informal carers (see 12.4.3) in assessment.

In the light of this power (finally exercised in 2004) to issue directions on assessment, one judge has held that guidance on assessment – even statutory guidance made under s.7 of the Local Authority Social Services Act 1970 – is of limited value. It has only to be taken account of; this is because the legislation clearly envisages that it is directions rather than guidance that would carry real weight in determining how assessment is to be carried out (*R(B&H) v Hackney LBC*).

However, in many other cases, the courts appear to have attached importance to policy guidance on assessment. One such example, *Community Care in the Next Decade and Beyond* (DH 1990), has been referred to and given weight many times in community care legal cases. For example, this guidance underlay findings of breach statutory duty for failing to take account of a person's preferences (*R v North Yorkshire CC, ex p Hargreaves*) and failure in a care plan (*R v Islington LBC, ex p Rixon*). More recently, the court made extensive reference to, and appeared to place considerable weight on, 'fair access to care' guidance (LAC (2002)13), concerning the setting and application of eligibility criteria for the purpose of assessment (*R v Sheffield CC, ex p Heffernan*).

## 6.2 DUTY TO ASSESS DISABLED PEOPLE

If during the s.47 assessment it appears to the local authority that the person is disabled, the local authority has a duty to make a decision as to whether services referred to in s.4 of the Disabled Persons (Services, Consultation and Representation) Act 1986 are required. The services referred to in the 1986 Act are those listed in s.2 of the Chronically Sick and Disabled Persons Act 1970.

Were a local authority somehow attempting to avoid this duty being triggered during the s.47 assessment, then s.4 of the 1986 Act anyway remains freestanding. In other words, under s.4, a disabled person (or his or carer) can make a freestanding request that a decision be made as to whether his or her needs call for any of the services contained in s.2 of the 1970 Act. The local authority then has a duty to comply with that request. In one case, a request for assistance by a mother in respect of her disabled child was accepted by the court as a request for a s.4 decision under the 1986 Act. It might not have been a formal request, but the court (and the local authority) had to look at the reality of the situation (*R v Bexley LBC, ex p B*).

Local authorities will inevitably make priorities in terms of how quickly they assess people (see 6.18). However, this strong duty of assessment does not mean that disabled people with a less urgent, lower priority can simply be ignored – as the local ombudsman has pointed out:

**Closing waiting lists for assessment: failure to assess disabled people.** A local authority had long waiting lists for occupational therapy assessments. The ombudsman investigated the case of one woman who had had to wait 56 months for assessment. The problems were such that waiting lists were closed.

The ombudsman found serious failures and maladministration. He noted: 'The law makes no distinction between the Council's duty to make an assessment in "urgent" and "non-urgent" cases. Any disabled person is entitled to request an assessment and to expect that the request is met within a reasonable time. In my opinion the Council may be failing to discharge their duties under the Chronically Sick and Disabled Persons Act 1970, and I am concerned that they did not seek legal advice on this matter before the lists were closed... The majority of the service users are elderly people suffering from severe disabilities who may not be able to make repeated enquiries to find out whether the list has been reopened in their area. Many of these people may not approach the Social Services Department a second time for assistance, and may continue to live in conditions of extreme discomfort and potential danger' (*Hackney LBC 1992a*).

The following illustrates how a local authority failed to assess a disabled woman under the 1986 Act; it effectively screened her out by means of a letter. For the local ombudsman this was maladministration:

**Screening out a disabled person.** A woman lived in a council house and received income support and mobility allowance. She was in poor health, had difficulty in walking and was entirely reliant on a neighbour to go shopping or to other facilities such as the local library. In order to alleviate these problems, she had bought an electric wheelchair but now required a shelter for it for protection against the weather and vandals. She had identified a prefabricated store costing £1000, and a charity had given her £600 towards the cost. She hoped to enter into an agreement with the supplier to pay the rest by instalment but was concerned that this financial commitment was beyond her means.

The council had some years ago provided a hardstanding and pavement crossing for the woman when she still had a car (since given up). However, now it claimed that it had 'no budgetary provision' for storage facilities for wheelchairs. It further argued that no legal duty arose under s.2 of the Chronically Sick and Disabled Persons Act 1970 'in the absence of any suggestion of personal danger or serious inconvenience'. The council's files held no record of any assessment of the woman's need. The council wrote to the woman, stating that 'a request had been made for her needs to be assessed, but that from the information received she did not appear to meet the Council's criteria for a service and would not therefore receive a visit'. Enclosed with the letter was a copy of the council's criteria of eligibility; the letter did state that the woman should contact the council if she felt that she had missed out important details from her application.

The ombudsman found maladministration. First, the council had made no assessment at the outset, and had then on reconsideration decided that she did not merit a visit (an assessment) because she did not meet the criteria it had sent her. Furthermore it had set out its criteria in an 'exhaustive list'. All this meant that the council was in breach of its duty to decide – on a request made under s.4 of the Disabled Persons (Services, Consultation and Representation) Act 1986 – whether services under s.2 of the Chronically Sick and Disabled Persons Act 1970 were needed (*Sheffield CC 1995*).

## 6.3 REFERRAL, SCREENING AND INITIAL ASSESSMENT

Given the demands made on them, local authorities adopt various types of 'screening' procedures, in order to determine whether a particular person is eligible for assessment – and, if so, what priority should be accorded in terms of how quickly the assessment should be carried out. However this screening is carried out, it needs to be understood in the context of the statutory duty to carry out an assessment under s.47 of the NHS and Community Care 1990. Local authorities must in principle attempt to distinguish between (a) screening a person out from assessment altogether and (b) carrying out a simple assessment of a person and then explaining that he or she does not qualify for services because the need is insufficiently high.

In the first case, people would be 'screened out' because they do not appear to be in need of community care services. In the second, they would be potentially in need of community care services, and would then be assessed as coming beneath the authority's threshold of eligibility and so not be entitled to services. Since the threshold for assessment is low (*R v Bristol CC, ex p Penfold*), it is likely that many more people will fall into the second category than the first; that is, be eligible for some sort of assessment, even if they are probably not going to be eligible for services. The following court case exposed the dilemma for the local authority:

**Assessment or not?** A local authority had been unable to make up its mind whether legally it should say that it had refused to carry out an assessment – or that it had carried out an assessment, albeit a simple, informal one. In the event, a letter written by the assessor, that it would have been preferable to maintain that an assessment had been carried out, gave the game away; the judge concluded that it had in fact not been carried out.

The judge added that, if he was wrong in this conclusion, then the authority had still acted unlawfully since any assessment it claimed to have carried out would have been in breach of policy guidance which talks of a comprehensive and flexible procedure able to determine appropriate responses to requests for assessment. The implications of this were that an assessment is directed at a particular person, and should fully explore need in relation to services which the authority has the legal power to supply (*R v Bristol CC, ex p Penfold*).

The local ombudsman, too, has found maladministration associated with an administrative system for screening out disabled people from obtaining access to home adaptations. The identified inadequacy was made worse by its application to both housing and social services legislation:

**Self-completion questionnaires.** When people applied for disabled facilities grants under the Housing Grants, Construction and Regeneration Act 1996, they were asked to complete a questionnaire; the application of priority points was based entirely on the replies. If a person was awarded fewer points than the threshold figure, the request was not considered further. Until the person reached that threshold (at a later date), he or she would not be seen by a professionally qualified assessment officer. The questionnaire replies were handled by an administrative assistant. This was maladministration.

However, the council was using the same system also to determine its potential responsibilities to people under the Chronically Sick and Disabled Persons Act 1970. There was no separate assessment in terms of social services responsibilities for adaptations. This too was maladministration (*Neath Port Talbot County BC 1999*).

The courts have not explicitly stated whether or not 'telephone' assessments are unlawful or not. What they have said is that the simplicity or complexity assessment must be proportionate to the potential needs of the person (*R v Bristol CC, ex p Penfold*). Nevertheless, it is undeniable that the less and the more cursory the contact the local authority has with a person, the more likely it is to make a mistake:

**Inadequacy of telephone.** In one ombudsman investigation, concerns about the way in which 'first level assessment' operated in determining a person's priority led to a complaints review panel recommending that the referral form completed at this stage should be completed face to face and not just on the telephone (*Ealing LBC 1999*).

### 6.4 LEVEL OF ASSESSMENT

Central government issued guidance in 1991, in anticipation of community care implementation. This referred to the fact that there would clearly be different levels of assessment, to be determined by the apparent potential needs of people being referred. Six levels were suggested, ranging from the simple to the comprehensive (SSI/SWSG 1991, para 2.18).

More recent guidance has been issued by central government on what it refers to as 'single assessment' for older people. It too envisages different assessment levels, but this time suggests only four: contact, overview, specialist and comprehensive (HSC 2002/001). This latter guidance does not explicitly supersede the 1991 guidance.

Any such guidance on assessment nevertheless has to be implemented in the context of the legislation. Thus a local authority must decide, in the case of a person clearly entitled to such an assessment, what level of assessment will reasonably satisfy this entitlement. The local ombudsman has criticised the notion of a 'single service' assessment for a significantly disabled person:

**Single service assessment not a proper assessment.** A man who was an amputee, wheelchair user, diabetic and doubly incontinent received what the local authority called a 'single service' assessment for home help. He was not offered an assessment of his potential need for any other service. He subsequently received a further single service assessment for a special chair. The ombudsman concluded that the local authority had failed properly to assess him as it was legally obliged to do under s.4 of the Disabled Persons (Services, Consultation and Representation) Act 1986 and s.2 of the Chronically Sick and Disabled Persons Act 1970 (*Westminster CC 1996*).

## 6.4.1 SCREENING AND ALLOCATING PRIORITIES FOR ASSESSMENT

The local ombudsman has pointed out that if there is to be screening, then it needs to be of an adequate standard:

**Screening and allocating priorities for assessment.** In one local ombudsman case a disabled housing association tenant applied for disabled facilities grant. She needed to be assessed by social services in order that the recommendation could be made. She was placed on a waiting list of 549 people, of whom 111 were deemed to be a priority; the average wait was a year. The social services assessment officer conceded that identifying priority assessments was 'hit and miss' because application forms contained inadequate information on which to base the decision. This was maladministration (*Bolton MBC 1992*).

Likewise, a poor response at the referral stage might result in a wait that is excessive in the circumstances:

**Improperly determined priority for a person suddenly blind.** A woman suffered a sudden and complete loss of sight. She was referred to the sensory disability team. She was considered not to have a high priority and should have been contacted within six weeks; however, a rigid three-month waiting time was being operated.

The local ombudsman found maladministration; furthermore, her priority had been improperly determined, since she had been at risk from burning and scalding and suffered injuries, which her doctor had seen. This had occurred because of the inadequacy of the original referral (based on a sparse report) and the failure of the sensory disability team to follow up subsequently with the woman what the issues and risks really were (*Stockport MBC 2003*).

In the following case, too, the ombudsman considered the adequacy of the referral process involving a customer services officer, in terms of training and competence:

**Inadequate treatment of referral and competence of customer services officer.** The father of a man who had a drinking problem and died subsequently of a heart attack complained that the local authority had not responded adequately to a request that his son be urgently visited. The ombudsman found that the customer services officer had been properly trained and was capable of reaching decisions about people's priority. Furthermore, although it could be argued that a trained social worker would be better placed to make such priorities, the council's wish to free its social workers for more urgent work were understandable. Nevertheless, the ombudsman found that the customer services officer who dealt initially with this referral did not give the request full and proper consideration. This was maladministration (*St Helens MBC 1998*).

Over-simple priorities or categories will also not do for the local ombudsman:

**Over-simple system of priorities.** A disabled child had to wait 15 months for new seating, including a 12-month wait for assessment. The assessment had been prioritised as complex, which meant that it was on a longer waiting list than existed for cases categorised as emergency or simple. The ombudsman concluded that the system of priorities was 'over-simple', because within the category of complex cases there was 'no provision for relatively simple solutions to tide people over until a full assessment' could be made. Furthermore, there was no provision for treating some cases more urgently within the 'complex' category, even though they were not emergency in nature. This over-simple system meant that the child's needs were not met promptly and was maladministration (*Rochdale MBC 1995*).

## 6.4.2 FORMALLY COMPLYING WITH DUTY OF ASSESSMENT

The courts will up to a point insist that the local authority explicitly complies formally, and is seen to comply, with duties of assessment and decisions about services in the correct logical order. This will be especially so if the shortcuts apparently taken in the assessment process lead to a misunderstanding of the legal questions that need to be asked before a final decision is made.

**Asking questions in the right order.** When deciding whether an autistic child qualified for a disabled facilities grant [see Chapter 15 in this book], the local authority should have first asked the question whether the proposed adaptation fell, in principle, within the purposes for which such a grant is mandatory (in this case the purpose of safety). Second, it then had to ask whether the adaptation would be 'necessary and appropriate' in respect of meeting need and minimising risk. Instead the local authority had stated that the works were not mandatory because they did not materially meet the child's needs. The court held that this was collapsing two questions into one and was consequently unlawful (R(B) v Calderdale MBC).

However, the courts will not always take this exacting approach if they think that in substance the assessment has been performed adequately:

**Assessment and completing all the boxes.** When a local authority offered care home accommodation to an elderly couple but not ordinary accommodation in the community, the court accepted that the local authority had not filled in every box on the assessment forms relating to unmet needs. However, in the context this did not indicate that it had failed to take account of those needs. In the particular situation, the reasons why only one option was offered was because this was the only reasonable option (R(Khana) v Southwark LBC).

**Formal assessment and tidy mindedness.** In a case about housing for a family, the court dismissed the argument that – irrespective of the housing legislation – proper assessments should be carried out under the Chronically Sick and Disabled Persons Act 1970, the Children Act 1989 and the Carers (Recognition and Services) Act 1995. It 'did not accept that at all. There have been numerous assessments in this case… It may be that some are better than others. It may be that some do not explicitly state under what statute or statutes they have been made… The judge exercised his discretion properly…with eminent good sense, when he said that "What this lad needs and what his parents need is a new home"…any correction of a lack of formal assessment in the past would simply be a bit of tidy minded putting the files in order and would not assist resolution of the real problem' (R v Lambeth LBC, ex p A).

**Going through the right steps in assessment.** A dispute arose about whether a 34-year-old man with severe epilepsy was entitled to have an adaptation for an upstairs lavatory, because of the danger of using the stairs. The local authority occupational therapist's report concluded that he did not qualify, because use of a commode at night would be appropriate, and because his able-bodied partner could empty the commode during the night. The court found that the local authority's assessment had not clearly followed the three-stage process demanded by the legislation, in terms of deciding whether the person might be in need of services, then assessing, then deciding whether needs call for services. The court accepted that there had been no 'formalistic' assessment, but was not minded to intervene since there was no prospect of the decision turning out any differently. This was because the council had in substance, if not in form, asked the right questions (R v Sheffield CC, ex p Low).

## 6.5 HEALTH AND HOUSING NEEDS IDENTIFIED DURING ASSESSMENT

If, during an assessment, it appears that the person may have health or housing needs, the local authority must invite the health authority, NHS primary care trust or housing authority (if different to the assessing social services authority) to participate in the assessment. The local authority must then take account of what either the NHS or housing authority is likely to provide, when making its decision about what services the local authority should provide (NHS and Community Care Act 1990, s.47).

The courts have pointed out that local authorities should not be wary of this duty to identify housing needs, simply because they fear that they themselves may have ultimately to meet them – if the housing authority is unable or unwilling to. The courts will be slow to impose a duty on social services to provide ordinary housing (*R(Wahid) v Tower Hamlets LBC*), even though a duty will sometimes arise (see 8.2.1).

There is no explicit, specific duty either on the NHS or on the housing authority to respond to this invitation to assist in the assessment. Indeed the courts have pointed out that the implications of s.47 are precisely not that housing authorities are under a statutory obligation to cooperate (*R v Lewisham LBC, ex p Pinzon*).

Even so, it is arguable that the social services response must be reasonable, in terms of what the NHS or housing authority is likely to provide. The following case, though not concerning s.47 of the 1990 Act, exposes a case of unrealistic reliance by social services, on what a housing authority might do, in order to avoid providing services:

**Unreasonably declining to assess.** A seven-year-old autistic boy lived in temporary accommodation with his mother. The need for alternative accommodation had been recognised by the council, but there was no indication as to when it might be forthcoming. However, the social services department refused to assess, on the grounds that the family might move shortly. The court held that, given the uncertainty over any such move, the needs of the child and the burden on his mother, the local authority should carry out an assessment under the Carers and Disabled Children Act 2000 and s.17 of the Children Act 1989 (*R(J) v Newham LBC*).

## 6.6 COMMUNITY CARE SERVICES

Community care assessment concerns people's potential need for community care services. Such services are defined in s.46 of the NHS and Community Care Act 1990, by reference to other legislation. This consists of Part 3 of the National Assistance Act 1948, Chronically Sick and Disabled Persons Act 1970 (s.2), Health Services and Public Health Act 1968 (s.45), NHS Act 1977 (schedule 8), and Mental Health Act 1983 (s.117). This legislation covers a wide range of non-residential and residential services (see Chapters 8 and 10).

## 6.7 NEEDS CALLING FOR SERVICE PROVISION

Having carried out the assessment, the local authority must decide whether the assessed needs call for provision of services by the local authority (NHS and Community Care Act

1990, s.47). Logically, this clearly implies that some needs may call for services, whilst others may not. There are probably three categories of need that will not call for services.

The first category comprises needs that might be met by another organisation such as the NHS, housing authorities or voluntary organisations – or even by relatives. For instance, some needs may occupy a 'grey area' such that they may legitimately be classed as relating to social care, housing or health care. In such circumstances, if another organisation meets the need, there is clearly no call on the local social services authority to do so. One such example would be where a housing authority will meet a person's needs by provision of a disabled facilities grant under the Housing Grants, Construction and Regeneration Act 1996 to adapt the home (see Chapter 15).

The second category relates to community care services, which the local authority has a power, but no duty, to provide. In this case, the local authority would not be obliged to provide such services, and therefore could conclude that the assessed needs do not call for services. For instance, certain services for older people falling under s.45 of the Health Services and Public Health Act 1968 (see below) entail only a power but no duty (see Chapter 10).

Even some of the duties within community care legislation are of the weaker, 'target', rather than the individual or specific, type (see 4.1); in which case enforcing provision may be problematic. For instance, duties to provide welfare services for disabled people under s.29 of the National Assistance Act 1948 (see 4.1.1) have been so characterised; the individual duty of assessment under s.47 of the NHS and Community Care Act 1990 – which overlays s.29 of the 1948 Act – has been held not to transmute the generality of the s.29 duty into a more specific, individual, enforceable one (*R v Islington LBC, ex p Rixon*).

The third category comprises those needs that are assessed as coming beneath the local authority's threshold of eligibility; in which case they will in principle be deemed not to call for services.

## 6.8 ASSESSMENT OF PREFERENCES AS OPPOSED TO NEEDS

A decision as to whether a person's needs satisfy the threshold of eligibility presupposes that the person has needs. It is the word 'need' that potentially triggers a duty. A mere preference will not do. The courts have identified the important distinction:

**Need or preference?** A local authority disputed whether a young man with learning disabilities really needed to go to a more expensive care home; it maintained that a cheaper one would be adequate to meet his needs. Thus, it argued, the more expensive home represented a mere preference. However, on the facts of the case, the judge held that the overwhelming evidence (through expert views given to a complaints review panel) was that going to the more expensive home constituted a psychological need, not just a preference. The more expensive cost would therefore 'simply be paying what the law required' (*R v Avon CC, ex p M*).

Likewise, the court found on the assessment evidence that the need of a man with mental health problems – for accommodation in a street house in a residential street, rather than in a flat in a large housing estate – constituted a need, not a preference (*R v Richmond LBC, ex p H*).

Therefore, a person's preferences may coincide with what the local authority recognises as a need. In theory this ought to be a not uncommon occurrence, since a whole range of guidance from central government states the importance of placing the individual person and their views at the centre of the assessment. This includes community care policy guidance (DH 1990, para 3.16), guidance on the 'single assessment process' for older people (HSC 2001/1, annex A), and guidance on 'fair access to care' and eligibility criteria (LAC(2002)13, para 35). Furthermore, to enable people to participate in assessments, local authorities should take 'positive steps' in respect of the communication difficulties faced by people with sensory impairments, mental incapacity or other disabilities (DH 1990, para 3.21).

In principle, if not always in practice, this would seem to make it more likely that preferences will coincide with needs. Of course distinguishing preference from need might be no easy matter for the local authority, when, for example, it is assessing an elderly woman who had suffered a bad experience in respite care – and whose preference now was expressed, on file, in terms of her having threatened to kill herself rather than go into residential care (*Cambridgeshire CC 2002*: an ombudsman investigation).

The local authority has to show that it has taken full account of a person's preferences, not necessarily that it has followed them:

**Unlawfully not taking account of preferences.** When assessing a woman with learning disabilities for respite care, the social worker had failed to obtain the views of the woman herself but only spoken with her brother. This breached Department of Health policy guidance (DH 1990, paras 3.16, 3.25) to the effect that preferences be taken account of. The court held that the assessment was therefore unlawful (*R v North Yorkshire CC, ex p Hargreaves*).

It is the local authority, rather than service user, that has the final say, since the legislation refers explicitly throughout to decisions being the local authority's responsibility. Department of Health guidance makes this very point when it states that, having weighed the views of all the relevant parties, it is the assessing local authority practitioner who is responsible for defining a person's needs (SSI/SWSG 1991, para 3.35). More recent guidance states that, in case of disagreement, the matter should be handled sensitively, safeguarding the best interests of both the service user and carer; and that in many cases it might be appropriate for a solution to be sought through independent or statutory advocacy (LAC(2004)24, para 2.4).

## 6.8.1 UNMET NEED
There can in principle be no unmet, eligible need. In other words, if a need is assessed by the local authority as coming above its threshold of eligibility (in terms both of level and coming under legislation that triggers absolute duties: see 4.1), then the need must be met within a reasonable period of time (*R v Gloucestershire CC, ex p Barry*).

First, true unmet need is non-eligible need; that is, need coming beneath the eligibility threshold, or need that comes under legislation that does not create an enforceable, absolute duty. Thus those local authorities that still instruct their staff not to mention the term 'unmet need' in any circumstances for fear of the legal consequences are often labouring under a misapprehension. Indeed, Department of Health practice guidance has always stated that unmet need should be referred to in care plans (SSI/SWSG 1991, para 4.37).

Second, it is nevertheless sometimes the case that the service required to meet an eligible need is simply not available, however much money the local authority is prepared to spend. In which case, unmet need arises. In such circumstances, the courts (and the local ombudsmen) do not demand miracles, but they will expect all reasonable efforts to be made to arrange the service. Therefore, allowing a situation to drift will not do, as the three following examples illustrate:

**Recreational facilities.** A severely disabled man was assessed as needing to access recreational facilities. Such facilities were unavailable. However, the court found that the local authority had appeared simply to take the existing unavailability of such facilities as an insuperable obstacle to further attempts to provide. The lack of a day centre had been treated, however reluctantly, as a complete answer to the question of provision (R v Islington LBC, ex p Rixon).

**Inadequate respite care.** A woman with severe mental and physical disabilities received respite care; her parents complained to the local ombudsman about the care she received, including injuries suffered. The local authority had only one respite house available for women in the north of the city. This had no ground floor bathing facilities, and was still being adapted 21 months into use; and reliance was being placed on staff from an agency about which doubts had been expressed by council officers. The facilities were unsatisfactory; this constituted maladministration (Manchester CC 1996b).

**Inadequate day services.** The complainants to the local ombudsman claimed that the council had failed to assess, and to make adequate day care provision, for the needs of their physically disabled, 25-year-old son. The ombudsman found that the council had 'failed properly to investigate and put in place adequate day provision'. It had not seriously explored the possibility of day services outside the district – indeed it had no policy on the funding of such services, despite recognition that provision for young disabled people was very limited within its own area. Eventually, it was the parents who arranged attendance for their son at a suitable centre. This was maladministration (Trafford MBC 1996).

On the other hand, the courts have held that a local authority may legally be entitled to refuse to provide a service, if it simply will not meet sufficiently the safety of either the person or others:

**Refusal to provide accommodation for released prisoner.** A local authority refused to make arrangements for residential accommodation for a person being released from prison. He had been assessed as being at extremely high risk of violent reoffending. His psychopathic disorder was not treatable and so he could not be admitted under s.47 of the Mental Health Act 1983 as a secure patient; he had a need for 'high secure' accommodation.

The local authority attempted to find such accommodation throughout the country but hospitals would not admit him unless he was sectioned under s.47 of the 1983 Act. It argued that it was under no statutory obligation to meet the man's needs by any other means, because less secure accommodation would likely create danger both for the man and other people. The man brought a case arguing breach of s.21 of the National Assistance Act 1948; the court rejected his application, and agreed that no obligation arose under s.21 (R v Swindon BC, ex p Stoddard).

Third, local authority staff sometimes refer to an additional category of unmet need. This occurs when a person is assessed as having eligible needs, the required services are available locally, but the local authority delays provision for financial reasons. In effect this relates to the question of waiting times for services (see 6.18).

## 6.9 ABSOLUTE DUTY TO MEET ELIGIBLE NEEDS

The courts have ruled that if a need for community care services is assessed as coming above a local authority's eligibility threshold, then in some circumstances it must be met, irrespective of the local authority's resources. This is therefore an 'absolute' or enforceable duty (*R v Gloucestershire CC, ex p Barry*).

However, such a duty is in principle triggered only if the needs and services relate to certain legislation. This comprises s.2 of the Chronically Sick and Disabled Persons Act 1970 (non-residential services), the duties as opposed to the powers under s.21 of the National Assistance Act 1948 (residential accommodation), and s.117 of the Mental Health Act 1983. The courts have specifically confirmed the existence of such a duty in relation to this legislation (*R v Gloucestershire CC, ex p Barry; R v Sefton MBC, ex p Help the Aged; R v Kensington and Chelsea RB, ex p Kujtim*).

**Significance of identifying community care needs in a care plan.** A local authority assessed a person (with a family) with significant mental health problems. It stated in his care plan that he required spacious, secure, ground-floor accommodation. The social services department of the authority had hoped that the housing department of the same authority would meet this need under the Housing Act 1996. However, the family had to wait a considerable length of time on the housing register. The court held in effect that if the housing department could not meet such needs, then the social services department would have to. This was because the need for accommodation was an assessed need and had been included in the care plan as a community care need; this gave rise to a duty under s.21 of the National Assistance Act 1948 (*R v Islington LBC, ex p Batantu*).

Some social service managers instruct their staff not to reveal the real reason for not providing services, for fear of unlawful practices being exposed. For instance, in some local authorities it is impressed upon staff that they must not use the terms 'waiting lists' or 'resources', even if these are the real reasons for delay or non-provision. However, all too often staff still tend to give straightforward and what they consider to be honest explanations to service users – but not, as should be the case, in terms of a person's assessed need being judged to come below the threshold of eligibility, but in far simpler terms of resources and financial crises. Such explanations will sometimes be indicative of unlawful decision making.

**Refusing to provide services in the 'financial freeze'.** A complaint was made to the local ombudsman that when a man with HIV/AIDS had requested a telephone, his request was refused on the basis that he lived with a carer and that he could use the caretaker's telephone (despite a past breach of confidence by the caretaker). However, the social worker conceded that she had referred to the lack of resources as a significant reason for the refusal and to the 'freeze' until the next financial year. The council also later confirmed that its telephone budget had been spent. In the interim, the man's carer installed a telephone at his own expense. This was maladministration since it confused funding with need (*Salford CC 1996*).

Similarly, a reduction in service to people with learning disabilities appeared to the local ombudsman to have been taken, in the language of the case notes, purely on grounds of resources – rather than by a proper consideration of individual need (*Derbyshire CC 2004*).

In contrast, if the needs and services required relate to other community care legislation containing either a general duty or simply a power then there is arguably no absolute duty, even if there is otherwise an apparently 'eligible need'. Such target duties or powers are to be found in s.21 of the National Assistance Act 1948 (residential accommodation) alongside the more specific s.21 duties, in s.29 of the 1948 Act (non-residential services for disabled people), in s.45 of the Health Services and Public Health Act 1968 (services for older people) and in schedule 8 of the NHS Act 1977 (range of non-residential services for illness, home help and laundry facilities).

Confusingly, central government guidance on 'fair access to care' (LAC(2002)13: see below) does not acknowledge, and was apparently written without an awareness of, these distinctions within community care legislation. It simply suggests that all need coming above the relevant threshold need must be met. However, even central government guidance cannot turn powers into duties.

## 6.9.1 VARYING THE THRESHOLD OF ELIGIBILITY

The courts have ruled, in the context of the Chronically Sick and Disabled Persons Act 1970, s.2, that the threshold level for eligibility can lawfully vary between local authorities, and that resources are a relevant factor in determining that level. However, resources are not the only factor – the relative cost of providing services should be balanced against the benefit of doing so. It is a question of matching severity of condition or seriousness of people's needs against the resources available to the authority (*R v Gloucestershire CC, ex p Barry*).

In the case too of s.21 of the National Assistance Act 1948 (residential accommodation), the Court of Appeal reluctantly accepted this principle, although felt that the scope for taking resources into account when deciding whether a person was in need of care and attention was decidedly limited (*R v Sefton MBC, ex p Help the Aged*). This could mean, as one law lord put it, that the needs of disabled people in Bermondsey may differ from those in Belgrave Square (*R v Gloucestershire CC, ex p Barry*). Furthermore, a local authority could lawfully vary the threshold level from time to time. However, such variation would have to be achieved formally at local authority social services committee level (*R v Gloucestershire CC, ex p Barry*). Thus it would not be lawful for individual social services teams informally to vary the threshold from month to month depending on the state of the local team budget.

The need for formality of decision making in setting criteria is also spelt out in Department of Health guidance. It states that eligibility thresholds should be determined for given periods, and be reviewed in line with local authorities' usual budget cycles – unless major or unexpected changes necessitate the bringing forward of such a review. Furthermore, there should be consultation with users, carers and appropriate local agencies, and criteria should be published in local charters and made readily available and accessible (LAC(2002)13, paras 19–20).

Assuming such formalities are complied with, the courts have indicated their reluctance to interfere, on grounds of unreasonableness, with the strictness of eligibility criteria for community care services. They have stated that a local authority's decision would be extremely difficult to review, and that the courts cannot second guess the way in which a local authority spends its limited resources (*R v East Sussex CC, ex p Tandy*). In similar vein, the Department of Health's practice guidance on eligibility criteria states that if resources are scarce locally, then the local authority could decide to assist only those people deemed to be in critical need (DH 2003h, para 3.9).

Thus, the courts have made clear that resources can play a role in setting the threshold for eligibility for services – that is, at what point assessed needs will call for services. However, the courts have gone further and stated that in determining what need is itself, local authorities can take account of resources. This was distinctly controversial, a point made by the two law lords in the minority in the *Gloucestershire* case; they noted that needs should be determined by the professional judgement of a social worker, not by the availability of resources. After all, a child either needs a new pair of shoes or does not; resources are irrelevant to that judgement. However, of the majority law lords, one emphasised that resources could affect the setting of eligibility criteria for need; another that resources would come into play when setting criteria for determining the necessity to meet the need (*R v Gloucestershire CC, ex p Barry*).

The second approach, that is determining necessity to meet need (but not need itself) with reference to resources, is to be preferred for obvious reasons. This second approach anyway accords with the Department of Health's subsequent guidance on eligibility criteria and 'fair access to care' (LAC(2002)13).

### 6.9.2 IMPROPERLY MANIPULATING THE THRESHOLD OF ELIGIBILITY

The implication of the rules set out by the courts is that resources are relevant to the setting of eligibility criteria but not to their application in any one case. Once a need has been assessed, either a person is judged to come over the threshold of eligibility for service provision, or not; either way, resources should not come into it. However, as the following local ombudsman investigation demonstrates, knowledge of the law does not always translate into practice:

**Assessment of residential placement.** A local authority assessed whether to place and pay for a residential placement for a person with learning disabilities. Its policy was legally correct; a decision about eligibility would follow an assessment of need but before a decision about affordability. However, this was not the practice; the chairwoman of the complaints review panel involved had expected to see a detailed assessment report of the young man's needs. Instead it was her view that the council's decision and supporting paperwork had been based solely on the fact that it did not want to pay for residential care. This was maladministration (*Kent CC 1998*).

A second type of improper manipulation occurs when a local authority provides inadequate resources to support the threshold of eligibility that it has set. In other words, if the threshold is 'too generous' in relation to resources, the local authority will be assessing 'too many' people as having eligible needs. The relevant budgets will then be at risk of being overspent; yet managers are frequently warned that it is 'more than their job is worth' to exceed their financial allocations. In which case, individual team managers sometimes instruct their staff 'secretly' to assess eligibility at a threshold significantly higher than that formally adopted and published by the social services committee. This is likely to be unlawful.

For instance, the local ombudsman found an instruction issued to officers stating that they were 'not to spend unless a situation had become critical and inescapable' – irrespective of service users who had been assessed as having eligible needs:

**Published eligibility and real eligibility threshold.** A woman with learning disabilities lived with her elderly parents, aged 77 and 75 years. She needed assistance with most aspects of daily life, including assistance with medication, avoiding certain foods, assistance in getting out of bed, supervision and guidance in meal and preparation, assistance with personal hygiene and bathing, assistance with communication, assistance and support with household tasks, shopping and the use of money, support to go anywhere outside the home. The parents found it increasingly difficult to cope; the GP had written a letter outlining poor hygiene, inappropriate reactions to problems, giving 'considerable cause for alarm'. She was assessed as being in eligible need of a residential placement because she was at major risk of harm – scored against the council's formal, published matrix of need.

Nevertheless, provision was not made until the requirement was eventually recorded as being 'inescapable'. This was significant because staff were under an informal instruction (i.e. not part of the official eligibility framework) not to spend unless a situation was 'critical and inescapable'. Nevertheless, it had taken from August 1998 to November 1999 for funding to be offered.

The local ombudsman found that three months would have been reasonable; therefore the woman had lived in conditions assessed by the council as 'utterly unsuitable' for 11 months longer than she should have done. This was maladministration (*Cambridgeshire CC 2001*).

Third, a significant number of local authorities utilise funding panels or equivalent (e.g. a supervising manager) to restrict spending. Such panels come in various guises and nomenclature, such as a 'Caring for People Panel' (*Liverpool CC 1998b*), 'Star Chamber' or 'Starlet Chamber' (*Camden LBC 1993*).

The funding panel process is sometimes used, in effect, to manipulate the threshold as it is applied both to individual people and to classes of person. Sometimes panels do not challenge the assessment of eligible need, but simply allocate waiting times. However, on other occasions they query the results of the professional assessment of need and put very considerable pressure on the assessor to alter his or her conclusions; alternatively the panel simply alters the decision itself.

There would perhaps be no objection where the panel is genuinely scrutinising whether a competent assessment has been carried out. However, on many occasions, it appears financial anxiety wholly drives the process and this can lead local authorities into unlawful territory, as the court uncovered in just such a case:

**Unlawfully backtracking on a decision.** A complaints review panel recommended that the council find larger accommodation for a family with three teenage boys who were severely mentally handicapped and had behavioural problems. This would be under s.21 of the National Assistance Act 1948 and s.17 of the Children Act 1989. A social services officer visited the family and made it clear that the authority had accepted the recommendation. The local authority subsequently changed its mind when the cost implications became clear. The court ruled that from the point of the social services officer's visit, the local authority had a duty to provide the accommodation. The subsequent change of heart was unlawful. He ordered the property to be identified within three months and made available within six (*R v Wigan MBC, ex p Tammadge*).

Local authorities must not allow such panels to obscure legal responsibilities for decision making. They should also be aware that the courts are more than capable of detecting improper short cuts, and sham proceedings where the panel has made up its mind in advance of a case:

**Panel usurping local authority's legal duty.** It was the function of a local continuing care panel to make recommendations to the local authority about the level (and funding) of care required by service users. The panel's role was advisory only.

In one particular case, the panel relied on the views of a doctor, who himself had not seen the woman involved. The panel also failed to consider all the relevant issues (e.g. a detailed social work team manager's report coming to the opposite conclusion to the doctor). The panel's recommendations were therefore flawed. Yet, in turn, the local authority relied on the panel's recommendations.

The court held that the local authority had failed to make a lawful decision as it was required to do, following a full, up-to-date community care assessment and taking account of all the relevant issues. One of the panel members had 'plainly made up her mind' before an (anyway) flawed meeting; the decision as a whole was simply pre-determined.

The court also took particular exception to an improper letter written by that panel member to the doctor, which indicated that it was only the daughter (as a 'lone voice', unsupported by professional opinion) who was opposing her mother's placement in a nursing home – when this was clearly not the case (*R(Goldsmith) v Wandsworth LBC*).

A safeguard for both staff and service users is for assessing staff to put forward well-evidenced and well-reasoned assessments, the conclusions of which are expressed in the relevant terminology – for instance, that of the 'fair access to care' eligibility criteria that local authorities apply. This makes it much more difficult for funding panels or senior managers to set aside assessment on spurious grounds. Indeed, Department of Health practice guidance clearly envisages that staff should be able to argue cases on an individual basis. First, it points out that what is 'vital' (a word used in the risk to independence framework: see 6.11) for one person might not be for another. Second, it states that assessment relies on person-centred conversations; 'frameworks, case examples and the like can only ever support the exercise of person-centred competent judgement' (DH 2003h, paras 3.6, 3.14).

All this is not theoretical; in one case, a comprehensive and well-documented assessment came to the rescue of an elderly woman, whom the local continuing care panel was attempting to remove from a care home, on the basis of partial and inadequate information (*R(Goldsmith) v Wandsworth LBC*; see 3.9 for details).

### 6.9.3 MEETING ASSESSED NEED: RELEVANCE OF RESOURCES OF SERVICE USERS

Department of Health guidance states that if a person has both the mental and financial (i.e. has resources over the 'capital threshold': see 9.6) capacity to arrange and pay for residential accommodation, then the local authority is not obliged to make the care home placement.

However, for non-residential services, guidance states the opposite, namely that local authorities should arrange services to meet eligible needs – irrespective of a person's financial capacity – if that is what the person wants (DH 2003h, para 8.5). This approach appears to be in line with the original community care policy guidance, which states that the provision of services should not be related to the ability of the people or their families to meet the costs (DH 1990, para 3.31).

Nevertheless, one of the law lords has stated that it might not be necessary for the local authority to make arrangements for non-residential services under the Chronically Sick and Disabled Persons Act 1970, s.2, if the person was 'wealthy enough to meet his needs out of his own pocket' (*R v Gloucestershire CC, ex p Barry*). Even were it lawful to take account of a person's resources in deciding whether to provide (as opposed to what to charge the person), the local authority would have to ensure that it was taking a reasonable approach on a case-by-case basis, rather than employing a blanket rule. In terms of good administration at least, this was the view of the local ombudsman:

**Taking account of a person's resources in deciding whether to provide a service.** A woman applied for help with a hardstanding and shelter for her outdoor, powered wheelchair. The local authority stated that such outdoor mobility needs should be met through her mobility allowance (a social security benefit) and not through the local authority. The local ombudsman accepted that 'an individual's private means may be relevant as to whether or not the Council itself needs to make any provision'. Nevertheless the council had raised this argument only 'very late in the day' – and had in any case apparently made no effort to establish what the mobility allowance was already being spent on in reality (*Sheffield CC 1995*).

This approach would seem to be supported by a judicial decision that in certain circumstances at least, the resources of the parents of two disabled children could be taken into account, when the local authority was deciding whether to provide assistance under the Chronically Sick and Disabled Persons Act 1970 (*R(Spink) v Wandsworth LBC*). It would seem at least arguable that if the resources of a third party can be taken into account, then so too could those of an adult himself or herself.

## 6.10 MEETING NEED COST-EFFECTIVELY

The courts have consistently ruled that if there are two or more options to meet a person's eligible assessed needs, the local authority can offer the cheapest, so long as that particular option genuinely meets those needs.

**Cost-effective options to meet need for residential accommodation**. In two Court of Appeal cases, it was lawful for the local authorities concerned to offer care home accommodation, even though the service users wished to be supported in the community. This was essentially because the care home accommodation would meet the assessed needs (*R v Lancashire CC, ex p RADAR; R(Khana) v Southwark LBC*). The Human Rights Act 1998 has not affected this general principle; the second of these cases (*Southwark*) was decided after the Act came into force.

On the other hand, if there were no resource implications in the difference between two options – both of which would meet the person's needs – then it might be unreasonable for the local authority not to offer the option of choice (*R(Khana) v Southwark LBC*).

**Mobility needs of a disabled woman at a day centre**. The court stated that a local authority was entitled to take account of resources in deciding how to meet a seriously disabled woman's need for assistance with mobility at a day centre; the choice was between human walking assistance, her walking alone (if the parents agreed to her wearing protective headgear), or use of a wheelchair and rollator (*R v Cornwall CC, ex p Goldsack*).

**Differentiating need from services: stairlift dispute**. In a dispute about provision of a vertical lift or stairlift, the court pointed out that need should be differentiated from the means to meet it. The requirement of the stairlift fell into the latter, but not the former, category. Therefore it was 'impossible to regard the provision of a stairlift at home as "the need"'. Instead the need was 'for the applicants to get in and out of the premises' – for which the authority could review various options and take account of cost. Indeed, the authority was 'perfectly entitled to look to see what is the cheapest way for them to meet the needs which are specified' (*R v Kirklees MBC, ex p Daykin*).

**Review of services and options for people with learning disabilities**. The applicant was a 50-year-old man with learning disabilities, poor eyesight and requiring assistance in looking after himself. In order to save money, the local authority was conducting a review of its care arrangements – and transferring the provision of care for some people to cheaper providers. The social worker was supposed to go down the list, starting with the cheapest, until he or she found a provider who was able to provide the care that was needed. This entailed a change of provider for the applicant – from a male support worker to a female carer – a change he did not want. The authority was accused of fettering its discretion in only making exceptions when the change in provision would be 'significantly detrimental' – and of making resources the prevailing or predominant consideration.

The judge did not find a fettering of discretion, and stated that the authority could take account of resources up to a point. He accepted that the changes were resource led in that they would not have been made unless there was a need to cut costs – but they were not on that account unlawful, so long as the 'correct balancing exercise' had been carried out in reassessing individual needs. The reassessment exercise had in fact resulted in 7 out of 13 users remaining with the more expensive care agency. Consequently there was nothing 'to indicate that resources were regarded as paramount or that the Council manifestly got the balance wrong' (*R v Essex CC, ex p Bucke*).

The courts have commented that a certain degree of specificity in how need is assessed and is to be met is clearly required; equally over-specification in every case might mean that even slight changes to services would trigger formal reassessments, and would be excessively cumbersome (*R v Cornwall CC, ex p Goldsack*).

Nevertheless the courts have also warned local authorities against allowing so-called 'best value' principles (under s.3 of the Local Government Act 1999) to interfere with the basic duty to meet people's assessed community care needs (*R (Bodimeade) v Camden LBC*). In other words, a local authority must ensure that it 'never forgets that the needs of the user are to be regarded as of greater importance than the need to save money' (*R v Essex CC, ex p Bucke*). Thus, where assessed needs call for a more expensive option, the local authority must find the resources; best value affects how a duty is performed, not whether to perform it. For instance, the refusal to place a person with learning disabilities at a residential home – which the local authority regarded as excessively expensive (and would have provided services in excess of his needs) – was unlawful, because the authority had made the decision before any suitable, cheaper alternatives had been found (*R(A) v Bromley LBC*).

Notwithstanding this, local authorities sometimes deprive themselves of the opportunity to decide which option really will meet a person's needs, typically by imposing rigid restrictions or ceilings on what they are prepared to consider – as the two following local ombudsman investigations reveal:

**Considering exceptional needs of a woman and the option of remaining at home.** A local authority operated a ceiling on home care packages for older people. It argued that this did not represent a fettering of discretion because it had a 'Caring for People Panel' that considered exceptions.

Applying this policy, the council refused to exceed the ceiling in the case of a woman who was blind and deaf, had diabetes, arthritis, hypertension and a heart problem, and was incontinent and depressed. She had become increasingly confused and had a loss of short-term memory. Her mobility was very restricted and she communicated by hand signing. The daughter explained (a) that given that her mother had 'no quality of life' but just existence, her going into a nursing home would mean that she would lose love, affection and understanding and that she could not abandon her mother in that way; and (b) that her mother's needs were exceptional since she required constant one-to-one attention day and night including constant reassurance and stimulation, changing, frequent strip washing (particularly important because of bowel and kidney problems), safety measures (she would crawl around the floor like a baby) – and so on.

The local ombudsman found a fettering of discretion, coming to the conclusion that there was no evidence that the 'Caring for People Panel' ever made exceptions. This was maladministration. The ombudsman also criticised the ceiling as discriminating against older people (*Liverpool CC 1998b*).

In the next case, the rigid restriction imposed by the local authority would, perversely, probably have resulted in greater expense than if an exception had been made and the service user's need met more appropriately:

**Providing services in the last days.** A man complained to the local ombudsman about the last days of his parents and the putting to bed service they received. The father was 90 with Parkinson's disease, arthritis and spinal kyphosis; his wife, who was 92, and his main carer, was blind and had angina. The father had been assessed as needing assistance with getting up and going to bed. Evening and weekend cover was provided by an agency.

On 1 Feb, the agency informed the council it was withdrawing weekend service because it could not recruit staff. On 2 March, the council informed the couple that they might have to attend respite care at a residential home instead; meanwhile district nurses provided the weekend cover on a temporary basis. The agency then informed the council that the evening service would be withdrawn from 26 March. On 24 March, the wife became ill, went into hospital and died on 16 May. The husband went into residential care and died on 21 April. All this had been very stressful; extracts from the woman's journal revealed this.

The council had been unable to find another agency to provide the putting to bed service unless it would pay travel costs of staff, above the flat rate fee for the service, and this was against council policy.

The local ombudsman found maladministration, reminding the council of the importance and sensitivity of its services to vulnerably elderly people. The council should have seized the offer from another home care contractor, even at a higher rate. The man's home care was 'entirely sacrificed to maintain the purity of the councils' contractual arrangements'. No one seriously thought of making an exception to the policy, even though the cost of the weekend respite care would probably exceed by far the costs of the agency staff even with extra travel costs. This was a classic case of the council fettering its discretion and of maladministration (*Essex CC 2001*).

### 6.10.1 FINDING THE MONEY WHEN THERE IS NONE

Hard-pressed local authority managers often ask the legitimate question of how they are meant to perform a legal obligation if their budgets are effectively inadequate. The answer is that when a duty arises, it arises not in respect of a particular local authority budget but in respect of the local authority as a whole. Thus the courts have considered and answered this very question directly, by stating that the money must be found from somewhere else within the local authority – that is, taken from other functions not subject to an absolute duty that demands expenditure.

**Finding the money to perform a duty.** Referring to education legislation, the court (House of Lords) stated that while the local authority might not want 'to bleed its other functions of resources so as to enable it to perform the statutory duty', nevertheless it could divert money from other discretionary functions. Thus, the 'argument is not one of insufficient resources to discharge the duty but of a preference for using the money for other purposes. To permit a local authority to avoid performing a statutory duty on the grounds that it prefers to spend the money in other ways is to downgrade a statutory duty to a discretionary power.' Indeed, if 'Parliament wishes to reduce public expenditure on meeting the needs of sick children then it is up to Parliament so to provide. It is not for the courts to adjust the order or priorities as between statutory duties and statutory discretions.' At an earlier stage of the same case the Court of Appeal pointed out that a local authority might have to save on non-mandatory items such as a proposed leisure centre or football ground (*R v East Sussex CC, ex p Tandy*).

Indeed, Department of Health guidance on assessment and eligibility criteria makes just this point when it states that local authorities 'should not adhere so rigidly to budget headings for specific services that resources cannot move from one budget heading to another, if necessary' (LAC(2002)13, para 23).

### 6.11 FAIR ACCESS TO CARE: ELIGIBILITY CRITERIA

The Department of Health has issued guidance to local authorities on what it calls 'fair access to care' in respect of adult social services. This guidance, although it does not explicitly acknowledge it, builds upon the rules set out in legal cases such as *R v Gloucestershire CC, ex p Barry*.

Although it is only guidance, and as such does not amount to law, it is nevertheless stronger rather than weaker and should generally be followed by local authorities unless there are very good reasons for not doing so. This is because it is made under s.7 of the Local Authority Social Services Act 1970, and thus constitutes what is sometimes called 'statutory guidance' (see 4.1.6). Certainly the courts have afforded it considerable attention (*R v Sheffield CC, ex p Heffernan*). The guidance states that when local authorities assess people's needs, evaluation of risks should focus on:

- autonomy and freedom to make choices; health and safety including freedom from harm, abuse and neglect, housing and community safety
- ability to manage personal and other daily routines
- involvement in family and wider community life, including leisure, hobbies, unpaid and paid work, learning and volunteering (LAC(2002)13, para 40).

In order to assist them to do this, the guidance states that local authorities should use a framework in terms of risk to independence. Risks to independence should be categorised as being critical, substantial, moderate or low. Each local authority should then set a threshold of eligibility, above which such risks (when translated into needs) will be eligible for service provision, and below which they will not. Local authorities have not been told where to set the threshold within the framework. It appears that many have set it either between the substantial and moderate, or between the moderate and low categories. The guidance also states that the same eligibility threshold should be operated across all services (LAC(2002)13, para 3). The framework is as follows, setting out four different categories of risk to independence (LAC(2002)13, para 16):

- **Critical risk to independence**.
  - Life is, or will be, threatened; and/or
  - significant health problems have developed or will develop; and/or
  - there is, or will be, little or no choice and control over vital aspects of the immediate environment; and/or
  - serious abuse or neglect has occurred or will occur; and/or
  - there is, or will be, an inability to carry out vital personal care or domestic routines; and/or
  - vital involvement in work, education or learning cannot or will not be sustained; and/or
  - vital social support systems and relationships cannot or will not be sustained; and/or
  - vital family and other social roles and responsibilities cannot or will not be undertaken.
- **Substantial risk to independence**.
  - There is, or will be, only partial choice and control over the immediate environment; and/or

- ○ abuse or neglect has occurred or will occur; and/or
- ○ there is, or will be, an inability to carry out the majority of personal care or domestic routines; and/or
- ○ involvement in many aspects of work, education or learning cannot or will not be sustained; and/or
- ○ the majority of social support systems and relationships cannot or will not be sustained; and/or
- ○ the majority of family and other social roles and responsibilities cannot or will not be undertaken.

- **Moderate risk to independence.**
  - ○ There is, or will be, an inability to carry out several personal care or domestic routines; and/or
  - ○ involvement in several aspects of work, education or learning cannot or will not be sustained; and/or
  - ○ several social support systems and relationships cannot or will not be sustained; and/or
  - ○ several family and other social roles and responsibilities cannot or will not be undertaken.

- **Low risk to independence.**
  - ○ There is, or will be, an inability to carry out one or two personal care or domestic routines; and/or
  - ○ involvement in one or two aspects of work, education or learning cannot or will not be sustained; and/or
  - ○ one or two social support systems and relationships cannot or will not be sustained; and/or
  - ○ one or two family and other social roles and responsibilities cannot or will not be undertaken.

The guidance stipulates that prevention should be built in to the application of this framework (LAC(2002)13, para 22). A glance at the indicators within each category makes it clear that assessment should be about far more than physical risk. Certainly, under the critical category, reference is made to threat to life, significant health problems, little or no choice and control over vital aspects of the immediate environment, serious abuse or neglect, and vital personal care or domestic routines. But beyond such issues, reference is made also to vital involvement in work or education or learning, vital social support systems and relationships, vital family and other social roles and responsibilities.

All this indicates that the scope of assessment under this guidance should be wide, taking an 'independent living' or 'social model of disability' approach. For instance, when disabled parents are assessed, parenting as well as other needs should be covered; something that apparently does not always occur (Morris 2003, p.14).

Further, practice guidance states that local authorities should not vary the wording of this framework (DH 2003h, para 3.1), a point the courts have picked up on:

**Unlawfully varying the guidance on eligibility.** When a local authority differentiated between 'major health problems' in the critical category, and 'significant health problems' in the substantial category, the court found the authority to be in error. In turn, this had the consequence that any needs related to a health condition should properly have been assessed as falling into the critical category. The local authority had assessed matters such as cleaning, shopping, and attendance at appointments as representing a moderate risk to independence only. However, because they were related to the man's health care condition, they should all have been placed in the critical category and so provided by the local authority (R(Heffernan) v Sheffield CC).

The guidance states that once eligibility of need is established, a duty arises to meet it (para 43). (However, unhelpfully, the guidance does not distinguish between different pieces of community care legislation and the fact that some of it entails only powers or target duties, neither of which give rise to enforceable legal obligations: see 4.1).

Practice guidance further complicates matters by reminding local authorities that the framework in the guidance refers to 'risk to independence', whereas it is only 'need' that triggers a legal duty to provide services. Therefore, it suggests that needs associated with eligible risk should only themselves be deemed eligible needs if 'through addressing them, risks are ameliorated, contained or reduced' (DH 2003h, para 3.12).

Overall, the breadth and scope of assessment, as set out in the guidance, is consonant with the implications of the community care legislation, such as the Chronically Sick and Disabled Persons Act 1970 (see 10.2), which covers a wide range of needs and services. It is also supported by the approach of the law courts in a number of community care cases, in terms of the potentially wide range of relevant factors that must be taken account of in assessments (see 6.12).

## 6.11.1 BLANKET POLICIES

The guidance expressly states that local authorities should not have blanket policies not to provide particular services (LAC(2002)13, para 23). There are at least four good reasons for the guidance to take this stance.

First, such policies will unlawfully fetter a local authority's discretion, as they would amount to excessive rigidity (see 4.2.2). Second, such policies might prevent lawful assessment because staff will not bother to carry out a full assessment for a service they know will not be provided (see 6.1.1). Third, this in turn might signify poor professional practice. Fourth, it is an unfair way of rationing services, because it is then based not on the level of people's needs, but on arbitrary decisions about which services will or will not be provided. The local ombudsman was thus concerned about such a blanket policy involving cleaning services:

**Prioritising shopping over cleaning.** Local authority staff applied a policy of prioritising shopping over cleaning services, whenever demand for services exceeded the local authority's capacity to deliver services. A man complained about this. He was an amputee, wheelchair user, diabetic and doubly incontinent. He was concerned that his health and indeed his life were placed at risk by this policy, which meant he did not receive a regular and reliable cleaning service.

The local ombudsman found maladministration, since there was no evidence that the local authority had considered the man's medical circumstances and whether they justified the maintaining of a cleaning service. Furthermore the policy had not been put to members of the social services committee, nor were there guidelines about how to apply it (*Westminster CC 1996*).

Indeed, Department of Health guidance concerned with the provision of assistance for carers states that local authorities that have decided not to provide or commission certain services as community care services – such as 'shopping only' or 'cleaning only' services – 'should review their positions' (DH 2001b). Restrictive policies on assistance with bathing are also not uncommon within local authorities; one such was criticised by the local government ombudsman:

**Restrictive policy on bathing and showering.** An 84-year-old man had suffered a stroke; he suffered greatly reduced mobility, and could walk only in a shuffling gait with a walking frame. He could no longer get into his shower and he requested a level access shower. Initially he was refused because the local authority's policy limited eligibility for such a shower to people with a skin condition, incontinence or arthritis (where the person was under a hospital consultant). The ombudsman commented that it would be unreasonable to set criteria so tightly that people obviously in need do not qualify; yet on the face of it the man had a need but did not meet the criteria (*Castle Morpeth BC 2003*).

Certainly, it is not clear how such restricted eligibility for showering or bathing, as a matter of policy, is consonant with the type of full, 'person-centred' assessment urged by the Department of Health's 'fair access to care' guidance (LAC(2002)13: see 6.11) – under which there would surely be many other possible reasons why a person's need for access to shower or bath might be categorised as associated with, for example, a critical or substantial risk to independence.

## 6.12 TAKING ACCOUNT OF LEGALLY RELEVANT FACTORS IN ASSESSMENTS

The courts' interpretation of what would constitute an adequate assessment is consonant with the breadth and scope of assessment set out in the 'fair access to care guidance'. The following cases, involving matters such as medical or therapy advice, cultural factors, preferences, distress, dignity, etc. are illustrative:

**Failing to obtain medical advice.** When reassessing a woman with multiple sclerosis, the local authority failed to obtain advice from the woman's general practitioner – advice that the local authority had itself identified as necessary. Nevertheless, it concluded the assessment and reduced the woman's care package. This was unlawful (*R v Birmingham CC, ex p Killigrew*).

**Cultural needs.** When offering to place an elderly Iraqi-Kurdish couple in a care home, against the husband's and wider family's wishes, the court was concerned to ascertain whether the local authority had taken account of the relevant cultural and language matters. It found that it had, and that the decision was lawful (*R(Khana) v Southwark LBC*).

**A person's preferences.** A local authority assessed a woman with learning disabilities for respite care. During the assessment, the social worker spoke only to the woman's brother, who was her main carer. Although the brother might have been obstructive, it was still incumbent on the local authority to ascertain what those preferences were (*R v North Yorkshire CC, ex p Hargreaves*).

**Fear, distress, dignity.** In a case about the manual handling requirements of two women with profound physical and learning disabilities, the court stated that the local authority would have to take account of the emotional, psychological and social impact on two women with learning and physical disabilities. This would be in terms of their wishes, feelings, reluctance, fear, refusal, dignity, integrity and quality of life. The context was about how to effect physical transfers of the two women, and whether they should be hoisted (R(A&B) v East Sussex County Council (no.2)).

The local government ombudsmen, too, look to ensure that all relevant factors have been considered:

**Failing to seek advice from occupational therapist and physiotherapist.** A man had suffered a stroke, substantially paralysing his right arm and leg. He had diabetes, hypertension, ulcerative colitis, coronary disease and deformities to his right hand and foot. When reducing a care package from 31 hours a week to 14 hours, the local authority's reassessment failed to obtain advice from a physiotherapist and occupational therapist as to whether the reduced package would still meet his needs. This was maladministration (Southwark LBC 2001).

**Reduction of care for woman with severe osteoporosis.** In 1997, the local authority proposed to reduce the weekly package of care for a woman with severe osteoporosis; she suffered constant pain, fear of new fractures, actual new major and micro-fractures, headaches, drug-induced side effects. She had a high risk of developing heart disease and was seriously underweight. She argued for a case review on the grounds that the reduced package would not meet her needs. The review identified the need for specialist advice from an occupational therapist and a consultant physician. The council made no sustained attempt to get the consultant's advice; yet without it, the reassessment could not be completed. There was gross delay. New care plans were issued in 1998 and 1999, altering the level of service but without completed reassessments. All this was maladministration (Croydon LBC 2000).

A Court of Appeal decision in 2004 notably illustrates the importance of relevant factors, and their role in achieving fairness in decision making:

**Taking a manifestly flawed and defective decision.** The local authority decided that a 95-year-old woman could not continue to live in her previous residential home, but would have to go into a nursing home. Her daughter opposed this decision. The court severely criticised the local authority. Amongst other things, it had failed to take account of a critical piece of information, namely the impressive and comprehensive assessment report of the social work team manager, who knew the woman best. For this and other reasons, the decision was manifestly flawed and failed to consider all the relevant factors (R(Goldsmith) v Wandsworth LBC).

## 6.12.1 RELEVANT FACTORS: CORRECT WEIGHTING

The courts and the ombudsman normally look only so far as to see whether relevant factors have been taken account of. Unless the decision-maker has taken an irrational or unreasonable decision, the courts will not interfere. To go further would run the risk of pronouncing on the merits of a particular decision; this would in turn run counter to the notion of the courts' 'supervisory jurisdiction' in judicial review (see 4.2.1) and to the statutory prohibition on the local government ombudsman to question matters of professional judgement (Local Government Act 1974, s.34).

Nevertheless, particularly where human rights are in issue, the courts might sometimes go beyond considering only the presence of relevant factors, and look to see whether the decision-maker has struck the correct balance (*R(AandB) v East Sussex CC (no.2)*). This is connected with what is sometimes called the principle of 'proportionality', such that even if the decision is not outlandish in terms of irrationality or unreasonableness, nevertheless the courts might decide whether the decision was a balanced one. This approach might sometimes have the effect of appearing to stray into a questioning of the merits of decisions and of professional judgements.

## 6.13 GIVING EXPLANATIONS AND REASONS

Community care legislation for the most part does not contain duties to give reasons for decisions; and there is no general common law duty to give them (see 4.2.6). However, local authorities would be well advised to have properly recorded reasons for decisions, since their absence may lead the courts to query the lawfulness of a particular decision; and a lack of reasons anyway constitutes maladministration in the eyes of the local ombudsman.

Thus, in measured exasperation, the courts in one case criticised a local authority decision about the needs of a disabled boy, finding a flawed decision-making process: 'Unless the repetition of an assertion is to be regarded as a proper manifestation of a reasoning process, there was none here' (*R v Ealing LBC, ex p C*). In another, the absence of explanation as to why services were being reduced led the court to conclude that the decision was an unlawful one (*R v Birmingham CC, ex p Killigrew*).

**Withdrawing services without relevant evidence of change of need.** When night sitter services were withdrawn from an 86-year-old woman on the basis of her no longer needing them – but without evidence of change of circumstance or need – the court stated that there was a very strong argument that the authority was acting irrationally or unreasonably (*R v Staffordshire CC, ex p Farley*).

In a futher case, the Court of Appeal struck down a local authority's purported decision to place a woman in a nursing home. The court pointed out that had the decision taken account of all relevant issues, had it been properly recorded with reasons, and had those reasons been communicated to the woman's daughter – then the local authority's decision would probably not have been susceptible to judicial review (*R(Goldsmith) v Wandsworth LBC*).

## 6.14 SELF-ASSESSMENT

As already noted, Department of Health guidance stresses the importance of the service user being at the centre of, and fully participating in, the assessment (see 6.8). Local authorities sometimes ask people to fill out 'self-assessment' forms in order to help achieve this. As part of a wider assessment, there is nothing objectionable in this. However, sometimes authorities go one step beyond, appearing to rely wholly on such self-assessment. It is difficult to see how this could be a lawful assessment under s.47 of the NHS and Community Care Act 1990, since it is the local authority that has to take the final decision; it could not give this duty up and hand it over entirely to the service user.

(Perhaps any such self-assessment schemes could be regarded as coming under s.29 of the National Assistance Act 1948 [non-residential services for disabled people] and s.45 of the Health Services and Public Health Act 1968 [non-residential services for older people]. If taken as freestanding, neither of these two Acts explicitly refers to assessments of, or decisions about, need. If this were not permissible, then perhaps such schemes could be regarded as coming under general local government legislation, such as s.111 of the Local Government Act 1972 or s.2 of the Local Government Act 2000.) In any event, the following local ombudsman investigation illustrates the confusion that can arise:

**Self-assessment system.** A council operated a system of providing home adaptations on the basis of what it termed self-assessment. Consequently a disabled woman assessed that she required an extra bedroom. The council then argued that it had no obligation to provide this, since its apparent willingness at one point to provide the extension did not translate into a legal duty to do so. The ombudsman accepted this but found the council's apparent undertaking had been misleading, leading to acute disappointment and frustration. This was maladministration (*Manchester CC 1994*).

In another context, that of housing allocation based on the 'additional preferences' identified by tenants themselves, the court pointed out that self-assessment would not identify priorities and different degrees of need. This was because the 'individual is inevitably concerned only with his or own situation and may not on any reasonably objective view have greater need' (*Lambeth LBC v A*).

## 6.15 REVIEW AND REASSESSMENT

From time to time service users will need to be reassessed. The trigger might be, for example, (a) a review date becoming due; (b) needs and circumstances anyway changing (perhaps before a scheduled review date); (c) a change in the local authority's threshold of eligibility.

**Failing to reassess on change of need.** A complaint was made to the local ombudsman concerning a man with learning disabilities who had in 1991 been placed in a care home jointly by social services and the NHS. In 1998, he was diagnosed as suffering from high functioning autism. However, he was not reassessed by the local authority until February 2003 and not provided with additional services until June of that year. The local ombudsman found maladministration (*Cambridgeshire CC 2004*).

In the legislation, there is no explicit duty of review or reassessment. However, reassessment is in effect covered by s.47 of the NHS and Community Care Act 1990; it is assessment all over again against potential (changed) need.

The importance of review is stressed by recent guidance, including that on 'fair access to care' (LAC(2002)13, paras 57–64) and on the 'single assessment process' for older people (LAC(2002)1, annex E). The guidance stipulates that reviews should be undertaken on a routine basis, within three months of services first being provided or of major changes to services, and after that annually or more frequently if necessary. It adds that 'one-off pieces' of community equipment do not need review after initial confirmation of suitability and safety, although major items should be reviewed for suitability and safety annually, or more frequently if recommended by manufacturers (LAC(2003)13, paras 60, 63; LAC(2002)1, annex E).

In practice, reviewing people's services would appear to have been a longstanding problem for local authorities. At the outset of community care, central government guidance acknowledged this (SSI/SWSG 1991, para 7.1); the local ombudsmen continue to identify the issue:

**Failure to reassess.** In July 1995, the local authority entered a contract with a voluntary organisation to provide services at a day centre, which two brothers with learning disabilities had been attending for years. The contract expressly stipulated that the services were to be for adults with sensory impairment, physical and invisible disabilities. Reference to learning disabilities was not included. The contract also stated that reassessment of all current service users would be undertaken within six months. However, this did not occur for 18 months, a delay of a year. The local ombudsman found maladministration (*Hackney LBC 1998*).

**Failure to review.** A woman complained on behalf of her mother, concerned amongst other things about her care in a care home including sitting in urine soaked clothing, assistance with feeding (she lost over four stone in weight) and inappropriate medication. The mother was 81 years old, had rheumatoid arthritis, angina, was occasionally incontinent and displayed early signs of dementia. Amongst her findings the local ombudsman criticised the failure to carry out a six-monthly review. She pointed out that had a review taken place, the weight loss could have been investigated and dealt with that much earlier (*Wigan MBC 2001*).

## 6.15.1 CONDITIONS FOR LAWFUL WITHDRAWAL OR REDUCTION OF SERVICES

Services can in some circumstances be lawfully changed, reduced or withdrawn by the local authority. First, there must be an individual reassessment (*R v Gloucestershire CC, ex p Mahfood*; see also Department of Health guidance, CI(92)34, para 31, arguably withdrawn, but still, in 2004, referred to in legal cases: e.g. *R(S) v Leicester CC*; also LAC(2002)13, para 58). Then, generally speaking, one of the following conditions must be met:

- the assessed needs have changed
- the needs can be met in a different way
- the authority's eligibility criteria have changed such that the person's needs no longer command the same level of service provision
- the person no longer wishes to receive the same services
- there is unreasonable behaviour on the part of the service user.

If such conditions are absent, then generally speaking the local authority's decision runs the risk of being unlawful. This follows from the fact that assessed eligible need must generally be met (*R v Gloucestershire CC, ex p Barry*: see 6.9).

## 6.15.2 WITHDRAWAL OF SERVICE AND REASSESSMENT

The courts have stated that a person's services cannot be reduced, withdrawn or significantly altered unless an individual reassessment has first taken place:

**Reassessing on individual basis.** When a local authority contemplated withdrawing or reducing home help services from up to 1500 people, the court ruled that it had to reassess each of them on an individual basis. It could not simply take a blanket decision (*R v Gloucestershire CC, ex p Mahfood*).

**Changing services.** When 13 service users were reassessed, 6 were allocated a cheaper service provider, 7 kept the original more expensive one. This balanced outcome reassured the court that individual reassessments had taken place, and that decisions had not been wholly determined by resources. The court accepted that the local authority could take account of resources in respect of the changes, so long as it never forgot that the needs of service users were more important than money (*R v Essex CC, ex p Bucke*).

Furthermore, the courts have also made clear that, particularly because of the vulnerable nature of community care service users, a local authority must make reasonable efforts to effect that reassessment:

**Making reasonable efforts to reassess.** A local authority was reviewing and reassessing people's needs for services they were currently receiving. The local authority wrote to service users offering a reassessment if they replied in the affirmative. If they did not, the implication was that they might anyway have their service reduced or withdrawn. The court found that this approach was not adequate in the community care context of vulnerable people, where the duty of assessment did not rely on a request. This contrasted with other contexts, where people might be better able to look after their own interests. Although effective reassessment could not be undertaken without a degree of cooperation from the service user, nevertheless such a letter would not be enough (*R v Gloucestershire CC, ex p RADAR*).

The ombudsman has expressed the view that if a change of service introduces no material difference in terms of meeting assessed needs, then a reassessment is not required; this was in a case involving a change of day centre. However, if the service user then withdrew, as she was entitled to if she was unhappy about the change, the local authority did then have a duty to reassess in order to identify an alternative (*Harrow LBC 2004*). In another ombudsman case, the fact that records showed that a visit was made by local authority staff in order to inform service users about a reduction in service did not mean that it could be assumed that a reassessment took place (*Derbyshire CC 2004*).

Central government practice guidance originally seemed to suggest that review would be face to face, since it stated that it might be appropriate to conduct the core part of it in the service user's own home (SSI/SWSG 1991, para 7.5). More recent Department of Health policy guidance is more direct, stating that other than in exceptional circumstances, reviews should be face to face, conducted by a competent professional and should not be delegated to the care provider (LAC(2002)13, paras 61–62).

### 6.15.3 WITHDRAWAL OF SERVICE AND CHANGE IN THRESHOLD OF ELIGIBILITY

If a local authority's threshold of eligibility has changed, it might be the case that certain service users might no longer be entitled to (the same level of) services, even though their own needs remain unchanged. In such circumstances, the courts have held that it is lawful to withdraw or reduce services following individual reassessments (*R v Gloucestershire CC, ex p Barry*).

However, central government guidance points out that caution must nevertheless be exercised, for example, where people may have developed such a dependency on the service that they would not cope without it (LAC(2002)13, para 66). Put another way, such a dependency would, in individual cases, have to be assessed as part of a person's eligible need. This might require a period of adequate notice, as the local ombudsman thought in the following case:

**Gradual withdrawal/change**. A local authority had been funding psychotherapy sessions for a woman, following the ending of her placement in a therapeutic community home. With no proper assessment or review, the local authority suddenly withdrew the service without adequate notice. The local ombudsman found maladministration; this warranted the local authority paying to the woman the money she owed on some of the sessions she had continued to have, as well as the travel expenses she had occurred and £1250 for distress caused (*Brent LBC 1994*).

The courts have stated their reluctance in principle to interfere with the severity of eligibility criteria under legislation such as the CSDPA 1970. Thus, on the withdrawal of services following reassessment, they may hesitate to interfere, even if they feel the revised package of care has been pared to the bone.

**Reassessment of man with multiple sclerosis**. A man with multiple sclerosis was reassessed, with the consequence that a package of care, that had effectively constituted 24-hour-a-day assistance, was reduced to five hours a day.

The judge decided that the reassessment and revised care plan did not constitute legal unreasonableness or irrationality since, on the evidence available, the authority had not 'taken leave of its senses'. Nevertheless, he did say that he had 'grave misgivings as to whether 5 hours per day of care plus meals on wheels and domiciliary nursing can meet the applicant's needs consistent with the [authority's] resources'. He went on to give an example of an authority taking leave of its senses and the high threshold necessary to warrant judicial intervention. Under its housing allocation system, an authority had awarded 0 points, on a scale from 0 to 250, to a woman with possibly recurrent cancer and gross breathing difficulty. Two consultants at London teaching hospitals had said in categorical terms that were she to climb stairs this would endanger her life. In such circumstances a court could 'properly but most exceptionally' conclude that the authority must have taken leave of its senses (*R v Haringey LBC, ex p Norton*).

Likewise, in another legal case – involving persistent efforts by the local authority to reduce or to keep to a minimum services for a person with Still's disease (a form of rheumatoid arthritis characterised by high spiking fevers) suffering serious flare-ups and almost totally blind – the judge remarked that the package was not generous, but then legally it did not have to be. The package was not perverse, but the judge would not have been surprised if a reassessment revealed the need for more hours of care (*R(Heffernan) v Sheffield CC*).

### 6.15.4 WITHDRAWAL OF SERVICE AND CHANGE IN NEED

If a person's needs have changed then clearly a change in service might be justified, but any such decision should be based on a proper reassessment, as the courts have emphatically stated:

**Reassessment and reduction of service.** Following a manual handling assessment of a woman with multiple sclerosis, a local authority provided two personal assistants for six hours instead of one for twelve hours. The local authority could not show (a) that this reduction equated to a change in the woman's assessed, eligible needs; or (b) that the needs were to be met in a different way (there was apparently no question of the eligibility threshold had changed).

In particular, the judge found no 'careful assessment' or proper analysis of the whole situation, if the time allotted were to be halved. He noted that it was 'important that the reduction to six hours' care was not driven by the need to have two carers to carry out the task'. The reduction could only be justified if there was no continuing need for 12 hours of care.

The judge held the decision to be unlawful and ordered that the local authority carry out its assessment again. In addition, he found a separate ground of unlawfulness; the assessor knew she ought to discuss matters with the woman's general practitioner, yet failed to do so. This was because the woman had just changed GP and the new GP did not yet feel able to offer any information. This was not good enough; it meant up-to-date medical information was not taken into account, when it should have been (*R v Birmingham CC, ex p Killigrew*).

Alternatively, there might simply be no formal assessment at all, in which case the courts will simply hold the local authority's decision to be unlawful:

**Change of residential placement.** A 35-year-old woman with autism had been placed by her local authority some years before in a further education placement in Newcastle. Subsequently, she moved out of the hall of residence to a residential address operated by the managers of the college. Seven years from the date of the original placement, the local authority sought to move the woman back to Leicestershire into an alternative residential placement. A letter to this effect was sent to the woman's mother, stating that this move would be for her daughter's long-term health, security and happiness.

However, the judge held that there had been no specific assessment for three and a half years since June 1999, and an assessment had to be carried out with a degree of formality prior to any change of placement. Furthermore he was not prepared to hold that the subsequent greater scrutiny of the woman's needs, which took place through the complaints procedure (when the mother complained), remedied this defect. This was particularly because the independent complaints investigator had first of all taken the approach that because a Leicestershire placement would be more suitable, therefore the Newcastle one was unsuitable. Yet logically this need not follow. Second, there had been an incorrect assumption that the health care services the woman required would not have been available in Newcastle. Thus, the local authority's decision was unlawful and the council would have to start again (*R(S) v Leicester City Council*).

Thus, without a change of need or other relevant circumstance, decisions run the risk of being unlawful:

**Reassessment and withdrawal of night sitting service.** An 86-year-old woman was reassessed. She suffered from severe arthritis and had poor mobility and a very weak bladder, which meant that she needed assistance from chair or bed to commode or toilet throughout the day and night. This resulted in an altered care plan and the loss of the night-sitting service which had previously been provided. The night-sitting service under the original care plan involved a person in attendance between 10pm and 7am to help with undressing, ensure that she was properly provided for and able to visit the toilet frequently during the night. The revised care plan involved only a person in attendance between 10pm and 10.30pm, to undress the woman, make her a drink and see that she was comfortable for the night. An interim injunction was sought – and obtained – to prevent this, pending a full judicial hearing.

The judge noted that nothing in the new care plan suggested a change either in the woman's needs or in any other relevant circumstances. This strongly suggested that the apparent decision, that she no longer needed night care, was based on no evidence whatsoever. This would make it irrational or unreasonable. He added that she was indisputably very infirm; and attempts by her to go to the toilet would result in physical problems, danger and possible extreme physical discomfort. To expose her to that sort of indignity and risk would, in the court's judgment, have been inhumane (*R v Staffordshire CC, ex p Farley*).

## 6.15.5 WITHDRAWAL OF SERVICE AND DIFFERENT WAY OF MEETING NEED

If a local authority can genuinely meet a person's need in another way, or if another organisation or person is prepared to meet the need, then a withdrawal or change in service may be lawful. Nevertheless, local authorities have to be able to demonstrate this; in neither of the two following examples could they do so:

**Emergency need.** When a local authority reassessed a woman with multiple sclerosis, it substantially reduced the daytime assistance she received. One of the purposes of this assistance had been to ensure that a carer was on hand in case an emergency arose. The new assessment and care plan did not deal with the issue of how an emergency need, in case of epileptic fit, would be met. This was one of the grounds on which the reassessment was held by the judge to be unlawful (*R v Birmingham CC, ex p Killigrew*).

Similarly, the local ombudsman will consider whether a reliable alternative exists:

**Unreliable alternative.** A local authority reassessed a man and stated that the need for recreational trips could in future be met through a local voluntary organisation rather than the local authority. Yet there was no evidence that the organisation could reliably supply the volunteers that would be required to assist him. The local ombudsman found maladministration (*Southwark LBC 2001*).

Furthermore, the general condition of reassessment – including participation of, and consultation with, the service user – must still be adhered to:

**Change in visiting arrangements.** A woman with severe learning disabilities had been placed in the care of a foster family. Arrangements for fortnightly Saturday visits home by the sister were agreed. These were subsequently being cancelled at short notice. The local authority proposed a change of day (Wednesday), and informed the mother who disagreed. The council went ahead and confirmed the change. Changing the day without consultation, and confirming the change against the family's wishes, was held by the local ombudsman to be maladministration (*Manchester 1996a*).

## 6.15.6 EXPLICIT REFUSAL BY SERVICE USER

In the case of adults with the capacity to take the relevant decision, community care services cannot be provided without their consent. In other words, such a person is obviously at liberty to refuse a service. Sometimes the person simply refuses a service; the question might then arise as to whether or not the service offered was reasonable, and whether the refusal was unreasonable – and thus whether the local authority should offer other options. For instance, in the following case, the court did not consider the refusal unreasonable:

**Unreasonable refusal of services?** A family occupied a two-bedroom flat on the twelfth floor of an 18-floor block. The man suffered from severe depression and pain in his knees that prevented him from negotiating stairs. He had psychotic symptoms and some features of post-traumatic stress disorder, and had been preoccupied with suicide and intrusive hallucinations. His wife had become significantly depressed.

Social services assessed and concluded that a ground-floor property was required with enough space for the rest of the family. A care plan was drawn up, stating that he needed a safe, secure, easily accessible and spacious environment in which to live so he had space away from his family, could access the dwelling and reduce the risk of self-harm. The man rejected the idea of short-let private property in principle due to lack of security of tenure and private sector rent rates, and argued that social services still had a duty to meet his needs.

The local authority argued that the refusal was unreasonable and that it had discharged its duty. The court accepted that a local authority does not have a duty 'willy-nilly' to provide accommodation under s.21 regardless of a person's willingness to accept it. However, in this case, the refusal of private, short-let accommodation, and of a three-bedroom flat with a number of unsuitable steps, meant that the man had not begun to stretch the duty 'to the point of willy-nilly'. The refusal was not unreasonable (R(Batantu) v Islington LBC).

The following court case provides a clearer example of unreasonableness on the part of the local authority, and indeed of a person's inability to refuse, reasonably or unreasonably:

**Refusal of hostel accommodation.** A woman with physical and mental health problems was evicted from home on neighbour nuisance grounds. The local authority housing department decided she was homeless but intentionally so. She was told of her right to a review of this decision under the Housing Act 1996. A request for a review was made three days outside of the statutory 21-day time limit (which expired on 21 May), after the Official Solicitor had been appointed to act (9 May) for her because of her mental incapacity. The council's housing department refused to accept the review request. On April 28, without an assessment, the social services department had offered hostel accommodation to the applicant under s.21 of the National Assistance Act 1948, which she had refused. Social services now stated that it could do nothing more.

The court found that the local authority should have extended the time for review; not least because evidence concerning the woman's mental illness would bear on the question of whether she was intentionally homeless under the Housing Act. The social services department should have assessed the woman; furthermore, the apparent refusal of accommodation by a psychiatrically ill applicant could not put an end to the continuing duty to provide accommodation under s.21 of the 1948 Act (R(Patrick) v Newham LBC).

The local ombudsman has warned that local authorities should not give up too readily when a person apparently refuses services:

**Refusal of services: taking this at face value.** A man with learning disabilities and autism had rejected offers of service from the local authority; he preferred to rely on his brother (who was however struggling to cope as carer). The local ombudsman accepted that, whilst a local authority cannot 'force services upon an unwilling person', nevertheless it must sometimes be cautious about taking a refusal of service at face value. The ombudsman considered that the local authority should have questioned whether the refusal constituted an informed decision. It should also have found a way to work both with the man and his brother; this was clearly possible because a community nurse, a psychologist and a worker from a voluntary organisation had all successfully interacted with the man; in which case, why could not the local authority do the same? (*Sheffield CC 2004*).

Even where a local authority is entitled to conclude that it has made a reasonable offer of a service, nevertheless refusal by a person of a particular option under one piece of legislation might not preclude continuing responsibilities under another. For example, an offer to an elderly couple of a care home place, which would have fully met their needs under s.21 of the National Assistance Act 1948, was refused. The court held that that it was a lawful and reasonable offer. However, the question then arose as to whether the local authority should still provide – notwithstanding this refusal of residential accommodation – other non-residential services, such as meals on wheels or laundry services, under s.29 of the 1948 Act. The court answered in the affirmative, since the accommodation duty under s.21 was one matter; the duty to provide services under s.29 another (*R(Khana) v Southwark LBC*).

## 6.15.7 UNREASONABLE BEHAVIOUR OF SERVICE USERS

Local authorities are often faced with the difficult decision of when to withdraw or withhold a service in the light of difficult or unreasonable behaviour by service users. The duty to meet assessed, eligible need should not be dismissed lightly; and where a person's behaviour stems from the type of need that local authorities are under obligations to meet (e.g. mental health problems), the courts have stated that caution is required in determining what constitutes unreasonable behaviour:

**Threats of violence and withdrawal of service.** An asylum seeker was being provided with hotel accommodation by the local authority. As a result of violence towards hotel staff, the local authority warned him that they would assist once more. However, if further such problems arose, they would cease to assist. A recurrence took place at different premises and the authority consequently withdrew its assistance.

The court held that the duty of the local authority under s.21 of the National Assistance Act 1948 was not absolute in the sense that it had a duty 'willy-nilly' regardless of the person's behaviour. The duty would be dependent on the cooperation of the person to occupy the accommodation in accordance with reasonable conditions – in terms of health and safety, preventing injury, nuisance or annoyance.

Nevertheless, the court stated that to the extent that s.21 of the 1948 Act was a safety net, the local authority should not lightly refuse to perform its duty; it would have to be satisfied of persistent and unequivocal refusal to comply with reasonable requirements.

Furthermore, such persistent and unequivocal refusal would be unlikely to be identified if the person's behaviour stemmed from a depressive condition associated with the very ill-treatment that had led him to seek asylum. The local authority would be expected to make reasonable efforts to identify a person's needs, although not to conduct a 'CID investigation' (*R v Kensington and Chelsea RBC, ex p Kujtim*).

Yet a point might sometimes be reached where the courts hold that it is reasonable and lawful to withhold a service in the light of threatening behaviour:

**Aggressive, abusive and threatening behaviour.** District nurses regularly visited a woman at home, suffering from disseminated sclerosis, unable to walk, use her arms and hardly able to do anything herself. The nurses were regularly subject to aggressive, abusive and threatening behaviour by the husband. He refused to give an undertaking not to behave in this way. The health authority warned him that it would withdraw the nursing service if this behaviour persisted. The woman challenged this in court, arguing that the authority was obliged to continue to provide nursing, and that husband and wife should be regarded separately. The Court of Appeal rejected this, stating that the authority was doing everything it could, that husband and wife could not be separated for this purpose, and that while the unreasonable behaviour continued, there was no duty to secure the attendance of nurses (*R v Hillingdon AHA, ex p Wyatt*).

Similarly, a local authority arranged accommodation for an asylum seeker; he failed to take up the offer of the accommodation on the grounds that he could not live in the same house as a Muslim; the council in turn refused to offer alternative accommodation. The court found the local authority's position perfectly reasonable (*R(Panic) v Secretary of State for the Home Department*).

Where exclusion from a service is applied, the local ombudsman has stated that there needs to be fair procedures in terms of the exclusion and reinstatement:

**Exclusion from a day centre.** The case concerned the exclusion of a person with mental health problems from a day centre, following disputes between her and other attenders about the way the centre was run. (At monthly meetings, increasingly more decisions were being taken by users of the centre – one of the complainant's objections concerned this development.)

The local ombudsman stated that if people were excluded from a service on which they rely, then 'natural justice' required that they be told promptly (a) why, (b) the duration of the exclusion, (c) what action was planned to facilitate re-entry, (d) who would decide about re-entry, and (e) how to appeal. Yet none of these requirements was fulfilled.

Managers had not been given clear guidance on how to manage or record difficult events – foreseeable at such centres – and this was maladministration. Also maladministration was the focus on the complainant's background and history in the investigation report produced in response to her complaint, because the 'purpose of a complaint is, first and foremost, to scrutinise the actions of the Council' (*Cornwall County Council 1996*).

If there are such procedures, it is important that they are adhered to and that staff are given appropriate guidance:

**Exclusion for smoking marijuana.** The case concerned aftercare for a man with schizophrenia under s.117 of the Mental Health Act 1983. He had been discharged from a hostel for people with mental health problems because he had been smoking marijuana. (About a year later he fell to his death from a tower block.) The parents claimed that the council had not dealt properly with the discharge.

The local ombudsman concluded as follows. As the council accepted and its procedure stipulated, the events leading to the discharge were grounds for an emergency review, but not an immediate discharge. However, staff had been given no clear written guidance about the procedure, nor about obligations under s.117 of the 1983 Act. The discharge amounted to maladministration (*Hounslow LBC 1995*).

Local authorities also have to bear in mind on the one hand their duty to meet the needs of vulnerable adults, but on the other their duties to their own staff. For example, a failure to protect their staff from racial discrimination, or the detrimental effects of it, could result in proceedings before an Employment Tribunal. The following employment tribunal case is particularly notable insofar as the unreasonable, discriminatory behaviour was not that of the patient:

**Racist behaviour by child's mother.** A very young child with cystic fibrosis had regularly to attend a hospital as an inpatient. The child's mother was known to have difficulties with drink, was dependent on drugs and known to be violent. The mother had approached a consultant, told him that she was racist and did not want a black person to care for her child. The black person in question was a specialist paediatric nurse of Afro-Caribbean origin and of exemplary character.

Thereafter, over an extended period of years, the staff acceded to the mother's wish and the child was moved between wards, or from one end of the ward or the other, to satisfy the mother.

Some years later, another child was admitted and its mother made the same racist request; however, this request was not acceded to by the senior sister. Furthermore, there was no evidence that the first mother had threatened to remove her child if she had not got her way; and if there had been genuine fears that she would and that the child would suffer, the courts or social services could have been involved. The Tribunal therefore had no hesitation in holding that the nurse had been discriminated against and that she had suffered substantial detriment in terms of being hurt, distraught, ashamed to tell her family, injury to feelings. An award of £20,000 was made (*Purves v Southampton University Hospitals Trust*).

Similarly, where violence is threatened, local authorities have duties towards their own staff under health and safety at work legislation; under the guise of what is 'reasonably practicable' to protect them, authorities will have to balance the meeting of service users' need with the safety of their employees (see 21.1.2).

## 6.15.8 CLOSURE OF LOCAL AUTHORITY CARE HOMES

Closures of local authority care homes, and transfers of residents elsewhere, are an example of a change in service provision. A considerable number of such closures have been challenged in the law courts. Despite some cases in which the courts notably reached decisions that the proposed closure was unlawful, the majority of such challenges have failed. A similar pattern has emerged in respect of closures of NHS facilities as well.

Nevertheless, in the case of the NHS there is a specific duty of consultation on health authorities, primary care trusts and NHS trusts. These relate to the planning and provision of services, changes to services, and decisions that affect the operation of services (Health and Social Care Act 2001, s.11). In addition, regulations made under s.7 of the 2001 Act place a duty on the NHS to consult with the overview and scrutiny committee of the local authority about substantial developments or variations in the provision of health services in the area (SI 2002/3048, r.4).

### 6.15.8.1 Home closures and individual assessment

The courts have sometimes insisted that for care home closures to be lawful, there must be individual assessment to ensure that the move and alternative provision will adequately meet people's needs.

**Assessing people with learning disabilities.** A health authority wished to close a long-stay hospital for people with profound learning disabilities and physical disabilities such as lack of mobility, incontinence and eating problems. Primary responsibility for the residents would be transferred to the social services authority. In the context of people with learning disabilities and guidance from central government (HSG(92)42) the court stated that individual assessment was required. This meant a detailed assessment had to be undertaken before any decision could be taken to move them out of NHS care (*R v Merton, Sutton and Wandsworth HA, ex p Andrew*).

Likewise, a health authority had to demonstrate, when deciding to close a purpose-built complex for people with learning disabilities, that it was proceeding on the basis of individual need – and not wrongly applying government policy by attempting to discharge all such patients into the community (*R(Collins) v Lincolnshire Health Authority*).

However, detailed individual assessment of need and how it will be met will not always have to take place before the decision to close has been taken (*R v North and East Devon HA, ex p Coughlan*). Sometimes it will be enough if it is carried out at a later stage when a decision about individual alternative placements is made (*R(Rowe) v Walsall MBC*). Alternatively, it might be permissible for the process to be in two stages, namely to take a decision in principle to close – to be confirmed only after a full assessment of the impact on the residents (*R(Cowl) v Plymouth CC*).

### 6.15.8.2 Home closures and consultation

The courts have stipulated that adequate consultation must take place:

**Adequate consultation.** Adequate consultation meant that the residents needed to know well in advance of the final decision about the proposed closure; to be given a reasonable amount of time to object; and to have had their objections considered by the local authority. The residents did not necessarily have a right to be consulted individually face to face; meetings held with residents generally could suffice (*R v Devon CC, ex p Baker*).

**Consultation containing misleading information.** The local authority proposed to close two residential homes. However, the court found the consultation process flawed because the health and safety reasons given for closure were not the true reasons, which in fact related to resources, strategic changes to services and best value (*R(Madden) v Bury MBC*).

**Consultation with residents of other homes.** The courts held that the duty of consultation extended not only to the residents of the particular home to be closed, but also to those properly interested in the council's other homes (*R v Wandsworth LBC, ex p Beckwith (no.2)*).

The courts will give some latitude to local authorities or the NHS in terms of how far the final decision must exactly reflect the options put forward in the consultation:

**Exhaustiveness of options.** The fact that the consultation put forward four options, and that an NHS trust decided to adopt a fifth, was not necessarily fatal to adequate consultation. In the particular case, involving a reduction of NHS services at a particular site, the court held that the fifth option was not so different from the fourth proposal that had been consulted on. And, in any case, the fifth option emerged from the consultation exercise and so there was no duty to consult again on it (*R v East Kent Hospital NHS Trust, ex p Smith*).

Conversely, however, a failure to consider a particular option by excluding it from the consultation exercise was not in itself unlawful (*R(Rowe) v Walsall MBC*).

The Cabinet Office (2004) has offered general guidance on consultation by public bodies, stating that a minimum of 12 weeks should be allowed for written consultation at least once during the development of a policy. In any event, it was entirely inadequate when residents were informed of the proposed closure of their care home eleven days, and relatives six days, before the relevant council committee meeting that voted on closure (*Redcar and Cleveland CBC 1999*).

### 6.15.8.3 Promises of a home for life

Residents of care homes and of NHS premises have sometimes been 'promised' that they have a home for life. On occasion, a court may feel that such a promise is so explicit and specific that it carries enough weight to militate against closure, unless there is an overriding public interest (*R v North and East Devon HA, ex p Coughlan*). At the very least, if such a promise has been made, then the courts will demand that the local authority's decision-making process must show that it has properly been taken account of:

**Failing to take account of the promise of a home for life.** Residents of a local authority home were given a booklet, which contained a heading of 'home for life'. When the local authority proposed to close the home, it had not taken this into account. It had therefore not considered all relevant matters, and the decision could not stand on its present basis (*R(Bodimeade) v Camden LBC*).

However, clear evidence of such a promise will be required:

**No promise of home for life in interim accommodation.** An NHS trust proposed to close an accommodation lodge in which the four claimants with mental health problems were currently living. They argued that they had received a promise of a home for life. The court rejected their claim, not least because the evidence was that the trust had not made such a promise, but had instead made clear that the accommodation had only ever been intended as interim accommodation (*R v Brent, Kensington and Chelsea and Westminster Mental Health NHS Trust, ex p C*).

On the other hand, the assessed needs and interests of residents in moving into the community may outweigh such a promise, and indeed outweigh the preferences of the residents not to move (*R(Collins) v Lincolnshire Health Authority*).

Where the promise has been made by an independent care home itself, which then proposes closure, the legal obstacles for residents to overcome in opposing closure are more formidable still:

**Independent care home closure**. Residents of a care home had received promises of a home for life, so long as their need did not deteriorate to the point where nursing care was required. The owner of the care home, a charitable housing association, maintained that all that had been stated both orally and in its brochure amounted to aims or objectives but not assurances. The judge rejected this interpretation; assurances, amounting to a promise, had been given.

Nevertheless, the judge held that, as an independent provider, the housing association was not open to judicial review, since this applies to public bodies only. Judicial review would of course apply to the local authority, but in this case it was not the local authority that had made the promises. The consequence was therefore that judicial review, in respect of the promise, lay against neither the care provider nor the local authority. The latter would meet its obligations by offering to meet the assessed community care needs of the residents elsewhere (*R v Servite Houses, ex p Goldsmith*).

In the *Servite* case, the judge did express his concerns about the outcome, pointing out that it constituted an inadequate response to the residents. However, the response was inevitable because Parliament had permitted public law obligations to be discharged by private law arrangements, thus attenuating the residents' potential rights and remedies. The *Servite* case was heard before the coming into force of the Human Rights Act 1998; however, a subsequent home closure case confirmed that neither judicial review nor human rights challenges could lie against an independent care home provider, notwithstanding that the residents had been placed in the home by the local authority or the NHS in performance of public law functions (*R(Heather) v Leonard Cheshire Foundation*).

### 6.15.8.4 Home closures and human rights

For the most part, human rights arguments have failed to prevent care homes or NHS facilities from closing. Even so, in one notable case, where there was an explicit promise to NHS residents (without an overriding public interest justification), the courts did find a breach of article 8 (right to respect for home and family life) of the European Convention on Human Rights (*R v North and East Devon HA, ex p Coughlan*). But otherwise the courts have tended not to find a breach of article 8; indeed in some cases they have doubted whether it was involved at all, let alone breached:

**Article 8 human rights**. Breach of an explicit promise of a home for life for a number of severely disabled residents in an NHS unit constituted a breach of article 8 (*R v North and East Devon Health Authority, ex p Coughlan*). In another case, the effect of closure on social ties, familiarity with surroundings, and proximity to friends and relatives did not interfere with article 8 rights (*R(Rowe) v Walsall MBC*). In a third case, the judge suggested that article 8 added little because he could not envisage a breach of article 8, so long as the council was acting compatibly with its relevant common law and statutory obligations (*R(Cowl) v Plymouth CC*: High Court stage).

When the NHS wished to close an accommodation lodge for people with mental health problems, the courts stated that any rights under article 8 were inextricably bound up with the trust's obligation to provide medical care. The proposal by the trust was desirable for the benefit of the claimants; furthermore the closure and then refurbishment would benefit other members of the community to whom the trust owed a duty and who enjoyed rights and freedoms the trust had to respect (*R v Brent, Kensington and Chelsea and Westminster Mental Health NHS Trust, ex p C*).

Likewise when a health authority sought to close a purpose-built complex for people with learning disabilities, the European Court of Human Rights held that the decision to move one of the residents into alternative social care gave proper consideration to her interests and was supported by relevant and sufficient reasoning in relation to her welfare. Indeed the court declared the application inadmissible to advance to a full hearing (*Collins v UK*).

In some cases, the courts have systematically considered and then rejected arguments based on more than one human right, namely right to life (article 2), right not to be subjected to inhuman and degrading treatment (article 3), and article 8:

**Care home closure and human rights generally (1).** An independent care home proposed to close. The Human Rights Act did not apply directly to the care provider, and the local authority was not in a position to prevent an independent concern from closing. However, the judge assumed for the purpose of argument that human rights did bear on the matter. In terms of what steps the local authority should take, the court considered articles 2, 3 and 8.

Article 2 (right to life) was not in issue because the council was taking the necessary steps to minimise the impact of the stress on the residents of a move. There was insufficient evidence on the risks to the claimants' lives. Furthermore, the courts give public bodies considerable latitude to decide a fair balance between the interests of the individual and the wider community. For similar reasons, the high threshold required to engage article 3 (inhuman and degrading treatment) had not been reached. The article 8 claim also failed because, first, there was no cogent evidence of disruption of home or family life or interference with physical integrity. Second, the financial resources of the council were an important element, and the council was entitled to consider the care home's fees disproportionately high. Third, the council was entitled to considerable deference in how it allocated its resources.

Throughout, the judge referred to the importance of the precautions taken by the council in order to manage the move, including the preserving of friendship groups (*R(Haggerty) v St Helens MBC*).

**Care home closure and human rights generally (2).** In another case, the article 2 argument was dismissed because no particularised medical evidence revealed a serious risk to the life of any resident. To bring the case under article 3 would be to strain language and common sense and to trivialise the article and the important values it protects. That article 8 was relevant at all was a generous assumption; if it was, then the court would be slow to interfere with decisions involving the allocation of resources (*R(Dudley) v East Sussex CC*).

Decided on similar lines was *McKellar v Hounslow LBC*, when residents unsuccessfully applied for an injunction preventing their removal from a local authority care home.

And, in a third case, assuming there was an interference under article 8.1, then the closure would be justified on grounds of the 'economic well being' of the council (*R(Rowe) v Walsall MBC*).

### 6.15.8.5 Grounds for rejecting challenges to home closures

It seems that most challenges to home closure have failed, and the courts – in addition to rejecting human rights arguments – have based their decisions on various grounds, in addition to those already outlined immediately above.

**Best interests decision.** In one case, the court pointed out that the issue in dispute was not in fact a public law issue, concerning the propriety of a public body's decision to close certain premises – but was one relating to the taking of a decision in the best interests of a person lacking capacity to decide for herself. The court declined to rule on the lawfulness or otherwise of a proposed closure, and instead held that a case should be taken to the Family Division of the High Court to seek a best interests declaration (*R(Payne) v Surrey Oakland NHS Trust*).

In some cases, the courts have not even given permission for a full judicial review hearing to take place:

**No permission to challenge closure.** In one case, where permission was sought to bring a judicial review case about transfer of local authority homes to an independent trust, it was argued that the local authority had failed (a) to take account of the consequences of the decision; (b) to include a particular option in the consultation exercise; and (c) to analyse the costs of the transfer of the home. The court found that (a) the consultation paper had considered both 'advantages' and 'disadvantages' of the transfer; (b) the additional option was simply not in the consultation paper and so not adopting it was perfectly proper; and (c) an analysis of costs would have been premature at this stage. Permission to bring the case was refused (R(Hands) v Birmingham CC; see also R(Rowe) v Walsall MBC).

Alternatively, the courts have simply shown a disinclination to become involved:

**Using the complaints procedure instead of the courts.** A number of residents opposed the closure of a home run by the council. Aged between 77 and 92 they were all frail and in poor health. They claimed that lawful and comprehensive assessments had not been carried out. The Court of Appeal stated that the local authority's complaints procedure should have been used, since the parties did not have a right to judicial review if an alternative procedure existed that would resolve a significant number of the issues (R(Cowl) v Plymouth CC).

The local authority subsequently appointed an extraordinary complaints panel that produced a thorough report, including an appendix containing draft guidelines meant to assist other local authorities when they consider whether to close a home (Plymouth CC 2002).

In subsequent legal cases, the courts have given these guidelines short shrift. For instance, the panel set up by Plymouth had no authority 'to promulgate guidelines for the world at large' (R(Dudley) v East Sussex CC); and the report was simply specific to the particular home closure in Plymouth, and it would be wrong to attach much weight to its views in other contexts (R(Haggerty) v St Helens MBC).

## 6.16 URGENCY

If a person's needs are perceived to be urgent, the local authority may provide services on a temporary basis before carrying out an assessment. If it does so, it should then carry out an assessment as soon as practicable (NHS and Community Care Act 1990, s.47). The courts have confirmed the meaning of this reference to urgency:

**Urgent provision of temporary accommodation.** The claimant was an asylum seeker, destitute and suffering from hepatitis B. The local authority argued that it had no power to provide accommodation under s.21 of the National Assistance Act 1948 until it had carried out a s.47 assessment. The court held that there was a strong case for arguing breach of duty, in the light of the terms of s.47(5). Also, as originally enacted, s.21 of the National Assistance Act 1948 did not require that an assessment take place before temporary accommodation is provided and gave local authorities an unfettered power to provide such. Far from introducing the need for assessment, s.47(5) merely confirmed it was not required (R(AA) v Lambeth LBC).

## 6.17 ASSESSMENT OF CHILDREN WHEN THEY LEAVE SCHOOL

Legislation provides for the assessment by local authorities of children or certain young people who have had statements of special educational needs – when they leave school or further or higher education institutions (Disabled Persons (Services, Consultation and Representation) Act 1986, s.5). In summary:

- Education authorities must obtain an assessment from the local authority social services department – for 15-year-old pupils who already have statements of special educational needs – as to whether or not the pupil is disabled. This is done by notifying the 'appropriate officer' appointed by the local social services authority for this purpose; he or she has to give an opinion as to whether or not the child is disabled. Likewise this duty of notification applies in respect of a child over 14 years old without a statement, but who then has one made for the first time.
- In either case, the education authority must inform the appropriate officer of the date when the child will no longer be of compulsory school age, and whether (and where) he or she intends to remain in full-time education – at least 8 but not more than 12 months before that date.
- In addition, further education or higher education institutions, or the Learning and Skills Council, are obliged to notify the local social services authority in writing at least 8, but not longer than 12, months before a pupil with a statement of special educational needs, who has been assessed as disabled, will cease to receive full-time education. This duty applies where the pupil is over compulsory school age, but under the age 19 years and 8 months.
- Once the above has taken place (in respect of school, further or higher education), the local social services authority must then carry out an assessment of the person's needs. This is to determine whether the local authority has a duty to provide services under Part 3 of the National Assistance Act 1948, s.2 of the Chronically Sick and Disabled Persons Act 1970, schedule 8 of the NHS Act 1977, or Part 3 of the Children Act 1989.
- The assessment must be carried out within five months of the date of notification. If a disabled student has ceased to receive full-time education or will cease to do so within less than eight months, and no notification has been made to the social services authority but should have been, then the education authority must notify in writing social services – who must then carry out the assessment as soon as reasonably practicable, and in any case within five months.

The intention of notifying the local social services authority is so that a smooth transition can take place and appropriate arrangements be made. However, this does not always work as well as it should, and the local ombudsman has investigated several cases in which the local authority has failed the disabled person adult involved:

**Failure to assess and budget for meeting need.** A young man with multiple disabilities was profoundly deaf, partially sighted, and able to communicate only by means of sign language and a computer. From the age of 16 on (statutory school-leaving age), the education authority considered whether he should continue to remain at a specialist residential boarding school. When he was 19 in 1990, it decided that it would cease funding, but that social services might wish to support him for a further period at the school.

Records from 1990 showed that social services had no planned budget for the man, that a newly formed resource centre could not meet his needs and that he should be given priority for assessment. No assessment took place, and some months later in January 1991, the man began attending the resource centre – even though it was recognised from the start that it was not able to meet his needs and that staff could not communicate with him. By 1993, he was still attending the centre, was also attending a local college of further education, and had been assessed by a national deaf association (in February 1993). Social services finally completed its overall assessment by August 1993.

The local ombudsman found various failings including (a) no assessment of need in 1990 as promised; (b) despite the council's knowing about the person since 1986, there had been no planning ahead and budgetary provision made; (c) the placement at the resource centre went ahead despite the unhappiness amongst both its own staff and the mother – and without it being made clear to the mother whether there were any alternatives; (d) a proper assessment had not taken place until 1993 (when the man's own views were finally sought) and this was an unreasonable delay. This was all maladministration which caused distress, anxiety and trouble to both mother and son; the ombudsman recommended that £1000 and £2000 be paid respectively to them (*East Sussex County Council 1995b*).

**Leaving the assessment too late.** A 19-year-old man with learning disabilities had attended a residential school outside Knowsley; in August 1993, the school wrote to the social services department inviting an officer to attend in March 1994 the last annual review of the man's statement of special educational needs. It was expected that he would spend the 1994 summer holidays at home with his parents and then move into local accommodation in September.

Despite the council's assurance that an 'appropriately supported living arrangement' would be in place by the time he left school, this did not happen. Apart from one attempt in May 1994 consisting of shared accommodation (the man realised he did not wish to share with the particular man in question), accommodation was not available until November 1995, and there was no evidence that priority had been given to resolving the situation. The council had failed to carry out an adequate assessment of need and to draw up a proper care plan (the council had maintained that a full assessment could not be completed until the man was back in the community).

Consequently, the mother had suffered great emotional and physical strain which had affected the relationship with her son. Feeling unable to accept interim provision in the form of domiciliary support or a hostel, she had given up her job and incurred financial loss.

The local ombudsman commended the council for reviewing its arrangements for transition from school to adult services, and recommended it pay £500 in compensation for anxiety, stress and trouble – but not for the mother's financial loss (since it was her decision to reject the temporary solution of hostel accommodation or domiciliary support) (*Knowsley MBC 1997*).

**Failure to assess and provide on leaving school and for two years after.** This was a complaint about the assessment and arrangements for a young man leaving school, who was initially thought to have mild learning disabilities and a stress-related physical condition, and was later diagnosed as schizophrenic.

First, the local ombudsman found that it was maladministration for the council not to assess him before he left school – as it was required to do under s.5 of the Disabled Persons (Consultation and Representation) Act 1986. However, it was not an injustice, because the ombudsman considered that, at this time, it was most unlikely that the person would have been assessed as disabled – in which case there would have been no automatic involvement of social services.

Second, following a community care assessment (two years after he had left school), nothing was done for nine months. This was 'too long'; the man had 'to wait longer for remedial help in overcoming his reclusiveness and…his family had to go longer than was necessary without practical support'. This was maladministration.

Third, it was also maladministration for the council not to have given the parents a copy of the assessment report when requested – even though no injustice flowed from this because the services, which a written report would have recommended, were in fact obtained.

Fourth, a delay in allocating the case to an officer following transfer to another team led to inadequate provision for seven months; this was maladministration.

Fifth, it was maladministration when a particular officer failed to keep appointments with the father, or to tell him sooner about problems with the appointments; this led to the father taking time off work unnecessarily (*Liverpool CC 1997a*).

## 6.18 WAITING TIMES FOR ASSESSMENT

Timescales are absent from community care legislation in terms of assessment (and provision of services) with one or two exceptions. One concerns the Community Care (Delayed Discharges) Act 2003 in relation to the discharge from hospital of patients from acute hospital beds (see 16.10). Even in the context of the 2003 Act, failing to assess (and discharge) a person within the relevant time limit is not an actionable breach of duty; it merely entails the payment of money, for the 'blocked' bed, by the local authority to the NHS. There is also a timescale in terms of assessments by local authorities when disabled pupils leave education (see 16.17).

Otherwise, in the absence of timescales set out in legislation or in central government guidance, the legal expectation is for a local authority to perform its duty within a reasonable period of time or without undue delay. In terms of maladministration, the local ombudsmen take a similar approach and have put it as follows in this 2004 example:

**Principle of waiting times.** The local ombudsman has stated that people must be assessed in a reasonable time; and a reasonable time in any particular case depends on the circumstances and urgency of the client's needs. First, there should be well-defined criteria for assessing priorities. Second, the criteria should be applied after proper consideration and reassessed promptly in the light of any relevant new information. Third, people in need and their advisers should be informed of the criteria, timescales, of their allocated priority, of council services and of reputable alternative suppliers (*Wakefield MDC 2004*).

What constitutes a reasonable period of time will generally depend on all the circumstances of the case. This somewhat vague principle is not as unhelpful as it might appear, since it depends very much on individual need. For example, a one-month wait for assessment may be acceptable for one person, but highly detrimental to another.

Central government in England has set certain targets for assessment in terms of 'performance indicators' which are used to measure and evaluate the performance of local authorities (see 3.2.2). However, the courts will not necessarily accept that government 'targets' or performance indicators equate to, or are even relevant to, the performance of a statutory duty.

### 6.18.1 ADEQUATE STAFFING

Staffing levels are not infrequently cited by local authorities as the reason for delay in assessments. Legislation does state that the local authority must provide the director of social services with adequate staff (Local Authority Social Services Act 1970, s.6: to be known in future as 'director of adult social services'; see the Children Act 2004, schedule 2 amendment to s.6). The minutes of social services committee meetings might provide useful evidence that s.6 of the 1970 Act has been breached, although the duty is usually regarded as rather vague and so difficult to enforce. The case of *R v Hereford and Worcester CC, ex p Chandler* was brought in relation to a breach of s.6(6) of the 1970 Act, given leave to proceed to a full judicial review hearing, but subsequently settled in favour of the applicant (Clements 2004, p.14).

The local ombudsmen have investigated the adequacy of staffing on a number of occasions and are generally, but not always, unsympathetic to local authorities that use this excuse.

**Waiting times and staff shortages**. For instance, if authorities are unable to provide an assessment through their occupational therapists within a reasonable period of time, then they should look at other ways of providing the assessment (*Wirral MBC 1993d*).

Maladministration might be found where problems have long since been reported to, and known by, the social services committee, and yet 'wider failure' in service delivery has continued, including a lack of monitoring and inadequate records of waiting lists (*Redbridge LBC 1993a*; *Redbridge LBC 1993b*).

On the other hand, if councils face 'particular resource and staffing difficulties' and have made attempts to remedy the situation, the ombudsmen might not find maladministration. For example, one council responded 'positively and creatively' to staff shortages, offered a recruitment and retention package, set up a special assessment clinic, and seconded health authority staff (*Lewisham LBC 1993*). Likewise, a five-month delay in assessment for a woman allocated a medium priority was not maladministration, given the priorities necessitated by the difficulty of recruiting and deploying occupational therapists (*Islington LBC 1995*).

Even so, in one case, a three-month wait for assessment of a 19-year-old woman seriously ill with Asperger's Syndrome (a form of autism) – for attendance at a day centre – was found to be maladministration. She had been allocated to a particular officer on grounds of the latter's expertise (even though the officer had no experience of the relevant condition: autism). The officer was absent for a considerable period, but the case had not been reallocated. The ombudsman did not 'consider that staff shortages or a departmental reorganisation can ever justify a failure to respond to repeated requests of this seriousness for help' (*Sheffield CC 1994*).

Similarly, a ten-month delay in assessing a woman unable to use her upstairs bathroom was maladministration. Shortage 'of money, communication and administration problems do not absolve the Council from their statutory duty' (*Bolton MBC 1992*).

A related issue is the degree to which a local authority insists on reserving certain tasks for certain types of staff; justified or not in the particular circumstances, this is a form of professional exclusivity. The local ombudsman has considered this matter on a number of occasions:

**Waiting times and professional exclusivity.** The local ombudsman will not necessarily defer to professional exclusivity. Following two amputations to a man's foot, it took five months for an occupational therapist to assess him, even though he was deemed to be of 'A' priority and should have been assessed within five days. He subsequently contacted the council again on a further matter, in relation to his bathing needs. This time he was categorised as 'B2' priority and should have been assessed in four months; this time it took eight. The ombudsman stated that in order to assess people within a reasonable time, the local authority should have taken a pragmatic approach. Its reluctance to employ locum staff, as opposed to permanent staff, was apparently based at least partly on financial consider-ations. This was unacceptable, given that it contributed to the target time for assessment being exceeded by 100 per cent (*Bridgend CBC 2004*).

A failure to assess for 21 months was deemed maladministration; in the absence of professional occupational therapists, the council 'should have sought other means to ensure that people did not wait an unacceptable length of time for an assessment'. When 'disabled people ask the Council for as-sistance in providing adaptations to their homes, they have the right to expect that assistance is pro-vided with reasonable speed' (*Wirral MBC 1992c*; see also *Middlesbrough BC 1996, Wirral MBC 1992a, Wirral MBC 1993d*).

Similarly, in another case the ombudsman stated that postponement of assessment for a year was not an option, and that an alternative channel for assessment should have been found (as the local au-thority had now done) if early use of occupational therapists was not possible – even though it would of course be ideal if professional advice were always to hand (*Sheffield CC 1989*).

In one authority, by the end of 1991, disability services were receiving 500 referrals per month and had over 1000 people awaiting assessment. Reorganisation and recruitment recommendations, made in a report to the social services committee, were thwarted shortly afterwards by a morato-rium. This was imposed on financial grounds and affected the recruitment of non-qualified staff. Indus-trial action added to the three-year delay the complainant suffered. The ombudsman still found maladministration in that the local authority should have addressed both the resourcing problems and staffing levels long before (*Newham LBC 1993b*).

Of course, staffing shortages should not be confused with administrative deficiencies, which mean that existing staff are not being utilised properly.

**Waiting times and administrative inefficiency.** A request by a registered blind person (also at risk of falling and with a rare degenerative disease) for equipment was not passed promptly to the sensory impairment team by an assistant director of social services. A nine-month delay resulted; the local ombudsman found maladministration (*Haringey LBC 1993*).

In another case, the local ombudsman accepted that the failure to carry out a survey for over a year in relation to a disabled facilities grant was due to a huge increase in workload rather than maladministration, but the social services department was still at fault for failing to check matters with the housing department and to refer the case properly (*Barking and Dagenham LBC 1998*).

The local ombudsman has also criticised the phenomenon of 'double queuing'. This sometimes results not just in the service user having to wait longer or negotiate more bureaucratic obstacles, but will also result in poor use of staffing resources, by virtue of the duplication involved.

**Waiting times and double queuing.** The local ombudsmen are likely to disapprove of double queuing; that is, where the administrative hoops of a local authority require that a person queues twice on the waiting list. For instance, when one man was originally classified as priority but then reclassified as high priority, he did not benefit as quickly as he should have because he was given a new 'start' date and so went to the end of the high priority list. This was maladministration (*Barking and Dagenham LBC 1998*).

Maladministration also occurred in relation to the double queuing when people applied for both disabled facilities and a renovation grant (*Liverpool CC 1996/1997*) or for two occupational therapy as-sessments, the first for equipment, the second for adaptations (*Waltham Forest LBC 1994*).

When a seriously ill and immobile man was referred to the occupational therapy service in August he was put on a waiting list for assessment. However, some of the recorded potential needs (such as cooking) at the referral stage should have triggered the involvement of the physical disability team as well. However, the duty occupational therapist did not refer these matters on to that team at that point; this only occurred later. This meant that there was a delay of five months or so in receiving an assessment and services for these other needs. This was maladministration (*Hackney LBC 1998a*).

After a man had been assessed as needing a level access shower, conditional on him finding a bungalow to live in, he was visited by an occupational therapist who confirmed the bungalow was suitable for the shower. But he was referred back to the occupational therapy waiting list for assessment. He should then have been assessed within four months instead of the six it actually took; exceeding this target by over two months was maladministration. In addition, the local ombudsman questioned not just the reasonableness but also the lawfulness of this further wait, since the person's need for a shower had already been assessed. The person should have gone straight onto the adaptations waiting list, instead of being subjected to a delay of seven months in joining that list (*Nottinghamshire CC 2000*).

## 6.18.2 WAITING TIMES FOR ASSESSMENT AND THE COURTS

The courts have barely explored what constitutes a reasonable wait for assessment. They may consider that such questions are best decided through complaints procedures or the local government ombudsman. Indeed, there seem to have been no community care legal cases purely on waiting times for assessment, although there have now been a few concerning waiting times for services (see 7.3.2). Nevertheless, in one case the courts identified a spurious ground for refusal of assessment that had resulted in a vicious circle:

**Failure to assess.** The local authority refused to carry out an assessment of need for an autistic child aged seven years old under s.17 of the Children Act 1989; and of his mother's ability to care under Carers and Disabled Children Act 2000. The local authority's explanation was that the family might soon be rehoused; and it would be a waste of resources to assess now, when circumstances might soon change.

The court held that if the change of accommodation was going to occur within one or two months, a postponement might have been justifiable; but on the evidence, there was no indication as to when the accommodation would be found. The local authority was therefore obliged to carry out both assessments, and the s.17 assessment within 35 days (*R(J) v Newham LBC*).

## 6.18.3 WAITING TIMES FOR ASSESSMENT AND THE LOCAL GOVERNMENT OMBUDSMEN

In contrast to the courts, the local ombudsmen have investigated delays in assessment many times. The ombudsmen have applied a sharper edge to waiting than the health service ombudsman, arguably because of the specific individual duties of assessment that apply to local authorities – under s.47 of the NHS and Community Care Act 1990 and s.4 of the Disabled Persons (Services, Consultation and Representation) Act 1986. There are no equivalent, specific duties applying to the NHS.

The following are but examples covering issues such as the ombudsmen's general approach, setting of priorities for assessment, higher and lower priorities, administrative inefficiency, staff shortages, identity of assessing staff, inconsistencies, double queuing, excessive waiting times.

**Waiting times and local ombudsmen's general approach.** The local ombudsmen consider the particular circumstances of each case, and so do not necessarily arrive at an easy rule of thumb of what constitutes a reasonable waiting time: it all depends. Nevertheless, faced with sometimes large numbers of complainants in a similar position, they have sometimes considered generally the question of what reasonable waiting times might look like.

For instance, in relation to disabled facilities grants, they suggested in 1997 two months for urgent, four months for serious, and six months for non-urgent cases (*Liverpool CC 1996/1997;* see also *Sheffield CC 1997a* and *Sheffield CC 1997b*). Otherwise, the ombudsmen might work out in specific cases what a reasonable waiting time would have been, measure the excess and then assess the resulting injustice, if any (e.g. *Wirral MBC 1992a*).

When local authorities have their own policies on waiting times, the local ombudsman has an additional lever to consider whether there has been maladministration over and above what might otherwise have been reasonable (had there been no policy). This is because significant breach by a local authority of its own policy is itself an additional ground of maladministration:

**Breach of own policy on waiting times.** In one case, even had a wait for assessment of six months been reasonable, the wait was 50 per cent longer than the local policy stipulated; the local ombudsman found maladministration. Likewise, an elderly person – in poor health and a wheelchair, living on the ground floor of her home, using a commode and bathing at a relative's house – should have been assessed within 60 days. It took instead more than seven months (some 215 days). This was maladministration (*Wakefield MDC 2004*).

The ombudsman found maladministration when a joint social services/housing department assessment should, according to policy, have been made within seven days from receipt of referral – but instead took place six weeks later (*Camden LBC 1993*).

Since waiting times have been an inescapable part of the community care landscape, and have been accepted up to a point as an unavoidable evil, the local ombudsmen will also look hard at how local authorities can mitigate the effects. One such type of mitigation is for the local authority at least to inform people about what is happening in terms of the wait. Thus, the local ombudsmen find maladministration when local authorities give people inadequate information about waiting times – whether or not the waiting times themselves are faulted (e.g. *Hackney LBC 1997c, Liverpool 1996/1997, Rotherham MBC 1995, Wirral MBC 1994c*). Even worse is where a local authority knowingly publishes unrealistic waiting times, misleading people almost by intention (*Ealing LBC 1999*).

Another form of mitigation, identified by the local ombudsmen, is that a priority system should mean that the waiting time for any individual person is in some measure proportionate to his or her perceived degree of need.

**Waiting times and priorities.** When local authorities handle applications for disabled facilities grants by date order, the ombudsmen criticise them on the grounds that such a system cannot take account of differing levels of need or of exceptions; it is 'insufficiently sophisticated' (e.g. *Leicester CC 1998*). Thus, the lack of a priority system, a failure to publicise it when it was adopted and inability to award priority at an early stage are all maladministration (*Liverpool CC 1996/97*). The consequences could be that an adaptation (stairlift) is not installed before the applicant dies (*Liverpool City CC 1996/1997*).

In another case the housing authority carrying out adaptations stated that it did not prioritise referrals from social services as it did not have the competent staff (i.e. occupational therapists) to do this. However, the social services authority making the referrals stated that it was not its task to prioritise on behalf of a housing authority. Nevertheless, the ombudsman found the absence of a system of priorities to be maladministration (*Castle Morpeth BC 2003*).

A local authority had a waiting list of 392 people waiting for occupational therapy assessments. It operated three priority groups. 360 of those waiting fell into priority group 2. The ombudsman found this to be maladministration because it meant the system of prioritisation was ineffective (*Halton BC 2002*).

Once there is a reasonable system of making priorities, the further question arises as to how long people should wait, once their priority has been determined. Inevitably, longer waiting times tend to be experienced by people deemed to have needs of a 'lower priority'; but the local ombudsmen have pointed out that this does not mean that they can be kept waiting endlessly.

**Waiting times for assessment: lower and medium priority needs**. A woman with cerebral palsy lived alone. She had arthritis in her right side, and weakness in both sides. She was unable to cope with shopping and domestic tasks. She worked full time as a teacher. At a first level assessment, a social work assistant stated that she needed a second level assessment, and she was given a priority 2 rating. This should have been completed within three months, the longest waiting time allowed. In fact it took nearly 18 months. This was maladministration (*Ealing LBC 1999*).

In one local authority, the waiting times for the highest priority was some four months, but for people given priorities 2 and 3, they were up to three years. A woman aged 86 applied for adaptations. She suffered from arthritis, asthma and sciatica and had fallen and broken her hip. She had not been able to use the bath for two of the three years she had spent awaiting assessment. The ombudsman's finding was maladministration, the delay being 'totally unacceptable' even though it was a 'relatively low priority' application. The assessment should have started within six months of the first approach to the local authority (*Redbridge LBC 1993a*).

The local ombudsman has stated that it is 'not acceptable that a client may wait up to two years for an assessment, whatever the outcome of that assessment'. This was maladministration, though she did commend the council for implementing a system of gathering information at an early stage so as to determine quickly whether it could assist the person (*Wirral MBC 1993c*).

Even allowing for shortage of staff, and the fact that a person is not within the 'at risk' category, the local ombudsman might find that 'it cannot be acceptable for a client in need to face a two-year wait before their needs are even quantified' (*Wirral MBC 1992d*).

Following a stroke, a man was discharged from hospital, awarded 'medium priority' and told that there would be a four-month wait for an assessment; his appalled wife had the bath removed and installed a shower and grab rails. The failure to assess in that time amounted to maladministration (*Barking and Dagenham LBC 1997*).

Even people placed in a higher priority for assessment sometimes wait excessive lengths of time, and this will be maladministration for the local ombudsmen:

**Waiting times and 'higher priority' people.** An elderly woman, placed initially in the second highest and then later in the highest category, had to wait 20 months for an assessment. This was 'totally unacceptable' according to the local ombudsman (*Redbridge LBC 1993b*).

In another case, a woman regarded as high priority had also to wait 20 months; it had taken six months even to get as far as allocating her priority. This was maladministration (*Hackney LBC 1997a*).

It was maladministration when the clearing of a backlog of assessments for people with non-urgent needs affected adversely those with more urgent needs (*Wirral MBC 1993e*).

When a roofer became paralysed after a fall and was discharged from hospital, the local authority was at fault in taking ten weeks to produce a draft community care assessment, despite having information from the hospital (*Avon CC 1997*).

Sometimes, the length of wait simply disappears 'off the scale' and turns into not being seen and assessed at all:

**Excessively long waits and never seeing people.** A wait for assessment of four years and eight months in one case was not even exceptional in that authority; the local ombudsman noted that a number of other people had been similarly affected (*Hackney LBC 1992a*). The severe criticism levelled at the local authority did not prevent it some years later from keeping the same woman waiting 20 months, when she requested a reassessment because of worn equipment and of additional needs in relation to looking after her two-year-old son; the local ombudsman found maladministration all over again (*Hackney LBC 1997a*).

Long waiting times can turn into never seeing people. In the first of the two cases referred to immediately above, the ombudsman found that the 'non-urgent' waiting lists had been closed indefinitely and believed that this might represent a failure of the council to discharge its statutory duty under s.2 of the Chronically Sick and Disabled Persons Act 1970 (*Hackney LBC 1992a*). The ombudsman might recognise the national problem of shortage of occupational therapists to carry out assessments, commend the practice of establishing priorities, but nevertheless find that 'it cannot be acceptable that those with the lowest priority may never be seen by an OT and thus never have their case considered' (*Wirral MBC 1992a*).

Even if a potentially acceptable system of priorities exists, the local ombudsmen will also be keen to see that it is applied equitably within a local authority, such that people with similar needs are not treated inconsistently – even if the inconsistency arises, for instance, from the 'soft-heartedness' of local authority staff in individual cases. (Although it should be noted that about variations in waiting times between local authorities the ombudsmen can do nothing.)

**Inconsistent application of priority for waiting.** It could not be fair that an applicant should wait a few weeks for a renovation grant in one part of the borough, but for years in another (*Newham LBC 1997b*).

In another finding of maladministration, one of the 'serious failures' was that a person who had waited four years and eight months for an assessment might have waited only five months had she lived a few hundred yards away in the same authority (*Hackney LBC 1992a*). In another case, disabled people's needs for adaptations depended on the competing demands of local area repair budgets from week to week. This meant the ombudsman could not be certain that people with similar needs were dealt with in a similar way; there should have been a borough wide system of prioritisation (*Camden LBC 1993*).

Another investigation found that a council had been misapplying its priority criteria: five people in a sample of 45 cases had been given priority incorrectly ahead of the particular complainant. The case illustrated the difficulties facing local authority staff such as occupational therapists. The reasons for the 'incorrect' decisions included 'soft-heartedness' in the case of a woman with asthma, emphysema and osteo-arthritis who could just about manage indoor steps and stairs indoors. A second person 'had great difficulty getting up from a sitting position, and could not bathe without aids, was unable to get in and out of the bath, and lived alone'. Two sisters, aged 82 and 81, with various problems including Crohn's disease, arthritis, osteo-arthritis in spine, hips and knees, were both unable to bathe. They should not have been given priority – but were given it, probably because of their joint needs and previous requests. Yet still the misapplication of priority criteria amounted to maladministration (*Lewisham LBC 1993*).

By the same token, if there is consistent and equitable application of priorities, then even significant waiting times will not necessarily constitute maladministration.

**Equitable application of priorities for waiting.** A six-month delay in assessment for home adaptations was not criticised, since the local authority had applied a system of priorities which took into account relevant factors and had fairly treated the complainant's priority as relatively low (*Ealing LBC 1993*).

Similarly, a 15-month delay was not unreasonable in the circumstances, because the authority had adopted a policy of priority categories as they were entitled to (especially given particular staffing and resource problems) – and the complainant had been properly dealt with under that policy (*Lewisham LBC 1993*).

A two-year wait might not draw the ombudsman's criticism if resources and staff restrictions mean that greater priority is given appropriately to those in greater need (*Wirral MBC 1994c*).

# Care plans and provision of services

**KEY POINTS**

Following a decision about what services will be provided, various guidance (but not legislation) states that a care plan should be drawn up containing details about objectives, services, agencies involved, costs, needs which cannot be met, date of first review, and so on. The form and complexity of a care plan will vary greatly depending on the level and types of service involved. The law courts have held that either a failure to follow, or at least to have proper regard to, this guidance can amount to unlawfulness.

Care plans are often implemented by independent care providers with whom the local authority contracts, rather than by the local authority directly. The way in which contracts are placed – their content, terms and conditions, and monitoring and review of performance – will therefore bear on how well, and sometimes whether, service users' needs are met. Unfortunately, the contracting out of services is sometimes seen by local authorities as an escape route from potential obligations; they see it as a further uncertainty in the system (see Chapter 3) which is to be exploited. However, ultimately local authorities remain responsible for the meeting of people's needs in a reasonable and safe manner; therefore an 'out of sight, out of mind' approach is misplaced.

In practice, waiting times affect the provision of a range of services, for instance residential care placements, day services, domiciliary services, community equipment. Keeping people waiting for services is obviously a major plank in the attempts of local authorities to control expenditure; waiting times therefore represent a major potential 'escape route' from obligations, as outlined in Chapter 3. However, some waiting times are likely to be lawful and remain within the ambit of good administration; whereas others will err toward the unlawful and constitute maladministration.

In the absence of timescales in either legislation or Department of Health guidance, the legal expectation is that a duty to meet needs will be performed within a reasonable period of time; and that what is reasonable will depend on all the circumstances of the case. The courts have seemed generally reluctant to become involved in such questions, although have done so on some occasions; in contrast, the local government ombudsmen have investigated on many occasions.

**Note: Wales, Scotland and Northern Ireland**. This chapter applies in broad principle to Wales, Scotland and Northern Ireland. Care plans do not feature in the relevant legislation, but as in England the emphasis upon them in community care has stemmed from guidance issued on assessment and care management; for example in Wales (WO 1991 and NAFWC 9/02), in Scotland (SWSG 11/1991, SSI/SWSG 1991 and CCD 8/2001) and in Northern Ireland (DHSS 1991).

## 7.1 CARE PLANS

Once a local authority has assessed a person and identified eligible needs, it will generally have a duty to provide services (see 6.9). If services are to be provided, a care plan will be drawn up. Care plans are not referred to in legislation, although community care guidance places considerable emphasis on them (see generally DH 1990, para 3.24 and SSI/SWSG 1991, paras 4.1–4.37). Policy guidance states that care plans should follow assessment and it lists, in order of preference, a number of types of care packages, from support for people in their own homes to institutional long-term care (DH 1990, para 3.24).

Practice guidance states explicitly that users should receive copies of their care plans and goes on to list what their content should be. Guidance issued in 1991 identifies the following as key elements of a care plan. These were:

- overall objectives
- specific objectives of users, carers, care providers
- criteria for measuring these
- services to be provided
- cost to the user
- other options considered
- points of difference
- unmet needs

- named person responsible for implementation
- date of first planned review (SSI/SWSG 1991, para 4.37).

Later policy guidance contains more or less the same list, although explicitly refers also to contingency plans to manage emergency changes (LAC(2002)13, para 47). Yet further guidance, on the 'single assessment process' for older people, refers to:

- summary of eligible need referring to intensity, instability, unpredictability, complexity, risk to independence, rehabilitation potential
- note on whether the service user has agreed the plan and has consented to information sharing
- objectives
- summary of how services will impact on need
- what the service user will do to meet need
- risk management details
- what carers are willing to do
- description of level and frequency of help, specifying the agency responsible
- details of charges
- nursing plan where appropriate
- level of registered nursing care contribution where relevant
- name of coordinator
- contact number for emergencies and contingency plan
- monitoring arrangements and review date (HSC 2002/1, annex E).

The courts have held in more than one case that failure – without good reason – to draw up a care plan approximating in form to that set out in the 1991 guidance is unlawful.

**Inadequate care plan.** The case concerned a 25-year-old man with Seckels syndrome. He was blind, microcephalic, virtually immobile, doubly incontinent and mostly unable to communicate. He also suffered from severe deformities of the chest and spine, a hiatus hernia and a permanent digestive disorder. His weight and size were those of a small child, his dependency that of a baby.

The care plan drawn up by the local authority was inadequate to meet his assessed recreational needs; it had not sufficiently attempted to adjust what it was prepared to provide, in order to meet those needs.

The court also held that his care plan breached, without good reason, Department of Health policy guidance (DH 1990, para 3.24) stating that the objective of social services interventions should be recorded. In addition, the plan breached practice guidance (SSI/SWSG 1991, para 4.37) in respect of its contents, specification of objectives, agreement on implementation, leeway for contingencies and the identification and feedback of unmet needs. Practice guidance did not, the judge explained, carry the force of the policy guidance, but even so, the authority should have had regard to it: 'Whilst the occasional lacuna would not furnish evidence of such disregard, the series of lacunae…does, in my view, suggest that the statutory guidance has been overlooked' (R v Islington LBC, ex p Rixon).

Furthermore, the courts have pointed out that a care plan generally provides evidence of a person's eligible needs, of the consequent duty on the local authority, and of the way in which the duty will be performed. On this basis, it follows that a significant failure to provide services in accordance with a care plan could well indicate a breach of statutory duty on the part of the local authority (R v Islington LBC, ex p Rixon).

A significant discrepancy between assessed need and the care plan is likely to be unlawful and also to constitute maladministration in the eyes of the local ombudsman.

**Significant discrepancy in one-to-one support.** A man with dual sensory impairment and ataxia was assessed in 1994 as needing significant one-to-one support because of very high dependency, special needs due to a combination of learning disability, physical disability, blindness, partial hearing, and communication difficulties. However, the care plan did not reflect this assessment and the appropriate level of one-to-one support was not provided. He only received two hours per week for some time. In 1999, the council offered an increase to six hours, which his mother found unacceptably low. It was only by 2001 that he was receiving 33 hours per week from a deaf-blind communicator. In addition, Independent Living Fund funding was obtained in 2000 for 27 hours a week care at home; this increased to 41 hours a week in October of that year.

The ombudsman concluded that for a number of years, the local authority had 'failed by a wide margin' to implement the 1994 assessment (*Hertfordshire CC 2002*).

The failure to produce a care plan, even if an assessment of sorts has been carried out, might lead to costly recommendations by the local ombudsman.

**Failure to produce proper care plan for a woman with learning disabilities.** A young woman with learning disabilities was in a residential placement. On a visit to her family at Christmas, she decided she wished to live nearby and not return to the placement. The council failed to produce a care plan, relying wrongly on assumptions about what the father wanted. It had now lost the relevant records. However, on the basis of other evidence, it should have been reasonably clear to the council by April that the father was expecting the council either to provide the care or to secure that it be funded with direct payments and Independent Living Fund money if necessary (which eventually happened). It offered only some day centre activity.

The failure to have in place a care plan by April was maladministration. The father had subsequently to look after his daughter for some two years; full local authority funding was not in place for two and a half. As a result, the father had been caused significant financial loss, distress and frustration. The local ombudsman recommended £80,000 by way of remedy to be paid to the father; the council agreed to this (*Hertfordshire CC 2003*).

Not passing a care plan on to the relevant care provider will also be regarded as maladministration:

**Care plan not given to care home.** When a 101-year-old woman was admitted to a care home, where she subsequently developed a chest infection and pressure sore, the local ombudsman found no evidence that her care plan or any other similar documentation was given to the care home manager. Yet the care plan was an 'important document' and drew attention to significant issues of washing and medication, including treatment for her leg ulcer. This was maladministration (*Kent CC 2001*).

## 7.1.1 CARE PLANS: INTERRUPTIONS TO SERVICE PROVISION

Interruptions to, or unreliability of, service provision will not always be unlawful or constitute maladministration. It will depend on the degree and the circumstances.

**Discontinuity in home care service.** Following meetings, conversations and visits from local authority staff, the applicant had been informed that his home care service might suffer from discontinuity in certain circumstances (e.g. when home carers were ill or on leave). The applicant complained about the discontinuity that duly followed.

The judge found that the council had (a) performed a proper balancing exercise 'taking into account resources and the comparative needs of the disabled in their area'; (b) given clear notice about the possible interruptions to the service; (c) provided what they had undertaken to provide and what had been assessed as needed; (d) at no time withdrawn the service; (e) not interrupted a service to a person for whom any interruption of the service would have been intolerable. For instance, missing a day's meal would not have been acceptable, but missing a day's cleaning would have been (*R v Islington LBC, ex p McMillan*).

Equally, that food is important for obvious reasons was recognised in a local ombudsman investigation:

**Meals.** The ombudsman criticised the period of two or three months which it took the council to respond to the request from the man's general practitioner and to change the type of meal he received – this was important because of his medical condition. He required meals for people controlling diabetes by diet (copper coded), rather than by insulin (red coded). Despite the request, red coded meals continued to be delivered for some time. This was maladministration, caused injustice and warranted a compensation payment of £150.

The man also complained about the irregular visiting times of his home help service; however, the ombudsman accepted that it might take a little time to establish a regular visiting time, and it would be unrealistic to expect visits to be made at exactly the same time each week (*Kensington and Chelsea RLB 1992*).

Nevertheless, the court's observation in the particular circumstances of the *McMillan* case, comparing cooking with cleaning, should not be taken as a general dismissal of the importance of cleaning. Thus, in one case the local ombudsman found maladministration, because a local authority had prioritised shopping over cleaning without taking account of the individual circumstances of the service user. He was an amputee, diabetic and doubly incontinent with an undoubted need for cleaning (*Westminster CC 1996*).

If home help services fail significantly the local ombudsman will find maladministration:

**Irregular home help service.** Over the course of a year, a man had frequently less than his planned three home help visits a week; no sufficient reason was given for this failure, and the local authority anyway had no system to tell people about cancellation or delay. This was maladministration (*Westminster CC 1996*).

In another case, the care plan stated that a woman with osteoporosis should receive 14.5 hours a week care; yet the council conceded that it had been providing only 12 hours. This was maladministration (*Croydon LBC 2000*).

### 7.1.2 CARE PLANS: SERIOUS DISCREPANCIES IN PROVISION

Substantial failures in the delivery of services will anyway attract criticism from the local ombudsman, and may relate to the quality of service provision, including the competence of staff, as well as to amount or quantity of service.

**Serious shortcomings in services in hostel.** A woman with epilepsy, severe learning difficulties, behavioural problems and urinary incontinence was placed in a hostel by the local authority under s.21 of the National Assistance Act 1948. The placement failed; the local ombudsman found serious shortcomings. These included the care plan not being fully in place when she moved in, insufficient monitoring of the placement, chronic understaffing, inadequate training, lack of proper evaluation of the woman's needs (*Hackney LBC 1992b*).

**Serious failures in provision of support to a person in a care home**. The local authority placed a man with severe learning disabilities in one of its own hostels. The parents complained of poor staffing, their son's sleep disturbance through sharing a room with a man who required attention several times a night, personal belongings being stolen or destroyed, lost laundry, missing lavatory seats, their son being left with tooth pain. The ombudsman found serious failures and maladministration. Although a support worker was provided, there was a lack of precision in setting, working toward and recording the meeting of targets; this, too, was maladministration – as was a failure on several occasions to administer the medication necessary for his epilepsy (*Manchester CC 1993*).

The courts in one case were prepared to challenge the competence of staff:

**Competence of staff**. A dispute arose over the competence of a supply teacher who had been taken on to teach an autistic child. The child's statement of special educational needs required that she be taught by a teacher experienced in teaching children with significant learning difficulties and autism and communication disorders. The court expressed its reluctance to intervene except when a decision appeared legally irrational. However, in this case, the judge found that the local authority could not reasonably have characterised the teacher as 'experienced'. Thus the authority was in breach of its duty to arrange the special educational provision specified in the statement of need (*R v Wandsworth LBC, ex p M*).

Serious failures in care plans might not only mean that people's needs are not met, but be maladministration – and be associated with, if not necessarily proved to have caused, serious consequences including death:

**Death of woman with learning disabilities**. The case concerned a woman in her thirties who, the coroner found, died accidentally by drowning (perhaps following an epileptic fit or cardiac arrhythmia) in the bath at a six-person residential care unit run by the council.

The woman had an 'Individual Programme Plan', but the ombudsman criticised the fact that it still contained an objective about learning certain skills – despite the fact that the officer with responsibility for the 'Goal Plan', designed to achieve such an objective, said that the woman was not capable of learning those skills. The absence of a formal decision to relax the requirement about these skills was maladministration. More specifically: 'No formal decision was ever taken that Anne had reached a stage where she could safely be left to bath alone. I can understand staff's concern to maximise her privacy and independence. Such concerns needed to be balanced against the needs of safety. It may be that, had a proper assessment been made, a decision could have been properly reached that Anne was able to bath alone but this is not what had happened and no such decision was conveyed to [the parents].'

This, together with a temporarily reduced staffing level, was maladministration, although the ombudsman – in line with the findings of the coroner – did not conclude that it had resulted in the woman's death. However, the staffing level was a factor that delayed discovery of what had happened. The ombudsman concluded that there was maladministration in the way in which the woman was cared for (*Cleveland CC 1993*).

In a similar type of case, considered judicially, the court concluded that the absence of the issue of bathing from the care plan, even if negligent (in civil law), was not sufficient to warrant a charge of manslaughter (in criminal law) on the grounds of gross negligence (*Rowley v DPP*; see 17.8.2).

If accidents involving bathing seem to be regularly reported, so too do incidents of 'wandering'; complaints might be made to the local ombudsman:

**Death of elderly man with Alzheimer's disease.** An 82-year-old man was admitted on 25 April for respite care to one of the council's residential homes. He suffered from Alzheimer's disease but was otherwise fit. He was prone to wandering off and had difficulty finding his way home in an unfamiliar area. Undetected by staff, he left the home on 29 April; he was found dead six weeks later.

The ombudsman found no fault in the local authority's original assessment of the need for respite care. However, it was at fault for not properly checking that the care home could meet his needs. Furthermore, there had already been a 'wandering' incident on 27 April before the final disappearance; the family should have been informed of the incident, invited to think again about the placement and involved in the risk assessment process. In addition, the care home should have reconsidered the suitability of the placement when it finally found and opened his assessment documents on 26 April; ensured that all its staff were aware of his needs and propensity to wander; recorded the 27 April incident; and ensured he was adequately supervised. This was all maladministration (*Hounslow LBC 1999*).

## 7.2 PROVISION OF COMMUNITY CARE SERVICES: CONTRACTS

Since community care was formally introduced in April 1993, a so-called 'mixed economy of care' has meant that local authorities make extensive use of independent care providers (both voluntary organisations with charitable status and private sector organisations) to deliver community care services. This involves a large scale of contracting, for instance, for residential accommodation (under s.26 of the National Assistance Act 1948) and for non-residential services (under s.30 of the National Assistance Act 1948).

However, overall, it is the local authority that retains statutory responsibility for meeting a person's community assessed care needs and for ensuring that a person's care plan is adhered to. In addition, local authorities retain health and safety at work responsibilities even where services have been contracted out. Therefore, they have to pay serious attention to contracting matters such as the tendering process, allocating sufficient money to contracts, terms and conditions within the contract, penalty clauses, monitoring and review of contract performance – and so on.

### 7.2.1 CONTRACTS AND SERVICE USERS

When health or social care is provided by the NHS or by local authorities, the courts have hitherto declined to identify the existence of a private law contract created between provider and service user. This is despite the emphasis in community care on individual care plans, which sometimes bear the language of agreement and are signed by all parties. Users of services and local authority staff sometimes imagine that enforceable contracts are being created.

The courts generally hold that the existence of statutory arrangements preclude the free negotiation and bargaining that are meant to be the hallmarks of a genuine contract. In this case, there will be no contract between the user of a statutory service and a statutory provider. This might be so even when money changes hands – as in a case concerning an NHS prescription charge, when the House of Lords stated that the transaction was governed by statutory obligations and not by contract (*Pfizer Corporation v Ministry of Health*).

Another obstacle to the identification and enforcing of contracts by users of services arises in relation to independent providers. This is the rule in English law called privity of contract. This means that a third party (i.e. the service user) cannot enforce a contract by two other parties (the local authority and the independent provider), even if it has been made for his or her benefit. The Contracts (Rights of Third Parties) Act 1999 was passed in order to enable third parties to enforce, in certain circumstances, a contract made between two other parties. However, whether the courts would interpret the Act as effective in the case of statutory social care and health care services is doubtful.

Of course some people fund themselves and enter directly into a contract with independent care providers, in which case contractual obligations exist directly between care provider and service user.

## 7.2.2 LOCAL AUTHORITY AND CARE PROVIDER CONTRACTS

Under regulations, passed under the Care Standards Act 2000, care providers are obliged to have care plans in respect of each individual service user – for instance in respect of domiciliary care (SI 2002/3214, r.14) and care homes (SI 2001/3965, r.15). This duty is expanded upon further in standards published for the purpose of registration and inspection of such providers – for example standard 7 of both the *Domiciliary Care National Minimum Standards* (DH 2003c), and of the *Care Homes for Older People National Minimum Standards* (DH 2003b). Nevertheless, the overall duty of the local authority to draw up a care plan and ensure that it is implemented remains.

### 7.2.2.1 Contracted out services: out of sight, out of mind?

Local authorities must beware of improperly shedding their duty to ensure that the needs of service users are met, as the local ombudsmen have concluded:

**Failing to reassess on change of need.** A man with learning disabilities was in 1991 placed in a care home jointly by social services and the NHS. In 1998, he was diagnosed as suffering from high functioning autism. He was not reassessed by the local authority until June 2003. The authority tried to excuse itself by arguing that it did not know of changes in the man's needs during this time, and had no record of recommendations apparently made by the care home in 1998.

The local ombudsman pointed out that the local authority was jointly responsible for the placement and for proper reviews of the man's needs and services. No such reviews had been in place; this was maladministration (*Cambridgeshire CC 2004*).

Some local authorities fail to include sufficient specification in their contracts with independent care providers, and to monitor and review the performance of such contracts. One consequence is that care providers might in some cases not adhere to individual care plans drawn up originally by the local authority – always assuming the local authority had itself drawn up an adequate care plan. Potentially, this would put the local authority in breach of its duty to meet people's needs; it might also make the local authority legally vulnerable in respect of human rights or health and safety at work issues.

**Tube feeding and manual handling by untrained staff.** The dangers – legal and otherwise – of local authorities' contracting with apparently substandard, independent domiciliary care providers was revealed in a *Panorama* programme shown in 2003 on BBC1 (*A Carer's Story*, broadcast Sunday 16 November 2003 at 10.15pm).

Seemingly severe shortcomings in training and working practices appeared to result in significant detriment to service users. Two of the situations shown concerned the tube feeding of one person, and the complex manual handling required to transfer an older woman with advanced dementia. The programme seemed clearly to reveal that people's care plans were not being properly implemented (assuming they had been adequately drawn up in the first place). This would mean that the local authorities concerned were potentially in breach of their community care duties to meet people's needs; and might be vulnerable also to challenges on human rights and various health and safety at work grounds.

Inadequate monitoring by the local authority might be associated with, if not directly cause, highly unfortunate outcomes for service users, and be maladministration:

**Care home placement and death.** A woman was placed in a nursing home by the local authority (before the introduction of free nursing care in 2001 and the implementation in 2002 of the Care Standards Act 2000). She subsequently died as a result of pressure sores. The woman's grandson brought separate complaints against the local authority, the health authority and the private company that ran the home.

As far as the local authority was concerned, it argued that it had no obligation to monitor the standards of nursing care provided in the home; it had to rely on the nursing home staff and the health authority's registration and inspection unit. The ombudsman took a different view, since it was the local authority that had placed her, with a view to meeting its statutory obligation to meet her needs. It therefore had to put in place arrangements to satisfy itself that those needs were indeed being met. If it felt that it was unable to do so with its own staff, it should have come to an arrangement for the health authority to do it under s.113(1A) of the Local Government Act 1972 (under which NHS staff can be made available to a local authority) (*Bexley CC 2000*).

**Death of young man addicted to alcohol.** A local authority placed a young man addicted to alcohol on a residential rehabilitation course in the area of another local authority. The man discharged himself and died shortly afterward from a drug overdose. The ombudsman did not conclude that the local authority was to blame for the death. However, he did find maladministration insofar as the authority failed to make proper checks with the registration and inspection unit of the local authority, within whose area the home was; failed to ensure that a proper contract was in place; and failed to keep in touch with the man (even on the telephone) (*Nottinghamshire CC 1999*).

Alternatively, a failure in the contracting process might lead to health and safety at work problems for the staff of the contractor and to prosecution of the local authority (see

22.5). Thus local authorities should not take an 'out of sight, out of mind' approach when services are contracted out. The following example illustrates what can happen when a local authority fails properly to take responsibility for the needs of a person it has contractually placed with a care provider. The upshot was a protracted dispute, the service user's needs not being met and a finding of maladministration by the local ombudsman:

**Care home placement and manual handling dispute.** A local authority placed a man in a residential home and paid an extra amount, to cover additional personal assistance for him. This included manual handling by way of assisted transfers. The care home manager subsequently refused to provide such assistance and insisted instead that the man use a hoist. The manager argued that two carers had been injured while manually handling the man; the man argued that they were in fact injured when assisting other residents. The manager supported his position with a risk assessment, which did not accord with that of the local authority.

The man refused to be hoisted. The manager told him that he would have to stay in bed. His elderly parents began to visit to provide their son with the personal assistance he needed. The man contacted his social worker, who told him that he would have to stay in bed if he refused to use a hoist. This was despite the fact that there was medical evidence that both hoist use and staying in bed would be detrimental.

The subsequent local government ombudsman investigation concluded that there was convincing evidence that the man could safely be given assisted transfers. He also found that the local authority had been in breach of its duty to meet the man's assessed needs (*Redbridge LBC 1998*).

Conversely, if a local authority does have adequate monitoring and review, it will not necessarily attract criticism from the local ombudsman if things do go wrong.

**Monitoring of domiciliary support.** Solicitors acting for a severely disabled man's grandmother complained that he had not received adequate care and that she had not been supported properly as a carer. Domiciliary support had been contracted to a care agency. Various complaints were made about the standard of care, financial and security lapses, and violence by a carer. However, the ombudsman found that the local authority initially had no reason to doubt the care agency's ability to provide satisfactory care, and had had adequate monitoring procedures in place through regular meetings with the man and his family (*Liverpool CC 1997b*).

Similarly in negligence cases, if a local authority takes reasonable care in procuring services from an independent provider, the fact that something then goes awry will not necessarily result in liability:

**Contracted out services: negligence liability.** The Ministry of Defence made arrangements with a London hospital, for the hospital in turn to contract for treatment of army personnel in Germany. The question arose as to whether the hospital should be liable for negligent treatment subsequently given in Germany. The court concluded that the London hospital's duty of care did not extend to ensuring directly that reasonable care and skill were used for hospital treatment in Germany. However, the London hospital might have been liable had it carelessly selected a provider, and mismanaged the contract such that an unsafe regime were permitted and injury to patients caused.

The Court of Appeal upheld this decision, which in effect identified the NHS duty as an 'organisational' duty to use reasonable care that the hospital staff, facilities and organisation provided were appropriate to provide safe and satisfactory medical care. This duty was not breached. Such a duty differed from a duty to ensure that the treatment actually given was administered with reasonable care and skill; however, this latter duty was not applicable (*A Child 'A' v Ministry of Defence*).

In another negligence case, concerning the checking of a contractor's insurance, the NHS was likewise found by the court not to be liable in negligence for the accident that had occurred:

**Contracted out 'splat wall' for fair in hospital grounds.** An NHS Trust organised a fair in its grounds. It contracted with 'Club Entertainments' for a splat wall, which allowed people to bounce from a trampoline and stick to a wall by means of velcro. The equipment was negligently set up and the claimant was injured. The court found that the Trust had a duty to satisfy itself about the competence of the contractor. This included factors such as experience, reliability and insurance. The Trust was therefore obliged to enquire about insurance, which it did – but not to demand actually to see the policy (which had in fact expired prior to the accident). The Trust was therefore held by the court not to be liable (*Gwilliam v West Hertfordshire Hospital NHS Trust*).

Of course the maintenance of standards applies to 'inhouse' providers, as well as to independent providers, as illustrated in the following health service ombudsman investigation:

**Respite care.** A woman was admitted for respite care to a residential home managed by an NHS Trust. She suffered a spiral fracture of her lower right leg. The health service ombudsman found a lack of effective leadership and appropriate supervision, and non-compliance with Trust policy on moving handling, safe bathing and personal care (*Surrey Oaklands NHS Trust 2002*).

### 7.2.2.2 Reliance on registration and inspection body

Reliance by a local authority on the registration and inspection body (e.g. the Commission for Social Care Inspection) will not necessarily be enough to discharge its duty to monitor and review in respect of individual service users – as the local ombudsman held in an investigation concerning the standard of nursing care in a care home:

**Death in care home.** A resident had died as a result of pressure sores. The local authority had sought to rely on the health authority (which had at the time responsibility for registration and inspection of the home) for monitoring the welfare of the residents placed by the local authority. The local ombudsman found that it was maladministration for the local authority not to have taken steps to check the welfare of the resident, in particular her nursing care (*Bexley LBC 2000*).

Furthermore the health service ombudsman, in a separate investigation of the same case, upheld a complaint against the health authority; its registration team had failed to look adequately into the care home's provision of staff, equipment, or precautions against accidents to residents. The ombudsman also criticised the looseness of the arrangements that the health authority had in dealing with the home (*Bexley and Greenwich Health Authority 1999*).

In another local ombudsman investigation, the local authority arranged a residential/rehabilitation placement for a person with an alcohol problem. The doubtful ability of the home to meet his needs was not picked up by inspection unit staff, who had no background in work with such service users, and did not recognise the different needs of residents of rehabilitation units (as in this case) from those in homes for elderly and mentally infirm people generally (*North Somerset CC 1999*).

### 7.2.2.3 Terms, conditions, standards

The courts have held that there is in principle nothing to stop a local authority imposing contractual terms that exceed what is demanded by national regulatory legislation such as the Care Standards Act 2000 (*R v Cleveland CC, ex p Cleveland Care Homes Association*). Furthermore, although the Human Rights Act 1998 does not apply directly to independent care providers, because they are not public bodies, nevertheless local authorities could impose a contractual obligation on such care providers to comply with human rights (*R(Heather) v Leonard Cheshire Foundation*).

Indeed, a local authority's insistence on high contractual standards, beyond regulatory requirements, coupled with firm and economical means of enforcing them, was held by the courts to be an essential means of balancing statutory requirements to meet needs and the fiduciary duty not to waste taxpayers' money (*R v Newcastle upon Tyne Council, ex p Dixon*). In similar vein, the local ombudsman held that it was within an authority's discretion to run an approved provider scheme and to give a higher council subsidy to such approved providers. To the extent that this might in practice mean higher subsidy being given to council-owned, rather than privately run, care homes, the ombudsman stated that it was not for him to determine; although the district auditor might take an interest (*Isle of Anglesey CC 1999a, 1999b; Neath Port Talbot CBC 2000*).

At the same time, the courts have stated that terms should not be so unreasonable as to threaten the ability of care providers to survive, and thus the ability of potential residents to exercise a choice of home, as envisaged by the community care legislation (*R v Cleveland CC, ex p Cleveland Care Homes Association*). Such factors must be taken into account when a local authority approves the terms of such contracts (*R v Coventry City Council, ex p Coventry Heads of Independent Care Establishments (CHOICE) and Peggs*).

In addition, there is implied – even if not explicitly written – into every contract that a service will be delivered with reasonable care and skill (Supply of Goods and Services Act 1982, s.13). Where a contract does not contain adequate specification within it, this principle may be of assistance if one party is not providing a reasonable level of service.

In terms of trying to ensure standards are adhered to and that the needs of service users are likely to be met, the courts held in one case that a local authority was not acting beyond its powers or unreasonably when it asked to see the full, rather than the abbreviated, accounts of a home – when it was contracting with the home. This was to check the financial viability of the home and its ability to provide long-term care and accommodation (*R v Cleveland CC, ex p Ward*).

### 7.2.2.4 Cost-effectiveness and 'best value'

'Best value' authorities must exercise their functions, having regard to a combination of economy, efficiency and effectiveness (Local Government Act 1999, s.3). Thus, best value is not meant to be about always finding the cheapest option; furthermore, it is essentially about *how* local authorities carry out their duties and not *whether* they should carry them out. In other words, best value cannot negate legal duties, whether performed through the provision of in-house services or contracted services. The courts have made this point:

**Not confusing best value with meeting people's needs.** In a case about closure of a care home, the courts reminded the local authority that best value did not override the meeting of people's assessed community care needs (*R(Bodimeade) v Camden LBC*).

In other words, the financial temptation to contract cheaply with care providers who cannot meet people's community care needs must be avoided. Similarly, if a local authority holds itself hostage to its rigid policies in the name of best value, this might be at the expense of performing its legal obligations to meet people's assessed community care needs. This will lead to findings of maladministration by the local ombudsman:

**Best value policy preventing the meeting of a person's needs.** A local authority had a list of approved home care providers; it would not go outside of this list. This was in the name of best value; previously 40 to 50 providers had been used. Now, in the cause of quality control, there were four to five approved providers in each area only. However, a particular approved provider could not provide the two carers that a risk assessment had identified as required to meet the assessed need of a woman to be hoisted in and out of bed. The provider had at first stated that it would not take on situations requiring two carers (because of the logistical difficulty of coordinating their whereabouts during the day); it later corrected this by stating that it would 'double up' its own carers, but would on no account have its carers double up with carers from another agency.

By rigidly refusing to go outside of its approved provider list to enable 'spot purchasing', and by also anyway imposing a £360 weekly limit on how much it would spend, the local authority was found to have 'fettered its discretion' and failed in its duty to meet a person's assessed need. The ombudsman pointed out that in the final analysis it was the needs of individuals that should have determined the council's response and not its contractual arrangements (*Cambridgeshire CC 2002*).

At the same time, ensuring that a service provider delivers services in accordance with the contract is of course a best value matter and indeed might interest the district auditor:

**Treatment day centre, value for money, health and safety.** The complainant to the local ombudsman was the mother of an autistic man who attended a day centre run by a voluntary organisation but paid for (including transport) by the council. She became concerned over various incidents, including her son (a) returning from the centre with injuries to the top of his legs (commensurate with a badly fitting climbing harness); (b) drinking river water and being sick; (c) stripping in public; (d) opening the doors of the moving minibus in which he was being transported; (e) going to a park and a carer's home to watch television when he should have been participating in a one-to-one care programme.

The mother had also complained to the district auditor that the council was paying for a service that the centre was not delivering; in response to the auditor's enquiry, the council said it would try to recover money from the centre. Additionally, the Health and Safety Executive had become involved in respect of opening the doors of the minibus; such an incident had occurred more than once and the Executive threatened enforcement in case of recurrence (*Liverpool 1998a*).

Another instance that could result in financial detriment to either local authority or the service user (if the latter is paying for his or her domiciliary care) concerns health and safety at work policies. Thus, some care providers (both independent and 'inhouse') operate blanket manual handling policies to the effect that there must always be two paid carers present in the case of many manual handling tasks. But because they are blanket in nature, the policies are applied to every individual service user, irrespective of the risk posed in any individual case. This could mean that a service user (or the local authority) is then charged by the care provider for having two carers, even when both are not actually required in that particular case. Indeed, a service user might anyway be upset if she saw her domiciliary care charges rise from £35 per week to £182, partly because she now had to pay for each of two carers needed to lift her (Thompson and Mathew 2004); how much worse if she were paying unnecessarily.

## 7.3 WAITING TIMES FOR SERVICES

Community care legislation contains no time limits on the delivery of services, other than the situation in which people should be discharged from acute hospital beds (Community Care (Delayed Discharges) Act 2003). Even in that case, exceeding the time limit imposed by an NHS discharge notice does not result in a breach of duty; it merely creates a duty on the local authority to pay money to the NHS for the 'blocked' bed. Likewise, government sets targets, by means of performance indicators, for service delivery; but the courts will not necessarily regard such targets as relevant to ascertaining whether undue delay has occurred.

As already noted (see 6.18), if legislation is silent on the time within which a duty must be performed, then the courts take the approach that it must be performed within a reasonable period of time. That means without undue delay. This will depend on the circumstances of the case. The courts and the local government ombudsmen have considered delay on a number of occasions. They are more likely to do so in the context of social services than the NHS, because the duties on local authorities to provide services to individuals are in some circumstances of the specific, 'absolute' and enforceable type – unlike, by and large, NHS duties.

### 7.3.1 INTERIM PROVISION

Department of Health guidance points out that interim provision will sometimes be required, for example when the care home place of choice is not yet available (LAC(98)19, para 11). Or, for instance, interim provision might be required in terms of assistive equipment and personal assistance in a person's home, while he or she is waiting for major adaptation works to be carried out or to move house.

**Waiting times: interim provision of equipment.** The local government ombudsman has referred on a number of occasions to interim provision: for example, a bath aid during a wait for alternative accommodation (*Barnsley MBC 1998a*); and provision of a commode by the social services department, while a person waits for a disabled facilities grant from the housing department, which might discharge the authority's duty under s.2 of the Chronically Sick and Disabled Persons Act 1970 (*Barnsley MBC 1998b*; see also *Liverpool CC 1996/1997, Tower Hamlets LBC 1997*).

However, the courts have reminded local authorities that the interim provision should not become an end in itself (*R v Sutton LBC, ex p Tucker*).

## 7.3.2 INVOLVEMENT OF THE COURTS

In large part, the courts might be reluctant to become involved in the question of waiting times for services.

**Judicial reluctance to rule on waiting times.** A child had entered a psychiatric unit for assessment. The doctor decided that a special foster placement was required as soon as possible, the accommodation and care to be provided under s.20 of the Children Act 1989. This had proved difficult and the child was still, nearly a year later, in the unit. The judge held that it was not appropriate for the court to make a declaration that the authority had not acted with reasonable diligence and speed. This would not be appropriate in the context of judicial review, because the court could not investigate the precise circumstances of the situation. Instead, it was more appropriate that the complaints procedure under s.26 of the Children Act 1989 be used (*R v Birmingham CC, ex p A*).

Nevertheless, in some more recent cases, the courts have in particular circumstances been prepared to refer to timescales.

**Delay in care plan.** A woman with learning disabilities was assessed as ready for discharge from NHS premises in July 1994. By 1996 she was still there. The judge found the local authority to be in breach of s.47 of the NHS and Community Care Act 1990, since it had still not decided about what services to provide (*R v Sutton LBC, ex p Tucker*).

In a Scottish case, the court also found breach of duty in respect of a considerably shorter timescale than was involved in the *Tucker* case.

**Delay funding care home place.** A 90-year-old man was admitted to a care home, the need for which the local authority had accepted. He had extremely poor short-term memory, restricted mobility and liability to fall, deafness in both ears, regular confusion, and inability to dress and look after himself. The local authority placed him on a waiting list for funding (in the mean time, his family were in effect being forced to pay the fees). The judge held that placing the man on a waiting list for several months was an abdication of the local authority's responsibility and was unlawful (*MacGregor v South Lanarkshire Council*).

Furthermore, in the *MacGregor* case, the court stated – just as the ombudsman has on many occasions in respect of waiting times for assessment (see 6.18.3) – that even if waiting lists had some legitimacy, they should not be operated simply in date order. Instead, they should be applied on the basis of priority being allocated according to the degree of individual need.

## 7.3.3 LOCAL GOVERNMENT OMBUDSMEN

Just as for waits for assessments (see 16.8), the local ombudsmen have investigated delays in services on a number of occasions. Much might hinge on the individual circumstances:

**Undue delay and the individual case.** The local ombudsman is likely to consider the circumstances of each case in deciding what a reasonable waiting time should have been. For instance, in one investigation, the local authority claimed, in relation to s.2 of the Chronically Sick and Disabled Persons Act 1970, 'that although they may be under an obligation to provide a facility they do not consider that they have an obligation to provide the facility immediately. Thus, they argue some delay is acceptable.' The ombudsman stated that 'whether or not any particular delay is so excessive as to constitute maladministration will depend on the facts of the individual case' (*Wakefield MDC 1992*).

Waiting times might afflict not just one stage of assessment and provision, but several, turning into a catalogue of delay:

**Catalogue of delay.** A woman with learning disabilities and autism had completed a university degree in deaf studies and sign language and now required some form of residential placement as she did not wish to return home to live with her father on a permanent basis. The local authority carried out an assessment of need in July 1997; in February 2000 the need still had not been met, through a catalogue of delay and lack of urgency in obtaining relevant information, holding meetings and making decisions. Even when a decision to provide a tailored assessment had been made, it took seven months from the date of the decision to hold a care planning meeting, and a further five months to request the extra funding that had been identified as needed. All this was maladministration for the local ombudsman (*Wakefield MDC 2000*).

Delay, amounting to maladministration in the judgement of the local ombudsman, might come in both long and short forms, whether a matter of days, weeks, months or years.

**Long and short waiting times**. When a man with paraplegia (following an accident) was discharged home from hospital, it took the local authority 16 months to put a complete care package in place; this was too long (*Avon CC 1997*).

A delay of two or three months in changing the meals-on-wheels for a person with special dietary needs and following a request from the man's general practitioner was maladministration (*Kensington and Chelsea RB 1992*).

It was maladministration also when cleaning and laundry services promised for February did not materialise until late March for a man discharged from hospital after a stroke – and when there was a failure to place straightaway and mark as urgent an order for a gas fire with top controls, given that he was blacking out when bending down to use the existing controls (*Kirklees MBC 1993*).

Delay in providing services of nine months, following the assessment of a young man who had just left school (and was later diagnosed as schizophrenic), was maladministration (*Liverpool CC 1997a*); as was a delay of 12 months in making arrangements for an alternative care package, after heavily supported independent living in a bungalow had failed (*Liverpool CC 1997b*). Even a ten-day wait for a visit to be made following the discharge of a man from hospital – when normally a visit would have been made next day – was blameworthy (*Sheffield CC 1996*).

Allowing situations to drift will attract criticism from the local ombudsman:

**Avoiding drift**. Delay in payment of a housing (renovation) grant could not be justified by the absence of the 'one person' who could make it, even in the absence of an authorised deputy (*Kirklees MBC 1997*). When a stairlift company was being slow in responding to the council's request that it assess and estimate the cost of installing a stairlift, the council should have been monitoring the situation and pursuing the company (*Liverpool 1996/1997*).

In order to identify blameworthy, as opposed to justifiable, delay, the local ombudsmen sometimes break down the whole process of referral, assessment and service provision into separate stages. They then give to each a reasonable time that is then measured against what actually occurred.

**Breaking down waiting times.** In establishing a blameworthy period of waiting (18 months), the ombudsman considered the time involved for each of the following: request for assessment, assessment, occupational therapist's report and request for costing, preliminary inspection and completion of grant enquiry form, stairlift estimate, test of resources, sending and return of application package, grant approval (*Liverpool CC 1996/1997*). Work arranged by the social services department to replace a bath with a shower, which took five months instead of only one, constituted maladministration (*Liverpool CC 1996/1997*).

# Residential accommodation

**KEY POINTS**

Local authorities have both duties and powers to arrange residential accommodation of various types under s.21 of the National Assistance Act 1948. Under s.26 of the 1948

Act, such accommodation may be arranged through the independent sector. The fundamental conditions that must be satisfied are:

- a person must be at least 18 years old
- have a need for care and attention
- this need must arise from age, illness, disability or any other circumstances
- the care and attention required must not be available otherwise than by the provision of accommodation under s.21.

Whether in respect of people subject to immigration control, or others in various types of need, s.21 of the 1948 Act continues to be legally scrutinised as to its meaning and scope. Notwithstanding its age, the courts have confirmed that it is a prime example of legislation that is 'always speaking'. Therefore, it should be interpreted in a way that continuously updates the meaning of wording, in order to allow for changes to society since the legislation was originally drafted. This was one reason why the courts have held that the term 'residential accommodation', whatever it might have meant in 1948, could now refer not just to institutional, but ordinary housing.

The flexibility of s.21, and this requirement that it be interpreted to keep pace with changing social circumstances, means that uncertainties flourish at times when pressure is put upon the Act because of those changing social circumstances and needs. For instance, s.21 continues to be closely scrutinised in the case of asylum seekers and other people subject to immigration control (see Chapter 13), and in respect of how far it creates obligations to provide 'ordinary housing'.

Note: Wales, Scotland and Northern Ireland. This chapter applies in principle to Wales; the primary legislation is the same and for the most part there are equivalent directions and guidance; for example, directions and guidance on residential accommodation under the National Assistance Act 1948 (WOC 35/93), and on choice of accommodation (WOC 12/93). However, the detail differs; for instance, NHS financial responsibility for the registered nursing care element of care home placement is calculated differently than in England.

The position in Scotland is different; the wording covering care home placements in the legislation differs significantly (Social Work (Scotland) Act 1968, ss.12,13A and 59) from that in England. There is nevertheless similar guidance on choice of accommodation (SWSG 5/93), and also additional guidance on choice and hospital discharge (CCD 8/2003).

In Northern Ireland, the legislation governing care home placements again reads differently than in England; there is far less specificity (Health and Personal Social Services (Northern Ireland) Order 1972). This became evident when the High Court in Northern Ireland held that the 1972 Order did not create the same sort of strong duty to provide accommodation for a person that was created by s.21 of the National Assistance Act 1948 in England (Re Margaret Hanna). Brief guidance on choice of accommodation was outlined in the original Northern Ireland policy document on community care (DHSS 1990, p.46).

## 8.1 NEED FOR CARE AND ATTENTION

The need under s.21 of the National Assistance Act 1948 is for care and attention, but the only service that can be provided is residential accommodation (together with associated amenities and requisites). There would thus appear to be something of a mismatch between the need and the service. The explanation is that the accommodation itself is not the care and attention but is the only means by which the requisite care and attention, or 'looking after', can be provided (*R(Wahid) Tower Hamlets LBC*).

Furthermore, the courts have made the point that a local authority should look ahead to some extent, if the circumstances are such that a person is not in immediate need of care and attention but is likely soon to be so (*R v Newham LBC, ex p Gorenkin*).

The courts have reluctantly conceded that, in formulating eligibility criteria about when a person is to be deemed to be in need of care and attention, local authorities may up to a point (a 'limited subjective element') consider their resources (*R v Sefton LBC, ex p Help the Aged*).

## 8.1.1 AGE, ILLNESS, DISABILITY OR ANY OTHER CIRCUMSTANCES

The care and attention required must be due to age, illness, disability or any other circumstances. Age, illness and disability are not defined. The term 'any other circumstances' means precisely what it says. The following two court cases illustrate this in terms of destitution and domestic violence both being relevant circumstances (although the law was subsequently altered in respect of destitution: see 13.2.1).

**Any other circumstances: asylum seekers.** The Court of Appeal ruled, upholding a decision of the High Court in relation to asylum seekers, that the term 'any other circumstances' did not necessarily have to be of a kind with age, illness or disability (the other conditions for assistance). However, the court also stated that even if it were wrong and it did have to be of a kind with these other terms, it was clear that the circumstances of the asylum seekers – without food and accommodation, inability to speak the language, ignorance of Britain, and stress – could result in illness or disability, thus establishing potential eligibility through these terms rather than 'any other circumstances'. Nevertheless, this did not mean that s.21 was a safety net for just anyone who happened to be short of accommodation and money (*R v Westminster CC, ex p A*: decided before the 1999 and 2002 Acts relating to immigration and asylum).

Similarly, domestic violence could be a relevant 'other circumstance' when a local authority considers whether the needs of an asylum seeker stem from destitution alone or something more (*R(Khan) v Oxfordshire CC*).

The open-ended, though not limitless, nature of 'any other circumstances', and the subsequent history of how the term has been applied, was indeed foreseen in 1948 at the time the Bill was passed in Parliament. It was described as not concerning age or infirmity (the original criteria in the section) but was to cover the difficult or marginal case, such that its absence might 'run us into trouble'. At the same time, it was not intended to place 'indefinite responsibility' on local authorities (*John Edwards: Standing Committee C, 21/1/1948, col.2498*). (Thus, for example, in a later 2004 case, the High Court held that a local authority did not simply have to accommodate en masse a group of Chagossian islanders who had arrived in England claiming to be destitute. However, it would have to accommodate some of the islanders if need were demonstrated in individual cases: *R(Selmour) v West Sussex CC.*)

## 8.1.2 TAKING ACCOUNT OF A PERSON'S RESOURCES

In deciding whether care and attention is otherwise available, the local authority must disregard the person's capital resources beneath the relevant capital upper threshold applying to care home fees (National Assistance Act 1948, s.21(2A) (see 9.6).

Even before the National Assistance Act 1948 was amended to put this beyond doubt, the Court of Appeal had held that to treat a person as able to make her own arrangements for residential accommodation – once her capital had fallen below the relevant threshold – was not lawful. The local authority had in fact been pursuing a policy that allowed a person's resources to fall to £1500 – far below the capital threshold – before it would assist (*R v Sefton MBC, ex p Help the Aged*).

In similar vein, the local ombudsman has stated that, where people are already in residential care and their capital dips below the capital threshold, a policy of delaying council funding and not back dating it would be likely to be unlawful and was in any case maladministration (*Cumbria CC 2000*).

**Undue delay in funding decision for person already in a care home.** A local authority told the wife of a self-funding resident of a care home to contact the local authority when his resources fell below the capital threshold. She did so, assuming that as soon as this point was reached, the council would contribute to the funding. In fact, from the point of the wife contacting the council, it took the local authority a total of 17 weeks to decide on the funding. The local ombudsman felt that seven weeks would have been reasonable; this meant that there were ten weeks of undue delay. This was maladministration (*Staffordshire CC 2000*).

However, the local ombudsman in one case suggested that the effect of the *Sefton* judgment was limited to those already in residential care; and that this still left open the question of whether waiting lists for those people in hospital or in their own homes are lawful – even where savings are below the capital threshold (*Liverpool CC 1999*). In fact, the effect of the *Sefton* judgment seems not to be limited to those already in residential care; the court's conclusions appear to be couched in such a way as to affect any person assessed to be in need of care and attention, not just a person already in a care home. Furthermore, central government subsequently amended the relevant regulations to make it quite clear that the rules concerning the test of resources applied not just to residents but also to prospective residents (SI 1992/2977, r.1).

Conversely, central government guidance points out that the effect of this rule does not mean that people who do have capital over the threshold will necessarily have to make their own arrangements. This was because, in some circumstances, the person might be unable to make their own arrangements; in which case, the local authority would still have a duty to do so (albeit then charging the person). Likewise if a person were to become 'self-funding' through sale of his or her property, the local authority should only sever its contract with the care home if the person is able to manage their own affairs or has assistance in doing so (LAC(98)19, paras 10–11).

This same principle applies in relation to the 12-week disregard rules (see 9.8.3), whereby for the first three months of a permanent stay in a care home arranged by the local authority, the value of a person's home is disregarded. Guidance points out that, at the end of the period, the local authority will have to consider whether the value of the resident's assets mean that council support is no longer needed and that the authority's contract with the care home should be terminated (LAC(2001)10, para 12). But the proviso concerning the ability of a potential self-funder to manage his or her affairs is equally applicable.

## 8.1.3 PROVISION DIRECTLY BY THE LOCAL AUTHORITY
Local authorities may directly provide residential accommodation themselves under s.21 of the National Assistance Act 1948, rather than contract with the independent sector.

## 8.1.4 MAKING ARRANGEMENTS THROUGH THE INDEPENDENT SECTOR
Under s.26 of the 1948 Act, the local authority may arrange for provision of residential accommodation by entering into arrangements with independent sector providers. The courts have held that a s.26 arrangement is only in place when the local authority is paying (i.e. has a contract with) the independent provider (see e.g. *Chief Adjudication Officer v Quinn; Steane v Chief Adjudication Officer*). For instance, providing somebody with advice on entering a care home (where the person would pay his or her own fees), and even providing transport to it, would not constitute 'making arrangements' under s.26. This principle was reiterated more recently in a county court case:

**No community care services being provided in the absence of a s.26 agreement.** Responsibility for certain residents of a care home, with 'preserved rights' and funded by social security benefits, was transferred to the local authority. The residents remained in the home, and the authority made payments based on the previous (social security) rate with some adjustments. However, no agreement under s.26 of the 1948 Act was in place. The care home subsequently sought more money for the care provided; the local authority argued that it was providing community care services and was obliged to pay only up to its usual cost level for such care. The court found that community care services were not being provided, given the absence of a s.26 agreement; and therefore the care home proprietor might have an arguable case to claim a 'reasonable sum' for the care provided (*Yorkshire Care Developments v North Yorkshire CC*).

## 8.1.5 EDUCATIONAL PLACEMENTS
Sometimes the question arises about responsibility for funding what are sometimes called specialist college placements for people aged 18 years or over. In particular, the question sometimes arises whether a placement should be made through the local social services authority, the local education authority department or through the Learning and Skills Council. In summary the position appears to be broadly as follows.

First, the Learning and Skills Council (LSC) has general duties in respect of securing the provision of proper facilities for people aged 16 to 18 years, and of reasonable facilities for those aged 19 years or over (Learning and Skills Act 2000, ss.2–3). In carrying out those general duties, the Learning and Skills Council must have regard to people with learning difficulties (s.13). However, there are two further particular duties and one power in respect of residential placements for people with learning difficulties:

- **Duty to under-19-year-olds.** For a person with learning difficulties and under 19 years old, if the LSC cannot secure sufficient (in quantity) and adequate (in quality) education or training without securing also boarding accommodation, then it must secure provision of boarding accommodation as well.
- **Duty to those aged 19 to 24.** For a person with learning difficulties who is 19 years old or over but under 25, if the LSC is satisfied it cannot secure the provision of reasonable facilities for education or training unless it also secures provision of boarding accommodation, then it must secure the provision of boarding accommodation for him.
- **Power in respect of those aged 25 years or over.** For a person who is 25 years old or over, if the LSC is satisfied that it cannot secure the provision of reasonable facilities for education or training for a person with a learning difficulty who is 25 or over unless it also secures the provision of boarding accommodation for him, it may secure the provision of boarding accommodation for him.

In respect of all placements, the Learning and Skills Council imposes a number of conditions, and applies additional criteria to determine whether a residential placement is appropriate (LSC 02/14).

Second, education authorities have a power to secure the provision of further education for people who are 19 years or over; in exercising this power, authorities must have regard to the needs of people with learning difficulties (Education Act 1996, s.15B).

Third, as to social services responsibilities, the courts have from time to time grappled with the issue. In one such case, the judge did make a general comment on the dividing line between what should be regarded as education or as community care:

**Community care or educational need.** A 20-year-old man with learning disabilities was due to take up a residential college placement. However, neither the local authority nor the Further Education Funding Council (FEFC: since superseded by the Learning and Skills Council) would agree to fund the placement.

In the event, the court dismissed the case against both local authority and the FEFC. For some reason that is perhaps not entirely clear, the court referred only to social servces legislation covering non-residential services (National Assistance Act 1948, s.29; Chronically Sick and Disabled Persons Act 1970, s.2) – and not to s.21 of the 1948 Act covering residential accommodation. Nevertheless, the judge considered whether educational and community care needs were mutually exclusive.

He concluded that formal instruction in an academic sense would obviously not correspond to a community care need. For a person with a learning difficulty, teaching him or her to read or the basic principles of mathematics (addition, subtraction, multiplication and division) would obviously be purely educational. However, instruction on how to deal with money or to read or how to recognise certain signs (e.g. on food labels or on male and female facilities) could amount to community care needs, notwithstanding an educational element. There would sometimes be overlap; but the correct approach – where the real purpose was to meet a community care need – was to regard it as welfare provision, notwithstanding its educational content.

However, this approach might not necessarily apply to a 'quite additional educational content for which statute provides a duty or power to provide' (*R v Further Education Funding Council and Bradford Metropolitan District Council, ex p Parkinson*).

The following local ombudsman case illustrates the confusion and maladministration that can arise when responsibilities are not clarified and funded:

**Funding specialist college placements**. In 1999, at the age of 21, a young man with learning disabilities started his final year at an out of county residential college specialising in providing services to people with a variety of learning disabilities, for developing life skills and work skills. His first year was funded fully by the Further Education Funding Council (FEFC: since superseded by the Learning and Skills Council). This funding was progressively reduced and by the final year the local authority paid the fee with contributions from state benefits. Another charity-run further education college was identified for him to move to, to where a number of his friends were moving on as well. He was offered a place there; but the council delayed for some months in approving funding; by which time he had lost his place. The consequence was that he was without appropriate care for two years, before his parents themselves funded a residential placement, located such that their son could still benefit from the day services of the charity-run further education college.

The ombudsman found maladministration; had the council made the funding available at the appropriate time, he would have been placed at the second college. Having accepted the need and the duty to meet it, the council should have made specific budgetary provision more quickly. The ombudsman recommended that the council pay £30,000 to the man or to his parents on his behalf (*East Sussex CC 2003*).

## 8.2 DIFFERENT TYPES OF RESIDENTIAL ACCOMMODATION

The 1948 Act refers to the need to provide for different types of accommodation and to have regard to the welfare of residents (s.21). However, the courts have held that this does not mean that local authorities are obliged themselves to provide or manage care homes; they can contract with other care providers instead (*R v Wandsworth LBC, ex p Beckwith*).

The duty as to different types of accommodation has been construed widely, both legally and in practice. For instance, local authorities typically place people in care homes and sometimes hostels, bed and breakfast and hotels where necessary (often in cases of urgency and temporarily); but the courts have held that s.21 is capable of extending also to ordinary accommodation.

**Different types of accommodation**. In certain circumstances, the courts have ordered local authorities to arrange (and pay for) ground floor flats or four- or five-bedroom houses for people with mental health problems or physical disabilities (e.g. *R v Islington LBC, ex p Batantu; R(Bernard) v Enfield LBC*). In other circumstances, small flats and bed and breakfast accommodation for asylum seekers were accepted as coming within s.21, since board and any other services required did not necessarily have to be part of provision under s.21 (*R v Newham LBC, ex p Medical Foundation for the Care of Victims of Torture*).

These cases clearly indicate that accommodation without board or personal care can be arranged under s.21 of the National Assistance Act 1948. However, conversely the provision of food without accommodation would not be lawful (*R v Newham LBC, ex p Gorenkin*).

Where care home accommodation is provided with nursing or personal care, as referred to in s.3(2) of the Care Standards Act 2000 (Chapter 24), then it must be registered under the 2000 Act (National Assistance Act 1948, s.26(1A)).

## 8.2.1 PROVIDING ORDINARY ACCOMMODATION

Some local social services authorities have been surprised by the courts' insistence that in some circumstances they must provide ordinary accommodation – and thereby made anxious that they are being asked to take on the role of housing providers. In summary, the legal position appears to be as follows. The courts recognise the importance of the distinction between provision of accommodation under the Housing Act 1996 and under s.21 of the National Assistance Act 1948. They are astute to the danger of people attempting to 'queue jump' and obtain ordinary accommodation more quickly through the social services authority than through waiting on the register of a housing authority (*R(Wahid) v Tower Hamlets LBC*).

However, it appears that if ordinary accommodation has been assessed as a community care need, and that the need cannot be met in any other way, then the social services authority may nevertheless have a duty to arrange the accommodation – in the absence of anybody else doing so. In particular, for example, the housing authority may not meet the need either at all or sufficiently speedily. One reason for this might be that the person has been lawfully judged to be intentionally homeless, and therefore not be eligible for accommodation under the Housing Act 1996. Another might be that the person will have a long (relative to his or her needs) but lawful wait on a housing register for the type of accommodation required.

Nonetheless, if the wait is, in the circumstances of the case, unduly long – and if there is no other way of the community care needs being met – the courts have held that a duty might arise for the social services authority itself to arrange the accommodation under s.21 of the National Assistance Act 1948.

**Provision of ordinary housing by local social services authority.** A local social services authority assessed a man with mental health problems and stated, as part of his care plan, that he required spacious, secure, ground-floor accommodation. After many months he was still waiting on a housing register with no real indication about when the housing department of the same local authority would be able to offer suitable accommodation under the Housing Act 1996. The court held that the responsibility now fell on the local authority social services department under s.21 of the National Assistance Act 1948, because of its assessment and care plan (*R v Islington LBC, ex p Batantu*).

In a second case, a local authority occupational therapist had assessed a woman (who had suffered a stroke) as requiring suitably adapted accommodation. The present accommodation could not be made suitable by adapting it. The housing department of the same local authority would not assist under the Housing Act 1996, because it had made a finding of intentional homelessness on grounds of rent arrears; this decision had been upheld by the courts. Thus, it was for the local authority, under its social services functions, to find a suitable house under s.21 of the 1948 Act (*R(Bernard) v Enfield LBC*).

Nevertheless, in the following example, the local authority successfully argued that the person's community care needs could be met through means other than a change of accommodation:

**Social services not obliged to provide ordinary accommodation.** A 53-year-old man suffering from schizophrenia lived with his wife and eight children in a two-bedroom flat on the ground floor of a council block of flats. He had refused alternative accommodation on grounds of unsuitability offered by the housing department under the Housing Act 1996. A psychiatric nurse wrote to a social services team leader, arguing that the man's mental stability could only be maintained in a more congenial and relaxed environment.

Social services refused to arrange alternative accommodation. The team leader conceded that better accommodation was required; but social services had to consider whether he needed care and attention under s.21 of the National Assistance Act. It concluded that he did not, since he was currently in good mental health, better in fact than for many years. He also argued that the man (and two of his adult sons) had unreasonably rejected offers of alternative accommodation by the council. He also concluded that the chances of mental breakdown from the overcrowding were small.

The court accepted this reasoning; it also referred to the effect of s.21(8) of the 1948 Act which precluded provision that could or must be made under another Act. Thus, ordinary housing needs that fall under the Housing Act 1996 could not come under s.21 of the 1948 Act. Lastly, it pointed out that social workers, traditionally strong advocates for clients, should not be deterred from identifying needs that properly come under other services – for fear that social services will have to meet them (R(Wahid) v Tower Hamlets LBC).

The 'anti-duplication' provision (in s.21(8) of the National Assistance Act 1948), referred to in the *Wahid* case, is potentially a significant obstacle to social services authorities providing prdinary housing, and one likely to be raised in future cases.

Sometimes the need for provision of ordinary accommodation arises for a family with members both 18 year old or over and under 18 years old – that is, both adults and children. The National Assistance Act 1948 s.21 applies on its face only to those over 18 years old. Although not ruling out the provision of accommodation for family members under 18 years old, the courts have stated that in normal circumstances s.21 should not be taken to apply to people under 18 years old (R(O) v Haringey LBC).

Thus in some cases, where provision is both for a disabled adult and a child in need, both s.21 of the 1948 Act and s.17 of the Children Act 1989 (general duty to safeguard and promote the welfare of children in need) should apply. Where the provision is primarily related to a child in need, s.17 of the 1989 Act would in principle suffice because of the provision it contains for providing for other family members and not just the child (e.g. R v Birmingham CC, ex P Mohammed). Nevertheless it would be as well for s.21 of the 1948 Act to be argued (at least in respect of adults) since the courts have read into s.21 a significantly stronger duty (R v Sefton MBC, ex p Help the Aged) than they have into s.17 of the 1989 Act (R(G) v Barnet LBC).

## 8.2.2 PROVIDING ACCOMMODATION WITH NURSING

Arrangements for accommodation together with nursing can only be made with the consent of a primary care trust or health authority (National Assistance Act 1948, s.26(1C)).

**Return to care home with or without nursing?** A 94-year-old woman wished to be discharged from hospital, following a fall and fracture of femur, back to a flat in a registered residential care home. Differing professional views emerged about whether her needs could continue to be met at the home – or whether she would require a place in a care home that provided nursing care. The High Court ruled that, quite apart from being entitled to rely on a particular medical doctor's expertise, the local authority had no choice but to accept the decision he had made on behalf of the NHS. This was because of s.26(1C) of the National Assistance Act 1948 (R(Goldsmith) v Wandsworth LBC: High Court).

Strictly speaking, the logic of this last judicial point appeared open to some doubt, since s.26(1C) applies only where it is proposed to place a person in a care home with nursing. Where the proposal is simply a care home without nursing (in this care, the woman's current care home), then s.26(1C) does not, explicitly at least, apply.

In fact the High Court's decision was duly overturned, when the Court of Appeal found that the decision about whether or not the woman should return to her original care home was for the local authority to take. The doctor's advice was given to the local continuing care panel. It was for the panel in turn to advise the local authority, but not to usurp the latter's duty to take the final decision. In fact the doctor's advice was anyway based on only limited information, and the panel's reasoning also left out of account a detailed report by a social worker which was at variance with the doctor's view (R(Goldsmith) v Wandsworth LBC: Court of Appeal).

## 8.2.3 AMENITIES ASSOCIATED WITH RESIDENTIAL ACCOMMODATION

The provision of residential accommodation under s.21 of the 1948 Act does not refer necessarily only to the provision of bare accommodation. Accommodation is defined to include reference to board and to other services, amenities and requisites provided in connection with the accommodation – except where in the opinion of the authority managing the premises their provision is unnecessary (National Assistance Act 1948, s.21(5)). Likewise, a local authority has a power to provide, where it considers appropriate, transport to and from the accommodation, and also to make available on the premises any services that appear to it to be required (s.21(7)). Directions made under s.21 of the 1948 Act state that local authorities must make arrangements, in respect of residents for whom accommodation has been provided under s.21:

- for their welfare
- for the supervision of hygiene
- to enable residents to obtain medical attention, nursing attention or the benefit of other NHS services (but the local authority is not required to provide anything that is authorised or required to be provided under NHS Act 1977)
- for provision of board and other services, amenities and requisites provided in connection with the accommodation, except where in the opinion of the authority managing the premises their provision is unnecessary
- to review regularly the provision made and to make necessary improvements (LAC(93)10, appendix 1).

Such obligations parallel those placed on care home providers by the Care Standards Act 2000 and regulations made under it (see Chapter 24).

In one case, the council claimed that in arranging accommodation for asylum seekers under ss.21 and 26 of the 1948 Act, it could offer accommodation only if it included also a package of services such as food, laundry and personal hygiene facilities. Because, it argued, there was no such accommodation in Newham, it would therefore have to offer accommodation to asylum seekers in Eastbourne. The court ruled that the effect of ss.21(5) and 26(1A) was that residential accommodation without board and personal care could in some circumstances be offered (*R v Newham LBC, ex p Medical Foundation for the Care of Victims of Torture*).

However, the reverse situation of providing food without accommodation under s.21 has been held to be unlawful. In another case (also concerning asylum seekers), the High Court ruled that because the need for care and attention was a condition for arranging residential accommodation, a local authority was not empowered under s.21 to provide food (vouchers) alone without accommodation (*R v Newham LBC, ex p Gorenkin*).

**Welfare, hygiene, medical attention.** The local ombudsman has investigated arrangements for welfare, hygiene and medical attention provided in a council hostel, finding serious failures relating to, for example, sleep interruption, theft, missing lavatory seats, lost laundry, failure to observe a resident's pain and need for dental treatment – and a failure to provide the required medication for epilepsy on several occasions (*Manchester CC 1993*).

On the other hand, although the courts have held that food is an amenity provided in connection with accommodation, they have also held that clothes or toiletries, for instance, have nothing to with accommodation (*R(Khan) v Oxfordshire CC*).

## 8.3 DUTIES AND POWERS TO PROVIDE RESIDENTIAL ACCOMMODATION

If the care and attention condition is satisfied, consonant with the application of a local authority's eligibility criteria, then the local authority has to consider whether it has a power or a duty to arrange the accommodation. The Act gives central government the power to issue directions and approvals under s.21; from these flow duties and powers respectively.

It should be noted, however, that there is a prohibition in the making of arrangements for people subject to s.115 of the Immigration and Asylum Act 1999 (i.e. people subject to immigration control excluded from welfare benefits), if their need arises through destitution, or the physical effects (actual or anticipated) of destitution (s.21(1A)). See Chapter 13.

### 8.3.1 DIRECTIONS AND DUTIES

Directions have been issued so as to create a duty in the case of people who are ordinarily resident within the area of the local authority, who are in urgent need, or who have a mental disorder of any description (LAC(93)10, appendix 1).

### 8.3.2 APPROVALS AND POWERS

A power arises where a mere approval, rather than a direction, has been issued by central government. The approvals issued apply to a person: (a) who is of no settled residence; (b) who is ordinarily resident in the area of another authority but who has been discharged from hospital and is now in another authority's area; (c) who is ill; (d) who is dependent on drugs or alcohol; (e) who is an expectant or nursing mother (LAC(93)10, appendix 1).

### 8.3.3 SPECIFIC, ENFORCEABLE DUTY

Where a duty is established against an assessed eligible need (i.e. against the local authority's eligibility criteria), the courts have accepted that the duty is absolute in the sense that it must be met irrespective of resources (see e.g. *R v Sefton MBC, ex p Help the Aged; R v Kensington and Chelsea RBC, ex p Kujtim*).

This is notwithstanding that the actual language of both the Act and the directions is more suggestive of a general target duty than an individual enforceable duty (see 4.4 for the distinction). The courts seem to have sensed that s.21 is such a fundamental provision that a specific duty is to be read into it.

## 8.4 ORDINARY RESIDENCE

The ordinary residence and no settled residence conditions, referred to within the directions and approvals, are further defined in s.24 of the National Assistance Act 1948 (see Chapter 14).

## 8.5 CHOICE OF RESIDENTIAL ACCOMMODATION

Directions issued by the Department of Health state that a local authority should make arrangements for the residential accommodation of a person's choice – if certain conditions are satisfied. These are as follows. The person must have an assessed, eligible need. The preferred accommodation must be suitable for the person's assessed needs and be available. The cost of the placement must be within the usual cost level for the degree of need (LAC(92)27, direction 3). Department of Health guidance makes clear the importance of local authorities giving people information in order to allow them to express choice; of encouraging the presence, wherever possible, of a relative, carer or advocate; and of keeping a written record of the conversation and in particular of decisions taken and preferences expressed (LAC(2004)20, para 7.2). Thus, a failure to consult and indicate choice will be maladministration for the local ombudsman:

**No consultation and no choice.** The grandson and main carer of a 101-year-old woman received a telephone call from the local authority stating that a placement had been arranged in a particular nursing home; while the grandson was being told this on the telephone, a van arrived to collect his grandmother. The local ombudsman found that the failure to consult and indicate any sort of choice was maladministration (*Kent CC 2001*).

Department of Health guidance gives examples of reasons why a local authority might have to incur higher than usual costs, in order to meet a person's assessed needs. These include specialist care for specific user groups with high levels of need, special diets or additional facilities required for medical or cultural reasons (LAC(2004)20, para 2.5.8). Likewise if a person's assessed needs mean that it is necessary to place him or her in a care home in another area, where the costs of placement exceeded the authority's usual cost level, the authority should nevertheless meet the additional cost (para 2.5). This last point is illustrative of the difference between an assessed need, which will trigger an obligation to pay a higher cost, and a 'mere' preference, which will not – as the courts have confirmed:

**Preference, psychological need and more expensive accommodation.** The case involved a 22-year-old man with Down's syndrome, for whom the local authority was under a duty to make arrangements for residential accommodation under s.21 of the National Assistance Act 1948. The man had an 'entrenched' wish to go to a particular home, whilst the Council had decided to place him in a cheaper one which would still, it claimed, meet his needs. The dispute went to the complaints procedure review panel, which recommended that the Council make arrangements for provision at the man's home of choice. The panel found, having consulted expert opinion, that the assessment should be based on current need including psychological, educational, social and medical needs. The entrenched position of the man formed part of his psychological need. The social services committee of the Council, worried about setting costly precedents, rejected the panel's findings.

The judge stated that needs 'may properly include psychological needs' – and that the authority was not therefore being forced to pay more than it otherwise would have normally (something it was not required to do under the Choice of Accommodation Directions in LAC(92)27): it would 'simply be paying what the law required'. He also referred to guidance (LAC(92)15) on adults with learning disabilities, which stated that services should be arranged on an individual basis, 'taking account of age, needs, degree of disability, the personal preferences of the individual and his or her parents or carers, culture, race and gender' (*R v Avon CC, ex p M*).

Similarly when a local authority refused to place a person with learning disabilities at a residential home – which the local authority regarded as excessively expensive (and would have provided services in excess of his needs) – the court found the decision to be unlawful, because it was made before any suitable alternatives had been found (*R(A) v Bromley LBC*). Conversely, the courts have in other circumstances avoided the question:

**Choice of accommodation for asylum seekers.** The case concerned whether asylum seekers had a right to exercise their entitlement to choice of accommodation (i.e. so that they could remain in London instead of being sent to the south coast). The court stated that the dispute (a) was suitable for referral to the Secretary of State with a view to exercise of the default powers (see 5.6); and (b) was primarily factual (as to whether or not there was alternative accommodation in London) and was a matter which could not be resolved one way or another by legally deciding about the existence and nature of the duty imposed by the directions on the local authority (*R v Westminster CC, ex p P*).

## 8.5.1 TOPPING UP CARE HOME FEES

The principle of topping up is that, over and beyond exercising a reasonable choice of which care home to enter, a resident could enter a more expensive one (i.e. more expensive than necessary to meet assessed needs) – if a third party were willing to pay the difference. Regulations allow for this; likewise they allow for self topping up (by the resident) in the case of the 12-week disregard of a person's property (see 9.8.3) or in a deferred payment agreement (see 9.8.5).

### 8.5.1.1 Third party topping up

The regulations concerning third party top-ups state that a local authority may place a person in more expensive accommodation if (a) a third party other than a liable relative (see 9.5.1) agrees to make up the difference between the usual cost level and the actual fee; (b) the third party can reasonably be expected to make the additional payment (SI 2001/3441, made under s.54 of the Health and Social Care Act 2001). This does not therefore amount to a duty on the local authority to allow such third party contributions. For instance, in the following example, the local authority, quite lawfully, had serious doubts about the ability of the third party to do so:

**Refusing to allow a third party top-up.** An 81-year-old woman applied for permission to apply for judicial review. In October 1999 she had indicated her preferred care home accommodation; her daughter had agreed to pay the difference between the local authority's usual cost level and the actual fees charged by the care home. Two years later, the daughter ceased to pay the top-up; the council then had to pay the full cost. The daughter then issued proceedings against the council for repayment of the top-up amounts she had paid for the two years. The grounds were that she had been induced into the agreement by unlawful duress and misrepresentation on the part of council officers. The county court proceedings had not yet been decided.

In January 2004, the woman was assessed as now needing nursing home care; her preferred accommodation cost £520 a week, which contrasted with the local authority's usual cost level of about £450. The daughter offered to pay the top-up; the local authority refused on the grounds that it was entitled to take into account what had happened previously – at least until the county court proceedings had been resolved.

The court refused to hold that the local authority was – at least pending the outcome of the county court proceedings – acting unlawfully by refusing to enter into the top-up agreement (*R(Daniel) v Leeds CC*).

However, the principle of topping up appears to have been seriously undermined in those local authorities that offer such a low usual cost level that there is little choice (if any) of care home at that cost. In which case, it seems that families are pressured into topping up, in order to meet not additional preferences but those basic needs that should properly be met by the local authority. Such practices are likely to be unlawful.

Department of Health guidance points out that residents should not be asked to pay more because of market inadequacies or failures in local authority commissioning. Thus, where a resident has not expressed a preference for more expensive accommodation but, for whatever reason, there is no place available at the authority's usual cost level – then the local authority must pay the more expensive cost (LAC(2004)20, para 2.5.5).

Low usual cost levels paid by local authorities might mean in practice that care homes have to limit the number of local authority-funded residents they take, unless third party top-ups are demanded as a matter of course – or otherwise take privately-funded residents who are then charged more for the same facilities. For instance, in one local ombudsman investigation the owner of the care home explained that for a council-funded resident the fee was £215 per week; for privately-funded residents it was between £260 and £320 (*Kent CC 2001a*).

Excessively low usual cost levels have not in general been successfully challenged either in the courts or through the local ombudsmen, but this does not mean that local authorities cannot be challenged in individual cases. For instance, the following local ombudsman case exposed the practice of some local authorities of not providing clear information for people and their carers, relatives or friends; of paying a usual cost level that meant that the choice of home is in reality restricted; and of failing to exercise their discretion (or arguably perform an obligation) to exceed the cost level in individual circumstances:

**Failure to exceed usual cost level.** A 98-year-old woman lived on her own. She was finding it increasingly difficult to cope. A friend, whom she had looked after when a child, had remained in close touch. In September 1994, the friend identified a care home that would be suitable for the woman. In March 1995, the council assessed the woman as eligible for a care home placement. The social worker's assessment recommended the placement at that same care home; however, it was some £33 more expensive per week than the council's usual cost level. The friend would have to top up; she was prepared to do this. However, when the woman found this out, she refused to take up the placement; she wouldn't hear of her friend making up the difference. Her health deteriorated; she was admitted to hospital in September 1995.

In October, the friend searched for suitable homes charging at the council's usual cost level. She found none; the council then decided it was willing after all to pay up to £285, that is above its usual cost level. The ombudsman found, amongst other things, that the council had failed to explain the choice of accommodation rules properly; and had fettered its discretion by not considering at the outset whether the circumstances meant that it should exceed its usual cost level in the particular circumstances (*Merton LBC 1999*).

### 8.5.1.2 Third party topping up and usual cost levels

It is not clear to what extent, if at all, the courts are prepared generally to interfere with the levels of payment offered by local authorities to independent care home providers. Nevertheless, they have stated that the various factors – including payment levels – that affect the availability of care home places must be taken account of by the local authority (see variously *R v Cleveland CC, ex p Cleveland Care Homes Association; R v Coventry City Council, ex p Coventry Heads of Independent Care Establishments (CHOICE) and Peggs*). More recently, the courts have displayed a distinct reluctance to get involved in such matters:

**Local authority cost levels**. A consortium of care homes in Birmingham challenged the rate at which the council would pay for placements of residents in those homes. It was principally contended that this rate would result in home closures and therefore undermine the council's ability to meet needs under s.21 of the National Assistance Act 1948 and to afford people some choice of care home. The council had partially accepted the results of a Laing and Buisson report that it had commissioned – but not wholly. In particular it had not accepted the recommended rate of return/profit for care homes.

The court found that the case was not made out; that, except in case of a statutory duty specifically compelling expenditure, decisions about affordability and allocation of resources were for the local authority. Furthermore the courts should be slow to intervene where there had been a long process of consultation and there was in effect contractual negotiation in train between local authority and care providers (*R v Birmingham CC, ex p Birmingham Care Consortium*).

An alternative avenue of approach to challenging local authority 'usual cost' levels appeared to beckon in the form of the Office of Fair Trading (OFT). However, as the following case demonstrates, this did not bear fruit:

**Complaint about usual cost levels to the Office of Fair Trading**. In connection with arguments that local authorities were abusing their dominant position in the market under the Competition Act 1998, by setting unfairly low cost levels for placements in independent care homes, a complaint was made to the Office of Fair Trading (OFT). The complaint concerned the fees paid for care home accommodation by the North and West Belfast Health and Social Services Trust. The OFT rejected the complaint on the basis that the Trust was not an undertaking for the purposes of the Act.

On appeal, the Competition Commission Appeal Tribunal then ruled that such contracting did constitute 'economic activity', and that the Trust was therefore a relevant undertaking. The complaint was remitted to the OFT (*BetterCare Group v Director General of Fair Trading*).

Nevertheless, the OFT subsequently rejected the complaint (identifying in effect a vicious circle that precluded it from interfering). It held that the Eastern Health and Social Services Board, which commissions services through health and social services trusts, was not itself an undertaking for the purpose of the Act. It then held that the Trust, which was of course a relevant undertaking, could not be committing an abuse even if it was paying excessively low prices. This was because it did not set the prices; the prices were set by the Eastern Health and Social Services Board. In any case, the OFT went on: (a) there was insufficient evidence that the prices were excessively low; (b) excessively low prices were likely to amount to an abuse only in exceptional circumstances; (c) there was no reason to believe that there were exceptional circumstances (*BetterCare Group v North and West Belfast Health and Social Services Trust*).

The Office of Fair Trading launched in 2004 a market study of care homes, to focus on how and in what circumstances people choose homes, and the transparency of pricing and contracts.

### 8.5.1.3 Self topping up of care home fees

In addition to third party top-ups, it is possible for residents themselves to make top-up payments either during the 12-week property disregard (see 9.8.3), or where a deferred payment agreement is in place (see 9.8.5) (SI 2001/3441).

### 8.5.1.4 Topping up and rises in fees

Guidance further explains that a home's fees and the local authority's usual amount of contribution might change. But they might not change at the same rate. Thus, Department of Health guidance states that authorities should tell residents and third parties that there cannot be a guarantee that increases in the accommodation's fees will be automatically shared between the local authority and the third party; the accommodation's fees might rise more quickly than the authority's usual cost level (LAC 2004(20), para 3.5.7).

Nevertheless, the following case illustrates this principle taken too far, resulting in what the local ombudsman referred to as an absurdity. It involved a local authority operating different usual cost levels, and therefore exacting unjustifiably variable 'top up' contributions from relatives of residents:

**Unacceptable variable usual cost levels.** A local authority's policy meant that the relatives of a resident who had lived longest in a care home contributed more to charges (by way of topping up) than the relatives of more recently placed residents. This was because up-ratings to the authority's usual cost level, its standard rate of payment, did not necessarily apply to existing residents. This had come about because the local authority was not contractually bound to the care home to increase the rate to such residents; and so long as the care home was receiving fees from somebody, it would not object.

However, the ombudsman found maladministration. First, she pointed out that Department of Health guidance (LAC(92)27) stated that such usual cost levels can only vary in response to assessed, individual need. Second, an absurd situation was created whereby had the resident moved to a different home (or even been discharged and readmitted to the same home), she would have been entitled to a higher standard rate, with a lower third party contribution involved (*Bolton MBC 2004*).

### 8.5.1.5 Topping up: ultimate responsibility for payment of fees

Department of Health guidance makes quite clear that when a local authority places a person in an independent care home under s.26(3A) of the National Assistance Act 1948, the local authority is responsible for the full cost of the accommodation. Even if an agreement had been reached, by which the resident and the third party paid their contributions direct to the care home, nevertheless in case of default the local authority would remain liable (LAC(2004)20, para 3.5.2).

### 8.5.2 CROSS-BORDER PLACEMENTS WITHIN THE UNITED KINGDOM

See Chapter 14.

## 8.6 CARE HOME PLACEMENTS: OTHER ARRANGEMENTS

### 8.6.1 NHS AND FREE NURSING CARE

If local authorities place people in care homes registered to provide nursing, the NHS is responsible for funding the registered nursing care element that the person requires (see 16.8). The local authority remains responsible for the accommodation, board and personal care.

### 8.6.2 NHS AND CONTINUING HEALTH CARE STATUS

In some circumstances, the NHS places in care homes people who are deemed to have continuing NHS health care status. In this case, the NHS is responsible, under the NHS Act 1977, for funding the entire placement in terms of accommodation, board, personal care, registered nursing care and any other health care required (see 16.7).

### 8.6.3 MENTAL HEALTH ACT AFTERCARE SERVICES: JOINT NHS AND LOCAL AUTHORITY RESPONSIBILITY

Under s.117 of the Mental Health Act 1983, certain patients must be provided with after-care services when they are discharged from hospital. The duty of provision is a joint one, placed on both local authority social services departments and the NHS. Aftercare services can include both residential accommodation and non-residential services and either way must be provided free of charge to the resident (see 10.5.8).

### 8.6.4 COMMUNITY HEALTH SERVICES IN CARE HOMES

The provision of NHS community health services in care homes has long been a vexed question; it is highly variable in type and quantity (see 16.9).

CHAPTER 9

# Charging for residential accommodation

## KEY POINTS

When local authorities arrange to place people in care homes under Part 3 of the National Assistance Act 1948, they are obliged to apply a statutory test of resources, or means test. This is to determine what contribution, if any, the resident must pay toward the cost of the accommodation. This is in contrast to charging for non-residential services, which is discretionary only and not governed by detailed legislative rules. Broadly, the charging rules for residential accommodation are as follows:

- **Test of resources**. If a local authority places a person in residential accommodation under s.21 of the National Assistance Act 1948, it has a duty to apply a test of resources in order to ascertain what, if anything, the resident should have to pay toward the accommodation, board and personal care.
- **Registered nursing care**. However, the registered nursing care element of the care provided, in a care home providing nursing, is the responsibility of the NHS and is thus free of charge to the resident (see 16.8).
- **Continuing health care**. If a resident has been deemed by the NHS to be of continuing health care status, then the NHS should fund the accommodation, board, personal care and nursing care – all of which will then be free of charge to the resident (see 16.7).
- **Mental health aftercare services**. If a person is placed in residential accommodation by way of aftercare provision under s.117 of the Mental Health Act 1983, then provision is free of charge to the resident (see 10.5.8).
- **Self-funding**. In some circumstances, if a person is assessed as having resources over the relevant threshold, and as having the ability (mental and physical) to make his or her own arrangements, then the local authority may decline to place the person. If the person then makes his or her own arrangements, he or she is known as 'self-funding'. However, when his or her resources are reduced to the relevant threshold, the local authority may then become responsible for making the placement.

The rules are detailed and complicated; the following represents an outline only. Reference should be made to the full, original sources of legislation and guidance, to expert advice or to specialist publications. The application of these rules sometimes proves controversial when people's savings or homes have to be used to pay for residential or nursing home accommodation – or when assets, which have previously been made a gift of to somebody else (e.g. another family member), are nevertheless taken account of in the means test.

**Note 1**. The extracts in the following chapter are drawn in the main from the National Assistance Act 1948, the National Assistance (Assessment of Resources) Regulations 1992 (SI 1992/2977), and the Charging for Residential Accommodation Guide (CRAG 2004), a looseleaf, regularly updated manual of guidance available from the Department of Health. The Regulations frequently cross-refer to, and rely on, the Income Support (General) Regulations 1987 (SI 1987/1967); however, CRAG helpfully summarises the effects of the cross-referencing.

Other sources of information include, for example, the Child Poverty Action Group's *Paying for Care Handbook* (CPAG 2003, 4th edn), the Child Poverty Action Group's *Welfare Benefits and Tax Credits Handbook 2004–2005* (CPAG 2004), or the *Disability Rights Handbook 2004–2005* published by the Disability Alliance (2004). Age Concern England produces helpful fact sheets.

There are also more specialist publications that consider how to protect the family's assets from being paid over to a local authority (Couldrick 2002; Neilson 2003). As both publications make clear, specialist advice is required.

**Note 2. Wales, Scotland and Northern Ireland**. This chapter applies in principle to Wales; the main legislation (National Assistance Act 1948, s.22 and the principal regulations, SI 1992/2977) is the same as in England. The guidance *Charging for Residential Accommodation Guide* is issued separately by the National Assembly for Wales, although is in effect the same as that issued by the Department of Health for England (CRAG 2004).

This chapter also applies in principle to Scotland; the main legislation (s.22 of the 1948 Act and SI 1992/2977) is the same as in England; and the Scottish Executive also issues the same guidance (CRAG 2004).

Likewise, the chapter applies in principle to Northern Ireland, where the rules are similar. The main legislation comprises the Health and Personal Social Services (Northern Ireland) Order 1972 (a.36) and principal regulations (SR 1993/127); and the Department of Health, Social Services and Public Safety publishes the CRAG guidance.

## 9.1 OVERALL DUTY TO CHARGE

Generally speaking, local authorities have a duty to apply a test of resources to each person for whom they make arrangements for the provision of residential accommodation (National Assistance Act 1948, s.22).

If the authority is providing the accommodation directly, then the charge should be at a standard rate and represent the full cost to the local authority of provision. However, if the authority is satisfied, according to the statutory test of resources (see below), that a person cannot afford to pay at the standard rate, then it must assess the person's ability to pay, and charge a lower rate accordingly (National Assistance Act 1948, s.22).

In the case of independent care providers, the charging procedure is more or less the same: the local authority pays to the provider the cost of the place, and the resident repays the authority the amount he or she has been assessed to pay (National Assistance Act 1948, s.26).

## 9.2 PERSONAL EXPENSES ALLOWANCE

In calculating the weekly amount payable by a resident, the authority must assume that he or she will require a certain amount of money for personal requirements: the personal expenses allowance (PEA; National Assistance Act 1948, s.22). The amount of this is determined by regulations and is currently (2004–5) set at £18.10 per week (SI 2003/628). It is proposed that this be increased to £18.80 from April 2005 (DH 2004m). Department of Health guidance states that its purpose is to allow residents to have money to spend as they wish, and that it should not be spent on services that have been contracted for, or that have been assessed by the local authority or the NHS as necessary to meet a person's needs (CRAG 2004, para 5.001).

The amount of the PEA can be varied (National Assistance Act 1948, s.22): for instance, in the case of less dependent residents (see 9.4.1); where the person in the residential accommodation has a dependent child; where the resident is in receipt of an occupational pension and is paying it to his or her partner, but is not married (so that the statutory disregard of half of the pension has not been triggered); or where the person is responsible for a property (and consequent associated costs) that is disregarded in the test of resources (CRAG 2004, para 5.005).

Guidance also states that residents must be left with the full PEA, following the test of resources (CRAG 2004, para 5.002); in other words it should not be used toward paying care home fees.

### 9.2.1 ADEQUACY AND MISUSE

Blatant misuse of personal expenses allowance is sometimes reported in practice. For instance, it has been suggested that owners or managers of care homes sometimes retain the allowances paid for individuals, and then pool them to be spent collectively. This means that individual residents not only lose control of their money, but that there might not even be an itemised account of how it has been spent (Office of Fair Trading 1998, p.26).

**Pooled 'extras account' in care home.** A man complained to the local ombudsman about his mother's placement in a council care home. Part of the complaint related to a pooled general 'extras account' operated by the home to cover personal items not included in the care home fees. This resulted in his mother effectively being charged for newspapers that she was unable to read, as well as for piano tuning, aquarium maintenance and plants for the garden. The ombudsman found this to be maladministration, insofar as items to be charged for were not clearly identified to residents in advance and some, such as piano tuning, were arguably not the responsibility of residents anyway (*Hampshire CC 2001*).

If people do not have their needs for incontinence pads (see 16.14) met by the NHS in care homes, they might end up spending their personal expenses allowance on the pads (Baroness Masham, House of Lords Debates, 26/4/2001, col.360).

Quite apart from improper erosion of the allowance by one means or another, a thorough study – providing a salutary reminder of the 'modest-but-adequate' living standard that residents reasonably require – concluded that the allowance should anyway, even in 1997, have been nearer £40 than the £14 it was at that time:

**Personal expenses needs of residents.** A study considered the recurrent cost of items including personal food (fruit, biscuits, tea/coffee, sugar, milk, soft drinks), alcohol (e.g. glass of sherry to give a visitor), clothing, personal care (e.g. plasters, cough mixture, aspirin, hairbrush, shampoo, bath oil, sponge bag, walking stick, watch, small mirror), household goods (e.g. furniture, linen, electrical appliances, crockery, batteries, shoe brushes), household services (e.g. postage, telephone call, footwear repair, dry cleaning), leisure goods (e.g. television, radio, newspapers, magazines, books, games, knitting, embroidery), leisure services (e.g. cinema, keep-fit classes, dancing, social club), transport (e.g. to dentist, optician, hairdresser, shopping, cinema, dancing, keep fit classes) (Parker 1997).

Department of Health guidance also stresses that local authorities should ensure that an individual resident's need for continence supplies or chiropody is 'fully reflected' in their care plan; and that neither local authorities nor care homes have the right to require residents to spend their PEA in particular ways (LAC(2004)9, annex).

## 9.3 TEMPORARY RESIDENTS

When people stay no more than eight weeks in accommodation, the local authority has a discretion, subject to reasonableness, to limit what it charges (National Assistance Act 1948, s.22). In other words, it is not obliged to follow the statutory test of resources in these circumstances. This gives local authorities considerable discretion in charging for respite care or short-term breaks.

Beyond eight weeks the local authority is obliged to apply the statutory charging procedure, subject to special rules applying to 'temporary residents'. A temporary resident is a person whose stay is unlikely to exceed 52 weeks or, in exceptional circumstances, is unlikely substantially to exceed 52 weeks (SI 1992/2977, r.2).

Guidance explains that if a stay which was thought to be permanent turns out to be temporary, then it would be 'unreasonable' for the authority to continue to apply the permanent residence rules to the resident. Conversely, if what was expected originally to be a temporary stay turns out to be permanent, the permanent residence rules should only be applied from the date of this realisation, not from the outset (CRAG 2004, paras 3.004–4A).

**Informing relative of change status of mother.** A complaint was made to the local ombudsman about a woman with senile dementia who had been placed in a care home on a temporary basis. Following a meeting, the local authority decided that her status had changed to that of permanent resident. However, the son was not informed until nine months later, when he was also notified that there were accumulated arrears (representing the difference between temporary and permanent resident charges).

This was maladministration. Furthermore, because the son would have sold his mother's house that much earlier, it meant that interest had been lost on the sum that would have been realised. The ombudsman recommended that the council pay £3300 in lost interest; and that it issue clear guidance to its staff (*Humberside CC 1992*).

### 9.3.1 DISREGARDING CERTAIN ASSETS

When applying the test of resources for temporary residents, the local authority must disregard certain assets. These include, for example: (a) the person's own home; (b) the home commitment element of income support/pension credit; (c) housing benefit; (d) housing support charges under 'Supporting People' arrangements; (e) reasonable home commitments not covered fully by income support/pension credit, housing benefit or Supporting People payments; (f) reasonable home commitments where income support/pension credit, housing benefit or Supporting People payments are not in payment; (g) cash payment made in lieu of concessionary coal; (h) attendance allowance and disability living allowance, care component (SI 1992/2977, schedule 3).

### 9.3.2 INTERMEDIATE CARE

A care home placement, made as part of intermediate care, must be free of charge up to six weeks (see 16.12).

## 9.4 LESS-DEPENDENT RESIDENTS

For people classed as less-dependent residents, authorities are explicitly given the option of not applying the normal charging rules. A less-dependent resident is defined as a person for whom accommodation is provided in premises not registered under the Care Standards Act 2000 (SI 1992/2977, rr.2, 5). Factors the local authority should take account of include the resident's commitments (in relation to necessities such as food, fuel, clothing), independence, and incentive to become more independent (CRAG 2004, para 2.010).

## 9.5 ASSESSMENT OF COUPLES

Legislation does not authorise the financial assessment of the joint resources of a couple; and even though spouses have a duty to maintain one another, local authorities are not empowered to apply the statutory means test under regulations (SI 1992/2977) to ascertain the potential liability of the spouse of a resident (CRAG 2004, para 4.001).

Each person entering residential care should be assessed individually – although the liability of a married person to maintain their spouse should be taken into account (CRAG 2004, paras 4.001, 4.003). This refers to s.42 of the National Assistance Act 1948, under which spouses have an obligation to maintain each other. Such liability applies only to husband and wife, and not to unmarried couples.

### 9.5.1 LIABLE SPOUSE

Guidance states that under ss.42 and 43 of the National Assistance Act 1948, local authorities may ask a spouse to refund all or part of the authority's expenditure on residential accommodation for his or her husband or wife (as well as on other non-residential services under the Act). However, it states that this does not mean that an authority can demand that a spouse provide details of his or her resources. It should not use assessment forms for the resident that require information about the means of the spouse.

According to the guidance, the authority should instead use 'tact' in explaining to residents and spouses the legal liability to maintain and point out that the extent of the liability is best considered in the light of the spouse's resources. In each case the authority should decide if it is worth pursuing the spouse for maintenance, and what sum would be appropriate. This will involve discussion and negotiation with the spouse, and will be determined to a large extent by his or her financial circumstances in relation to his or her expenditure and normal standard of living. It suggests that following such negotiation, the local authority should, if appropriate, secure a retrospective contribution from the spouse.

The guidance also states that, in the Department of Health's view, it would not be appropriate, for example, necessarily to expect spouses to reduce their resources to Income Support/Pension Credit levels. In any case, it concludes by saying that, ultimately, only the courts can decide what is an 'appropriate' amount (CRAG 2004, paras 11.001–6). It is expected that the liable relative rules will be abolished in the foreseeable future; an Age Concern England study pointed out the defects, which included:

- lack of operational policies in many local authorities
- arbitrary nature of whether a spouse is pursued for payment
- England-wide, only a small number of spouses are anyway being pursued
- where pursuit did take place, Department of Health guidance was breached and spouses were asked for financial details on the same form used for the financial assessment of the spouse entering the care home
- huge variations in the approach to establishing a 'reasonable' spouse contribution
- finance officers struggling to apply the rules, which most felt were unclear
- some spouses, unaware of the local authority policy, had felt intimidated into agreeing a level of payment, unaware that they could negotiate a reasonable level of payment
- the rules apply only to spouses, not to unmarried couples, and so are inequitable (Thompson and Wright 2001).

## 9.6 ASSESSMENT OF CAPITAL

Resources are assessed in terms of both capital and income. If a resident individually has more than a prescribed upper capital figure, then he or she will automatically pay the whole amount due and receive no financial support from the local authority. This means that there is then no call to assess income. However, beneath that upper figure but above a lower prescribed figure, any capital over the lower figure is deemed to produce a (clearly unrealistic) weekly tariff income of £1 for every £250. At the time of writing the upper and lower figures are £20,000 and £12,250 respectively (SI 1992/2977, r.20). It is proposed that these be increased to £20,500 and £12,500 from April 2005 (DH 2004m).

## 9.6.1 WHAT IS COUNTED AS CAPITAL

Capital is not defined in legislation. Guidance gives a non-exhaustive list. Included are buildings, land, national savings certificates, premium bonds, stocks and shares, capital held by the Court of Protection or a receiver it has appointed, building society accounts, bank accounts, SAYE schemes, unit trusts, trust funds and Cooperative share accounts. The guidance states that the position concerning investment bonds is complex, and that local authorities should seek legal advice (CRAG 2004, para 6.002). Income from capital is generally treated as capital (not income), except in the case of certain disregarded capital (SI 1992/2977, r.22).

## 9.6.2 JOINT BENEFICIAL OWNERSHIP

For joint beneficial ownership of a capital asset, except for an interest in land, the total value should be divided equally between the owners (SI 1992/2977, r.27).

## 9.6.3 DISREGARDED CAPITAL
### 9.6.3.1 Capital disregarded indefinitely

Certain capital is disregarded indefinitely including property (in some circumstances: see below). Such disregarded capital includes, for example, surrender value of life insurance policies and annuities, payment of training bonus up to £200, age-related payments to pensioners (under the Age Related Payments Act 2004), payments in kind from charities, personal possessions (unless bought to reduce the accommodation charge payable), payments from the MacFarlane Trusts, Skipton Fund payments, the Fund (payments for non-haemophiliacs infected with HIV) or Independent Living Funds, Social Fund payments, funds held in trust or administered by a court (e.g. Court of Protection) following payment for personal injury, value of a right to receive income (under an annuity, personal injury trust, life interest or life rent, occupational pension, rent), ex gratia payments paid to former Japanese prisoners etc. (SI 1992/2977, schedule 4).

Where the capital to be disregarded is by way of funds held in trust or by a court following payment for personal injury, the disregard applies to the whole of the capital – as the courts have confirmed:

**Disregarding all the capital of personal injury payments held in trust by a court.** It was argued in one court case that the capital disregard for personal injury payment held in trust by a court should only apply to the part of the compensation payment awarded for pain, suffering and loss of amenity – not, for example, to the part covering future care costs or loss of earnings. If this were so, the local authority could take account of at least some of the personal injury payment capital, for the purpose of charging for the residential care being provided to the person involved. (He had sustained a severe head injury at a textile mill, when retrieving a cricket ball from the roof of a shed.)

The case centred on a reference to 1987 Income Support Regulations, which referred to disregard of a payment 'for' personal injury, as opposed to the term 'in consequence of' personal injury. It was argued that the 'for' implied damages only for the pain, suffering and loss of amenity; and not damages for the cost of care and loss of earnings. The court rejected this argument, and found that whole of the capital fell to be disregarded (*Firth v Ackroyd*; see also *Bell v Todd*, and subsequent confirmation of this approach by the Court of Appeal in *Sowden v Lodge*).

The frustration this rule causes local authorities can be seen from the following court case in which the local authority attempted to hold an NHS trust liable for the costs of residential accommodation:

**Circumventing rule about personal injury trusts.** A local authority incurred costs of some £81,000 for the residential accommodation of a person who had suffered a stroke due to the negligence of an NHS trust. The damages award resulted in a structured settlement, with £40,000 payable annually into the Court of Protection. This sum had to be disregarded by the local authority under the charging rules. Instead, it sought to reclaim the costs from the NHS trust, on the basis that the latter could reasonably have foreseen that the consequences of its negligence would be a personal injury settlement paid into trust (and therefore to be disregarded); and also that the situation was unjust.

The case failed; the court held that the NHS trust could not reasonably have foreseen that the damages would be paid to the Court of Protection or a trust fund. It also held that the relevant charging rules were a necessary consequence of the interface between central government and local authority; and it was an abuse of language to call the consequence a gross injustice (*Islington LBC v University College London Hospital NHS Trust*).

### 9.6.3.2 Capital disregarded for 26 weeks
Other capital is disregarded for up to 26 weeks or more, including the assets of a business owned or part-owned by the resident in which he or she intends to work again; money acquired for replacement of the home or repairs to it – or premises which the resident intends to occupy but to which essential repairs or alterations are needed; premises for which the resident has commenced legal proceedings to obtain possession; the proceeds of the sale of a former home which are to be used to buy another home; money deposited with a housing association and to be used to buy another home; or a grant obtained under housing legislation to buy a home or to repair it, so as to make it habitable (SI 1992/2977, schedule 4).

### 9.6.3.3 Capital disregarded for 52 weeks
Yet other capital is disregarded for 52 weeks, for example arrears or compensation in relation to non-payment of a range of state benefits, payments or refunds in relation to the NHS (dental treatment, spectacles and travelling expenses), free milk, vitamins or prison visits (SI 1992/2977, schedule 4).

### 9.6.3.4 Other disregarded capital
The assets of a business – owned or part-owned by the resident who is no longer a self-employed worker in it – must be disregarded for a reasonable period, so that the resident can dispose of the business assets (SI 1992/2977, schedule 4; CRAG 2004, para 6.031).

Payments made, in respect of variant Creuzfeldt Jacob Disease, to a victim's parent should be disregarded for two years from date of death of the victim. If made to a dependent child or young person, the payments should be disregarded until the person is no longer a member of a family (i.e. until they leave school between 16 and 17) but in any case for at least two years (SI 1992/2977, schedule 4; CRAG 2004, para 6.030A).

## 9.7 NOTIONAL CAPITAL

In certain circumstances, a resident may be assessed as possessing capital – even though not actually in possession of it. This is called notional capital and might be capital (a) of which the resident has deprived himself or herself in order to decrease the amount payable for the accommodation; (b) which would be payable if he or she applied for it; or (c) which is paid to a third party in respect of the resident.

However, the rule that capital, which would be available on application by the resident, should be treated as belonging to him or her does not apply where that capital is held in a discretionary trust, a trust derived from a personal injury compensation payment (or a court administered sum arising from personal injury compensation), or a loan that could be raised against a capital asset (e.g. the person's home) which is being disregarded (SI 1992/2977, r.25; CRAG 2004, para 6.052–3).

### 9.7.1 SHOWING DEVPRIVATION OF CAPITAL

A local authority can treat a resident as still possessing a capital asset, and thus possessing notional capital, if it believes that the resident has deprived himself or herself of it, in order to reduce accommodation fees (SI 1992/2977, r.25 and CRAG 2004, para 6.057).

Guidance states that avoiding the charge 'need not be the resident's main motive but it must be a significant one'. Furthermore, it would not be reasonable for the authority to identify such deprivation of income if the resident was, at the time of the disposal, 'fit and healthy and could not have foreseen the need for a move to residential accommodation' (CRAG 2004, para 6.064).

The courts in England and Scotland (where the deprivation rules are roughly the same) appear to have taken a different approach to what is required to show a significant motive. Effectively the Scottish courts have tended toward an objective (and arguably harsher) approach; the English toward a more subjective one.

**Inference of motive for giving the house away.** An elderly woman, aged 78 years, transferred her house in early 1995 to her granddaughter for love, favour and affection, though retaining a right to live there. She also executed a power of attorney in favour of her son. A year or so later, she fell, breaking her arm; by June 1996 her physical and mental condition had deteriorated such that she entered a nursing home. The son indicated, before admission to the home, that his mother had deteriorated over the past few years and had harboured paranoid ideas regarding a neighbour. The local authority could not show directly that the woman's motive for the transfer had been avoidance of future care home costs. However, it received no explanation as to why the woman had not left her house in her will, as opposed to transferring it in life.

The court held that the local authority was entitled to draw inferences on the basis of all the material available to it; furthermore, it did not have to make a specific finding as to the exact state of knowledge or intention of the woman (*Yule v South Lanarkshire Council (no.2)*).

In another Scottish case, the courts took a similar, arguably even harsher, line, because there was no evidence that at the time of the transfer anybody either knew or suspected that the person had begun to suffer from senile dementia:

**Transfer of home.** An elderly woman transferred to her children, for love, favour and affection, her home, but continued to live there. It was argued that this was in part to discourage the pestering of her brother who wished to come to live with her. The head of the local authority's social work department stated that he was not satisfied that this was a satisfactory explanation; and that it appeared to him that the property was transferred at least in part for the purpose of reducing residential accommodation charges. The local authority succeeded on this point in both the Outer and then, on appeal, the Inner House of the Court of Session (*Robertson v Fife Council*).

The above Scottish cases seemed to place considerable burden on the service user to provide an explanation, and gave considerable latitude to the local authority to draw inferences. They appear to contrast markedly with the approach taken by the English High Court, which emphasised the importance of the subjective state of knowledge of the person transferring the asset:

**Giving the house away.** A man had a stroke in March 1997 at the age of 90. Discharged from hospital a month later, he went home 'on a wing and a prayer' (as a social worker put it), receiving intensive home care three times a day including personal care, meal preparation, shopping, cleaning and laundry. He had been in receipt of home care for some years eight years previously, comprising assistance with domestic tasks for three hours a week. In April 1997, a week after hospital discharge, he transferred his house to his son by deed of gift. This was later explained with reference to the fact that his son's 24-year marriage had broken down, and that he was concerned that his son would become homeless. The father had no thought of dying anywhere else than in his own home.

In April 1999, the man was admitted to hospital in a state of collapse and exhaustion. He returned home in May, was readmitted to hospital in August – and in September assessed by social services as requiring residential care. Social services decided that he had deprived himself of an asset which would have funded his residential care. The son complained, and the complaint reached the final complaints review panel stage. The panel rejected the son's complaint, and the director of social services accepted the panel's findings. One of the panel members at one stage pointed out that ignorance of the law was no defence.

The court found the local authority's decision to be unlawful. The test to be applied was meant to be a subjective one in terms of the father's state of mind. If the son's evidence was rejected on this point, the panel had to explain why with adequate reasons. The absence of such reasons suggested the panel was not applying the right test. The 'ignorance of the law' comment betrayed a misunderstanding of that test (*R(Beeson) v Dorset CC*, High Court).

## 9.7.2 DEPRIVATION OF CAPITAL AND CONSEQUENCES

If deprivation of capital is shown, the local authority can attempt to recover the assessed charge owing from either the resident as normal – or, if the resident cannot pay, then in some circumstances from the third party to whom the asset was transferred (see 9.11; SI 1992/2977, r.25; CRAG 2004, para 6.067).

If notional capital is taken into account, it must be regarded by the local authority as reduced each week by the difference between the (greater) amount the resident has been assessed to pay because of the notional capital, and the (lesser) amount he or she would have paid but for the notional capital (SI 1992/2977, r.26). There is no rule about how long ago the deprivation must have occurred, although the greater the period between the 'deprivation' and the entry into the care home, the more difficult it is likely to be for the local authority to argue relevant motive.

**Notional capital and timescales.** In one Scottish court case, where the rules are the same in England, the petitioner claimed that the power to take account of notional capital conferred by r.25 of SI 1992/2977 was limited to disposals of assets only up to six months before entry into residential accommodation – a limit deriving from s.21 of the Health and Social Services and Social Security Adjudications Act 1983. However, the court confirmed what had been widely supposed to be the case, that there was no such time limit (the limit of six months applying only when an authority wishes to make liable a third party, to whom the asset in question had been transferred) (*Yule v South Lanarkshire Council*).

Of course demanding payment, notwithstanding deprivation, will not be greatly to the authority's benefit if the resident does not have sufficient actual, as opposed to notional, capital. If the asset was transferred to a third party more than six months before the resident entered the care home, the rules are that the authority cannot legally hold the third party liable (see 9.11).

An incentive for identifying notional capital would be for the local authority then to argue that it has no duty to contract for the care home placement at all. This would be on the basis that notionally, if not actually, the person had sufficient resources to make his or own arrangements. In practice the local authority might seek to rely on the third party (e.g. a family member), who now had the actual property or other asset, to pay the fees. However, there would be no legal (as opposed to moral) obligation on that third party to do so, always assuming the six-month rule is not relevant. In which case, so the argument runs, the person would have to remain in the care home until his or her resources (actual rather than notional) ran out. At which point, he or she could in principle be evicted for non-payment and end up actually, or metaphorically, on the street. The Scottish courts were prepared to countenance this happening. However, the House of Lords overturned the decision and ruled that in Scotland at least this would not be lawful; and that local authorities are obliged to continue to fund the care home placement, notwithstanding the existence of notional capital (*Robertson v Fife Council*).

There is a degree of uncertainty about the extent to which this Scottish judgment applies to England. This is because some of the court's reasoning referred to elements of the Scottish legislation that differ from the English. Possibly there is material in the *Robertson* case to argue the position either way. Ultimately, however, it is doubtful whether the English courts would allow a vulnerable, disabled person (particularly without, but maybe even with, the mental capacity to decide or arrange welfare matters for himself or herself) to be abandoned by both care home and local authority and 'put out on the streets'.

## 9.7.3 INSOLVENCY PROCEEDINGS
Alternatively, the local authority may consider insolvency proceedings in respect of what it considers to be a deprivation of capital (see 9.13).

## 9.8 ASSESSMENT OF REAL PROPERTY (HOUSE OR LAND)

In some circumstances, a resident's property might be disregarded in the assessment of assets, but otherwise it is fully taken account of.

### 9.8.1 TEMPORARY RESIDENTS

The value of one dwelling of a temporary resident will be disregarded if he or she intends to return to the dwelling or is taking reasonable steps to dispose of the property in order to acquire another more suitable one to return to (SI 1992/2977, schedule 4).

Guidance notes that if a person's stay was thought to be permanent, but turns out to be temporary, he or she should be treated as if the stay were temporary from the outset (CRAG 2004, para 7.002).

### 9.8.2 PROPERTY AND OCCUPIED BY OTHER PEOPLE

#### 9.8.2.1 Property occupied by other people: mandatory disregard

The value of the resident's home must be disregarded if it is occupied, whether wholly or partly, (a) by the resident's partner or former partner (except in case of divorce or estrangement); (b) by a lone parent who is the claimant's estranged or divorced partner; (c) by a relative or member of the family who is at least 60 years old, or is under 16 years old and is liable to be maintained by the resident, or is incapacitated (SI 1992/2977, schedule 4; CRAG 2004, para 7.003).

Guidance points out that 'incapacitated' is not defined in the regulations, but that a reasonable test might be whether the person receives, or could receive, a disability-related social security benefit (CRAG 2004, para 7.005).

#### 9.8.2.2 Property occupied by other people and discretionary disregard

Outside the mandatory disregard, if anybody else is living in the home, local authorities have a discretion to disregard the property, if they 'consider it would be reasonable' (SI 1992/2977, schedule 4). Guidance suggests that it might be reasonable where, for example, 'it is the sole residence of someone who has given up their own home in order to care for the resident, or someone who is an elderly companion of the resident particularly if they have given up their own home'. However, it would be for the authority to decide when or whether to review the exercise of any such discretion – for example, when the carer has died or moved out (CRAG 2004, paras 7.007–8). It should be noted that the example given in the guidance is just that; the discretion is a wide one – although in the following court case, the local authority had lawfully decided not to exercise it:

**Discretion to disregard value of house.** In 1991, a man gave up his job in Australia (as a welfare officer working with Aboriginal Australians) to return to England to look after his mother; she was suffering from Parkinson's disease and had been forced to go into residential care. On his arrival, she returned to her own home, and he looked after her with constant assistance and support. However, she suffered a series of strokes and was admitted to hospital in July 1993. In March 1994, the son returned to Australia to resume his job; but this did not work out and he had returned by July.

In May 1994, his mother had been discharged from hospital to a nursing home. In April 1997 she died. There was a shortfall in the payments she had made to the local authority for this nursing home care; the local authority decided to take account of her home in the test of resources. During this period, it did not force the son to sell the house, but created a charge of £500 a month on it. The mother died with a bill of £25,000 outstanding – and interest began to accrue from date of death. The authority would not enforce the charge (i.e. force a sale) until the son ceased to occupy the property.

The judge decided that 'in all the circumstances of the case it was not unreasonable to take account of the house'. One factor – though not the only one – in the overall decision was that the son had returned to Australia after his mother had gone into residential care for the second time, in order to attempt (unsuccessfully) to resume his career. This meant that on his second return to England, occupation of the house had become attributable not to the need to look after his mother, but to the decision to give up the job and accommodation in Australia. Overall, the judge was satisfied that the decision had been taken by the local authority's officer within the ambit of the regulations, was 'properly based on conclusions of fact to which he was entitled to come on the material which he had to consider', and 'was based on full and proper assessment of all the facts and circumstances of the case' (R v Somerset CC, ex p Harcombe).

Nevertheless, even if the local authority is entitled to take account of the house, it needs to provide clear information; a failure to do so means a finding of maladministration by the local ombudsman:

**Misleading advice about taking account of the value of the house.** A son lived with his elderly mother. The council wrongly advised him that if she moved into a care home, the value of her house would not be taken into account when calculating her contribution to the care home fees. Four and a half months after she had entered the care home, the local authority told the son that the house would after all be taken into account and that there was now a legal charge on the property. The son stated that had he received proper advice at the outset, he would have given up his job to care for his mother at home – something he had done for relatively long periods in the past.

The ombudsman found maladministration in that the local authority failed to give clear written advice and took far too long in carrying out its financial assessment. The council agreed to waive £2000 from the charge and not insist on a sale of the property (although the mother had now died). Nevertheless, the ombudsman did not recommend that the charge on the property be lifted, since the mother had received the residential care, the cost of which was property recoverable (Cumbria CC 2001).

**Wrong information.** The local authority assessed, wrongly, an elderly woman's liability for residential care fees in December 1995. In April 1997, when it gained the information to correct the error it did not do so; it only did so in September 1999 (the delay being because of insufficient procedures to pursue the debt). By now there was £13,500 owing. All this was maladministration. The son claimed he would have taken more urgent action regarding the house, either selling it earlier or renting it out (Kent CC 2001a).

### 9.8.2.3 Legal and beneficial ownership of property

There will be some circumstances in which the local authority might have difficulty taking account of the value of a property where somebody else is living, if the person has a beneficial interest. Guidance points out that legal owner means the person in whose name a property is held; beneficial owner means the person entitled to receive the proceeds or profits of the property. Normally the two will be one and the same. However, this is not always so. Where the care home resident is a legal owner of a property but has no beneficial interest in it, the property should not be taken into account for charging purposes. However, if the resident has a beneficial interest in the property, then the property should be taken into account, even though he or she is not the legal owner (CRAG 2004, paras 7.009–11).

The guidance goes on to suggest that the law of equity might resolve doubts about beneficial ownership, by considering the original intentions involved between the parties (CRAG 2004, para 7.014A). The following court case was about a beneficial type of interest or ownership:

**Beneficial interest of lodger as against local authority's interest.** A relatively fit and healthy couple had a lodger. Their physical and mental capabilities declined into frailty, helplessness and incontinence; the lodger in effect became an unpaid live-in carer, until they went into a care home. Although he stopped paying rent at a certain point, the lodger had been providing substantial personal care and incurred out-of-pocket expenses of £1700. The lodger claimed that the couple had repeatedly assured him that he would have a home for life.

After the couple had both died, the lodger resisted sale of the property by the executors of the will, on the grounds that he had a right to live there. The court found that he had a claim in equity under the principle of proprietary estoppel. The couple had, through assurances, induced the lodger to act as he did, and he then acted to his detriment (the level of care he provided was greater than could be accounted for by friendship and a sense of responsibility). The claim amounted not to a right to live there for life but instead to a sum of £35,000; and this claim ranked ahead of the local authority's charge (£64,000) that it had placed on the home for the couple's residential care (*Campbell v Griffin*).

Purchase of council houses has sometimes given rise to legal dispute in respect of a local authority attempting to take account of a person's house for the purpose of care home fees:

**Purchase of council house.** A secure tenancy of a council property passed from a woman's father to her mother when he died. The mother then exercised her right to buy; the property was worth £120,000 but it attracted a discount of £50,000. The daughter funded the whole purchase by means of a mortgage; she and her mother became joint legal owners. Just before the transfer the mother went into hospital and was subsequently discharged to a care home; she then died. The local authority subsequently registered a caution against the property by way of seeking a contribution to the care home fees. The daughter argued that the property had only ever been intended for her use and not her mother; she had paid the entire purchase price; and her mother had only joint legal title, but no beneficial interest.

The court held that on the evidence it was not clear that the mother had no beneficial interest. There was no express declaration by the mother and daughter concerning the beneficial interest at the time of purchase. In the absence of such declaration, the court would normally decide that the joint purchasers held the property on a resulting trust for themselves in proportion to their original contributions (as in *Springette v Defoe*). In this case, this would mean the mother holding a beneficial interest of 5/12 of the property (representing the £50,000 discount value attributable to her being the tenant), compared to the £70,000 contributed by the daughter. 

The court ruled that it was not unlawful for the local authority to have registered the caution; but that further proceedings could be brought by the daughter to try to show specific evidence of com-

mon intention by herself and her mother – to displace the presumption of the existence of the resulting trust (*R(Kelly) v Hammersmith and Fulham LBC*).

### 9.8.2.4 Joint ownership and willing buyer

In the case of land, the resident's share should be valued at an amount equal to the price
which his interest in possession would realise. However, this would be on the basis of it
being sold to a willing buyer, and taking into account the likely effect on that price of any
incumbrance secured on the whole beneficial interest (e.g. somebody in occupation with
a beneficial interest). The price would also be less 10 per cent (SI 1992/2977, r.27).

However, this rule means that the value of a property might therefore have only a
nominal value if a co-owner is still living in it, since in reality there may be no willing
buyer to purchase the resident's interest. In some circumstances the value could therefore
be nil. For example, no other relative (or anybody else) might be willing to buy the resident's interest, if the financial advantages did not significantly outweigh the risks and
limitations involved of somebody else having part ownership (CRAG 2004, para 7.014).

In one case concerning income support, the Court of Appeal held that in the case of
father and daughter who had a beneficial interest in the family home, the value of the father's interest was to be taken by reference to the current market value (minimal), not to
his share of the beneficial interest taken as a whole (*Chief Adjudication Officer v Palfrey*).

In a more recent case a local authority attempted to circumvent this rule, by approaching the question on the basis of a hypothetical 'open market value' that effectively assumed the existence of a willing buyer, by ignoring the 'real circumstances'. The property
in question was jointly owned by the care home resident and his son; the latter had intended to move in when he retired. The local ombudsman found that the council's approach was inconsistent with both Department of Health guidance and legal case law.
Without significant evidence or opinion to support such a contrary position, this was
maladministration (*Lincolnshire CC 2004*).

However, in the context of income support, a 2004 decision by the Social Security
Commissioner suggested, without deciding, that it should not be assumed that in every
such case the resident's share of the value is little or nothing. For example, it might have
value for inheritance tax purposes (the resident was now deceased). In the particular case,
however, the Commissioner accepted that the resident's share (one-third) of the house
(the other two-thirds owned by her daughter) was minimal (CIS/3197/2003).

### 9.8.3 12-WEEK DISREGARD OF PROPERTY

The value of a person's dwelling is disregarded for the first 12 weeks of a permanent resi-
dency (SI 1992/2977, schedule 4). It is therefore important to note that this does not affect the disregarding of the dwelling during a temporary stay (see 9.3); if a stay then
becomes permanent, the dwelling is disregarded for a further 12 weeks (LAC(2001)10,
annex).

### 9.8.4 INTENTION TO OCCUPY PROPERTY

If the resident has acquired a home that he intends to occupy, then it should be disregarded for up to 26 weeks or a longer period if reasonable (SI 1992/2977, schedule 4, para 18; CRAG 2004, para 7.006).

### 9.8.5 PROPERTY AND DEFERRED PAYMENTS

Local authorities have the power to make deferred payments (Health and Social Care Act 2001; SI 2001/3069). This means that, where a local authority would be otherwise entitled to take account of a resident's home, it will not do so (SI 2001/3067). Instead, it can agree not to force the sale of the house, but instead place a progressively increasing land charge for an agreed period (i.e. until the person dies or for some other period). The purpose is so that people do not have to sell their homes during the period of the agreement. Guidance stresses a number of points.

- Local authorities have only a discretion, not a duty, to enter a deferred payment agreement.
- Authorities should ensure that the resident will have sufficient assets eventually to repay the money owing and meet other commitments (e.g. mortgage payments).
- If an authority enters into a high value agreement with one person, it might affect its ability to enter agreements with others.
- A deferred payment agreement would only take effect after the 12-week mandatory property disregard (see 9.8.3).
- Such agreements should not supplant the use of the discretion not to take account of the property at all, where there is somebody (such as a former carer) still living in it (see 9.8.2.2).
- An agreement lasts until the end of the exempt period, that is 56 days after the resident dies or when it is otherwise terminated by the resident. The authority cannot terminate the agreement of its own accord. The debt is only payable, and interest only chargeable, from the day after the exempt period ends.
- Authorities should distinguish the placing of a charge on the property under a deferred payment agreement (Health and Social Care Act 2001) from placing a charge on a property when the resident is simply failing to pay an assessed charge (under the Health and Social Services and Social Security Adjudications Act 1983) (LAC(2001)25, annex).

## 9.9 ASSESSMENT OF INCOME

A payment of income (other than earnings: see below) is generally distinguished from capital on the basis that it is made in relation to a period and is part of a series (regular or irregular) of payments (CRAG 2004, paras 8.001–2). As with capital, income might be wholly or partly disregarded, or taken fully into account. Residents may also be assessed as having notional income if, for example, they have deprived themselves of income in order to reduce the charge payable.

### 9.9.1 NOTIONAL INCOME

A resident may be treated by the local authority as having notional income, even though he or she does not actually receive it, if it is income: (a) paid by a third party as a contribution towards the cost of the accommodation; (b) which would be available on application; (c) due but not yet paid; (d) of which the resident has deprived himself or herself 'for the purpose of decreasing the amount that he may be liable to pay for his accommodation' (SI 1992/2977, r.17; CRAG 2004, paras 8.059–70A).

However, the rule that income, which would be available on application by the resident, should be treated as belonging to him or her does not apply where that income is payable under a discretionary trust, a trust derived from a personal injury compensation payment, or a loan that could be raised against a capital asset which is being disregarded (SI 1992/2977, r.17; CRAG 2004, para 8.070).

In respect of deprivation, guidance states that there 'may have been more than one purpose of the disposal of income, only one of which is to avoid a charge, or a lower charge. This may not be the resident's main motive but it must be a significant one.' The authority can then attempt to recover the assessed charge owing from either the resident as normal – or, if the resident cannot pay, from the third party to whom the asset was transferred (CRAG 2004, paras 8.077–82). (See discussion of notional capital at 9.7 above.)

### 9.9.2 INCOME FULLY TAKEN ACCOUNT OF

Income fully taken account of includes most social security benefits, annuity income, cash in lieu of concessionary coal (permanent residents only), child support maintenance payments (if the child is accommodated with the resident under Part 3 of the 1948 Act – i.e. mother and baby unit), ex gratia incapacity allowances from the Home Office, income from certain disregarded capital (e.g. from property or business assets which have been disregarded), insurance policy income, income from certain sublets, occupational pensions, income tax refunds, payments made by third parties, trust income, and war orphan pension (SI 1992/2977, r.15).

Although capital in personal-injury-related trusts is disregarded, the income actually paid is to be taken into account (SI 1992/2977, schedule 3; CRAG 2004, para 8.015), unless it is held by the Court of Protection, in which case it is treated as capital which falls to be disregarded (*Ryan and Liverpool City Council v Liverpool Health Authority*).

Third party top-up payments (see 8.5.1.1) will be counted as income of the resident. Where the resident is topping up from his or her own resources during the 12-week disregard period (see above) or as part of a deferred payments agreement, the value of the top-up should be taken into account – unless it is being added to the deferred contribution (SI 1992/2977, r.16A; CRAG 2004, paras 8.018–8.019C).

### 9.9.3 INCOME PARTLY DISREGARDED

Income partly disregarded includes a £10 disregard for payments made under German or Austrian law to victims of National Socialist persecution, war disablement pension, war widow's pension and civilian war-injury pension. There is also a savings disregard.

In addition, various amounts are disregarded including occupational pensions, personal pensions and retirement annuity contract payments; some charitable payments; annuity income from a home income plan; subletting income; income from boarders; insurance policies for mortgage protection; income from certain disregarded capital, for example disregarded might be the element of the income representing mortgage repayments, council tax or water rates (CRAG 2004, paras 8.021–37; SI 1992/2977, schedule 3).

### 9.9.4 INCOME FULLY DISREGARDED

Income fully disregarded includes income support/pension credit, home commitments of temporary residents (see above); Supporting People housing support payments; some charitable and voluntary payments; child support maintenance and child benefit payments (unless the child is living with the resident in accommodation: i.e. mother and baby unit); child tax credits, Christmas bonus associated with certain benefits; payments from the Macfarlane Trusts, Independent Living Funds, Eileen Trust and the Fund, council tax benefit, disability living allowance (mobility component), mobility supplement for war pensioners; dependency increases associated with some benefits; gallantry awards; income in kind or frozen abroad; social fund payments; some payments made to trainees; special payments to war widows; work expenses paid by employer, expenses payments for voluntary workers (CRAG 2004, paras 8.038–56; SI 1992/2977, schedule 3).

## 9.10 RESPONSIBILITY FOR PAYMENT OF FEES

The ultimate responsibility for paying an independent provider of accommodation is the local authority as a party to the contract. However, the resident can make payment direct to the provider if this is agreed by the authority, the provider and the resident. Where this is agreed, but the resident fails at some point to make the required payment, the local authority is obliged to pay the shortfall to the provider (National Assistance Act 1948, s.26(3A); CRAG 2004, para 1.023).

## 9.11 PURSUIT OF DEBT

Local authorities are empowered under the National Assistance Act 1948, without prejudice to any other method of recovery, to recover money owing for care home fees, as a civil debt. However, proceedings must be brought within three years of the sum becoming due (National Assistance Act 1948, s.56).

## 9.11.1 PURSUING THIRD PARTIES FOR FEES

Local authorities are empowered to pursue money owing to them from a third party, to whom the resident transferred assets not more than six months before entry into residential accommodation. This must have been done knowingly and with the intention of avoiding charges for the accommodation. The transfer needs to have been at an under-value or for no consideration at all (Health and Social Services and Social Security Adjudications Act 1983, s.21).

This six-month rule is only triggered where the local authority has assessed the person as needing residential accommodation under Part III of the 1948 Act, and has arranged a placement. The rule does not apply if the resident is self-funding in an independent sector home, has not been assessed, and has not had his or her placement arranged by the local authority. Even if the requisite conditions are met, the rule applies only to assets that would have been taken into account when assessing the charge (CRAG 2004, annex D).

This would mean valuation at time of transfer, namely the amount that would have been realised on the open market by a willing seller. However, debts secured on the asset would have to be taken into account together with a reasonable amount in respect of the expenses of a sale (CRAG 2004, annex D).

## 9.12 PLACING A CHARGE ON LAND OR PROPERTY

If a resident fails to pay assessed charges for accommodation, the local authority is empowered to place a charge on any land or property in which the resident has a beneficial interest. The legislation states that such a charge will only bear interest from the day after the resident dies. The rate of interest should be a reasonable one as directed by the Secretary of State; otherwise, as the local authority determines (Health and Social Services and Social Security Adjudications Act 1983, s.24). Guidance states that the local authority should advise or assist the resident to consult a solicitor (CRAG 2004, annex D).

The Department of Health believes that because a specific power to create a charge is contained in the 1983 Act, local authorities cannot decide instead to use other general powers contained in s.111 of the Local Government Act 1972 in order to be able to charge interest during the person's lifetime (CRAG 2004, annex D).

The placing of a charge on property when a resident fails to pay should be distinguished from the situation of deferred payments; the placing of the charge occurs in different circumstances and under different legislation; by mutual agreement under the Health and Social Care Act 2001 in respect of deferred payments; but, where there is a lack of agreement and the resident fails to pay, under the HASSASSA 1983.

## 9.13 INSOLVENCY PROCEEDINGS

If local authorities attempt to enforce charges, but the person being pursued has no or little money left (e.g. following a deliberate deprivation of resources), they clearly have a problem. However, authorities might consider utilising provisions under the Insolvency Act 1986 to enable them to pursue debts that are owing.

First, steps might be taken (under ss.339–341 of the 1986 Act) to have the resident declared bankrupt, in which case any of the resident's transactions made at an undervalue in the past two years can be set aside (or in the last five years, in the unlikely event that the resident was already insolvent at the time of the transaction).

Second (under ss.423–425), a gift, no matter how long ago it was made, can be set aside if the court is convinced that the purpose (not necessarily sole or even dominant, but at least substantial) of the gift was to place the assets beyond the reach of a possible creditor or otherwise prejudice a creditor's interests (i.e. to avoid paying residential care charges). However, this test does not necessarily mean that a transaction designed to minimise tax liabilities would fall foul of s.423, as the following legal case illustrates:

**Tax planning not to be equated with avoiding potential creditors.** A successful businessman and solicitor had for many years put his assets, as he accrued them, into his wife's name. He was subsequently investigated by the Law Society for breaches of accounting rules. The man died. The Law Society sought to recoup £283,000 in costs incurred by its intervention, relying on s.423 of the Insolvency Act 1986 to do so. The court rejected the Law Society's arguments; stated that the evidence clearly showed that the transfer of assets to the wife was based on the advice of his accountant for the purpose of minimising tax liability; and that the Society should not have engaged in speculative litigation against an elderly lady (*Law Society v Southall*).

## 9.14 CARE HOMES: PERSONAL FINANCIAL ISSUES

Possible or actual need for residential or nursing home accommodation raises various financial issues for people and their families including how to raise capital on their own home, making gifts and transferring assets to avoid possible charges. Fearful that they will in effect be forced by local authorities to sell their home in order to pay residential or nursing home fees, some people contemplate making a gift of their home – for example, to close family – so as to put the property out of the reach of the local authority. However, there exist a range of possible complications, and it is clear that expert advice should be sought by those considering gifts of property or other assets, or other forms of alienating them (such as trusts). This is the first point made in a Law Society (2000) publication concerning gifts of property in the context of paying for long-term care. The following two legal cases are cautionary reminders of how things can go wrong in the case of lifetime transactions within families:

**Undue influence of great nephew on elderly man.** An elderly man contributed (£43,000) towards the purchase (for £83,000) of a house by his great-nephew (and in the latter's sole name) in return for living in it for the rest of his life. The nephew defaulted on the mortgage repayments, and the man tried to retrieve his money ahead of the mortgage lender. This was not without complications; eventually the Court of Appeal ruled there had been undue influence exercised, and that he could recover a proportion, but not the whole, of the original amount. This was because the house was sold for only £55,000. The man could not recover his original £43,000, but only an amount (£28,700) corresponding to the proportion (i.e. 43:40) he had contributed to the original purchase price (*Cheese v Thomas*).

**Sharing of house, breakdown of arrangements.** A man provided the money (£33,950) towards purchase of a house for his son and daughter-in-law. He would then live there rent free for the rest of his life. The arrangement broke down when the son accused the father of sexually molesting the latter's young granddaughter; it was subsequently clear that the accusation was unfounded and made without reasonable grounds. The High Court ruled that the full sum was recoverable on the basis of a doctrine known as proprietary estoppel (basically about a person's expectation, which has arisen because he or she has acted to his or her detriment in reliance on a promise or assurance).

However, the Court of Appeal ruled that the expectation lost was not the full sum, but the value of the father's expectation to live in the house rent free for the rest of his life. This would be a smaller amount than the original sum he had contributed (*Baker v Baker*).

CHAPTER 10

# Non-residential services

## KEY POINTS

A substantial range of non-residential community care services is contained in various community care legislation. Access to these services is governed in the main by assessments conducted under s.47 of the NHS and Community Care Act 1990, covered in Chapter 6. However, these services are not contained within the 1990 Act itself, but are instead scattered under five other pieces of legislation. These are the National Assistance Act 1948, s.29, Chronically Sick and Disabled Persons Act 1970, s.2, Health Services and Public Health Act 1968, s.45, NHS Act 1977, schedule 8, and Mental Health Act 1983, s.117: covering both non-residential and residential services.

It is apparent that, in practice, local authority staff and managers are frequently unfamiliar with this legislation, and thus not always aware of just how wide the range of services is that they have legal duties and powers to provide. For instance, services referred to in the legislation include social work services, advice, support, holidays, practical assistance in the home, assistance to take advantage of educational facilities, recreational activities, additional facilities (equipment), home adaptations, holidays, night sitter services, home help, laundry service, visiting services, assistance in finding accommodation etc.

The very extent, overlap and fragmentation of the legislation governing non-residential services feeds the type of uncertainty outlined in Chapter 3; not only are service users unaware of what services could or must be provided, but so too sometimes are managers and staff.

**Note: Wales, Scotland and Northern Ireland**. This chapter applies in principle to Wales, where the legislation is the same and equivalent directions and guidance have been issued (under WOC 35/93).

In Scotland, the Social Work (Scotland) Act 1968 reads differently to the English legislation in terms of community care services listed. However, the Chronically Sick and Disabled Persons Act 1970 (s.2) applies in Scotland by virtue of the Chronically Sick and Disabled Persons (Scotland) Act 1972. Also s.4 (assessment request) and s.8 (having regard to carer) of the Disabled Persons (Services, Consultation and Representation) Act 1986 apply in Scotland as they do in England.

In Northern Ireland, the Health and Personal Social Services (Northern Ireland) Order 1972 reads differently to the English legislation in terms of services listed. However, the equivalent of s.2 of the Chronically Sick and Disabled Persons Act 1970 and ss.4 and 8 of the Disabled Persons (Services, Consultation and Representation) Act 1986 are present in Northern Ireland in the form respectively of the Chronically Sick and Disabled Persons (Northern Ireland) Act 1978 and the Disabled Persons (Northern Ireland) Act 1989.

As to mental health aftercare services (for England and Wales, in s.117 of the Mental Health Act 1983), mental health legislation differs in Scotland (Mental Health (Scotland) Act 1984 and Mental Health (Care and Treatment) (Scotland) Act 2003) and in Northern Ireland (Mental Health (Northern Ireland) Order 1986).

## 10.1 NATIONAL ASSISTANCE ACT 1948, S.29: NON-RESIDENTIAL SERVICES FOR DISABLED PEOPLE

Under s.29 of the National Assistance Act 1948, various non-residential services are listed in respect of disabled people. However, s.29 states that the provision of such services is subject to either approval or direction by the Secretary of State.

### 10.1.1 NON-RESIDENTIAL WELFARE SERVICES: DUTIES

By means of directions issued under s.29, there is a general duty to arrange various services for disabled people who are ordinarily resident within the area of the local authority. For disabled people who are not ordinarily resident, arranging these services is a power only (LAC(93)10, appendix 2). The duties, created by the directions, are:

- compiling and maintaining a register of disabled people
- providing a social work service and such advice and support as is needed for people at home or elsewhere
- providing, whether at centres or elsewhere, facilities for social rehabilitation and adjustment to disability including assistance in overcoming limitations of mobility or communication
- providing, either at centres or elsewhere, facilities for occupational, social, cultural and recreational activities – and, where appropriate, payments to persons for work they have done.

Although the directions effectively create a duty, the courts have held that the duty under s.29 is of a target, general nature only. This means that in the event of non-provision of a service, it is likely to be extremely difficult legally to enforce provision for any one individual. For instance, in one case the court stated that it would be impermissible to adjudicate on the s.29 target duty with reference to an individual case (*R v Islington LBC, ex p Rixon*; see also *R v Cornwall CC, ex p Goldsack*).

**Walking assistance at a day centre.** The court concluded that the walking assistance being given to a young disabled woman at a day centre was being provided under s.29 of the 1948 Act rather than under s.2 of the CSDPA 1970. It might have been provided under s.2 if it had been closely associated with meeting her recreational needs, but this was not so in the particular case (*R v Cornwall CC, ex p Goldsack*).

Even so, there have been a number of local ombudsman investigations concerning s.29 services. For instance:

**Social work services.** In one investigation relating to support and advice given to people entering or resident in nursing homes (before April 1993, when social services departments assumed responsibility for nursing home funding), the local ombudsman stated that a social work service should in principle be available to 'all those living in their area', i.e. residents of private nursing homes should not be excluded (*Buckinghamshire CC 1992*).

In another, the ombudsman found maladministration because, in considering whether to provide social work support, the authority had not balanced the views of relevant professionals against the resources it had available (*Tower Hamlets LBC 1993*).

**Advice.** On more than one occasion the local ombudsman has found maladministration because of a failure on the part of local authority staff to provide directly — or at least to ensure provision of (e.g. by pointing people to other sources) — adequate advice about welfare benefits (e.g. *Devon CC 1996; Stockton-on-Tees BC 1997; Wakefield MDC 1993*).

In one case, the ombudsman pointed out that either the council should offer adequate training to social workers to enable them to give proper advice, or it should instruct them to advise clients to obtain advice elsewhere (*Devon CC 1996*).

**Social rehabilitation and adjustment to disability.** A person with learning disabilities was placed in a residential home by the local authority. The authority provided, in addition, a support worker for 30 hours a week, in order to meet his developmental needs (under s.29 of the National Assistance Act 1948) by way of social rehabilitation and adjustment to disability. The amount of time allocated seemed reasonable to the ombudsman; however, the lack of precision in setting, working towards and recording the meeting of targets was maladministration (*Manchester CC 1993*).

### 10.1.1.1 *Registration of partially sighted or blind people*

The duty to keep a register of disabled people is one that has by and large not been rigorously carried out by local authorities. Nevertheless, in the case of partially sighted people, local authorities are notified by means of a form known as the Certificate of Vision Impairment (CVI) 2003, signed by a consultant ophthalmologist (DH 2003g). This notification should then trigger registration of the person by the local authority; this in turn makes the person eligible for certain benefits, for example a television licence.

For hearing impairment, Department of Health guidance states that there is no formal examination procedure for determination, under s.29, as to whether a person is deaf or hard of hearing (LAC(93)10, appendix 4).

Department of Health guidance asks local authorities to keep registration data under three main headings: very severe handicap, severe or appreciable handicap and other persons (for example, people with a less severe heart or chest condition or with epilepsy). The first two of these categories are themselves further explained (LAC(93)10, appendix 4):

- **Very severe handicap** includes those who:
  - 'need help going to or using the WC practically every night. In addition, most of those in this group need to be fed or dressed or, if they can feed and/or dress them-

selves, they need a lot of help during the day with washing and WC, or are incontinent'
- ○ 'need help with the WC during the night but not quite so much help with feeding,
  washing, dressing, or, while not needing night-time help with the WC, need a great
  deal of day-time help with feeding and/or washing and the WC'
- ○ 'are permanently bedfast or confined to a chair and need help to get in and out, or
  are senile or mentally impaired, or are not able to care for themselves as far as normal
  everyday functions are concerned, but who do not need as much help' as the above
  two categories.
- **Severe or appreciable handicap** includes those who:
  - ○ 'either have difficulty doing everything, or find most things difficult and some im-
    possible'
  - ○ 'find most things difficult, or three or four items difficult and some impossible'
  - ○ 'can do a fair amount for themselves but have difficulty with some items, or have to
    have help with or two minor items'.

## 10.1.2 NON-RESIDENTIAL WELFARE SERVICES : POWERS

By means of approvals issued by the Secretary of State under s.29, there is a power to arrange a further range of services for disabled people irrespective of whether they are ordinary residents in the area or not (LAC(93)10, appendix 2). The services are:
- providing holiday homes
- providing free or subsidised travel for people who do not otherwise qualify for other
  travel concessions
- assisting a person to find accommodation which will enable him or her to take
  advantage of arrangements made under section 29
- contributing to the cost of employing a warden in warden-assisted housing, and to
  provide warden services in private housing
- informing people to whom s.29 relates about services available under that section
- giving instruction to people at home or elsewhere in methods of overcoming effects
  of their disabilities
- providing workshops where such people may engage in suitable work and for
  providing associated hostels
- providing suitable work in people's own homes or otherwise, and to help people
  dispose of the produce of their work.

The power to give instruction to people at home or elsewhere in relation to overcoming
their disability is clearly a wide one. However, instruction is not the same as education; in
*R v Further Education Funding Council, ex p Parkinson,* the court held, in its attempt to separate out the education and social services functions of the local authority, that instruction
could not include a service that was 'purely educational'.

The House of Lords has in the past confirmed (in a rating valuation case) that
s.29 could not authorise the arranging of residential accommodation (*Vandyk v Oliver
(Valuation Officer)*).

## 10.1.3 DEFINITION OF DISABILITY

A basic condition of eligibility for the provision of non-residential welfare services under s.29 of the National Assistance Act 1948 (and under the Chronically Sick and Disabled Persons Act 1970, s.2) is that the person be disabled – namely blind, deaf, dumb; have a permanent and substantial handicap through illness, injury or congenital deformity, or have a mental disorder of any description (s.29).

The definition is elaborated upon in longstanding guidance. The approach advocated by the guidance, and by the government during the passing of the NHS and Community Care Act 1990, appears to be a generally inclusive one, thus discouraging local authorities from setting narrow definitions of disability in order to exclude people from eligibility for services. (The definition applies also to the Disabled Persons (Services, Consultation and Representation) Act 1986, s.4, and it is also found in the Housing Grants, Construction and Regeneration Act 1996 and in almost identical form in s.17 of the Children Act 1989.)

Department of Health guidance points out that registration of disability is not a condition for provision of service; the question is whether or not the person is to be regarded as having a hearing, vision or speech impairment or is substantially and permanently handicapped by illness, injury or congenital deformity (LAC(93)10, appendix 4, para 5).

For people with blindness or partial sight, the guidance refers to the established procedure of medical certification and local authority registration (see 10.1.1.1). For people with hearing impairment, it states that the 'deaf' category should include people who are deaf with speech, deaf without speech, or hard of hearing (that is, those who, with or without a hearing aid, have some useful hearing and whose normal method of communication is by speech, listening and lip-reading (LAC(93)10, appendix 4).

The guidance then states that it is not possible to give precise guidance on the interpretation of the phrase 'substantially and permanently handicapped'. However, it asks local authorities to give a wide interpretation to the term 'substantial', which should always 'take full account of individual circumstances'. With regard to the term 'permanent', it states that authorities would wish to interpret this 'sufficiently flexibly to ensure that they do not feel inhibited from giving help under s.29 in cases where they are uncertain of the likely duration of the condition'. However, the guidance does suggest registration categories and gives examples of 'very severe' and 'severe' handicap (see 10.1.1.1; LAC(93)10, appendix 4).

Nevertheless, despite the urging of the guidance to adopt an inclusive approach, it appears that in practice some local authorities, faced with what they perceive to be excessive demand for services under the Chronically Sick and Disabled Persons Act 1970, are tempted to restrict what they mean by 'substantial handicap'. Those authorities might, for instance, attempt to exclude certain groups of older people on the grounds that they might be frail, but that they are not disabled. It is then argued that those people are not eligible for services under s.29 of the National Assistance Act 1948 and s.2 of the Chronically Sick and Disabled Persons Act 1970. In which case, they might at best qualify for services for 'aged' or 'old' people under either the weaker duty contained in schedule 8 of the NHS Act 1977, or for services under the Health Services and Public Health Act 1968, which an authority has a power but no duty to provide. However, such an approach carries the risk of discriminating against older people and being potentially unlawful, by implying that the effects of frailty and age do not 'count' as disability, even if the consequence is that those persons are in fact significantly disabled in daily life. Indeed, Department of Health guidance (LAC(93)10), providing examples of 'substantial handicap' refers to handicap in terms of function, not of condition or of age (see 10.1.1.1). And frailty would often be associated with an 'illness' such as arthritis (so as to bring it within the overall s.29 definition which refers to illness, injury or congenital deformity).

Alternatively, some local authorities may take 'permanent' to mean, strictly, for the rest of a person's life. Others, more generously, tend to draw on definition of the words 'long term' in the Disability Discrimination Act 1995, and state that a disability likely to last longer than 12 months constitutes a 'permanent' disability. The interpretation of 'substantial and permanent handicap' appears never to have arisen directly in a legal case.

### 10.1.3.1 Other definitions of disability

In addition to the term 'substantial and permanent handicap' under s.29 of the 1948 Act, related terms also apply under other legislation:

- The term 'handicapped' is one of the conditions governing community care services arranged under schedule 8 of the NHS Act 1977. There is a question as to whether this term (a condition for receipt of home help services or laundry facilities) is to be construed as including the whole class of so-called handicap (i.e. both mild and substantial) or only the mild. The correct construction is probably the former, inclusive of both mild and substantial disability.
- 'Disability' is one of the qualifying conditions for provision of residential or nursing home care under s.21 of the National Assistance Act 1948, where, however, it is not defined.
- The term 'illness' is used in s.3 of the NHS Act 1977 in respect of health care and in schedule 8 in respect of certain community care services; as defined in s.128 of the 1977 Act, it includes 'disability' requiring medical or dental treatment.
- The definition applied by the 1948 Act should be distinguished from the definition in the Disability Discrimination Act 1995, although there are some similarities. The 1995 Act definition does not supplant the s.29 definition in the 1948 Act. Arguably though, to the extent that a local authority is using its discretion to interpret the s.29 definition, it could, or perhaps should, seek to utilise the 1995 Act definition.

### 10.1.4 PAYMENTS AND PROHIBITIONS

There are two express prohibitions contained in s.29 of the 1948 Act.

### 10.1.4.1 Prohibition on payments

The payment of money to disabled people is prohibited (except in relation to workshops and provision of suitable work). However, the effect of this prohibition is now reduced in the light of the existence of direct payments made under the Health and Social Care Act 2001 (see 12.1); and also the possibility of making 'third party' payments under s.30 of the National Assistance Act 1948 (see 12.1.10).

### 10.1.4.2 Anti-duplication provisions

Also prohibited is the provision under s.29 of any accommodation or services required to be provided under the NHS Act 1977. This latter provision has caused some confusion. For example, in one case it was argued that because home help can be provided by a local authority under schedule 8 of the NHS Act 1977, it could therefore not be provided under the Chronically Sick and Disabled Persons Act 1970 (in the guise of practical assistance in the home). This would be because the 1970 Act was in effect an extension of s.29 of the 1948 Act. The judge rejected this, stating that what authorised services under s.2 of the 1970 Act was precisely s.2 of the 1970 Act – and not s.29 of the 1948 Act. This decision may appear straightforward and pragmatic, but does not sit easily with the Court of Appeal's decision, in another context, that s.2 of the 1970 Act is not freestanding and is firmly hitched to s.29 (*R v Powys CC, ex p Hambidge*).

Two further uncertainties arise. The first concerns whether the prohibition refers (a) only to a service which a *local authority* has a duty to provide under the 1977 Act (i.e. under schedule 8 of that Act); or (b) to a service which either a *local authority or the NHS* has a duty to provide under the 1977 Act. The second interpretation is clearly very much wider than the first, and makes better sense in terms of drawing a line of demarcation between social care and health care.

Second, the term 'required to be provided' is suggestive of a duty. However, as far as NHS provision goes under the NHS Act 1977 as a whole, not many services are listed in the Act (medical, nursing, ambulance and services in relation to illness are explicitly referred to in s.3 of the Act). So it becomes difficult to discern what exactly is 'required' to be provided by the NHS under the 1977 Act.

It is clear that social services legislation is not capable of being used to provide registered nursing care, because this is legally prohibited. However, registered nursing care is limited to those services provided by a registered nurse and involving the provision, planning, supervision, or delegation of care – so long as the nature of the services and the circumstances of their provision is such that they need to be provided by a registered nurse (Health and Social Care Act 2001, s.49).

Other than registered nursing care in care homes, one way of pinpointing NHS, as opposed to social services, responsibilities might be to scrutinise relevant Department of Health guidance and identify the services listed in it. For instance, guidance on NHS continuing health care (see 16.7.3) and on NHS services in nursing homes (see 16.9.1), in residential homes (see 16.9.2) and in people's own homes (see 16.9.3) lists various services (HSC 2001/15).

Particularly where a type of service is not listed in such guidance, or where it is a service that could clearly be regarded either as social care or health care (e.g. bathing services or occupational therapy services), another approach might appear to be consideration not of the service itself but of the purpose for which it is needed. This approach was taken in the following case, albeit in a different context, in which the court solved a similar problem and prohibition by stating that incontinence pads were not necessarily 'medical' items:

**Incontinence pads as non-medical items.** The Social Fund (a social security agency) was prohibited, legally, from providing assistance with medical items. On the basis that incontinence pads were medical items provided by the NHS, a Social Fund officer had denied a 26-week supply of pads to a woman who was incontinent, arthritic and had asthma. The relevant health authority did provide free incontinence pads in principle, but in practice its criteria were so stringent – regular double incontinence or terminal illness – that the woman did not qualify. Hence her application to the Fund.

The judge found that the decision of the Social Fund officer, that the pads were medical items and thus excluded by the Social Fund rules, was wrong. She had asked whether the pads were needed for a medical problem and were thus necessarily a medical item. However, it was 'quite clear that a handkerchief might not be needed, but for a severe attack of a runny nose in a heavy cold. It is quite clear that a bowl might not be needed unless there was a medical problem of a severe bout of vomiting but nobody would think of those articles, the handkerchief or the bowl, as medical items' (R v Social Fund Inspector, ex p Connick).

On the same basis, the Social Fund sometimes helps on occasion with powered wheelchairs (normally the statutory responsibility of the NHS). Whatever the answer, it is clear that local authorities argue all the more about divisions of responsibility when they are short of resources; and then tend to take decisions improperly and in a hurry – as the local ombudsman found:

**Provision of psychotherapy services.** The local authority had, from 1987, been making up the difference between the charges of a residential therapeutic community home and the DHSS (as it was then) funding available for a woman with mental health needs. When the placement came to an end, the authority agreed to fund psychotherapy sessions for the woman. The dispute arose around the authority's subsequent attempt to stop such funding, and its rather belated attempt to suggest that such provision was health, rather than social, care – and so was properly an NHS responsibility.

The local ombudsman concluded that whatever view the authority took in hindsight, it had obligations to the woman. Although it was entitled to reduce or stop the funding, it had to take into account the woman's needs as well, not focus solely on an overspent budget, and to make the 'promised assessment' of the benefit and value of the therapy. Had a proper review been carried out, the authority might have decided to stop the payments earlier than it did. However, the failure to carry out proper review and assessment meant that the authority made a sudden decision to withdraw without giving adequate notice.

Once the director of social services had decided that these were health rather than social care needs, no approach was made to the health authority about alternative sources of funding.

All of this was maladministration; the ombudsman recommended that the council pay the woman (a) the amount she owed to the psychotherapist for the sessions in 1993 that had not yet been paid for; (b) travel expenses; (c) £1250 for distress caused and for the time and trouble in pursuing the complaint with both ombudsman and council (*Brent LBC 1994*).

Also suggestive of fluid statutory boundaries was the local ombudsman's doubt in one investigation, about whether the local authority social services department simply had no responsibility for the provision of powered wheelchairs under s.2 of the Chronically Sick and Disabled Persons Act 1970 (*North Yorkshire CC 1993*).

## 10.1.5 EMPLOYMENT OF AGENTS

For the purpose of arrangements for welfare services under s.29 of the 1948 Act, local authorities are empowered to employ, as agents, voluntary organisations or any other person carrying on, professionally or by way of trade or business, activities that consist of or include the provision of such services. This is so long as the organisation or person in question appears to the local authority to be capable of providing the relevant services (National Assistance Act 1948, s.30).

## 10.2 CHRONICALLY SICK AND DISABLED PERSONS ACT 1970, S.2: NON-RESIDENTIAL SERVICES FOR DISABLED PEOPLE

Under the Chronically Sick and Disabled Persons Act 1970 (CSDPA), a local authority has a duty, if certain conditions are met, to arrange non-residential services for disabled people. The conditions are:

- that the local authority has functions under s.29 of the 1948 Act (i.e. that the person is disabled)
- that the person is an ordinary resident in the authority's area
- that the person has a need
- that it is necessary, in order to meet that need, for the local authority to arrange services.

The section also states that, in carrying out its functions under s.2, a local authority must act under the general guidance of the Secretary of State issued under s.7(1) of the Local Authority Social Services Act 1970. (For the ordinary residence condition, see 14.2.3.) The services are listed as follows:

- **practical assistance**: provision of practical assistance for the person in his or her home
- **recreation**: provision for the person of, or assistance to that person in obtaining, wireless, television, library or similar recreational facilities
- **recreation/education**: provision for the person of lectures, games, outings or other recreational facilities outside his home or assistance to that person in taking advantage of educational facilities available to him or her
- **travel**: provision for the person of facilities for, or assistance in, travelling to and from his home for the purpose of participating in any services provided under arrangements made by the authority under the said section 29 or, with the approval of the authority, in any services provided otherwise than as aforesaid which are similar to services which could be provided under such arrangements

- **adaptations and additional facilities**: provision of assistance for the person in arranging for the carrying out of any works of adaptation in his or her home or the provision of any additional facilities designed to secure his greater safety, comfort or convenience
- **holidays**: facilitating the taking of holidays by the person, whether at holiday homes or otherwise and whether provided under arrangements made by the authority or otherwise
- **meals**: provision of meals for that person whether in his home or elsewhere
- **telephone**: provision for that person of, or assistance to that person in obtaining, a telephone and any special equipment necessary to enable him to use a telephone.

## 10.2.1 STRONG DUTY UNDER THE CSDPA

The duty to arrange these services, unlike the duty in s.29 of the National Assistance Act 1948, has been held judicially to be a strong one, amenable to enforcement by an individual service user. The courts have held under s.2 of the CSDPA 1970 that once a person is deemed to have an eligible need (that is, to have been assessed above the authority's threshold of eligibility: see 6.9), then performance of the duty to meet that need will not be excused by a lack of resources (R v Gloucestershire CC, ex p Barry).

The reason for this strength of duty lies in the fact that s.2 of the 1970 Act refers to 'any person' and states that, once the local authority is satisfied that it is necessary to meet the need of that person, it must do so by providing any or all of the services listed.

## 10.2.2 NEED, NECESSITY AND THE LOCAL AUTHORITY'S RESOURCES

A number of matters concerning the assessment of a person's needs have already been covered in Chapter 6. In the Gloucestershire case, one of the law lords held that a local authority could set a threshold of eligibility as to what it meant by need, in relation to the resources it had available. Another law lord took a different view, emphasising the relevance of resources to setting criteria in respect of the necessity to meet need (but not in respect of need iself). This second approach is more in line with central government guidance on 'fair access to care' (LAC(2002)13: see 6.11); although guidance issued in 1970 in association with the CSDPA 1970 stated that criteria of need were matters for authorities to determine in the light of resources (DHSS 12/70, para 7).

The courts have subsequently added that they would be very slow in interfering with the level of strictness of an authority's threshold of eligibility under s.2 of the 1970 Act. This was because once the reasonableness of an authority's actions depends on a decision about the allocation of scarce resources, it becomes extremely difficult for the courts to review that decision by second-guessing the local authority about how it spends those resources (R v East Sussex CC, ex p Tandy). Nevertheless, the effect of this judgment, delivered before the implementation of the Human Rights Act 1998, would be tempered by human rights considerations. For instance, if the severity of the criteria were such as to breach a person's article 3 rights in respect of inhuman or degrading treatment, then the courts might feel obliged to interfere after all.

### 10.2.3 NECESSITY: RELEVANCE OF A PERSON'S OWN RESOURCES
This is discussed above (see 6.9.3).

### 10.2.4 NECESSITY: AVAILABILITY FROM OTHER SOURCES
If a person's needs could readily be met from other sources, then there would clearly not be a necessity for the local authority to meet the need. For instance, a need for home adaptations might be met by the local housing authority under the Housing Grants, Construction and Regeneration Act 1996, by means of a disabled facilities grant.

### 10.2.5 CSDPA 1970: SERVICES
The range of services listed in s.2 of the CSDPA 1970 is extensive.

#### 10.2.5.1 Practical assistance in the home
Practical assistance in the home is a broad term that could range from a small amount of home help each week, to full-scale personal assistance 24 hours a day. The major community care case of *R v Gloucestershire CC, ex p Barry*, already referred to, concerned the provision and withdrawal of such practical assistance. The need for local authorities to avoid acting unlawfully, for instance by ruling out as a matter of policy cleaning or shopping services, has been considered by the local ombudsman (see 6.11.1). In the case of *R(Heffernan) v Sheffield CC*, the court held that the local authority was obliged to provide such services.

#### 10.2.5.2 Wireless, television, library or similar recreational facilities
In 1971, an apparent example of a local authority deciding that it was not necessary to provide a radio was given in Parliament: a severely disabled man, using an environmental control system with an interface for a radio, wished to take an educational degree and required a radio. The local authority refused because he already had one; so he had, but he could not operate it because he was completely paralysed (*Lewis Carter-Jones: House of Commons Debates*, 21/5/1971, col.1667). The Department of Health has issued no guidance on the provision of radio or television.

**Note.** In Northern Ireland, following the passing of the Chronically Sick and Disabled Persons (Northern Ireland) Act 1978, the Department of Health and Social Services (DHSS) gave guidance on the provision of televisions by health and social services boards (HSSBs). The person had to be housebound and living alone, or confined to a room that meant that a television was needed in that particular room. As well as providing the sets, the licence fees of eligible applicants could also be paid (HSS(PH) 5/79). The Northern Ireland DHSS also issued guidance stating that HSSBs should provide batteries free of charge for people who had radio sets provided by the British Wireless Fund for the Blind (HSS(OS5A) 4/76).

### 10.2.5.3 Lectures, games, outings or similar recreational facilities

When a local authority ruled out, as a matter of policy, providing for a person's social, recreational and leisure needs, stating that he could arrange these for himself by approaching a local resource centre, the court found that it had acted unlawfully.

**Not providing for social, recreational and leisure activities as a matter of policy.** Following a reassessment, a man with multiple sclerosis received a letter from the local authority. It outlined the care plan, which would only cater for the man's personal needs; the letter explained that in relation to the man's social, recreational and leisure needs, he could approach a local resource centre himself. The authority was unable to meet these needs because it was not in a position 'to meet or address all the demands made [and so was] forced to make decisions upon prioritising need and working within existing resources'.

The judge held that it was 'impermissible to carry out the reassessment by putting social, recreation and leisure needs on one side and saying, "I would be happy to provide you with details of the Winkfield Road Resource Centre." The care package that should have been assessed...had to be a multi-faceted package. This Applicant has been able to overcome or at least live with some of the most awful characteristics of his illness by the social intercourse achieved in recreational facilities such as the playing of bridge, swimming, etc. A reassessed care package should have comprehended such matters and should not have discriminated in the manner that it did' (R v Haringey LBC, ex p Norton).

In another court case, a local authority similarly failed to meet a person's recreational needs:

**Failure to meet recreational needs of person.** The case concerned a 25-year-old man who suffered from Seckels syndrome and who was blind, microcephalic, virtually immobile, doubly incontinent and mostly unable to communicate. He also suffered from severe deformities of the chest and spine, a hiatus hernia and a permanent digestive disorder. His weight and size were those of a small child, his dependency that of a baby. The dispute concerned the provision for his social, recreational and educational needs; having left a special needs school, the applicant had requirements which the local authority could not meet because, it pleaded, it was short of resources.

The judge found that the local authority had failed to provide for the person's recreational needs under s.2 of the Chronically Sick and Disabled Persons Act. The duty under the Act was 'owed to the applicant personally' to provide 'recreational facilities outside the home to an extent which Islington accepts is greater than the care plan provides for. But the authority has, it appears, simply taken the existing unavailability of further facilities as an insuperable obstacle to any further attempt to make provision. The lack of a day centre has been treated, however reluctantly, as a complete answer to the question of provision' (R v Islington LBC, ex p Rixon).

The local ombudsman, too, has found local authorities improperly excluding consideration of people's recreational needs on reassessments, in the attempt to reduce packages of care (Southwark LBC 2001).

### 10.2.5.4 Taking advantage of educational facilities

Taking advantage of educational facilities, under s.2 of the CSDPA 1970, has been held by the courts not to include actually making arrangements for the provision of education, but merely to take advantage of what was already potentially available (R v Further Education Funding Council, ex p Parkinson). This very point was made in guidance issued in 1970 in connection with the CSDPA (DHSS 12/70, para 7). Likewise, in the *Parkinson* case, the court also stated that the power under s.29 of the National Assistance Act 1948 to give instruction to disabled people in their own homes (see 10.1.2) could not be read into the duty regarding educational facilities in s.2(1)(b) of the 1970 Act.

Department of Health guidance has stated that such assistance could cover, for instance, personal care that might be required to assist a person study. This could be in addition to any educational disabled student allowance that a person might already be receiving (LAC(93)12, paras 9–10). The following local ombudsman investigation illustrates the potential difficulty that sometimes afflicts the meeting of a person's education-related needs – in this case a communication aid:

**Loss of college placement.** A young person with moderate learning difficulties, poor fine and gross coordination and some mobility problems had the use of a communication aid at school from the age of 6 onward. He subsequently had a 'light-writer', with a lightweight keyboard, a voice synthesiser and two-sided visual display. The cost of such an item was £2000 plus VAT. On leaving school, he was accepted on a course at a post-16 further education college. The education authority allowed him to keep the communication aid for a few months, but then stated that it must be returned. Funding was sought all to no avail from the general practitioner, the health authority and the Further Education Funding Council (since superseded by the Learning and Skills Council). The local authority stated that its duty extended only to giving advice on sources of funding, and that the CSDPA 1970 was never intended to be used for such aids.

However, without the aid, the young person would lose his place on the college course; he felt he had 'lost his voice'. Eventually, the local authority agreed to loan a communication aid under the Children Act 1989. The ombudsman concluded that communication aids fell within a 'grey area', and that central and local government needed to produce a clear, unambiguous statement of responsibilities (*Kingston upon Hull C 2000*).

In the above case, the local ombudsman appears to have accepted that the local authority social services had no potential duty to provide such equipment. Nevertheless, this conclusion is questionable, given the reference in s.2 to assistance with education, the absolute duty to meet eligible need – and more recently the reference in Department of Health guidance on eligibility criteria to 'vital involvement in education' (LAC(2002)13: see 6.11). If the assistance under s.2 might have to cover personal assistance (as stated in guidance: LAC(93)12, paras 9–10), why not equipment?

### 10.2.5.5 Assistance in arranging for the carrying out of any works of adaptation

The duty to make arrangements in relation to home adaptations is qualified by a lengthy chain of wording: '…making arrangements for the provision of assistance for that person in arranging the carrying out of adaptations'. This suggests to some local authorities that direct provision is not contemplated.

The correct view is probably that in some circumstances an arm's-length approach might legitimately be taken, but if the need cannot be met in any other way then the local authority is probably committed to some form of direct arrangement (always assuming that the applicant has surmounted both the need and necessity tests: see above). This view would also be consonant with the judicial approach taken to the word 'facilitate' in the context of holidays (see immediately below). For a full discussion, see 15.6.2.

### 10.2.5.6 Additional facilities for greater safety, comfort or convenience

Local authorities might be tempted to focus only on safety and regard comfort and convenience as surplus. However, they should beware not to cut words out of the legislation.

**Safety, comfort or convenience**. In one case, the local ombudsman referred not only to the potential danger, but also to the 'extreme discomfort' and the 'inconvenient' accommodation, in which a disabled woman had to live – whilst waiting four years and eight months for the simple aids that eventually made such a difference to her life (*Hackney LBC 1992a*).

On the other hand, an authority might maintain that its priorities or criteria conform, albeit strictly, to the statutory wording by referring to safety in terms of 'personal danger' and to convenience as the absence of 'serious inconvenience' (*Sheffield CC 1995*).

### 10.2.5.7 Facilitating the taking of holidays

The provision of holidays has been examined in several court and local ombudsman cases:

**Privately arranged holidays**. The local authority had – in order to save money – adopted a blanket policy of only providing assistance with holidays which it had arranged itself. The judge found this blanket policy to be 'quite wrong', since the legislation expressly contemplated that authorities might assist with holidays 'otherwise arranged'. The local authority's policy had prevented it asking the question of whether the person's needs were such that they required to be met through a privately arranged holiday (*R v Ealing LBC, ex p Leaman*).

**Not assisting fully with a holiday**. The local authority argued in court that its role under s.2 of the CSDPA 1970 was not to relieve poverty, and that it would only assist with the extra costs (such as special accommodation or transport expenses) of a disabled person's holiday arising because of disability – in other words, not with the ordinary travel and hotel expenses which everybody has to pay when they go on holiday. It also argued that the term 'facilitate' precluded it from paying for the full cost. The judge found that the policy fettered the local authority's discretion and was not consistent with the wording of the legislation (*R v North Yorkshire CC, ex p Hargreaves (no.2)*).

**Inadequate arrangements for holiday**. A complaint was made to the local ombudsman; a local authority had been assisting an older woman with learning disabilities to take a holiday. She arrived at the hotel, but such serious problems arose in relation to her behaviour that the hotel owners drove her home again that same evening (a distance of 115 miles). The council complained to the local tourist information centre and the English Tourist Board, and wanted the money for the holiday refunded by the hotel both to itself and to the woman. However, the hotel owners consulted a solicitor and themselves demanded an apology and compensation.

The local ombudsman concluded – from the 'total absence' of records about how the hotel was identified and about the taking up of references – that the 'proper degree of care' in arranging the holiday had not been exercised. The hotel owners had not been given the 'full and accurate information' about the needs of the woman to which they had been entitled. This was all maladministration, as was the precipitate complaint to the tourist organisations before the hotel owners had had the opportunity to put their case (*Buckinghamshire CC 1998*).

### 10.2.5.8 Telephones and related equipment

The Department of Health has issued no guidance on the provision of telephones and related equipment. Their provision has sometimes been subject to inappropriate application of policies and criteria, as in the following local ombudsman case:

**Minicom telephone equipment.** A local authority was restricting provision of minicoms (telephone equipment for deaf or hearing impaired people) to people who already had a telephone; the local ombudsman agreed with the British Deaf Association that this criterion was a legally irrelevant consideration (*Wakefield MDC 1992*).

**Telephone line rental payments.** The local authority decided in 1994 to pay telephone rental charges for the complainant. In 1996, it decided not to pay them for new applicants. In 1999, as part of the 'budget making process', it ceased to pay the charges even for the existing 1000 or so recipients. Although minuted, no written report was presented to the social services committee, which took the decision. The council argued that it had received legal advice that such payments were unlawful; however, it refused to provide the ombudsman with a copy of the advice and to identify who gave the advice. It referred to s.29(6) of the National Assistance Act 1948, which prohibits cash payments. Subsequent legal advice from leading counsel stated that the original advice was wrong.

 The ombudsman declined to express a view on the correctness of either set of legal advice. However, he found maladministration of a fairly serious nature because (a) the decision to withdraw the payments implied that many other councils, and Haringey up to that time, had been acting unlawfully; (b) therefore a clear written report backed up by considered opinion was required; (c) in reality the decision seemed to have been taken without any proper consideration by the committee (*Haringey LBC 2000*).

**Note.** In 1971, the Association of County Councils (ACC) and Association of Metropolitan Authorities (AMA) – now both part of the Local Government Association (LGA) – issued a joint Circular (note: not a government Circular). In summary, people would qualify if, in the view of an authority, they lived alone, or were frequently alone – or lived with a person who was unable, or could not be relied on, to deal with an emergency or maintain necessary outside contacts. In addition to this, the person either (a) would have a need to get in touch with a doctor, other health worker or helper and would be in danger or at risk without a telephone; or (b) be unable to leave the dwelling in normal weather without assistance or have seriously restricted mobility – and need a telephone to avoid isolation. Also, there should be no friend or neighbours willing and able to help (ACC, AMA 1971). Guidance on telephones was issued in Scotland and Northern Ireland and contained similar criteria to the AMA/ACC guidance (SW7/1972; HSS(OS5A)5/78).

## 10.2.6 CSDPA 1970, S.2 AS AN EXTENSION OF S.29 OF NATIONAL ASSISTANCE ACT 1948

The reference in s.2 of the Act to the exercising of functions under s.29 of the National Assistance Act 1948 has given rise to dispute in the law courts. This is not just a theoretical dispute, since it has focused on, for instance, (a) whether CSDPA services are legally 'community care services' at all under s.46 of the NHS and Community Care Act 1990; (b) whether local authorities are empowered to charge for CSDPA services under s.17 of the Health and Services and Social Security Adjudications Act 1983. The problem is that s.2 of the CSDPA 1970 is listed in neither the 1990 nor the 1983 Act at the relevant place; and if s.2 were to be regarded as 'freestanding' and not embraced by s.29 of the National Assistance Act 1948, then services under s.2 could be neither community care services nor capable of being charged for.

In fact, the Court of Appeal ruled in 1998 that s.2 of the CSDPA 1970 is not freestanding (*R v Powys CC, ex p Hambidge* about charges). This confirmed the High Court ruling in the same case, another Court of Appeal judgment of nearly 20 years before (*Wyatt v Hillingdon LBC*), and the House of Lords finding that s.2 of the 1970 Act was clearly embodied in the whole of the community care regime (*R v Gloucestershire CC, ex p Barry*).

## 10.2.7 MAKING ARRANGEMENTS FOR SERVICES

The term 'make arrangements' does not entail that the authority make direct provision under s.2, since the National Assistance Act 1948, s.30 authorises the employment by local authorities of agents to deliver services. When a local authority chooses neither to make direct provision nor to make a direct payment nor to employ another as agent to do so – but to give advice instead – it would probably be doing so under s.1 of the CSDPA 1970 (provision of information) or under s.29 of the National Assistance Act 1948 (duty to provide advice and support). This is because the person would be going on to make his or her own arrangements for services, or have them made by somebody else other than the local authority.

## 10.2.8 INFORMATION FOR INDIVIDUAL DISABLED PEOPLE

Local authorities have a specific duty under s.1 of the CSDPA 1970 to inform existing service users about other services which the authority thinks relevant and which it knows about. This is a strong duty that a local authority has towards individual people, not just a general duty. Failure to provide this information might give clear grounds for challenge, although even this duty is qualified since it depends on the authority's opinion about other relevant services and on its having particulars of those other services.

Nevertheless, the local ombudsman does sometimes find maladministration in relation to the giving of information by local authorities in specific instances – for example, poor advice about social security benefits, or unclear information about disabled facilities grants.

**Provision of information.** The local ombudsman has on occasion considered provision of information under s.1 of the CSDPA 1970, finding maladministration when inaccurate advice is given, for example about entitlement to state benefits (*East Sussex CC 1995a*), or when a social services authority fails to discuss the possibility of home adaptations available through a housing authority with a disabled person (*Leicester CC 1992b*). However, in another case, there was no maladministration in respect of information provision. First the complainant had been given a range of leaflets in response to his request for information. Then, following a complaint the man had made, a council officer visited him to go through the relevant legislation and to leave copies with him (*North Yorkshire CC 1993*).

## 10.3 HEALTH SERVICES AND PUBLIC HEALTH ACT 1968, S.45: NON-RESIDENTIAL SERVICES FOR OLDER PEOPLE

Under s.45 of the Health Services and Public Health Act 1968, local authorities may (if approved by the Secretary of State) and must (if directed by the Secretary of State) make arrangements for promoting the welfare of old people. The Secretary of State has only ever approved the making of arrangements by local authorities for the following services (DHSS 19/71: approvals):

- **meals and recreation**: to provide meals and recreation in the home and elsewhere
- **information**: to inform the elderly of services available to them and to identify elderly people in need of services
- **travel**: to provide facilities or assistance in travelling to and from the home for the purpose of participating in services provided by the authority or similar services
- **finding accommodation**: to assist in finding suitable households for boarding elderly persons
- **visiting and advice**: to provide visiting and advisory services and social work support
- **practical assistance, adaptations, additional facilities**: to provide practical assistance in the home including assistance in the carrying out of works of adaptation or the provision of any additional facilities designed to secure greater safety, comfort or convenience
- **wardens**: to contribute to the cost of employing a warden on welfare functions in warden assisted housing schemes and to provide warden services for occupiers of private housing.

Department of Health guidance states that the purpose of s.45 is to enable authorities to make other approved arrangements for services to the elderly who are not substantially and permanently handicapped. This would promote the welfare of the elderly generally and so far as possible prevent or postpone personal or social deterioration or breakdown (DHSS 19/71, para 2). It refers to home help, including laundry services and other aids to independent living, social visiting organised and coordinated by the local authority but largely undertaken by voluntary workers and meals-on-wheels (para 10).

### 10.3.1 SERVICES FOR OLDER PEOPLE: POWER ONLY

Section 45 of the 1968 Act gives central government the ability to issue directions and thereby turn these services into a duty, or to issue approvals that would confer a power rather than duty. Despite the potential value of providing such services for older people, no government in over 30 years has had the financial courage to issue directions and thereby create a duty. Instead the approvals issued in 1971 make the provision of these services a mere power.

It is possible that if, in developing its community care policies and services, a local authority could be shown not even to have taken account of the approvals and guidance in respect of s.45, then a case might be arguable in the law courts. Local authorities should at least have regard to guidance (see 4.1.6); and even in respect of powers, should beware of fettering their discretion (*British Oxygen v Board of Trade*).

Exercise of the powers is not restricted to those elderly people ordinarily resident in the area of a local authority; and the powers are capable of being used creatively. Indeed, to the extent that, for example, local authorities extend adult protection activity to vulnerable older people (who may not be disabled), s.45 would arguably constitute the legal underpinning.

### 10.3.2 EMPLOYMENT OF AGENTS

For the purpose of arrangements for welfare services under s.45 of the 1968 Act, local authorities are empowered to employ, as agents, voluntary organisations or any other person carrying on, professionally or by way of trade or business, activities that consist of or include the provision of services for old people. This is so long as the organisation or person in question appears capable of providing the service to which the arrangements apply (s.45).

### 10.3.3 PROHIBITIONS

There is an anti-duplication provision in s.45 of the 1968 Act that precludes the making available of any accommodation or services required to be provided under the NHS Act 1977 (see 10.1.4.2) for discussion of such a provision. Likewise there is a prohibition on the making of cash payments: but this prohibition is tempered by the provisions for making direct payments under the Health and Social Care Act 2001 (see 12.1).

A further prohibition is the making of arrangements for people subject to s.115 of the Immigration and Asylum Act 1999 (i.e. people subject to immigration control excluded from welfare benefits), if their need arises through destitution, or the physical effects (actual or anticipated) of destitution (s.45).

## 10.4 NHS ACT 1977, S.21 AND SCHEDULE 8: NON-RESIDENTIAL SERVICES

Local authorities may (if the Secretary of State approves) or must (if the Secretary of State directs) make arrangements for various non-residential services (NHS Act 1977, schedule 8). These services relate to expectant and nursing mothers; and to the prevention of illness, the care of people who are suffering from illness and the aftercare of people who have been so suffering (schedule 8). In addition there is a general duty to provide home help services and a corresponding power to provide laundry facilities.

One prohibition is the making of arrangements for people subject to s.115 of the Immigration and Asylum Act 1999 (i.e. people subject to immigration control excluded from welfare benefits), if their need arises through destitution, or the physical effects (actual or anticipated) of destitution (schedule 8).

A further proviso is that such provision is subject to s.3 of the NHS Act 1977, under which the NHS has functions in relation to such services; in other words, this would appear to be an anti-duplication provision, such that schedule 8 social care provision should not duplicate health care provision by the NHS under s.3. There is no ordinary residence condition stipulated.

Illness is defined as including 'mental disorder within the meaning of the Mental Health Act 1983 and any injury or disability requiring medical or dental treatment or nursing' (NHS Act 1977, s.128).

## 10.4.1 NON-RESIDENTIAL SERVICES FOR ILLNESS AND MENTAL DISORDER

A major part of schedule 8 deals with non-residential services for the prevention of illness, the care of people who are ill, the aftercare of people who have been ill – including specific duties towards people with a mental disorder. Both directions and approvals have been made in respect of these services; the directions relate only to illness in the form of mental disorder; the approvals refer simply to illness and so are not confined to mental disorder.

### 10.4.1.1 Directions: illness, mental disorder

By means of directions issued under schedule 8, there is a general duty to arrange various non-residential services for people with a mental disorder (LAC(93)10, appendix 3). The duty is to arrange for:

- the provision of centres (including training centres and day centres) for the training or occupation of such people
- the appointment of sufficient approved social workers
- the exercise of their functions towards people received into guardianship under Part 2 or 3 of the Mental Health Act 1983
- the provision of social work and related services to help in the identification, diagnosis, assessment and social treatment of mental disorder and provide social work support and other domiciliary and care services to people living in their homes or elsewhere.

However, because these services appear to be covered only by a general, target, rather than a specific, duty (see 4.1), it is likely that legally enforcing provision for any one individual would be difficult.

### 10.4.1.2 Approvals: illness generally

In addition, by means of approvals issued under schedule 8, there is a power to arrange a further range of services in respect of illness. The services comprise arrangements for the provision of:

- centres or other facilities for training or keeping people suitably occupied, to equip and maintain such centres, and for the provision for those people of ancillary or supplemental services

- meals at centres and at other facilities, and meals-on-wheels for housebound people (not already provided for under s.45 of the Health Services and Public Health Act 1968, or schedule 9 of the Health and Social Security Adjudications Act 1983)
- the remuneration of people engaged in suitable work at centres or at other facilities
- social services (including advice and support) in order to prevent the impairment of physical or mental health of adults in families where such impairment is likely, or to prevent the break-up of such families, or for assisting in their rehabilitation
- night sitter services
- recuperative holidays
- facilities for social and recreational activities
- services specifically for alcoholic or drug-dependent people.

### 10.4.2 HOME HELP AND LAUNDRY FACILITIES

Local authorities have a general duty to arrange, on a scale adequate for their area, home help – and a power to provide or arrange laundry facilities – for households where it is required because there is somebody who is ill, lying in, an expectant mother, or aged or handicapped as a result of having suffered from illness or congenital deformity. The power to arrange the laundry facilities is dependent on the household either receiving, or being eligible to receive, the home help (NHS Act 1977, schedule 8).

Assistance is for the household, suggesting that it could be made for other members of the household, not just the disabled, aged or ill person. The duty is probably to be regarded as a general, target one and therefore difficult to enforce in individual cases (see 4.1).

### 10.4.3 SERVICES FOR EXPECTANT OR NURSING MOTHERS

Through approvals made under schedule 8 of the 1977 Act, local authorities have the power to make arrangements for the care of expectant and nursing mothers, other than for residential accommodation.

## 10.5 MENTAL HEALTH ACT 1983, S.117: AFTERCARE SERVICES

NHS primary care trusts or health authorities, and local social services authorities – in co-operation with voluntary organisations – have a duty to provide aftercare services, when certain categories of patient detained in hospital under the Mental Health Act 1983 are discharged from hospital. The duty also applies to those patients on leaving hospital, even if they had previously ceased to be detained, but had remained in hospital for a while as informal patients.

This duty persists until the primary care trust or health authority, and the local authority, are satisfied that such services are no longer required. However, they cannot be withdrawn if a person is under supervised aftercare: see below (Mental Health Act 1983, s.117).

## 10.5.1 APPLICABILITY OF AFTERCARE SERVICES

The people covered by s.117 are those who have been detained under the 1983 Act, under s.3 (treatment), s.37 (convicted offenders with hospital or guardianship orders), or s.47 and s.48 (prisoners – serving a sentence, on remand, civil prisoners, people detained under the Immigration Act 1971 – for whom a transfer direction has been made). Aftercare services under s.117 do not apply to informal mental health patients. However, they have been held to apply to a person granted leave of absence under s.17 of the 1983 Act – and to a person who has been transferred into guardianship (via s.19 of the 1983 Act), having originally been detained under s.3 (*R v Manchester CC, ex p Stennett*: High Court stage).

## 10.5.2 RESPONSIBLE AUTHORITIES FOR AFTERCARE SERVICES

The responsible primary care trust, health authority and local authority are those for the area in which the person is resident or for the area to which he or she is sent on discharge (s.117). This has been taken by the courts to mean that the responsible bodies are those where the person was resident at the time of detention. However, if there was no place of residence at the time of detention, then the responsibility would lie with those relevant bodies in the area to which he or she is discharged under s.117 (*R v Mental Health Review Tribunal, ex p Hall*: High Court stage).

## 10.5.3 AFTERCARE UNDER SUPERVISION

In certain circumstances aftercare under supervision orders may be made under s.25A–25J of the 1983 Act. The two key conditions are as follows. First, that there would be a substantial risk either of serious harm to the health or safety of the patient or to the safety of other persons or of the patient being seriously exploited, if s.117 aftercare services were not to be provided. Second, that being subject to aftercare under supervision is likely to help to secure that he or she receives those s.117 aftercare services (Mental Health Act 1983, s.25A–25J).

## 10.5.4 SETTING UP AFTERCARE SERVICES

The Mental Health Act Code of Practice (DH 1999: made under s.118 of the Mental Health Act 1983) states that in establishing a care plan for aftercare, a number of professionals should be involved in the discussion. These are the person's 'responsible medical officer', a hospital nurse involved in caring for the person, a social worker specialising in mental health work, the person's GP, a community psychiatric nurse, a voluntary organisation representative (where appropriate and available), the person (if he or she wishes) or a nominated relative or other representative.

The issues particularly to be considered should be the patient's own wishes and needs; those of relevant friends, relatives, supporters; agreement of any other health authority to be involved, involvement of other agencies, care plan, key worker, and identification of unmet need. The Code itself explains that it imposes no additional duties on statutory authorities. Instead it explains that it provides guidance, and although there is no legal duty of compliance, a failure to follow the Code could be relevant to legal proceedings (DH 1999, p.1).

### 10.5.4.1 Setting up services before discharge

Despite a previous finding in one case that the local authority and health authority were obliged to complete a multidisciplinary assessment before a mental health review tribunal hearing (*R v Mental Health Review Tribunal, ex p Hall*), the courts have subsequently held that this is not a legal requirement, although there would be nothing to stop them making plans before a tribunal sat if they wished (*R(W) v Doncaster MBC*).

## 10.5.5 RANGE OF AFTERCARE SERVICES

Services under s.117 are effectively undefined and so can be wide in scope covering both residential and non-residential services. The Mental Health Act Code of Practice lists the following non-exhaustively: daytime activities or employment, appropriate accommodation, outpatient treatment, counselling and personal support, assistance with welfare rights and managing finances (DH 1999, para 27.10). The courts have rejected the argument that s.117 itself contains no services and is merely a gateway to the services contained in other community care legislation (*R v Manchester CC, ex p Stennett*).

## 10.5.6 STRENGTH OF DUTY TO PROVIDE AFTERCARE SERVICES

In 1993, the courts interpreted s.117 of the Mental Health Act as placing a strong duty (towards individuals) on health authorities and local authorities – contrasting it with the less specific duty in relation to aftercare owed by the health authority under s.3 of the NHS Act 1977 (*R v Ealing DHA, ex p Fox*). By the same token, the duty placed by s.117 on local authority social services departments is likewise a stronger duty (towards individuals) than the general duty to provide aftercare for mentally disordered people under schedule 8 of the NHS Act 1977.

Even so, it should be noted that although the judge in this case emphasised the strength of the s.117 duty, he also seemed deliberately to exclude from the ambit of his judgment the situation where authorities plead lack of resources for non-performance of duty. The strength of the duty was subsequently referred to in a later case, when the courts stated that s.117 did not constitute an absolute duty, but merely a duty to exercise best endeavours (*R(IH) v Secretary of State*). In an earlier case, the courts had referred to 'reasonable endeavours' (*R(K) v Camden and Islington Health Authority*).

**Local authority failing to find hostel under s.117.** The patient suffered from schizophrenia and had a long history of mental illness. In 1994 he had stabbed at a woman with a knife. He was hospitalised under ss.37 and 41 of the Mental Health Act 1983. By 2000, he had improved dramatically. A mental health review tribunal recommended his discharge on condition that he received psychiatric treatment, supervision from a social worker and that he live at appropriate accommodation approved by both doctor and social worker. The local authority faced 'perfectly genuine difficulties'. These related to professional concerns about a proposed placement, lack of necessary staff at the placement, lack of support for the placement by the treating psychiatrist, other suitable placements not being identified. The man was therefore not discharged over a certain period. He argued that the local authority had breached s.117 of the 1983 Act, as well as breaching article 5 of the European Convention by committing the tort of false imprisonment.

The court rejected the claim, pointing out that the s.117 duty was to use best or reasonable endeavours only. It pointed out that there was neither a bottomless pit of funds nor an adequate supply of suitable accommodation and support in relation to difficult cases. Local authorities and health authorities had to do the best they could; the former faced particular difficulties in finding out-of-area placements (R(W) v Doncaster MBC).

However, it can be seen that the *Doncaster* case concerned the practical difficulty in arranging the aftercare services. In neither case was the NHS trust or local authority refusing to make suitable aftercare arrangements on the simple grounds of lack of resources in financial terms. It would therefore seem, the *Fox* case nothwithstanding, that simple lack of resources (i.e. unwillingness to pay as opposed to genuine non-availability of facilities) would not be a defence to not performing the s.117 duty. The Court of Appeal has also pointed out that s.117 imposes a duty to provide aftercare facilities, but that the nature and extent of those facilities would to a degree fall within the discretion of the health authority, which must have regard to other demands on its budget (*R(K) v Camden and Islington Health Authority*).

In summary, these cases would appear to bring the s.117 duty into line with the other strong community care duties – s.2 of the CSDPA 1970 and s.21 of the National Assistance Act 1948 (see 6.9 and 6.10). That is, finance alone would not be a defence for non-performance of the duty, but financial resources can lawfully be a factor as to how (but not whether) to provide aftercare services.

## 10.5.7 ENDING PROVISION OF AFTERCARE SERVICES

The legal requirement not to charge for s.117 services (see 10.5.8) means that there is sometimes an incentive for a local authority to discharge s.117, but nevertheless to continue to provide services through other legislation under which charges can be made. Nevertheless, it is clear from local government ombudsman investigations and judicial comments in a legal case that caution is required.

First, the decision to discharge s.117 is a joint one. It arguably cannot be made unilaterally. Therefore a local authority would be acting erroneously if it were to base its decision solely on what the NHS stated, since it must make its own reasoned decision as a social services authority. This was the reasoning of the local ombudsman:

**Social services decision making.** A local authority decided to discharge s.117 services in the case of a woman in a residential care home, even though she was to continue to live in a specialist care home for elderly, mentally infirm people. The council had argued that the decision was a medical one, and it had followed the NHS decision to withdraw. This was maladministration because the local authority had a responsibility to come to its own decision (*Clwyd CC 1997*).

Second, local authorities have in the past sometimes taken the view that s.117 could be discharged if the service user had 'stabilised' in the community and was unlikely to require readmission/detention to hospital. This would be a suspect ground, because clearly the fact that the aftercare services are meeting that need does not mean they are no longer required. Furthermore, the courts have stated that so long as a person's mental disorder persists, then so too must the s.117 services.

**Discharging s.117 provision of services.** The court explained in one case that, on leaving hospital (following s.3 detention under the Mental Health Act 1983), the local authority would owe a duty under s.117. It considered that there might be cases where accommodation would no longer be required for a person's mental health condition (under s.117), but still be needed for physical disabilities (under s.21 of the National Assistance Act 1948). In this situation the person could then be charged for services. However, the court stated that in the case of a person with dementia, it was difficult to see how such a situation could arise in practice (R v Manchester CC, ex p Stennett, High Court).

The local ombudsman, too, has come to a similar conclusion:

**Discharge of s.117, despite worsening dementia.** A local authority decided to discharge s.117 services in the case of a woman in a residential care home, even though she was to continue to live in a specialist care home for elderly, mentally infirm people. This would enable the local authority to charge her under the National Assistance Act 1948. Nevertheless, at the time of the discharge she was assessed; her dementia was getting worse, she was extremely paranoid and suffered from hallucinations. The discharge therefore was maladministration (Clwyd CC 1997).

The local ombudsmen have thus underlined that local authorities cannot casually recategorise services being provided under s.117 as suddenly coming under other community care legislation, with a view to imposing financial charges (which are barred under s.117). They have therefore criticised those local authorities that have attempted to discharge s.117 in retrospect, in order to justify charging, and have failed to consult the person and his or her carer in accordance with Department of Health guidance (HSC 2000/3).

**Retrospective discharge of s.117.** A woman was detained under s.3 of the Mental Health Act 1983; she was discharged to a care home under s.117 of the 1983 Act. The council charged her, from May 1995, for the next few years' care a sum of £60,000. Yet by March 1996, the local authority had received legal advice that such charging was likely to be unlawful; however, the policy was not changed for over two years. This was maladministration.

On reviewing matters in 1998, the council argued that since July 1996 the woman had been self-funding and had effectively been discharged from s.117 at that point. The ombudsman found no scope for retrospective judgements, since discharge had to be based on proper review at the time and (under the Mental Health Act Code of Practice: DH 1999, section 27) consultation with others who were involved with the person. This too was maladministration; her care costs should be reimbursed to her (Wiltshire CC 1999).

In another case, the local authority decided only after a person's death that she had in fact been previously discharged from s.117, and that thus part of her estate should be paid to meet the charges. Yet the ombudsman quoted Department of Health guidance (HSC 2000/3) that the patient and his or her carer should always be consulted. As the ombudsman pointed out, the woman (who was dead) could not be consulted about the retrospective decision. She had therefore been in receipt of s.117 aftercare to the day of her death (*Leicestershire CC 2001*).

Decisions to cease aftercare services are likely to become all the more problematic when staff are anyway uninformed about what s.117 entails. This is maladministration for the local ombudsman:

**Absence of guidance for staff on s.117.** A man with schizophrenia had been discharged from a hostel with mental health problems for smoking marijuana. A year later he fell to his death from a tower block. The parents complained about how the local authority had dealt with the discharge. The local ombudsman found maladministration, since staff were given no written procedural guidance about the requirements of s.117 of the Mental Health Act 1983 (*Hounslow LBC 1995*).

Lastly, some local authorities have in the past set a rigid time limit for discharging s.117 – for instance, after six or twelve months in all cases. As can be seen from the above points, such a policy would be legally indefensible.

## 10.5.8 CHARGING FOR AFTERCARE SERVICES

The courts have held that it is unlawful to make charges for services, residential or non-residential, provided under s.117 of the 1983 Act. They have rejected the argument that s.117 contains no services itself, and was instead merely a gateway duty to other community care legislation, under which services could be provided (and charged for).

However, it was also argued that this created an inequitable anomaly: namely that a mentally disordered person who had been sectioned under the Mental Health Act would receive free aftercare services; whereas an informal but compliant patient, with a similar disorder, would be charged for services on discharge from hospital. The courts rejected this argument, pointing out that s.117 arises from the use of compulsory powers under the 1983 Act. Thus, in some cases patients would not be voluntarily availing themselves of aftercare services; this would be a good policy reason for not charging them (*R v Manchester CC, ex p Stennett*).

However, during the judicial review proceedings, it became clear that many local authorities had been charging for such services over a long period of time. As a consequence of the courts' decision, they potentially owed substantial sums of money to relevant service users. For instance, in one local government ombudsman investigation, the ombudsman recommended that the local authority reimburse £60,000 to one person whom it had wrongly charged for s.117 aftercare (*Wiltshire CC 1999*). In another instance, the ombudsmen have reported that the amount owing to an individual service user was £294,000 (CLAE 2004, p.7).

The local ombudsmen were aware that local authorities were in some cases attempting to avoid making retrospective payments either by retrospectively discharging people from s.117, or employing restrictive cut-off dates for money owing. As a consequence, they issued their own guidance on how local authorities should go about things (CLAE 2003):

- Local authorities should in general not carry out retrospective assessments to remove aftercare services from an earlier date.
- Any such retrospective assessments that have taken place should be reviewed.
- Out-of-time complaints should not be rejected (for 12 months from July 2003).
- Where aftercare was improperly ended, financial restitution with interest was appropriate.
- No generally applicable date should be applied when repayments were being calculated.
- Local authorities should put in place mechanisms to identify those people who had been improperly charged.

**Note**. A draft Mental Health Bill published in September 2004 proposes to alter the rules concerning charging for aftercare services, by allowing charging in some circumstances after a period of six weeks, and in others straightaway (DH 2004k, cl.68).

CHAPTER 11

# Charging for non-residential services

**KEY POINTS**

Unlike the case of residential accommodation (see Chapter 9), local authorities do not have a duty to charge for non-residential services. Instead, they have only a power to do so (Health and Social Services and Social Security Adjudications Act 1983, s.17: HASSASSA). Although local authorities generally exercise powers (as opposed to duties) sparingly, the power to charge is perhaps the one power that is employed extensively.

For non-residential services, local authorities can charge if they wish (although they do not have to) but only (a) if the charge is a reasonable one; (b) to the extent that they are satisfied that it is 'reasonably practicable' for the individual person to pay it. In addition to the legislation, the Department of Health has issued guidance that effectively sets out elements of what it considers to be a reasonable charging system. Significant points in the guidance include not reducing people's weekly income to income support levels, not taking account of earnings, and – where a person's disability related benefits are being taken

244

into account as income – carrying out an assessment of that person's disability related expenditure. If people do not pay the charges for the services they have been assessed as needing, the guidance states that local authorities should not legally withdraw services but do have the power to pursue the ensuing debt.

The local government ombudsmen have investigated charging systems on a number of occasions, setting out what they consider a reasonable system to be, especially in terms of formulating, consulting on and providing information about the system, and how decisions can be challenged.

As the boundaries between health and social care blur, the redefining of certain services as 'social' rather than 'health' care can result in services such as bathing or respite care, previously provided free of charge by the NHS, now being charged for by local authorities. It makes it all the more important therefore that, despite central government's insistence on joint working and 'seamless' services, there is clarity as to which part of a care package is health care and which social care. Such clarity will avoid unlawful charging for those health care services that should be free.

In 2000, the Audit Commission issued a critical report about home care charges, identifying significant inconsistencies and also disadvantages suffered by those service users on the lowest incomes and with the highest costs related to their disability (Audit Commission 2000a). In response, the Department of Health's guidance was issued in 2001 with a view to achieving greater consistency. It was to be implemented partly by October 2002 and fully by April 2003.

In April 2004, an Age Concern England research report was published. It concluded that the guidance had resulted in greater consistency for poorer service users, but otherwise there remained large inconsistencies between authorities – in how they set their maximum charges, what they charge per hour and what they allow in terms of disability related expenses (Thompson and Mathew 2004). Thus, charging for non-residential services remains one of those significant uncertainties inherent in the community care system referred to in Chapter 3 (see 3.1).

**Note: Wales, Scotland and Northern Ireland.** The legislation covering charging for non-residential services is the same in Wales as in England. The National Assembly for Wales has issued similar guidance to that issued in England (NAFWC 28/02). However, the Welsh policy is in transition because the Assembly intends to introduce 'free personal care' into Wales, following the Scottish example (NAFWC 10/2004). However, the National Assembly for Wales has not passed the equivalent regulations to those in England (made under the Community Care (Delayed Discharges) Act 2003), that have made intermediate care, equipment and adaptations costing under £1000 free of charge.

In Scotland, the position is different, although the rules concerning the reasonableness and reasonable practicability of charges are the same as in England (Social Work (Scotland) Act 1968, s.87). However, the Scottish Executive has pursued a policy of free personal care (not just free registered nursing care) for older people (Community Care and Health Scotland Act 2002), and its charging guidance (CCD 5/2003) thus reads differently to that in England. In respect of non-residential services that can still be charged for (i.e. are not personal care for older people), older Scottish Office guidance (SWSG 1/97) has not yet been updated.

would then be disregarded from the calculation of a person's income available for paying charges). In doing so, it applied a 'family member' rule that meant that allowance would not be made for any payments made to family members – unless there were cultural issues (i.e. it would be unacceptable to have somebody other than a member of the family providing care), or other (so the council claimed, though did not state in its policy document) exceptional circumstances. This policy was on the basis that provision of care by a family member was generally by choice, except in a particular cultural situation where it might be due to necessity, because it would not be acceptable to have a non-family member undertaking the caring role. In which case an exception might be made in respect of making allowances for any payment made.

*Payment to daughter.* The claimant paid her daughter, an experienced nurse, £45.00 a week for a range of assistance (laundry, ironing, correspondence, finances, some housework, toe-nail cutting, outings) – over and above that which the council carers provided. Her daughter had reduced her working week as a nurse, in order to spend more time with her mother. To compensate her for loss of earnings, her mother paid her.

*Choice as opposed to necessity.* The court held that this distinction between choice and necessity in relation to paying family carers was not an irrational policy – and that, other than in cases of necessity, support offered by a family member could reasonably be expected to be provided without charge (indeed it was only the mother who insisted on making the payments). Furthermore there were other legitimate justifications for the policy: prevention of fraudulent claims, the impracticality of investigating claims of payments to family members, and the otherwise possible effect that family members would be increasingly tempted to charge for the caring they provided.

*Human rights.* The judge also rejected an argument that article 8.1 of the European Convention on Human Rights was breached in terms of interference with family life. This was because the policy did not prevent a person being cared for by a family member, but merely prevented any payment being treated as disability related expenditure. Furthermore, the local authority could anyway treat any case as exceptional and thus make an exception to the rule. In any case, even if family life were being interfered with under 8.1, it was an interference that could be justified under 8.2 in terms of prevention of crime or the economic well-being of the State.

*Discrimination.* The judge also rejected the argument that the woman was being discriminated against under the Race Relations Act 1976, since s.35 of the Act states that it is not unlawful to afford facilities or services in order to meet the special needs of people belonging to a particular racial group.

*Equipment.* The woman had bought disability equipment costing some £1800 (reclining bed and chair, and bath lift). The local authority treated it as having a lifespan of ten years and so assessed (i.e. made allowance for) her expenditure on it at £3.46 per week over that period. The woman argued that the lifespan of the equipment should have been regarded as only five years, thus her weekly expenditure should have been assessed at over £6.00. The court held there was no evidence put forward (e.g. from manufacturers) that the ten-year estimate was irrational.

However, it did not appear to the court altogether rational for the local authority to regard repair costs in the same way by 'amortising' the costs over the estimated lifetime of the equipment. Likewise, it was not rational to defer treating repair costs as disability related expenditure until the next accounting period, instead of considering them as they arose (*R(Stephenson) v Stockton-on-Tees Borough Council*).

## The local ombudsman has criticised arbitrariness in rules on charging:

**Unreasonableness: arbitrariness in charging.** The local ombudsman has questioned the reasonableness of a charging policy when the council (a) failed to give careful thought as to how much a person receiving income support could be expected to pay; (b) adopted a threshold above which charges would be automatically exempted, but only if weekly expenses exceeded income by £10 – a criterion which was 'quite arbitrary' and not well thought out (*Essex CC 1991*).

The courts have in one case identified irrationality:

**Unreasonably charging for daytime services.** It was unlawful, unfair and irrational for a local authority to take account of that part of disability living allowance (higher rate) paid in respect of night care – in order to assess the amount to be charged for day care (*R(Carton) v Coventry CC*).

If staff are not made aware of the local authority's local charging policy, that too is maladministration: for example when invalid carer's allowance and carer's premium was taken account of contrary to the local policy (*Durham CC 2000*).

## 11.4 REASONABLE PRACTICABILITY OF PAYING THE CHARGE

If a person satisfies the local authority that it is not reasonably practicable for him or her to pay a charge, the authority should only charge an amount that appears to it to be reasonably practicable for the person to pay (HASSASSA 1983, s.17).

The courts have stated that it is for the service user to 'discharge his burden of persuasion' by showing that he or she had insufficient means to pay (*Avon CC v Hooper*). In the same case the court also gave a wide interpretation of 'means':

**Reasonable practicability of paying a charge.** Under the legislation, the person had to show that he has insufficient means. The time at which he has to do this is the time when the local authority is seeking to charge him for the service. If his means have been reduced, as might be the case with a businessman whose business had run into difficulties after his being injured, the reduction in his means is something upon which he would be entitled to rely as making it impracticable for him to pay, even though at an earlier date he might have been better off.

The court also stated that the word 'means' in s.17 of the 1983 Act referred to more than just cash, since as a 'matter of the ordinary use of English, the word "means" refers to the financial resources of a person: his assets, his sources of income, his liabilities and expenses. If he has a realisable asset, that is part of his means; he has the means to pay… If he has an asset which he can reasonably be expected to realise and which will (after taking into account any other relevant factor) enable him to pay, his means make it practicable for him to pay' (*Avon CC v Hooper*).

The local ombudsman considers that the word 'hardship' is not a simple substitute for 'reasonable practicability', implying that the latter is of wider scope (*Gateshead MBC 2001*). In determining reasonable practicability, the local ombudsman will look for reasoned decision making:

**Arbitrary decision making.** A failure to explain how a decision is reached on reasonable practicability – beyond expressing scepticism of the parents' breakdown of expenditure in relation to their adult children with learning disabilities – suggested arbitrary decision making by officers not familiar with the specific care needs of those individuals concerned. This was maladministration (*Gateshead MBC 2001*).

One way in which the service user can discharge this burden is to take advantage of appeal procedures, about which the local ombudsman has commented on a number of occasions. Even if the burden is on the service user to convince the local authority about reasonable practicability, a local authority should provide adequate information and procedures to enable that burden to be discharged, according to the local ombudsman:

**Information and appeals procedure.** The local ombudsman has pointed out that for people to be able to exercise their statutory right to satisfy the authority that they cannot afford charges: (a) they must be informed that the local authority has the discretion to waive charges; (b) a proper appeals procedure must exist in order to assess people's cases (*Greenwich LBC 1993*).

**Decision letters.** The fact that an appeals procedure existed in principle, but that the decision letters made no clear reference to it, was maladministration (*Derbyshire CC 2004*).

**Information and appeals procedure.** In another investigation, the ombudsman stated that essential to the appeals procedure was (a) the application of clear, thought-out criteria; (b) accurate and sufficient information on which decisions were based; (c) information about how to challenge the outcome of the appeal; (d) clear reasons explaining decisions. In particular, criteria should have been relevant – for example, they should have related to ability to pay (as demanded by s.17 of the 1983 Act) and not to a reassessment of degree of need – and been applied consistently. The information on which appeal decisions were based should have been of good and consistent quality (*Essex CC 1991*).

In another case, the ombudsman likewise referred to the need for simple and transparent procedures, information about them, and clear reasons for decisions. All this was very difficult if a new charging system was implemented before the appeal criteria were formally adopted; in which case service users had 'no idea' of the factors that would support their case or be taken into account (*Gateshead MBC 2001*).

## 11.4.1 TAKING ACCOUNT OF THE SERVICE USER'S RESOURCES IN DECIDING WHETHER TO PROVIDE THE SERVICE

The question of charging for providing a non-residential service should not be confused with the taking account of a person's resources in order to decide not what to charge, but whether to provide a service in the first place (see 6.9.3).

## 11.5 DEPARTMENT OF HEALTH GUIDANCE ON CHARGING

After many years of failing to issue clear and formal guidance, the Department of Health finally did so in 2001 (LAC(2001)32; with attached guidance that was slightly amended in 2003: DH 2003j). The guidance was issued under s.7 of the Local Authority Social Services Act 1970, which makes it of the stronger, policy variety (see 4.1.6). The main points include the following:

- **No presumption of charging.** The guidance makes no presumption that local authorities will charge for non-residential social services, since the 1983 Act creates only a power, not a duty (para 4).
- **Discretion on local policies.** The guidance notwithstanding, local authorities retain substantial discretion as to how to implement local charging policies, so long as they are consistent with the clear objectives set out in the guidance (para 5).
- **Income Support levels.** Local authorities should not charge people on levels of income equal to basic levels of Income Support plus 25 per cent. For service users with higher income levels, charges should not be imposed that have the effect of reducing the person's income below those Income Support levels plus 25 per cent (para 20).

- **Taking account of disability benefits**. Some disability benefits may be taken into account as income, namely the Income Support severe disability premium, attendance allowance, disability living allowance, constant attendance allowance, and exceptionally severe disablement allowance. War pensioners' mobility supplement and the mobility component of disability living allowance may not be taken into account (paras 30–31) and likewise age-related payments to pensioners under the Age Related Payments Act 2004 (LAC (2004) 25).

- **Assessment of disability-related expenditure**. If disability benefits are taken into account, the service user must not be left without the means to pay for other necessary care and support or for other costs arising from their disability. In order to ensure this happens, local authorities should specifically assess the disability related expenditure of any service user, whose disability benefits are being taken into account (para 33).

- **Disability-related costs**. The guidance gives a non-exhaustive list of disability-related expenditure, needed for independent living. The list includes payment for community alarm system, costs of privately arranged care services, specialist washing powders or laundry, special dietary needs, special clothing or footwear, additional bedding costs (e.g. because of incontinence), additional heating costs, reasonable costs of domestic tasks (maintenance, cleaning, domestic help) where the assistance is required because of the disability, disability-related equipment costs (e.g. purchase, maintenance, repair, hire) and other transport costs over and above the mobility component of DLA (para 46).

- **Day and night care services**. When assessing a charge for daytime services, local authorities should avoid taking account of, as income, the element of benefits that are payable for night care. This reflects the case of *R(Carton) v Coventry CC*: see 11.3. The guidance suggests that normally it would be reasonable to treat the difference between, DLA care component high rate and middle rate as representing the element paid for night care (although this might not always be so) (paras 35–43).

- **Taking account of savings**. Service users with savings over the upper capital threshold used for the residential accommodation test of resources may be asked to pay the full cost of the service. The guidance suggests that the same approach to capital should be taken as for residential accommodation (para 58).

- **Taking account of capital**. Various types of capital can be taken account of in line with the test of resources for residential accommodation; however, the person's home should be disregarded (para 59).

- **Parents and other members of the family**. Under s.17 of the 1983 Act, only the service user's means may be assessed, not those of other members of the family. However, the guidance then goes on to suggest that in some circumstances the service user may have a legal right to share in the value of an asset, even if the asset is not in his or her own name. This may be through statutory or equitable rights (para 64).

- **Earnings**. All earnings should be disregarded as income. This is so that a disincentive to work is not created (para 72).

- **CJD**. No charges should be made for people suffering from any form of Creutzfeldt Jakob Disease (para 75).
- **Full cost of the service**. The maximum charge must not exceed the full cost of providing the service, which cannot include costs associated with the purchasing function or costs of operating the charging system (para 77).
- **Notional costs**. If the costs of services vary within a local authority's area (e.g. because of diverse provider charges), it is for the local authority to decide whether to set a notional average (e.g. to avoid people in rural areas being disadvantaged, para 79).
- **Carers**. If informal carers are being charged for carers' services under the Carers and Disabled Children Act 2000, then the local authority should take account of costs that the carers may have borne, before deciding what to charge. For example, private purchase of care (to allow short breaks), adaptations to the carer's home (e.g. where the disabled person has moved in), additional transport costs (e.g. taxis because there is not time to use public transport), and additional costs relating to the person's disability (see above) that the carer meets (para 83).
- **Direct payments**. Direct payment recipients are to be charged in the same way as if they had received the equivalent services from the local authority (para 86).
- **NHS payments**. If a person's community care services are being in effect paid for by NHS money, transferred to the local authority via s.28A of the NHS Act 1977, service users could still be charged up to the full cost of the service. However, s.17 of the 1983 Act is not a revenue raising power. In joint working generally, charging arrangements must be clear, because there is no power to charge for NHS services (para 88).
- **Refusal to pay charge**. A service should not be withdrawn because a person refuses to pay a charge; however, the debt could be pursued through the civil courts (para 97).
- **Refusal to disclose resources**. If a person refuses to disclose their resources, it may be reasonable to charge them the full cost of the service (para 97).
- **Consultation**. Changes to charging policies, including increases, should be consulted on with users and carers (para 98).
- **Scope of review in considering reasonable practicability**. The fairness of the charge should be considered in the light of individual circumstances. The review may need to go beyond consideration of the terms of the council's policy, since the policy is unlikely to make provision for all conceivable personal circumstances (para 101).
- **Information about a review**. Users must be provided with information making it clear that they can seek a review of the charge or can make a formal complaint (para 102).

Certain parts of the Department of Health guidance merit discussion; some may be open to question. First, in one breath, the guidance acknowledges that the mobility supplement of disability living allowance (DLA) should be disregarded as income (para 30); but in the next there is a suggestion that the disability-related expenditure assessment should consider travel costs 'over and above the mobility component of DLA' – apparently implying that it should be taken into account (para 46). This seems to be contradictory.

Second, caution must be exercised in setting notional averages for certain types of expenditure being assessed as disability related expenditure. For instance, setting such a notional weekly amount for single or double incontinence would run the risk of (a) generally being set anyway too low; and (b) even if it was not set unduly low, and represented a reasonable average, it would still not represent everybody's expenditure – since one person's incontinence needs might necessitate considerably greater expenditure (in terms of both quality and quantity) than another's. In fact further guidance alludes to this very pitfall, stating that to a limited degree it might be possible to set standard allowances for costs such as laundry, but that the main emphasis should be on each individual's verifiable expenditure (DH 2002a, para 48).

There is a particular need for caution in practice because of the potential considerable discrepancy between maximum state benefits payable and the actual expenditure faced by disabled people. For example, a 2004 report concluded that, for 'high to medium' needs, the weekly benefits payable amounted to £235, but that budgetary requirements (excluding personal assistance) were £467, resulting in a weekly shortfall of £232 (Smith *et al.* 2004, p.77).

(An Age Concern England report (Thompson and Mathew 2004, p.57) revealed the rough, ready and arbitrary nature of how some local authorities were assessing disability related expenditure. For instance, disallowed were vitamin drinks (because not prescribed by the doctor), heating costs (not great enough to qualify), plastic bags to put incontinence pads in, chiropody (simply not 'allowable'), hairdresser who visits (because this was not in the care plan), incontinence pads bought from the chemist because the woman found those from the district nurse too bulky, transport to day centre and physiotherapy sessions, and special transport to take her husband (who had had a stroke) on holiday.)

Third, the guidance claims that even if services are being provided through money given by the NHS to the local authority (under s.28A of the NHS Act 1977), so that the services are not costing the local authority anything, nevertheless the local authority could still charge the person up to the full cost of the service (para 88). This may seem controversial; but although s.17 of the HASSASSA 1983 is not a general revenue-raising power, nevertheless all it says is that the authority may recover such a charge as it considers reasonable. It says nothing about recovering the actual overall cost to it of providing the service to any particular service user.

Fourth, as far as taking account of disability benefits as income is concerned, the courts have held that charging a person receiving disability benefits more than a person who does not receive them is not contrary to the Disability Discrimination Act 1995 (*R v Powys CC, ex p Hambidge (no.2)*).

Fifth, the question of whether in some circumstances the resources of other members of the family (partner, parents etc.) could be taken into account, at least in some circumstances, is to some extent unclear. In two cases concerning the provision of home adaptations under s.2 of the Chronically Sick and Disabled Persons Act 1970, the courts declined to answer the question of whether other people's resources could be taken account of in deciding what to charge. One case concerned the resources of the partner of the disabled person(*R(Fay) v Essex CC*), the other the resources of the parents of a disabled child (*R(Spink) v Wandsworth LBC*).

(Although it is not commonly realised, the 'liable spouse' rules (see 9.5.1), under ss.42 and 43 of the National Assistance Act 1948, appear to apply (in principle at least) to non-residential services provided under the 1948 Act, as well as to residential accommodation. The rules involve the liability of a husband or wife to support the other – and the power of the local authority to ask one spouse for payment in respect of services provided for the other spouse.)

## 11.6 CONSULTATION WITH SERVICE USERS ABOUT CHARGING

The courts have confirmed that where fundamental changes are being made to the charging structure, fairness requires that proper consultation should take place. Uprating and adjustment of charges is one thing, but quite another are changes to the policy and rules that result in significant differences for service users; this latter requires consultation (*R(Carton) v Coventry CC*). On any view, introducing a charging system from scratch marks a significant change, making it all the more imperative that consultation take place; a failure to ensure this was maladministration (*Derbyshire CC 2004*).

The *Coventry* case appears to contrast with a previous one, in which the courts stated that a failure to consult service users about significant increases in charges was not procedurally unfair – since each service user had the right to an individual review under s.17 of the HASSASSA 1983 (*R v Powys CC, ex p Hambidge (no.2)*: High Court).

## 11.7 CHARGING AND PERSONAL INJURY COMPENSATION PAYMENTS

In principle, there is nothing in the HASSASSA 1983 to prevent a local authority taking account of a personal injury compensation payment (not just the income, but also the capital and right to income), even where it is held in trust. This contrasts with the explicit rules for charging for residential accommodation which prevent the capital, and value of the right to receive income (although not the actual income), being taken into account (see 9.6.3.1).

However, there are two notes of caution. First, the Department of Health guidance (DH 2003j, para 59) states that the same approach to capital should be taken for non-residential charges as for residential accommodation. This would then preclude taking into account trust-held personal injury compensation sums. Second, the local authority would anyway need to consider the precise purposes for which the compensation was paid, and whether it was reasonable in the all circumstances to demand payment against the compensation sum.

## 11.8 PLACING A CHARGE ON THE HOUSE

Some local authorities, when assisting people with home adaptations under s.2 of the CSDPA 1970, place a charge on the person's house, with the consent of the person. The value of the charge is then payable if and when the house is sold. There may be three possible objections to this.

First, it would appear to be taking account of the home for the purpose of charging under s.17 of the HASSASSA 1983 contrary to the Department of Health policy guidance (DH 2003j, para 59). Second, it might be arguable that the local authority has no legal power to do this anyway under s.17 of the 1983 Act. For instance, placing a charge on the house is expressly contemplated in the case of residential accommodation for pursuing a debt (HASSASSA 1983, s.22) or in the case of deferred payments (Health and Social Care Act 2001, s.55); in the absence of express provision, there could be doubt as to the lawfulness of placing such a charge in the case of non-residential services. Third, it would place home owners at a considerable disadvantage compared, for instance, to a tenant; in the latter case the question of a charge on the property could not arise.

## 11.9 CLEAR POLICY ON CHARGING

The local ombudsman has in the past put great emphasis on a local authority having a clear policy and information about its charging system.

**Having a clear policy on charging.** The local ombudsman has found maladministration when a local authority has failed to have (a) 'a properly recorded policy on financial assessment'; (b) 'a statement of the criteria for the basis of assessing financial resources and need'; (c) 'advice and explanation of this together with information on what information must be submitted for the assessment'.

In this particular case, part of the problem had arisen because the local authority refused to disregard charitable pledges obtained by the applicants for adaptations for their daughter. The applicants claimed that this was inconsistent with the purpose of the pledges, which were designed to bridge the shortfall between the authority's contribution and the actual cost of the works. The ombudsman did not fault the authority for wanting to practise 'prudent' budget management, but for the lack of policy and criteria for such practice, and of advice and explanation (*Hertfordshire CC 1992*).

## 11.10 PEOPLE WHO REFUSE TO PAY

There seems to be nothing in legislation to suggest that authorities can withdraw, or refuse to provide, services solely on the grounds that a person will not pay. However, the legislation empowers authorities to recover charges as a civil debt (in a magistrates' court), without prejudice to any other method of recovery (HASSASSA 1983, s.17).

The generally accepted legal view seems to be that if an authority has a duty to provide a service, then non-payment of a charge cannot justify withdrawal of the service. Certainly this is the stance taken by guidance (DH 2003j, para 97). This is on the assumption that a duty (to provide a service) cannot be overridden by a mere power (to make a charge). Nevertheless, this approach would appear to leave open the possibility that a service provided under a mere power (e.g. for an older person under the Health Services and Public Health Act 1968) could be withheld lawfully if the person refused to pay.

The local ombudsman has questioned the dividing line between a service user declining services, in reaction to charges being imposed, and the local authority withdrawing them – particularly where both staff and service user were ignorant of the legal position on withdrawal of services.

**Suspending or withdrawing services for non-payment?** Faced with difficulty in meeting the charges being demanded, a man suspended the local authority care being provided to his wife. Local authority staff had not explained to him that the authority had a duty to continue to provide the services even if he did not pay. However, staff were unaware of the authority's guidance that explained this point. This was maladministration. In such circumstances the ombudsman also questioned whether the man's decision to suspend care was in fact the equivalent of withdrawal of care by the local authority (*Durham CC 2000*).

The problem for local authorities lies in deciding in what circumstances to pursue such debts, especially given the sensitivity and potentially adverse publicity surrounding the legal pursuit of disabled, elderly or vulnerable people. In deciding whether to recommend pursuit of a debt, local authority staff might be faced with difficult decisions and react in ways little related to the law – as the following study revealed:

**Moral judgements about whether to pursue a debt**. Social care practitioners might react in various ways when faced with a man with learning disabilities who owes money to the local authority, who has recently won several thousand pounds through a lottery, but who refuses to reduce the debt. Some practitioners might inform the finance department and urge that the debt be pursued for the sake of equity (i.e. having regard to other users of services).

Also in the name of equity, practitioners might even suggest that, since services cannot legally be withdrawn on non-payment (see above), they should instead be withdrawn by means of a reassessment and a downward adjustment of assessed need and service provision. Others might wish to preserve confidentiality and not pass on the information; yet others still might decide to keep quiet because to do otherwise would be 'snitching' and taking away the luck that had come the client's way (Bradley and Manthorpe 1997, pp.70–73).

## 11.11 GENERAL LOCAL GOVERNMENT LEGISLATION AND CHARGING

Some local authorities have considered making use of another statutory route for making charges, namely s.111 of the Local Government Act 1972. This enables authorities to do things to facilitate, or which are conducive or incidental to, the discharge of any of their functions. However, the courts have sounded a clear warning against use of this section by local authorities to make charges for services (*McCarthy v Richmond LBC*).

Likewise, any attempt to circumvent restrictions on charging by utilising s.93 of the Local Government Act 2003 would almost certainly be unlawful. First, this would be because it only applies to discretionary services as opposed to services that a local authority has a duty to provide. Second, even if discretionary services could be identified (e.g. provided for older people under s.45 of the Health Services and Public Health Act 1968), s.93 of the 2003 Act cannot be used if there is a power outside of s.93 to charge for those discretionary services (see ODPM 2003, paras 11–13). There is of course just such a power: in s.17 of the HASSASSA 1983.

CHAPTER 12

# Direct payments, carers, families with children in need, and other specific groups of people

**KEY POINTS**

DIRECT PAYMENTS

If certain conditions are met, local authorities have a duty to make direct payments to people, so that the latter can purchase their own non-residential community care services – rather than have the local authority provide or arrange the services. The conditions are, in summary, that the person has an assessed eligible need, that the service to be purchased will reasonably meet that need, that he or she consents to the payment, and that he or she is able to manage the payment with or without assistance. The overall purpose of direct payments is to give service users greater independence and control over their daily lives.

CARERS

Various pieces of legislation now make provision for carers. In summary, informal carers providing substantial and regular care, and who request an assessment, have a right to have their ability to care assessed and may be provided with services. Additional 2004 legislation means that carers' involvement in (or wish to do) work, training, education or a leisure activity must also be taken into account in the assessment.

CHILDREN IN NEED AND THEIR FAMILIES

Under the Children Act 1989, local authorities owe a general duty toward children in need (including disabled children) and may provide services also for any member of the child's family. Therefore, in considering the legal basis for meeting the needs of disabled children and their families, or disabled adults with children, local authority staff will sometimes have to carry out assessments under both adult community care legislation and under the Children Act.

OTHER GROUPS OF PEOPLE

The Department of Health has issued specific guidance in relation to specific groups of people; these include, for example, deaf-blind people, people with learning disabilities, people with HIV and people with drug or alcohol problems.

Note. Wales, Scotland and Northern Ireland. The direct payments legislation is effectively the same as in these three countries as in England, although there have been different rates of implementation in extending payments to all the relevant groups of people. In Wales, direct payments come under the Health and Social Care Act 2001 as in England, but are being implemented through separate regulations (SI 2004/1748). In Scotland they come under the Social Work (Scotland) Act 1968, s.12B; and in Northern Ireland under the Carers and Direct Payments (Northern Ireland) Act 2002 and a.18C of the Children (Northern Ireland) Order 1995.

The legislative provisions for informal carers are effectively the same in Wales, although the National Assembly for Wales has issued its own guidance (e.g. NAFW 2001). In Scotland, the provisions are similar (but not the same) under s.12AA of the Social Work (Scotland) Act 1968 and under s.24 of the Children (Scotland) Act 1995. However, in Scotland, the legislation does not provide for explicit provision of services for carers. In Northern Ireland, similar provisions to those in England are to be found in the Carers and Direct Payments (Northern Ireland) Act 2002, and articles 17A and 18A of the Children (Northern Ireland) Order 1995. Guidance has been issued in Scotland (CCD 2/2003) and Northern Ireland (DHSSPS 2003) also. The duty to have regard to the carer contained in s.8 of the Disabled Persons (Services, Consultation and Representation) Act 1986 applies to Wales and Scotland; and its equivalent is found in the Disabled Persons (Northern Ireland) Order 1989.

For children in need (including disabled children), the legislation is the same in Wales as in England (Children Act 1989, s.17); the equivalent provisions in Scotland and Northern Ireland are to be found respectively in s.22 of the Children (Scotland) Act 1995, and in a.18 of the Children (Northern Ireland) Order 1995.

## 12.1 DIRECT PAYMENTS: OVERALL PURPOSE

Legislation obliges local authorities to give service users money, by way of 'direct payments' to purchase their own services, rather than have the local authority arrange the services. This obligation is triggered if certain conditions are met in any individual case. Department of Health guidance states that the overall purpose of direct payments 'is to give recipients control over their own life by providing an alternative to social services provided by a local council' (DH 2003d, p.3).

The duty to make direct payments extends to older people as well as other groups of service users; however, a study published in 2004 questioned the extent to which such payments were making possible greater independence when compared with payments made to other groups of service users. This was because older people's social and leisure needs were not deemed by local authorities as essential or 'eligible' as they would be for other adult groups; despite the fact that this was contrary to Department of Health guidance (LAC(2002)13, para 12) on 'fair access to care' that cautioned against such discrimination (Clark *et al.* 2004, p.56).

More widely, the Commission for Social Care Inspection found in 2004 that the uptake of direct payments in general was slow due to lack of clear information, unawareness on the part of local authority staff, restrictive or patronising professional attitudes, inadequate advocacy and support services, inconsistency between the legislation and local practice, excessive paperwork – and difficulties in the recruitment, employment and retention of personal assistants, and in assuring quality (CSCI 2004, p.5).

## 12.1.1 ELIGIBLE GROUPS OF PEOPLE FOR DIRECT PAYMENTS

Eligible for direct payments are all community care service users aged 18 or over with an assessed eligible need and informal carers aged 16 or over for whom the local authority has decided services are called for (Health and Social Care Act 2001; SI 2003/762). Also eligible are the parents of disabled children, disabled parents of children, and children aged 16 or 17 years old. In the last three categories, the child in each case has to be a child in need under s.17 of the Children Act 1989, for whose needs the local authority has decided services are called for (Children Act 1989, s.17A; SI 2003/762).

**Note**. There are a number of exclusions relating to mental health and criminal justice legislation. These include guardianship under the Mental Health Act 1983, but do not include aftercare under s.117 of the 1983 Act, unless it is aftercare under supervision.

In summary, the exclusions are: (a) patients detained under mental health legislation on leave of absence; (b) conditionally discharged detained patients subject to Home Office restrictions, status; (c) patients subject to guardianship under mental health legislation and those receiving aftercare under supervision; (d) people receiving aftercare or community care that is part of a care programme initiated under a compulsory court order; (e) offenders serving a probation or combination order, or offenders released on licence, subject to an additional requirement to undergo treatment for a mental health condition, or drug or alcohol dependency; (f) people subject to equivalent restrictions in Scottish mental health or criminal justice legislation (DH 2003d, annex C; see SI 2003/762 for details).

## 12.1.2 CONDITIONS TO BE MET FOR DIRECT PAYMENTS

The conditions that have to be met are as follows:

- The person has to have an assessed, eligible need (Health and Social Care Act 2001, s.57; Children Act 1989, s.17A).
- The local authority must be satisfied that the service can meet the relevant need or, in the case of child-related services, that the welfare of the child concerned will be safeguarded and promoted (SI 2003/762).
- The person must consent (Health and Social Care Act 2001, s.57; Children Act 1989, s.17A). This implies both ability or capacity to do so and willingness.
- The person must be able to manage the payment with or without assistance (SI 2003/762).

If all these conditions are met, a duty arises. The prior requirement that the local authority must first have decided that services are called for in the individual case – that there must first be an assessed, eligible need – indicates that direct payments are not a 'back door' route to services, which the person would not otherwise be eligible for. In other words the normal rules of assessment and eligibility apply (see Chapter 6).

Department of Health guidance points out that blanket assumptions should not be made about whether certain categories of person will or will not be able to manage direct payments. The guidance goes on to state that assistance might include, for instance, keeping records, management of day-to-day relationships with staff or using a payroll service; the assistance itself might be bought in (DH 2003d, paras 47, 52). Therefore the question would be whether, overall, the recipient could control what was happening, even if he or she could not necessarily handle the day-to-day administration.

**Managing a direct payment with assistance.** A complaint was made to the local ombudsman. A woman with learning disabilities visited the family home at Christmas and decided not to return to her residential placement. The father wanted the council to pursue the possibility of a direct payment in combination with Independent Living Fund money so that she could live nearby. The council initially refused direct payments on the ground that she lacked the capacity to manage such payments without assistance. This was maladministration (*Hertfordshire CC 2003*).

The organisation Values into Action provides pointers to thinking through the question of consent and control in the case of people with learning disabilities; although it also makes the point that direct payments are not the only way of people achieving greater independence (Bewley 2002, p.5).

If a person does not agree with the council about his or her capacity to manage, the guidance states that the person should have access to an advocate and that arbitration should be available (DH 2003d, para 54). In addition, it might be that a person could manage some services and not others (or simply wish to manage some but not others). This would not prevent the making of a direct payment, since a person's needs could be met in part by the making of a direct payment, and in part by directly provided services arranged by the local authority (DH 2003d, para 50).

The guidance also states that, in its view, a person operating an enduring power of attorney could continue to receive direct payments on behalf of a person who had already consented (before loss of the requisite capacity). However, such an attorney could neither provide the original consent nor continue to receive the direct payments if, on review, services change (DH 2003d, para 59). This is because enduring powers of attorney relate only to property and financial affairs, not to welfare decisions. However, this position will change if and when the Mental Capacity Bill 2004 becomes law (see Chapter 18).

Local authorities thus need to pay attention to these rules; a failure to do so could result in the local authority being deemed to have employer responsibilities. The following employment tribunal case, albeit drawn from a slightly different context, is illustrative:

**Local authority as employer.** Two people with learning disabilities ostensibly had a contract with a personal assistant, who was paid with money from the Independent Living Fund (a grant giving body) and from a local authority social work department.

The assistant was bringing a case against her employer, based on allegations of sex discrimination and breach of contract, but was unsure who her employer really was. An employment tribunal held that because the local authority retained overall control of the situation in a number of respects, and that conversely the two people with learning disabilities appeared to take little responsibility, the local authority was in reality the employer. In other words, with or without assistance, the disabled people were not managing the payment. The tribunal's decision was upheld on appeal (*Smith v South Lanarkshire Council*).

Lastly, it should be noted that the condition of consent implies not only capacity to decide to receive direct payments, but also willingness: people should not be 'forced' into them, as the local ombudsman noted:

**Only offering direct payments for domiciliary care.** The local ombudsman criticised a local authority, when it would only offer home care for an elderly woman by way of direct payments; otherwise only permanent residential care or temporary (institutional) respite care was offered. The woman rejected both these options; she was on file as having threatened suicide rather than enter a care home and had previously had a bad experience in respite care. She reluctantly accepted the direct payments option in order to be able to stay at home; but, as the local ombudsman pointed out, direct payments 'are not something that everyone can reasonably be expected to take on' (*Cambridgeshire CC 2002*).

## 12.1.3 RELEVANT SERVICES FOR DIRECT PAYMENTS

Direct payments are available for non-residential services including community equipment. They may also be used for residential accommodation but only on a limited basis. This is that the accommodation be provided for no more than four continuous weeks in any period of 12 months. Stays of shorter duration are to be added together, unless they are separated by a period of four weeks or more. However, they must anyway not exceed 120 days a year (SI 2003/762). Thus substantial, regular respite care throughout the year is possible under these rules, so long as there are four-week gaps and the 120-day mark is not exceeded.

The direct payments legislation (Health and Social Care Act 2001, s.57; Children Act 1989, s.17A) covers social services, but not NHS or housing services. This means that under the direct payments legislation at least, the NHS cannot make direct payments in respect of health care services that it provides. Nevertheless, the NHS could, under s.28A of the NHS Act 1977, make money available to social services to bolster a direct payment. However, the services in question could not be health care services, since s.28A payments must be in respect of local authority (i.e. in this context social services) and not health care functions.

Even given such apparent restrictions, there remains a significant 'grey area' of uncertainty as to what constitutes health or social care. Clearly to the extent that a service (e.g. bathing) could be regarded as either, then for the purpose of direct payments it could be labelled as social care (i.e. a social services function) and be eligible. For recipients of direct payments, it may seem advantageous to have all, or at least the greater part of, their needs met through the flexibility of direct payments. However, two further issues arise.

First, the more services are categorised as coming within social services functions, the more they are subject to charging (the NHS is not empowered to charge for most services). Second, the extent to which local authorities have a legal power to provide 'health care' type services is governed in part by a prohibition in s.29 of the National Assistance Act 1948 (see 10.1.4.2). One study considered the very question of the dividing line between social care and health care in the context of direct payments. It found that in practice:

- health professionals considered that tasks such as simple surgical dressings, giving suppositories and regular physiotherapy exercises could be performed by non-professionals; they lay in the grey area between health and social care (and so could arguably be included in direct payments)
- health professionals considered the following type of task as not suitable for non-professionals (and so, arguably, should not be included within direct payments): care of leg ulcers or deep tissue wounds, assessing effectiveness of treatment, giving bladder washouts, tube feeding, enemas, manual bowel evacuation, colostomy care, tracheal suction, other aspects of tracheostomy care, changing urinary catheters (Glendinning *et al.* 2000).

## 12.1.4 USING DIRECT PAYMENTS TO PURCHASE SERVICES FROM CLOSE RELATIVES OR LOCAL AUTHORITIES

A direct payment recipient may not use the money to pay close relatives living in the same household, unless this is necessary in order for the recipient's needs to be met satisfactorily – or, in respect of a child-related direct payment, it is necessary for promoting the welfare of the child. The list of relatives comprises parent or parent-in-law, son or daughter, son-in-law or daughter-in-law, stepson or stepdaughter, brother or sister, aunt or uncle, grandparent, spouse, or any person living as spouse with anybody on this list (SI 2003/762).

The local authority may also make a direct payment subject to whatever other conditions it thinks fit, including that it should not be used to purchase services from a particular person (SI 2003/762). Such conditions might also relate to financial procedures, including methods of payment, monitoring procedures and accounting procedures; guidance has been published by the Chartered Institute of Public Finance and Accountancy on such matters (CIPFA 2004).

The Department of Health in the past stated that it would not be possible for a direct payment to be used to purchase services from a local authority itself. Whether or not this was merely policy, or reference to a perceived legal obstacle, is not entirely clear. In Scotland, there appears to be no impediment, legal or policy wise, since the Scottish Executive's guidance makes it quite clear that direct payments could be used to purchase services from a local authority (CCD4/2003, para 64).

## 12.1.5 AMOUNT OF DIRECT PAYMENT

The local authority must make the payment at a rate that it estimates 'to be equivalent to the reasonable cost of securing the provision of the service concerned' (Health and Social Care Act 2001, s.57). Department of Health guidance emphasises that the payment should be sufficient to enable the recipient 'lawfully to secure the service of a standard that the council considers is reasonable to fulfil the relevant needs'. There should be 'no limit on the maximum or minimum amount' of the amount of care to be purchased, or of the value of the direct payment (DH 2003d, para 82). The guidance also states that a local authority can pay a higher amount if the benefits of doing so outweigh the costs and 'best value' is still adhered to (para 85). Thus financial ceilings imposed as a matter of policy – for example, on the total weekly amount, or on the hourly rate that the direct payment will cover – are likely to be unlawful. Certainly the local ombudsman criticised a ceiling of £360 per week offered by way of direct payment, to pay for the two evening carers a woman needed; that amount was insufficient for the purpose (*Cambridgeshire CC 2002*).

The payment might also include, for instance, an amount to cover recruitment costs, national insurance, statutory holiday pay, sick pay, maternity pay, employers' liability insurance, public liability insurance and VAT (DH 2003d, paras 82–83).

In some circumstances, the reasonable cost might appear to the local authority to be more expensive than directly provided services. For instance, in the case of personal assistance or equipment, the local authority might benefit from bulk contracts. If so, the personal assistance hourly rate or the equipment per item might be cheaper for the local authority to purchase than the individual with the direct payment.

Thus, some local authorities are tempted to argue 'best value' or cost-effectiveness as a reason for not making the payment, or at least not making it up to the reasonable amount required for the person to purchase the service. However, this would seem legally dubious. First, the duty is to ensure that the person can meet his or her needs through direct payments. A failure to make the payment at all or up to the reasonable amount would breach this duty and run the risk of reducing it to a mere power. Second, best value would normally be relevant to *how* a duty is performed, not to *whether* it is performed. Nevertheless, there might still be an element of uncertainty as to how the courts would respond where a particular direct payments package was markedly and demonstrably more expensive than direct provision by the local authority. In this uncertain vein, guidance from the Chartered Institute of Public Finance and Accountancy states that if the cost of a direct payment is greater than the cost to the local authority of providing the service itself, then a direct payment does not have to be given (CIPFA 2004, para 5.1).

### 12.1.5.1 'Charging' for direct payments

The reasonable amount the local authority must estimate is a gross payment. However, it can make a 'net' payment; that is, it can reduce the payment if it is satisfied that it is reasonably practicable for the recipient to make a contribution toward the cost of the service. Alternatively, even where it is reasonably practicable for the recipient to make a contribution, the local authority can still make the gross payment, but then seek reimbursement of that assessed contribution (Health and Social Care Act 2001, s.57; SI 2003/762).

### 12.1.6 COMMUNITY EQUIPMENT

Department of Health guidance makes clear that direct payments apply to equipment, as well as to other community care services. It states that the recipient should be supported by adequate expertise, especially where major items of equipment are concerned. The local authority should also clarify responsibilities for ongoing care and maintenance, as well as what should happen when the person no longer needs the equipment (DH 2003d, paras 78–81).

### 12.1.7 TOPPING UP DIRECT PAYMENTS

If a direct recipient wishes to purchase a service or equipment to a standard over and beyond that which the local authority judges necessary for the meeting of the need, there would seem to be nothing to stop a recipient 'topping up' with their own, or a third party's, resources – so long as other relevant conditions are met and the local authority agrees.

However, as with the case of topping up in respect of residential accommodation (see 8.5.1), local authorities, or perhaps rather service users, must beware of the following trap. This would consist of the local authority not just allowing a person to top up to obtain a service over and beyond their assessed need, but by awarding too low an amount of direct payment to allow the person reasonably to purchase the basic service required. This would then 'force' the person to top up in order to meet the basic assessed need. In turn, this would be likely to be unlawful.

### 12.1.8 DIRECT PAYMENTS, AND HEALTH AND SAFETY

Some local authorities tend to express concerns over health and safety issues in the context of direct payments. For example, a disabled person might on occasion use the payment in such a way as to give rise to serious health and safety concerns on the part of the local authority. If, in response, the local authority takes a 'hands-off' approach it is likely to be anxious about negligence litigation in respect of any accident that occurs – even if the recipient has, as a condition of the direct payment, taken out insurance. In addition to a claim against the disabled person, a local authority would still represent an additional and tempting target for litigation because of its relatively deep financial pocket. In some circumstances, the disabled person might anyway argue that the accident was the local authority's fault (e.g. because of lack of information or poor initial risk assessment) and so to try to deflect the litigation away from himself or herself on to the local authority.

In such circumstances, the local authority might be legally vulnerable because, overall, it remains statutorily responsible for assessing need and making a direct payment in order that the need be met. Yet, an excessively 'hands-on' or interventionist approach would risk undermining the whole purpose of direct payments, which is to give people greater choice and control over their own lives.

Department of Health guidance states that recipients should be given information about health and safety and also the results of any risk assessment carried out. In addition, recipients should be encouraged to develop strategies on manual handling. However, the guidance clearly states: 'As a general principle, local councils should avoid laying down health and safety policies for individual direct payment recipients' (DH 2003d, para 96).

This guidance would appear unequivocally to represent a hands-off approach. It is an approach consistent with the underlying purpose of direct payments, namely to give disabled people more control, including responsibilities. Even so, in case of accident, it is possible that local authorities could in some circumstances be legally vulnerable not only to negligence litigation, but also in respect of possible breach of s.3 of the Health and Safety at Work Act 1974 (see 22.5).

Perhaps the term 'general principle' contained in the guidance should be better interpreted to mean that, at least in some circumstances, local authorities should consider intervening. In any event, in the absence of any legal case law directly in point, it would seem that local authorities would be well advised to steer a middle course, not intervening excessively, but nevertheless intervening constructively if they have serious health and safety concerns.

Certainly, local authorities arguably have the power ultimately to withhold payments (and instead arrange services themselves for the person) if they are not being used in a reasonable manner (see 12.1.10).

## 12.1.9 HEALTH AND SAFETY AT WORK LEGISLATION

It is probable that because of the effect of s.51 of the Health and Safety Work Act 1974, health and safety at work legislation does not apply as between a direct payment recipient who acts as employer and his or her employees. However, the employee could still bring negligence litigation if necessary; in other words the recipient has a common law duty of care to his or her employees. The local authority would still potentially have health and safety at work responsibilities toward both the recipient and any employee employed by the recipient – since both would be 'non-employees' of the local authority for the purpose of s.3 of the Health and Safety at Work Act 1974 (see 22.5).

If the recipient contracts with an agency, then the agency has duties toward its employees under s.2 of the Health and Safety at Work Act 1974 and various regulations relating to, for example, manual handling (SI 1992/2793) – and toward the recipient under s.3 of the 1974 Act. The employees have duties towards themselves and others under s.7 of the 1974 Act and other related legislation.

If the personal assistants supplied through an agency are not employees of the agency but are genuinely self-employed, then the agency has a s.3 duty toward them as non-employees and likewise to the direct payment recipient. Self-employed persons, too, have duties towards themselves and others under s.3 of the 1974 Act and related legislation.

## 12.1.10 WITHDRAWING OR WITHHOLDING A DIRECT PAYMENT

The effect of the legislation is to allow a local authority to withdraw a direct payment if any of the relevant conditions are no longer being satisfied – for example, in relation to need not being met or capacity to manage the payment (SI 2003/762).

Department of Health guidance states that councils should encourage people to plan for the unexpected and be prepared to step in to provide services, or to help a person continue to manage his or her own care, particularly if the problem is temporary or unforeseen (DH 2003d, para 154). Indeed, the legislation itself states that if a person is unable, temporarily, to manage the payment, the local authority can continue to make the payment if somebody else is prepared to accept and manage it, and the service provider agrees to accept payment from that other person (SI 2003/762).

In addition, the legislation allows the local authority to seek repayment if the money involved has not been used to secure a relevant service, or if a condition of the direct payment agreement has been breached (SI 2003/762). However, Department of Health guidance states that this power to recover money should not be used to penalise honest mistakes, or to seek repayment where the recipient has been the victim of fraud (DH 2003d, para 161).

## 12.1.11 THIRD PARTY OR INDIRECT PAYMENTS

Where a person clearly lacks capacity to consent or to manage the payment with or without assistance, a direct payment cannot lawfully be made to the person. However, there are ways around this involving what are variously referred to as third party or indirect payments, and may involve what has been termed a 'user independent trust'. This became clear during the course of a manual handling dispute that ended up in court:

**Manual handling and user independent trust.** One legal case concerned two women with profound physical and learning disabilities cared for by their parents at home. The local authority and parents engaged in an extended dispute about manual handling for the two women. It was accepted by all involved that direct payments would not be possible because of the two women's inability to consent or to manage the payment with or without assistance.

However, the judge stated that it would be possible for a 'user independent trust', in the form of a registered company, to be formed. The local authority could make payments (sometimes referred to as 'indirect' or third party payments) to the trust, which in turn would purchase personal assistance including manual handling assistance. The arrangements would lie not under direct payments legislation but under s.30 of the National Assistance Act 1948. If the judge was wrong about this possibility under s.30, then he suggested such an arrangement could come under s.111 of the Local Government Act 1972, that allows a local authority to do things to facilitate, or which are conducive or incidental to, the discharge of any of its functions. Alternative to either of these two, s.2 of the Local Government Act 2000 would also serve, under the power to promote or improve social well-being in the local authority's area (R(A&B) v East Sussex CC (no.2)).

It should be noted that the judge was astute to the above arrangement not simply being a covert or sham means of giving the parents the money. The trust would be in the form of a registered company, with five members on the trust board; this would mean the parents had neither a veto nor majority voting rights. The daughters could not have received direct payments in their own right because of their lack of relevant mental capacity. Had it been raised as a possibility, the parents (in their role of informal carers) could not have received carers' direct payments because such services cannot involve anything of an intimate nature (see 12.4.6).

## 12.2 VOUCHERS

Local authorities have a power to issue vouchers (Carers and Disabled Children Act 2000; SI 2003/1216). They can be issued in respect of the informal carer (16 years old or more) of an adult aged 18 years; or to the parent of a disabled child. Department of Health guidance describes the purpose of vouchers as offering flexibility in timing and choice of short breaks, giving service users and carers an alternative to direct payments or to direct provision of services. A key difference between direct payments and vouchers is that in the case of the former, the recipient of the payment takes on contractual responsibility; whereas with vouchers, the local authority retains that responsibility. Thus, for service users and carers, vouchers will be simpler to operate (DH 2003e, paras 4–5). They therefore represent something of a halfway house.

A voucher enables a person to obtain services which he or she would have otherwise have obtained through the local authority. A voucher is issued where a local authority agrees with an informal carer (including a parent) that a temporary break from caring would help him or her to care for the person being cared for (Carers and Disabled Children Act 2000, s.3; Children Act 1989, s.17B). Such breaks must not last longer than 28 days at any one time and cumulatively not exceed 120 days in any 12-month period (SI 2003/1216).

Vouchers may be expressed in terms of money or of time. A time voucher must specify the service for which it is valid; and it may, but does not have to, specify the supplier of services (Carers and Disabled Children Act 2000, s.3; Children Act 1989, s.17B; SI 2003/1216). In the case of community care services for adults, time vouchers may be issued either to the person cared for, or to the carer if the cared for person consents or lacks capacity to give that consent. In respect of children in need, they may be issued to the parent. However, money vouchers can be issued only to the person cared for or the parent of a child in need.

If the voucher holder wishes the care provider to provide additional or more expensive services over and above those covered by the voucher, a third party may pay the extra (i.e. 'top up'). However, vouchers must not be issued either to a cared for person or a carer who comes into any of the categories of people who are subject to certain criminal justice and mental health legislation and who are prohibited from receiving direct payments (see 12.1.1) (SI 2003/1216).

Department of Health guidance states that a local authority's normal charging system for non-residential services should be applied to the provision of vouchers (DH 2003e, para 25).

## 12.3 INDEPENDENT LIVING FUND

Grants are available to disabled people through a fund, paid for by central government, known as the Independent Living Fund. It is beyond the scope of this book to enter into detail. The following is a summary based on guidance notes produced by the Fund (ILF 2000).

There are two funds. The first has been closed to new applicants since April 2003 and is known as the Independent Living (Extension) Fund. Eligibility is basically in terms of the person being in receipt of the higher rate of care component of disability living allowance (or of attendance allowance), and having capital of less than £18,500. The maximum weekly payment available through the Extension Fund is £715.

The second fund is known as the Independent Living (1993) Fund for new applicants since April 1993. Eligibility is basically in terms of: the person being aged over 16 years, and under 66 years (at the time of first application); receipt of, or entitlement to, higher rate care component of disability living allowance or of attendance allowance; receipt of local social services authority support of at least £200 per week; capital of less than £18,500; an expectation of living independently at home for at least the next 12 months. In calculating the cost of care a local authority is contributing, the Fund considers the cost to the local authority, less any charge it is imposing on the service user (i.e. the £200 must be net of any charges made to the service user). The Fund can pay the money to a third party to administer it, usually where the disabled person is unable to manage his or her own money.

The 1993 Fund is primarily intended to pay for the cost of employing personal assistants, for personal and domestic care. The money cannot be used to employ/pay close relatives living in the same household. There are also a range of services on which the money cannot be spent; for example, holidays, care homes, wheelchairs, equipment, home adaptations, furniture, physiotherapy, etc. The maximum weekly payment available through the Fund is currently £420; the combined local authority and ILF contribution must be no more than £715 per week. If the £715 figure is subsequently exceeded (normally after the first six months), the ILF may be prepared to maintain or increase its contribution (but only up to its maximum of £420).

It will be seen, in the case of the 1993 Fund, that there is a close link with social services support (the £200 rule), which local authority staff therefore need to be aware of. Thus, when a local authority reduced a person's weekly care package, and told her that it would not affect her entitlement to ILF, this was incorrect and the local ombudsman found maladministration (*Croydon LBC 2000*).

## 12.4 INFORMAL CARERS

At least six pieces of legislation are directly relevant to informal carers in the community care context. These are the Carers (Equal Opportunities) Act 2004 (due to come into force in 2005), Carers and Disabled Children Act 2000, Carers (Recognition and Services) Act 1995, Children Act 1989 (s.17), Disabled Persons (Services, Consultation and Representation) Act 1986 (s.8), and the NHS Act 1977 (schedule 8).

### 12.4.1 RIGHT OF INFORMAL CARER TO AN ASSESSMENT

Under the Carers (Recognition and Services) Act 1995 and the Carers and Disabled Children Act 2000, informal carers are entitled, if certain conditions are met, to have their ability to care assessed by local authorities. Under the 1995 Act, for an informal carer to be entitled to an assessment, the local authority must be carrying out an assessment of the person cared for under s.47 of the NHS and Community Care Act 1990. In the case of a disabled child, there must be an assessment of that child under Part 3 of the Children Act 1989 or s.2 of the Chronically Sick and Disabled Persons Act 1970.

By contrast, under the 2000 Act, an assessment of the person being cared for is not a prerequisite; the condition for a carer's assessment is simply that he or she must be caring for a person for whom the local authority is satisfied that it has the power to provide or arrange community care services. In the case of a parent of a disabled child, the local authority must be satisfied that it has the power to provide or arrange services for the child and family under s.17 of the Children Act 1989. In other words, a carer's assessment under the 2000 Act may be an entitlement irrespective of whether an assessment of the person cared for has taken place. Whereas under the 1995 Act, a carer's assessment could not proceed unless associated with a community care assessment of the cared for person.

The remaining conditions are as follows. First, the carer must be providing substantial and regular care. Second, he or she must request the assessment. What legally constitutes a request is not always clear; the following two court cases are arguably inconsistent:

**Requesting a carer's assessment.** A local authority maintained that it had not carried out an assessment of the mother of a disabled child under the Carers (Recognition and Services) Act 1995, because it had not received a request to do so. The court held that a letter sent by the woman's solicitors, requesting a full enquiry into both mother and child's 'total needs', was not specific enough. So no request had been made, and there was no duty to assess (R(AB and SB) v Nottingham CC).

This rather restrictive judicial approach in the Nottingham case seems inconsistent with the approach taken in another case concerning the need for a request (by a disabled person or carer) to trigger an assessment of the disabled person under s.4 of the Disabled Persons (Services, Consultation and Representation) Act 1986. A mother had requested assistance for herself and her disabled ten-year-old son. The judge accepted that she had made no formal request for assessment, but held that the courts should look at the 'reality of the situation'; her request for assistance was in effect a request for assessment under the 1986 Act (R v Bexley LBC, ex p B).

However, as the local ombudsman has found, it is certainly easier if informal carers are informed about this right to request an assessment:

**Complete failure to inform carers about their right to an assessment.** A profoundly disabled girl was cared for by her parents; the local authority provided weekend respite care in a care home. The local ombudsman found that, over a period of several years, the authority had done absolutely nothing to inform the parents of the statutory provisions for the assessment of carers. Its efforts at publicising the 1995 carers' legislation fell far short of what government guidance stated should happen. Yet there could not have been another family whose need was more pressing. This was maladministation (*North Yorkshire CC 2002*).

With this very point in mind, the Carers (Equal Opportunities) Act 2004 will amend both 1995 and 2000 Acts so as to confer a duty on the local authority to inform carers about their right to request an assessment.

Any informal carer aged 16 years or over would potentially be entitled to an assessment under either the 1995 or 2000 Act. Aged under 16 years, as a young carer, he or she would be entitled to an assessment under the 1995 Act only. However, arguably such a child would also have a right to be assessed as a child in need under s.17 of the Children Act 1989.

Some local authorities continue to attempt to avoid carers' assessments; in one case, when an authority argued that it had fully assessed the family circumstances when assessing the disabled person, the local ombudsman found maladministration, insofar as a clear assessment of the carer's needs had not thereby been undertaken (*South Tyneside MBC 1999*), as in the following case also:

**Failure to assess the father of a woman with learning disabilities.** A woman with learning disabilities visited home at Christmas and decided not to return to her residential placement. She wanted to live close to her family; the father suggested direct payments and Independent Living Fund money. The council failed properly to assess and to draw up a care plan; as a result the father had to take responsibility for the care of his daughter for over two years. During this time, his needs as a carer were not assessed. The local ombudsman found maladministration (*Hertfordshire CC 2003*).

When a social worker failed to visit a couple – requiring help with cleaning and shopping needs – in order to carry out a community care assessment, the council was not in a position to consider properly whether a carer's assessment was required; this was maladministration (*Salford CC 2003*). And, in another local ombudsman investigation, the local authority failed to respond to a carer's request for assessment for over two years; and then unacceptably was impliedly critical of the carer wishing to discuss his mental health problems, which he felt were exacerbated by caring for his highly dependent brother who had learning disabilities and autism (*Sheffield CC 2004*).

## 12.4.2 INFORMAL CARERS: DEFINITION

Under both the 1995 and 2000 Acts, the definition of carer excludes both paid carers and volunteers for a voluntary organisation. Under the Disabled Persons (Services, Consultation and Representation) Act 1986 (see below), only paid carers, but not such volunteers, are excluded. It also appears that, under the 1986 Act, paid carers working for a voluntary organisation would also not be excluded (s.8 of the 1986 Act excludes only paid carers working for an organisation exercising functions under legislation – which a voluntary organisation would arguably not be doing).

## 12.4.3 SUBSTANTIAL CARE ON A REGULAR BASIS

Central government guidance states that local authorities should judge the condition of substantial and regular care from the point of view of the informal carer and the sustainability of his or her role (DH 2001a, paras 16, 19). This would mean that an over-simple criterion, such as the amount of time spent each week on the caring role, should not in itself be decisive. For instance, additional guidance states that factors to be considered would include physical and mental stress, anxiety, impact on other family responsibilities or employment; in other words, the whole caring situation needs to be considered. This guidance goes on to set out a framework of risk, similar to the 'fair access to care' framework (see 6.11) and consisting of critical, substantial, moderate and low categories; within this authorities should set a local threshold of eligibility (DH 2001b, paras 67–70).

### *12.4.3.1 Ability to care*

The assessment under both 1995 and 2000 Acts must be of a person's ability to care. The Carers (Equal Opportunities) Act 2004 will amend both Acts so as to oblige the local authority to consider, in addition, whether the carer works or wishes to work – or is undertaking, or wishes to undertake, education, training or any leisure activity.

## 12.4.4 RIGHT OF INFORMAL CARER TO BE HAD REGARD TO

If an informal carer of a disabled person does not wish for an assessment, or does not request it, the local authority is still obliged to take account of that carer's ability to care when deciding what welfare services to provide for the disabled person (Disabled Persons (Services, Consultation and Representation) Act 1986, s.8). However, this duty under the 1986 Act does not apply where a carer's assessment is carried out under either the 1995 or the 2000 Act. Furthermore, the proviso that the carer be providing substantial and regular care applies under the 1986 Act, just as it does under the 1995 and 2000 Acts.

## 12.4.5 SERVICES FOR CARERS: CARERS AND DISABLED CHILDREN ACT 2000

Under the Carers and Disabled Children Act 2000, in the case of the cared for person being 18 years or over (i.e. excluding disabled children), a local authority has a duty to consider:

- whether the carer has needs in relation to the care being or intended to be provided
- whether those needs could be satisfied wholly or in part by services that the local authority has the power to provide
- if so, whether or not to provide these services (Carers and Disabled Children Act 2000).

This threefold duty is expressed in a somewhat tortuous manner and in any case only seems to create obligations in terms of considering the question of whether to provide services. Actual provision of services appears to amount only to a power and not a duty.

Assuming that the provision of carers' services is merely a power, then this is clearly a potential weakness in the Act. Nevertheless, a potential strength is that services are not defined, and therefore a local authority would have very wide scope indeed. This is clear from examples of services given in Department of Health guidance. They include shopping, cleaning, a washing machine in the informal carer's own home (to deal with incontinence laundry), a travel warrant for the brother of a person with a psychotic illness to come and stay for a week (thus giving the mother a break), and trips to art galleries (for a 17-year-old carer to get a break while caring for his dying father) (DH 2001b, paras 80–102).

Providing instruction and training for informal carers could be another form of carer's service. For instance, it has been pointed out in the *Selfish Pig's Guide to Caring* that, in respect of the manual handling of disabled people, paid staff might receive training, specialist equipment and have assistants. In contrast, unpaid carers all too often receive no information, little equipment and have to lift alone (Marriott 2003, p.123). Furthermore, a local authority would unlawfully fetter its discretion (see 4.2.2), were it to adopt a blanket policy not to provide carers' services either at all, or to certain classes of person, or in terms of the type of carer's service that it was prepared in principle to provide.

The potential availability of services under the 2000 Act contrasts with the position in the past, when there was no explicit legal power to provide for carers. Thus, in a 1996 case, informal carers living in upstairs premises wished to apply for assistance with modification of their dwelling. This would help them better to care for the elderly family members they were caring for in downstairs premises. The judge pointed out that the assessment under the Carers (Recognition and Services) Act 1995 did not get anyone anywhere in terms of services, and that s.2 CSDPA 1970 anyway did not explicitly cover provision for carers (*R v Kirklees MBC, ex p Good*). This example contrasts with that given immediately above (from the Department of Health guidance) of installing a washing machine not in the cared for person's home, but in the (separate) home of the informal carer.

The power to provide services in the 2000 Act applies only in the case of carers aged at least 16 years old, who are caring for a person 18 years old or over. For parents (as carers) of disabled children, services would fall to be provided under s.17 of the Children Act 1989 (see 12.5.3).

## 12.4.6 SERVICES FOR THE CARER OR FOR THE CARED FOR PERSON
Some services will be capable of being characterised as either being for the disabled person or for the cared for person – for instance, a laundry service. However, there is an im-

portant proviso to this flexibility. Regulations made under the 2000 Act state that carers' services may not involve anything of an intimate nature in respect of the person being cared for (SI 2001/441). A service of an intimate nature is defined as involving:

- lifting, washing, grooming, feeding, dressing, bathing, toileting, medicine administration, or other forms of physical contact
- assistance in connection with washing, grooming, feeding, dressing, bathing, administering medicines or using the toilet
- supervision of the person while he or she is dressing, bathing or using the toilet.

Nevertheless, the regulations also contain an exception to this. During the delivery of what was meant to be a non-intimate service, the carer may deliver an intimate service:

- if the person providing the service is asked by the cared for person to provide a service of an intimate nature
- if the person cared for is likely to suffer serious personal harm if the intimate service is not provided and (a) the person cared for is unable to consent to the service; or (b) the person providing the service reasonably believes it is necessary to provide the service because the likelihood of serious personal harm is imminent.

## 12.4.7 DIRECT PAYMENTS FOR CARERS

Where the local authority has decided to provide a carer's service, the service could be provided or arranged by the local authority or by means of direct payments (see 12.1.1).

## 12.4.8 OTHER LEGISLATION FOR CARERS

Services for informal carers are also potentially available under at least three pieces of legislation other than the 1986, 1995 and 2000 Acts.

The first is the Children Act 1989, s.17, which contains a 'general duty' to safeguard and promote the welfare of children in need by provision of services for such children and their families.

The second is schedule 8 of the NHS Act 1977, which places a general duty on local authorities to provide home help for households (and a power to provide laundry facilities) where it is required owing to the presence in the household of a person who is ill, disabled, aged etc. (see 10.4.2). The way in which the duty is couched would appear not to exclude provision in respect of informal carers, since providing for a household could presumably mean providing for any person in that household.

The third concerns the provision, by the NHS and by other authorities, of services for informal carers. The NHS Act 1977, for instance, does not explicitly refer to carers at all; on the other hand, it is couched in such broad terms that there would be nothing to stop the NHS making plentiful provision for carers.

However, the Carers (Equal Opportunities) Act 2004 will impose a twofold duty of cooperation on other authorities, including the NHS. These other authorities are any other local social services authority, housing authority, education authority or NHS body (listed as special health authority, local health board, primary care trust, NHS trust or NHS foundation trust):

- If a local authority requests these other authorities to assist it in planning the provision of services – for carers entitled to assessment under the 1995 or 2000 Acts, and for those receiving substantial and regular care from those carers – the authority must give due consideration to the request (s.3).
- If a local authority is carrying out, or has completed, a carer's assessment, and believes that the carer's ability to care might be enhanced by services from another authority (as defined above), it can ask the other authority to provide the services. The other authority must give the request due consideration (s.3).

The term 'due consideration' is a relatively weak term; although the NHS could not simply operate a blanket policy of refusing local authority requests for assistance, nevertheless the duty is a far cry from imposing a strong duty to assist in the planning of, or to provide, services for carers. At time of writing, the 2004 Act is not yet in force.

## 12.4.9 COST-EFFECTIVENESS OF CARERS' SERVICES

Cost-effectiveness applies to an absolute duty in terms of how that duty is performed; but to a power it may apply to whether that power will be exercised at all. Carers' services are seemingly governed by a power only. Therefore in practice local authority staff are likely to have to support recommendations about such services with strong arguments about cost-effectiveness.

**Cleaning assistance: example from Department of Health guidance.** An older woman is caring for her husband. She carries out all the care, but would like help with cleaning. The local authority assessor understands the stress she feels at not being able to clean, and that this is undermining the sustainability of the whole caring situation. Her husband would be eligible for home care provided by the local authority but neither he nor his wife want this. The authority instead assists with the cleaning. This solution meets the couple's wishes and is more cost-effective (DH 2001b, para 81).

This example illustrates how useful a relatively small-scale service can be in a caring situation. It might even save the local authority money, since if the situation breaks down because the cleaning service is not provided, then the ensuing care package would be very much more expensive to provide. Department of Health guidance makes this very point, stating that carers sometimes approach local authorities, only to be told that they are entitled to expensive personal care (which they do not want) but not the cheaper cleaning service (which they do want). The guidance states that authorities who do not provide shopping-only, cleaning-only or other low level services should rethink their position – in the cause of genuinely assisting people and of cost-effectiveness (DH 2001b, para 80).

## 12.5 CHILDREN IN NEED AND THEIR FAMILIES

Local authorities have a general duty to safeguard and promote the welfare of children in need within their area. So far as it is consistent with that duty, they must promote the upbringing of such children by their families by providing a range and level of services appropriate to those children's needs (Children Act 1989, s.17). The section has notable strength and weakness. The strength essentially lies in the breadth and scope of provision that can be made; the weakness is that such provision is barely enforceable in any individual case.

### 12.5.1 DEFINITION OF CHILDREN IN NEED
A child in need is defined as:
- unlikely to (or have the opportunity to) achieve or maintain a reasonable standard of health or development without the provision of services
- one whose health or development is likely to be significantly impaired, or further impaired, without the provision of services
- disabled.

A disabled child in turn means a child who is 'blind, deaf or dumb or suffers from mental disorder of any kind or is substantially and permanently handicapped by illness, injury or congenital deformity'.

Development means 'physical, intellectual, emotional, social or behavioural development'. Health means 'physical or mental health' (Children Act 1989, s.17). A child is defined as being under 18 years old (s.105).

### 12.5.2 RANGE OF SERVICES FOR CHILDREN IN NEED
The duty under s.17 of the Children Act 1989 is couched in such general terms – accommodation, assistance in kind and, in exceptional cases, cash – that a wide range of services could in principle be provided. For the purpose 'principally of facilitating' the discharge of this general duty, a local authority has a duty to provide, as it considers appropriate, the following services (s.17):
- advice, guidance and counselling
- occupational, social, cultural or recreational activities
- home help (which may include laundry facilities)
- facilities for, or assistance with, travelling to and from the home, in order to take advantage of any other service provided under the 1989 Act or any similar service
- assistance to enable the child and family to have a holiday (schedule 2).

The local authority also has a duty to minimise the effect on disabled children within their area of their disabilities and to give such children the opportunity to lead lives that are as normal as possible (schedule 2).

Services may be arranged in the form of direct payments in respect of the parents of disabled children, disabled children aged 16 or 17 years old, or disabled parents of children – where the child concerned is deemed to be in need of s.17 services (see 12.1.1). In addition, the parent of a disabled child may obtain services designed to give him or her a short break, by means of time or money vouchers (s.17B: see 12.2).

### 12.5.3 PROVISION FOR THE FAMILY

Any service provided under s.17 of the 1989 Act may be provided for the child's family or any member of the family, so long as it is with a view to safeguarding and promoting the welfare of the child (s.17).

### 12.5.4 DUTY OF ASSESSMENT

There is no explicit duty on the local authority to assess a child in need under s.17 of the Children Act 1989; although the Act (schedule 2) does state that an assessment under s.17 may take place at the same time as an assessment under other legislation such as s.2 of the Chronically Sick and Disabled Persons Act 1970 (CSDPA).

However, policy guidance, *Framework for the Assessment of Children in Need*, assumes such a duty and sets out timescales of responding to referrals within one day, conducting an initial assessment within seven, and completing an in-depth, core assessment within 35 days (DH 2000a, paras 3.8–3.11). The courts have ruled that such guidance should be followed:

**Assessment of child in need.** The court stated that in terms of carrying out a core assessment of a child in need, the local authority had either to follow the guidance, or at least adopt a similarly systematic approach to achieve the same objectives. In the case of a core assessment this was to assess the child's developmental needs, parenting capacity, and family and environmental circumstances. It was then to identify the needs, produce a care plan and provide services. Failure to take this approach 'without good cause would constitute an impermissible departure from the guidance' (R(AB and SB) v Nottingham CC).

In another case, the court specifically ordered the local authority to carry out the s.17 assessment that it had been attempting to avoid, within 35 days (R(J) v Newham LBC).

Second, the courts have anyway confirmed that s.17 implies a duty of assessment of each child in need, whenever it appears necessary to assess (*R(G) v Barnet LBC*).

It should be noted that unlike much of the community care legislation, s.2 of the CSDPA 1970 applies to children as well as adults. There is a condition referred to in s.2 of the CSDPA that for s.2 to apply a local authority must have functions under s.29 of the National Assistance Act 1948 (welfare services for disabled adults). In the case of disabled children, this condition is substituted and replaced by a reference to Part 3 of the Children Act 1989 (CSDPA 1970, s.28A).

There is a duty, on request by the disabled child or a parent, to decide whether a disabled child's needs call for services under s.2 of the CSDPA 1970 (Disabled Persons (Services, Consultation and Representation) Act 1986, s.4).

### 12.5.5 DISABLED CHILDREN

The courts have pointed out that by contrast to s.17 of the Children Act 1989, an enforceable duty to provide for assessed, eligible need does arise in the case of a disabled child under s.2 of the Chronically Sick and Disabled Persons Act 1970. Therefore, artificial attempts to avoid providing for a disabled child, by arguing that the provision (a respite service) concerns s.17 of the 1989 Act rather than s.2 of the CSDPA 1970, are likely to be treated with scepticism by the courts (*R v Bexley LBC, ex p B*).

## 12.6 LEAVING CARE: CHILDREN PREVIOUSLY LOOKED AFTER

In some circumstances, local authorities retain specific responsibilities (both duties and powers) into adulthood for certain people, who as children were in the care of the local authority ('former relevant' children: Children Act 1989, s.23C). There are also other wider responsibilities toward not just people previously looked after as children by a local authority, but also those who as children were (a) formerly accommodated by a voluntary organisation or in a private children's home; (b) for a period of at least three consecutive months accommodated by an education authority, by the NHS, or in a care home or independent hospital; (c) privately fostered (Children Act 1989, s.24). The legislative provisions are complicated and the following is a broad summary only.

Where a child is a former relevant child or was otherwise looked after by a local authority, the responsible authority is the authority that last looked after him or her. Otherwise, it is the local authority in whose area the person now is (Children Act 1989, ss.23–24). Such responsibilities are known as 'leaving care' provisions; the duties amongst them are individual duties. They normally cease when a child has reached 21 years but can in some circumstances continue beyond that age (Children Act 1989, ss.23C, 24B).

For former relevant children, the duties include keeping in touch with the former relevant child (now an adult); continuing the appointment of an adviser to the person; keeping a 'pathway plan' under regular review; and giving assistance in terms of living or other expenses incurred in relation to employment, education or training. Other assistance, in kind or exceptionally cash, must be given to the extent that the person's welfare requires it (Children Act 1989, ss.23C, 24B). The courts have held that these duties, under the Act and relevant regulations (SI 2001/2874), apply as much to disabled children as to able-bodied children (*R(P) v Newham LBC*).

For other children, duties and powers include advising and befriending, providing assistance in kind (exceptionally accommodation or cash), living or other expenses in connection with education or training (Children Act 1989, ss.24A–24B).

The definition of 'looked after' excludes children who have received services under s.17 of the Children Act 1989 (see s.22 of the Act); however, Department of Health guidance warns that local authorities should not on that account artificially label the provision of accommodation as s.17 (rather than s.20) provision merely to avoid 'leaving care' obligations at a later date (LAC(2003)13). Identification of the responsible local authority, for the purpose of leaving care functions, is covered below (see 14.2.4).

## 12.7 OTHER SPECIFIC GROUPS OF PEOPLE

The Department of Health has issued various guidance relating to specific groups of people.

### 12.7.1 HIV SOCIAL CARE SERVICES

Guidance has been issued in respect of support grant for people with HIV/AIDS, which is provided by central government under the Local Government Grants (Social Need) Act 1969. The guidance lists matters that local authorities should consider taking into account. These include the need for:

- effective joint planning arrangements
- comprehensive population needs assessments to ensure that minority groups are not overlooked (including women, children, people from newly arrived minority ethnic communities, and men who have sex with men)
- flexible care management arrangements including direct payments
- eligibility being determined on basis of assessed need, not just HIV status
- assessment and support for informal carers
- integration of HIV services with those services for other service users, particularly children, families and people with drug-related problems
- review of continuing health care eligibility to ensure that people with HIV/AIDS have access to such services (LAC(2004)19).

### 12.7.2 DEAF-BLIND ADULTS

The Department of Health has issued guidance in respect of deaf-blind adults. This is in recognition of the particular impact of dual sensory loss; and of the fact that such dual loss does not necessarily mean profound deafness coupled with profound blindness. Even separately milder sensory loss can cause difficulty in combination (LAC(2001)8). The guidance states that local authorities should:

- make contact with and keep a record of deaf-blind people in their catchment area
- ensure that assessment is carried out by a specifically trained person or team in respect particularly of the need for one-to-one contact, assistive technology and rehabilitation
- ensure that services for deaf-blind people are appropriate, since mainstream services or those aimed at people who are either blind or deaf (but not both) may not be of benefit to deaf-blind people
- ensure that deaf-blind people are able to access one-to-one support workers where this is an assessed need
- ensure that a senior manager includes amongst his or her responsibilities responsibility for deaf-blind services.

### 12.7.3 PEOPLE WITH LEARNING DISABILITIES

Department of Health guidance issued in 1992 set out three basic service principles for people with learning disabilities (LAC(92)15, paras 9–15):

- People with learning disabilities should be treated as individuals and thus services should be provided on an increasingly individual basis, taking account of age, needs, degree of disability, personal preference of the person or his or her parents or carers, culture, race gender.
- Parents and carers should be fully involved in decisions about services; conciliation and counselling should be offered in case of conflicts between parents/carers and people with learning disabilities – but generally the views of the person with learning disability should be respected.
- Local authorities should give assurance that people's essential needs would be met on a lifelong basis, for instance to reassure aging parents about continuity of service in the future for their sons or daughters with learning disabilities.

In 2001, central government published a White Paper, entitled *Valuing People*. It set out what it called four key principles: rights, independence, choice and inclusion. It referred to improving 'life chances', enabling more choice and control (e.g. through use of direct payments), improving health, more options for housing and education and employment, better quality of services, and partnership working by agencies (DH 2001d).

Subsequent implementation policy guidance told the chief executives of local social services authorities to set up Learning Disability Partnership Boards. Representation on the boards should include social services, NHS bodies, housing, education, Employment Service, Jobcentre Plus, independent providers and voluntary organisations. The boards should promote effective arrangements for enabling young people with learning disabilities to move smoothly from children's to adult services in respect of all relevant agencies. Directors of social services should ensure the existence of good links between children's and adult's services in local authorities (LAC(2001)23).

The guidance stated that boards should also collate information about advocacy services to inform decisions on the funding of advocacy; foster the development of support services and schemes so that more people with learning disabilities benefit from direct payments; recommend procedures for dealing with the exclusion from services of people with learning disabilities. Boards should, amongst other things, also ensure that arrangements were in place to enable people currently in NHS long-stay hospitals to move to more appropriate accommodation by April 2004; introduce a 'person-centred' approach to planning services by spring 2003; begin to modernise day services; and have a local housing strategy for people with learning disabilities etc. (LAC(2001)23).

Person-centred planning was described in subsequent guidance as an approach based on what is important to a person from his or her own perspective, with a view to the person's fuller inclusion in society. It was to be distinguished from community care assessment and care plans under s.47 of the NHS and Community Care Act 1990 (DH 2001b).

## 12.8 DRUGS AND ALCOHOL

The Department of Health issued guidance in 1993 in respect of misuses of drugs and alcohol (LAC(93)2). Some of the main points include:

- **Priority**. Local authorities are expected to attach a high priority to alcohol and drug misusers in community care (para 1).
- **Special circumstances**. Misusers of alcohol and drugs present a particular challenge. Assessment procedures must be capable of identifying alcohol or drug misuse. People might have complex needs, move between areas frequently, and have no settled residence. They might self-refer to agencies in areas in which they are not resident, avoid contact with statutory services, and require services several times before they bring the misuse under control. Their behaviour might be unpredictable, and they might require rapid responses to avoid deterioration (paras 12–13).
- **Eligibility criteria**. Local authorities should ensure that eligibility criteria are sensitive to the circumstances of alcohol and drug misusers (para 14).
- **Assessment by the independent sector**. Local authorities should consider involving the expertise of the independent sector in the assessment process, although ultimate responsibility for the decision to provide services remained with the local authority (paras 16–17).
- **Out of area placements**. Generally, local authorities, within certain financial bounds, must attempt to give people a choice of residential accommodation. There might be 'therapeutic benefit in referring people to a residential area away from the area in which they are experiencing their alcohol and drug problems... LAs should ensure that resources can be identified for out of area placements' (para 23).
- **Probation service**. For people who misuse drugs or alcohol and who might require residential or non-residential care, local authorities should liaise with probation services (para 25).

Despite the firm tone of the guidance, it should be noted that where needs are seen to arise from drugs or alcohol use, community care legislation contains only powers rather than duties, whether in respect of residential accommodation (National Assistance Act 1948, s.21: see 8.3.2) or non-residential services (NHS Act 1977, schedule 8: see 10.4.1.2). Nevertheless, if the need of the user of alcohol or drugs can be equated with more than just the substance misuse, then a duty could be identified – for instance, if the person has in addition, or as a consequence of the substance misuse, a mental disorder, an illness or a disability.

CHAPTER 13

# Asylum seekers and other people subject to immigration control

**KEY POINTS**

The law as a whole relating to people subject to immigration control is beyond the scope of this book. Therefore the following is a summary only, designed to give a few pointers on matters relating to community care. Much of the legal case law revolves around s.21 of the National Assistance Act 1948; therefore this chapter should be taken in conjunction with Chapter 8.

Since about 1996, a significant part of community care for some local authorities has concerned the provision of services for asylum seekers and others who are subject to immigration control. The relevant law continues to be in a continual state of flux and uncertainty; a situation reflected in the very large volume of legal case law on immigration matters generally, a significant part of which has involved local social services authority responsibilities. This represents an additional and unexpected layer of complexity in the community care system, which even in its basic form has uncertainty enough (see 3.1).

The reader should be aware that at the time of writing the case law continues to provide new twists and turns from one month to the next; and further legislation came into force in December 2004: the Asylum and Immigration (Treatment of Claimants) Act 2004. Under s.9 of that Act, schedule 3 of the Nationality, Immigration and Asylum Act 2002 is amended. This means that failed asylum seekers with dependent children may be denied support even before they have failed to comply with a removal direction. However, the children would still be eligible to receive support from the local social services authority.

Thus, provision of welfare support (including community care) for asylum seekers and others subject to immigration control is an especially complex and specialist area. This chapter attempts to give a number of pointers only; but reference should also be made to other specialist sources of information – such as *Support For Asylum Seekers: A Guide To Legal and Welfare Rights*, published by the Legal Action Group (Willman 2004), which sets out the detailed position most helpfully.

**Note: Wales, Scotland and Northern Ireland**. The asylum and immigration legislation (Immigration and Asylum Act 1999, the Nationality, Immigration and Asylum Act 2002, and the Asylum and Immigration (Treatment of Claimants) Act 2004) referred to in this chapter applies to Wales, Scotland and Northern Ireland. The particular prohibitions, relating to community care, contained in this legislation are therefore applied to the relevant community care legislation in each country. In Northern Ireland, specific policy guidance has been issued on access to health and social services by asylum seekers and refugees (DHSSPS 2004).

## 13.1 IMMIGRATION CONTROL: BACKGROUND

Unexpectedly, asylum seekers and people subject to immigration control have featured prominently in community care since at least 1996. In attempts to deal with this, something of a 'cat-and-mouse' situation seems to have developed between central government, local government and the courts. Parliament has passed a great deal of legislation. Because of the fundamental issues involved, the courts have closely scrutinised the legislation for loopholes. Because of the potential financial implications, local authorities have made relatively sustained attempts to avoid responsibilities that they feel for one reason or another to be unfair.

The immediate background is that in 1996 regulations were introduced to deny certain classes of asylum seeker access to income-related benefits including income support and housing benefit. The courts struck down these regulations as unlawful in the light of the rights implicit in the Asylum and Immigration Appeals Act 1993 (*R v Secretary of State for the Home Department, ex p Joint Council for the Welfare of Immigrants*).

Central government reacted via the Asylum and Immigration Act 1996, so as to restore the effect of the regulations that the courts had just held to be unlawful. Consequently, certain asylum seekers were deprived of accommodation, funds, benefits and permission to work (for at least six months). A possible last resort was then identified; namely s.21 of the National Assistance Act 1948 and the duty of social services authorities to arrange residential accommodation in certain circumstances for those in urgent need of it. The 1948 Act had not been on the list of exclusions contained within the 1996 Act.

Faced with potential unexpected and significant expenditure, the affected local authorities resisted and fought out several issues in the courts, including whether s.21 was relevant at all to asylum seekers (*R v Westminster CC, ex p A*: it was), whether cash payments could be made to those being provided with residential accommodation (*R v Secretary of State for Health, ex p Hammersmith and Fulham LBC*: they could not), whether food vouchers could be given under s.21 even if residential accommodation was not being provided (*R v Newham LBC, ex p Gorenkin*: they could not), whether accommodation alone – without food, laundry and other facilities for personal hygiene – could be provided (*R v Newham LBC, ex p Medical Foundation for the Care of Victims of Torture*: it could), or whether choice could be exercised in relation to where the accommodation was arranged (*R v Westminster CC, ex p P*: the question was not answered).

One case was particularly significant. The Court of Appeal emphasised that the plight of the asylum seekers was horrendous and that the National Assistance Act 1948 was a prime example of legislation that was 'always speaking' to respond to changing social circumstances (*R v Westminster CC, ex p A*). It should also be noted that up to October 2000, this type of case was decided before the Human Rights Act 1998 had come into force. The courts instead referred on several occasions to an 1803 case (*R v Inhabitants of Eastbourne*), in which the 'law of humanity, which is anterior to all positive laws', had been invoked and which obliged that relief be given to prevent poor foreigners from starving (see e.g. reference in *R v Westminster CC, ex p A*: High Court).

By 1998, it was clear that the pressure on some local social services authorities had become considerable. In 1999 and 2002 further major legislation was passed to give the present position (see below). During 2004, yet further legislation was passed. The 1999 legislation was apparently designed to shift the burden of asylum seekers away from local social services authorities; the subsequent case law and judicial interpretation suggests that the Act did not achieve this to the extent intended. The 2002 legislation was designed to reduce substantially the assistance given by social services authorities to other people subject to immigration control.

### 13.2 IMMIGRATION CONTROL: SOCIAL SERVICES, PRESENT POSITION
The following paragraphs outline the present position concerning responsibilities in the community care context, to asylum seekers or other people subject to immigration control.

## 13.2.1 DESTITUTION TEST

People to whom s.115 of the Immigration and Asylum Act 1999 applies (those subject to immigration control including asylum seekers) may not be provided with community care services by local authorities, if the need for care and attention arises solely (a) because the person is destitute; or (b) because of the physical effects, or anticipated physical effects, of destitution.

Basically, s.115 applies to people who are denied a wide range of social security benefits because they are subject to immigration control. A person is subject to immigration control if he or she is not a national of an EEA state and (a) requires leave to enter or remain in the United Kingdom but does not have that leave; (b) has leave to enter or remain on condition of not having recourse to public funds; (c) has leave to enter or remain as a result of a maintenance undertaking by another person; (d) during an appeal concerning leave.

The prohibitions on community care services are contained in the National Assistance Act 1948 (s.21(1A NAA)), the Health Services and Public Health Act 1968 (s.45(4A)) and the NHS Act 1977 (schedule 8, para 2A). It should be noted, however, that s.117 of the Mental Health Act 1983 is not listed. Nor is s.29 of the 1948 Act, or s.2 of the Chronically Sick and Disabled Persons Act 1970; this is presumably because it is assumed that the various disabilities required to trigger this legislation (see 10.1.3) would not normally be regarded as solely destitution related.

A person is defined as destitute if he or she does not have adequate accommodation or any means of obtaining it (whether or not other essential living needs are being met); or he or she does have adequate accommodation or has the means of obtaining it, but cannot meet other essential living needs (Immigration and Asylum Act 1999, s.95).

**Ineligible for assistance through destitution.** The applicant was a 51-year-old British citizen, holder of a British passport with right of abode in the United Kingdom. He was ineligible for social security benefits because he was not classed as habitually resident in the UK and did not speak English. The manager of a night shelter – where the man had been staying, but which was now closing – wrote on his behalf, seeking for residential accommodation to be provided by the local authority under s.21 of the National Assistance Act 1948.

An assessment was carried out by the local authority, with the conclusion that, though without benefits and homeless, the man was able-bodied and had worked previously as a ship's captain and cook, was not physically disabled except for dental problems for which he could receive NHS treatment, and was aware of his situation. On this basis his application was refused.

The judge held that it was not 'perverse' of the local authority to have refused assistance. For instance, the present applicant was not ineligible from seeking accommodation under homelessness legislation, was not 'under any physical or mental disability', was able-bodied and of working age. He also referred to the Court of Appeal's judgment in R v Westminster CC, ex p A, which emphasised that s.21 of the 1948 Act was not a safety net for anybody short of money or accommodation. Nor could the judge fault the local authority's assessment, finding that it was 'not arguable that they left out of that consideration any material matter' (R v Newham LBC, ex p Plastin).

However, the courts have held that a disabled asylum seeker might be eligible for provision of accommodation under s.21 of the National Assistance Act 1948, but nevertheless have other essential living needs (e.g. for clothing) unrelated to the accommodation or to the amenities and requisites that go with it (see 8.2.3). In which case, the Home Office (through the National Asylum Support Service) might have potential responsibility under s.95 of the 1999 Act for meeting those additional needs (*R(O) v Haringey LBC*).

In the case of various categories of people subject to immigration control other than asylum seekers, there are further prohibitions in respect of community care services – even if their needs are not solely related to destitution (see 13.2.6).

## 13.2.2 ADULT ASYLUM SEEKERS

The effect of the legislation and court cases is that if an adult asylum seeker has a community care need going beyond destitution, then he or she will be eligible for community care services. This will be so, even if the level of need falls below the normal threshold of eligibility applied by the local authority (see 6.9).

Where the local authority has such an obligation, the Home Office is precluded from assisting under its own scheme to assist asylum seekers. This is because of the effect of s.95 of the1999 Act, which allows Home Office provision only if the person is destitute; which the person will not be if he or she is eligible for assistance with accommodation and essential living needs from a local authority under its social services functions.

Thus, in relation to the provision of residential accommodation under s.21 of the National Assistance Act 1948, an asylum seeker is eligible for assistance from the local authority if his or her need for care and attention (arising from destitution) is to a material extent made more acute by age, illness, disability or any other circumstances (i.e. the reasons why care and attention must be required under s.21).

The legal test is as follows, formulated in a court case not involving asylum seekers but others subject to immigration control – but nevertheless applicable now to asylum seekers also:

**Differentiating need solely caused by destitution from need otherwise caused.** In a case involving two people subject to immigration control, the court considered two possible approaches. The first was to ask whether the applicant would still need assistance under the 1948 Act, even were he or she not destitute. The second was to ask whether the applicant's need for care and attention was to any material extent made more acute by some circumstance other than the mere lack of accommodation and funds. The court was in no doubt that the second, more inclusive, approach was to be preferred. This was because the 1948 Act had been the last refuge for the destitute; and if there were to be immigrant beggars on the streets, 'then let them at least not be old, ill or disabled' (*R v Wandsworth LBC, ex p O*).

Although concerning non-asylum seekers, the test as formulated in the above case is applied also to asylum seekers to determine whether or not they are in need of care and attention (e.g. *Westminster CC v NASS*). The consequence is that the normal test of eligibility for community care services (see 6.9) is not straightforwardly applicable to asylum seekers. Instead the test has been replaced by the blunt question of whether the need for care and attention is to a material extent made more acute by circumstances other than lack of accommodation or funds (*R v Wandsworth LBC, ex p O*). Put another way, the question is whether a person needs care and attention for any reason other than destitution (*Westminster CC v NASS*).

Furthermore, the courts have stated that this means that entitlement to s.21 assistance does not depend on a need for care and attention of a kind only available through the provision of residential accommodation. In other words, assistance is not confined just to those asylum seekers who would otherwise be eligible for s.21 accommodation (even if they did not have a need related to immigration status). So asylum seekers have a substantially better chance of qualifying for s.21 accommodation than their 'indigenous counterparts' (*R(Mani) v Lambeth LBC*). It has been argued that it is absurd that local authorities, rather than the Home Office, should have to support people who are eligible only because they are asylum seekers, rather than because they are in 'eligible' need, as normally understood, for s.21 accommodation. The courts, whilst acknowledging the substance of such concerns, have declined to say more (*Westminster CC v NASS*).

The following court cases illustrate the test as to whether a person's need is to a material extent made more acute for some reason other than lack of accommodation or funds:

**Eligibility for accommodation.** An infirm, destitute asylum seeker had spinal cancer; she required accommodation that was wheelchair accessible. The local authority argued that, had she been an ordinary resident rather than an asylum seeker, she would not have required, or been eligible for, accommodation under s.21 of the 1948 Act. She would have had her own accommodation, at which other services could have been provided if required. The court disagreed and stated that she was eligible under s.21 (*Westminster CC v NASS*). Likewise, a destitute asylum seeker who had a leg abnormality needed help with bed-making, hoovering and heavy shopping; he too was eligible for s.21 accommodation (*R(Mani) v Lambeth LBC*).

**HIV status and destitution.** A local authority took a decision without medical evidence to decide that a person with HIV was not in need over and beyond destitution – and so was ineligible for assistance under s.21 of the 1948 Act. In other words, it was not the case that all people with HIV would automatically be eligible. However, the court stated that in the light of subsequent medical evidence, there would be at least a strong case for the local authority to reassess and find that the woman would be in need of care and attention (*R(J) v Enfield LBC*).

In another case, the court stated that the fact that an asylum seeker who was HIV positive required medical treatment was sufficient to show that he was more vulnerable than somebody who was able-bodied and destitute. He therefore required care and attention for a reason that related to more than destitution; he was thus the responsibility of the local authority under the 1948 Act, and not of the Home Office (*R(M) v Slough BC*).

The threshold set by the courts is therefore a low one. Furthermore, the conditions in s.21, that might take an asylum seeker out of the 'destitution only' category, include not only age, illness and disability, but also 'any other circumstances', the ambit of which is potentially wide.

**Domestic violence.** A woman had been granted leave to enter the United Kingdom from Pakistan to join her husband. She was subjected to violence; he tried to strangle her and threatened her with a knife; she was kidnapped and locked up in a house. She escaped. The local authority now considered whether it had a duty to accommodate her. Under s.115 of the Immigration and Asylum Act 1999 she was subject to immigration control, because her condition of entry was that she did not have recourse to public funds. This meant that unless she could show her needs stemmed from more than just destitution, she would not be eligible for local authority assistance under s.21 of the 1948 Act.

The court accepted that a background of domestic violence could be a relevant 'any other circumstance' for the purpose of showing this. Thus the local authority had to show that it had genuinely considered, when rejecting her application for assistance, whether the woman's needs stemmed solely from destitution or whether she was more vulnerable because of such a background. In fact, the local authority could show this and the court would not interfere with its reasoning (R(Khan) v Oxfordshire CC).

Nevertheless, even with this low threshold, a need for care and attention not otherwise available still needs to be demonstrated in order for the legal duty to provide residential accommodation to be triggered:

**Care and attention otherwise available from wife or family overseas**. The court found that the local authority was acting lawfully in the following circumstances. A United States citizen with mental health problems was not currently living with his wife (a British citizen, who was disabled and suffering from epilepsy) because, following his discharge from hospital, she did not feel she could cope living with him. However, they were on good terms. He also had family in the United States. He was in the country lawfully but subject to immigration control insofar as he had leave to remain so long as he did not have recourse to public funds. He therefore came under s.115 of the Immigration and Asylum Act 1999. This in turn meant that the local authority would be prohibited from assisting him under s.21 of the 1948 Act, if his need for care and attention arose solely from destitution or the physical effects of destitution.

However, apart from contesting the question of destitution, the local authority also argued that care and attention was otherwise available to him either from his wife or from his family in the United States. The court held that the local authority was entitled to take this stance, both in principle and on the facts of the case (R(P) v Camden LBC).

In sum, it can be seen therefore that there has been considerable incentive for dispute between local authorities, the Home Office and asylum seekers.

### 13.2.3 ASYLUM SEEKERS WITH CHILDREN

If an asylum seeker eligible for social services assistance (under s.21 of the National Assistance Act 1948 because of a need relating to more than destitution) has a child, then the Home Office is normally responsible for supporting the child under s.95 of the Immigration and Asylum Act 1999. The Home Office discharges this responsibility through the National Asylum Support Service (NASS). To avoid fragmented practical arrangements, with the local authority providing for the adult and the NASS for the child, the courts have suggested that the NASS could come to an agreement with the local authority, whereby the local authority would make arrangements for the child on behalf of the NASS (R(O) v Haringey LBC).

This issue was considered in the case of a woman, who was an asylum seeker and was HIV positive, with two children aged three and five years old. The following points were made (*R(O) v Haringey LBC*):

- Local social services authorities cannot provide assistance under s.17 of the Children Act 1989 for children of asylum seekers or their families, if they are eligible for assistance under s.95 of the 1999 Act (Immigration and Asylum Act 1999, s.122).
- The family would be eligible under s.95, only if its accommodation and essential living needs could not be met elsewhere (Immigration and Asylum Act 1999, s.95).
- The court held that s.17 of the Children Act 1989 contained such a vague duty (because it was not enforceable) that it could not be relied upon as evidence of accommodation being otherwise available for the family (nor were ss.20 or 23 of the Children Act 1989 relevant to deciding the issue).
- The National Assistance Act 1948, s.21, placed an obligation on the local authority to provide for the adult (whose needs were more than just destitution related); but there would be no entitlement or enforceable expectation under s.21 of the 1948 Act that children would be accommodated with their parents.
- Thus the family as a whole was destitute under s.95 of the 1999 Act, essentially because the child had no other reliable means of support. The family was therefore eligible for NASS support; however, the mother's eligibility under s.21 of the 1948 Act had to be taken into account.
- Therefore the NASS would have to provide support for the children under s.95 of the 1999 Act, whilst the local authority would provide the accommodation for the mother under s.21 of the 1948 Act. However, to avoid fragmented arrangements, the NASS would request the local authority to make arrangements for the child on the NASS's behalf and at the NASS's expense.

If the child is disabled, but the adult asylum seeker parent is not, then the effect of the legislation is that the NASS has responsibility for the whole family under s.95 of the Immigration and Asylum Act 1999.

The courts have also held that 'adequate accommodation' for a disabled child, under s.95 of the Immigration and Asylum Act 1999, should be suited to the disabled child. The National Asylum Support Service had argued that, even in the case of a disabled child, adequacy should be tested with reference only to able-bodied children (*R(A) v National Asylum Support Service*).

## 13.2.4 UNACCOMPANIED CHILDREN

Local social services authorities have potential responsibilities toward all unaccompanied children in need who are subject to immigration control (including asylum seekers). Such support is prohibited neither in s.122 of the Immigration and Asylum Act 1999 nor in schedule 3 of the Nationality, Immigration and Asylum Act 2002.

An unaccompanied child will be the potential responsibility of the local authority under the Children Act 1989. Faced with the possible choice of different sections in the Children Act under which assistance could be given, local authorities have received guidance from the Department of Health. This states that there will be a presumption that accommodation provided for unaccompanied asylum seeking children will be under s.20 of the 1989 Act (thus attracting the 'leaving care' provisions: see 12.6) rather than s.17 (which does not bring a child into the leaving care provisions). A local authority that took the opposite position (that s.17 was the norm) would be potentially in breach of the guidance and acting unlawfully (*R(Berhe) Hillingdon LBC*).

Local authorities should also take care when making a decision about an unaccompanied asylum seeking child's age. For instance, they should not simply follow the Home Office's view but come to their own conclusions, should explain the purpose of the interview to the person and give him or her an opportunity to address the issues (*R(B) v Merton LBC*).

**Age of asylum seeker: not taking account of material considerations.** An immigration and asylum adjudicator had concluded that an asylum seeker was only 17 years old, and the Secretary of State for the Home Office had accepted this, giving her leave to remain in the United Kingdom until her 18th birthday.

The local authority now reached a different decision to the adjudicator. It might have been entitled to this, but it was unable to show that it had taken account of the relevant considerations. It failed actually to ask the asylum seeker from Angola, who had suffered horrific experiences there, why it was that she was maintaining that she was under 18 years old. It failed also to take account of the report of a consultant paediatrician, or of the views of the Child Guidance team and of the person's mental health worker. In addition, the questioning of the person was unduly hostile; this led her to 'clam up' and to the local authority assessors wrongly disbelieving her evidence (*R(T) v Enfield LBC*).

## 13.2.5 OTHER ACCOMPANIED CHILDREN

In respect of asylum seekers, the position is as set out above (13.2.3). If the parent with a child is not an asylum seeker, but nevertheless subject to immigration control, support or assistance can be given by a local social services authority to the child but not to the family (Nationality, Immigration and Asylum Act 2002, schedule 3, paras 1–2). However, regulations have been made to allow the provision of temporary accommodation for such a parent and dependent child (see 13.2.7).

## 13.2.6 PEOPLE SUBJECT TO IMMIGRATION CONTROL (OTHER THAN ASYLUM SEEKERS): ADULTS

For adults who are subject to immigration control, but who are not (or are no longer) asylum seekers, social services are barred from providing support or assistance under nearly all the community care legislation (Nationality, Immigration and Asylum Act 2002, schedule 3).

This prohibition covers the National Assistance Act 1948 (ss.21 and 29 and by implication s.2 of the Chronically Sick and Disabled Persons Act 1970), Health and Services and Public Health Act 1968, s.45, section 21, and schedule 8 of the NHS Act 1977. Also listed is the Children Act 1989, insofar as provision can be made for adults under ss.17, 23C, 24A and 24B.

It should be noted, however, that s.117 of the Mental Health Act 1983 is not listed; and children in their own right are likewise not excluded from assistance. Furthermore, assistance is not prohibited if there would otherwise be a breach of human rights or of European Community treaties.

This prohibition further means that, whereas previously the courts had stated that a local social services authority should concern itself with meeting people's community care needs and leave it to the Home Office to determine immigration status (*R v Wandsworth LBC, ex p O*), now local authorities have an obligation to make efforts to comply with this prohibition.

The prohibition applies to (a) people who have refugee status abroad; (b) certain people who are members of a European Economic Area state other than the United Kingdom (but see 13.2.9); (c) failed asylum seekers who are not cooperating with removal directions; (d) any other person, not an asylum seeker, who is in breach of the immigration laws (defined in s.11 of the Act); (e) failed asylum seekers with dependent children who, according to a certificate issued by the Security of State, have failed without reasonable excuse to take reasonable steps to leave the United Kingdom voluntarily.

**Failure to comply with removal order.** In one legal case (heard prior to the 2002 Act), a man who had originally been granted political asylum in the United Kingdom was subsequently convicted of drug offences and imprisoned. A deportation and removal order was made, but Sweden would not permit his re-entry. The court pointed out that the applicant had served a lawful prison sentence and was unable to leave through factors entirely beyond his control. He was therefore not exercising a choice not to comply with the deportation order (*R v Lambeth LBC, ex p Sarhangi*).

## 13.2.7 PEOPLE SUBJECT TO IMMIGRATION CONTROL: ADULTS WITH CHILDREN

The prohibitions placed on a local authority's ability to provide support for an adult subject to immigration control (other than an asylum seeker) does contain an exception – if he or she is accompanied by a dependent child. This is possible through regulations issued under schedule 3 of the 2002 Act – the Withholding and Withdrawal of Support (Travel Assistance and Temporary Accommodation) Regulations 2002 (SI 2002/3078). These regulations give local authorities the power to accommodate a person unlawfully in the United Kingdom, with a dependent child, so long as he or she has not failed to comply with directions for removal.

Although it is only a power that is conferred, a failure to exercise it could result in separation of the parent from the child, with the child alone then being cared for under s.20 of the Children Act 1989. But this could potentially infringe the right to respect for family life under article 8 of the European Convention on Human Rights (*R(Grant) v Lambeth LBC*; see also *R(M) v Islington LBC*).

The same regulations confer on local authorities a power to make travel arrangements for an adult and child to return to their country of origin only in the case of nationals of European Economic Area (EEA) Member States and those with refugee status in such an EEA state. Otherwise, paradoxically, a local authority could not make such travel arrangements, but instead have to consider providing accommodation under the regulations. Alternatively, the courts have held that a local authority could offer instead to make travel arrangements under s.2 of the Local Government Act 2000 (see 13.2.10), in order to avoid breach of human rights – for a family for whom it could not make travel arrangements under the regulations themselves. (*R(Grant) v Lambeth LBC*).

## 13.2.8 HUMAN RIGHTS

The prohibitions placed on social services authorities in schedule 3 of the 2002 Act do not apply if a person's human rights (or rights under European Community law) would otherwise be breached. Likewise the prohibitions placed on Home Office assistance under s.55 of the Act (see 13.2.11).

**Human rights and assistance for an illegal overstayer.** In a case heard prior to the Nationality, Immigration and Asylum Act 2002, the courts considered whether a local authority should assist a Brazilian man with advanced HIV/AIDS who had illegally overstayed on his six-month visa. In making its decision, it had to decide whether or not he was fit to travel back to Brazil to receive care and treatment. If not, the local authority had to consider the effect of the absence of shelter and accommodation. This could in turn give rise to considerations under articles 2 and 3 of the European Convention on Human Rights (*R v Brent LBC, ex p D*).

There have been many court cases argued concerning whether human rights would be breached if no assistance were given. Many of these have hinged on article 3 of the European Convention and the question of inhuman or degrading treatment – in relation to denial of support by the Home Office under s.55 of the 2002 Act.

**Human rights generally.** An asylum seeker denied support under s.55 had shelter, sanitary facilities and some money for food. He was not entirely well but did not require medical treatment. There was no breach of article 3 (*R(S) v Secretary of State for the Home Department*).

In another case, the outcome of which was subsequently overruled, specific proof was required to indicate that a claimant had no charitable support and could not fend for himself or herself. No home, no income, few or no possessions, little or no money, being a stranger, not speaking English, loneliness, anxiety, vulnerability – all these factors were not normally enough to trigger article 3. Food from a charity and access to hygiene facilities could extend the period of time before a person began to cross the article 3 threshold (*R(Zardasht) v Secretary of State for the Home Department*).

In yet another case (*R(Limbuela) v Secretary of State for the Home Department*), the Court of Appeal subsequently disapproved and therefore overruled the approach taken previously in the above *Zardasht* case. The court now stated that the test to be applied was that already applied by the Court of Appeal in *R(Q) v Secretary of State for the Home Department*. In that case, the court had stated that article 3 would be breached not just if there was a 'real risk' of degradation, but if it was clear that charitable support was not being provided and that the individual was incapable of fending for himself or herself such that his or her condition would verge on the severity required under article 3. Thus, in the present case, this test was used to find that article 3 would be triggered if a person had no charitable support and could not support himself or herself (*R(Limbuela) v Secretary of State for the Home Department*: Court of Appeal).

This Court of Appeal decision that overturned the *Zardasht* judgment at the same time upheld two other High Court decisions. The first of these stated that – where a person had taken reasonable steps to get support, had to beg for food and support, and was living for days on end in the same clothes – the a.3 threshold would normally be crossed. Winter provided additional danger to health (R(Limbuela) v Secretary of State for the Home Department: High Court). In the second, sleeping rough on the streets for a month, one charity meal a day but no money or other charitable support, and evidence that the person was unlikely to secure accommodation from charities also meant article 3 was triggered (R(Adam) v Secretary of State for Home Department).

## 13.2.9 EUROPEAN ECONOMIC AREA NATIONALS

Not all people from the European Economic Area are excluded from support under schedule 3 of the 2002 Act. For example, some will have a right to reside in the United Kingdom and be classed as a 'worker'; and a refusal to provide community care services could then result in a breach of the relevant regulations (SI 2000/2326). A note of clarification from the Department of Health explains that, generally speaking, European Economic Area nationals who have worked or work in the United Kingdom, their families, self-employed and former self-employed people and students are eligible for assistance from social services (DH 2003f).

The guidance explains that this is because of European Community law on freedom of movement and the enjoyment of social advantages in other EEA states. Other EEA nationals who have entered the United Kingdom on the understanding that they had sufficient resources so as not to become a burden in terms of social welfare should not be provided with support – beyond temporary support. The guidance goes on to suggest that local authorities could seek to determine such matters by examining documents such as P60 forms in the case of employed (or formerly employed) people. Establishing self-employment status might, the guidance concedes, be difficult (DH 2003f).

## 13.2.10 CIRCUMVENTING PROHIBITIONS

Apart from utilising the Human Rights Act 1998 to test the various prohibitions placed on local authorities from assisting asylum seekers and others subject to immigration control, some attempt has been made to use the Local Government Act 2000. In particular s.2 of this Act allows a local authority to do anything it thinks will achieve the promotion or improvement of the social well-being of the area. However, this power does not enable a local authority to do anything that other legislation prohibits, restricts or limits (s.3).

In a case where a person subject to immigration control under s.115 of the Immigration and Asylum Act 1999 was not eligible for residential accommodation under s.21 of the National Assistance Act 1948 (because her need was essentially destitution related), the courts took a fairly restrictive approach to use of the 2000 Act. They held that the rules under s.21(1A) of the Act (see 13.2.1) constituted a prohibition on the provision of accommodation for such a person – and on the provision of the amenities and requisites provided in connection with the accommodation (such as food). However, clothes or toiletries, for instance, had nothing to with the accommodation; so s.2 would give the local authority a power to provide such items (R(Khan) v Oxfordshire CC).

In another case, it was accepted that under schedule 3 of the Nationality, Immigration and Asylum Act 2002, the local authority was precluded from assisting a Jamaican woman and her children, unless to avoid a breach of human rights. It could avoid such a breach by exercising a power to provide temporary accommodation under the Withholding and Withdrawal of Support (Travel Assistance and Temporary Accommodation) Regulations 2002 (SI 2002/3078). Alternatively, the court accepted that the local authority could make travel arrangements back to Jamaica under s.2 of the Local Government Act 2002, use of which was not prohibited in order to avoid a breach of human rights, even though such travel arrangements could not lawfully be made under the 2002 regulations themselves (R(Grant) v Lambeth LBC).

## 13.2.11 HOME OFFICE RESPONSIBILITIES: ASYLUM SEEKERS

The Home Office has a discretion to support asylum seekers by providing adequate accommodation and for essential living needs, if they do not have those or the means of obtaining them (Immigration and Asylum Act 1999, ss.95–96). This support is provided by the National Asylum Support Service.

However, the Home Office is prohibited from providing this support if the asylum seeker has not claimed asylum as soon as reasonably practicable after arriving at the United Kingdom (i.e. at port of entry). This prohibition does not apply if a person's human rights would otherwise be breached (Nationality, Immigration and Asylum Act 2002, s.55). The asylum seeker who is given no assistance can still pursue his or her asylum claim, albeit with the difficulty of potentially having no shelter or food.

Nevertheless, at the time of writing (December 2004), following the major decision by the Court of Appeal in R(Limbuela) v Secretary of State for the Home Department (see 13.2.8) – about the circumstances in which those human rights would be breached – the Home Office is taking a less harsh approach under s.55. It is not attempting to deny asylum seekers support if they lack access to alternative sources of support (Home Office 2004). However, the Limbuela case is due to go on appeal to the House of Lords during 2005.

In addition to provision of support under s.95 of the 1999 Act, support may also be provided for asylum seekers by the Home Office (through the National Asylum Support Service) in 'hard cases' (Immigration and Asylum Act 1999, s.4). And some 'merely' destitute asylum seekers continue to be supported directly by local authorities under interim regulations passed in 1999 (SI 1999/3056). These provide for authorities to continue to support asylum seekers whom they had been supporting between 1996 and 1999 under s.21 of the National Assistance Act 1948 or s.17 of the Children Act 1989 (and thus prior to implementation of the 1999 Act which removed from local authorities the responsibility for merely destitute asylum seekers).

**Making decisions fairly.** The courts have stated that proper directions need to be given to case-workers, interviewers need to ascertain reasons for the delay in a person claiming asylum, interviewing skills beyond standard form questionnaires are required, the interviewer and decision-maker should be the same person, claimants should be given the chance to rebut suggestions of non-credibility, etc. (R(Q) v Secretary of State for the Home Department).

The discretion to provide support under s.95 does not apply in the case of any asylum seeker who is eligible for social services assistance because his or her needs amount to more than destitution or destitution-related need. If such a person is eligible for social services assistance, he or she is not destitute for the purpose of s.95. In which case the Home Office discretion does not arise (Westminster CC v NASS).

## 13.2.12 EXCEPTIONAL LEAVE TO REMAIN

Outside of the normal rules on immigration, the Secretary of State had under the Immigration Act 1971 discretion to grant 'exceptional leave to remain'. In April 2003, this type of leave was replaced for asylum seekers by policies (under the same general provisions of the 1971 Act) labelled 'humanitarian protection' and 'discretionary leave'. In addition, in cases other than asylum seekers, a residual discretion still remains to grant leave to remain (APU 1/2003).

In one case, under the previous discretion governing exceptional leave to remain, the courts found that the discretion should be properly exercised:

**Leave to remain.** A Polish couple in their sixties came to the United Kingdom to care for their ageing mother. Their leave to remain was extended so that they could care for the wife's brother, a British citizen who suffered from epilepsy, had learning difficulties and spoke no English. They again applied for leave to remain, with the support of Hackney Council, which pointed out that the alternative of residential care was very costly, not acceptable to the brother and in its view not an appropriate solution. The Secretary of State refused the application.

The judge stated that the critical issue was that the brother was a British citizen who was entitled to remain in the United Kingdom and to be cared for in accordance with the policies and duties (i.e. in relation to community care) applying to citizens in general. First, he drew a parallel with another immigration case in which the Secretary of State had not performed the appropriate balancing exercise in comparing immigration issues with the rights of British citizens. Second, there was no evidence supporting the Secretary of State's assertion that he was satisfied that alternative arrangements could be made for the brother. In fact, the government's community care policy, to enable people to remain in their own homes, was consistent in this case with domiciliary care provided by the family rather than residential care. He concluded that the Secretary of State's decision was unreasonable and should be overturned (R v Secretary of State for the Home Department, ex p Zakrocki).

## 13.2.13. DECISION ABOUT ASYLUM OR LEAVE TO REMAIN

Subject to a duty not to breach the Human Rights Act 1998 or European Community Treaties, the following rules apply in relation to community care services – following decisions about people's right to remain in the United Kingdom.

If adult asylum seekers, who have already been receiving community care services, have their applications for refugee status rejected by the Home Office, then they will continue to be eligible for community care services until they refuse to cooperate with removal directions (Nationality, Immigration and Asylum Act 2002, schedule 3). Alternatively, if their applications are successful, continuing eligibility for community care services will depend on a reassessment and whether they are eligible for services under the local authority's 'normal' test of eligibility for community care – as opposed to the special rules concerning asylum seekers and destitution (see 13.2.2).

If asylum seekers have dependent children, and have their application for refugee status rejected, they (although not their dependent children) must be denied support by the local authority, if the Secretary of State issues a certificate that they have not taken reasonable steps to leave the United Kingdom (schedule 3).

If unaccompanied children lose their application for asylum, they would continue to be eligible for local authority assistance under the Children Act 1989 until they reach their 18th birthday; and thereafter, as adults, only until they fail to cooperate with removal directions (at which point assistance would be prohibited, see schedule 3). Alternatively if such children succeed in their application, the local authority would have to decide whether they have a continuing need for support under the Children Act 1989. The local authority might anyway have a duty to provide some continuing assistance under 'leaving care' Children Act provisions (by way of a pathway plan and other support, see 12.6) at least up to the age of 21 years. On the child's reaching the age of 18, the local authority would have also to assess him or her against the normal eligibility rules for community care (see 13.2.2).

If a child or adult asylum seeker is granted humanitarian protection or discretionary leave to remain, then the local authority would have to assess whether or not they are respectively a child in need under the Children Act 1989 – or eligible for community care services under the normal rules (see 13.2.2).

## 13.3 NHS SERVICES AND OVERSEAS VISITORS

In April 2004, the government amended the relevant regulations (SI 1989/306) and issued new guidance concerning the provision in England of hospital services to overseas visitors (DH 2004b). The main rules, as set out in the guidance, are as follows:

- **Normal residence**. The NHS, in respect of hospital services, has a duty to establish whether a person is normally resident in the United Kingdom, to assess liability for charges and to charge those liable to pay.
- **Immediately necessary treatment**. This should not be delayed in order to establish chargeable status of patient (delay could breach the Human Rights Act 1998). However, 'emergency' treatment (unless given in an accident and emergency department) does not itself exempt a person from charges. If payment is unlikely, treatment should be confined to that which is clinically necessary to enable the person to return to his or her own country. Such treatment would not normally be routine treatment, unless it was to avert to a life threatening condition.
- **Urgent treatment**. Where the treatment cannot wait for the person to return to their home country. The patient should be booked in for treatment, and the intervening period used to establish chargeable status.

- **Non-urgent treatment**. Where the treatment could wait until the person returns to their own country. The patient should be placed on a waiting list, but not until a deposit equivalent to the cost of the treatment has been obtained. The guidance maintains that this is not a refusal to provide treatment, merely a requirement that the payment condition be met before treatment can be commenced.
- **Accident and emergency departments**. Treatment given in such departments (or at walk-in centres providing similar treatment) is free of charge for everyone, but exemption ceases once the patient is admitted to a ward or becomes an outpatient.
- **Primary medical care services**. At the time of writing these are free (e.g. services from a district nurse employed by a GP would be free, but chargeable if employed by an NHS trust). At the time of writing the Department of Health has proposed to remove this exemption (DH 2004c).
- **Family planning services**. Free for everyone.
- **Public health**. Treatment for certain diseases in order to protect the wider health.
- **HIV/AIDS**. The exemption from charging applies only to initial diagnostic test and associated counselling.
- **12-month residence**. Anyone who has lived lawfully in the United Kingdom for at least 12 months previous to the treatment is exempt from charges.
- **Overseas visitor definition**. An overseas visitor is defined as a person not ordinarily resident in the United Kingdom. Ordinary residence is not defined and thus lies in the common law interpretation provided by the courts (see 14.2.3).
- **Overseas visitors, exemptions**. There is a long list of other exemptions from charging.

In respect of degrees of urgency of treatment, the above guidance would seem in general principle to be in accord with what the law courts have found, albeit under the previous version of the regulations and guidance (and before the implementation of the Human Rights Act 1998):

**Dialysis treatment for overseas visitor.** A Nigerian overseas visitor suffered renal failure and required dialysis three times a week. This had been paid for in advance by a company, of which the man's father was an employee. The company would not now make further payments to the London hospital concerned; however, treatment was available in Nigeria. The hospital would continue to treat him, so that he was fit to return to Nigeria for continuing treatment. Furthermore, the court noted that if non-treatment were to lead to an emergency, then on humanitarian grounds the hospital could exercise its discretion to treat without insistence on a deposit or advance payment (*R v Hammersmith Hospitals NHS Trust, ex p Reffell*).

# Residence and eligibility for services

## KEY POINTS

This chapter considers the issue of residence in a number of contexts involving both local authorities and the NHS. The question of a person's ordinary residence is a recurring one in community care. The reason for this is that various duties are conditional on a person being an ordinary resident within the area of the local authority; and the resource implications might be considerable. Local authorities thus see arguments about a person's ordinary residence as one of the possible escape routes (referred to in Chapter 3) away from unwanted obligations and expenditure.

**Note: Wales, Scotland and Northern Ireland**. Guidance similar to the English guidance on ordinary residence for social services (LAC(93)2) has been published in Wales (WOC 41/93) and in Scotland (SWSG 1/96). Section 14.4 of this chapter covers cross-border placements within the United Kingdom.

## 14.1 RESIDENCE: OVERVIEW

Some local authority obligations to provide community care services (both residential and non-residential) depend on whether a person is 'ordinarily resident' in the authority's area. If a person is not ordinarily resident, then the relevant duty might not exist, and instead be converted to a mere power.

Should a dispute arise between local authorities about where a person really lives, Circular guidance makes it clear that assessment and service provision should anyway not be delayed or prevented. The decision about which authority is responsible for arranging and paying for services should be made subsequently. If a person has housing and health care needs as well, there is scope for uncertainty because social services, housing and NHS rules for residence and responsibility differ.

## 14.2 ORDINARY RESIDENCE: SOCIAL SERVICES

14.2.1 COMMUNITY CARE LEGISLATION AFFECTED BY ORDINARY RESIDENCE

Community care legislation affected by the ordinary residence condition comprises the National Assistance Act 1948 (s.21: provision of residential accommodation and s.29: welfare services) and the Chronically Sick and Disabled Persons Act 1970 (s.2: welfare services). For instance, what might be a duty towards an 'ordinary resident' to arrange a care home placement might be a power (discretion) only towards a non-resident of the area (s.21 of the National Assistance Act 1948 and directions made under it: see 8.3.1). Under s.29 of the 1948 Act, a general duty to provide certain services for disabled people is rendered a power only in the case of those not ordinarily resident (see 10.1.1). And s.2 of the Chronically Sick and Disabled Persons Act 1970 anyway extends to ordinary residents only, there not even being a power to provide those services to disabled people who are not ordinarily resident (see 10.2).

14.2.2 MEANING OF 'ORDINARILY RESIDENT'

There is no statutory definition of 'ordinarily resident' and it is ultimately for the courts to decide what it means. Department of Health guidance states that the term should be given its ordinary and natural meaning subject to any interpretation by the courts. It states that the concept of ordinary residence involves questions of fact and degree, and factors such as time, intention and continuity in the particular context (LAC(93)7, para 2). A number of court cases that have considered 'ordinary residence' are cited in the guidance (paras 12, 13):

- *R v Barnet LBC, ex p Shah*: 'abode in a particular place or country which he had adopted voluntarily and for settled purposes as part of the regular order of his life for the time being, whether of short or long duration'
- *R v Waltham Forest LBC, ex p Vale* and *R v Redbridge LBC ex p East Sussex CC 1992*.

Of these last two court cases, one involved provision for autistic twins who had apparently been abandoned by their parents:

**Ordinary residence (1).** A dispute arose between two local authorities about which authority had a statutory responsibility for making arrangements for two autistic twins with learning disabilities. Their parental home had been in Redbridge but they had attended a residential Rudolf Steiner school in East Sussex. The parents then sold the house in Redbridge and returned to Nigeria. The imminent closure of the school subsequently sparked the dispute between the two councils about which would be responsible for making arrangements for the provision of residential accommodation under s.21 of the National Assistance Act 1948.

The judge, referring to the case of *R v Barnet LBC, ex p Shah,* found that the parents' departure and sale of the family home meant that the twins had ceased to be ordinarily resident in Redbridge, and that the duty to make provision fell to East Sussex (*R v Redbridge LBC, ex p East Sussex CC*).

The second case concerned the ordinary residence of a woman with learning disabilities:

**Ordinary residence (2).** The person concerned was 28 years old and mentally handicapped from birth. In 1961 she had moved to Ireland with her parents where she lived in residential homes. Her parents returned to England in 1978 to live in Waltham Forest; she returned in 1984 and lived for one month with her parents before being placed in a home in Buckinghamshire. Waltham Forest now denied financial responsibility for the placement on the grounds that she had been ordinarily resident in Ireland and that the stay with her parents had been merely temporary.

The judge disagreed. First, the woman concerned was so mentally handicapped that she was totally dependent on her parents and was in the same position as a small child. Concepts such as 'voluntarily adopted residence' or 'settled purpose' – used in *R v Barnet LBC, ex p Shah* – were irrelevant to the case. Therefore, the woman's ordinary residence was that of her parents, which was not her 'real home' (a concept rejected in the *Shah v Barnet LBC* case) but her 'base'. Should he have been mistaken in this view, the judge went on to state that in any case the one-month stay with her parents was sufficient to constitute ordinary residence – since the *Shah* case made clear that ordinary residence could be of short duration. Thus, responsibility lay with Waltham Forest and not Buckinghamshire (*R v Waltham Forest, ex p Vale*).

### 14.2.3 COMMUNITY CARE RESIDENTIAL ACCOMMODATION AND ORDINARY RESIDENCE

The rules concerning ordinary residence and the provision of residential accommodation – where due to age, illness, disability or any other circumstances, care and attention is not otherwise available for a person – are contained in s.24 of the National Assistance Act 1948, together with directions. Central government has also issued guidance on the matter. In substance, the position is as follows:

- **Ordinarily resident**. A local authority has a power to provide residential accommodation to a person ordinarily resident in the area (this is turned into a duty by directions: see 8.3.1).
- **No settled residence**. A local authority has a power to provide residential accommodation for people with no settled residence and for people ordinarily resident elsewhere but who are in urgent need of accommodation. (In the case of urgency, or mental disorder, this is converted to a duty by directions: see 8.3.1.)
- **Provision on behalf of another local authority**. A local authority has a power to provide residential accommodation for a person ordinarily resident in the area of another authority with the consent of that other authority.

- **Placement in another area**. If a person is provided with residential accommodation, he or she is deemed to be ordinarily resident in the area in which he or she was ordinarily resident immediately before the residential accommodation was provided.
- **NHS patient**. An NHS patient is deemed to be ordinarily resident, for local authority purposes, in the area (if any) he or she was living in immediately before entering hospital.

Department of Health guidance advises that when a person states that he has no settled residence or describes himself as having no fixed abode, the social services authority where he presents himself should normally accept responsibility (LAC(93)7, para 16).

The guidance also states that if a person is placed in a care home by one local authority in the area of another local authority, then it is the former that retains responsibility. However, if by 'private arrangement' the person then moves, he or she 'may' become ordinarily resident in the area of the second authority, 'depending on the specific circumstances'. If the person makes his or her own arrangements to enter a care home in a different local authority's area, and subsequently requires social services assistance, he or she will normally be ordinarily resident in the second authority's area (LAC(93)7, paras 7,10).

## 14.2.4 ORDINARY RESIDENCE: LOOKED AFTER CHILDREN
The 'leaving care' provisions under the Children Act 1989 place certain responsibilities (duties and powers) on local authorities in respect of people formerly looked after as children by the local authority, or otherwise accommodated as a child. The responsibilities are usually up to the age of 21 years of the person, but may extend beyond (for details of the leaving care provisions, see 12.6).

In the case of a disabled person requiring, for example, non-residential community care services under s.2 of the Chronically Sick and Disabled Persons Act 1970 (CSDPA), uncertainties could arise concerning responsibility – if that person were subject to the leaving care provisions.

Where the person (as a child) was looked after by a local authority (as opposed to another body: see 12.6), but is now in the area of another authority, the original authority retains certain responsibilities and duties, including the provision of assistance 'in kind' (see 12.6).

Therefore any uncertainties about responsibilities (between the former authority and the present authority) might centre on the individual case, and on the interpretation placed by the courts on the word 'assistance' in the leaving care provisions. It is possibly unclear whether the courts would hold that the assistance referred to in the leaving care provisions extends to the services contained in s.2 of the CSDPA 1970. Section 23B(4) of the Children Act 1989 might suggest not, since it refers to a leaving care assessment as being separate from a CSDPA assessment. If this is right, the present authority would retain its responsibilities under s.2 of the CSDPA to the person, who is now ordinarily resident within its area; whilst the former authority would retain the leaving care responsibilities. Guidance issued by the Department of Health on inter-authority arrangements for care leavers does not explicitly clarify this issue in respect of disabled persons (LASSL(2004)20).

### 14.2.5 HOMELESSNESS AND HOUSING ISSUES

Social services and housing authorities apply different tests to establish the 'ordinary residence' of homeless people. Therefore the responsible housing authority will not necessarily be the same as the responsible social services authority. The test for 'local connection' in the context of homelessness legislation is to be found in s.199 of the Housing Act 1996 and covers normal residence (past or present), employment, family associations or special circumstances.

Department of Health guidance states that when a person states that he or she has no settled residence or fixed abode, the social services authority where he presents himself should normally accept responsibility. This is because, for a person in urgent need, that social services authority cannot argue that the possible existence of a 'local connection' elsewhere excuses it from its duty to assess and provide necessary services. In particular, the guidance warns against using the housing rules to identify ordinary residence for social services purposes (LAC(93)7, para 16).

### 14.2.6 ORDINARY RESIDENCE OF PEOPLE IN HOSPITAL, NURSING HOMES, PRISON AND SIMILAR ESTABLISHMENTS

The legislation states that people in hospital are to be regarded by local authorities as ordinarily resident in the area (if any) they were ordinarily resident in before entering hospital (National Assistance Act 1948, s.24). Department of Health guidance suggests that local authorities could reasonably apply this approach to other situations, such as people leaving prisons, resettlement units and other similar establishments. These people would be without a permanent place to live and require social services involvement at the time of their discharge (LAC(93)7, para 14).

### 14.2.7 ORDINARY RESIDENCE DISPUTES AFFECTING SERVICES

Uncertainty and disputes about ordinary residence sometimes arise between local authorities. Circular guidance states that delay in assessment and service provision should not occur: 'If there is a dispute about the ordinary residence of a person in need of services it should be debated after the care assessment and any provision of service' (LAC(93)7, summary and para 3). A failure to follow this guidance will attract judicial censure:

**Washing hands of responsibility.** A 28-year-old woman with learning disabilities lived in Camden. Her relationship with her husband broke down. She went to live with a boyfriend in Hackney. She had been receiving community care services in Camden, including a vocational training placement. Camden proposed to withdraw the services in the context of a dispute with Hackney about her ordinary residence. Neither council was prepared to accept responsibility for her. Pending resolution of the dispute, the courts granted an injunction obliging both authorities to provide her with accommodation for people with learning disabilities – at accommodation where she had previously lived. Eventually the woman anyway moved back to Camden, which resumed its community care responsibilities toward her.

In a subsequent court case concerning a dispute about legal costs, the court criticised both authorities for 'plain breach of the guidance'; the wrangling between the authorities over a period of months meant the woman was left in limbo (the training placement was interrupted for eight months). Both authorities 'washed their hands' of the woman. Since there was no good reason for the departure from the guidance, this meant that the authorities had acted unlawfully (*R v Hackney LBC, ex p J*).

Similarly the local ombudsman will find maladministration in this respect:

**Dispute concerning responsibility.** Two questions arose about responsibility and ordinary residence in the case of a man currently in a care home, in a different local authority area to his previous residence. The first complication was that he had moved to the care home on his own initiative and only sought funding from his original authority after the event. The original authority therefore questioned its responsibility, since it had not placed him there. The second question concerned responsibility for a community care package, were he to leave the care home to live in the community in the second local authority's area. Whatever the correct answer, the maladministration lay in the delay of a year, before a determination from the Secretary of State was sought (*Redbridge LBC 1998*).

## 14.2.8 RESOLUTION OF DISPUTES ABOUT ORDINARY RESIDENCE

Guidance refers to the fact that disputes about ordinary residence under Part III of the National Assistance Act 1948 are ultimately to be determined by the Secretary of State under s.32 of the same Act.

Disputes about ordinary residence could relate to non-residential services under s.29 of the 1948 Act, as well as to residential services under s.21. The guidance states that each case has to be considered on its own facts; that the Secretary of State's decision is final subject only to judicial review; that the question of establishing ordinary residence is essentially a legal one; and that authorities must have agreed provisional liability for service provision before the dispute is referred to the Secretary of State. The guidance describes the procedure to be followed by local authorities (LAC(93)7, paras 24–28).

The Secretary of State's powers of dispute resolution under s.32 of the National Assistance Act 1948 do not apply to s.117 of the Mental Health Act 1983 (aftercare for discharged patients) (LAC(93)7, para 24). There is however reference to the residence issue within s.117, and the courts have interpreted how the rules should be applied (see 10.5.2).

The courts have also held that the s.32 resolution procedure does not apply to disputes concerning ordinary residence under s.2 of the Chronically Sick and Disabled Persons Act 1970 (*R v Kent County Council, ex p Salisbury*). This is another example of the strained relationship between s.29 of the 1948 Act and s.2 of the 1970 Act; sometimes the courts hold that they function separately as in this instance, and in the case of *R v Islington LBC, ex p McMillan*. Yet in other respects, for example for the purpose of charging, the courts have held that they are firmly hitched together (*R v Powys CC, ex p Hambidge (no.2)*):

## 14.3 NHS: RESPONSIBLE COMMISSIONER

The legal framework regarding NHS commissioning responsibilities is set out in regulations (SI 2002/2375) concerning Primary Care Trusts (PCTs). Such trusts are in England now responsible for commissioning most health services for the population in each of their areas. Guidance issued by the Department of Health includes the following points (DH 2003a):

- **Delay or refusal of treatment**. Treatment should not be delayed or refused because of uncertainty or ambiguity in funding responsibility relating to a person's place of residence.
- **Basic test**. A PCT is responsible for commissioning services for people registered with a general practitioner (GP) associated with the PCT; and also for people usually resident in the area or non-UK residents present in their area – who are not registered with a GP, or otherwise are not registered with a GP (e.g. because they are in prison). In summary, the responsible PCT is identified by the GP with whom a patient is registered or, where not applicable, by the person's usual address.
- **Specific services**. Some services must anyway be provided for the benefit of anybody within the PCT's area (e.g. accident, emergency, ambulance, sexual health, etc.).
- **Changing place of residence**. If a person moves residence during a course of treatment, the same basic test applies as above (i.e. depending on GP registration). However, the guidance suggests the original PCT may wish to continue to provide the treatment on behalf of the new PCT for a certain length of time.
- **Overseas visitors**. See 13.3.
- **Prisoners**. From April 2003, the PCT within whose area a prison is located is responsible for commissioning services for the prisoners.
- **Mental Health Act**. For people detained for treatment, the basic test applies. If GP registration or residential address cannot be established, the responsible PCT would be determined by the location of the mental health unit.
- **Continuing NHS health care**. At the time of writing, the basic test would apply as above (i.e. person's GP registration or usual address). However, the guidance refers to future legislation that would mean that the original, placing PCT would remain responsible. However, in the meantime, the guidance urges a flexible approach in order to ensure continuity of care.
- **Registered nursing care**. If a person is placed in a care home outside the original PCT, it is the receiving PCT that becomes responsible – albeit after being informed by the original PCT.
- **Disputes**. Ultimately, the responsibility for resolving disputes lies with the Secretary of State, although he or she would expect full attempts at local resolution first.

## 14.4 RESIDENCE: CROSS-BORDER RESPONSIBILITIES

Uncertainty commonly arises concerning cross-border issues, that is between England, Wales, Scotland and Northern Ireland, in respect of both health and social care responsibilities.

### 14.4.1 CROSS-BORDER SOCIAL SERVICES PLACEMENTS IN CARE HOMES

The position as to the placement of people in care homes across the borders of the four United Kingdom countries is a confused one. The following is a broad summary of the apparent position.

The original Choice of Accommodation Directions (in LAC(92)27) issued in 1992 contained an error by referring to the placing of people by English local authorities in care homes anywhere in the United Kingdom. An amendment was quickly made to the directions in 1993, limiting the choice to England and Wales, and the guidance accompanying the amending direction (in LAC(93)18) further clarified the position – which was reiterated in guidance (LAC(2004)20) issued in 2004 on choice of accommodation. The 2004 guidance replaced the guidance (but not the directions) in LAC(92)27 (but did not replace the guidance contained in LAC(93)18). This reflects s.26 of the National Assistance Act 1948, which restricts placement to homes in England and Wales, because residential accommodation providing personal and nursing care must be registered under the Care Standards Act 2000 (which applies to England and Wales only).

In the case of Scottish local authorities wishing to place people in English or Welsh care homes, the position is not as clear. First of all s.13A of the Social Work (Scotland) Act 1968 apparently prohibits such placements in respect of care homes that provide nursing, although the wording is not without possible ambiguity. However, under s.59 of the 1968 Act, covering placements in care homes not providing nursing, there is apparently no prohibition on such placements (see e.g. Scottish Executive 2001, paras 31–35).

The Health and Social Care Act 2001 provides for regulations to be made to rectify this situation and to allow English (and Welsh) local authorities to place people in residential homes in Scotland, Northern Ireland, the Channel Islands and the Isle of Man (s.56). There is a similar Scottish provision in the Community Care and Health (Scotland) Act 2002 (s.5); when passed, the position of Scottish local authorities placing people in England and Wales will in any event be clarified. However, at the time of writing, neither English nor Scottish regulations have been made.

In the absence of such regulations, the Department of Health's 1993 guidance appears still to hold good. It states that Scottish authorities have a discretion to arrange residential accommodation for people resident in England and that where prospective residents wish it, English authorities are expected to approach Scottish authorities to exercise this discretion (LAC(93)18). In which case, although the contract for care would be between the Scottish local authority and the care home, an arrangement between the two authorities concerned should allow for the Scottish authority to be reimbursed by the English one.

In the case of Scottish local authorities wishing to place people in English care homes, the position would be the same in reverse (LAC(93)18; and see also equivalent Scottish guidance: SWSG 6/94). The statutory provisions allowing such reimbursement in both directions lie in the National Assistance Act 1948, ss.32–33; and s.86 of the Social Work (Scotland) Act 1968. However, in the light of the uncertainty in Scotland referred to immediately above, it appears that in practice some Scottish local authorities simply place people directly in English care homes anyway, believing that they have the legal power to do so.

The Department of Health guidance states that such reimbursement arrangements would not be possible in respect of Northern Ireland; that is, for English authorities to arrange to pay for residential care in Northern Ireland or for health and social services boards in Northern Ireland to pay for residential accommodation arranged by English authorities (LAC(93)18, para 11).

### 14.4.2 CROSS-BORDER NHS RESPONSIBLE COMMISSIONER

The Department of Health has issued guidance on cross-border responsibilities within the United Kingdom (DH 2003a). It is based on the relevant legal framework and in particular the NHS (Functions of Strategic Health Authorities and Primary Care Trusts and Administration Arrangements) (England) Regulations 2002 (SI 2002/2375). The guidance states:

* **Moving to England**. If a patient moves from Scotland, Wales or Northern Ireland to England, there is an expectation that he or she will register with a general practitioner (GP). This would then determine the responsible PCT (DH 2003a).
* **Living in Scotland with English general practitioner**. In Wales, Scotland and Northern Ireland, the responsible authority for health care is determined by where the person is usually resident, and not by general practitioner registration. Therefore, if a person is registered with an English GP but lives in Scotland, the responsible commissioner will be Scottish.
* **Living in Wales or Northern Ireland but with English general practitioner**. If a person is resident in Wales or Northern Ireland but registered with a GP in England, both Wales/Northern Ireland or England could be held responsible as commissioner; it would be up to local organisations to come to an agreement about this.
* **Living in England, but registered with a GP elsewhere**. If a person is resident in England, but registered with a general practitioner in Wales, Scotland or Northern Ireland, the responsible commissioner is the English PCT (DH 2003a).

### 14.4.3 CROSS-BORDER REGISTERED NURSING CARE

A protocol developed by the National Assembly for Wales and the Department of Health concerning registered nursing care includes the following principles: first, that the level of funding provided will be that of the destination (i.e. receiving) PCT (in England) or Local Health Board (LHB in Wales); second, that the PCT or LHB within which the home is located will arrange the funding for the registered nursing care (DH/NAFW 2003).

## 14.5 RESIDENCE AND DISABLED FACILITIES GRANTS

Housing authorities have in some circumstances a duty to award disabled facilities grants for home adaptations under the Housing Grants, Construction and Regeneration Act 1996 (see Chapter 15). The residence condition relates not to the local authority's area but to whether the dwelling in question is the disabled occupant's only or main residence. For instance, it is likely that the courts in most ordinary circumstances would hold that a person could not have more than one only or main residence. This would rule out the provision of disabled facilities grants for two dwellings (e.g. in the case of shared care).

However, this residence condition is to be contrasted with that in s.2 of the Chronically Sick and Disabled Persons Act 1970, which also covers home adaptations. The 1970 Act refers to ordinary residence in the area of the authority, and not to only or main dwelling. Therefore, in the case of shared care, home adaptations might be possible (where the needs call for it) in two dwellings via both a disabled facilities grant under the 1996 Act and assistance under s.2 of the 1970 Act. (Two sets of adaptations are typically required in the case, for example, of split care arrangements for disabled children.) This assumes that a duty on social services to fund such a second adaptation could be made out: see 15.6 and 10.2.5.5.

PART III

# Housing, home adaptations, NHS services and joint working

CHAPTER 15

# Housing and home adaptations

## KEY POINTS

It is beyond the scope of this book to cover housing legislation in general. This chapter therefore makes only passing reference to the interface between housing and social services legislation in terms of provision of accommodation and also the Supporting People initiative. The chapter does however set out in more detail the law concerning home adaptations, provision of which overlaps in several significant respects with social services legislation. Adapting people's homes was recognised in the original community care policy guidance as a key method of enabling people to remain in their own homes (DH 1990, para 3.24).

However, the system of home adaptations is subject to considerable complexity, relying as it does on continual cooperation between local social services authorities and local housing authorities, and on more than one set of legislation. Local housing authorities operate a system of disabled facilities grants (DFGs) under the Housing Grants, Construction and Regeneration Act 1996; whilst social services authorities have a responsibility for adaptations under s.2 of the Chronically Sick and Disabled Persons Act 1970.

The system of adaptations has been beset by funding problems in relation to demand, and consequently by long waiting times. Local housing authorities in some areas attempt to weaken their strong duty to approve disabled facilities grants by deploying a range of restrictive policies, a significant number of which are probably unlawful. This is because the strong duty to award such grants does not allow as many lawful, as opposed to unlawful, 'escape routes' as other weaker legislation might do (see 3.1). Alternatively, both local housing and social services authorities attempt to exploit their divided responsibilities for home adaptations, by engaging in disputes and passing the buck from one to another.

The courts have considered few cases on disabled facilities grants, although in 2004, one case did reach the Court of Appeal (*R(B) v Calderdale MBC*). However, the local government ombudsmen have investigated the provision of home adaptations on many occasions.

**Note: Wales, Scotland and Northern Ireland**. The Housing Grants, Construction and Regeneration Act 1996 governs the provision of disabled facilities grants (on DFGs) for home adaptations in England and Wales. However, the National Assembly for Wales now passes its own regulations under the Act; as a result one distinction between the two countries is that the maximum grant of £25,000 in England is in Wales £30,000. The National Assembly for Wales has published substantial guidance (NAFWC 20/02).

In Northern Ireland, disabled facilities grants come under the Housing (Northern Ireland) Order 2003 and associated statutory rules (SR 2004/8). There are some differences; in Northern Ireland, discretionary disabled facilities grants are still available (for welfare, accommodation or employment purposes); these were abolished in England and Wales by July 2003, by means of the Regulatory Reform (Housing Assistance)

(England and Wales) Order 2002. Also in Northern Ireland the financial test of means applied to disabled facilities grants has been removed in the case of disabled children.

Scotland operates a different system of home improvement grants under the Housing (Scotland) Act 1987 with mandatory grants limited to adaptations concerning the provision of, or provision of access to, standard amenities (lavatory, wash-hand basin and sink (with hot and cold water), shower, bath). Grants for other purposes are discretionary; a means test operates under regulations (SI 2003/461).

## 15.1 PROVISION OF HOUSING ACCOMMODATION

Principal duties in terms of allocating public sector housing and providing accommodation for homeless people lie under the Housing Act 1996. Nevertheless, in a number of cases local social services authorities have been found unprepared for the courts' findings that, in certain circumstances, they too have a duty to provide 'ordinary' accommodation under s.21 of the National Assistance Act 1948. In other words, some local social services authorities have in the past assumed that any duties in respect of ordinary accommodation might extend to making referrals to housing authorities (e.g. under s.47 of the NHS and Community Care Act 1990), but not to social services authorities themselves providing the accommodation. The courts have not always shared this view (see 8.2.1).

## 15.2 COOPERATION BETWEEN HOUSING AND SOCIAL SERVICES AUTHORITIES

Various legislative provisions entail cooperation between social services and housing authorities. For instance, s.47 of the NHS and Community Care Act 1990 entails a duty on the social services authority to invite a housing authority to assist in a community care assessment (see 6.5). In addition, local social services authorities have a duty of cooperation with housing authorities in respect of housing allocation and homelessness generally, and particular cooperation duties in respect of children (Housing Act 1996, ss.213–213A). Likewise housing authorities have a duty of cooperation with social services authorities under s.27 of the Children Act 1989; and social services authorities have a duty to assist a housing authority with the formulation of a local homelessness strategy and to take it into account when exercising their functions (Homelessness Act 2002). Nevertheless, such duties of cooperation only go so far, as the following court case illustrates:

**Duty of cooperation.** A housing authority decided that it had no duty to secure permanent accommodation for a homeless family (because it judged that the homelessness was intentional). The social services authority then declined to exercise its power to give assistance in cash to the family – as part of its duty to safeguard and promote the welfare of the children – under s.17(6) of the Children Act 1989. Instead it tried to rely on s.27 of the 1989 Act which stated that it had the power to request the assistance of other authorities, who 'shall comply with the request if it is compatible with their own statutory or other duties and obligations and does not unduly prejudice the discharge of any of their functions'. The housing authority, unsurprisingly, having already assessed the application in the negative, now refused to offer long-term accommodation.

On the issue of cooperation between authorities, the House of Lords stated that the 'two authorities must cooperate. Judicial review is not the way to obtain cooperation. The court cannot decide what form cooperation should take. Both forms of authority have difficult tasks, which are of great importance and for which they may feel their resources are not wholly adequate. The authorities must together do the best they can… In this case the housing authority were entitled to respond to the social services authority as they did' (R v Northavon DC, ex p Smith).

## 15.3 SUPPORTING PEOPLE

During the 1990s, a number of challenges were made as to the type of service that could legitimately be covered by housing benefit (e.g. *R v North Cornwall DC, ex p Singer; R v St Edmundsbury Housing Benefit Review Board, ex p Sandys*: concerning counselling and support services).

As a consequence, changes were made to the housing benefit system, and a number of housing support services that used to be covered by housing benefit are now available through a central government funded scheme, administered by local authorities. Entitled Supporting People, it should be distinguished from community care services, since it is not part of a local authority's social services functions.

The basic legal framework consists of the Supporting People (England) Directions 2003, the Supporting People Programme Grant and Grant Conditions, Supporting People Grant (England) Guidance 2003 and the Local Authorities (Charges for Specified Welfare Services) (England) Regulations 2003 (SI 2003/907: to be replaced by the charging powers contained in s.93 of the Local Government Act 2003).

As far as charging goes, there has been transitional protection for certain tenants; and people receiving short-term services are exempt from charges. A short-term service is one that aims at bringing about independence within two years, or at least aims to increase capacity for independent living through time limited support of up to two years. However, it is not a short-term service if it aims to maintain a limited degree of independence which is not expected to increase and may diminish over time (ODPM 2003a, para 20).

Guidance explains that eligible services are defined as being housing-related support services, concerning housing aspects of supporting independence; they are to be distinguished from general health, social services or statutory personal care services. For instance, included would be life skills such as cooking or budgeting, or the general support of a visiting support worker to give the person confidence to sustain his or her own home. The guidance states that Supporting People services are about the long-term development of more independent living skills, or the maintenance of skills critical to sustaining an independent living arrangement. 'Occasional welfare services' can also be included – for instance, arrangements for tidying the garden of an elderly person; though as with handyperson schemes, the payment would be for arranging the work, not for the work itself (ODPM 2003a, paras 48–53).

Supporting People services are not aimed at the general public but at people at risk of losing their own home due to an inability to cope, for reasons such as homelessness, rough sleeping, previous imprisonment, mental health problems, learning difficulties, domestic violence, teenage pregnancy, vulnerability due to age, drug and alcohol problems, physical or sensory disability, HIV or AIDS, and being a refugee (ODPM 2003a, para 52).

Specific exclusions are residential care, the type of service provided by a registered care provider, personal or nursing care, services that local authorities have a statutory duty to provide, building works (other than advice and personal support services), equipment (e.g. stairlifts or specialist adaptations), psychological therapy or therapeutic counselling, services to enforce court of law requirements, and general housing management services (ODPM 2003a, para 59).

However, the guidance states that community care packages may contain an element of housing-related support; but such support must be identified so that only it, and not other services, attracts Support People payments (ODPM 2003a, para 60). The need to draw this dividing line became clear in the following case, in which the court held that a number of services being provided should have come under community care legislation and not Supporting People:

**Relationship between Supporting People and community care services.** A local authority assessed a person with significant health problems related to Still's disease (a form of rheumatoid arthritis) involving frequent, painful and highly debilitating flare-ups; he was also nearly blind. It had categorised some of his needs as moderate only, in particular cleaning, shopping, and attendance at appointments. This meant that under the authority's 'fair access to care' eligibility criteria, those needs would not attract social services support. Instead these needs were met through the Supporting People scheme. However, because they were related to the man's health care condition, the court held that these needs should all have been assessed as coming within the critical category of the eligibility framework, and so been provided as community care services, and not through Supporting People (*R(Heffernan) v Sheffield CC*).

## 15.4 HOME ADAPTATIONS: DISABLED FACILITIES GRANTS (DFGS)

Under the Housing Grants, Construction and Regeneration Act 1996 (HGCRA), housing authorities have a duty, if certain conditions are met, to approve applications for disabled facilities grants for the carrying out of home adaptations.

The conditions are basically that (a) the adaptation in question falls into one of the purposes in the Act that attract mandatory grant; (b) if so, that it is necessary and appropriate, and also reasonable and practicable. It is important that the two questions are asked and answered logically and discretely; not to do so has been held by the courts to be unlawful:

**Collapsing two questions/answers into one.** In one case involving a loft conversion to provide an extra bedroom for a boy with autism, the local authority's reasoning in effect stated that the works were not necessary and appropriate because there was no clear case for a mandatory grant. The court held that this was impermissibly to collapse the first question about the mandatory nature of the grant with the second question as to whether it was necessary and appropriate (*R(B) v Calderdale MBC*).

15.4.1 PURPOSES FOR MANDATORY GRANT

The 1996 Act lists a number of purposes that will in principle attract mandatory grant. These are to facilitate access by the disabled occupant:

- **dwelling**: to and from the dwelling
- **family room**: to a room used as the principal family room
- **sleeping room**: to, or providing for the disabled occupant, a room used or usable for sleeping
- **lavatory**: to, or providing for the disabled occupant, a room in which there is a lavatory – or facilitating its use by the disabled occupant
- **bath, shower**: to, or providing for the disabled occupant, a room in which there is a bath or a shower (or both) – or facilitating its use by the disabled occupant
- **washhand basin**: to, or providing for the disabled occupant, a room in which there is a washhand basin – or facilitating its use by the disabled occupant (s.23).

Other purposes are:

- **safety**: making the dwelling or building safe for the disabled occupant and other persons residing with him
- **cooking**: facilitating the preparation and cooking of food by the disabled occupant
- **heating**: improving any heating system in the dwelling to meet the needs of the disabled occupant or – if there is no existing heating system or an existing system is unsuitable for use by the disabled occupant – providing a heating system suitable to meet his needs
- **use of power, light, heat**: facilitating the use by the disabled occupant of a source of power, light or heat by altering the position of one or more means of access to, or control of, that source – or by providing additional means of control
- **disabled occupant as carer**: facilitating access and movement by the disabled occupant around the dwelling in order to enable him to care for a person who normally resides in the dwelling and needs such care (s.23).

As detailed immediately above, the legislation, together with the guidance (see below), provides a firm base from which to answer the question as to whether the proposed works will in principle attract mandatory grant. Yet it is perhaps surprising how many local authority policies concerning DFGs appear not to be based on either the legislation or the guidance. Examples of such doubtful policies are given in the following paragraphs.

15.4.2 SAFETY IN THE DWELLING

Guidance from central government gives examples of adaptations relating to safety. These include provision of specialised lighting, adaptations to minimise the danger if a disabled person has behavioural problems, enhanced alarm system in connection with cooking facilities, fire escapes, toughened or shatterproof glass, fire or radiator guards, reinforcement of floors, walls or ceilings, and cladding of exposed surfaces and corners to prevent injury (ODPM 2004, annex B, para 18–20). The examples indicate just how wide the safety purpose goes. The Court of Appeal has considered the implications of the safety purpose in the circumstances of the following case:

**Safety.** The parents of a boy with autism applied for a loft conversion. The boy had for the last few years subjected his younger brother, with whom he shared a bedroom, to dangerously inappropriate horseplay and to violent interference with his sleep, day after day, night after night. The local authority declined to approve the application on the ground that the danger to the younger brother was confined to the shared bedroom; therefore an extra bedroom would still not make the dwelling safe for him. The High Court upheld the local authority's argument; the case went to appeal (*R(B) v Calderdale MBC*).

This judgement was overturned by the Court of Appeal, who ordered that the local authority re-take its decision. This was on the basis that the works could not necessarily be expected to make the premises completely safe for the disabled person and other people he lived with. The question was whether it was enough if the works simply made the premises (a bit) safer, or whether there was some threshold of safety that the works would have to get over, in order for them to be deemed necessary and appropriate:

**Reducing risk.** The Court of Appeal found that there was a threshold, namely that the proposed works must minimise the material risk — in other words reduce it as far as is reasonably practicable, if it could not be eliminated. In turn, this would mean that it would be immaterial even if there were other areas of risk that the grant did not (*R(B) v Calderdale MBC*).

A number of local authorities apparently operate policies that effectively state that they will never approve applications for works to the garden. However, logically, such policies are unlikely to be lawful if applied in every case. This is because dwelling is defined in s.101 of the 1996 Act to include garden; and the mandatory purpose relating to safety is stated to apply to the dwelling. Therefore it would seem to follow that to bar all such works would be to prevent the housing authority coming to a proper decision on the individual facts of the case, and be a fettering of its discretion. It should also be noted that the Act refers to the safety of the disabled occupant and other people living with him:

**Safety of other people.** The court held that so long as the safety of the disabled occupant is involved in some way, a grant would not be precluded; there was not a requirement that the principal purpose of the works be the safety of the disabled person. For example, a fire escape or cooking alarm might benefit several other occupants of a dwelling, and not just the disabled occupant. Thus, the fact that the disabled occupant (who might injure himself) was the immediate and direct source of danger did not preclude a grant; by the same token the danger could arise from a person's behaviour, and not just the condition or lack of facilities in the dwelling (*R(B)v Calderdale MBC*).

## 15.4.3 SLEEPING ROOM

Guidance states that provision of a room usable for sleeping should only be undertaken if the adaptation of an existing room in the dwelling (upstairs or downstairs) or the access to that room would be unsuitable in the particular circumstances. Where the disabled occupant shares a bedroom, grant could be given to provide a room of sufficient size, in order that normal sleeping arrangements be maintained (ODPM 2004, annex B, para 21).

## 15.4.4 BATHROOM

Guidance points out that, compared to the previous legislation containing DFGs (Local Government and Housing Act 1989), the 1996 Act separated the provisions relating to lavatory and washing, bathing and showering facilities. This was to make clear that 'a disabled person should have access to a wash-hand basin, a WC and a shower or bath (or if more appropriate, both a shower and a bath)'. Therefore DFG should be given 'to provide a disabled person with each of these facilities' and to facilitate their use (ODPM 2004, annex B, para 22).

## 15.4.5 FOOD, PREPARATION AND COOKING

Guidance states that eligible works would include the rearrangement or enlargement of a kitchen to ease manoeuvrability of a wheelchair and specially modified or designed storage units, gas, electricity and plumbing installations.

However, it also states that where most of the cooking and preparation of meals is carried out by somebody else, it would not normally be appropriate to carry out full adaptations to the kitchen. Nevertheless, certain adaptations might still be appropriate, to enable the disabled person to do some things, such as prepare light meals or hot drinks (ODPM 2004, annex B, paras 23–24).

## 15.4.6 HEATING, LIGHTING, POWER

Guidance states that people with limited mobility who remain in one room for long periods usually need more warmth than able-bodied people. Where there is no heating system or where the existing heating arrangements are unsuitable to meet his needs, a heating system may be provided. However, the works should not involve adaptation or installation of heating in rooms that are not normally in use by the disabled person. Installation of central heating should only be considered where the disabled person's well-being and mobility would otherwise be adversely affected.

As far as operating heating, lighting and power, power points could be relocated, and suitably adapted controls provided (ODPM 2004, annex B, paras 25–26). Local authorities should beware of adopting restrictive approaches, as highlighted in a court case:

**Policy on central heating too narrow.** In a dispute about a person's needs for central heating, the local authority conceded that its existing policy was unlawfully rigid. It had stipulated that the applicant must (a) be receiving home kidney dialysis and the treatment room be inadequately heated; (b) have a medical condition that made a constant temperature, 24 hours a day, necessary; or (c) have been assessed by social services as requiring extended bedroom/bathroom facilities that required heating (*R v Birmingham CC, ex p Mohammed*).

The local ombudsman has identified too limited an approach:

**DFGs and assessment for central heating: restrictive approach.** The social services occupational therapy service considered that it could only provide assessments for heating if the need arose from a severe functional loss or if there was a risk of injury: that is, risk of burning because of the dysfunction, or inability to control the existing heating where the person lived alone (or was frequently left alone for four hours or more). The occupational therapy service did not consider that it should assess when poor housing conditions (e.g. damp and cold) affected people with a medical condition. The local ombudsman concluded that the council did 'have a duty to consider a request from one of its tenants for installation of central heating on medical grounds and to reach a decision'.

After consulting with the Department of Environment, Transport and the Regions, he concluded that the criteria used by the occupational therapy service for assessing heating requests amounted to maladministration because they 'placed a narrow construction on legislation and guidance about the circumstances in which grants might be awarded for heating improvements... I can understand the difficulty for the occupational therapy service; its concern is with functional loss. But if that service is not able to advise on applicants with medical need, the Council should have some other mechanism which can' (*Hackney LBC 1997b*).

## 15.4.7 DISABLED OCCUPANT

A person is disabled if (a) his sight, hearing or speech is substantially impaired; (b) he has a mental disorder or impairment of any kind; or (c) he is physically substantially disabled by illness, injury impairment since birth or otherwise.

A person is also to be taken to be disabled if he or she is registered under s.29 of the National Assistance Act 1948 (see 10.1.3), or is a person for whom welfare arrangements have been made under that Act or in the opinion of the social services authority might be made under it (HGCRA 1996, s.100).

## 15.4.8 DFG FOR ONLY OR MAIN DWELLING

Unlike for social services or the NHS (see Chapter 14), the residence qualification for DFGs is given in terms of dwelling rather than area of residence. The dwelling must be the person's only or main residence, either as owner (s.21) or occupier of a houseboat or caravan (HGCRA 1996, s.22A).

### 15.4.8.1 Owner's application for DFG

A certificate is required that the applicant has or proposes to acquire a qualifying owner's interest, and that the disabled occupant will live in the dwelling or flat as his only or main residence throughout the grant condition period, or for such shorter period as his or her health and other relevant circumstances permit (s.21). The grant condition period is ten years. In the case of an applicant who proposes to acquire a qualifying owner's interest, the application must not be approved until he or she has done so (HGCRA 1996, s.24). Repayment is not required in case of breach of the time condition.

### 15.4.8.2 Tenant's application for DFG

A certificate is required that the applicant intends that he (if he is the disabled occupant) or the disabled occupant will live in the dwelling or flat as his or her only or main residence throughout the grant condition period, or for such shorter period as his or her health and other relevant circumstances permit. The grant condition period is five years. Unless it is unreasonable in the circumstances, a tenant's certificate must be accompanied by an owner's certificate (HGCRA 1996, s.22). Replayment is not required in case of breach of the time condition.

One drawback identified by the local ombudsman involved the case of a man who had to accept the offer of a council tenancy before he was eligible for a disabled facilities grant. However, the house would not be habitable until the works were complete. This meant that he had to pay for two dwellings for an indeterminate period (*Birmingham CC 2002*). This situation arose because although a prospective (rather than actual) owner can apply for a DFG, it appeared that only an actual tenant, as opposed to a prospective tenant, could apply (HGCRA 1996, s.19). However, guidance issued subsequently by central government states that the offer and acceptance of a tenancy in principle, subject to the completion of adaptations, should be treated as a residence qualification for the purpose of DFG (ODPM 2004, para 6.6).

### 15.4.8.3 Caravan and houseboat applications for DFG

An 'occupier's certificate' must certify that the applicant intends that he or she (if he or she is the disabled occupant) or the disabled occupant will live in the qualifying houseboat or caravan as his or her only or main residence throughout the grant condition period (five years) or such shorter period as his or her health or other relevant circumstances permit. Repayment is not required in case of breach of the time condition.

However, unless it is unreasonable in the circumstances to require such a certificate, the local authority cannot consider an application unless a consent certificate is received from a person who is entitled to possession of the premises at which the houseboat is moored or the land on which the caravan is stationed – or who is entitled to dispose of (sell) the houseboat or park home (s.22A).

Qualifying park home was restrictively defined in the HGCRA 1996 (s.58) so as to exclude, for example, disabled people living on gypsy sites, as well as various others. An amendment contained in the Housing Act 2004 changed the reference from qualifying park home simply to caravan, as defined in Part 1 of the Caravan Sites and Control of Development Act 1960 – and thus widened its application.

### 15.4.9 DFG MUST BE NECESSARY AND APPROPRIATE

The works must be necessary and appropriate. This is a decision for the housing authority to take, but if the housing authority is not itself also a social services authority, then it is under an obligation to consult the latter about this issue (s.24). The dangers of losing control of this process of recommendation were illustrated in the following local ombudsman investigation:

**Loss of control of assessment and recommendation for a DFG.** Following treatment for cancer, a woman living alone had difficulties in managing at home. Supported by Macmillan nurses to some extent, she needed more help and wished to have an additional room in which a carer could stay overnight.

The social services department purportedly assessed her and made a recommendation to the district council that such an adaptation/extension was necessary and appropriate, and so qualified for a disabled facilities grant. The district council refused to provide one, explaining that the proposed adaptation did not come under the mandatory category of grant, but only under the discretionary; and the council had a policy of not awarding discretionary grants.

Relying on guidance from central government, which stated that in such circumstances (i.e. rejection by the district council of a social services recommendation) the social services authority had a continuing duty to meet the person's needs, the woman asked the social services authority for help. In the course of refusing, the authority disowned its previous recommendation to the district council.

It transpired that, at the relevant time, the occupational therapy assistant originally involved had no substantial support or supervision from a qualified occupational therapist; and the possibility of using NHS therapists had been rejected on grounds of cost. As a consequence, and unknown at the time to the director of social services, the original assessment had been delegated to another organisation altogether (a home improvement agency) – and the recommendation, made without the use of qualified staff (e.g. therapists), had been forwarded as the council's own and without question by the social services department to the district council.

Amongst other findings, the ombudsman found maladministration insofar as social services had throughout failed to assess the woman's needs properly (*Dyfed CC 1996*).

Some councils might avoid even getting to the stage of properly considering an application for a DFG and whether works might be necessary and appropriate. This will be maladministration for the local ombudsman:

**Self-completion questionnaires.** When people applied for disabled facilities grants, they were asked to complete a questionnaire; the application of priority points was based entirely on the replies. If a person was awarded fewer points than the threshold figure, the request was not considered further. Until the person reached that threshold (at a later date), he or she would not be seen by a professionally qualified assessment officer. The questionnaire replies were handled by an administrative assistant. This was maladministration (*Neath Port Talbot County BC 1999*).

Social services and housing functions might come under one roof (e.g. in a unitary or metropolitan local authority) or separate roofs (e.g. county council and district council). Previous guidance (now superseded) stated that, in the case of unitary authorities, the housing department should still consult the social services department (DoE 17/96, annex I, para 37).

The previous guidance also stated that if 'both the social services and housing authorities collaborate effectively it should be a rare occurrence where a housing authority determines not to approve particular adaptations recommended by a social services authority' (DoE 17/96, annex I, para 4).

The replacement guidance states that local housing authorities, having consulted social authorities about what is necessary and appropriate, must then decide what action to take on the basis of the advice provided by social services. The decision must be taken in respect of the statutory provisions for mandatory DFG under s.23 of the HGCRA 1996 (ODPM 2004, annex B, para 34). The guidance goes on to make a number of points about assessing the need for adaptations including (ODPM 2004, Chapter 5):

- Occupational therapists will generally assess for adaptations, but others who may be involved include occupational therapy assistants – and specialist staff working with people with sensory impairments, learning disabilities or mental health problems.

- Disabled people must be involved in the assessment of needs and carefully listened to, since they are the experts on their own needs (this includes children, young persons and their parents).
- 'Self-assessment' may be part of the consultation with the disabled person.
- Particular materials may have to be used or avoided in the adaptation for the protection of a person with learning disabilities or of other people living in the dwelling.
- Adaptations might be required for the protection (from harm or from intrusions provoking their problems) of people with mental health problems.
- People with autism may require additional quiet space, without which serious adverse consequences may occur.

The guidance refers to three sets of guidance as containing the 'general principles' of social care assessment, namely on 'fair access to care' (LAC(2002)13), on the single assessment for older people (HSC 2002/001), and on the assessment framework for children in need (DH 2000a). However, elsewhere the guidance reminds local authorities that they cannot straightforwardly apply to DFG decisions the social care eligibility rules under the social services 'fair access to care' guidance (ODPM 2004, para 4.7, see 15.4.9.1).

Some councils in practice apply quite restrictive policies in this respect. For example, they might insist that the adaptations must make the whole dwelling 'barrier free', in order for adaptations to be necessary and appropriate. Applying such a policy, they then refuse to carry out adaptations to the bathroom, for example, on the grounds that access to the dwelling will remain difficult for the disabled occupant. However, the pointers given in the guidance do not necessarily equate to a completely 'barrier free' dwelling. Given the variety of needs, circumstances, reasons (and care plans), in respect of which people might need adaptations, such policies are excessively restrictive. They almost certainly run the risk of being held to be unlawful or to be maladministration if applied in blanket fashion.

Similarly councils that state that they will 'never' build extensions or extra space run the risk of acting unlawfully or with maladministration. This is because if an adaptation is deemed to be necessary and appropriate, and there is no reasonable way of achieving it through use of existing space, then an extension might be the only option for meeting the need. Indeed, the guidance states that sometimes an extension will be necessary where existing space cannot be reasonably used (see 15.4.3).

### 15.4.9.1 Relevance of resources to necessity and appropriateness

The courts have stated that the decision about whether works are necessary and appropriate is 'directed to a consideration of a technical question'. Local housing authorities were therefore not entitled to take resources into account (*R v Birmingham CC, ex p Taj Mohammed*).

The courts distinguished the rules under the 1996 Act from those under s.2 of the Chronically Sick and Disabled Persons Act 1970. The latter allows local authorities to set a threshold of eligibility, at least partly based on the local authority's resources, to determine the sort of circumstances in which it is necessary to meet them (*R v Gloucestershire CC, ex p Barry*). The *Birmingham* case appears to state that such an approach is not legally permissible under the 1996 Act.

In the light of this judicial decision, both social services and housing authorities must especially guard against applying the rules for one set of legislation to another. For instance, there is a danger that social services authorities will apply the eligibility rules for community care legislation (including 'fair access to care': see 6.9 and 6.11) to the recommendation about whether a DFG is necessary and appropriate under housing legislation. Legally this would appear to be impermissible, since it would in effect be collapsing two quite distinct sets of legislation into one. Guidance points out that a person might be eligible for DFG assistance but not for social services assistance (ODPM 2004, para 4.7).

**Collapsing two Acts into one.** The local ombudsman found maladministration because a local authority had collapsed into one procedure the dealing of applications for assistance with adaptations under both the HGCRA 1996 and the Chronically Sick and Disabled Persons Act 1970. The situation was exacerbated by the inadequacy of the self-assessment questionnaire that was used to make a judgement about a person's priority under both Acts (*Neath Port Talbot CBC 1999*).

The distinction is by no means academic, since it is quite conceivable that in some circumstances a person could be eligible for a DFG but not for social services assistance. This is because the decision made in respect of social services can be influenced by resources (in terms of the threshold of eligibility), whereas that made by housing cannot. This might particularly occur where a social services authority has set its 'fair access to care' threshold of eligibility at a high level (see 6.11).

Equally, in some circumstances, eligibility could be in reverse in that a person might be eligible for social services assistance but not for housing assistance (*Neath Port Talbot CBC 1999*). For instance, the adaptation in question might be one that does not come under one of the DFG mandatory purposes; in which case it might fall to social services to consider whether to assist under the CSDPA 1970. Again, in order to come to a proper decision, favourable or otherwise, the two Acts would need to be distinguished.

Where people have deteriorating conditions, housing authorities often hesitate to approve adaptations. Some tend to impose blanket-type conditions that the adaptation must be likely to be of use for a certain length of time, if the works are to be deemed necessary and appropriate. Guidance states, however, that the fact that an adaptation might be appropriate for only a limited period of time, should not of itself be regarded as 'sufficient reason' for delaying or withholding provision (ODPM 2004, para 5.22). For instance, an adaptation might be required to enable a middle-aged father to spend his last year or so of life at home with his family. The fact that he is likely to die within a year or two does not mean that the adaptation would not be of immense benefit and be 'necessary and appropriate'.

## 15.4.10 DFG MUST BE REASONABLE AND PRACTICABLE

In addition to deciding whether a proposed adaptation is necessary and appropriate, housing authorities must also decide whether it is reasonable and practicable in relation to the age and condition of the dwelling. Central government guidance gives examples of issues that relate to this condition. These include:

- architectural and structural characteristics of the dwelling
- practicalities of carrying out adaptations to smaller properties with narrow doorways, halls and passages which might make wheelchair use difficult or, for example, steep flights of steps making access for wheelchair use difficult and continued occupation of the dwelling open to question
- conservation considerations and planning constraints
- the impact on other occupants of proposed works which would affect existing facilities in the dwelling (ODPM 2004, annex B, para 37).

The courts have indicated that resources might in some circumstances legitimately inform the decision.

**Reasonable practicability and relevance of resources.** The court stated in one case that it might not be a 'sensible use of resources to make a DFG to improve an old dilapidated building, or a dwelling which was not fit for human habitation' (R v Birmingham CC, ex p Taj Mohammed).

Indeed, in deciding whether to approve a DFG application, the 1996 Act explicitly states that the local authority must take into account whether the dwelling would be fit for human habitation. The fitness standard, currently contained in s.604 of the Housing Act 1985, has been described in guidance as applying, as a matter of principle, to the physical characteristics of a dwelling and not to the occupants and the way the dwelling is occupied (DoE 17/96, annex A). The statutory of definition of fitness will be amended when part one of the Housing Act 2004 is implemented.

Therefore it would seem legally suspect for housing authorities simply to argue that a DFG is not reasonable and practicable because the budget cannot cope. Instead, the rejection of an application must relate (a) to the individual case; and (b) genuinely to the age and condition of the dwelling in question. Thus, it was arguably incautious of a council to state simply that the reasonable practicability test was related to the 'public purse', without mention of the age and condition of the particular dwelling (Harlow DC 2000: although the local ombudsman did not comment on this particular statement).

## 15.4.11 RECOVERY AND MAINTENANCE OF EQUIPMENT

The Housing Grants, Construction and Regeneration Act 1996, s.52, allows local authorities to impose additional conditions on grants – subject to consent from the Secretary of State. One such consent allows local authorities to recover 'specialised' (removable equipment such as stairlifts), when it is no longer needed. They should consider carefully the condition of recovery to be imposed if the applicant has made a significant contribution to the equipment (i.e. pay the current value of the proportion of the equipment corresponding to the person's original contribution); and also make good damage to the property. It states that in practice social services are best placed to recover the equipment so that it can be reused by other people. However, where it is clear that the equipment will not be reused because of its age or condition, the local authority may waive its right to recovery (ODPM 2004, annex B, para 65 and Housing Renewal Grants (Additional Conditions) (England) General Consent 1996).

Some adaptations such as stairlifts or through-floor lifts require regular maintenance. Guidance states that it is good practice for such maintenance (and repair) arrangements to be put in place at time of installation. Thus the cost of an extended guarantee or service contract should be included in the calculation of the DFG payable (ODPM 2004, para 8.1).

## 15.4.12 SERVICES AND CHARGES

The cost of a range of various charges and services can be included within a DFG; for example, relating to design, advice, assistance in completing forms, surveys, supervision of works, application for building regulations approval – and the services of an occupational therapist (SI 1996/2889).

## 15.4.13 ELIGIBILITY ACROSS DIFFERENT HOUSING SECTORS

Eligibility for DFGs extends to all owner-occupiers, tenants or licensees who meet the criteria in ss.19–22 of the 1996 Act. This has been emphasised in guidance (ODPM 2004, para 3.21).

### 15.4.13.1 Council tenants

Notwithstanding the legislation, and the emphasis by guidance that it is 'not lawful for persons in any tenure to be obstructed in' applying for disabled facilities grants (ODPM 2004, para 3.26), some councils in practice deny this option to their tenants.

Guidance makes clear that a local authority could carry out required adaptations to its own stock from its own resources, rather than through the DFG system (ODPM 2004, para 3.21). If it does so, it would presumably be acting under the Housing Act 1985 by considering housing conditions and needs with specific regard to disabled people (s.8 together with s.3 of the Chronically Sick and Disabled Persons Act 1970); and by altering, enlarging or improving its housing stock (s.9).

Nevertheless, the works should be carried out on terms as advantageous as if a DFG had been awarded (ODPM 2004, para 3.21). The following case clearly illustrates the local ombudsman's view of the disadvantages that might accrue if an individual council tenant is not offered a DFG or at least its equivalent – even though the alternative procedure offered by the council might have been generally more advantageous for other tenants than a DFG would have been:

**DFGs and assessment for central heating**. The case concerned the application for central heating by a council tenant who had been diagnosed in 1988 as HIV positive and was receiving income support. A complaint was made to the local ombudsman.

*Original request.* In August 1991, the Hackney Energy Audit Project wrote to the estate manager pointing out that the underfloor heating for the block in which the man lived had been defective since 1976, leaving tenants to heat their flats by using peak-rate electricity. The letter requested that affordable heating be installed for him and included supporting letters from the hospital and from an occupational therapist. The estate officer replied that there was no programme to fund central heating in individual cases, and that the man should apply for a transfer. However, the man did not wish to do this because of his network of friends and possible carers in the area.

*Different procedure.* In June 1992, the man applied for both renovation and disabled facilities grants; he was sent information, but this did not explain that there was a special procedure for council tenants. By the end of 1992, the housing department had not agreed to fund the heating, so in December social services agreed to do so from its own budget. After some uncertainty about whether storage heaters should be installed rather than central heating (pending refurbishment of the whole estate), the heating was installed together with an electric shower in June 1993 at a cost of £3393.60 – though without thermostatic radiator valves. The man complained that radiators in two of the bedrooms were too small; the contractors confirmed that this was so and replaced them in February 1994.

*Offering a choice of DFG or alternative.* The local ombudsman congratulated the council on offering to its own tenants a procedure that was often better than the statutory procedure for disabled facilities grants. However, applicants should still have been given the choice between the two procedures; and if the council's own procedure was to be used, then it should 'be followed smoothly and without delay'. Neither of these things happened. Eventually, following confusion amongst council officers, the man had been told that he could not apply for a disabled facilities grant; his case was dealt with under the council's own procedure without his agreement being obtained. Furthermore, it took seven months for funding to be agreed and five months for the heating to be installed; this was 'too long' and was maladministration.

*Disadvantage in time and nature of the adaptation.* The injustice was that, had the council not made mistakes, the heating would have been installed by June 1992 rather than June 1993. In addition, the heating system installed was not what the man wanted (and which would have been specified if a disabled facilities grant had been awarded): there were no thermostatic valves, the water tank was wrongly positioned and the pipework not boxed in.

*Important issue of public interest.* The ombudsman recommended that the council check the heating against 'design temperatures', replace the valves, pay the man £700 compensation in respect of the delay, time and trouble – and review its procedures to enable council tenants to apply for disabled facilities grants, as is their statutory right. This last was an important issue of public interest: 'When a statutory entitlement exists and a Council considers that an alternative, non-statutory scheme would be preferable, the Council should publicise and explain both in an even-handed way and should leave the choice between the two schemes to the individual beneficiaries' (*Hackney LBC 1995*).

Thus, the local ombudsmen have in the past been highly critical of councils that have effectively prevented their own tenants applying for DFGs:

**Not offering DFGs to council tenants**. The local ombudsman has found maladministration when local councils fail to inform their own tenants of their right to apply for DFGs (e.g. *Hackney LBC 1995; Humberside CC 1996; Barnsley 1998a, 1998b*) or are not even themselves sure what the position is (*Durham CC 1993; Bristol CC 1998*).

Likewise, when a council does offer adaptations to its own tenants, but simply manages the resulting demand by excessive waiting times, the local ombudsman will find maladministration:

**Excessive demand in coal mining area.** Three council tenants were kept waiting – for two years in two cases and over one and a half years in the other – for showers and stairlifts. The council explained that demand exceeded its budget; and that the demand was particularly high because it was an area formerly dominated by coal mining with the resultant problems of ill-health and disability. Nevertheless, the ombudsman refused to accept that lack of resources excused the excessive delays in helping people whose needs had been clearly assessed and accepted (*Bolsover DC 2003*).

### 15.4.13.2 Housing associations/registered social landlords

Housing associations, or registered social landlords, have the power to carry out home adaptations for their tenants. However, they are not under an obligation to carry out such adaptations for individual tenants; such individual obligations lie with housing and social services authorities.

Housing association tenants are eligible to apply for disabled facilities grants, a point stressed in guidance (ODPM 2004, para 3.26). It appears that in practice some local authorities adopt policies that preclude such applications; yet, as with council tenants, this would appear to be denying housing association tenants their statutory right (as the guidance states, it is 'not lawful': para 3.26).

Sometimes there are other options for housing association tenants; for works over £500 a grant might be available to the housing association, from the Housing Corporation under the Housing Act 1996, s.18, which gives a power to make grants. Alternatively, for minor or more major works, housing associations may pay for works out of their own revenue or reserves. In some areas, difficulties appear to arise when all concerned indulge in buck-passing and funding is not forthcoming from the Housing Corporation, the housing association, the local housing authority, or the local social services authority.

In some circumstances, when local authorities have transferred council housing to housing associations, part of the agreement has been that the housing association will carry out a certain level of adaptations for its disabled tenants. Such transfers are sometimes known as 'large-scale voluntary transfers'. In such circumstances, housing authorities sometimes then refuse to approve DFGs for any of those tenants. This would seem to be a spurious ground for refusal, since any breach of an agreement concerning adaptations is a matter between local authority and housing association; the right of a disabled tenant to apply for a DFG is unaffected.

### 15.4.13.3 Rehousing

Increasingly in practice, it seems that local authorities are encouraging people to move rather than have adaptations carried out. This often occurs in the case of council tenants but sometimes also in the case of private tenants.

When local authorities make such a decision, they need in principle to be able to justify it against the terms of the 1996 Act. For instance, in the individual case, the works might be judged not to be necessary and appropriate or not to be reasonable and practicable. Guidance states that if a dwelling is unfit, to the extent that it is unreasonable and impractical to proceed with the proposed adaptations, the housing authority should, together with social services, consider alternatives. This might be renovation of the dwelling first, a reduced level of adaptations that would still meet the person's needs and considerations of practicality, or alternative accommodation (ODPM 2004, annex B, para 36).

More controversial, and sometimes legally suspect, is where the adaptation is judged to be necessary and appropriate, and reasonable and practicable, but the local authority simply refuses to countenance a DFG – instead offering rehousing only, because it judges that this is the cheaper option. First, the 1996 Acts says nothing about people having to move house (in either public or private sector housing), simply because it would be cheaper than an adaptation. Second, *even were this approach legally arguable* (and it may not be), it would still need to be shown that the person's needs were being met by the rehousing to the extent that they would have been met by the DFG – and that the person was not in other ways being significantly disadvantaged by the move.

Yet the following examples reveal that rehousing might be far from straightforward. For instance, loss of a local support network might mean that a move would simply not meet a person's needs. The financial consequences of having to move might be highly significant (including moving costs, cost of a higher mortgage, effect on benefits entitlements). In any case, rehousing might take a substantial length of time, before a suitable dwelling is identified – longer than a DFG would have taken. In which case it might be arguable that the rehousing option is less advantageous and so not a suitable alternative to adaptations. The local ombudsman was in no doubt that it was maladministration in the following case to force the woman to move council house:

**Trying to force a disabled woman to move: loss of support network.** A couple had lived in a council house for 30 years. The woman was a permanent wheelchair user and depended on her husband for assistance. Three of their children lived in the same village and provided a support network. The woman was assessed as having no access to basic facilities such as toilet and bath; the occupational therapist considered the situation unacceptable and highly distressing to the woman. Adaptations were recommended. The council did not permit council tenants to apply for DFGs; it did carry out works to its own stock but allocated only £40,000 for these for the whole year. As the works would have used up a quarter of this budget, the council declined approval. Instead it would offer to move them to a nearby village; provide new purpose-built accommodation in the same village in some three years' time; or fund a third of the cost of the works, and expect the couple to find charitable funding for the remaining two thirds.

The failure to approve the adaptations was maladministration. First, government guidance stated that council tenants should be eligible to receive home adaptations either through a DFG, or at least on the same terms as in the private sector. The ombudsman was in no doubt that, had the couple been owner-occupiers, they would have received a 100 per cent mandatory DFG. Second, the budgetary allocation was irrelevant to this mandatory duty. Third, the availability of alternative accommodation in another village was an irrelevant consideration given the couple's reliance on a local support network (*North Warwickshire 2000a*).

The ombudsman also recommended a total of £4500 compensation. The council agreed to carry out the adaptations, but refused to pay the compensation because the couple had refused to move and because the money would have to come from the DFG budget and thus delay other applicants. The ombudsman found this to be irrational. There was no reason why their reasonable decision not to move should be used against the couple; likewise no reason why the compensation should not come out of another budget (*North Warwickshire BC 2000b*).

The following local ombudsman investigation reveals a situation that was anything but clear, and highlights the problems arising from imposing a highly restrictive policy in respect of DFG funding, in terms of a financial ceiling (£15,000) well below the statutory figure of £25,000 (up to which housing authorities have a duty to award DFG):

**Restrictive policy on adaptations.** A local authority had a policy that for any adaptation costing over £15,000 there was an expectation that rehousing would be offered as the only alternative to meeting the need. Only exceptionally, where a suitable alternative adapted property owned by the council or housing association (that could be nominated by the council) was not available, would adaptations over £15,000 be considered. This policy was applied in the case of a family in their own house with a disabled child. The family were prepared to move to another private property within the area; but would have to increase their mortgage, which they could not afford to do. They asked whether social services financial assistance to move might be available.

The family was also concerned about a move to council-owned property; the money realised would be taken into account in relation to their entitlement to benefits. In fact the council housing option that would have meant knocking two properties into one was anyway a remote possibility. Even so the local authority delayed in reaching the decision, and in producing a feasibility report (that was inadequate) for a through-floor lift. This led the council to approve a ground floor extension that was then judged not to be feasible. Further delay ensued while the council considered whether to financially assist the family with the purchase of another private property. In other words, the council was not considering all the relevant facts on each option. This was maladministration (*Kirklees MBC 2003*).

Likewise, the offering of alternative accommodation might not be straightforward, and result, after substantial delay, in reoffering a DFG:

**Offering rehousing: confusion and delay.** A complaint was made to the local ombudsman concerning a man who had early onset Alzheimer's disease, epileptic fits, and Parkinson's disease. He had had a heart attack, stroke, and transient ischaemic attacks. He was unable to feed himself, walk any distance or use the toilet unaided; he required care around the clock. His wife provided it, although she had back problems and had developed osteo-arthritis. Initially, an assessment concluded that certain adaptations would not meet his longer term needs. Other adaptations might have, but the district council miscalculated the couple's contribution, which put them off pursuing the application. The council then suggested council rehousing, but it took eight months for them to make clear that the couple would not be eligible; this was because the money from the sale of their existing house would exclude them from the council's allocation scheme. All this caused confusion and delay and was maladministration. The council subsequently reoffered a disabled facilities grant (*Maldon DC 2000*).

The local ombudsman in the next case uncovered a protracted rehousing process and a failure in the meantime to meet people's needs:

**Failure to adapt and rehousing**. When a couple applied to be rehoused, the local authority offered in early 1998 a two-storey property with a bathroom and toilet upstairs. This was maladministration since, on the medical evidence, the slightest exertion made the wife breathless, and there would be a problem with the stairs. Further rehousing took until April 2002. Yet a downstairs toilet was assessed as required in June 1998; this was not provided, although a chemical toilet downstairs was supplied to mitigate the situation. By October 1999, the council stated that the downstairs toilet would not meet the longer term needs, therefore it had no obligation to adapt. Nevertheless the ombudsman criticised the fact that the council had previously stated that the toilet was required; it was maladministration not to have carried out the adaptation as required in 1998 – because of lack of funding (*Salford CC 2003*).

People sometimes find themselves caught within a 'vicious circle'; having applied for rehousing, they are as a matter of policy then excluded from being on the adaptations list. Although defensible on a case-by-case basis, applied as a policy this can result in some cases in significant problems. Things are made even worse if there is then confusion amongst staff about whether or not there is such a policy (*Barking and Dagenham 2000*). Such policies can lead to patent absurdity, as became apparent in a Court of Appeal case:

**Refusing to carry out adaptations**. A local authority awarded 'nil points' to a mother who had applied for a council house transfer for herself and her two children, one of whom had been assessed as significantly disabled. This decision would have effectively ruled out a move in the foreseeable future; yet the council stated that while the mother remained on the housing transfer list, no adaptations could be carried out. The council in fact backed down, and the court suggested that the award of nil points could anyway have been susceptible to judicial review (*R v Ealing LBC, ex p C*).

Lastly, it is worth noting that even in a case where the court suggested that an elderly disabled couple's needs could in principle be lawfully met either by means of a stairlift or by 'removing' them to another house, the judge referred to the potential complications of such a move:

**Difficulty of moving house**. The judge stated that the local authority was bound to take into account that the couple should remain in the area, to ensure continuity of service. Any new premises would have to be suitably adapted. Likewise there was a risk that, because of medical evidence as to the vulnerability of the couple, whatever was done would be fatal to the husband (both medical specialist and the GP said he was not fit to move house). Even so the judge (with some regret) was not prepared to state that a move to alternative accommodation was legally irrational – but did state that the local authority would have to reconsider the matter carefully about whether such a move should take place (*R v Kirklees MBC, ex p Daykin*).

(In the *Daykin* case, the court did not apparently consider the Housing Grants, Construction and Regeneration Act 1996; reference was made only to social services legislation (Chronically Sick and Disabled Persons Act 1970, etc.). Had the court been referred to the 1996 Act, with its specific duties in respect of adapting people's homes, its conclusions might have differed and come down in favour of adapting the home.)

## 15.4.14 LANDLORD CONSENT

Landlord consent is a significant obstacle to the carrying out of adaptations, since it will effectively prevent the work being carried out. However, central government guidance states that every attempt should be made to gain the approval of landlords. This would include, in 'appropriate circumstances', the local authority giving an assurance to the landlord that the authority will 'make good' when the adaptation is no longer needed by the tenant (ODPM 2004, para 6.3). Apart from potential refusal by private sector landlords, the question of landlord consent has in some areas assumed greater significance in respect of council tenants. It seems that, separate from any question of whether an adaptation is necessary and appropriate (and reasonable and practicable), some local authorities are in practice simply refusing consent as landlord as a matter of policy in respect of their own tenants. In other words, they are in principle allowing applications by their own tenants, but then refusing landlord consent wholesale. This is likely to be unlawful, since it would represent a systematic undermining of the DFG system by a local authority that is both legally responsible for DFGs and is landlord.

Other local authorities apparently regularly refuse landlord consent to their own tenants in individual cases (rather than wholesale) on grounds of overcrowding or under-occupation. Such grounds probably cannot be brought under the 'reasonable practicability' condition, since that relates to the age and condition of the dwelling: see 15.4.10). Sometimes local authorities attempt to connect overcrowding with the 'necessary and appropriate' condition; effectively stating that the need for extra space or an extra facility is not related to the need of the disabled occupant but to the whole family's situation. However, caution is again required:

**Extra bedroom and overcrowding.** When the parents of an autistic child applied for conversion of the attic into an extra bedroom, the local authority at one point suggested that this was simply an overcrowding issue. However, the parents rejected this, pointing out that if it were not for the child constantly attacking his brother with whom he shared a bedroom, the two boys could happily continue to share. Therefore the extra bedroom was disability, and not overcrowding, related. This point was not pursued by the local authority (*R(B) v Calderdale MBC*, High Court).

The local ombudsman has questioned undue application of the overcrowding argument:

**Overcrowding.** When adaptations were sought by the parents of a severely disabled girl, the council argued that the major problem was overcrowding. However, the ombudsman pointed out that although the daughter did not have her own bedroom, the family was not statutorily overcrowded; furthermore, the lack of a separate bedroom was only one reason why the home was not satisfactory. The ombudsman saw no evidence that the authority had adhered to its own policy on this matter; this was maladministration (*Sunderland CC 2002*).

The ground of under-occupancy is commonly used by local authorities to refuse consent to council tenants. How relevant, and indeed lawful, it is in respect of such DFG applications is perhaps unclear. The question would seem to boil down to whether the courts would view strategic use of stock as a valid reason for refusing landlord consent; whatever the answer, it would almost certainly be complicated because of the local authority's dual role as landlord and DFG provider.

The HGCRA 1996 carries no obligation that a landlord should not unreasonably refuse consent to an adaptation. Likewise, the Disability Discrimination Act 1995 (DDA) imposes no explicit duty on landlords not to refuse consent unreasonably. Consequently, it has been strongly recommended that the DDA be amended (Joint Committee 2004, para 321); however, it appears that central government will not accept this recommendation.

The Landlord and Tenant Act 1927 (s.19) does place some potential limitations on the right of a landlord to object to an 'improvement', although this only operates where there is a provision in the lease or tenancy agreement allowing the tenant to make improvements with landlord consent. Where there is an absolute prohibition on such improvements, s.19 of the 1927 Act does not apply. It has been suggested that the failure of a landlord to remove such a prohibition could in future be challenged (once the DDA has been amended: see Chapter 21), if it represented an unreasonable failure to change or waive the term of the lease in question (see discussion in Joint Committee 2004, para 311). It should also be pointed out that s.19 allows for the landlord to demand payment of a reasonable sum from the tenant for a diminution in the value of the premises. This might be significant because not every adaptation required by a disabled person enhances the value of a dwelling.

## 15.4.15 GIVING REASONS AND TIME LIMITS

Reasons must be given if applications for DFGs are refused, and applications must be approved or refused within six months from the date of application. If approved, payment must be made no longer than 12 months from the original date of application (ss.34–36). Guidance states that the 12-month limit should be used sparingly, especially where hardship or suffering would be caused (ODPM 2004, annex B, para 54).

Local authorities often run preliminary application schemes including waiting lists. They sometimes do this when they are short of resources; the intention is to limit the annual expenditure on grants (as the local authority admitted in *Qazi v Waltham Forest LBC*). Such schemes tend to spin out the application process; and the statutory six months do not start to run until the application is finalised.

Previous guidance (now superseded) stated that local authorities 'should not use pre application tests as a way of delaying applications or avoiding their statutory duty to process applications within 6 months' (DoE 17/96, annex I). Nevertheless, the local ombudsmen have in the past stated that they might not be 'critical of councils which have, in effect, introduced a rationing system for limiting the number of applications they approve provided that the system has been designed fairly and operates fairly, and provided that the council concerned has done what can reasonably be expected to secure the resources needed to meet its responsibilities in this area' (CLAE 1994, p.24). Even so, the courts have, in passing, expressed some doubt about the lawfulness of this approach suggested by the local ombudsmen:

**Preventing formal applications for grant.** In a court case concerning waiting times for the processing of renovation and disabled facilities grants applications, the court held that restricting access to mandatory grant aid could be unlawful. The alleged approach of the local authority in that case included not indicating to applicants that they had not submitted a formal application, and not indicating the difference between an enquiry and an application. The court also expressed surprise that the local government ombudsman should have described as 'administratively unavoidable and proper' a queuing system that restricted access to mandatory grant (*Qazi v Waltham Forest LBC*).

The local ombudsmen have anyway condemned queuing on other occasions.

**Preliminary enquiry system.** Local authorities might operate preliminary enquiry systems; but preventing people from submitting formal applications or not telling that they have a right to do so is maladministration (e.g. *Walsall MBC 1996*).

More bluntly, the ombudsman found maladministration in a local authority's general approach of queuing disabled applicants at the enquiry stage for long periods, in order to avoid processing applications within the six-month statutory period. Lack of resources was not an acceptable reason for excessive delay in helping people whose needs had been clearly assessed and accepted (*Cardiff CC 2004*).

**Withholding or failing to process application forms.** When a council claimed that it could not process an application for a renovation grant because the woman had not submitted a certificate of owner occupation, the ombudsman found that technically this was correct. However, the situation had come about because the council had deliberately withheld the documents necessary for the woman to complete her application; this was maladministration (*Manchester CC 1998*).

Simply putting on hold a recommendation received from the social services department – so that the adaptations were not ready almost two years after referral – was maladministration (*North Yorkshire CC 1993*).

Where there are waiting lists and waiting times, the local ombudsman has stated that at the very least a process of prioritisation should take place; date order would not be acceptable.

**Priority systems and information.** The local ombudsman has set out various steps necessary in relation to applications for housing grants, including making known the details of priority systems to enquirers and applicants in a consistent and uniform way (e.g. by leaflet or information sheet), and treating requests for information with 'helpful and meaningful responses' (*Merthyr Tydvil 1994*).

It is maladministration if an authority fails to keep adequate records of information given to enquirers, and to explain clearly (a) the priorities; (b) the difference between initial enquiry and formal application; (c) the necessity of a council survey; (d) the importance of not starting works before grant approval (*Newham LBC 1997b*). Failure to publish criteria about priority and to tell enquirers about them is maladministration, as is adopting a policy about priority without being able to produce a record of its formal adoption (*Dinefwr BC 1995*).

Whether or not delay itself is reasonable, failure to notify people about what is going on might be found by the local ombudsman to be maladministration. For example, a borough council's 'failure to notify [the applicant] formally of the decision to delay the work and then its failure to notify him formally of its schedule for carrying out the work…was maladministration'. Similarly, in the same case, the failure to notify the applicant about the fluctuations in the authority's views of what the applicant's needs really were was maladministration (*North Yorkshire CC 1993*).

**Methods of prioritisation.** The local ombudsman has disapproved of systems in which applicants are treated solely in date order, because this prevents priority being given to those in greater need (*Liverpool CC 1996/1997*) – but has accepted that local authorities should adopt priorities and that this means people will have to queue (*Newham LBC 1997b; Walsall MBC 1996*). Furthermore, giving priority for grants (renovation and disabled facilities) to certain groups such as disabled people or those with houses with dangerous structures is not a fettering of discretion when room is left to consider exceptional cases. However, if waiting lists are uneven in different areas of the authority and priority criteria are applied inconsistently, this is maladministration (*Newham LBC 1997b*).

## 15.4.16 DWELLING (INCLUDING GARDEN)

Dwelling means a building or part of a building occupied or intended to be occupied as a separate dwelling, together with any yard, garden, outhouses and appurtenances belonging to it or usually enjoyed with it (s.101). Likewise, the definitions of houseboats and park homes (caravans: see 15.4.8.3) include such yards, garden, outhouses and appurtenances (s.58). These definitions are sometimes overlooked when, for instance, applications are made in respect of gardens. Some housing authorities reject these out of hand on the mistaken view that the definition of the word 'dwelling' does not include the garden.

Nevertheless, the definition does mean that DFGs cannot be used for works outside the boundary of the dwelling; this can lead to complications and delay in organising and finding funding for such work (e.g. pavement vehicle cross over and dropped kerb: *Birmingham CC 2002*).

## 15.4.17 MAXIMUM MANDATORY GRANT

If all the relevant conditions are met, housing authorities are obliged to approve applications for DFGs up to a certain maximum, currently £25,000. Central government has offered the advice that this maximum is to be applied before, rather than after, the assessed contribution of the applicant (see 15.4.18) has been deducted from the amount of grant payable (DTLR 3/2002). If this is the correct interpretation of both the 1996 Act and the relevant regulations (SI 1996/2890), it results in less generous provision of grant. For instance, if the works cost £30,000, and the applicant is assessed to contribute £5000, the grant awarded will be only £20,000 (i.e. £25,000 less £5000) rather than £25,000 (i.e. £30,000 less £5000).

Housing authorities have a discretion, but not obligation, to exceed this maximum amount of grant by exercising their separate, general discretion under the Regulatory Reform (Housing Assistance) (England and Wales) Order 2002 (see 15.5). Local authorities should beware of the importance of following regulations rather than making up their own, unlawful, rules:

**Making up the rules.** Before renovation grants were abolished (from July 2003), the legislation listed specific and exclusive factors that authorities had to take into account when deciding how much

grant to give (just as there are for DFGs). Nevertheless, the authority had added its own rule that effectively limited the maximum grant payable to 20 per cent of the total cost of the works.

The judge found nothing in the Act which gave the Council a discretion 'to impose some
arbitrary limit on the amount payable or to take account of financial resources or their absence'.
Express language in the legislation would have been required to sanction such a policy (R v Sunderland
CC, ex p Redezeus).

## 15.4.18 TEST OF RESOURCES

Once an application has been approved, the applicant will be subject to a test of resources
in order to determine his or her contribution to the cost of the works. The test is similar to
that applied to housing benefit applications. In the case of an adult, only that adult's resources, and those of his or her partner, will be taken into account. In the case of children,
the test of resources is applied to the parents. In the case of a child aged over 16 but under
19 who is receiving in his or her own right an income-related benefit and is not in receipt
of any advanced education, it is the resources of the child rather than the parents that are
taken into account (SI 1996/2890).

It should also be noted that where it can be shown that a couple no longer live as husband or wife, but are still living in the same dwelling, the resources of the applicant's
spouse/partner would not be assessed (see, for example, the situation in R(Fay) v Essex
CC). The sort of test to be applied is well known to social security law; it would involve
matters such as independent financial arrangements, separate eating arrangements, independent arrangements for the storage and cooking of food, no evidence of family life,
separate commitment to housing costs (CPAG 2004, p.799).

Probably the greatest criticism levelled at this means test is that it takes no account of
outgoings. This can severely affect some applicants who have an income such that they
have to pay a contribution, but whose essential (disability-related or otherwise) outgoings
mean that they cannot afford to meet their contribution by means of a loan or otherwise.
Parents of disabled children have been affected in particular; to the extent that in Northern Ireland (but not England and Wales) the equivalent legislation (under the Housing
(Northern Ireland) Order 2003) has been amended and the DFG test of resources is no
longer applied in respect of disabled children.

Under s.51 of the HCGRA 1996, housing authorities may, with the consent of the
Secretary of State, impose a condition requiring an application for DFG to pursue a legal
claim for damages, or insurance claim relating to damage to the property. The Secretary of
State has made a general consent in relation to s.51 claims (Housing Renewal Main
Grants (Recovery of Compensation) General Consent 1996). Guidance states that
authorities should consider imposing such a condition where such a legal claim is made
and the cost of works to the property is part of the claim (or where the applicant has made
or could make an insurance claim in respect of damage to the property). If the applicant
receives the payment against the legal (or insurance) claim, he or she should use it to repay
the authority, 'so far as is appropriate' (ODPM 2004, annex B, paras 59–62).

### 15.4.18.1 Successive applications and 'nil grant' applications

Guidance recognises that, for disabled people with degenerative conditions, more than one application might be required over time; the legislation imposes no express restriction on successive applications. Any previously assessed contribution will be taken account of in a new application; this is why it is worthwhile for applicants to follow an application through to completion even when they receive 'nil grant' because their contribution equals or exceeds the cost of the works (ODPM 2004, annex B, para 11). Their contribution will then be taken account of in any future application within five or ten years (depending on whether the applicant is tenant or owner). Thus, the failure of a local authority to advise applicants of the advantages of pursuing such a nil grant application will constitute maladministration (*Cardiff CC 2004*).

## 15.5 HOME ADAPTATIONS: REGULATORY REFORM ASSISTANCE

Under the Regulatory Reform (Housing Assistance) (England and Wales) Order 2002, housing authorities have a wide discretion to assist with housing in their locality. The assistance can include acquiring living accommodation but also adapting or improving it. This discretion could clearly cover the adaptation of people's homes.

The assistance may be provided in any form; it may be unconditional or subject to conditions, including repayment of, or contribution to, the assistance. The housing authority could take security, including a charge over the property.

Housing authorities must, under the Order, have a local, published policy, explaining what assistance it is able to give. Central government guidance points out that in order to avoid fettering their discretion (see 4.2.2), authorities should have a mechanism to consider individual requests, even if they fall outside the scope of the local policy (ODPM 5/2003, para 4.5).

**Discretionary grants.** The court held that a policy of never providing a particular type of discretionary grant (in this case a renovation grant) would amount to an unlawful fettering of discretion (R v Bristol CC, ex p Bailey).

An explanatory document issued by central government gave examples of how people with disabilities could be assisted. For instance, housing authorities could offer disabled applicants a choice of means-tested mandatory DFG or the option of a non-means-tested loan; the latter would avoid the need for the applicant to divulge their financial details. If the applicant was anyway not eligible for a DFG, the authority could offer assistance through a loan. Assistance could also be given toward relocation (rehousing) of a disabled occupant, where this would be a preferred option – for instance, if the existing dwelling was in a state of severe disrepair or adaptation would be unsuitable (DTLR 2001a, pp.11, 27–29).

Otherwise, a consultative government paper suggested that the discretion could in principle be used, for instance, to assist a disabled person with small-scale adaptations to avoid the complexity of DFGs, to top up mandatory DFGs (e.g. where the works are particularly expensive or an applicant cannot afford contribution, or where some of the works are not mandatory – such as more satisfactory internal living arrangements for the disabled occupant), garden access if that is not already mandatory, a safe play area for a child, where a disabled occupant is receiving specialised care or medical treatment and where he or she is responsible for the works, or a 'complete solution' for the disabled person's needs (examples taken from DTLR 2001, para 9.7).

Finally, guidance issued in late 2004 stated that, since mandatory DFG would not be adequate to deal with all likely requests for assistance, it would be 'very important' for the published policies of local authorities to include what additional assistance was available for adaptations for disabled people (ODPM 2004, para 2.25). It also reiterates that there is no restriction on the amount of discretionary assistance that can be given either as an addition or alternative to mandatory DFG (para 2.23).

Examples of such assistance given in the guidance are small scale adaptations to meet needs not covered by mandatory DFG or in order to avoid the procedural complexity of DFG; provision of top-up assistance for mandatory DFG where the local authority believes that the DFG assistance is inadequate to meet the needs of the disabled person and family; or assistance in acquiring alternative accommodation, if the authority believes this will benefit the disabled occupant as much as improving or adapting his or her existing accommodation (para 2.24).

## 15.6 HOME ADAPTATIONS AND SOCIAL SERVICES AUTHORITIES

Central government guidance has always envisaged that local social services authorities have a significant part to play in the provision of home adaptations under s.2 of the Chronically Sick and Disabled Persons Act 1970. Views are sometimes expressed that the wording of s.2 does not place extensive obligations on social services to assist. However, it seems likely that in individual cases, where need cannot be met in any other fashion, a duty to provide substantial assistance will arise (see 10.2.5.5).

Guidance states that, even when an application has been made for a DFG, social services authorities might be asked to assist when (a) the assessed needs of the person exceed the scope of DFGs; (b) the person has difficulty meeting the assessed contribution for a DFG. In such circumstances, once social services have confirmed eligible need, it remains their duty to assist, even when the housing authority has either refused, or is unable to approve, the application (ODPM 2004, para 2.8).

Likewise, in other cases, the courts appear to have accepted – admittedly without it being argued to the contrary – that social services authorities might have substantial responsibility for adaptations under the Chronically Sick and Disabled Persons Act 1970 (*R v Kirklees MBC, ex p Daykin; R v Kirklees MBC, ex p Good; CD(A Child) v Isle of Anglesey CC; R(Fay) v Essex CC; R(Spink) v Wandsworth LBC*).

Similarly, under the Northern Ireland version of the 1970 Act, the Chronically Sick and Disabled Persons (Northern Ireland) Act 1978, the courts have assumed that adaptations in the form of a heating system could come under s.2 of the 1978 Act (*Re: Teresa Judge*). And in another case brought in Northern Ireland concerning the provision of heating for a disabled person, the court held that it was quite acceptable for the health and social services trust to pass the matter on to the housing authority (the Northern Ireland Housing Executive). However, if the Executive could not satisfactorily deal with the problem, then the trust would retain 'overall statutory responsibility' for 'ensuring that the necessary requirements' of the person were met (*Withnell v Down Lisburn Health and Social Services Trust*). In other words, if a person's need for adaptations could be met through another channel, a duty would not arise for the trust to do so under the Chronically Sick and Disabled Persons Act. However, if the needs could not otherwise be met, then obligations would arise under that Act.

### 15.6.1 SOCIAL SERVICES: TEST OF ELIGIBILITY

The main ways in which social services could arguably be called on to assist are as follows. First, the adaptation required may simply not come under the purposes listed in the Housing, Grants, Construction and Regeneration Act 1996. Second, a person may, under the DFG test of resources, have to contribute an amount that he or she cannot reasonably afford. Third, the works required may exceed the £25,000 maximum that housing authorities are obliged to approve. In the latter two cases, social services might be asked to 'top up'; in the first, to assist with the whole of the cost.

When requested, social services authorities would be obliged to assess whether the person's needs come above their threshold of eligibility (see 6.9 and 6.11). They would also be entitled to take into account whether the person could reasonably afford any contribution he or she may have been asked for under the DFG test of resources. If social services authorities were not legally entitled to do so, every DFG applicant could as a matter of course demand that social services authorities make up the shortfall. This would in turn undermine, and indeed make redundant, the test of resources under the 1996 Act. Certainly the local ombudsman appears in the past to have accepted the reasonableness of this approach:

**Inability to afford DFG contribution.** It was maladministration when a council took two years to agree to provide an interest-free loan as part of its 'continuing duty', following the inability of a person to meet the contribution which had been assessed by the housing authority (*Wirral MBC 1994b*). Again, the ombudsman has doubted a council's initial view (later reversed) that once it had assessed the need for a disabled facilities grant, it had done its duty under s.2 of the Chronically Sick and Disabled Persons Act. What it failed to do in this particular case was to establish whether the applicants could actually afford their contribution to the adaptations themselves, and if not, possibly offer an interest free loan (*Wirral MBC 1994a*).

Thus the courts held that, when the parents of two disabled children were assessed to pay a large contribution toward a DFG, the social services authority could take account of the parents' resources when deciding whether or not to assist with the adaptations under the CSDPA (*R(Spink) v Wandsworth LBC*). Whatever the precise extent of the duty to top up, the local ombudsman will in any case find maladministration if decisions are made arbitrarily because of the absence of a policy on such topping up (*Hertfordshire CC 1992*).

## 15.6.2 NATURE OF CONTINUING SOCIAL SERVICES DUTY

The local government ombudsmen have considered the question of social services responsibilities for home adaptations.

**Continuing social services responsibility.** Maladministration was found, when having identified a need for a downstairs extension, social services failed to act for 20 months – after the housing authority had offered a grant which the applicant family could not accept because it could not afford the contribution. The 'Council appear to have ignored the fact that their statutory responsibility to provide assistance did not come to an end with the offer of a grant [by the housing authority]' (*Salford CC 1993*).

Likewise, the local ombudsman has found that when a housing authority 'is not immediately able to provide the necessary funding, the Council must meet the costs of making provision under the terms of the Chronically Sick and Disabled Persons Act by other means in its capacity as Social Services Authority' (*Wirral MBC 1992a*).

**Interim provision by social services.** The duty on social services might in some circumstances be simply to make interim provision such as a commode (*Barnsley MBC 1998b*), until a grant is forthcoming (see e.g., *Liverpool CC 1996/1997c*; also *Tower Hamlets LBC 1997*).

**Drawing a veil over the social services duty.** Some social services departments appear to draw a veil over any continuing involvement, not even telling the person what its recommendation is and lacking a system of responding if the housing department does not act on that recommendation (*Durham CC 1993*).

**Closing files or disowning assessments.** Closing files prematurely also attempts to avoid continuing duties, but is maladministration (*Durham CC 1993; Gravesham BC 1987*). Alternatively, the social services department, when confronted with the continuing duty, might simply try to disown its original assessment of need (*Dyfed CC 1996*).

**Expenditure moratorium and social services responsibilities.** The ombudsman found that the housing authority had imposed a moratorium on expenditure having discovered half way through the financial year that finance was 'tighter than anticipated'. The need for a stairlift identified by social services therefore remained unacted upon for a long period. Social services in turn did not act (as it might have, given the continuing duty potentially incurred). The ombudsman found maladministration which had caused a two-year wait (*Camden LBC 1993*).

In other investigations, the ombudsmen seem not to have been quite so certain of social services responsibilities, stating in one that 'the Chronically Sick and Disabled Persons Act 1970 does not place a statutory obligation on the council to make a financial contribution' (*Hertfordshire CC 1992*). In another, the ombudsman did not necessarily disagree with authorities who claim that advice and assistance might suffice in place of direct provision (*Wirral MBC 1992a*); and in a third that, likewise, alternative accommodation would obviate the need for adaptations (*Manchester CC 1994*).

And in a Northern Ireland legal case, there was a wait for the Northern Ireland Housing Executive to carry out an adaptation for a tenant in one of its properties. This was to replace an open fire with a non-manual heating system. During this period of delay, the court held that the health and social services trust's responsibility under s.2 of the Chronically Sick and Disabled Persons (Northern Ireland) Act 1978 – equivalent to s.2 of the CSDPA 1970 – had been discharged satisfactorily by means of interim provision. This consisted of the provision of a home help service to clean out, light and refuel the fire during the day, while the woman's sons would be expected to take responsibility on evenings and weekends (*Re Teresa Judge*).

15.6.3 DIVISION OF RESPONSIBILITIES FOR HOME ADAPTATIONS

The division of responsibility for adaptations between social services and housing authorities is by no means clear. Up to a point it is fluid. Central government guidance has in the past stated that social services authorities would normally provide equipment that could be easily installed and removed with little or no structural modification to the dwelling. Whereas larger adaptations, involving structural modification, would be the responsibility of housing authorities and attract DFG. However, it went on to state that ultimately it was for housing and social services authorities to decide how to meet people's needs, and that a disabled person's needs remained paramount (DoE 17/96, para 7.6).

Nevertheless, joint working has sometimes led precisely in the opposite direction and to a non-meeting of a person's need, as the local ombudsman has sometimes exposed:

**Collusion in delay or non-provision.** Sometimes, housing and social services departments apparently collude in strategies of delay – for instance, by the former asking the latter to suspend assessment visits, thereby creating waiting lists and taking the pressure off the housing grants budget. However, such an approach might in turn lead to the social services department's failing to assess within a reasonable time and to a finding of maladministration (e.g. *Bolton MBC 1992*).

In another investigation, given the problems the housing department was having, the social services department suggested that baths at a day centre rather than a shower were the solution in apparent misunderstanding of the law (*Humberside CC 1996*).

*15.6.3.1 Cost threshold to determine responsible authority*

In practice, local housing and social services authorities often come to local agreement about divisions of responsibility, on the basis of cost. Under a certain financial threshold, the social services authority normally takes responsibility, over that threshold the housing authority is expected to consider a DFG. Since June 2003, the figure of £1000 is sometimes used to mark this threshold. This is because of the regulations effective since then, which state that if a social services authority provides an adaptation (as a community care service), costing £1000 or less, then it is to be regarded as 'minor' and cannot be charged for. Over that figure, social services authorities retain the power to charge (SI 2003/1196). Use of £1000 as a line of demarcation is convenient but is not explicitly demanded by the regulations; they are concerned with charges, not with divisions of responsibility.

Indeed, both housing and social services authorities should take care not to be rigidly bound by such a threshold. The reason for this is that not all adaptations costing over a certain threshold (whether £1000 or any other figure) will necessarily attract mandatory DFG. For example, an adaptation required to enable a person to work, but which did not otherwise come under the mandatory grant purposes (see 15.4.1), would not attract DFG. On the other hand, it might attract a social services duty, since vital involvement in work is indicated in central government guidance as constituting a critical risk to independence (see 6.11).

Conversely, some adaptations falling under the financial threshold figure (whatever it may be) might not attract social services assistance because the person's needs are not sufficiently high to come over the local threshold of eligibility (see 6.11). However, in some cases, there could still be eligibility for a DFG. Indeed, although the bureaucracy of the DFG process should as a matter of practicality generally be avoided in the case of lower cost adaptations, there is no lower cost threshold beneath which DFGs are prohibited. (Nevertheless deliberate referral of adaptation requests costing under £1000 – for DFG rather than social services funding, in order simply to be able to charge people – could possibly be interpreted as a deliberate, unlawful undermining of the purpose of the regulations.)

Central government concludes that in practice it is likely that minor adaptations (under £1000) will be provided free of charge either through social services or through local housing authority discretionary powers (see 15.5) (ODPM 2004, para 6.21).

### 15.6.4 HOME ADAPTATIONS UNDER NHS LEGISLATION

The NHS is not normally associated with home adaptations, but in certain circumstances it may be potentially responsible. First, central government guidance issued in 1974 stated that home adaptations required for home renal dialysis should be funded by the NHS; it would be responsible for adaptation of people's homes to provide suitable accommodation for dialysis (HSC(IS)11). This guidance was reaffirmed in 1993 (HSG(93)48).

Second, the NHS has continuing health care responsibilities towards certain categories of patient (see 16.7), including some patients in their own home. It is arguable that, just as for renal dialysis, equipment and home adaptations required directly in relation to the continuing health care treatment or services should likewise be the responsibility of the NHS.

## 15.7 HOME ADAPTATIONS: GENERAL

In practice, the system of home adaptations can be fraught with complications, and it would seem that it has often not worked well, in particular in relation to major, as opposed to minor, adaptations (Heywood 2001, p.38). Guidance was issued by central government in England in 2004, in order to highlight good practice. It included reference to: proper application of the legislation, flexibility, equity, 'one-stop shops', self-assessment, interim help, use of agencies to facilitate adaptations, disability housing registers, involving service users, and time targets (ODPM 2004).

The same guidance emphasises that it is not acceptable for a disabled person to be left for weeks or months without interim help, if the process of adaptation is likely to be lengthy. Such interim help could include equipment, temporary works or practical and financial assistance to find 'decent' accommodation during the wait (ODPM 2004, paras 5.40–5.44). It also states that, for people with deteriorating conditions, consideration should be given to 'expedited procedures' (para 5.21).

Over the years, there has been a relatively large number of investigations conducted by the local government ombudsmen involving home adaptations; some of these are illustrated in the following paragraphs.

### 15.7.1 DELAY IN HOME ADAPTATIONS

The system of home adaptations has generally been afflicted not just with the inevitable delay associated with major works to a dwelling, but with the potentially avoidable delay that comes with lack of resources or poor administration by local authorities. The courts have barely considered the issue of waiting times either in this context, although have commented on at least one occasion (*Qazi v Waltham Forest LBC*; see 15.4.15).

In contrast, the local government ombudsmen have investigated such delay on many occasions. They have often been very critical; yet on some occasions they appear to have recognised the mismatch between demand and available resources and not found maladministration – even though the delay arguably breached the time limits set out in legislation. Sometimes the delay is simply cumulative, occurring at several stages:

**Cumulative delay.** The fact that a complex system requires considerable communication and cooperation between different departments and agencies does not mean that the local ombudsman will overlook administrative deficiencies. For instance, a 19-month period between application and final assessment was maladministration, including as it did insufficient record keeping, possible lost papers and the applicant's consequent uncertainty throughout the period about what was going on (*Wirral MBC 1994a*). A four-year wait for home adaptations, made up of a series of delays, was 'entirely unacceptable' (*Gravesham BC 1987*).

A considerable lapse of time caused by obtaining medical opinion, drawing up plans and getting planning permission might be reasonable in the eyes of the ombudsman. However, once all this was done, a delay in approving and submitting plans was maladministration; as was inadequate monitoring by the council of a contractor whose defective work caused further delay (*Wirral MBC 1992b*).

Opportunities missed to progress works when finance was available and despite pressure from the hospital, the lack of finance when the application was submitted, a priority request not being progressed, availability of funding not checked, and misunderstanding between an occupational therapist and surveyors all constituted maladministration (*Tower Hamlets LBC 1992*).

Local authorities might have impressive policies but simply fail to follow them:

**Not following own policy.** The authority's policy was to raise an order (for a stairlift) within seven working days of an assessment visit; in practice, this did not happen for 22 months and was maladministration (*Camden LBC 1993*).

While there are many examples of effective arrangements between social services and housing departments, lapses also occur leading sometimes to findings of maladministration:

**Housing and social services' lack of coordination**. Things can go wrong in relation to different councils (*Durham CC 1993*), or even where social services and housing are different departments in the same council (*Camden LBC 1993*); and a breakdown in communication can result in nothing happening for months on end (*Leicester CC 1992a*).

When attempts by senior officers to discuss delay with their opposite numbers in social services failed, 'officers in both departments should have taken responsibility to ensure such discussions took place'. Not to do so was maladministration (*Newham LBC 1993b*). Inadequate coordination between departments leading to delay in the meeting of assessed needs for equipment or adaptations was not acceptable; the council should 'exercise proper management to ensure that no unreasonable delays occur before those needs are met' (*Wirral MBC 1992a*).

In yet another investigation, the 'process of establishing what needs were to be met, the drawing up of plans, the obtaining of grant aid, and the granting of planning permission involved three different departments of the Council (and two separate sections of one of those departments). If such a process is to work properly, then different parts of the Council must work together more effectively than happened in this case. The failure of officers to coordinate their activities led to the submission and processing of an unacceptable planning application and consequent delay. The Council's failure to co-ordinate their activities was maladministration' (*Salford CC 1993*).

The problems between housing and social services may come in the form of disagreement, simply unaccountable delays and problems of tracking correspondence:

**Disagreements, delays, tracking correspondence.** Allowing a disagreement, between the social services and housing departments about central heating for a man with AIDS, to drag on for over a year was maladministration; as was the concern about resources and about setting an unwanted precedent, which meant that genuine technical problems in installing the heating were identified only belatedly (*Tower Hamlets LBC 1997*). Delay caused by the seeking of medical advice will not be faulted; but subsequent failure to visit for three months, and a further three-month delay in approving a revised plan, would be (*Wirral MBC 1992b*).

Problems of correspondence in a large organisation did not make it 'right that a Council should rely on a service user to follow up delays caused by non-arrival of internal mail. It should not be beyond the capability of the Council to devise a system of keeping track of applications such as this' (*Liverpool CC 1992*). Thus, communication failure between a social worker and housing officer meant that a message was never received and led to a two-month delay; this was maladministration (*Rotherham MBC 1995*).

Again, a failure in coordination working between housing and social services can result in a catalogue of disasters and duplication:

**Catalogue of disasters and duplication**. The eight-month delay, between the approval and the placing of the order for an adaptation, was regarded as not unusual and with 'apparent equanimity' by the council. This was maladministration (*Wirral MBC 1993e*). Lack of 'effective liaison' between the social services and housing authority, resulting in delay for adaptations, was maladministration (*Camden LBC 1993*); the same fault might result in an occupational therapist's recommendations being omitted from a schedule of works drawn up by a technical officer – or in a 'catalogue of disasters and duplicated work' as well as the disappearance of an application in the architect's department (*Liverpool City CC 1996/1997*). A wait of seven and a half months between receipt of instructions from social services and the housing department's sending of a preliminary form to the applicants was also maladministration (*Wirral MBC 1994b*).

Delay arising from lack of clarity or workload levels on staff might also constitute maladministration:

**Workload and information**. Failure to provide clear information to clarify the exact works involved and the amount of contribution required of an applicant is maladministration (*Nottinghamshire CC 1998a*). Workload might explain part of the delay in installing a shower, but the fact that an order marked urgent did not appear to have received the appropriate priority was maladministration (*Islington LBC 1988*).

Of course not all delay will necessarily constitute maladministration. Sometimes, the sheer complexity or unexpected problems might make it unavoidable:

**No maladministration**. An 18-month wait for major adaptations following assessment, including design and construction taking a year, was deemed by the local ombudsman not to be 'unreasonable delay' (*Ealing LBC 1993*). The ombudsman did not criticise a council for failing to predict construction, foundation and drainage problems; nor the council's inability to get the work finished quicker by a contractor (*Cumbria CC 1992*).

   Similarly, the council was not at fault when delay occurred because of disagreement between the person and council officers, the seeking of advice by the applicant from a doctor, and an indication by the applicant, without good cause, that she wished for no further help because of the delays. In addition, it was not the council's responsibility that the person had bought a home which was difficult to modify (*Wirral MBC 1993f*).

   When an initial financial assessment was incorrect but was followed quickly by the formal assessment which correctly worked out the applicant's potential contribution, there was no evidence that the applicants were substantially misled (*Wirral MBC 1994b*).

   The fact that a lift obtained through a disabled facilities grant broke down 16 times, the door was defective, it marked the wall when in use and turned out to be too small was not in the circumstances maladministration, though the ombudsman had some sympathy for the complainants. However, in the same case, the amending of the original recommendation for a shower to a smaller model (because of cost) meant that the shower was too small for the shower chair used by the disabled person; in addition the shower leaked and the water temperature varied too quickly. The failure to ensure provision of a satisfactory shower was maladministration (*Leeds CC 1995*).

Alternatively, even if the process is going awry, the local ombudsman sometimes sympathises with those local authorities that are managing nevertheless still to act fairly:

**Acting fairly**. Although the local ombudsmen have in the past been critical of delay in processing grants, they have also recognised the difficulties facing councils who have to operate a demand-led system of DFGs with insufficient resources. Thus, lack of resources leading to a failure to comply with housing grants legislation might not in itself necessarily be maladministration (*Cyngor Dosbarth Dwyfor 1994*).

   Whilst breach of the timescale is maladministration (*Newham LBC 1993*), nevertheless the ombudsmen might accept that councils get into financial difficulty because of increased demand for grants; if complainants have not suffered injustice 'above and beyond' others in the same position, the ombudsmen might not recommend any remedy or compensation (*Middlesbrough BC 1996*; also *Newham LBC 1997b*) – other than that the council should get on and do all it can to eliminate delays (*Sheffield CC 1997b*).

Furthermore, the service user has certain responsibilities, as the local ombudsman has pointed out:

**Responsibility of service users.** It is the responsibility of grant applicants to obtain estimates, choose surveyors, choose contractors, etc., a point made by the local ombudsman when people complain after things have gone wrong (e.g. *Hounslow LBC 1994*). The council's role has been described by the local ombudsman as being about the monitoring of adaptations proceeding by way of grant to ensure that public money is spent wisely and building regulations adhered to; its inspections are therefore to protect the public revenue and not grant recipients. It is the latter's responsibility to ensure that works are carried out to a high standard (*Newham LBC 1995*). However, if a council is offering its own agency services to facilitate the adaptation, then it clearly takes on more responsibility (*Leicester CC 1992a 1995*); but in any case it should at least make clear to people the responsibilities they are taking on in relation to a grant (*Hounslow LBC 1994*).

# NHS services and joint working

## KEY POINTS

COMMUNITY CARE AND THE NHS

Basically, the duties of the NHS remain unchanged by community care legislation and are indeed for the most part not covered by it. This creates an anomaly: the essential and pivotal duty of community care, which is to assess people's needs, does not apply directly to the NHS. That said, there are some duties to cooperate, and central government has been encouraging joint working between local authorities and the NHS – including a 'single assessment process', in respect of the social and health care needs of older people. In addition, joint working could result in an NHS body – for example, an NHS primary care trust – carrying out community care functions on behalf of a local authority.

## NHS PROVISION OF SERVICES

The NHS has a general duty which includes the provision of medical and nursing services as well as the prevention of illness, care of people who are ill, and aftercare for people who have been ill. The duty is a general one only (towards the local population, but not towards individuals) and extends only to providing services 'necessary to meet all reasonable requirements'. The effect is that the duty is far from absolute and is carried out within the resources which NHS bodies have available and according to priorities which they set.

The law courts have generally, although not always, denied a remedy to applicants complaining about the rationing or withholding of services, and have avoided the sort of close scrutiny they have brought to bear in some other welfare fields such as housing, education and to some extent community care. The NHS has been left by the courts with very considerable discretion to ration services.

The discretion has been checked sometimes by the health service ombudsman, and by Department of Health guidance, of which blatant disregard might attract the censure of the courts. However, by and large, NHS bodies have had more to fear from public outcry than from serious legal challenge. For patients, the situation is one of considerable uncertainty. Service provision can vary greatly from place to place, which means that what services people get can depend on where they live. Even within the same area, provision could lawfully be uneven from week to week and from month to month, depending on the resources and facilities available. Thus, not only will there many be escape routes (see 3.1) for the NHS in terms of restricting expenditure, but many of them will be lawful, since concrete obligations are so hard to find.

## NHS CONTINUING HEALTH CARE

Service users with sufficiently complex, unpredictable, unstable or intense needs may qualify for what is called NHS continuing health care. This enables them to receive NHS services in hospital, a care home or in their own home. Apart from benefiting from the services themselves, there can be very substantial financial advantages for service users. For example, if the person is in a care home, the NHS would then be responsible for funding, free of charge, the accommodation, board, personal care and nursing care. This would compare to a care home resident who was deemed not to be in need of NHS continuing health care; he or she would receive only a certain amount of nursing care free of charge. The rest would be subject to a local authority means test that could result in the resident paying and having to sell his or her own house.

The Department of Health guidance on the rules about continuing health care is unclear and difficult to understand and has been so for a decade or more. The health service ombudsman repeatedly, and the courts on one occasion, have pointed this out; the Department of Health has persistently failed properly to clarify, although it has made the odd token gesture. The resulting situation is a classic example of the sort of uncertainty that riddles the community care system generally (see 3.1). However, this particular uncertainty is one that the Department of Health, to all appearances at least, seems quite deliberately to have fostered and encouraged.

## HOSPITAL DISCHARGE
Hospital discharge is now subject, in respect of acute beds, to time limits under the Community Care (Delayed Discharges) Act 2003. If these are not adhered to then, in some circumstances, local social service authorities have to make payments to the NHS by way of reimbursement for the 'blocked bed'.

## NHS SERVICES PROVIDED IN CARE HOMES AND IN PEOPLE'S OWN HOMES
In principle, the NHS is responsible for providing a range of health care services, to people in care homes and to people in their own homes. In practice, however, provision tends to be highly variable; this flows largely from a lack of both resources and lack of legal entitlement to such services. However, it should be noted that, as a result of guidance issued by the Department of Health, incontinence supplies should not be rationed in respect of people's assessed needs, if they are resident in a care home that provides nursing.

## INTERMEDIATE CARE
Under guidance issued by the Department of Health, the NHS and local authorities provide intermediate care services, which are designed either to prevent admission to hospital or other institution, or alternatively to enable people to return home by means of (usually up to six weeks) provision of rehabilitation or other services.

## SINGLE ASSESSMENT PROCESS
Guidance on a single assessment process for older people provides for the NHS and local authorities to streamline and integrate health and social care assessments, and to organise it in terms of four levels: contact, overview, specialist and comprehensive assessment.

## NATIONAL SERVICE FRAMEWORKS
The Department of Health has published a number of national service frameworks that amount to guidance (rather than legislation) and apply to both the NHS and local authorities. Two of particular relevance to community care concern older people and mental health. A further framework on long-term conditions is in the process of development.

## JOINT WORKING
Department of Health policy is to encourage joint working between the NHS and local authorities, and a number of legislative provisions allow for this. For instance, the Health Act 1999 allows for pooled budgets, lead commissioning of services and transfer of func-

tions (e.g. where an NHS primary care trust discharges community care duties on behalf of the local authority).

**Note: Wales, Scotland and Northern Ireland**. The basic duties to provide a health service contained in the NHS Act 1977, governing England and Wales, are reflected in the NHS (Scotland) Act 1978 and in the Health and Personal Social Services (Northern Ireland) Order 1972. Beyond that however, in terms of regulations, policy and guidance, there is a range in each country, some of which is common in approach and content and some of which is not. It is beyond the scope of this note to provide a complete breakdown.

The Community Care (Delayed Discharges) Act 2003 applies to England and Wales only; but the National Assembly for Wales has chosen not to implement it so far. Nevertheless, for example, Scotland, to whcih the Act does not apply, has instead issued guidance on hospital discharge times (CCD 8/2003).

Guidance on continuing NHS health care has been published in Wales (WOC 47/95) and in Scotland (NHS MEL(1996)22), but not in Northern Ireland.

Free registered nursing care is covered in Wales by the same legislation as in England (Health and Social Care Act 2001, s.49) and by guidance issued by the National Assembly for Wales (NAFWC 12/2003 and NAFWC 34/01). In Northern Ireland, it comes under s.1 of the Health and Personal Social Services (Northern Ireland) Act 2002 and guidance issued by the Department of Health, Social Services and Public Safety (DHSSPS BP 436/2002). The payment levels for registered nursing care however are different in Wales and Northern Ireland than in England. In Scotland there is no direct equivalent of the free nursing care guidance, since in Scotland a different approach is taken; both personal care and registered nursing care are free for older people under the Community Care and Health Scotland Act 2002; the Scottish Executive has issued guidance (CCD 5/2003).

In respect of joint working, the Health Act 1999 applies in Wales, albeit with separate regulations spelling out the detail (SI 2000/2993). In Scotland, the joint working provisions, equivalent to those in the Health Act 1999, lie in the Community Care and Health (Scotland) Act 2002 (ss.13–17). In Northern Ireland health and social services are already combined in health and social services boards and trusts.

## 16.1 NHS BASIC DUTIES AND RESOURCES

The statutory duties of the NHS remain basically unchanged by community care legislation. The main duties in the NHS Act 1977 that ultimately underlie the provision of service for individual people are as follows:

- The Secretary of State has a general duty to continue the promotion of a comprehensive health service designed to secure improvement (a) in the physical and mental health of the population; (b) in the prevention of, diagnosis and treatment of illness, and for that purpose provide or secure the effective provision of services (s.1).
- The Secretary of State has the power (a) to provide such services as he or she considers appropriate for the discharge of any duty in the NHS Act 1977; (b) to do any other thing to facilitate, or which is conducive or incidental to, the discharge of such a duty (s.2);
- The Secretary of State has a duty, to such extent as he or she 'considers necessary to meet all reasonable requirements', to provide:
  - ○ hospital accommodation or other accommodation for the purpose of any service provided under the Act
  - ○ medical, dental, nursing and ambulance services
  - ○ other services for the care of expectant mothers and young children as he or she considers appropriate as part of the health service

○ facilities for the prevention of illness, the care of persons suffering from illness and the aftercare of persons who have suffered from illness – such as he or she considers are appropriate as part of the health service (s.3).

The above functions are exercisable by strategic health authorities and NHS primary care trusts.

In the attempt to work out what the above duties mean for the provision of services to an individual patient in any particular place on any particular day, there are at least two points to note. The Act does not contain a detailed list of services, such as continence services, community nursing, stoma care, palliative care, respite care, physiotherapy, speech and language therapy, physiotherapy, chiropody – the sort of services that are so important for community care and for enabling people to remain in their own homes.

Second, these duties are anyway expressed to be towards the population generally and have been characterised by the courts as target or general duties, barely amenable to enforcement by individual service users (*R v Inner London Education Authority, ex p Ali*). Such duties are to be contrasted with specific duties towards individual people that are to be found in some of the community care legislation (see 4.1). Accordingly, the NHS has a very wide discretion to make priorities and allocate resources locally. Such is this discretion that the general duty to provide services under s.3 of the NHS Act 1977 is sometimes seen, in respect of any particular service, to be in effect a power only and as representing the absence of a right to health care (Brazier 1992, p.23).

## 16.2 GENERAL PRACTITIONERS

Community care policy guidance states that, as a matter of good practice, general practitioners (GPs) will wish to make a full contribution to community care assessments. It also reminds local authorities that GPs are not always best placed to assess on behalf of a local authority, since GPs have a personal duty and relationship with their patients; in which case, local authorities might wish other practitioners to act in that capacity (DH 1990, paras 3.47–48).

Under their contractual terms, GPs have to provide a consultation at the request of a person at least 75 years old, who has not had such a consultation in the previous 12 months. The inquiries and examinations to be undertaken are such as appears to the GP to be appropriate in all the circumstances (SI 2004/291, schedule 6). A GP may demand or accept a fee from any statutory body for services rendered for the purpose of that body's statutory functions (schedule 5).

## 16.3 NHS LEGAL CASES AND SCARCE RESOURCES

One of the legal consequences of the general duties contained in ss.1 and 3 of the NHS Act 1977 is that the NHS has been highly successful in legally defending the non-provision of services, if it has argued a lack of resources as the reason. This has become clear in a series of legal decisions over a period of some two decades, involving orthopaedic patients who had been waiting some years for treatment (*R v Secretary of State for Social Services, ex p Hincks*), children with heart conditions requiring operations (*R v Central Birmingham HA, ex p Collier; R v Central Birmingham HA, ex p Walker*), a child with leukaemia (*R v Cambridge Health Authority, ex p B*) and women wishing for fertility treatment (*R v Sheffield HA, ex p Seale*).

**Lack of resources for orthopaedic treatment.** Some people in Staffordshire who had been on a waiting list for NHS orthopaedic treatment for some years sought a declaration that the Secretary of State was not providing a comprehensive health service. The applicants had waited for periods longer than 'medically advisable'; the delay occurred because of a shortage of treatment facilities that was due partly to a decision not to build a new block on the grounds of cost. They claimed that the Secretary of State, regional health authority and area health authority had all breached their statutory duties under both s.1 and s.3 of the NHS Act 1977.

One of the judges (Lord Denning) stated that s.3 of the NHS Act 1977 did not impose an absolute duty, since it was inevitably governed by resources. Indeed, the only way it could be read was to supply extra words which did not actually appear in the Act at all. These were as follows (italics added): 'duty to provide throughout England and Wales, to such extent as he considers necessary to meet all reasonable requirements *such as can be provided within the resources available*'. He went on to point out that it 'cannot be supposed that the Secretary of State has to provide all the latest equipment [or] to provide everything that is asked for… That includes the numerous pills that people take nowadays: it cannot be said that he has to provide all these free for everybody.'

Another of the judges, sounding a cautionary note, added that he felt 'extremely sorry for the particular applicants in this case who have to wait a long time, not being emergency cases, for necessary surgery. They share that misfortune with thousands up and down the country. I only hope that they have not been encouraged to think that these proceedings offered any real prospects that this court could enhance the standards of the National Health Service, because any such encouragement would be based upon manifest illusion' (*R v Secretary of State for Social Services, ex p Hincks*).

A more recent case was decided in similar fashion:

**Refusing potentially lifesaving treatment for a child.** A health authority refused to provide possibly lifesaving treatment for a ten-year-old child suffering from leukaemia. One of the grounds for the refusal was that the proposed treatment would not be an effective use of resources. The Court of Appeal, on the same day, overturned the High Court's decision that the health authority should think again.

On the question of resources, it stated that it was not for the law courts to take decisions about the optimum – that is, utilitarian – allocation of resources. It was 'common knowledge that health authorities cannot make ends meet. They cannot pay their nurses as much as they would like; they cannot provide all the treatments they would like; they cannot purchase all the extremely expensive equipment they would like… Difficult and agonising judgements have to be made as to how a limited budget is best allocated to the maximum advantage of the maximum number of patients. That is not a judgement which the court can make.'

In addition, the court dismissed the argument that if the health authority had money in the bank which had not been spent, 'then they would be acting in plain breach of their statutory duty if they did not procure this treatment'. Indeed, 'it would be totally unrealistic to require the Authority to come to the court with its accounts and seek to demonstrate that if this treatment were provided for B then there would be a patient, C, who would have to go without treatment. No major Authority could run its financial affairs in a way which would permit such a demonstration' (*R v Cambridgeshire HA, ex p B*).

The chief reason for the failure of such cases is that the courts are generally (and understandably) not prepared to interfere with how the NHS allocates resources. As the Court of Appeal put it in the *Cambridge* case, difficult and agonising judgements had to be made in allocating resources to the maximum advantage of the maximum number of patients; and it was not for the courts to make them.

An alternative legal avenue has more recently been explored. This was to see whether, in case of undue delay in the provision of NHS services, patients who sought the required treatment in other European Community countries would then be entitled to reimbursement from the NHS. (Any such entitlement would not arise directly under the NHS Act 1977, but under a.22 of Council Regulation 1407/71 and a.49 of the European Community Treaty.) Given the significant implications of the case, the Court of Appeal referred the matter to the European Court of Justice (*R (Watts) v Bedford Primary Care Trust*). It seems unlikely that the European Court will return a radical decision that would significantly undermine the policy of rationing services in the United Kingdom.

Lastly, the implementation of the Human Rights Act 1998 was seen by some as likely to trigger a change of approach by the courts in relation to the rationing of health services. However, this has not generally happened to date; instead human rights have arisen in some specific instances.

**Human rights.** In one case (not ostensibly about rationing), the court did warn against the dangers of a breach of human rights. This was in the context of ensuring that a man with learning disabilities (and mentally incapable of giving or withholding consent) was not given less satisfactory treatment than a person who understood the risks, pain and discomfort of major surgery: 'To act in any other way would be contrary to the rights of a mentally incapacitated patient both under our domestic law and under the European Convention' (*An Hospital NHS Trust v S*).

In a second case, which arguably was about rationing and resources, the courts found a breach of article 8 (albeit prior to the Human Rights Act 1998 coming into force) when the NHS proposed to close a specialist disability unit, without sufficient reason and in breach of an explicit promise that the unit would be a home for life (*R v North and East Devon HA, ex p Coughlan*).

The health service ombudsman, like the courts, will generally not tackle the matter of resources directly, but might nevertheless in some circumstances find fault with resource-related matters. For instance, he has criticised a two-year wait for an assessment at a hearing clinic; and also the fact that the trust had not developed a coherent strategy for trying to remedy such long waits for this service (*Southampton University Hospitals NHS Trust 2003*).

## 16.4 NHS LEGAL CHALLENGES ON GROUNDS OTHER THAN RESOURCES

The NHS has sometimes been legally challenged successfully, when the ground of challenge was not explicitly that of resources. For instance, central government guidance must be properly taken account of. A failure to do so in relation to drug treatment for multiple sclerosis meant that the health authority had acted unlawfully (*R v North Derbyshire Health Authority, ex p Fisher*).

The NHS is also subject to the common law principles of fairness applied by the law courts in judicial review cases (see 4.2).

**Fettering discretion: blanket NHS policies.** When a health authority applied a policy so rigidly such that it fettered its discretion, the Court of Appeal found that it had acted unlawfully. The health authority stated in one breath that exceptions could be made, but in another that the treatment in question, gender reassignment surgery, could never be clinically justified. This meant that there was therefore no genuine possibility of an exception; it was over-rigid application of a blanket policy (*R v North West Lancashire Health Authority, ex p G, A and D*).

The health service ombudsman will also look to see if blanket polices have been imposed and whether there was a genuine mechanism to consider exceptions, as in the following cases concerning powered wheelchairs, breast reduction, homoeopathic treatment and growth hormone treatment.

**Excessively rigid policies.** The health service ombudsman has found maladministration when the NHS had no genuine mechanism for considering whether to make exceptions in terms of provision of electrically powered indoor and outdoor wheelchairs (*Epsom and St Helier NHS Trust 2001*).

Likewise when a health authority applied an over-restrictive – indeed arguably 'perverse and wholly unreasonable' – policy on breast reduction surgery. The woman had a spinal disorder and back pain, but had been refused surgery as a matter of policy, because the policy only allowed such surgery for psychiatric morbidity. This refusal was despite support for the surgery from her GP, consultant and surgeon (*North Essex HA 2001*).

A policy not to fund homoeopathic treatment was not objectionable; but the policy was adopted without sufficient thought as to whether there might be circumstances that could justify departure from it. The patient in question had a chronic skin disease that had previously responded to homoeopathic treatment, when other treatments had failed. Although the health authority's extra-contractual referral panel did review the case, it was not clear what considerations it took into account, and no clear indication as to what sort of circumstances might have led to an exception being made (*East Sussex, Brighton and Hove Health Authority 1999*). The health service ombudsman made similar objections in the case of non-provision of growth hormone treatment for a woman whose consultant had recommended it. The request was refused because there were no exceptional circumstances; but the health authority could shed no light on what might constitute exceptional circumstances (*North Essex HA 2003*).

In another court case, a health authority misinterpreted its responsibilities to provide continuing health care services under the NHS Act 1977. It expected the local authority to act unlawfully by providing a level of nursing service that was beyond the legal power of a local authority to provide (*R v North and East Devon HA, ex p Coughlan*). In the same case, the health authority acted unlawfully in respect of a breach of promise and the dashing of people's legitimate expectations:

**Legitimate expectation.** The breaking of an explicit promise to a disabled person constituted, without an overriding reason, a breach of legitimate expectations. The claimant, together with other patients, had received an explicit promise that when she moved into a specialist residential unit for disabled people, she could remain there for life. A few years later, the health authority tried to close the unit. The proposed closure was held to be unlawful (*R v North and East Devon HA, ex p Coughlan*).

## 16.5 NHS DIRECTIONS AND GUIDANCE

Directions issued to the NHS, though not legislation, will in effect impose a duty; this will be in contrast with guidance that would have merely to be taken account of but not necessarily followed (*R v North Derbyshire HA, ex p Fisher*). The courts have stated that directions should be clearly labelled as such, although it might still be possible to find a direction contained in guidance – if it was expressed in sufficiently forceful language (*R v Secretary of State for Health, ex p Manchester Local Committee*). For instance, two sets of directions have been issued in respect of continuing NHS health care (see 16.7.2). Such directions are issued under ss.17, 17A and 126 of the NHS Act 1977.

## 16.6 NHS HEALTH SERVICE OMBUDSMAN INVESTIGATIONS AND RESOURCES

Legal challenges to the provision, or more accurately non-provision, of NHS services have been relatively few. This contrasts with the comparatively large volume of negligence cases brought against the NHS by service users who claim to have suffered harm as a result of carelessness in the provision of NHS services. This illustrates the point that it is legally 'safer' for the NHS to refuse to accept patients and to provide services at all, rather than to provide services but to a negligent standard (Brazier 1992, p.23).

By contrast, the health service ombudsman has considered the adequacy of NHS provision many times on community care related matters. The ombudsman has acknowledged that the NHS can reasonably argue lack of resources when it fails to meet a person's need; but this has not stopped the finding of fault on many occasions on other grounds. A number of examples of ombudsman investigations are contained within this chapter.

## 16.7 CONTINUING NHS HEALTH CARE

What has become known as continuing NHS health care illustrates as well as any the nebulous nature of NHS legal obligations. At heart is the matter of who is going to provide and pay for such continuing care: the NHS, the local authority or the service user. The difficulty has been to make clear in what circumstances the NHS is, or is not, responsible for providing such care. Continuing NHS health care can be provided in hospital, in a care home or in a person's own home. It is a significant matter, because it is about the provision of care to often highly vulnerable people who are often very ill and disabled or both. It is also about money. For instance, if a care home resident has continuing health care status, then the NHS is responsible for fully paying the fees of the care home. Without such status, the service user might have to pay most of the fees (other than for the nursing care), even if it means selling his or her house in order to be able to afford them.

## 16.7.1 CONTINUING NHS HEALTH CARE BACKGROUND

In order to understand the present position (see 16.4.2.), the background needs first to be understood. In 1994, the health service ombudsman published a report on the non-provision of continuing NHS health care by Leeds Health Authority:

**Failure to provide NHS care for people with neurological conditions.** A health authority had decided not to provide directly, or pay for elsewhere (e.g. a nursing home), continuing care for people with neurological conditions: the health authority neuro-surgical contract did not refer to institutional care at all. The person discharged was doubly incontinent, could not eat or drink without assistance, could not communicate, had a kidney tumour, cataracts in both eyes and occasional epileptic fits. There was no dispute that when he was discharged he did not need active medical treatment but did need 'substantial nursing care'. The health authority defended its position with reference to resources, priorities and national policy (which was being followed by other health authorities).

The health service ombudsman found a failure in service. He cited s.3 of the NHS Act 1977 at the beginning of the report, including s.3(1)(e) which refers to 'aftercare'. His findings read: 'This patient was a highly dependent patient in hospital under a contract made with the Infirmary by Leeds Health Authority; and yet, when he no longer needed care in an acute ward but manifestly still needed what the National Health Service is there to provide, they regarded themselves as having no scope for continuing to discharge their responsibilities to him because their policy was to make no provision for continuing care. The policy also had the effect of excluding an option whereby he might have the cost of his continuing care met by the NHS. In my opinion the failure to make available long-term care within the NHS for this patient was unreasonable and constitutes a failure in the service provided by the Health Authority. I uphold the complaint.'

The ombudsman recommended that the health authority reimburse nursing home costs already incurred by the man's wife and meet future costs; and also that it should review its 'provision of services for the likes of this man in view of the apparent gap in service available for this particular group of patients' (Leeds HA 1994).

In the wake of the Leeds case the following sequence has unfolded:

**1995 guidance.** In 1995, largely in response to the Leeds investigation, the Department of Health published specific guidance on continuing care in 1995 (HSG(95)8).

**1995–6: more ombudsman investigations.** By 1995 and 1996 the health service ombudsman was publishing further reports of highly restrictive policies being operated by health authorities – such as not contracting for continuing care nursing home beds, even though the authority's hospital beds were inadequate to meet continuing care needs (North Worcestershire HA 1995), simply not funding continuing care beds either in hospitals or nursing homes (Avon HA 1996), not informing patients and their families about continuing care (East Kent HA 1996), quite improperly making even partial continuing care funding dependent on whether the patient received income support (North Cheshire HA 1996), or prejudging people's continuing care status and simply not telling them about it (Buckinghamshire HA 1996).

**1999 Coughlan judgment.** In 1999, the Court of Appeal criticised the Department of Health's 1995 guidance, finding aspects of it both elusive and unclear. The court stated that the local authority should be responsible for nursing services in a care home, only if they were incidental or ancillary to the provision of the accommodation, or of a nature 'which it can be expected that an authority whose primary responsibility is to provide social services can be expected to provide'. Any other nursing care the NHS would be responsible for; in turn this would mean that a resident requiring such nursing care would be deemed to have continuing NHS health care status (*R v North and East Devon Health Authority, ex p Coughlan*).

**1999 interim guidance and inaction**. In response to the *Coughlan* judgment, the Department of Health then issued interim guidance in August 1999 (HSC 1999/180), stating that it would issue final guidance later in 1999; as a consequence the NHS and local authorities appeared to do little pending the imminent guidance. Unfortunately, it was almost a two-year wait before the guidance was issued. The health service ombudsman has since found evidence that during this time the Department of Health did little to encourage the NHS to review its practices; one letter sent out by a regional office of the Department could justifiably have been interpreted as a 'mandate to do the bare minimum' (HSO 2003, para 21). At one meeting with such a regional office, a health authority was told to 'duck and dive' for a while (*Suffolk HA 2003*).

**2001 guidance**. In 2001, in belated response to the *Coughlan* case, the Department of Health finally issued revised continuing care guidance (HSC 2001/15). Also in 2001, the Department of Health introduced what it termed 'free nursing care' and, in so doing, added an additional variable to the continuing care equation (not present at the time of the *Coughlan* case).

**2003 highly critical ombudsman report**. In 2003, the health service ombudsman published a special report on continuing care matters, this time severely criticising the 2001 guidance and the Department of Health's policy on continuing care. She found that the 2001 guidance was not only as unclear as the 1995 guidance (itself criticised by the Court of Appeal), but in fact was 'weaker'. This meant it would be even harder to judge under the 2001 guidance whether local NHS criteria were in line with the national guidance. She stated that any system should be 'fair and logical and should be transparent in respect of the entitlement of individuals'. Yet from what she had seen, 'the national policy and guidance that has been in place over recent years does not pass that test' (HSO 2003, paras 28, 31).

The ombudsman also recommended reimbursement of nursing home fees to all those service users who had as far back as 1996 themselves paid – when the NHS should have (HSO 2003, para 39). The Department of Health instructed the NHS to comply with this recommendation by conducting retrospective reviews. However, the Department of Health has to date signally failed to respond to the criticism of its guidance.

**2004 ombudsman report on person with Alzheimer's disease in own home**. In 2004, the health service ombudsman published a further special report on continuing care, this time concerning a man with advanced Alzheimer's disease in his own home (*Cambridgeshire HA 2004*).

**2004 directions**. In 2004, the Department of Health passed two sets of directions in respect of continuing care concerning assessment, the application of eligibility criteria and reviews (see immediately below).

**2004 further ombudsman report**. In December 2004, the health service ombudsman issued yet another report, pointing to the continuing difficulties, casting doubt on the process of retrospective reviews and reimbursement (see 2003 report above), and making the following recommendations for action to be taken by the Department of Health in respect of:

- the establishment of clear, national minimum eligibility criteria which are understandable by health professionals, patients and carers
- the development of a set of accredited assessment tools and good practice guidance to support the criteria
- supporting training and development to expand local capacity and thus ensure that continuing care cases are assessed and decided properly and promptly

- clarification of standards for record keeping and documentation
- seeking assurance that the retrospective reviews have covered all those who might be affected
- monitoring the progress of retrospective reviews.

**2004 Department of Health report.** A report commissioned by the Department of Health was published in December 2004, making a number of findings similar to that of the health service ombudsman's report of December 2004 (Henwood 2004).

**2004 Department of Health undertaking to publish further guidance.** In December 2004, a government minister (Stephen Ladyman) announced that he would commission a 'new national framework' on continuing care, although he still maintained (despite the health service ombudsman's withering criticisms) that the existing criteria were 'fair and legal' (DH 2004o).

## 16.7.2 CONTINUING HEALTH CARE DIRECTIONS ON ELIGIBILITY CRITERIA AND REVIEW PANELS

In 2004, the Department of Health passed two sets of directions in respect of continuing care, both of which impose specific duties on the NHS. One set, in respect of delayed patient discharges from hospital, stipulates that before the NHS gives notice to a social services authority to assess a person in relation to hospital discharge (under the Community Care (Delayed Discharges) Act 2003), it must first carry out such an assessment as it considers appropriate of the person's need for continuing care. This assessment must be, where the NHS considers it appropriate, in consultation with the relevant social services authority. The assessment must also be in consultation with the patient and, where it considers it appropriate, with the patient's carer (DH 2004). The second set of directions is as follows:

- Strategic health authorities must establish a single set of eligibility criteria to be applied in respect of continuing care; and appoint a standing chairman to act as chairman of a continuing care review panel. They must also establish a list of people (one from each local primary care trust and one from each local authority) to sit on the panel. The PCT and local authority members of the list must not sit on a panel in relation to a decision relating to their own PCT or local authority.
- The strategic health authority then has the power to refer a request for a review to such a review panel.
- A request for such review must be in relation to the procedure followed by a primary care trust or NHS trust in reaching a decision about continuing care criteria, or in relation to the application of the criteria.
- Primary care trusts must act in accordance with the eligibility criteria, and take reasonable efforts to ensure that an appropriate assessment is carried out in all cases where it appears that there may be a need for such services. They must inform the person about the decision and make a record of the decision. They must also inform the person about how to apply for a review of the decision.
- The review procedure and operation of the panel are matters for the standing chairman, having regard to guidance issued by the Secretary of State to the strategic

health authority. The guidance referred to is contained in HSC 2001/15, annex E; see 16.7.3.9.

- Having taken account of any advice from a review panel, the strategic health authority must give written notice of its decision with reasons to the applicant and to the primary care trust or NHS trust involved. Other than exceptionally, the notice must be given within two weeks of the request for a review being made (DH 2004a).

Thus, the above sets of directions might mean that, up to a point, decision making should be reasonably formal and transparent, something that the health service ombudsman has sometimes found to be lacking:

**Inadequate decision-making process.** The health service ombudsman has found fault when a continuing care decision was taken without sufficient explanation being given (*West Kent HA 2001*); or when a district nurse simply decided that a woman, who had had a foot amputated as a result of diabetes, and then suffered a stroke, was not eligible for continuing care, without telling the family anything about continuing care – and the family was not given any information about the financial consequences of the nursing home placement (*Central Manchester PCT 2003*).

The ombudsman has also expressed concern about decision making of the following type. A woman was assessed as being within the high band of registered nursing care, rather than continuing care. She was diagnosed with epilepsy, anaemia, contractures and fractures of her left arm and leg due to falls, and frequent urinary tract infections that made her confused and agitated. No evidence or rationale was presented to support the decision; only nine months later did the primary care trust give her husband a copy of the eligibility criteria against which his wife had been assessed. The trust undertook to 're-review' the case in June 2004, but did not do so until October 2004; the decision remained unchanged; the husband and daughter were told that they were not entitled to be present at the review panel meeting (HSO 2004b, para 20).

A social worker failed to set in motion an application for continuing care funding for a man with Alzheimer's disease. Despite the fact that the NHS officer who was head of continuing care stated retrospectively that the man would have qualified, the social worker involved seemed to doubt this at the time. No application was made. The local ombudsman found maladministration. In response to his draft recommendations, the local authority and health authority agreed to reimburse the nursing home costs in full which his wife had paid – over £26,000 (*Hertfordshire CC 2003a*).

Even so, the national guidance at the heart of continuing care assessments remains unclear and difficult to apply. Arguably therefore, the directions provide merely a veneer of orderly decision making, without getting to the heart of the problem. The health service ombudsman considers that they 'fall short' of what is required for clarity (HSO 2004b, para 43).

## 16.7.3 CONTINUING NHS HEALTH CARE PRESENT POSITION

As a consequence of the directions referred to immediately above (DH 2004a), there should be a set of eligibility criteria based on the national guidance (HSC 2001/15) issued by the Department of Health being applied within the area of each strategic health authority. The national guidance contains a number of points that at the very least should inform any decision made about continuing care, notwithstanding the health service ombudsman's severe criticism of this guidance (HSO 2003, paras 28–31).

The guidance sets out seven 'key issues' that the NHS should 'bear in mind' (although the ombudsman notes that this sort of language is of a distinctly weak variety: HSO 2003, para 31). They are (HSC 2001/15):

1. **Coughlan judgment.** 'The eligibility criteria or application of rigorous time limits for the availability of services by a health authority should not require a local council to provide services beyond those they can provide under section 21 of the National Assistance Act, as established in the *Coughlan* judgment.'

2. **Nature, complexity, intensity, unpredictability.** 'The nature or complexity or intensity or unpredictability of the individual's health care needs (and any combination of these needs) requires regular supervision by a member of the NHS multidisciplinary team, such as the consultant, palliative care, therapy or other NHS member of the team.'

3. **Specialist health care equipment.** 'The individual's needs require the routine use of specialist health care equipment under supervision of NHS staff.'

4. **Rapid deterioration, instability.** 'The individual has a rapidly deteriorating or unstable medical, physical or mental health condition and requires regular supervision by a member of the NHS multidisciplinary team, such as the consultant, palliative care, therapy or other NHS member of the team.'

5. **Terminal illness.** 'The individual is in the final stages of a terminal illness and is likely to die in the near future.'

6. **Registered nurse.** 'A need for care or supervision from a registered nurse and/or a GP is not, by itself, sufficient reason to receive continuing NHS health care.'

7. **Location.** 'The location of care should not be the sole or main determinant of eligibility. Continuing NHS health care may be provided in an NHS hospital, a nursing home, hospice or the individual's own home.'

In addition, the guidance lists a range of services that the NHS is responsible for funding and arranging, in order to meet people's continuing physical or mental health care needs in a care home or in their own home. These include primary care, assessment by doctors and nurses, rehabilitation and recovery (distinct from intermediate care), respite health care, community health services, specialist health care support, healthcare equipment, palliative care, and specialist transport services (HSC 2001/15, para 16).

### 16.7.3.1 Coughlan judgment

The *Coughlan* judgment (the first of the key issues in the guidance) stated that local authorities could lawfully provide nursing services if they were merely incidental or ancillary to the provision of residential accommodation under s.21 of the National Assistance Act 1948; and if they were of a nature which it could be expected that a local authority would provide under social services functions.

Although the *Coughlan* judgment continues to be frequently cited, it is by no means certain what its implications really are. The term 'incidental or ancillary' is exceedingly vague. In addition, the reference to the expectation of what a local authority should provide under social services functions is arguably circular. It begs the question that the court was meant to be answering of how precisely those expectations could be defined and applied in practice.

A further complication is that the *Coughlan* judgment was decided prior to the advent of 'free nursing care' in 2001 (see 16.8). This now means that the NHS would arrange registered nursing care required in a care home, and thus social services would not be obliged to provide the type of nursing care prohibited in the *Coughlan* case. In other words, at the time of the *Coughlan* case, the court was looking at two options: fully funded NHS care or fully funded social services care. There is now a third option that was not available at the time of the judgment: social services funded accommodation, board and personal care, in combination with NHS funded registered nursing care. Consequently, the health service ombudsman has expressed the view that the *Coughlan* judgment is now of less relevance (HSO 2003, para 23). It is therefore at least open to question whether the courts would decide a *Coughlan*-type case differently now than in 1999.

### 16.7.3.2 Nature, complexity, intensity, unpredictability of a person's needs

Local eligibility criteria for continuing health care should be based on the nature or complexity or intensity or unpredictability of health care needs (the second of the key issues). The guidance states that any combination of these will suffice for eligibility; therefore, even one would be enough. In other words, for example, although a person's needs might be relatively predictable and not complex, they might still be of an intense nature and thus eligible for continuing care status.

These terms are unsuitably vague; and the Department of Health has failed to adopt the health service ombudsman's 2003 recommendations that new guidance be issued with case examples of 'patterns of need likely to mean NHS funding should be provided' (HSO 2003, para 32). In the absence of more helpful guidance, a number of case examples can be given, where a person's condition led the health service ombudsman, and in one case (the second listed below) the courts, to deem that the person was of continuing care status.

**Substantial nursing care.** A man was doubly incontinent, could not eat or drink without assistance, could not communicate, had a kidney tumour, cataracts in both eyes and occasional epileptic fits. There was no dispute that when he was discharged he did not need active medical treatment but did need 'substantial nursing care'. Failure to provide continuing care was unreasonable and a failure in the duty to provide a service for a highly dependent person (*Leeds HA 1994*).

**More than incidental and ancillary.** A woman, who had been badly injured in a road traffic accident, was described as tetraplegic, doubly incontinent, requiring regular catheterisation, partially paralysed in respiratory function, subject to problems attendant on immobility and also to recurrent headaches caused by an associated neurological condition. Her nursing needs were held to be more than just 'incidental or ancillary' to the provision of accommodation, and were not of a nature that social services could be expected to provide (*R v North and East Devon HA, ex p Coughlan*).

**More than incidental and ancillary**. A woman had suffered several strokes, had no speech or comprehension, was unable to swallow and required feeding by a PEG tube into the stomach, and was doubly incontinent. Her needs were more than just incidental or ancillary to the provision of nursing home accommodation or of a nature that social services could be expected to provide; they were on a par with those in the *Coughlan* case, and should have attracted continuing health care funding (*Wigan and Bolton HA 2003*).

**Intensive and complex care package**. A woman had vascular dementia, confusion and challenging behaviour; she had been assessed as having multiple and complex nursing and medical problems. These required an 'intensive and complex' personal care package, well beyond the customary level of care offered by a nursing home. The ombudsman could not see how the nursing care required could be only 'incidental or ancillary' to the provision of accommodation, or of a nature that social services could be expected to provide (*Berkshire HA 2003*).

**Constant supervision**. A man with Alzheimer's disease was now living at home, being cared for by his wife and other personal assistants. He was totally reliant on others for his needs to be met. He was subject to epileptic seizures, muscular spasms, panic attacks and episodes of choking, visual spatial difficulties and hallucinatory experiences. He required constant supervision (*Cambridgeshire HA 2004*).

The health service ombudsman expressed concern in this last case, that the local eligibility criteria focused inadequately on aspects of dementia such as mood changes, delusions, hallucinatory experiences and visual spatial difficulties – causing staff to produce inappropriate assessments based only on physical need (*Cambridgeshire HA 2004*). The ombudsman has also pointed out that addition of a requirement in local eligibility criteria that there be 'specialist' intervention is an unduly restrictive interpretation of the Department of Health's guidance (HSO 2004, para 19).

### 16.7.3.3 Supervision of staff

Three of the seven key issues in the guidance refer to regular supervision by NHS staff. The health service ombudsman has picked up on this matter; for instance, the supervision in question does not just relate to hospital consultants:

**Supervision by consultants**. The health service ombudsman found failings where the local criteria emphasised the necessity of care provided under the direction of a consultant and normally in a hospital setting. In practice this meant that the need for consultant input was used as the sole criterion (*Wigan and Bolton HA 2003*).

The health service ombudsman has also considered what is meant by 'regular' supervision:

**'Regular' supervision**. The health authority had interpreted the need for 'regular' as entailing at least weekly review by a consultant or continual skilled health care supervision on a 24-hour basis. However, the ombudsman found that this was an over-restrictive interpretation of the guidance; and that it failed to reflect the *Coughlan* case, since there would a group of people not meeting this restrictive condition, but who would have needs for nursing care that was not just incidental or ancillary to the provision of accommodation (*Birmingham HA 2003*).

Similarly, the requirement in a case involving a woman with Alzheimer's disease of at least a weekly psychiatric review and daily specialist nursing management was held to be over-restrictive and to interpret the national guidance and the word 'regular' too narrowly (*Suffolk HA 2003*).

### 16.7.3.4 Routine use of specialist health care equipment

The health service ombudsman investigated a case involving a woman who had had a stroke, was unable to swallow and required to be fed through a gastric tube, and was discharged to a nursing home. There, she was charged both the nursing home fees (£375) and £25 per week extra for the feeding tubes. The health authority conceded that it had a duty both to pay for the woman's nursing home fees and the feeding tubes (*North Worcestershire HA 1996*).

### 16.7.3.5 Terminal illness and likely to die in the near future

The reference to terminal illness – the fifth of the key issues in the guidance – is vague. It seems that in practice the NHS in some areas applies very short timescales such as a few days or, at most, weeks.

Yet past guidance from the Department of Health sounded a warning to those health authorities operating very short time limits. It explained that the purpose of the 1995 guidance (HSG(95)8) was to give people likely to die in the very near future the choice of being cared for in NHS-funded accommodation. The crucial objective was to ensure 'sensitive discharge practice for this group of patients while recognising that clinical prognosis in many cases will be imprecise... Very short time limits (for instance of the order of a couple of weeks) are not appropriate and any time limits should be applied flexibly in the light of individual circumstances' (EL(96)8, section C). The government has more recently stated in a House of Commons command paper that it is 'inappropriate to apply rigid life expectancy criteria when assessing eligibility for NHS-funded continuing care' (Secretary of State for Health 2004, para 8).

Elsewhere, the current 2001 guidance states that people who require palliative care and are likely to die in the near future should be able to choose to remain in NHS funded accommodation (including a nursing home) or to return home with appropriate support (HSC 2001/15, para 18). Thus continuing NHS health care eligibility in case of terminal illness, in combination with the location of care (see below), is indeed a key issue. Not least because, on the Department of Health's own admission, evidence suggests that over 50 per cent of people wish to die in their own homes, but only 20 per cent are able to do so (DH 2004).

### 16.7.3.6 Registered nurse

The sixth of the key issues in the guidance states that the need for care or supervision from a registered nurse is not in itself enough for continuing care eligibility. The precise implications of this might not be entirely clear. It could reasonably be taken to mean that if, for example, the intensity, unpredictability or complexity of the person's condition necessitated the registered nursing, then eligibility would be established.

However, the Department of Health would appear not necessarily to take this view. Its guidance on free nursing care in care homes (see 16.8) suggests a distinction between the terms 'complex and unpredictable' used to determine a registered nursing contribution and the same terms used to determine a person's overall healthcare needs for the purpose of continuing care (HSC 2001/17, appendix 6). Whether the courts could make sense of this distinction and, if they could, uphold it as lawful must be open to some question. Furthermore, the need for registered nursing care should not necessarily be equated with a registered nurse:

**Eligibility for continuing care without input by a registered nurse**. One health service ombudsman case involved the care at home by a woman (and personal assistants) of her husband, who had Alzheimer's disease. One of the grounds on which the NHS had held that he was not continuing health care status was that he was not receiving regular care from registered nurses. Two of the senior staff involved in continuing care decisions (the manager and director, both nurses) stated that the wife was not providing nursing care, since nursing qualifications and skills could not be self-taught and took many years to acquire. Therefore the care being given by the wife could not be highly professional. Yet both an independent medical consultant and the consultant psychiatrist involved disagreed with this view; they said that the severity of the man's condition meant he had health care needs 'well beyond' anything that the average care worker was competent to deal with.

The consultant psychiatrist also gave the view that the care was being provided in a professional manner, and was equal to, if not superior to, the care the husband would have received on an NHS dementia ward. Indeed, the 'atmosphere was not one that could be replicated in a continuing care ward' (*Cambridgeshire HA 2004*).

If a health authority is going to argue that a person's nursing needs do not amount to continuing health care needs, then it has do so on the basis of adequate assessment:

**Inconsistency and lack of clarity**. A woman had suffered a stroke, was admitted to hospital and then discharged to a nursing home. She had insulin dependent diabetes, and had been left by the stroke immobile and unable to speak. Prior to her discharge, a feeding tube was removed. She was assessed as ineligible for continuing care.

The health service ombudsman criticised the decision, on the grounds that the assessment documentation was incomplete, and that the family had been neither given information about the eligibility criteria, nor been involved properly in the discharge process. The health authority's criteria had been reviewed in the light of the *Coughlan* judgment, but the support documentation for assessment had not been. This led to inconsistency and a lack of clarity (*Gloucestershire HA 2003*).

The health service ombudsman has further expressed disquiet that some NHS bodies simply view continuing care funding as a 'top band' above the high band of registered nursing care funding. This might then mean that they fail to consider the 'totality' of a person's health care needs, instead carrying out only nursing, rather than multidisciplinary continuing care, assessments. The ombudsman has found evidence of this occurring, and suggested that one causative factor might be the confusing similarity of wording in the registered nursing care guidance with the wording in the continuing care guidance (HSO 2004, para 22).

### 16.7.3.7 Location of care

The health service ombudsman has identified circumstances where the location of care, the seventh key issue in the guidance, was improperly determining eligibility.

**Equating hospital with continuing care**. The local eligibility criteria were being applied such that if a person could be cared for in a nursing home rather than an NHS facility, an assumption was made that the person would not be of continuing health care status. The ombudsman criticised this, notwithstanding that the criteria did in principle allow for exceptions; but in practice, this aspect of the criteria was 'likely to be missed by those interpreting the policy' (*Dorset HA 2003*).

**Undue emphasis on hospital care.** A health authority stated that people in specialist nursing home care could be eligible for continuing care funding. However, the criteria went on to state that this would only be where there was a constant availability of on-site specialist medical expertise 24 hours a day, or of highly complex or specialist medical equipment to maintain life. In reality, this was only possible in hospital; thus the issue of whether a person needed hospital medical provision was overly significant in the decision about eligibility for continuing care (*Berkshire HA 2003*).

**Respite care only as NHS inpatient.** In another case, the ombudsman criticised the fact that continuing care funding would only be available for respite care if the person concerned became an NHS inpatient, but would not be available in his own home, so as to give his main carer, his wife, a break (*Cambridgeshire HA 2004*).

**No continuing care other than in hospital.** The health authority had decided, as a matter of policy, not to contract for private nursing home places for continuing care needs. Yet the 24 long-stay hospital beds for continuing care were insufficient for that purpose. Therefore, in order to manage this shortfall, the authority's policy simply excluded NHS funding for the continuing care of younger, highly dependent patients not in need of hospital inpatient treatment. The health service ombudsman found this to be a failure to provide a service that it was a function of the health authority to provide (*North Worcestershire HA 1995*).

The guidance contains a potential anomaly. If a person is of continuing health care status in hospital or a care home, then the NHS effectively funds accommodation, board, personal care and nursing care. However, in a person's own home, the guidance states that the NHS will be responsible for health care needs only. Unfortunately this gives rise sometimes to unseemly wrangles between the NHS and local authorities about how to fund a package of services in a person's own home. The question is also to what extent, in the case of a care package in a person's own home, the personal care is 'severable' from the health care.

For instance, in one investigation, the health service ombudsman held that the NHS should be funding a certain level of respite care (one week in every five) for a man with Alzheimer's disease living in his own home (*Cambridgeshire HA 2004*). Following this decision, it appears that the NHS must have accepted that the respite care was not severable from the care being provided for the rest of the time (hitherto defined as 'personal care') and therefore reportedly took on responsibility for funding the whole care package (Revans 2004).

### 16.7.3.8 Reimbursement of money to people wrongly charged for care
Following the health service ombudsman's report of 2003 (HSO 2003), the Department of Health instructed strategic health authorities to conduct reviews of people who might have wrongly been charged for care, which should have been free as continuing NHS health care. Such reviews should have been directed not just at past nursing home placements, but also at situations where people at home might have been paying for services that should have been free from the NHS (see e.g. *Cambridgeshire HA 2004*).

The outcome of these reviews is that a great deal of money has to be repaid; although the health service ombudsman has since criticised the speed of the efforts being made (HSO 2004, p.13). Further criticism by the health service ombudsman at the end of 2004 pointed out that:

- the Department of Health had assured the ombudsman that retrospective reviews of cases would be finished by December 2003, but it was now clear that the backlog might not be dealt with even by the end of 2004 (HSO 2004b, Summary)
- the Department of Health had not collected central statistics relating to retrospective reviews since July 2004 and had no plans to do so (HS 2004b, para 5)
- in more than 50 per cent of review cases examined by the ombudsman, the assessments had not been carried out properly due to a lack of consistency of approach, variable quality of assessments, confused and inconsistent panel procedures (e.g. some lacked clinical or professional input), failure to record reasons for decisions, and poor communication with patients and relatives. There had also been delays in the payment of restitution following retrospective reviews (HSO 2004b, para 29)
- in the absence of support and leadership from the Department of Health and some strategic health authorities, the ombudsman's office was regularly receiving requests for advice, interpretation of the guidance and even training. However, it was for the Department of Health to clarify procedures, which it had itself initiated, rather than for the ombudsman to do so (HSO 2004b, para 32).

The scale of the problem of retrospective review and reimbursement is indicated by the number of reviews involved (nearly 12,000), the number of complaints made to the health service ombudsman (reported in December 2004 as numbering 4000 since February 2003), and the amount of money allocated by the Department of Health for restitution (£180 million). The ombudsman has further pointed out that she could not say with certainty whether all strategic health authorities had made extensive and comprehensive efforts to locate patients (and their relatives) eligible for retrospective review (HSO 2004b, paras 5, 40, 12).

**Note.** A memo from the Department of Work and Pensions confirmed that any such compensation would not retrospectively turn people into 'hospital inpatients' for the purpose of the relevant benefit regulations. Thus they will not be liable to repay benefits received during the relevant period (DWP 2004).

### 16.7.3.9 Continuing care assessment: review of decisions

The directions summarised above (16.7.2) provide for the operation of review panels in respect of decisions about continuing health care. The directions make reference to Department of Health guidance, which in turn makes a number of points about reviews:

- A review is to check that procedures have been followed and criteria have been properly and consistently applied.
- The review procedure is not suitable to challenge the content of criteria.
- Patients should be given clear information about the review procedure.

- All steps should be taken to solve the dispute informally.
- The patient, family or any carer may request a review.
- The health authority is not obliged to refer any individual case for a review where, for instance, the patient clearly falls well outside the criteria.
- While the review procedure is being conducted, the patient should remain in NHS funded accommodation; and any existing care package, whether hospital or community based, should not be withdrawn in any circumstances until the outcome of the review is known.
- The role of the panel is advisory only and its decisions are not binding. However, the Department of Health's expectation is that its recommendations will be accepted in 'all but very exceptional circumstances'. If a health authority decides to reject the panel's recommendation in an individual case it must put the reasons in writing to the patient and the chair of the panel (HSC 2001/15, annex E).

The principle of maintaining NHS funding, until a decision is reached, has been picked up by the health service ombudsman:

**Discharged improperly from NHS care despite request for review.** A woman with Alzheimer's disease was admitted to hospital in April. On 4 October her husband handed hospital staff a letter, dated 2 October, disagreeing with the proposal that she be discharged to a care home. He thought his wife was entitled to NHS care. On 10 October she was moved to a care home on a trial basis. The hospital wrote to him on 18 October telling him he could appeal, but not explaining how to do that. On 1 November, his letter of 2 October was accepted as a request for a review. On 9 January, the chair of the panel refused to convene a panel. The woman was held liable for charges for her stay in the care home from 10 October.

The health service ombudsman stated that the letter of 2 October should have been sufficient to trigger a review; and that NHS funding should have continued until the review procedure was complete on 9 January (*Barnet Healthcare NHS Trust 2000*).

The convening of a review panel is a power, not a duty; the directions state that a strategic health authority may refer an appeal to a panel, for the panel to give it advice on the case (DH 2004a). But the health service ombudsman has stated that the discretion should be exercised properly:

**Improperly not convening a review panel.** In respect of the discretion to convene a panel not being exercised, the health service ombudsman referred to the guidance (HSC 2001/15) that states that the decision not to convene should be confined to those cases where the patient falls outside the criteria or is otherwise clearly not appropriate for the panel to consider. In the particular circumstances, the ombudsman criticised the failure to convene a panel, although the woman involved could not be seen 'as anything other than borderline', given the 'scoring' she had received when assessed (*Herefordshire HA 1999*).

## 16.8 FREE REGISTERED NURSING CARE

With the introduction of what has been referred to as 'free nursing care' in October 2001, local authorities continue to make arrangements with care homes that provide nursing – but only in respect of the accommodation, board and personal care. The NHS has a duty to arrange the registered nursing care required, free of charge to the resident.

This was brought about by s.49 of the Health and Social Care Act 2001, which prohibits local authorities from providing, or arranging for the provision of, registered nursing care under social services legislation. Registered nursing care is defined as services provided by a registered nurse, including the provision of care or the planning, supervision or delegation of the provision of care. However, excluded from registered nursing care are services that, by their nature and in the circumstances in which they are provided, do not need to be provided by a registered nurse; such services will therefore continue to be the responsibility of the local authority, rather than the NHS.

The Department of Health subsequently issued a direction and guidance in order to implement the effect of the legislation (HSC 2001/17; HSC 2003/006). The key points in the guidance are as follows:

- **Assessment**. The registered nursing needs of a care home resident, and the appropriate level of NHS funding for that resident, should be determined by using the *NHS Funded Nursing Care Practice Guide and Workbook* (DH 2001e). All residents of care homes who are receiving registered nursing care are potentially eligible for the NHS contribution, whether they have been placed by a local authority or whether they are 'self-funding'.
- **Quality of assessment**. Primary care trusts (PCTs) must ensure that suitably skilled nurses are available to carry out registered nursing care assessments, covering the full physical and mental health needs of different groups of residents – including people with dementia or mental health needs, physical disabilities, head injuries, etc. The need for care in assessing people with dementia is particularly emphasised.
- **Level of NHS contribution to care home cost**. Registered nursing care contributions payable by the NHS will fall into one of three bands in England, high, medium or low, with different rates payable to the care home accordingly.
- **Intermediate care**. Free nursing care should not be confused with intermediate care (see 16.12), since the latter should be entirely free (i.e. accommodation, board, personal care and nursing care) whether it is made up of health care, social care or both.
- **Care plans**. Care plans should set out what services are to be provided. Residents should not have to pay for any NHS services specified in their care plans.
- **Continuing care**. Underlined in bold in the guidance is that the first consideration should be to decide whether the person meets the criteria for NHS continuing care, in which case the total funding for the care home placement, and not just the registered nursing care, would be met by the NHS (see 16.7).
- **Equipment in nursing homes**. See 16.13.
- **Incontinence pads and equipment**. See 16.14.
- **Identifying the responsible primary care trust**. See 14.3.
- **Cross-border placements**. See 14.4.
- **Reviews**. If individuals are dissatisfied with a decision about registered nursing care, it can be referred for review by a continuing care panel.

The guidance is not straightforward. The workbook (DH 2001e) to which the guidance refers, and to which nurses must work when assessing the NHS registered nursing care contribution, contains a number of examples. These are designed to illustrate whether a resident will come within a high, medium or low band – and indeed whether a resident is eligible for such a registered nursing care contribution as opposed to continuing NHS health care. For instance:

**Department of Health example of high band of registered nursing care.** One example given of the 'high band' of registered nursing care is of a 76-year-old man who has been diagnosed with dementia for five years. His 'multiple' needs are described as including assistance with:

- personal hygiene
- constant supervision because of wandering
- poor eye and hand coordination
- feeding problems and choking, disorientation in time, place and person
- unable to make himself understood
- weepy and frustrated
- restless and hard to distract
- erratic and disturbed sleep
- poor spatial awareness
- double incontinence
- physical aggression towards his wife.

He is assessed as coming within the high band on the basis of having an unstable and unpredictable condition that necessitated a high level of registered nursing care (DH 2001e, para 3.13).

This example in the guidance appears simply to be inconsistent with the approach of the health service ombudsman and the courts, in terms of whom they have identified as being eligible for continuing health care (see 16.7.3.2). In any case, the guidance attempts, wholly unconvincingly, to distinguish complexity and unpredictability in the context of registered nursing needs, and complexity and unpredictability in the context of 'overall healthcare needs' (HSC 2001/17, appendix 6). It would seem to border on absurdity for the guidance to insist that the needs of the man in the example above are not about his overall health care needs.

## 16.9 PROVISION OF COMMUNITY HEALTH SERVICES IN CARE HOMES AND PEOPLE'S OWN HOMES

As already explained at the beginning of this chapter, legal entitlement to NHS services is difficult to identify with any precision if at all. Department of Health guidance reflects this faithfully, when it describes entitlement to a range of health services in people's own homes or in care homes.

### 16.9.1 COMMUNITY HEALTH SERVICES FOR NURSING HOME RESIDENTS

Guidance on free nursing care puts the matter in a deceptively succinct manner. It states that physiotherapy and chiropody services should be made available to residents of care homes (that provide nursing) on the same basis as to people in other settings such as other types of care home and people's own homes. It then states that where such NHS services are not provided, the NHS has no obligation to provide those services (HSC 2003/6, para 29). In other words, there is no entitlement.

Other guidance less clearly states that people in nursing homes, but who are not receiving continuing health care, are entitled to a range of NHS community health services on the same basis as the rest of the population who are not NHS inpatients. It goes on to state that the only exceptions to this are 'some or all of the nursing care these people may need and the provision of continence services' (HSC 2001/15, para 19). The lack of clarity (and transparency) arises because the guidance does not properly explain that, under the free nursing care guidance, registered nursing care and continence services (HSC 2003/6) are the only reliable entitlement to NHS community health services in nursing homes – whilst entitlement to other services is illusory. This in turn is because the 'rest of the population' does not have a clear entitlement. The same guidance then goes on to list the range of community health services that should be available in principle for residents of nursing homes (HSC 2001/15, paras 23–25):

- access to GP and other primary care services
- nursing advice, for instance, on incontinence or stoma care
- physiotherapy, occupational therapy, speech and language therapy, dietetics and podiatry
- specialist medical and nursing equipment
- palliative care
- access to hospital care
- ambulances and specialist transport to and from hospital or hospice, emergency admission to a nursing home, non-emergency travel to and from health care facilities
- respite health care, including rehabilitation and intermediate care.

## 16.9.2 COMMUNITY HEALTH SERVICES IN CARE HOMES (NOT PROVIDING NURSING)

Department of Health guidance states that for people living in a care home (that does not provide nursing), the NHS should provide the same full range of primary and community health services as for people living in their own home. As with the guidance on health services in nursing homes, this guidance suffers from the same defect. It fails to spell out that the entitlement of people in their own homes to health services is not readily identifiable. The services listed include:

- access to GP and other primary care services (including community nursing)
- district nursing and other nursing services (e.g. continence advice and stoma care)
- physiotherapy, occupational therapy, speech and language therapy, dietetics and podiatry
- continence pads and nursing aids
- palliative care

- ambulances and specialist transport to and from hospital or hospice, emergency admission to a nursing home, non-emergency travel to and from health care facilities
- rehabilitation and intermediate care (HSC 2001/15, paras 28–32).

The sheer vagueness of this sort of guidance effectively means that the courts and the health service ombudsman can apparently do little, even in the face of clearly inadequate provision.

**Lack of speech therapy.** The health service ombudsman investigated a complaint about delayed and intermittent speech therapy provided by a health authority for a two-and-a-half-year-old child with severe communication difficulties. The ombudsman accepted the health authority's position. This was that, although the speech therapy service was understaffed and underfunded by national and regional norms, the health authority was well aware of and concerned about the situation. The 'HA have to balance the needs of the STS against other services and I am aware, from other investigations, of the problems health authorities face in deciding between competing demands. The HA is vested with the discretion to decide how to allocate its resources...and the legislation which governs my work does not permit me to question such a decision unless I find evidence of maladministration in the way it was reached' (HSO W.783/85–86).

### 16.9.3 COMMUNITY HEALTH SERVICES IN PEOPLE'S OWN HOMES

The guidance on health services in nursing homes immediately above (16.9.2) states that the list of services applies also to the 'rest of the population'. However, as already stated, the 'rest of the population' generally has no concrete legal entitlement to services, whether in their own homes or elsewhere (see 16.3). Nevertheless, even absent such absolute entitlements, the health service ombudsman might still find fault with the manner in which a decision not to provide a service is made, if not with the principle of non-provision itself:

**Withdrawal of chiropody services.** A woman received a regular home visiting chiropody service, involving dressing her feet and cutting her nails. At what she believed was a routine appointment, she was assessed that she was no longer eligible for home visits; she would no longer have her feet dressed, and the only service would be toenail cutting at four-monthly intervals. However, she was not told this; she only found out when she rang up the Trust when the chiropodist failed to arrive on the next agreed date. The ombudsman also criticised generally the lack of system for informing patients of the planned review of chiropody services and possibility of withdrawal of service; and also that there were no agreed criteria for judging which patients would be eligible and which would not be (*Thames Gateway NHS Trust 2001*).

## 16.10 DISCHARGE OF PEOPLE FROM HOSPITAL

Two main issues seem to arise around hospital discharge. The first concerns the decision in principle about how, when and to where discharge should be made. The second concerns the adequacy of the arrangements made (see 16.11).

In terms of the first, the Community Care (Delayed Discharges) Act 2003 (CCDDA) was implemented in January 2004. In terms of the second, the health service ombudsman has investigated on many occasions, whilst the Department of Health continues to issue exhortative guidance from time to time.

## 16.10.1 DELAYED DISCHARGES

In the light of what had come to be known increasingly as 'blocked beds', the Community Care (Delayed Discharges) Act 2003 was passed essentially in order to expedite hospital discharges. It involves social services authorities having to reimburse the NHS for such blocked beds. Key points, deriving (unless otherwise stated) from the Act itself and regulations passed under it (SI 2003/2277), are set out below.

## 16.10.2 DELAYED DISCHARGES OVERALL POLICY

Generally, the pressure on the NHS and local authorities to effect speedy discharge of patients is greater than ever. Clearly such a policy has, in principle, an acceptable rationale. First, hospital beds are a scarce resource and it is poor use of public money to use them wastefully. Second, prolonged hospital stays can be bad for people's health, whether in terms of loss of physical function and increased dependency, or of hospital-acquired infection. Equally, the danger of pressurised discharge is that the policy and practice might lurch too far in the wrong direction and work to the active detriment of service users.

For example, local authorities and the NHS might in the past have tended to allow a person to remain in hospital some days or weeks while a care home placement of their choice became available. Indeed, within certain limits, service users have the right to choose residential accommodation (see 8.5). Now, however, people are more likely to be placed in interim, or step-down, accommodation, so that reimbursement charges payable to the NHS by the local social services authority can be avoided.

For some people, such interim accommodation might be suitable and even more beneficial than remaining in hospital. However, for others it might be highly disruptive and detrimental to their physical and mental welfare. Even moving from ward to ward or hospital to hospital can be highly disruptive and upsetting for some patients; how much worse might be an inappropriate move to different interim accommodation altogether. In order to avoid such detriment, local authorities need to be aware that even an interim placement must legally meet a person's needs, as pointed out by Department of Health guidance. Thus, interim arrangements must be based 'solely' on the person's assessed need, and sustain or improve independence. If this cannot be achieved by an interim placement, the person has to remain in hospital and social services will be liable for reimbursement (HSC 2003/9, para 97). It should also be recalled that need might, for example, be psychological and emotional as well as physical (see 6.12).

A Commission for Social Care Inspection report issued in late 2004 identified both the positive effects of delayed discharge policies but also the more negative outcomes – for instance, where intermediate care and rehabilitation services are inadequate (CSCI 2004a, p.5).

## 16.10.3 DELAYED DISCHARGES FOR ACUTE CARE ONLY

At the time of writing, the rules under the Act apply in practice to acute care only. They do not cover paying patients, nor maternity care, mental health care, palliative care, intermediate care, recuperation or rehabilitation. However, there is a power in the Act to pass further regulations extending the applicability of the rules to other categories of patient.

Mental health care is defined as psychiatric services or other services for preventing, diagnosing or treating illness where a consultant psychiatrist is primarily responsible for those services (SI 2003/2276).

## 16.10.4 DELAYED DISCHARGE ASSESSMENT NOTICES

A 'section 2' notice must be given by the NHS to the social services authority, if it is unlikely to be safe to discharge the patient without community care services. The notice can be given up to eight days prior to a hospital admission. On the other hand, it can be given up to two days before the date of proposed discharge. The patient and, if reasonably practicable, the carer must be consulted before the notice is given.

The notice must be withdrawn in certain circumstances if (a) the NHS considers that it would no longer be safe to discharge the person; (b) it considers that the person needs NHS continuing care; (c) if it considers safe discharge will not be achieved without further community care services provided than those already proposed by the local authority; (d) if the patient's proposed treatment has been cancelled or postponed. Alternatively it must withdraw it if it becomes aware that the person is ordinarily resident in a different local authority.

The assessment notice must be in written form and dated. It must also include various matters including likely date of discharge, a statement that the patient and carer have been consulted – and that it has considered whether or not to provide continuing NHS health care and the result of that decision. It must refer to whether the patient has objected to the notice, and also to the name of the liaison person between hospital and social services (CCDDA 2003, ss.2 and 3 of the Act; SI 2003/2277).

## 16.10.5 CONTINUING CARE ASSESSMENT DIRECTIONS AND DISCHARGE

In order to emphasise the importance of taking a proper decision about possible continuing care status, directions (DH 2004) have been issued in addition to the Act and Regulations. The Directions place a duty on the NHS to do the following before serving an assessment notice on the local authority.

First, it must carry out an assessment as it considers appropriate of the patient's need for continuing care – in consultation, where the NHS considers it appropriate, with the local authority. Second, it must decide, having regard to the assessment and any relevant eligibility criteria, whether the patient's needs call for provision of continuing care by the NHS. Third, it must notify the patient of the decision and record it in the patient's notes –

and inform him that he may apply for a review of the decision (DH 2004). This would be through the same review panel procedure as applies to continuing care (see 16.7.3.9).

### 16.10.6 DUTY OF SOCIAL SERVICES AUTHORITY ON RECEIPT OF ASSESSMENT NOTICE

On receipt of a s.2 assessment notice, the local authority must carry out an assessment of a person's needs for community care services to achieve a safe discharge. After consultation with the NHS, it must decide which of those services to make available.

The local authority must also assess an informal carer with a view to identifying services which may be provided under the Carers and Disabled Children Act 2000 – and, after consulting the NHS, decide which of those services to make available. However, the duty to assess the carer only arises if the carer requests the assessment or, if within the 12 months before the section 2 assessment notice was given, has previously requested an assessment under s.1 of the Carers and Disabled Children Act 2000.

The local authority must also keep under review the patient's and carer's needs in relation to the services required for safe discharge. The local authority can alter its decision in the light of changed circumstances following the assessment (CCDDA 2003, s.4).

### 16.10.7 DUTY OF NHS FOLLOWING ASSESSMENT NOTICE

The NHS must consult social services before deciding what services it will provide on discharge. It must give social services notice of the proposed day of discharge (the relevant day). This notice may be withdrawn. The minimum interval between the giving of the notice and the discharge day is one day. Up to 31 March 2005 at least, Sundays and public holidays in England and Wales do not count as part of the minimum interval (CCDDA 2003, s.5; SI 2003/2277).

### 16.10.8 LIABILITY TO MAKE DELAYED DISCHARGE PAYMENTS

If the end of the relevant (discharge) day is reached and the patient has not been discharged because social services has failed (a) to carry out an assessment or to take a decision about what services are required; or (b) has not made available community care services it had decided to make available to the patient, or not made available carer's services it had decided to make available – then social services must make a payment for each day of the delayed discharge period. The delayed discharge period begins with the day after the relevant day and ends no later than the day of actual discharge (CCDDA 2003, s.6). Therefore, at the minimum a charge could not be made until three days after an assessment (and discharge) notice had been given (which at the minimum can specify 48 hours for assessment and arranging of services) (DH 2004, paras 76–79).

There are various rules about the timings – for example, s.2 assessment notices given on Sundays, public holidays or after 2pm on other days are counted as being given on the next day. For s.5 discharge notices, next day counting relates to notices given on Sundays, public holidays, after 2pm on a Friday or after 5pm on any other day (CCDDA 2003, s.5). However, if the reason for the delayed discharge is not solely due to the social services authority's failure, then the reimbursement duty does not arise (CCDDA 2003, s.6).

16.10.9 DELAYED DISCHARGE CRITERIA, DECISION MAKING AND REVIEWS
A person can challenge a discharge decision by means of the review panels set up to deal with continuing care decisions (see 16.7.3.9). The relevant directions have already been explained (see 16.10.5).

16.10.10 DISPUTE BETWEEN PUBLIC AUTHORITIES ABOUT DISCHARGE
In case of dispute between public authorities, those authorities may apply to the strategic health authority for the appointment of a panel. Legal proceedings cannot be brought until such a panel has made a recommendation (CCDDA 2003, s.9 and SI 2003/2277).

16.10.11 REFUSAL OF PATIENT TO LEAVE HOSPITAL
If a person has been deemed suitable for discharge, then, subject to any review requested or complaint made, the question inevitably arises about what to do if he or she simply refuses to leave hospital. The guidance on hospital discharge states that patients do not have the right to stay in an acute hospital bed if they no longer need the care (HSC 2003/9, para 96); in fact that principle applies to any bed. However, the guidance is notably silent on what to do in difficult cases.

**Refusal to enter a nursing home.** In one health service ombudsman investigation, a woman had wanted the NHS to fund the nursing home care of her husband who had Alzheimer's disease. The health authority was prepared to provide the health care element of his care, but the local authority would arrange the accommodation and meet the level of costs for which it would be liable in the light of its statutory test of resources. However, the woman refused a financial assessment, without which the local authority would not arrange the care. The health authority acknowledged it could not force the husband into a nursing home, but at the same time clinical advice prevented his discharge to his own home. He was cared for in a community hospital and funded by the health authority; the ombudsman found that the health authority had acted reasonably (*Oxfordshire HA 1996*).

## 16.11 HOSPITAL DISCHARGE PRACTICE
Apart from delayed discharges from acute care and reimbursement (see immediately above), community care legislation is silent about hospital discharge (other than in respect of aftercare services under s.117 of the Mental Health Act 1983).

16.11.1 HOSPITAL DISCHARGE PRACTICE GUIDANCE
The Department of Health has issued guidance on the 'pathway, process and practice' of hospital discharge. It is extensive and somewhat repetitive. Introducing itself as good practice guidance to assist the processes of discharge planning, it does not appear to be the type of guidance that carries legal weight or the 'badge of mandatory requirement' that a judge might search for (*R v North Derbyshire Health Authority, ex p Fisher*). That said,

there are specific points made in the guidance that might in any case be picked up on by the health service ombudsman or local government ombudsman, if not necessarily by the courts. Indeed one, concerning active engagement of the patient and carer, relates to the duty under directions (DH 2004) to consult with the patient and carer (see 16.10.5).

The 'key messages' made in the Foreword include, for instance: (a) ensuring that service users and carers are actively engaged in planning and delivering care (including provision of information); (b) recognising the important role of carers; (c) effective communication between primary, secondary and social care services; (d) ensuring all patients are assessed for a period of rehabilitation before decisions are made on care options (DH 2003m). Indeed, the original community care policy guidance states that patients should not leave hospital until at least essential community care services have been agreed with them and their carers (DH 1990, para 3.44). Such points are typically picked up in health service ombudsman investigations; for instance, lack of involvement of carers in discharge decisions:

**Discharge and suicide, inadequate consultation with relatives.** A woman with a history of mental ill health was granted temporary home leave, having been detained under the Mental Health Act 1983. A day later she committed suicide. The health service ombudsman criticised the inadequate care plan, inadequate consultation with relatives, poor documentation and an inappropriate decision to discharge (*Nottinghamshire Healthcare NHS Trust 2003*).

In another mental health discharge case, also ending in suicide, the ombudsman criticised the failure to appoint a community psychiatric nurse for a person with such complex mental health problems. The hospital consultant who was her key worker was also key worker for up to 30 patients, an arrangement that was 'not ideal' (*Newcastle, North Tyneside and Northumberland Mental Health NHS Trust 2001*).

The health service ombudsman has repeatedly found shortcomings in terms of information provided. For instance:

**Lack of information on discharge.** The health service ombudsman has found fault when: an 89-year-old woman moved to a care home without being informed of alternatives (*East Norfolk HA 1996*); a woman who had suffered a stroke moved to a nursing home with no clear information (oral or written) provided for the family on the costs involved (*North Worcestershire HA 1996*); a woman with a broken leg was discharged to a care home and faced a bill of £900 for a month's stay without being told about the fees (HSO W.524/92–93); a brain damaged man was discharged to a nursing home without his wife being informed about the fees (*Leeds HA 1994*).

The ombudsman also found fault when the daughter of a woman who had suffered several strokes was not informed about the fees for a nursing home. The hospital staff relied on social services to provide this, but neglected to refer some patients to social services if they thought they would be ineligible for assistance (*East Kent HA 1996*).

Closely allied to lack of information is serious failure in communication that can result in clearly inappropriate discharges because the required arrangements are not in place:

**Lack of communication resulting in inappropriate discharge arrangements.** The health service ombudsman found fault when a woman with Huntington's chorea was discharged by the consultant, before he had ascertained whether the local authority and voluntary organisations could provide the assistance required (HSO W.40/84–85); similarly when a consultant had not found out whether the equipment and home adaptations required on discharge would be available (HSO W.113/84–85). It was clearly unacceptable when the carer first knew about the discharge through a telephone call telling her that her mother was already on her way home; when no hospital 'key worker' had been identified; and also that discharge policy and procedures were not fully operational and unknown to some staff (HSO W.254/88–89).

In another case, the ombudsman placed a considerable burden on the hospital staff; it was not enough that they had decided that clinically a person no longer needed to be in hospital; they had to ensure that the discharge would be to a satisfactory environment. It was insufficient for them to hope that the outcome would be satisfactory and otherwise offer readmission if necessary (HSO W.420/83–84).

In yet another case, the hospital clinicians overlooked vital information from the GP about the domestic circumstances of the man to be discharged, and about the fact that this wife could not cope with her husband's twice-daily bathing needs. There was considerable doubt about the registrar's communications, little evidence of a multidisciplinary approach and no system of recording discharge arrangements on patients' notes (HSO SW.82/86–87).

In other cases, it appears that the arrangements are simply inadequate irrespective of communication issues, and will be criticised by the ombudsman. When an elderly man was admitted to hospital suffering from a head injury, multiple abrasions and confusion, he was discharged home later the same day – to his home where his dependent elderly wife lived – with no community nursing arrangements having been made. He was then readmitted to hospital because of subsequent community nursing concern, but discharged again without dressings for a pressure sore and again without arrangements for community nursing. He was then readmitted following an overdose; and died two days later, without his relatives being adequately informed about his deteriorating condition. This sequence of events had taken place over a period of about a month (Southend Hospital NHS Trust 2001).

## 16.11.2 TRANSFER OF FRAIL OLDER PATIENTS

The Department of Health has issued guidance on the transfer of frail older people from long-stay hospital settings. This followed a health service ombudsman investigation into one such transfer:

**Transfer against consultant's advice (ombudsman).** In 1996, the health service ombudsman published an investigation in which an elderly man with dementia was transferred from a hospital, in which he had been a patient for four years, to a private nursing home. He died 17 days after the transfer which was (a) opposed by the man's consultant but approved, in her absence, by a colleague who was aware of the consultant's opposition but believed there was no alternative; (b) as a result of a planned closure of the ward which had been brought forward by 21 months – a change of plan approved at a health authority meeting which had not been open to the public.

The ombudsman doubted whether the second consultant's acquiescence in the discharge amounted to sufficient authority to sanction the discharge and was particularly concerned that, given the first consultant's opinion, the second consultant made no entry on the clinical records. The NHS Trust did not comply with Department of Health discharge guidance (then HC(89)5) and drew the ombudsman's strong criticism, although he recognised that Winchester Health Authority's decision to speed up the closure gave the Trust little time to consult and make practical arrangements.

The ombudsman found it 'totally undemocratic that a public body should have considered it justifiable to discuss a policy matter of such importance to patients and their families at a meeting closed to the general public', and criticised the authority's calling the meeting informal. He concluded by stating that the circumstances of the complaint 'should serve as a grim warning to any health authority or trust planning the discharge of patients from hospital or elsewhere' (*North and Mid-Hampshire HA 1996*).

The subsequent Department of Health guidance covers consultation, a project plan, the needs of the individual and their relatives or carers, the process of transfer and role to be played by staff in the new setting, and follow-up and monitoring. In particular, a care plan for each patient should be drawn up, be subject to regular review before the transfer, involve consultation with relatives and carers, and include the patient's preferences in terms of diet, eating habits, bathing arrangements and idiosyncrasies. There should be a checklist of actions and tasks for each patient before and after the transfer. Information should be provided for patients, relatives and carers. Crucially, because a move can seriously threaten 'physical, psychological and social well-being', it is 'very important, therefore, to be aware of the risks, to handle the process sensitively and to be prepared to delay or halt a transfer if necessary' (HSC 1998/48, para 21).

The requirement in the guidance that a multidisciplinary risk assessment be coordinated was found to have been breached by the High Court in *R v North and East Devon HA, ex p Coughlan*, although the Court of Appeal in the same case overturned this finding.

This NHS guidance has since been held not to apply to the closure of local authority care homes for reasons such as: (a) its being issued to the NHS and not to local authorities; (b) its being aimed at NHS (not local authority) long-stay patients; (c) uncertainty about whether the guidance is anyway still extant or is now obsolete; (d) the Department of Health's decision not to issue such guidance to local authorities about this issue; (e) the guidance is anyway not statutory or mandatory in nature (see: *R(Dudley) v East Sussex CC; R(Haggerty) v St Helens Council*).

16.11.3 HOSPITAL DISCHARGE: DOCUMENTATION, ROUTINES, PROCEDURES

The health service ombudsman has investigated hospital discharge situations on many occasions. The sort of issue consistently identified includes the following. Poor documentation may lead to problems:

**Discharge after a stroke.** A man who had suffered a stroke was discharged to his daughter's flat. She had health problems and used crutches to walk. A care package was not provided for three days, during which time he could not move unaided. However, the daughter had informed the hospital staff about her health problems, but this had not been properly recorded. Had it been so, a proper care package could have been in place before discharge; the ombudsman criticised the standard of nursing documentation (*St Mary's NHS Trust 2002*).

Following discharge routine and procedure, but not varying this in the light of changes to the patient's needs and condition, might also result in poor discharge:

**Not responding to changing needs prior to discharge.** The health service ombudsman criticised a discharge when a man had suffered a fall the day before discharge at which time a chest infection was also identified – yet there had been no full physical examination prior to discharge (*West Sussex HA 2002*).

Similarly, a discharge took place on the basis of the nature of the person's previous admissions (for chemotherapy); whereas this time, the circumstances had been different but this had not been recorded in the nursing notes. This was faulted by the ombudsman (HSO W.286/86–87). The ombudsman criticised the progress of a planned discharge which was not adjusted to take account of the fact of changed circumstances – namely that the woman was now in severe abdominal pain, had been scalded and fallen on the morning of discharge (HSO W.24 and W.56/84–85).

The local government ombudsman too sometimes explores hospital discharge from the local authority's point of view:

**Failure to visit.** A man was discharged from hospital following a major operation. He had been told in hospital that help would be provided when he got home. Normally a local authority officer would have visited the next day. Instead it took ten days, during which time the man survived mostly on tinned food and managed to get to the shops with considerable difficulty. This was maladministration for the local ombudsman, although the man had not been entirely alone or completely immobile – and he could have contacted the council during the ten days, which he chose not to do (*Sheffield CC 1996*).

**Discharge to nursing home with pressure sore.** When a local authority arranged for a woman to be discharged from hospital to a nursing home, it was unaware of the full extent of the pressure sores from which she was already suffering, and which would eventually lead to her death some weeks later. However, the local ombudsman found that the hospital told neither the council nor the nursing home the full facts of her medical condition (the pressure sores had been concealed beneath bandage), and that therefore the council was not at fault in this particular respect (*Bexley LBC 2000*).

## 16.12 INTERMEDIATE CARE

Guidance was issued by the Department of Health in 2001 on what it called intermediate care (HSC 2001/01). Overall, the guidance stemmed from central government's concern about 'blocked' hospital beds; as such it was a forerunner of the legislation relating to delayed discharges. However, it also serves to a degree to support the concept of rehabilitation, although the six-week general limit will of course be relevant to some short-term rehabilitation only. The guidance states that intermediate care should be:

- for people who would otherwise face unnecessarily prolonged hospital stays or inappropriate admission to acute inpatient care, long-term residential care or continuing NHS inpatient care
- provided on basis of comprehensive assessment, resulting in a structured individual care plan involving active therapy, treatment or opportunity for recovery
- planned with an outcome of maximising independence and typically enabling people to live at home
- time limited, normally no longer than six weeks and frequently as little as one to two weeks
- inclusive of cross-professional working, with a single assessment framework, single professional records and shared protocols.

The guidance lists the following as constituting intermediate care services: rapid response, hospital at home, residential rehabilitation, supported discharge, day rehabilitation (HSC 2001/1).

It states that intermediate care should normally last no more than six weeks, but may sometimes be slightly longer (e.g. for stroke patients). In any event, it states that all individual care plans should have a review date specified within a six-week period; exceptional extensions should be based on full reassessment and authorisation of a senior clinician. It also stipulates that individual care plans should specify what care, therapy or support may be needed on discharge from intermediate care (HSC 2001/1).

The guidance recognises what was at the time the legal discretion of local authorities to charge for the social care element of non-residential intermediate care (and a legal duty to charge for residential elements) but stated that the Department of Health considered that intermediate care in either residential or non-residential form should be free of charge (HSC 2001/1).

However, since June 2003, the social care element of intermediate care must anyway be provided free of charge. For the purpose of these regulations, intermediate care is defined as a 'structured programme of care provided for a limited period of time to assist a person to maintain or regain the ability to live in his home'. The prohibition on charging applies to both residential and non-residential care. This prohibition on charging cannot exceed six weeks (SI 2003/1196).

## 16.13 COMMUNITY EQUIPMENT SERVICES

The provision of community equipment services has long been recognised as inadequate. Reports stretching back over three decades have repeatedly exposed a chaotic and inefficient system; these culminated in a highly critical Audit Commission (2000) report.

### 16.13.1 COMMUNITY EQUIPMENT SERVICES GUIDANCE

The Department of Health finally issued guidance in 2001, setting out 'action that should be taken' to improve provision of community equipment services. In particular, the guidance stated that local authorities should increase the number of people benefiting from community equipment services by 50 per cent and integrate local authority and NHS community equipment services by March 2004. In order to achieve this, central government stated that it was making extra funding available. For the NHS, this extra funding was quantified, but was not ring fenced; for social services authorities there was no quantification (HSC 2001/8). The result has apparently been that in a significant number of areas, the extra funding has been merely theoretical, and has instead been spent on other things. Community equipment cannot be charged for either by local authorities (see 11.2) or by the NHS (see 16.20).

### 16.13.2 RANGE OF COMMUNITY EQUIPMENT SERVICES

Further guidance (DH 2001) attached to HSC 2001/8 gives a non-exhaustive definition of community equipment. Although the list is useful, local authorities should bear in mind that it is non-exhaustive, and that obligations may arise to provide all sorts of equipment – depending on the assessed needs of a service user.

The guidance refers to home nursing equipment such as pressure relief mattresses, commodes and daily living equipment such as shower chairs and raised toilet seats. It also lists minor adaptations (e.g. grab rails, lever taps, improved lighting), sensory impairment equipment (e.g. liquid level indicators, hearing loops, assistive listening devices, flashing doorbells), communication aids, wheelchairs for short-term loan and telecare equipment (e.g. fall alarms, gas escape alarms, health state monitoring devices). Wheelchairs (16.3.4) were excluded from the ambit of the guidance and the 'reforms' being promulgated by the Department of Health.

### 16.13.3 COMMUNITY EQUIPMENT IN CARE HOMES

Regulations made under the Care Standards Act 2000 are vague concerning equipment provision in care homes, barely mentioning equipment. Likewise even the care standards made under the Act give little away. For example, the national minimum standards on care homes for older people refer only to the home providing grab rails, other aids, hoists, assisted toilets and baths, communication aids such as loop systems and storage areas for equipment (DH 2003b).

One of the consequences of this vagueness is uncertainty and sometimes dispute as to who should be providing particular items of equipment in a care home; the care home as part of its basic provision within its basic fee level, or the NHS or local authority.

Department of Health guidance on 'free nursing care' attempts to deal with the matter (HSC 2003/6). It states that a care home providing nursing would be expected (under the Care Standards Act 2000) to have basic handling, mobility and lifting equipment and adaptations. However, if an individual resident needs a particular item of equipment, the NHS should ensure that the care home provides it straightaway; should provide it on a temporary basis until the care home can do so; or provide it on loan to the individual until he or she no longer needs it. The guidance goes on to say that it would not be reasonable to expect care homes to provide equipment which would not be capable of being utilised by other care home residents – because the equipment's design, size and weight requirements are such that it is in effect specifically tailored to an individual (HSC 2003/6, para 30).

Nevertheless, the position is hazy. Indeed, the 2003 guidance reads much more restrictively than the 2001 guidance on free nursing care, which is not formally superseded; that is, both sets of guidance are relevant. The 2001 guidance refers to residents having access to the full range of community equipment services on the basis of assessed specialist need, in addition to equipment provided by the care home in accordance with the national minimum standards (see 24.4.3). This would include NHS provision of pressure relief equipment, aids to mobility and communication aids (HSC 2001/17, para 9). Local authorities, primary care trusts and care homes would therefore be well advised to ensure that local agreements and contracts make the position clear.

## 16.13.4 WHEELCHAIRS

The Department of Health has issued guidance on both the provision of electrically powered indoor/outdoor chairs, and on a voucher system for wheelchairs. The guidance on powered wheelchairs stated that the NHS should provide powered indoor/outdoor wheelchairs for severely disabled people, including children, who could benefit from them. Scooters were not to be included. Health authorities were told that they should formulate local eligibility criteria, which should be broadly based on the following three conditions:

- inability to propel a manual wheelchair outdoors
- ability to benefit, through increased mobility, from an improved quality of life
- ability to handle the chair safely.

It also states that if a person has such a powered wheelchair, but then moves to another area, where he or she would not be eligible, the wheelchair should not be withdrawn unless there is a good clinical reason for doing so (HSG(96)34).

Separate guidance set out the details of a wheelchair voucher scheme that should be offered by NHS wheelchair services. This involves the NHS giving a person a voucher equivalent to the cost to the NHS of providing a new wheelchair that, in the opinion of the assessing professional, would meet the clinical needs of the person. The person can then purchase a wheelchair with the voucher (the value of which the supplier can recover from the NHS), and 'top up' if he or she wishes.

Beyond this, there are two options. The 'independent option' involves the person becoming the owner of the wheelchair, being responsible for maintenance and repairs (and receiving those estimated costs for a specified period in the voucher). The 'partnership option' involves the NHS retaining ownership of the wheelchair, and also retaining responsibility for maintenance and repair.

The key principles of the scheme are described as universal eligibility (that is, anyone assessed as meeting the local eligibility criteria for a wheelchair); assessment and review of needs, followed by wheelchair prescription, in consultation with the service user; provision through agreed suppliers; and continued access in any event to NHS provision of special seating and pressure relieving cushions where required (HSG(96)53); the legal power to operate the voucher scheme is contained in regulations: SI 1996/1503.

### 16.13.4.1 Eligibility criteria for wheelchairs

The health service ombudsman has considered wheelchair eligibility criteria provision on a few occasions.

**Lightweight manual wheelchairs.** An NHS primary care trust operated additional eligibility criteria for the provision of lightweight manual wheelchairs. A woman with cerebral palsy was assessed by a charity as needing one, so that she could perform certain activities that she could not manage in her standard wheelchair. Her request was refused; the ombudsman found nothing wrong with the application of such additional criteria for lightweight wheelchairs, which were more expensive than the standard chairs (*Plymouth NHS Primary Care Trust 2002*).

However, in another case, the ombudsman found that the NHS trust had applied its criteria too restrictively:

**Applying guidance too restrictively.** A complaint was made by the parents of their disabled son, respecting provision for him of an electrically powered indoor/outdoor wheelchair. The ombudsman found that the NHS Trust had applied local and national guidance too restrictively and had not taken account of his previous experience of using such wheelchairs. It had also failed to consider whether he had exceptional needs not coming under the terms of the guidance (*Epsom and St. Helier NHS Trust 2001*).

## 16.13.5 COMMUNITY EQUIPMENT CASES

A number of the local ombudsman cases referred to elsewhere in this book, particularly concerning assessments and waiting times for services, concern community equipment. However, the health service ombudsman too has considered equipment on a few occasions:

**Four-month delay in equipment for man with dementia.** An elderly man suffered from multi-infarct dementia. At a care programme approach (CPA) meeting involving the senior consultant psychiatrist and GP, a number of recommendations were made for the provision of occupational therapy equipment. This took four months; the day after it was received, he fell and had to be admitted to a nursing home for rehabilitation. The health service ombudsman criticised the delay in implementing the recommendations; the ordering arrangements for equipment had been complex and unwieldy (*Wiltshire and Swindon Health Care NHS Trust 2002*).

**Delay in commode and toilet seat provision.** A complaint was upheld by the health service ombudsman when, despite the need for a commode and toilet seat extension having been assessed at least a week before discharge from hospital, they were not provided in time (HSO W.24 and W.56/84–85).

Rationing is generally assumed to take place on the basis of clinical priority:

**Rationing of crutches.** When the health service ombudsman investigated the non-provision of crutches for a patient leaving hospital, he found maladministration because the decision not to provide was not clinical but administrative, made as it was by a technician and founded on a shortage of crutches (HSO WW.3/79–80).

## 16.14 CONTINENCE SERVICES AND EQUIPMENT

The Department of Health has repeatedly stressed, in relation to incontinence supplies, that the NHS has the power to make priorities locally. All too often, looking to exercise this power, it appears that the NHS continues, at least in some areas, to view incontinence services, pads and other supplies as an 'easy target' when it wishes to save money.

Incontinence is a vexed issue not only because of the struggle over adequate funding for continence services. In addition, effects, both social and medical, are serious, and yet it – or the worst of its effects – often avoidable. Indeed, with the right input, be it surgical, bladder retraining, adjustment of the environment or provision of the right mobility equipment (people are wrongly labelled incontinent if they cannot get to the lavatory in time because of mobility difficulties), it can be wholly remedied.

The importance of making such remedies available, and of professionals understanding incontinence, becomes all the more important since incontinence is often cited as a reason why people have to enter care homes. The following dispute about what constituted 'incontinence' is informative:

**Incontinence and care homes.** A woman required a toileting regime (in order to get her to the toilet in time) in a care home (that did not provide nursing). Her daughter argued that this meant her mother was not incontinent. However, a medical doctor advising the local continuing care panel stated that, according to the local policy, a toileting regime meant that she was incontinent, and that therefore the mother required to be placed in a care home that provided nursing. The daughter maintained that her mother simply was not incontinent, since she passed urine on the toilet. The local authority for this, and other reasons, stated that the mother would have go to the nursing home. The court found this decision to be unlawful on various grounds, although it did not comment particularly on the incontinence point (*R(Goldsmith) v Wandsworth LBC*).

In addition, people may often be embarrassed to talk about incontinence, thus making the job of hard-pressed professionals that much more difficult.

## 16.14.1 CONTINENCE SERVICE PROVISION: BACKGROUND

A little background by way of a few examples will serve to highlight some of the issues concerning incontinence, and also illustrate the general point made earlier in this chapter about just how elusive are people's 'entitlements' to NHS services, especially the 'less glamorous' ones.

**1977: aids and equipment.** The Department of Health and Social Security wrote to nursing officers, having in mind 'positive action' even in the economic circumstances of the time. Although 'every effort should be directed towards maintaining continence, there are inevitably those whose control is so impaired as to make it necessary to meet as comprehensively as possible their need for the aids and equipment which will help to overcome this handicap' (CNO(SNC)(77)1).

**1987: concerns.** Restriction of services in some areas had led to considerable concern about the situation and a request being made by the Department to health authorities for information about their practices (D(87)45).

**1990: variability of provision.** Central government conceded that health authorities' provision of incontinence aids to people in their own homes and in care homes was variable (Stephen Dorrell: House of Commons Written Answers, 22/11/1990, col.32).

**1990: withdrawing continence aids.** Example quoted in Parliament of a health authority's consultation document, proposing to withdraw 'free incontinence aids' from 400 to 500 people living in independent sector residential homes, though still continuing to advise home owners and sell supplies to them at cost price (Stephen Dorrell: House of Commons Written Answers, 20/12/1990, cols.347–8).

**1990: pressure sores and dealing with faeces and urine – none too pleasant.** Baroness Masham reminded Members of the House of Lords about the realities of rationing of incontinence pads: 'The general public who are healthy and well have no idea that at such a basic level people who are incontinent are having many problems. They are having to buy pads or have them rationed or cut off. The mother of a spastic daughter who cannot speak and is doubly incontinent, living in a Cheshire Home, was told that she would have to pay for her daughter's incontinence pads as the Cheshire Home has nursing home status. The mother has to choose between supplying her daughter with pads or giving her a holiday. She cannot afford to do both. Other people have been told that they cannot have the pads which are the most suitable for them. If this goes on there will be an increase in pressure sores and all sorts of problems costing the health service millions of pounds. In addition to this, there are difficulties for carers who may find dealing with other people's urine and faeces none too pleasant. If people do not have adequate pads, life will become unbearable' (House of Lords Debates, 3/4/1990, col.1342).

**1990: failed legislative amendment.** Baroness Masham of Ilton attempted, unsuccessfully, to remedy the vagueness of the NHS Act 1977, by an amendment to the NHS and Community Care Bill: 'In carrying out its primary functions a District Health Authority shall provide a district wide incontinence service and shall identify a continence advisor and a consultant to take a special interest in incontinence.'

The government's reply simply reaffirmed health authorities' discretion: 'In this as in other areas of health care provision district health authorities should be left free to determine the pattern and level of service in their districts in the light of local needs and circumstances' (Baroness Blatch, House of Lords Debates, 24/4/1990, cols.546–550).

**1991: wide variations in provision.** Government acknowledged 'wide variations in the level of services to people with incontinence' (Stephen Dorrell: House of Commons Written Answers, 4/3/1991, col.22).

**1991: withdrawal of pads.** The Department of Health issued guidance stating that if local changes to the supply of incontinence pads were proposed, vulnerable patients or clients should not be exposed to anxiety; and there should be an assured alternative in place before withdrawal or reduction (EL(91)28).

**1991: Department of Health report.** Department of Health commissions a report on an 'agenda for action on incontinence services' (Sanderson 1991).

**1994: legal case illustrating rationing.** A court case illustrates how a woman had to seek assistance with incontinence pads from the Social Fund. This was because she did not meet her local health authority's strict eligibility for NHS provision: double incontinence or terminal illness (*R v Social Fund Inspector, ex p Connick*).

**2000: good practice guidance, but arbitrary rationing of pads irrespective of assessed need.** The Department of Health publishes *Good Practice in Continence Services*. It tells health authorities, primary care trusts and NHS trusts to work together to 'ensure that people with continence problems are identified, assessed and get the treatment they need' (DH 2000b). It pointed to geographical variations in people's eligibility for NHS continence services as well as in the range and quantity of treatment provided; it also noted with particular concern the 'gross difference' in NHS trust policies for supply of incontinence pads. Arbitrary rules and policies limited the supply of pads irrespective of the assessed needs of individual service users; there were also inflexible rules concerning the provision of either washable or disposable pads (p.8).

**2001: reusing paper sheets, and getting infections and pressure sores.** Parliament is reminded about how important continence supplies are: 'We know about the problems which arose when there was a hiccup or a cut-back in the community in relation to the incontinence service. People were reusing paper sheets, drying them on radiators. You end up with infections; your skin condition breaks down; and you may get pressure sores. If that happens, you then have to go into hospital because you cannot be looked after in a care home. Pressure sores cost the NHS millions of pounds per year' (Baroness Darcy de Knayth, House of Lords Debates, 26/4/2001, col.368).

**2001: issuing a direction about continence supplies in nursing homes.** A government minister undertakes in Parliament to issue a direction to the NHS about free continence supplies in nursing homes (Lord Hunt, House of Lords Debates, 3/5/2001, col.848). In the event, no such formal direction (which would have been stronger than guidance) is issued.

**2001 and 2003: guidance on continence supplies in nursing homes.** Department of Health guidance undertakes that incontinence aids should be free of charge to meet the assessed needs of residents in care homes providing nursing (HSC 2001/17, HSC 2003/6).

In 2004, it is apparent that continence supplies, at least in some areas, continue to be rationed arbitrarily (i.e. not according to assessed need) for people in their own homes, in care homes (not providing nursing) and, despite, Parliamentary undertakings and guidance issued to the NHS to the contrary, in nursing homes as well.

## 16.14.2 CONTINENCE SERVICES IN CARE HOMES PROVIDING NURSING

Although entitlement generally to continence services and equipment is vague, Department of Health guidance makes quite clear that the NHS is responsible for the supply of continence aids to meet the assessed needs of all residents of care homes that provide nursing care – where the residents are receiving NHS funded nursing care (HSC 2001/17, para 12).

In case there were room for doubt, guidance goes on to state that supplies of products should be related to the separate continence assessment of that individual (HSC 2003/6, para 31). Further, it states that residents should not pay for continence supplies that the NHS is already paying for; but that care homes can charge additionally for services that the NHS does not consider are appropriate (HSC 2003/6, para 32).

All this seems to bear the inescapable implication that the guidance is telling the NHS that it must meet, free of charge, all the assessed continence-related needs of a resident in a care home that provides nursing. In other words, the rationing of pads for such residents in nursing homes is not consistent with the guidance. This would be in contrast with such provision for people in other types of care home or in their own homes, where rationing is in principle possible. Nevertheless, it seems that in some areas at least the NHS continues to ration incontinence supplies not just to people in their own homes and care homes that do not provide nursing, but also to people in care homes that do provide nursing. In the light of the Department of Health guidance, which is written in reasonably strong terms, this sort of systematic rationing in nursing homes might arguably be unlawful.

## 16.15 SINGLE ASSESSMENT PROCESS

In 2002, the Department of Health issued guidance on what it named the single assessment process for older people (HSC 2002/1). The main thrust of the guidance is twofold. First, it urges that local authorities and the NHS should work jointly when older people are assessed. Second, it sets out what it considers to be an effective approach to assessment in terms of different levels of assessment, and what it calls contact, overview, specialist and comprehensive assessments.

Somewhat confusingly however, this guidance does not formally replace the plentiful guidance issued to local authorities (but not the NHS) on community care assessment over a decade before, and which itself had plenty to say about levels of assessment (DH 1990; SSI/SWSG 1991). Some of the salient points are as follows (HSC 2001/1):

- **Place of the older person in the assessment.** 'During assessment, care planning and other processes, the older person's account of their needs and their views and wishes must be kept at the centre of all decisions that are made... Agencies should remember that the person who is most expert in the care of an individual older person is that older person.'
- **Four levels of assessment.** Four levels of assessment are envisaged: contact, overview, specialist and comprehensive.
- **Contact assessment.** The guidance states that basic personal information can be collected or verified by trained, but not necessarily professionally qualified, staff. The exploration of potential needs should be undertaken by a trained and competent single professional (health or social care), whether qualified or not (HSC 2001/1).
- **Overview assessment.** The guidance describes an overview assessment as a more rounded assessment, in which some or all of the domains (see below) of assessment are explored. It suggests that the overview assessment could be carried out by a single health or social care professional, who need not necessarily be a qualified professional. However, it states that local agencies should nevertheless be clear as to just who is competent to carry out such an assessment.
- **Specialist assessment.** The guidance states that specialist assessments are to explore specific needs. Professionals should confirm the presence, extent, cause, likely development of a health condition or problem or social care need – and establish links to other conditions, problems, needs. Such assessments should rely on the involvement and judgement of appropriately qualified and competent professionals. The assessment should be administered and interpreted by the most appropriate professionals – with access to other professionals to contribute.
- **Comprehensive assessment.** The guidance states that comprehensive assessments should involve all or most of the domains of assessment, and a range of different professionals or specialist teams.
- **Domains of assessment.** The guidance describes 'domains' of assessment as comprising: the perspective of the service user, clinical background, disease prevention, personal care and physical well-being, senses, mental health, relationships, safety, immediate environment and resources.

## 16.16 NATIONAL SERVICE FRAMEWORKS

In addition to the general mass of guidance that it otherwise publishes, central government has also drawn up what it has called national service frameworks (NSFs), in order to target and improve specific types of service. Two of the frameworks drawn up are particularly relevant to this book and concern older people and mental health. Although the frameworks have received a significant amount of publicity, they are no more than guidance. It is also arguable that as far as social services authorities are concerned, these two frameworks are of the weaker variety of guidance (see 4.1.6), since no reference to s.7 of the Local Authority Social Services Act 1970 is to be found in either framework.

### 16.16.1 NATIONAL SERVICE FRAMEWORK FOR OLDER PEOPLE

The National Service Framework (NSF) for Older People applies across both health and social care and contains a number of standards (DH 2001c).

- **Age discrimination**. NHS services will be provided, regardless of age, on the basis of clinical need alone. Social care services will not use age in their eligibility criteria or policies, to restrict access to available services (standard 1).
- **Person-centred care**. NHS and social care services treat older people as individuals and enable them to make choices about their own care. This is achieved through the single assessment process, integrated commissioning arrangements and integrated provision of services, including community equipment and continence services (standard 2).
- **Intermediate care**. Older people will have access to a new range of intermediate care services at home or in designated care settings, to promote their independence by providing enhanced services from the NHS and councils to prevent unnecessary hospital admission and effective rehabilitation services to enable early discharge from hospital and to prevent premature or unnecessary admission to long-term residential care (standard 3).
- **General hospital care**. Older people's care in hospital is delivered through appropriate specialist care and by hospital staff who have the right set of skills to meet their needs (standard 4).
- **Strokes**. The NHS will take action to prevent strokes, working in partnership with other agencies where appropriate. People who are thought to have had a stroke have access to diagnostic services, are treated appropriately by a specialist stroke service, and subsequently, with their carers, participate in a multidisciplinary programme of secondary prevention and rehabilitation (standard 5).
- **Falls**. The NHS, working in partnership with councils, takes action to prevent falls and reduce resultant fractures or other injuries in their populations of older people. Older people who have fallen receive effective treatment and rehabilitation and, with their carers, receive advice on prevention through a specialised falls service (standard 6).

- **Mental health in older people**. Older people who have mental health problems have access to integrated mental health services, provided by the NHS and councils to ensure effective diagnosis, treatment and support, for them and their carers (standard 7).
- **Promotion of health and active life in older age**. The health and well-being of older people is promoted through a coordinated programme of action led by the NHS with support from councils (standard 8).

## 16.16.2 NATIONAL SERVICE FRAMEWORK FOR MENTAL HEALTH

The NSF for Mental Health (DH 1999a) applies across both health and social care and contains a number of standards. Standard 6 in particular is for social services authorities to take a lead on because it relates to the carers' legislation (see 12.4). In summary, the standards are as follows:

- Health promotion (standard 1).
- Identification and assessment of mental health needs, offering of effective treatments (standard 2).
- Round-the-clock contact with local services. Ability to use NHS Direct (standard 3).
- All service users on Care Programme Approach should:
  - receive care optimising engagement, preventing or anticipating crises and reducing risk
  - have a copy of a written care plan including action required in a crisis, advice to GP – and the care plan should be regularly reviewed
  - be able to access services 24 hours a day, seven days a week (standard 4).
- Each service user assessed as requiring a period of care away from home should have:
  - timely access to appropriate (hospital) bed, which is in the least restrictive environment consistent with self- and public protection, and is as close to home as possible
  - have a copy of a written care plan agreed on discharge setting out care and rehabilitation to be provided, identifying care coordinator and specifying action in a crisis (standard 5).
- All individuals providing regular and substantial care for a person on CPA should have:
  - an annually repeated assessment of caring, physical and mental health needs
  - have their own written care plan, given to them and implemented in discussion with them (standard 6).
- Health and social care communities to prevent suicides (standard 7) by:
  - promoting mental health for all (standard 1)
  - delivering high quality primary mental health care (standard 2)
  - ensuring people with mental health problems can contact local services (standard 3)
  - ensuring that people with severe and enduring mental illness have a care plan (standard 4)
  - providing safe hospital accommodation where needed (standard 5)
  - enable, by support, carers to continue caring (standard 6)
  - support local prison staff

- ○  ensure that staff are competent to assess the risk of suicide
- ○  develop local systems to audit suicide, to learn lessons and to take any necessary action.

## 16.17 CARE PROGRAMME APPROACH: MENTAL HEALTH

The Care Programme Approach (CPA) applies to the NHS and stems from guidance issued in 1990 concerning the management of people with mental health problems (HC(90)23). The four key elements identified were systematic assessment, a care plan, a key worker and regular review (para 10). Despite the emphasis placed by central government on CPA, it is not to be found in legislation.

Updated guidance was issued in 1999, the gist of which is as follows (DH 1999b). It states that even though the CPA is aimed at those most in need, nevertheless it should be applied to all service users in contact with the secondary mental health system (para 18). The four key elements remain the same as in the 1990 guidance (para 4). It refers to two levels of CPA: standard and enhanced.

It also states that people receiving aftercare services under s.117 of the Mental Health Act 1983 will be subject to the same principles as CPA, and the guidance recommends that the s.117 register should be a subset of the overall CPA register (para 71). Standard CPA is referred to as applying to people with some of the following characteristics:

- requiring support or intervention of one agency or discipline or only low key support from more than one agency/discipline
- being more able to manage their mental health problems themselves
- having active informal support network
- posing little danger to themselves or others
- being more likely to maintain appropriate contact with services (DH 1999b, para 57).

Enhanced CPA is referred to as applying to people with some of the following characteristics:

- having multiple care needs, including housing, employment, etc., requiring inter-agency coordination
- only being willing to cooperate with one professional or agency despite having multiple care needs
- being in contact with a number of agencies (including the criminal justice system)
- being likely to require more frequent and intensive interventions, perhaps with medication management
- being more likely to have mental health problems co-existing with other problems such as substance misuse
- being more likely to be at risk of self-harm or of harming others
- being more likely to disengage with services (DH 1999b, para 58).

The guidance states that the CPA should take account of the needs of the wider family, especially the needs of children and carers of people with mental health problems – in the light of social services carers' legislation (see 12.4) and the National Service Framework standard on carers (para 33). Ultimate responsibility for implementing the CPA lies with the NHS. However, the Department of Health has repeatedly stressed the importance of an integrated approach covering both CPA and social services assessment and care management under community care legislation. This is to minimise confusion and distress for service users and duplication (DH 1999b, paras 35, 38).

The guidance refers to a single point of referral, a unified health and social care assessment process, coordination of the roles and responsibilities of NHS and local authority, and single access process to health and social care services (DH 1999b, para 36). Nevertheless, care must be taken that, if health and social care assessment processes are integrated, it is on the basis of a proper legal understanding of the respective duties lying on social services and the NHS. Such integration approached in the wrong way can result not in helpful 'streamlining' of assessment and services, but depriving service users of proper assessment and services. In 2004, the courts effectively sounded a warning that joint working was not to be regarded as synonymous with legal shortcuts (*R(HP) v Islington LBC*; see 16.19.4).

## 16.18 MENTAL HEALTH ACT 1983

It is beyond the scope of this book to cover the Mental Health Act 1983 generally. Nevertheless, the book does refer to it in various places, in particular in respect of s.117 of the Act (aftercare services: see 10.5), of interventions potentially relevant to adult protection (see 17.5.2), and of examples of human rights legal cases (see Chapter 20).

## 16.19 JOINT WORKING BETWEEN NHS AND LOCAL AUTHORITIES

There has long been legislation allowing joint working between the NHS and local authorities and sometimes demanding it. However, more recent legislative provisions passed by central government are designed to facilitate such working and make it more prevalent.

The reasons for joint working would appear to be compelling, namely to simplify assessment and provision of services for service users, to reduce duplication of function – and to reduce the unseemly wrangling and cost shunting between local authorities and the NHS that sometimes results in delay in the provision, or even non-provision, of services. Thus, original community care policy guidance stated that the objective was to provide a service in which the boundaries between primary health care, secondary health care and social care did not form barriers from the perspective of the service user (DH 1990, para 1.9). Examples of previous legislation (as amended) allowing or demanding joint working include the following:

- **Cooperation**. Between NHS bodies (strategic health authorities, health authorities, special health authorities, primary care trusts, local health boards, NHS trusts, NHS foundation trusts) and local authorities (NHS Act 1977, s.22).

- **Arrangements with other organisations**. The NHS can arrange with any person or body, including a voluntary organisation for that person or body to provide, or assist in providing, any service under the NHS Act 1977; also the NHS may make available to such a person or body goods, materials, premises, etc. (NHS Act 1977, s.23).
- **Arrangement with local authorities**. The NHS must make available to local authorities services, facilities, etc., so far as is reasonably practicable to enable local authorities to discharge their functions relating to social services, education and public health (NHS Act 1977, s.26).
- **Local authority staff available to health authority**. A local authority has a duty to make available to NHS bodies the services of its employees in respect of social services functions, so far as is reasonably necessary and practicable to assist those NHS bodies to discharge their functions under the NHS Act (NHS Act 1977, s.28).
- **NHS payments to local authorities**. A health authority, special health authority, primary care trust or local health board may, if it thinks fit, make payments to various bodies including a social services authority, a housing authority and a voluntary organisation, in connection with those authorities' functions. Payments may also be made, if such an NHS body thinks fit, to a local authority in connection with any of that authority's functions if the NHS body believes that those functions have an effect on the health of any individuals, have an effect on or are affected by any NHS functions, or are connected with any NHS functions (NHS Act 1977, s.28A).
- **Local authority payments to NHS**. A local authority may, if it thinks fit, make payments to a health authority, strategic health authority or primary care trust (NHS Act 1977, s.28BB).
- **Agreements involving staff**. Local authorities and the NHS may enter into agreements involving the making of each other's staff available to each other (Local Government Act 1972, s.113).

## 16.19.1 JOINT WORKING AND THE HEALTH ACT 1999

Section 31 of the Health Act 1999 refers specifically to the pooling of budgets and to the delegation of functions. It does not impose a duty, but instead places a power on the NHS and local authorities to work jointly in this way. Section 31 empowers the Secretary of State to make regulations enabling prescribed NHS bodies and prescribed local authorities to enter into particular arrangements in relation to their respective functions. This is on condition that any such arrangements are likely to improve the way in which those functions are exercised. The section goes on to state that the prescribed arrangements may include (a) the establishment and maintenance of joint funds; (b) the exercise by an NHS body of prescribed health-related functions of a local authority and vice versa; (c) the provision of staff, goods, services or accommodation in connection with (a) or (b).

## 16.19.2 HEALTH ACT 1999: SERVICES INVOLVED

The relevant regulations spell out the detail of which bodies and services the joint working arrangements apply to. Relevant NHS functions are those under s.2 and s.3(1) of the NHS Act 1977, including rehabilitation services and those services intended to avoid admission to hospital. Also included are aftercare and supervised aftercare under ss.25A–25H and 117 of the Mental Health Act 1983. Excluded are surgery, radiotherapy, termination of pregnancies, endoscopy, Class 4 laser treatment, other invasive treatment and emergency ambulance services, medical and dental inspections of school age children – and advice, examination and treatment on contraception, substances and appliances (SI 2000/617).

Relevant local authority functions are many (with a few specific exclusions). The regulations were amended in 2003 to allow charging functions, for both residential and non-residential accommodation, to be included. Other local authority functions covered, in addition to social services functions, include education authority functions, and housing authority functions under both Part 1 of the Housing Grants, Construction and Regeneration Act 1996 (containing disabled facilities grants), and under Parts VI and VII of the Housing Act 1996 (housing allocation and homelessness).

The Regulations state that partners may establish and maintain a pooled fund, and that NHS bodies may exercise health-related local authority functions, and that local authorities may exercise NHS functions (SI 2000/617).

### 16.19.3 CARE TRUSTS
Joint working can take the form of a care trust, comprising an NHS trust or primary care trust that may exercise health-related functions of a local authority (Health and Social Care Act 2001, ss.45–48).

### 16.19.4 JOINT WORKING PARTNERS' LEGAL FUNCTIONS AND AVOIDANCE OF PITFALLS
The Health Act 1999 makes quite clear that any arrangements made under it affect neither the liability of NHS bodies or local authorities for the exercise of their functions, nor the powers or duties of local authorities to recover charges for services (s.31). Likewise, in respect of care trusts, the Health and Social Care Act 2001 states that existing functions of both NHS and local authority are not affected (s.45).

This is a cautionary reminder to those local authorities and NHS bodies who enter joint working agreements without an appreciation of the legal implications. When joint working takes place, it is sometimes forgotten that existing duties on each partner (local authority or NHS) remain unaltered. This can lead to unlawfulness where either partner improperly gives up its decision-making responsibilities. Single health and social care assessments are one thing, unduly restrictive assessment quite another. This was illustrated in a court case where the local authority improperly determined the outcome of its community care assessment with reference to NHS matters. It had therefore in effect lost its own legal identity:

**Fundamental error of local authority in giving up its decision-making responsibility.** An assessment was carried out as to whether a man was eligible for assistance through the Care Programme Approach, which is primarily an NHS responsibility. The final decision was that he was not eligible, because he did not have a severe and enduring mental illness. It was then concluded, on the basis of the CPA decision, that he was not eligible for community care services either. This was legally impermissible; before a decision was taken about community care, an assessment was required to investigate the risk, self-neglect and vulnerability to deterioration that had already been identified. There had never been a proper and comprehensive community care assessment; this was a demonstrable, fundamental and serious error (*R(HP) v Islington LBC*).

Likewise in another court case, reliance on health reports was not enough for the local authority to discharge its decision-making obligations:

**Local authority failing to take community care decision.** A medical doctor made recommendations to a local continuing care panel about whether a woman should be placed in a nursing home. They were based on the reports of health professionals during the woman's hospital stay. They took no account of the social work team manager's detailed assessment and report. However, the local authority simply followed the panel's recommendations, even though the latter's function was advisory only, and it had made those recommendations on the basis of limited or flawed information.

In deciding whether to place the woman in a nursing home, the final decision lay with the local authority; but it had to take account of all relevant factors, including an up-to-date community care assessment. This it had not done. The Court of Appeal held that the local authority's decision was manifestly flawed (*R(Goldsmith) v Wandsworth LBC*).

The apparent legal submersion of local authority community care responsibilities in such cases reflects at the same time professional concerns that joint working can lead to the 'over-medicalisation' of services (Bilson 2004). In addition, if joint working is to be effective it needs somehow to grapple with the cost shunting exercises that typically take place, as described by the local ombudsman when making a finding of maladminstration:

**Joint working and cost shunting.** A woman had severe physical and learning disabilities and challenging behaviour. Following a local authority's assessment of need, two years passed until she actually received the day care she needed. Over a year after assessing the need, the local authority attempted to persuade the NHS to fund it. However, there was no record that the woman's needs had changed from the previous year when the local authority had accepted that it had responsibility. Thus, it was clear that financial reasons lay behind the council's reluctance to secure a service.

The ombudsman found it was inappropriate for the council to attempt to shift the burden, given the additional delay this would cause; the failure to 'grasp the nettle' was maladministration. Furthermore, no strategy was developed to further joint working and ensure that gaps in care were filled and that a 'seamless service' existed. Instead the authority chose to place the woman in the 'grey area' of responsibility, rather than accepting the financial burden that the five-day care package would have entailed. The ombudsman recommended £15,000 compensation for this (*Calderdale MBC 1998*).

Further caution must be exercised when joint health and social care packages are delivered. This is because the NHS for the most part is unable legally to charge for services. Thus, however 'seamless' or joined up a care package is, a seam nevertheless needs to be identified in order to pinpoint the social care elements that can be charged for, and the health care that cannot be. A reminder of this is provided in Department of Health guidance (DH 2003, para 88).

## 16.19.5 JOINT WORKING WITHIN ORGANISATIONS

Although local authorities and the NHS are urged to work jointly across agency boundaries, nevertheless coordinated working may also be lacking within local authorities themselves. At times such fragmented working can bear consequences that will attract censure from both the courts and the ombudsmen:

**Lack of coordinated working within local authorities.** In one local authority, the social services and housing departments failed to meet the needs of a severely disabled woman over a period of two years. As a consequence she was left in a situation in the family home, such that her human rights (article 8 of the Convention) were breached. The judge found that one cause of this had been what he referred to as 'corporate failure' (R(Bernard) v Enfield LBC).

In another case, the lack of coordinated working between departments resulted in an 'outrageous' breach of an undertaking given to the court by the local authority:

**Lamentable and outrageous breach of undertaking to the court.** A local authority gave an undertaking to the High Court to carry out a community care assessment and not to enforce any warrant for possession of the premises. Six days later, in breach of the undertaking, the woman was evicted. The judge referred to this as lamentable and outrageous. The local authority explained this as an administrative oversight and lack of communication between departments. The undertaking had been given on behalf of social services, whereas the eviction had been arranged by the housing department. This division of responsibility was mirrored in the legal department of the council. For the court, this was a systematic inadequacy with the potential for disaster. What was required were procedures that were adequate, understood by relevant staff and rigorously enforced. The local authority appeared to 'fall down on every count' (R(Bempoa) v Southwark LBC).

Such occurrences seem not necessarily to be isolated. The local ombudsman investigated similarly:

**Corporate failure.** The local ombudsman identified corporate failure when the housing department served a possession order in respect of a person with mental health problems, vulnerable and unwell, but failed to inform social services, in particular the mental health division. Had this happened, the council's social workers would have been able to offer help to the man in managing his money and avert the eviction (Barnet LBC 2000).

In another case that resulted in the severe housing and social care needs of a disabled boy and his family not being met, the local ombudsman identified poor communication between housing and social services officers of the same council. This in turn meant that even those local authority officers who were attempting to help were rendered helpless by other officers responding to their own priorities (Bristol CC 1998). Likewise, following a failure to provide a stairlift that would have made the last two years of her life easier for her, the ombudsman found a 'sorry tale of confusion' within and between the two councils involved (Durham CC 1993).

Sometimes the failings are apparently trivial, but can result in an application for assistance being delayed for a year; for example, when an internal memorandum between the social services and housing department of the same council never arrived and there was no system for checking the safe arrival of internal mail (*Liverpool CC 1992*).

Unawareness of funding sources even within the same department of the same council may mean a person's needs are not met promptly, and exacerbate a fragmented approach to assessing and meeting people's needs. The local ombudsman found maladministration:

**Special fund for HIV/AIDS.** A social worker, involved in the assessment of a man with HIV/AIDS, was unaware of the special fund which the social services department had for people with AIDS. This caused delay. An occupational therapist subsequently visited; she recorded his serious condition and recommended various items including walking sticks, height adjusters and a sheepskin. These were delivered within days; a shower was later installed, paid for by the special AIDS fund, since the housing department said it had no resources. Between March and April, the man was assessed on three separate occasions by three different parts of the social services department – a fragmented approach which, the carer claimed, added to the stress the man was under in trying to obtain appropriate services. This was maladministration; the consequent delay meant that at a time when he was dying, appropriate and essential services had been denied him (*Salford 1996*).

Sometimes, unusual needs or uncertainty as to what the need is result in people 'falling between stools'. For instance, team or specialism boundaries may effectively exclude people from assistance, as the following local ombudsman investigation found:

**Team boundaries failing service users.** A man was born with physical problems (mild cerebral palsy) that remained undiagnosed until adulthood (1995, when a voluntary body carried out an assessment). He suffered throughout life from difficulty in defecating and micturition. He was caused great unhappiness, embarrassment and loss of confidence because of difficulty in keeping himself clean. He became socially withdrawn. His mother had in 1994 requested (when he was 17 years old) social services involvement; amongst other things a clos-o-mat was requested – i.e. an automatic washing/drying toilet.

Over an extended period, he was referred between the social services learning disability and physical disability teams, a consultant neurosurgeon, consultant psychiatrist and gastro-enterologist in an attempt to diagnose the problem. He seemed not to 'fit' into any team or any specialism. Social services had stated that it would not provide the clos-o-mat until the cause of the problem had been identified. However, by 1999 definite medical advice had still not been provided; social services finally decided to provide the clos-o-mat. The ombudsman accepted that the council had now agreed to review its procedures; this would include ensuring that boundaries between teams did not prevent people's needs from being met (*Northumberland CC 2000*).

Reflecting a similar type of issue, a report published by the Joseph Rowntree Foundation in 2004 highlighted the difficulties faced by people with both a physical disability and mental health problems; people's needs were treated unhelpfully and in fragmented fashion between physical disability and mental health teams (Morris 2004).

## 16.20 NHS AND CHARGES FOR SERVICES

Health services and equipment provided by the NHS, unless otherwise specified, are by default free of charge to patients (NHS Act 1977, s.1). Despite this relatively clear position, misunderstandings and illegal charges do sometimes occur; hence the Department of Health issues guidance from time to time, in order to remind NHS bodies of the legal position (e.g. EL(91)129; EL(92)20).

Generally speaking, the charges that are specified cover equipment and drugs prescribed by general practitioners; dental services and appliances; spectacles and contact lenses; and elastic hosiery, wigs, abdominal or spinal supports and surgical brassieres (SI 2000/620). There are further distinctions to be made depending on the status of a patient, since not even these charges apply to NHS inpatients (NHS Act 1977, schedule 12). There are anyway also exemptions from, or reductions in, payment depending on factors such as the age, condition and financial status of patients (SI 2000/620). In addition, separate rules govern charges for private patients (NHS Act 1977, s.62) and overseas patients (see 13.3).

Patients cannot be charged if there is a defect in the appliance as supplied (NHS Act 1977, schedule 12, para 1), but can be charged if the need for repair or replacement is required due to an 'act or omission' of the patient (NHS Act 1977, s.82; SI 1974/284).

**Improper charging policy for shoe repairs.** A man had severe lower limb problems (caused by thalidomide) that caused excess wear and tear on the several pairs of NHS supplied orthopaedic shoes that he required. The NHS Trust had a policy of making patients pay for the first two repairs per year per pair of shoes – on the basis that anyone using ordinary shoes might have to repair their shoes twice a year.

The health service ombudsman stated that this policy was inconsistent with the 1974 regulations, that only gave a power to charge for a repair caused by a specific act or omission of the patient (*North Bristol NHS Trust 2000*).

Although, therefore, the NHS does not have the same wide powers to charge as social services authorities, it does, ironically, have a wide discretion not to provide services at all. Sometimes confusion arises as to whether NHS patients have had to pay for NHS services or equipment (which would be unlawful) or been asked to purchase them privately (which would be lawful):

**People buying their own equipment.** The health service ombudsman investigated a case where the complainant had bought a transcutaneous nerve stimulator (TNS) for the relief of pain and wanted reimbursement from the hospital. The ombudsman accepted the hospital's explanation that normally it could not loan its own stock of TNS machines on a semi-permanent basis because of demand and a finite budget. One of the hospital staff explained that there was a point at which people 'had to look after themselves', since if they attended the hospital indefinitely, the system would grind to a halt. It transpired however that a long-term loan might have been possible from elsewhere, but that the hospital had not given a proper explanation of the possibilities; the ombudsman therefore found fault with the lack of information given to the complainant (HSO W.263/83–84).

**Non-provision of chiropody services.** Some 25 years ago, the health service ombudsman considered the use of a means test in relation to chiropody services. He found the authority's policy vindicated and quoted a DHSS letter to the authority: 'We know that many [authorities] do not have the manpower or other resources to provide a satisfactory service for even the elderly and have therefore decided to introduce their own criteria for determining priority amongst this and other groups…decisions as to level of provision rest with individual [authorities] and if your [authority] considers that a "means" type test is the best way of determining priority amongst those seeking treatment that is entirely a matter for the authority' (HSO W.68/77–78). One suspects that, given the sensitive nature of NHS rationing, such a policy would, if publicised, nowadays generate lively debate – if not in terms of the rationing itself, then of the criterion used to determine eligibility.

It is probable that unlawful charges are more widespread than is commonly supposed, and that there is some confusion about the true position.

In one case, the health service ombudsman found it unobjectionable that a hospital occupational therapy department had made a charge for a reaching stick; perhaps on the basis that responsibility lay with the local authority social services department, but the person (understandably) did not want to wait (HSO W.340/80–81). Though a probably helpful practice, its lawfulness might have been open to question. Indeed, a decade later, the health service ombudsman investigated unlawful charging for chiropody appliances:

**Charging for chiropody appliances.** A health service ombudsman investigation found that a health authority had improperly tried to make charges for chiropody appliances supplied to a 13-year-old girl. The attempted justification by the authority referred to local financial constraints; but such constraints could not permit either a health authority or NHS Trust to breach their statutory duties. Furthermore, Circular guidance had made clear that services, new or existing, should be planned within resources. Thus, the health authority could at its discretion decide to continue or discontinue altogether the bio-mechanics service; what they could not do was make unlawful charges for it. There were possibly 20 patients involved in such charging: the health authority was urged to investigate all 20 (HSO W.226/91–92).

It has been reported that some NHS trusts request deposits from £5 to £40 for the loan of equipment. In one case the NHS trust said that this was 'voluntary' but the notices to this effect were apparently unclear and in very small print (Clark *et al.* 1998, p.29). Such deposits are typically taken for items such as walking aids and wheelchairs. The Association of Community Health Councils expressed the view that such deposits amount to charges and are therefore unlawful (Ford, McLeish and Chester 2002, p.13).

PART IV

# Adult protection, decision-making capacity, information sharing, human rights, disability discrimination

CHAPTER 17

# Adult protection

## KEY POINTS

During the 1990s concern grew about the phenomenon of what has been termed adult abuse. In 2000, the Department of Health published guidance concerned with the protection from abuse of vulnerable adults. Such an adult is defined as a person 'who is or may be in need of community care services by reason of mental or other disability, age or illness; and who is or may be unable to take care of him or herself, or unable to protect him or herself against significant harm or exploitation'.

Abuse is referred to as physical, sexual, psychological, financial or material, neglect and acts of omission, discriminatory, institutional. Some abuse will constitute a criminal offence, for instance in relation to physical assault, sexual assault and rape, fraud, etc. However, substantially no new social services legislation was passed concerning adult protection, equivalent for example to child protection provisions contained in the Children Act 1989. Indeed, central government has failed to adopt proposals made by the Law Commission (1995) that local authorities should be given such protective powers in respect of adults. (Although at the time of writing, a disturbing report concerning the abuse of a group of people, in the care of a Scottish local authority both as children and adults (SWSI 2004), might lead to specific adult protection legislation in Scotland.)

Therefore, in order to understand the legal framework, a twofold approach is required. First, from the social services point of view, adult protection issues have to be set in the context of community care legislation and related guidance. Second, in order to understand how other agencies are able to act, an appreciation of other, non-social services legislation is needed. An appreciation of this wider legal framework will assist as a pointer to the identification of, and possible legal remedies for, certain types of abuse.

Thus the chapter includes reference to the protection of vulnerable adults list (POVA), criminal record certificates, removing people from their homes under the National Assistance Act 1948, mental health law interventions including guardianship, environmental health powers, civil wrongs (e.g. assault, battery, false imprisonment), criminal justice legislation (including sexual offences and theft), and the principle of undue influence in relation to financial abuse.

In addition, the exercise by the courts of their inherent jurisdiction to intervene in the case of people lacking capacity to take decisions for themselves has also become part of the legal armoury in tackling adult protection matters. One or two examples of this are given in this chapter (see 17.5.2.7), but otherwise the inherent jurisdiction is covered in the next chapter (see 18.8). Some of the matters and interventions covered in this chapter go beyond protection from other people and extend to situations of self-neglect as well.

**Note: Wales, Scotland and Northern Ireland**. The scope of this chapter is such that this note does not extend to detailing the equivalent legislation and guidance in Scotland and Northern Ireland. However, the legislation in this chapter applies to Wales, and the National Assembly for Wales has published its own guidance on adult protection (NAFW 2000), which is the equivalent of the *No Secrets* guidance published by the Department of Health in England (DH 2000).

## 17.1 DEPARTMENT OF HEALTH GUIDANCE

In 2000, the Department of Health published policy guidance under s.7 of the Local Authority Social Services Act 1970. Entitled *No Secrets*, it stated that local authority social services departments should take the lead in 'inter-agency' working to combat such abuse. It set out a framework only, on which local authorities could base more detailed local policies and procedures (DH 2000).

The guidance states that it is concerned with the protection from abuse of vulnerable adults. A vulnerable adult is defined as a person 'who is or may be in need of community care services by reason of mental or other disability, age or illness; and who is or may be unable to take care of him or herself, or unable to protect him or herself against significant harm or exploitation'. Abuse can be physical, sexual, psychological, financial or material, neglect and acts of omission, discriminatory, institutional. Some forms of abuse are criminal offences, for example physical assault, sexual assault and rape, fraud, etc.

The guidance stresses the importance of inter-agency working including the NHS and social services, sheltered and supported housing providers, regulators of services, polices and Crown Prosecution Service, voluntary and private sector agencies, local authority housing and education departments, probation service, DSS benefit agencies, carer support groups, user groups and user-led services, advocacy and advisory services, community safety partnerships, legal advice and representation services, and so on.

## 17.1.1 INFORMATION SHARING

The guidance also points out that, as part of inter-agency working, agreement on the sharing of information will be required, in order to balance on the one hand confidentiality, and on the other the importance of sharing information (even in the absence of consent). The guidance summarises the principles of sharing confidential information as follows (DH 2000, para 5.6):

- information must be shared on a 'need to know' basis only
- confidentiality should not be confused with secrecy
- informed consent should be obtained but, if this is not possible and other vulnerable adults are at risk, it might be necessary to override this requirement
- assurances of absolute confidentiality should not be given where there are concerns about abuse.

It also goes on to state that principles of confidentiality designed to safeguard and promote the interests of service users should not be confused with those 'designed to protect the management interests of an organisation' (DH 2000, para 5.8). Information sharing is covered in Chapter 19 of this book.

## 17.2 SOCIAL SERVICES LEGISLATION

Since no specific new legislation was passed to accompany central government policy as set out in the *No Secrets* guidance, local social services authority adult protection work primarily (though not wholly: see below in this chapter) rests on the existing community care legislation as set out previously in this book. Hence the reference in the guidance to a vulnerable adult having to be a person who may be in need of community care services. This is a direct reference to the condition in s.47 of the NHS and Community Care Act 1990, which is the legal trigger for community care assessment of a person's needs.

The absence of any specific adult protection legislation has in effect been recognised by the courts. In one adult protection case (concerning an assisted suicide), whilst acknowledging the *No Secrets* guidance, the judge held that a local authority's duties were limited to addressing the community care needs of the particular person as assessed by the authority. Any common law duties that it might owe 'did not extend the scope of the statutory duties' under the relevant community care legislation. Furthermore, such duties were not 'all-embracing' in the ways provided for children under s.33 and Part 3 of the Children Act 1989 (*Re Z*).

Community care legislation contains a wide variety of services that local authorities can potentially arrange for people (see Chapters 8 and 10) – and which may be relevant in the context of abuse. These include, for example, placing a person in a care home, as well as providing practical assistance in a person's own home, providing advice, support, visiting services, and so on. Such non-residential services referred to are available for both disabled people under the National Assistance Act 1948 (s.29) and the Chronically Sick and Disabled Persons Act 1970 (s.2). They are also available for older people generally, who are not disabled, under the Health Service and Public Health Act 1968 (s.45). One such example of a service provided under the 1968 Act was reported to the author as follows:

**Gardening services to prevent crime.** In one particular area, 'con men' were targeting older people by means of unkept front gardens. Where the householder did turn out to be elderly and vulnerable, they were performing small amounts of gardening and charging extortionate amounts of money. In consultation with the police, the local authority arranged for a gardening service for older people in that particular area, in order to remove the indicator (the unkept garden).

The carers' legislation, too, may be useful (see 12.4). For instance, where a potentially abusive situation is building up, an assessment and provision of a break for the carer, either as a carer's service under the Carers and Disabled Children Act 2000, or as community care service under the National Assistance Act 1948 or Chronically Sick and Disabled Persons Act 1970, might defuse the threat of abuse.

## 17.3 PROTECTION OF VULNERABLE ADULTS LIST
Under the Care Standards Act 2000, there is a duty on the Secretary of State to keep a list of care workers who are considered unsuitable to work with vulnerable adults because they have harmed, or placed at risk of harm, vulnerable adults – and the employer has, or would have, dismissed the person, or transferred him or her to a non-care position (s.81). The protection of vulnerable adults (POVA) list was started in July 2004.

### 17.3.1 DEFINITION OF CARE WORKER AND VULNERABLE ADULT
Care workers are defined as (Care Standards Act 2000, s.80):
- people who are or have been employed in a position giving them regular contact in the course of their duties with adults to whom accommodation is provided at a care home
- people with similar contact where prescribed services are provided by an independent hospital, independent clinic, independent medical agency or NHS body
- people who are or have been employed in a position concerned with the provision of personal care for persons in their own home who by reason of illness, infirmity or disability are unable to provide it for themselves without assistance
- people who have entered an agreement to provide support, care or accommodation by way of employment, for an adult (who is not a relative) [i.e. under an adult placement scheme].

Department of Health guidance points out that 'regular contact' should be given its 'ordinary everyday meaning', but that it implies contact with a constant or definite pattern, or which recurs at short uniform intervals or on several occasions during short periods of time such as a week (DH 2004e, para 9).

Vulnerable adult means (Care Standards Act 2000, s.80):

- a person for whom accommodation and nursing or personal care are provided in a care home
- a person for whom personal care is provided in his or her own home by a domiciliary care agency
- a person for whom prescribed services are provided by an independent hospital, independent clinic, independent medical agency or NHS body.
- a person provided with support, care or accomodation under an adult placement scheme.

Harm means (Care Standards Act 2000, s.120):

- in the case of an adult who is not mentally impaired – ill-treatment or impairment of health
- in the case of an adult who is mentally impaired – ill-treatment, or the impairment of health or development.

See 24.4.4 regarding personal care.

Department of Health guidance does not elaborate on what 'harm' might mean beyond its definition in the Act, although it does refer to other guidance on adult protection (DH 2000) for a fuller discussion of 'harm and abuse' (DH 2004e, para 50). But presumably, for example, the reference in the legislation to 'ill-treatment' could include financial abuse, as well as other forms of harm.

### 17.3.2 DUTY OF REFERRAL FOR INCLUSION ON LIST

There is a wide-ranging duty of referral placed on care home providers and domiciliary care providers (and on employment agencies and employment businesses). This is whether or not they run for profit (Care Standards Act 2000, s.121(5)). At the time of writing the POVA scheme has not been implemented in relation to the NHS and independent health sector, and will only be so on a longer timescale.

Such providers of care for vulnerable adults have a duty to refer a worker (paid or voluntary) to the Secretary of State for Health if the care provider has dismissed or transferred to a non-care position that worker on the grounds of misconduct that harmed or placed at risk of harm a vulnerable adult. The duty of referral applies even where there is only a suspension or provisional transfer on these grounds (Care Standards Act 2000, s.82).

The duty to refer also applies if such a dismissal or transfer would have occurred, or the care provider would have considered those steps, had the worker not already resigned, retired or been made redundant. Likewise if (a) the care provider has dismissed the worker, or the worker has resigned or retired or has been transferred to a non-care position; (b) information not available at the time of the dismissal, resignation, retirement or transfer has since become available; (c) the provider is of the view that, if that information had been available at that time, the provider would have dismissed him/her or considered doing so, on such grounds as mentioned above (harm or risk of harm to vulnerable adult

(Care Standards Act 2000, s.82). Corresponding duties are placed on employment agencies and employment businesses (s.83).)

Registration authorities (i.e. the Commission for Social Care Inspection) have the power to refer a care worker if they consider that he or she is guilty of the relevant misconduct and has not been referred to the Secretary of State (s.84).

## 17.3.3 INCLUSION OF WORKER ON THE LIST

The Secretary of State must consider the reference and information submitted and, if it seems that it may be appropriate to include the individual on the list, place the person on it provisionally. The worker must be invited to make observations. The Secretary of State must then either confirm inclusion on the list or remove the person from the list (s.82).

A worker included on the list (other than provisionally) may appeal against the decision directly to the Secretary of State or to the Care Standards Tribunal (s.86). The Tribunal must allow the appeal if it is not satisfied either that the individual is guilty of the misconduct, or that the individual is unsuitable to work with vulnerable adults. In addition, a person can apply to the Tribunal for removal from the list if he or she has been on the list for ten years (or five years if placed on the list when he or she was under 18 years old) and has not made such an application during that time. However, the Tribunal cannot give permission for the application to be made unless during that time the individual's circumstances have changed and the change is such that permission should be given (ss.87–88).

Cross-referral between the POVA list and the Protection of Children Act 1999 (POCA) list can be made (s.92).

## 17.3.4 DUTY TO CHECK POVA LIST

From 26 July 2004, care providers have a duty to check the POVA list, and must not offer employment if the prospective employee is included on the list (whether or not provisionally). This duty also covers existing employees who are moving or being transferred from a non-care to a care position. If the employer discovers that an existing employee is on the list, the employer must cease to employ the person in that care position (Care Standards Act 2000, s.89; DH 2004e, para 29).

The original intention was that when application for criminal record certificates under the Police Act 1997 was made to the Criminal Records Bureau (CRB), then the CRB would automatically check against the POVA list as well (Police Act 1997, ss.113(3C), 115(6B)). However, regulatory changes have meant that, exceptionally, new staff can start work in advance of a full CRB check, but only after a check has been made against the POVA list. This exceptional POVA check is referred to as a 'POVA First' check; it is intended that it be used only so that care providers can recruit staff quickly in order to ensure that statutory staffing requirements are met (DH 2004e, paras 40, 46).

It is an offence for a person on the POVA list (unless the inclusion is provisional only) to apply for, offer to do, accept or do any work in a care position.

The duty of referral applies only in respect of dismissals, resignations or other departures that occur after the POVA's scheme inception, on 26 July 2004. However, guidance states that care providers may (but are not obliged to) refer care workers in respect of such occurrences before that date, but would have to supply the necessary supporting information (DH 2004e, paras 56–57). The guidance goes on to set out a list of the various information that is required to support a referral to the Secretary of State (DH 2004e, para 68).

### 17.3.5 STRIKING THE RIGHT BALANCE

Care providers (and indeed the Secretary of State) need to strike a balance between protecting vulnerable service users and over-reaction. The ramifications of suspension or transfer to a non-care position – namely then having to refer the person for provisional inclusion on the POVA list – might pose a dilemma for care providers. For example, they might have, in the past, operated a policy of suspension or provisional transfer as a matter of course (erring on the side of caution), but might now hesitate to do so.

Perhaps with this sort of issue in mind, Department of Health guidance covers the matter of suspension or provisional transfer. First, it states sensibly that before a care worker is suspended the care provider should speedily try to establish whether the allegations of harm have substance. It points out that a precipitate suspension and subsequent referral to the POVA list, on the basis of groundless allegations, can cause significant upset (see e.g. case of *Gogay v Hertfordshire CC* immediately below).

Second, the guidance attempts to distinguish suspension (perhaps imposed as a matter of course and precaution) from the care provider's being satisfied of the substance of the allegations. It states that even if a care worker is suspended immediately, because the allegations of harm are particularly serious, a POVA list referral should only be made if the care provider is satisfied that the allegations have some substance (DH 2004e, para 53). Whether this distinction is sustainable is another matter; because presumably suspension should normally not take place unless there are good grounds for it.

A court case, albeit prior to the implementation of the POVA list, showed the potential legal consequences of what the courts might regard as an over-reaction leading to breach of the principle of good faith in employment contracts and to damages for psychiatric personal injury:

**Suspension, and breach of employment contract.** A residential social worker was suspended following potential allegations made by a child with learning and communication difficulties. Following a 'strategy meeting', a decision was taken to hold an investigation under s.47 of the Children Act 1989. The investigation concluded that the child had never disclosed any abuse in relation to any member of staff, and while in therapy had never said anything that could be construed as an allegation of abuse. The social worker was immediately reinstated; but by then she was ill and had by and large not worked since the suspension. She claimed loss of earnings and damages for personal injury caused by breach of contract; she now suffered from clinical depression caused by the suspension.

The court held that it was quite proper for the local authority to investigate and make inquiries; but it did not necessarily follow that a member of staff, who may have been implicated in the risk to the vulnerable person, had to be suspended. The question should be whether, in the individual circumstances, it was reasonable and proper to do so. The court thought not. The strategy meeting had itself recognised that the information was 'difficult to evaluate' and to describe it as an allegation of abuse was putting it 'far too high'. The court also asked whether there were not other alternatives, such as a short period of leave or a transfer to other useful work.

Instead there had been a 'knee-jerk' reaction. The local authority had seriously damaged the relationship of trust and confidence between employee and employer – a relationship implied into contracts of employment. The claimant was entitled to damages (*Gogay v Hertfordshire CC*).

In some instances, by contrast, the courts might be reluctant to intervene, particularly where a potential remedy is available through appeal to a care standards tribunal. In one case, concerning the 'consultancy index' (the forerunner of the Protection of Children Act (POCA) list – the children's equivalent of the POVA – the court declined to intervene when a local authority referred a care worker to the Secretary of State. The court held that, even if the care worker had been treated unfairly, the referral was not necessarily unlawful. On the facts of the case, the court held that the care standards tribunal was a better means of dealing with the case than the courts (*M v Bromley LBC*). In the event, the tribunal subsequently allowed the man's appeal because of the clear unreliability of the allegations made against him, and ordered that his name be removed from the list (*M v Secretary of State for Health*).

Other examples, although not related to the adult POVA list, also serve as reminders that care must be taken not to act unfairly to the detriment of care workers – for instance, as in this local ombudsman investigation:

**Unsubstantiated allegations and information disclosure procedures.** A local authority disclosed information to a woman's employer concerning unsubstantiated allegations made by a third party of financial abuse by the woman of a vulnerable adult. The local ombudsman investigated; the council agreed a settlement whereby it would send a letter of apology, make a token payment of £250, seek the woman's permission to send copies of the apology to her employer, review its policy and procedures on disclosure of information and inform her of the outcome. The local authority then delayed in changing its policy and procedures; and its failure to make any contact with the woman about this or with the ombudsman was inexcusable and maladministration (*Kirklees MBC 2002*).

Sometimes libel proceedings might result:

**Malicious actions of review team on child abuse.** The two claimants were nursery nurses. They had been suspended and then dismissed for gross misconduct for child abuse. They were acquitted at trial. The council anyway investigated and set up an independent review. The review concluded the two were guilty of serious abuse; 743 copies of the report were distributed by the council. The claimants brought libel proceedings. The judge found that the review team had acted maliciously by making a number of claims it would have known were untrue. The terms of appointment, and the methodology, of the review team were wholly unsuited to the task in hand. Elementary safeguards for the accused had been omitted, and the principles of natural justice had been overlooked. The claim succeeded against the review team, but not against the council (*Lillie v Newcastle CC*).

## 17.4 CRIMINAL RECORD CERTIFICATES

Under the Care Standards Act 2000 and associated regulations, care providers must obtain criminal record certificates from the Criminal Records Bureau (CRB) in respect of certain types of worker under the Police Act 1997. For example, such certificates must be obtained by care providers under the Domiciliary Care Agencies Regulations 2002 (SI 2002/3214, schedule 2) under the Care Home Regulations 2001 (SI 2001/3965, schedule 2) and under the Adult Placement Schemes (England) Regulations 2004 (SI 2004/2070, schedule 3).

An application for a standard or enhanced disclosure must be countersigned by a person registered with the CRB. However, it is possible for persons or bodies not so registered to find out such details, if they ask another registered body to countersign an application on their behalf. Another body acting in this way is known as an 'umbrella body' (CRB 2001, para 4).

### 17.4.1 LEVELS OF DISCLOSURE

The Police Act 1997 provides for three different levels of disclosure. The first is basic disclosure, which will contain details of convictions held in central police records that are not 'spent' under the Rehabilitation of Offenders Act 1974 (s.112). However, the CRB does not, at time of writing, issue such disclosures.

The second is standard disclosure, which contains details of spent and unspent convictions, but also cautions, reprimands, warnings, recorded centrally by the police. The disclosure will also indicate whether the person is on the POVA list (see above) and thus unsuitable to work with vulnerable adults (s.113).

The third level is enhanced disclosure, which contains the same information as a standard disclosure, but it can also contain additional 'soft', non-conviction information held in local police records – that a chief police officer considers may be relevant. The legislation states that the Secretary of State must request the chief police officer to provide any information relevant as to the person's suitability that the chief police officer thinks (a) ought to be included in the certificate; or (b) ought to be provided but not included in the certificate in the interests of the prevention or detection of crime (s.115).

### 17.4.2 ENHANCED DISCLOSURE: VULNERABLE ADULTS

In respect of community care services for adults, enhanced disclosure applies to workers who occupy a position involving regular care for, training, supervising or being in sole charge of people aged 18 or over – and enables the person to have regular contact in the course of his or her duties with a vulnerable adult. Under the legislation (Police Act 1997, s.115; SI 2002/446):

- A vulnerable adult is defined as a person receiving certain services, because of a certain condition resulting in disability.
- The services are listed as accommodation and nursing or personal care in a care home; personal care or nursing or support to live independently in a person's own

home; any services provided by an independent hospital, independent clinic, independent medical agency or NHS body; social care services; services provided in an establishment catering for people with learning difficulties.

- The conditions necessitating the provision of such services are listed as (a) learning or physical disability; (b) physical or mental illness, chronic or otherwise, including drugs or alcohol addiction; (c) reduction in physical or mental capacity.
- Disability is described as:
  - dependency on others in the performance of (or assistance in performance of) basic physical functions
  - severe impairment in ability to communicate with others
  - impairment in a person's ability to protect himself or herself from assault, abuse or neglect.

Nothwithstanding this clear statutory authority for disclosure of information, the question has arisen in the courts as to what extent a presumption of disclosure now applies to the police when providing the 'soft', non-conviction information – and how this might relate to the common law of confidentiality and human rights. The courts have held that the duty under s.115 of the Police Act 1997 has effectively displaced the common law presumption of non-disclosure:

**Enhanced criminal record certificate and soft information.** An enhanced criminal record certificate was issued under s.115 of the Police Act 1997 concerning an Afro-Caribbean social worker with no convictions. Certain 'soft' information was included, provided by the relevant local police force. This stated that it had been alleged that in December 2001 the social worker indecently exposed himself to a female petrol station attendant. It was alleged that he repeated the offence in May 2002. He was arrested and interviewed; he stated that he did not think he had committed the offence but he was suffering from stress and anxiety at the time. At that time he was employed by a Child Care company and was charged with two counts of indecent exposure. However, the alleged victim failed to identify the suspect during a covert identification parade. The case was subsequently discontinued.

In the High Court, the Chief Constable's decision to provide this information in the certificate was found to be unlawful, essentially on the grounds that the balance, in favour of disclosure, had been wrongly struck.

The High Court decision was subsequently overturned in the Court of Appeal. In particular the latter found that the common law principle of confidentiality, though generally entailing a presumption of non-disclosure, did not apply to the present case. The statutory framework created by the Police Act 1997 meant that the position was more positively in favour of disclosure – which had to be made unless there was a good reason for not doing so. Furthermore, the judge had also been wrong in stating that the police should have informed the man before disclosure and have given him an opportunity to make representations. This would place too heavy a burden on the police. As the information was being made available in accordance with the law, there was no breach of article 8 (right to respect for privacy) of the European Convention on Human Rights (R(X) v Chief Constable of West Midlands Police).

## 17.5 INTERVENTIONS

When abuse (or simply neglect without accompanying abuse) is identified or suspected, there is sometimes uncertainty about what interventions might be appropriate to protect the person involved. The general position is that a statutory intervention must be used – that is, an intervention based on a duty or power given in legislation. The intervention might be one based in social services legislation; it might alternatively be based elsewhere, for instance, in environmental health, criminal justice or family law.

If the person being abused is refusing assistance, further questions arise about which statutory interventions can be used irrespective of a person's wishes or ability to consent. For instance, in the case of a person lacking the capacity to decide, or consent to, the relevant matters, an additional intervention comes in the form of acting in common law, out of necessity, in that person's best interests – and if necessary seeking a declaration, or occasionally an injunction, from the courts in the exercise of their 'inherent jurisdiction' (see 18.8).

Even if a potentially appropriate intervention does exist, a further question might arise as to whether it is likely to achieve the desired outcome. For instance, a crime might have been committed but the Crown Prosecution Service (CPS) still has to decide whether it is in the public interest to prosecute.

**Prosecution for attempted murder of wife.** A distressed elderly man attempted to kill both himself and his wife following a dispute with a local authority over home care arrangements and manual handling. His wife suffered from Alzheimer's disease, was doubly incontinent and immobile. A prosecution for attempted murder was brought; the judge criticised the CPS for bringing the case, questioning whether it had been in the public interest to do so (R v Bouldstridge).

Furthermore, although witnesses can be compelled to give evidence, the CPS might weigh up in individual cases whether such compulsion is likely to succeed. For example, some reluctant prosecution witnesses, particularly in cases of domestic abuse (e.g. wife and husband, father and son), 'change their story' at the last moment and become in effect witnesses hostile to the prosecution.

In the following case, there was only so much the local authority could do; the judge set out what could be expected:

**Assisted suicide and adult protection procedures.** A woman was suffering from cerebellar ataxia; the condition was incurable and irreversible; it attacked that part of the brain controlling the body's motor functions. She had become increasingly disabled. She wished to be assisted to commit suicide; her family was initially opposed to this. Now, reluctantly, her family had decided to support her wishes. Her husband informed the local authority, which had been providing extensive support for his wife, that he was arranging to take her to Switzerland where assisted suicide is not a criminal offence.

The local authority applied to the courts for exercise of the inherent jurisdiction; an injunction was initially granted restraining the husband from removing his wife to Switzerland. The court then subsequently considered the situation. It concluded that the adult protection duties of the local authorities were as follows:

- to investigate the position of the vulnerable adult to consider her true position and intention
- to consider whether she was legally competent to make and carry out her decision and intention
- to consider whether (or what) influence may have been operating on her position and intention and to ensure that she had all the relevant information and knew all available options
- to consider whether to invoke the inherent jurisdiction of the courts to decide about the issue of her competence
- if she was not competent, to provide assistance in her best interests
- if she was competent, to allow her in any lawful way to give effect to her decision, although this should not preclude advice or assistance being given about what are perceived to be her best interests
- to inform the police if there were reasonable grounds for suspecting that a criminal offence would be involved
- in very exceptional circumstances only, to seek an injunction from the courts using s.222 of the Local Government Act 1972.

By the time of the hearing, it had become quite clear that the woman had legal competence to take the decision. The court concluded that the local authority's duties extended no further than the above list; and that the authority had no obligation to seek a continuation of an injunction under s.222; criminal justice agencies had all the powers. For its part, unless it was under an obligation, the local authority anyway did not wish to do so.

Nor would the court, of its own motion, continue the injunction where noone else with the necessary standing was seeking such an order, where the criminal justice agencies had the requisite knowledge and power, and where the effect of the injunction would be to 'deny a right to a seriously disabled but competent person that cannot be exercised herself by reason only of her physical disability' (Re Z).

## 17.5.1 NATIONAL ASSISTANCE ACT 1948, S.47: REMOVAL OF PEOPLE FROM HOME

Under s.47 of the National Assistance Act 1948, local authorities (district councils or borough councils) can by magistrate's order remove to institutional care people who:

- 'are suffering from grave chronic disease or, being aged, infirm or physically incapacitated, are living in insanitary conditions; and'
- 'are unable to devote to themselves, and are not receiving from other persons, proper care and attention'.

A medical officer of health (i.e. community physician) must certify to the authority that removal is necessary either in his or her own best interests, or for prevention of injury to the health of, or serious nuisance to, other people.

The authority can apply to a magistrates' court for an order that may authorise the person's detention for up to three months; although this may be extended by court order. Seven days' notice is required to be given to the person before a court can consider the application. The period of notice can be dispensed with under powers in the National Assistance (Amendment) Act 1951, if it is certified both by the medical officer of health and another registered medical practitioner that in their opinion it is necessary in the interests of the person that he or she be removed without delay.

However, the person does not have to be mentally incapacitated or mentally disordered for s.47 to operate. Thus, there exists a view that s.47 of the 1948 Act is simply contrary in principle to the Human Rights Act 1998. This would be on the basis that neglect is not a ground on which people may be deprived of their liberty under a.5 of the European Convention on Human Rights. The article refers to people of unsound mind, alcoholics, drug addicts or vagrants – but not to people who neglect themselves or are neglected, who have the mental capacity to decide where and how they want to live (and so are not of unsound mind), and who are not otherwise diagnosed as mentally disordered.

For instance, medical opinion is reportedly divided about intervention in the case of people who suffer from so-called Diogenes syndrome, which is characterised by extreme self-neglect, domestic squalor, social withdrawal and apathy and tendency to hoard rubbish. They often refuse assistance and have many physical problems including nutritional deficiencies, but may be content and survive without external support. Many might not be suffering from mental disorder, but have rejected normal standards of behaviour (Persaud 2003, pp.304–6).

Whether s.47 would be held to be contrary to human rights is not clear, given the case of *HM v Switzerland*, heard before the European Court of Human Rights (the United Kingdom courts must take account of, though not necessarily follow, the European Court's judgments).

**Removing a person from her own home.** Under the Swiss Civil Code, a person can be deprived of liberty on grounds of mental weakness or neglect.

A woman in her eighties was living at home, was fairly infirm and had leg sores, and was nearly blind but capable of making decisions for herself. She was receiving a home help service from a voluntary organisation. This service was withdrawn because of difficulties in the home – the son opening the door skimpily dressed and only after a delay, rubbish around the house impeding the home help workers, unheated rooms, chaos in the woman's bedroom, etc. The family did not respond to a request to ameliorate these conditions.

The local authority ordered that the woman be removed, against her will, for an unlimited period to a nursing home on the ground of serious neglect. She was not placed in the locked ward of the nursing home; she had freedom of movement and had social contacts with the outside world. The woman complained, arguing that she was able to wash and dress herself, that her son (also an invalid) could cook for her and that she did not want him left alone. The local authority disputed this. Both the Appeals Commission and Federal Court upheld the local authority's action.

She was removed on grounds both of neglect and 'vagrancy' (an article 5 term) and unsoundness of mind. Yet she had never been examined by a medical expert in respect of the latter issue, although one of the members of the Appeals Commission was a medical expert.

The European Court held that article 5 was not engaged because she had not been deprived of her liberty. This conclusion was based on the fact that she had been placed in the home in her own interests in order to provide her with the necessary medical care, as well as satisfactory living conditions and hygiene (*HM v Switzerland*).

Nevertheless, one of the judges strongly dissented in *HM v Switzerland*. He believed that article 5 had been breached on various grounds. Most important, and decisive for this dissenting judge, was the fact that the finding by the Appeals Commission that she effectively lacked capacity had been challenged by the woman and never confirmed by a medical expert; whilst the Federal Court had declined to examine the issue on the grounds that serious neglect would anyway justify removal.

### 17.5.1.1 Protection of property: s.48 National Assistance Act 1948

A duty to protect property arises if:

- a person is admitted to hospital, admitted to residential accommodation under s.21 of the 1948 Act, or removed under s.47 of the 1948 Act
- it appears to the local social services authority that there is danger of loss of, or damage to, any of the person's movable property by reason of his or her temporary or permanent inability to protect or deal with the property
- no other suitable arrangements have been or are being made.

If these conditions are satisfied, then the local authority must take reasonable steps to prevent or mitigate the loss or damage. The authority has the power, at all reasonable times, to enter the person's place of residence and to deal with any movable property in a reasonable way to prevent or mitigate loss or damage. The local authority can recover reasonable expenses either from the person concerned or anybody else liable to maintain him or her (National Assistance Act 1948, s.48).

Examples of reasonable steps might include, for example, securing the premises, informing the police about an empty property, taking an inventory, turning off utilities, disposing of perishable food, and arranging for pets to be cared for (Jones 2004, para D1–088).

## 17.5.2 MENTAL HEALTH ACT INTERVENTIONS

Where mental disorder is in issue, adult protection may be served by certain interventions under the Mental Health Act 1983. For instance, such interventions may serve to break or prevent a cycle of abuse or neglect. However, such grounds of intervention must be used properly and in this respect it will be noted that the threshold for intervention varies. For example, the grounds for s.2 detention include not just specified mental disorders, but also the wide ranging 'any other disorder or disability of mind'. In contrast, s.3 detention is limited to those more specific mental disorders. Awareness of higher and lower thresholds could mean the difference between intervention and no intervention. Nevertheless, such drastic interventions can only be exercised if the relevant statutory grounds are made out.

**Note.** In September 2004, a draft Mental Health Bill was published, which will, if it becomes law, replace most of the Mental Health Act 1983. Amongst other changes, it introduces a simplified definition of mental disorder – as an 'impairment of or a disturbance in the functioning of the mind or brain resulting from any disability or disorder of the mind or brain'. It also allows for formal powers to be used in the community as well as in hospital (DH 2004k).

### 17.5.2.1 Mental Health Act 1983: interventions and mental disorder

Mental disorder is defined in s.1 of the Mental Health Act 1983:

- **Mental disorder** is defined as mental illness, arrested or incomplete development of mind, psychopathic disorder and any other disorder or disability of mind and 'mentally disordered' shall be construed accordingly.
- **Severe mental impairment** means a state of arrested or incomplete development of mind, which includes severe impairment of intelligence and social functioning and is associated with abnormally aggressive or seriously irresponsible conduct on the part of the person concerned.
- **Mental impairment** means a state of arrested or incomplete development of mind (not amounting to severe mental impairment) which includes significant impairment of intelligence and social functioning and is associated with abnormally aggressive or seriously irresponsible conduct on the part of the person concerned.
- **Psychopathic disorder** means a persistent disorder or disability of mind (whether or not including significant impairment of intelligence) which results in abnormally aggressive or seriously irresponsible conduct on the part of the person concerned.

### 17.5.2.2 Limited detention for assessment (and treatment)

Under s.2 of the 1983 Act, an application for admission for assessment is made on two grounds, both of which must be made out:

- The 'patient' is suffering from mental disorder of a nature or degree that warrants his or her detention in a hospital for assessment (or for assessment followed by medical treatment) for at least a limited period (up to 28 days).
- He or she ought to be detained in this way in the interests of his own health or safety or with a view to the protection of other persons.

Thus, the following detention, although clearly designed for the protection of both mother and baby, was held to be unlawful:

**Unlawful detention.** A woman in the late stages of pregnancy was suffering from pre-eclampsia; there was a risk to the lives of both herself and the unborn baby. She fully understood the potential risks and clearly rejected medical intervention; she wanted the baby to be born 'naturally'. She was then sectioned (unlawfully as it turned out) under s.2 of the Mental Health Act 1983. This was because although mental disorder was present (depression), it was not of a type that warranted detention in hospital (*R v Collins, ex p S*).

However, it is arguable that the breadth of s.2 (mental disorder including 'any other disorder or disability of mind') could allow detention of a person with a learning disability even in the absence of abnormally aggressive or seriously irresponsible conduct – compared to s.3 (detention) or s.7 (guardianship), both of which require such conduct (Jones 2004a, p.29).

### 17.5.2.3 Longer term detention for treatment

Under s.3 of the 1983 Act, an application for admission for treatment is made on the following grounds, all of which must be made out in each case:

- The patient is suffering from mental illness, severe mental impairment, psychopathic disorder or mental impairment and his mental disorder is of a nature or degree which makes it appropriate for him or her to receive medical treatment in a hospital.
- In the case of psychopathic disorder or mental impairment, the treatment is likely to alleviate or prevent a deterioration of his condition.
- It is necessary for the health or safety of the patient or for the protection of other people that he should receive such treatment – and that it cannot be provided unless he is detained.

### 17.5.2.4 Entry and inspection of premises

Under s.115 of the Mental Health Act 1983, an approved social worker of a local social services authority may enter and inspect premises (not a hospital) in the area of that authority, if he or she has reasonable cause to believe that a mentally disordered person is living there and is not 'under proper care'.

This power to enter and inspect applies at all reasonable times after the social worker has produced, if asked to do so, some duly authenticated document showing that he or she is such a social worker. Although s.115 does not allow for force to be used, obstruction could constitute an offence under s.129 of the 1983 Act.

### 17.5.2.5 Warrant for search and removal

Under s.135 of the Mental Health Act 1983, a justice of the peace may issue a warrant authorising a constable to enter, using force if necessary, premises in order, if it is thought fit, to remove a person to a place of safety. This would be with a view to making an application under the Mental Health Act 1983 or other arrangements for care and treatment.

Such a warrant may be issued if it appears to the justice of the peace, from information received on oath by an approved social worker, that there is reasonable cause to suspect that a person believed to be suffering from mental disorder (a) has been or is being ill-treated, neglected or not kept under proper control; or (b) is unable to care for himself or herself and is living alone.

### 17.5.2.6 Removal of a mentally disordered person from a public place

Under s.136 of the Mental Act 1983, a constable may remove to a place of safety a person appearing to be suffering from mental disorder from a place to which the public have access. The constable may do this if (a) the person appears to be in immediate need of care and control; (b) the constable thinks it necessary in the interests of the person or other people. The person may then be detained for up to 72 hours in the place of safety, so that he or she can be examined by a medical practitioner and interviewed by an approved social worker, and so that necessary arrangements for treatment or care can be made.

### 17.5.2.7 Guardianship and the inherent jurisdiction

Under s.7 of the Mental Health Act 1983, a guardianship order can be made for a patient aged 16 years or over on the following grounds:

- that he or she is suffering from mental disorder in terms of mental illness, severe mental impairment, mental impairment or psychopathic disorder
- that the mental disorder is of a nature of degree that warrants his or her reception into guardianship
- that this is necessary in the interests of the welfare of the patient – or for the protection of other persons that the patient be so received.

Under s.8 of the Act, the guardian (either the local social services authority or other person) has the power:

- to require the patient to reside at a place specified by the authority or person named as guardian
- to require the patient to attend at specified places and times for medical treatment, occupation, education or training
- to require access to the patient to be given, at any place where the patient is residing, to any registered medical practitioner, approved social worker or other specified person.

Guardianship is a potentially useful tool in adult protection. Although there is no explicit power in the Act to convey the person to the place of residence, there is a power to return him or her, if he or she has absconded (Mental Health Act 1983, s.18). However, in practice, persistent non-cooperation generally might render guardianship ineffective. The courts have previously held that there is anyway an implied duty under s.7 of the 1983 Act to act generally for the person's welfare in ways not explicitly referred to in s.8 (*R v Kent CC, ex p Marston*: Court of Appeal stage).

Furthermore, in respect of some people with learning disabilities, for whom guardianship might be desirable, it is simply not available. This is because the definitions in the Act of impairment and severe mental impairment, which would apply to people with learning disabilities, include the requirement that the impairment be associated with abnormally aggressive or seriously irresponsible conduct. This requirement is likely to exclude many people with learning disabilities, since the courts have taken a restrictive approach to the term serious irresponsibility (*Re F (Adult Patient)*) and effectively excluded passive tolerance of neglect as evidence of serious irresponsibility (see discussion in Jones 2003, para 1–027). Thus neither a young person's wish to go home against a background of possible sexual exploitation (*Re F (A Child)*), nor a person's lack of road sense (*Newham LBC v BS*), constituted seriously irresponsible conduct.

This accounts for the courts being increasingly asked instead to exercise their inherent jurisdiction to declare where the best interests of people with learning disabilities lie:

**Protecting a young woman with learning disabilities.** A young woman, 18 years old, was in the care of the local authority. She had a level of intellectual functioning of a child aged five to eight years old. The local authority wished to control contact with her family and require her to live in local authority accommodation. The daughter had expressed a wish to return to her family. The local authority was concerned, because its view of the home situation was one of chronic neglect, lack of minimum standards of hygiene and cleanliness in the home, serious lack of adequate parenting, and worrying exposure to those engaged in sexual exploitation and possible sexual abuse (seven other younger children are now in the care of the local authority). The mother opposed the local authority, arguing that it had no legal power to supervise and restrict contact, and was breaching human rights.

The court had already ruled, when the woman was 17 years old, that guardianship under the Mental Health Act was not appropriate. This was because there was no abnormally aggressive or seriously irresponsible conduct; the local authority had argued the latter simply because the daughter wanted to return home to her mother. Yet the court could not characterise the wish of a child in care to return home as seriously irresponsible (Re F (A Child).

On the assumption that the daughter lacked the capacity to decide the issue for herself, the court held that it had the inherent jurisdiction to make a declaration as to the daughter's best interests in the terms sought by the local authority. In addition, article 8 of the European Convention of Human Rights would not be breached, since it contained not a right to family life, but a right to respect for family life. This meant an entitlement (within limits) to what was benign and positive in family life (Re F (Adult Patient)).

The inherent jurisdiction had likewise to be exercised in another adult protection related case, where guardianship was not available:

**Determining where an adult is to live.** A 19-year-old man had a chromosomal abnormality which resulted in him having the developmental level of a 2-year-old; he also had physical disabilities. He had always been cared for by his father. He had previously been placed on the child protection register, following concerns about him not being bathed properly and kept out of school. (The father blamed the local authority for the bathing issue, arguing that it refused to pay for a walk-in shower.)

Whilst still under 18, he had been physically injured by his father when the latter had lost his temper and placed in respite care. Now he was 18 years old, the local authority had brought the proceedings to determine where he should live. It argued that he should not live with his father because of the risk of physical and emotional abuse; that the father could not work cooperatively with the authority; that he should live in a specialist nursing home; and that he should have supervised contact with his father away from the father's home.

The court had to draw up a balance sheet weighing up potential benefits and disadvantages of the options. It had also to recognise the importance of family life under article 8 of the European Convention, whether (in the case of a mentally incapacitated person) the child is under 18 or over 18 years. Furthermore, other things being equal, the parent in such a situation will normally be the appropriate person to care for the child, rather than a public authority, however well intentioned.

Nevertheless, in this case the result of the balance sheet exercise pointed in favour of the local authority. Although the father was motivated by love and concern, he had buckled under the strain; had failed to accept responsibility for the incident in which he had injured his son; and there was a long history of disputes between him and the council due to his unreasonable demands (Re S (Adult patient)).

Thus it can be seen that relevant local authority staff need to be acquainted with the rules concerning guardianship:

**Inappropriate pursuit of guardianship.** A complaint was made to the local ombudsman, following a protracted dispute between the local authority and the family of a man with learning disabilities, about where he should live. The ombudsman criticised the local authority's persistent attempts to pursue guardianship. This was despite medical opinion each time that the conditions for guardianship were not met, in particular the absence of abnormally aggressive or seriously irresponsible conduct (Bury MBC 2000).

Neither the 1983 Act, nor the main Department of Health guidance on charging for residential accommodation (CRAG 2004), refers to residential accommodation provided for a person under a guardianship order (under ss.7–8 of the Mental Health Act 1983). It may therefore be unclear as to whether a person, subject to guardianship and required to live in a care home under s.8, should be exempt from charges or not.

The question might well hinge on whether the accommodation is to be regarded as actually provided under s.8 itself. If so, charges would probably not be lawful. If, however, it is merely the requirement to reside somewhere that comes under s.8, whereas the accommodation itself is to be regarded as provided under the National Assistance Act 1948, then charging might be lawful.

### 17.5.2.8 Informal mental health patients

There is nothing in the 1983 Act to prevent a person who needs treatment for mental disorder from being admitted to hospital without formal detention, nor from remaining in hospital informally following any formal detention (Mental Health Act 1983, s.131). The English courts have further held that in the case of a mentally incapable, but compliant, person, it is not necessary that he or she be formally sectioned under the 1983 Act. The common law of best interests and necessity suffices. However, the following court case exposes the consequences, namely the lack of safeguards for such informal patients:

**Removal to hospital.** A 48-year-old man had been autistic since birth. He was unable to speak and required 24-hour care, and unable to go outside alone. He had no ability to communicate consent or dissent to treatment or to express preferences as to where he should live. He was frequently agitated, had no sense of danger and had a history of self-harm. From the age of 13, for over 30 years, he was resident at a hospital. He was then discharged on a trial basis into the community, going to live with paid carers.

One day he was attending a day centre and became agitated and was banging his head against a wall, and hitting his head with his fists. The day centre got in touch with a local doctor who came and administered a sedative; the social worker with overall responsibility for him was contacted and recommended that he be taken by ambulance to accident and emergency. There, after further agitation, a psychiatrist assessed that he needed inpatient treatment. However, it was decided that he could be admitted informally, rather than making use of s.2 or s.3 of the 1983 Act, because he appeared to be fully compliant and did not resist admission. He subsequently remained in hospital for several months on this informal basis.

The House of Lords, overruling the Court of Appeal, held that it was permissible to admit informally to hospital (s.131 of the Mental Health Act 1983) patients who lacked the capacity to consent but who did not positively object. The court stated that the removal, care and treatment of the person had been in his best interests and was justified by the common law doctrine of necessity, which was not excluded by the provisions of the 1983 Act. Nevertheless, one of the law lords pointed out that this conclusion was not wholly satisfactory, since it meant that the formal safeguards contained in the Mental Health Act did not apply to this particular class of vulnerable informal patient (*R v Bournewood Community and Mental Health NHS Trust, ex p L*).

The case was then taken to the European Court of Human Rights, which found that both article 5.1 and 5.4 had been breached. The former (5.1: concerning lawful deprivation of liberty), because of the arbitrary nature, without fixed procedural rules, of his detention for a period of over three months (at which point he was actually formally detained). The latter (5.4: concerning entitlement to a speedy decision as to the lawfulness of detention) was also breached (*HL v United Kingdom*). The health service ombudsman had also, between the House of Lords and European Court decisions, separately criticised the prolonged 'detention' in this case, finding that the man should have been discharged back to the family the same, or following, day (*Bournewood Community and Mental Health NHS Trust 2002*). At the time of writing it is unclear whether the provisions contained in the Mental Capacity Bill 2004 (application to a new Court of Protection to challenge health and welfare decisions) will be sufficient to meet the European Court's concerns in the *HL* case.

In the light of the judgment of the European Court, the Department of Health issued guidance in December 2004 stating that it would be bringing forward proposals for appropriate procedural safeguards. However, until these were in place, the guidance makes clear that to provide care or treatment (whether in hospital or other residential settings) for a mentally incapacitated patient, amounting to a deprivation of liberty, is unlawful unless the person is detained under the Mental Health Act 1983. It suggests, amongst other things, that:

- the NHS and local authorities should ensure they have systems in place to assess whether a person is being deprived of his or her liberty;
- wherever possible to avoid situations in which professionals take 'full and effective control' of a person's care and liberty;
- decisions should be taken in a structured way;
- there should be effective, documented care planning;
- there should be consideration of alternatives to hospital admission or residential care, and that any restrictions placed on the person are kept to the minimum necessary in all the circumstances;
- both assessment of capacity and care plan should be kept under review, and an independent element to this may well be helpful;
- if it is concluded that there is no way of providing appropriate care without a deprivation of liberty occurring, then consideration should be given to use of the formal powers of detention under the 1983 Act.

However, the guidance also includes a note of caution, pointing out that not all patients, subject to restrictions amounting to deprivation of liberty, can be detained lawfully under the 1983 Act. For instance, their mental disorder might not warrant detention in hospital. In addition, there are dangers in using the Act simply to be on the 'safe side'; formal detention may be perceived as a stigma. Further, significant increased use of the 1983 Act would place considerable pressure on local authority approved social workers, second opinion appointed doctors (SOADs) and on the operation of Mental Health Review Tribunals (DH 2004n). The guidance merely reflects the legal uncertainty.

The lack of safeguards for such compliant patients lacking capacity was also illustrated in a local ombudsman investigation, which revealed that a young woman with learning disabilities had effectively been wrongly detained in hospital, informally, for some ten years:

**Woman wrongly kept in hospital for ten years**. At the age of 18 years, a woman with severe learning difficulties was received into guardianship by the local authority; she resided at a care home. Following concerns about her behaviour, she was admitted in March 1990 to hospital under s.3 of the Mental Health Act 1983; this compulsory detention replaced the guardianship order. Six months later in September 1990, the consultant psychiatrist wrote to the local authority, stating that a further stay in hospital was not warranted; the s.3 detention ceased. However, the local authority failed to put in place any plan for discharge because it was concerned about the cost of any such placement, and also argued with the NHS about who should be responsible for the funding.

The woman finally left hospital in 2001, having spent over ten years as an informal, compliant but incapacitated, patient. As a consequence, aftercare duties under s.117 of the 1983 Act were never triggered and the local authority never tested on its potential duties under s.117. The ombudsman concluded that if it had been, the authority would have 'fallen far short' of its responsibilities.

The evidence suggested that the woman did not need to be a long-stay patient. A consequence of this unnecessary stay in hospital was that the local authority had neither investigated, nor prevented, the abuse the woman suffered at the hands of other patients during her inappropriate hospital stay. For example, as early as 1991, a local authority mental health management officer wrote to the director of social services about the woman's deteriorating welfare, bites on her legs inflicted by another patient, and her shoddy clothing.

The ombudsman found the local authority had failed in its duties, notwithstanding legal uncertainties during some of the period about NHS 'continuing care' responsibilities; and recommended £20,000 compensation (*Wakefield MDC 2003*).

## 17.5.3 ENVIRONMENTAL HEALTH INTERVENTIONS

In the context of adult protection, gaining entry into domestic premises (via an appropriate legal channel) in cases of neglect is not necessarily easy. However, local authority environmental health departments do have various statutory powers to enter premises.

### 17.5.3.1 Environmental Protection Act 1990

Under the Environmental Protection Act 1990 (EPA), local authority powers of entry apply in respect of statutory nuisances. On the production of authority, an authorised person can enter premises at any reasonable time to ascertain whether a statutory nuisance exists, or to take action or execute work authorised under part 3 of the 1990 Act. In the case of residential property, then 24 hours' notice is required, unless it is an emergency such as danger to life or health (EPA 1990, schedule 3).

Statutory nuisance is defined as including premises that are in a state prejudicial to health or nuisance, smoke, fumes or gases emitted from premises so as to be prejudicial to health or a nuisance, any accumulation or deposit prejudicial to health or a nuisance, any animal kept in such a place or manner as to be prejudicial to health or a nuisance, and noise emitted from premises so as to be prejudicial to health or a nuisance (EPA 1990, s.79).

A local authority has a duty to serve an abatement notice if a statutory nuisance exists (EPA 1990, s.80). If the notice is not complied with, the local authority may itself abate the nuisance and recover expenses reasonably incurred (s.81).

### 17.5.3.2 Public Health Act 1936

Under the Public Health Act 1936, local authority powers of entry apply in respect of certain public health issues referred to in the Act (s.287). These include filthy, unwholesome, verminous premises (s.83); verminous person or clothing (including removal of person) (s.85); cleaning or destroying filthy or verminous articles (s.84). Also there is a power to require vacation of premises during fumigation (Public Health Act 1961, s.36). The usefulness of such powers, but also the need to exercise them carefully, was demonstrated in the following local ombudsman case:

**Cleaning of premises under the Public Health Act 1936.** A man was in poor health with limited ability to care for himself. His home became dirty and cluttered to the point where it required thorough cleaning in order to prevent a health and safety risk to himself and his care workers. His sister got in touch with the local social services authority; it then liaised with the environmental health department. Under s.83 of the Public Health Act 1936 the latter proposed to clean the flat, and explained to the sister that it would do the work and recover the cost from her brother. However, the council sent a very much larger bill (over £1100) than the cost (£300) the sister claimed had originally been advised by the local authority.

The ombudsman concluded that the council had not been clear enough in its explanation; the bill had also been wrongly calculated (it included VAT in error; and an inflated amount for environmental health officer time had been included). He recommended that the bill be corrected and then reduced by £300, that the sister receive £200 in recognition of her time and trouble, that the council review the wording of its letters about such work and charges for it, and that it check that all bills for such work carried out since January 2003 had been correctly calculated (*Ealing LBC 2004*).

## 17.5.4 POLICE POWERS OF ENTRY

A constable may enter premises in order, amongst other things, to recapture any person whatever who is unlawfully at large and whom he is pursuing – or to save life or limb or prevent serious damage to property (Police and Criminal Evidence Act 1984, s.17).

## 17.5.5 INTERVENTIONS ON GROUNDS OF NECESSITY AND BEST INTERESTS

In the adult protection context, and failing an appropriate statutory intervention, a local social services authority may sometimes have to fall back on the common law of necessity and best interests. This would be in order to intervene in a particular situation involving a person who lacks capacity to decide or to act in relation to the relevant matter. Sometimes it might involve applying to the courts to exercise their inherent jurisdiction in respect of people lacking the relevant capacity (see 17.5.2.7).

17.5.6 GAS AND ELECTRICITY OPERATORS

There are some powers of entry associated with utility companies: for instance, gas operators have such powers under the Gas Act 1995 (schedule 2B, paras 20–28) and Rights of
Entry (Gas and Electricity Boards) Act 1954.

## 17.6 CRIME AND DISORDER STRATEGIES

Under the Crime and Disorder Act 1998 (ss.5–7), 'responsible authorities' have certain
obligations. They are the local authority (county or unitary) and the following (any part
of whose area comes within that of the local authority: chief officer of police, police
authority, NHS primary care trust, and fire authority). These authorities must formulate
and implement a strategy for the reduction of crime and disorder and for combating the
misuse of drugs in the area. Guidance has been issued to primary care trusts about their
responsibilities (DH 2004j).

## 17.7 MULTI-AGENCY PUBLIC PROTECTION ARRANGEMENTS (MAPPA)

Under the Criminal Justice Act 2003, a duty is placed on 'responsible authorities' (chief
of police, probation board and on the Prison Service) to establish arrangements for assessing and managing risks in relation to certain offenders. The duty applies to certain specified categories of violent and sex offenders, as well to other people who have committed
offences and who the responsible authority considers pose a risk of serious harm to the
public.

In addition, other specified organisations must cooperate insofar as such cooperation
would be compatible with the exercise of their functions under any other legislation.
These organisations include local councils with social services responsibilities, primary
care trusts, other NHS trusts, strategic health authorities, Jobcentres Plus, local youth
offending teams, registered social landlords that accommodate MAPPA offenders, local
housing authorities, local education authorities, electronic monitoring providers (LASSL
(2004)3). Such cooperation may include the exchange of information (Criminal Justice
Act 2003, ss.325–327). Extensive guidance has been published (NPS 54/2004).

Department of Health guidance explains that there is a three-level structure of case
referral of people presenting a serious risk of harm. The first level involves a single agency
only, normally the Probation Service. The second will involve more than one agency because, even if the risk is high, management may not be complex. The third, dealing with a
few critical cases, will trigger meetings of the Multi-Agency Public Protection Panel
(MAPPP) meetings – in the case of the highest risks or highly problematic risk
management issues (LASSL(2004)3).

The question of information exchange has given rise, unsurprisingly, to legal dispute
about confidentiality and human rights. In the following case the courts held that a presumption against disclosure still obtained (see 19.3):

**Disclosure of information to manager of sheltered accommodation.** A 66-year-old man killed his wife. Six years later he was due to be released on licence on the recommendation of the Parole Board. Conditions were not set. The man wished to purchase and live in a flat in a sheltered accommodation complex. Under Multi-Agency Public Protection Panel Procedures (then under the Criminal Justice and Court Services Act 2000, ss.67–68), the National Probation Service carried out a risk assessment and disclosed the man's background to the manager of the accommodation. The court held that the risk assessment had been conducted carefully, but had approached the question of disclosure from the wrong starting point, namely a presumption of disclosure rather than one of disclosure. Furthermore the risk assessment had not addressed the man's rights, nor explicitly balanced the need for disclosure with the potential harm to the man (*R(A) v National Probation Service*).

This case was decided under previous legislation (Criminal Justice and Court Services Act 2000) before the relevant provisions were superseded in the 2003 Act, and before the express duty of cooperation, carrying with it a power (but not a duty) to exchange information, was added.

## 17.8 ASSAULT, BATTERY AND SEXUAL OFFENCES

Some forms of abuse may constitute a criminal offence. These include the following.

### 17.8.1 ASSAULT AND BATTERY

Assault means the apprehension or anticipation of any immediate and unlawful violence or touching (*R v Savage and Parmenter*). Battery means any intentional touching of another person without the consent of that person and without lawful excuse. It need not necessarily be hostile, rude or aggressive (*Faulkner v Talbot*).

### 17.8.2 MANSLAUGHTER

Gross negligence resulting in a person's death may constitute the basis of a criminal charge of manslaughter. The following is an example of a 1977 case relevant to the adult protection context:

**Informal carers guilty of manslaughter through gross negligence.** A partially deaf and almost blind man of low intelligence lived with a woman described as his mistress, who was described as ineffectual and inadequate – together with the man's mentally impaired son. The man's sister came to live in the house as a lodger, in one room without ventilation, toilet or washing facilities save for a polythene bucket.

The sister was morbidly anxious not to put on weight, denied herself proper meals and spent days at a time in the room. After three years, she had become helplessly infirm. The mistress, who took the sister food, tried to wash the sister with the help of a neighbour, who advised her to contact social services. Also, the licensee of a pub frequented by the mistress and the man advised her to get a doctor. The sister refused to give the name of her doctor, whom the man and mistress had attempted to locate. The man tried to get his own doctor to attend unsuccessfully. Neither the man nor the mistress made any further efforts to obtain professional assistance, not even mentioning anything to the social worker who visited the son.

Three weeks after the attempt to wash the sister, she died of toxaemia spreading because of infected bedsores, immobilisation and lack of food. Had she received medical attention during that three weeks, she would probably have survived.

The Court of Appeal upheld the conviction (although reduced the sentence) and described gross negligence in the following way: 'The duty which a defendant has undertaken is a duty of caring for the health and welfare of the infirm person. What the prosecution have to prove is a breach of that duty in such circumstances that the jury feel convinced that the defendant's conduct can properly be described as reckless, that is to say a reckless disregard of danger to the health and welfare of the infirm person. Mere inadvertence is not enough. The defendant must be proved to have been indifferent to an obvious risk of injury to health, or actually to have foreseen the risk but to have determined nevertheless to run it' (R v Stone).

More recently, the Court of Appeal displayed very much greater reluctance to consider manslaughter in the context of personal care when it refused to overturn a decision of the Crown Prosecution Service not to prosecute anybody for manslaughter, following the death by drowning of a disabled person in a local authority care home:

**Death in a care home: no prosecution for manslaughter.** A man with profound mental and physical disabilities, resident in a local authority care home, died by drowning in five inches of water. The police and Health and Safety Executive both concluded that there was inadequate evidence to prosecute. The Director of Public Prosecutions (DPP) concluded the same.

In the case of one of the care staff, it never crossed her mind that the man might be unsafe in the bath during the four to five minutes that he was left alone, since he had always kept his head out of the water in the past.

From an organisational point of view, there was a care plan, but it did not deal with the matter of bathing. The DPP had concluded that a formal policy on leaving a severely disabled person was not required because it was common sense. Furthermore, some risks were managed, some training was provided and staff were appropriately experienced. The DPP decided that it would be difficult to find a guilty 'directing mind' at organisational level, and that there was an absence of conduct so 'bad' as to be described as gross negligence.

The court held that even if there had been ordinary common law negligence, criminality or badness still had to be established for a manslaughter case. The presence or absence of subjective recklessness was a relevant issue and the DPP had applied the right legal test (Rowley v DPP).

### 17.8.3 MENTALLY DISORDERED PEOPLE: ILL-TREATMENT OR NEGLECT

It is an offence for employees or managers of a hospital, independent hospital or care home to ill-treat or wilfully neglect a person receiving treatment for mental disorder as an inpatient in that hospital or home; likewise, ill-treatment or wilful neglect, on the premises of which the hospital or home forms a part, of a patient receiving such treatment as an outpatient.

It is also an offence for any individual to ill-treat or to wilfully neglect a mentally disordered patient who is subject to his or her guardianship under the 1983 Act or otherwise in his or her custody or care. It is an offence for any individual to ill-treat or wilfully to neglect a mentally disordered patient who is subject to aftercare under supervision (Mental Health Act 1983, s.127). However, the section is arguably weakened by the fact that no proceedings can be brought under it for an offence unless the Director of Public Prosecution brings, or at least gives consent to, such proceedings.

### 17.8.3.1 People lacking capacity: offence if ill treatment or neglect

Under the Mental Capacity Bill 2004, an offence of ill-treatment or neglect is created in respect of people lacking capacity, who have been so treated by a person in whose care they are (cl.42).

### 17.8.3.2. Offence of causing death of vulnerable adult

The Domestic Violence, Crime and Victims Act 2004 will (it is not yet in force) introduce a new offence of causing or allowing the death of a vulnerable adult. In outline, it will apply when:

- the vulnerable adult dies as a result of an unlawful act
- the person who committed the act was a member of the same household and had frequent contact with the victim;
- the victim must have been at significant risk of serious physical harm by an unlawful act by such a member of the household
- the person either caused the victim's death, or was or ought to have been aware of the risk, failed to take reasonable steps to protect the victim, and the act occurred in circumstances that the person foresaw or should have foreseen.

For the offence to be made out, the prosecution does not have to prove whether the person actually did the act or instead failed to protect the victim. The purpose of the offence is to overcome the problem of showing which of two perpetrators committed the act when, for example, each is blaming the other and the evidence is otherwise inconclusive.

A person could be classed as a member of the same household even if he or she does not live there but visits so often and for such periods of time that it would be reasonable to regard him or her as such a member. A vulnerable adult means a person aged 16 or over whose ability to protect himself or herself from violence, abuse or neglect is significantly impaired through physical or mental disability or illness, through old age or otherwise (s.5).

### 17.8.4 SEXUAL OFFENCES

The Sexual Offences Act 2003 reformed the law on sexual offences. In relation to adult protection, there are, in addition to the basic offences (rape, sexual assault, etc.), a number of offences specifically related to mental disorder.

### 17.8.4.1 Sexual offences relating to mental disorder

The following constitute offences specifically related to mental disorder. Mental disorder bears the same meaning as in s.1 of the Mental Health Act 1983 (see 17.5.2.1).

### 17.8.4.2 Sexual offences, mental disorder, and inability to refuse

Sections 30–33 of the 2003 Act contain certain offences that rely on the victim being unable, on account of his or her mental disorder, to refuse the sexual activity. The inability to refuse must be on account of lack of capacity, either because the person does not understand the nature of, or reasonably foreseeable consequences of, the activity, or for any other reason. Alternatively, the inability must be because the mentally disordered person cannot communicate his or her choice. This set of offences also relies on the perpetrator knowing, or reasonably being expected to know, of the mental disorder and of the likely inability to refuse.

The offences are (a) sexual activity with a mentally disordered person; (b) causing or inciting a person with a mental disorder to engage in sexual activity; (c) engaging in sexual activity in the presence of a person with a mental disorder for the purpose of sexual gratification of perpetrator; (d) causing a person with a mental disorder to watch a sexual act for the purpose of sexual gratification of perpetrator (ss.30–33).

### 17.8.4.3 Sexual offences, mental disorder, no reliance on inability to refuse

A further number of offences do not require an inability to refuse on the part of the mentally disordered person. In other words, these offences would be more easily made out, insofar as consent issues are not relevant. However, they do still require the perpetrator to know or to be reasonably expected to know that the victim has a mental disorder.

These offences all concern inducement, threat or deception to (a) procure sexual activity with a person with a mental disorder; (b) cause a person with a mental disorder to engage in sexual activity by inducement, threat or deception; (c) engage in sexual activity in the presence, procured by inducement, threat or deception, of a person with a mental disorder; (d) cause a person with a mental disorder to watch a sexual act by inducement, threat or deception (ss.34–37).

### 17.8.4.4 Sexual offences, mental disorder and care workers

A third set of offences applies in the context of care workers and mentally disordered people. The offences do not rely on the inability of the victim to refuse; in effect they do not rely on the issue of whether there was consent. The perpetrator must have known or reasonably be expected to have known that the victim has a mental disorder. However, if it is proved that the victim has a mental disorder, then it is assumed that the care worker knew or should reasonably have known this, unless sufficient evidence is led to question such an assumption.

The offences apply to a care worker (a) engaging in sexual activity with a person with a mental disorder; (b) causing or inciting sexual activity; (c) engaging in sexual activity in the presence of a person with a mental disorder; (d) causing a person with a mental disorder to watch a sexual act (ss.38–41).

A care worker is defined as somebody having functions in the course of his or her employment that brings, or is likely to bring, him or her into regular face-to-face contact with the mentally disordered person in various circumstances. These include (a) in a care home, or (b) in the context of the provision of services by the NHS or an independent medical agency or in an independent hospital or clinic. Alternative to either of these is where, whether or not employed to do so, the perpetrator provides care, assistance or services to the victim in connection with the victim's mental disorder – and so has, or is likely to have, regular face-to-face contact with the victim (s.42).

The care worker offences do not apply where (a) the mentally disordered person is 16 years old or more, and is lawfully married to the care worker; or (b) a sexual relationship existed between the mentally disordered person and the other person worker immediately before the latter became involved in the care of the mentally disordered person (ss.43–44).

## 17.9 VULNERABLE WITNESSES AND SUSPECTS

The detention, treatment and questioning of vulnerable persons by police officers is governed by special provisions, in particular the provision of an appropriate adult under Code of Practice C, made under the Police and Criminal Evidence Act 1984 (Home Office 2003).

However, in addition, both legislation and guidance now seek to provide assistance for vulnerable witnesses as well. The Youth Justice and Criminal Evidence Act 1999 provides for special measures to be taken in the case of both vulnerable and intimidated witnesses. Eligibility includes the fact that the witness suffers from a mental disorder under the Mental Health Act 1983, or otherwise has a significant impairment of intelligence and social functioning (s.16). The special measures listed include screening the witness from the accused, evidence by live link, evidence given in private, removal of wigs and gowns, video recorded evidence in chief, video recorded cross-examination or re-examination, examination of witness through intermediary, and aids to communication (ss.23–30; see also the rules on special measures directions in respect of magistrates' courts and crown courts: SI 2002/1687 and SI 2002/1688).

In addition, the Home Office has published a set of guidance as part of its 'achieving best evidence' policy covering vulnerable or intimidated witnesses, including children. In particular, in respect of vulnerable adults, various aspects are covered. These include a definition and identification of vulnerable witnesses, and support for the witness in terms of planning for an interview, at interview, during the investigation, pre-court hearing, during the court hearing and after the hearing. In addition, court-based intermediaries are referred to, and issues around capacity (and oath taking) discussed (Home Office 2002a). Separate guidance has been issued on the use of therapy in relation to the welfare of the witness, and on precautions to be taken so that the therapy does not unnecessarily 'contaminate' the evidence to be given by the vulnerable witness (Home Office 2002b).

A vulnerable adult witness is defined as a person whose quality of evidence the court believes will be diminished by reason of (a) mental disorder or significant impairment of intelligence and social functioning; or (b) has a physical disability or is suffering from a physical disorder (Youth Justice and Criminal Evidence Act 1999, s.16).

The following court case shows the importance of a basic recognition of a person's ability to give evidence in the light of a disability:

**Making allowances for a vulnerable witness.** A man was conducting his own defence in respect of an alleged offence of failing to comply with a statutory notice under the Housing Act 1985. He had suffered a stroke, which had caused brain damage and affected his ability to work, concentrate and remember things. He waited all day in court before the hearing was held. He said to the judge that he was therefore physically and mentally unable to conduct his case due to the medical problems arising from the stroke. The judge insisted on proceeding. The Court of Appeal held that the man had not been given a fair hearing; the consequences of stress and fatigue on a person who had suffered a stroke had not been taken into account; the case would have to be reheard (*R v Isleworth Crown Court, ex p King*).

The question of the giving of evidence by people with some form of mental impairment or disorder has been considered by the courts on a number of occasions. Some of these cases have involved in particular:

- s.23 of the Criminal Justice Act 1988 (admissibility, as exception to hearsay rule, of a statement in a document by a person who is unable to attend court by reason of his or her bodily or mental condition)
- s.26 of the 1988 Act (whether any particular document should be admitted as evidence as a matter of justice)
- s.53 of the Youth Justice and Criminal Evidence Act 1999 (creates presumption that at all stages of criminal proceedings, a person of whatever age is competent to give evidence, unless it appears to the court that he or she is unable to understand questions put to him or her as a witness, or to give comprehensible answers)
- s.78 of the Police and Criminal Evidence Act 1984 (whether in all the circumstances, including how the evidence was obtained, it would be unfair to admit the evidence).

Two such court cases each involved the alleged rape of an elderly woman suffering from Alzheimer's disease and whether their video evidence should be admitted to court:

**Admissibility of video evidence given by women with Alzheimer's disease in rape trials.** The defendant was accused of attempting to rape and of indecently assaulting an 81-year-old woman who had longstanding delusional problems associated with early Alzheimer's disease. He attempted to have video testimony given by the woman excluded from the trial – partly on the grounds that the woman lacked capacity. The Court of Appeal upheld the judge's decision to admit the video, and confirmed that, though relevant, the woman's capacity was not decisive as to whether the video should at least be admitted as evidence. Its reliability could then be challenged by the defendant, through medical evidence as to the woman's capacity when the video was made (*R v D*). A similar outcome was reached in the case of *R v Ali Sed*.

In a third, unusual, case, it was one of the defendants who wanted the video evidence admitted:

**Admissibility of transcript made by social worker.** An elderly man, living with his disabled son, had shown kindness to a female heroin addict. She went round to his flat with an acquaintance; they stole money, a television set and video recorder. The elderly man was punched and kicked such that he died 16 days later. The woman was convicted of robbery and manslaughter. However, she denied this, arguing that she had not inflicted any injuries, that there had been no agreement about using violence and that she had acted under duress from her companion.

Her version of events was supported by the elderly man's son (who had since died), whose interview had been video-taped. The son had been severely disabled though with unimpaired mental faculties. He suffered from cerebral palsy, epilepsy, Parkinson's disease, severe speech difficulties and was confined to a wheelchair. He had acute difficulties in making himself understood, quite apart from a reluctance to speak to strangers. Only the social worker could understand what he was saying in what had been supposed to be a police interview; in fact the man did not answer the police officers, so the social worker asked all the questions. The social worker then made a transcript record of what the man had been trying to say. The court concluded that the video and transcript could be admitted; the question would then be to decide at trial how much weight to place on them (*R v Duffy*).

## 17.10 HARASSMENT

The Protection from Harassment Act 1997 creates both civil and criminal remedies. In summary, it states that a person must not pursue a course of conduct (a) which amounts to harassment of another; and (b) which he or she knows or ought to know amounts to harassment of the other (s.1). Harassment is not defined in the Act, and is capable of being interpreted widely depending on the particular circumstances.

The Act creates a criminal offence of harassment (s.2) and, more specifically, of putting a person in fear of violence on at least two occasions (s.4). It also creates a civil right to claim damages (s.3) and gives the courts the power to issue restraining orders in respect of a criminal offence, or a restraining injunction in respect of civil proceedings – breach of which itself is an offence (ss.3, 5).

## 17.11 NON-MOLESTATION ORDERS

Under the Family Law Act 1996, the court can issue non-molestation orders enforceable through contempt proceedings. (An amendment will make breach of non-molestation a criminal offence: Domestic Violence, Crime and Victims Act 2004, s.1, which adds s.42A to the 1996 Act.) The issue of molestation is not limited to violence or threats of violence. In relation to the adults concerned, there must be an association that in effect is a domestic connection. For a relevant association to apply, the adults must:

- be or have been married
- be cohabitants or former cohabitants, live or have lived in the same household (other than through one of them being the other's employee, tenant, lodger or boarder)
- be relatives
- have agreed to marry (whether or not the agreement has since been terminated)
- in relation to a child, be the parents or have parental responsibility, be party to the same set of family proceedings (s.62).

(An amendment will extend the definition of domestic connection, so as to include same sex relationships; and include people who, although they have never cohabited, have nevertheless had an intimate personal relationship of significant duration: Domestic Violence, Crime and Victims Act 2004, ss.3–4, which amends s.62 of the 1996 Act.)

The court has a discretion to make an order, and must have regard to all the circumstances including the health, safety and well-being of the applicant, the other party and any relevant child (s.42).

Non-molestation orders might sometimes be relevant in the context of adult protection, although in the following court case, the order was being sought against an adult who might himself have been classed as a vulnerable adult – namely a man whose mental condition meant that he had become abnormally jealous of his wife, violent and abusive toward her, and had been detained under the Mental Health Act 1983.

**Capacity to understand non-molestation order.** An 82-year-old man lived with a 62-year-old woman in the same house. They divorced, although both continued to live in the matrimonial home. The woman had brought in a lodger with whom she ended up sharing her bedroom. The woman sought a non-molestation order on the grounds that her former husband had behaved improperly toward her. A social worker gave evidence that he did not meet the criteria for residential care and that she had never found him to be aggressive. The man was having difficulty remembering things, as he was suffering from the early stages of dementia. The court held that, on the evidence, this was a borderline case; that the judge in the original case was entitled to have made the non-molestation order; but that now the evidence suggested that the man's mental capacity was such that the order could not be continued. This was on the basis of a previous case (*Wookey v Wookey*) in which it had been held that such an order should not be made against a person who was incapable of understanding the nature of such an order (*Harris v Harris*).

## 17.12 OCCUPATION ORDERS

Under the Family Law Act 1996 (s.33 and following), the courts have a discretion, and sometimes a duty, to issue occupation orders. The precise rules vary, depending on the entitlement to occupy the dwelling of the applicant or of the respondent respectively. There needs to be an association or domestic connection (see 17.11) between the applicant and the respondent.

### 17.12.1 APPLICANT WITH ENTITLEMENT TO OCCUPY DWELLING

If the applicant is entitled to occupy the dwelling house, then a court order can cover a number of matters that could be relevant to adult protection. These are (a) entitlement to remain in occupation; (b) requiring the respondent to permit the applicant to enter and remain in the dwelling house or part of it; (c) regulating the occupation of the dwelling house by both parties; (d) prohibiting or suspending or restricting the right of the respondent to occupy the dwelling (if he or she is otherwise entitled to do so); (e) if the respondent has matrimonial home rights, the restriction or termination of those rights; (f) requiring the respondent to leave the dwelling or part of it; (g) excluding the respondent from the specific area within which the dwelling lies.

The court has to have regard to the respective housing needs and resources of the parties and of any relevant child, financial resources of the parties, the likely effect of any order or of any court decision not to exercise its powers on the health, safety, and well-being of the parties and of any relevant child, and the conduct of parties to each other and otherwise.

The court's power turns into a duty if the applicant or any relevant child is likely to suffer significant harm. However, the order still need not be made if the respondent or relevant child is also likely to suffer significant harm if the order is made – and that harm would be as great as, or greater than, the harm attributable to the conduct of the respondent and likely to be suffered by the applicant or child, if the order is not made (Family Law Act 1996, s.33).

## 17.12.2 OTHER CATEGORIES

The court also has a power to make some occupation orders (but not all of those listed in 17.10.1 above) in relation to other categories of applicant. These are namely (a) former spouse with no right to occupy the dwelling; (b) one cohabitant or former cohabitant with no existing right to occupy; (c) neither spouse entitled to occupy; (d) neither cohabitant or former cohabitant entitled to occupy (ss.35–38).

## 17.13 CIVIL TORTS

Adult protection may give rise to questions about whether civil torts (i.e. wrongs) have been committed and whether civil actions for damages might arise. Two such torts are trespass to the person and false imprisonment.

Trespass to the person is the civil law equivalent of assault and battery in criminal law (see 17.8.1). In the following case, concerning an NHS trust's failure to withdraw a medical intervention on the request of the patient, the court concluded that the trust had acted unlawfully in terms of the tort of trespass to the person:

**Unlawful failure to withdraw ventilator and trespass to the person.** A former social worker suffered from a haemorrhage of the spinal column in her neck. At the time she executed a living will. This stated that if a time came when she could not give instructions, but was suffering from a life-threatening condition, permanent mental impairment or permanent unconsciousness, then she wished for treatment to be withdrawn. She subsequently suffered another major bleed and became tetraplegic; and had to use a ventilator in order to breathe. She asked for the ventilator to be switched off in March 2001; a year later, at the time of the court's judgment, it had still not been turned off.

Considering the evidence, the court started with the presumption of capacity; it considered that this had been displaced between April and August 2001. However, from August onward she had regained capacity; on the evidence the court concluded that she had in fact had capacity from August 2001 onward. The court criticised the NHS Trust's consistent failure for not attempting to resolve the dilemma urgently; the woman had been treated unlawfully by the Trust (i.e. trespass to the person), for which a small award of damages should be made. The court drew a distinction between the duties of the team of doctors and nurses and that of the Trust as a whole; it was unfair that the burden of decision and responsibility had remained in the hands of the former – when it was the Trust's responsibility to act (Re B (adult: refusal of treatment)).

Likewise in the following case, a caesarean section, carried out against a woman's will, constituted unlawful trespass to the person:

**Unlawful caesarean section and trespass to the person.** A woman in the late stages of pregnancy was suffering from pre-eclampsia; there was a risk to the lives of both herself and the unborn baby. She fully understood the potential risks and clearly rejected medical intervention; she wanted the baby to be born 'naturally'. After she had been detained in hospital unlawfully under the Mental Health Act 1983, the hospital then purported to act in her best interests from necessity – on the ground that she lacked mental capacity – by performing a caesarean section. It did so, having obtained an emergency declaration from the High Court, on the basis of inadequate and misleading informa- tion being given to the judge. She subsequently brought a legal case against the approved social worker and the hospital. On the evidence, she had had capacity to decide about the operation; in the event, she ceased to offer resistance. However, the court pointed out that this was not consent but submis- sion; thus the caesarean section, together with the associated medical procedures, constituted unlaw- ful trespass to the person (R v Collins, ex p S).

In an ostensibly similar case, the outcome was different. A 40-week pregnant woman was refusing to have a caesarean section, required because the baby was in the breech position. The court held that to perform the operation would be in her best interests. This was because she was rendered tempo- rarily incapable of making the decision by her all-pervasive fear of needles that dominated everything and overrode the consent she had given in principle to the operation (Re MB (caesarian section)).

## 17.14 PHYSICAL RESTRAINT

The physical restraint of adults, as well as of children, is of considerable concern to some practitioners. On the one hand, total prohibition on restraint might result in harm to both the service user and other people; equally improper restraint runs the risk of resulting in, for example, injury to the restrained or the restrainer, breach of human rights, the criminal offence of assault and battery, and the civil tort of trespass to the person.

In response to such concerns, the Department of Health issued guidance in 2002 on physically restrictive interventions for people with learning disabilities or autism in health, education and social care settings (DH 2002). In summary, the guidance emphasises that interventions are legally permissible in certain circumstances (e.g. self-harm or injury to others) – and that any interventions should be the least restrictive necessary. They should be planned as far as possible, result from multidisciplinary assess- ment and be part of a wider therapeutic strategy detailed in individual care plans. Preven- tion should be the primary aim, in order to avoid the use of restraint if possible. There should be clear organisational policies and adequate training (DH 2002).

Although aimed at people with learning disabilities or autism, the principles set out in the guidance would arguably apply to some other groups of people with a mental disorder where restraint is sometimes necessary. The Mental Health Act 1983 Code of Practice also contains guidance on restraint (DH 1999, paras 19.1–19.14). The health service ombudsman found fault in the following case, because of the absence of policy, planning, training and individual care plan:

**No policy or care plan for restraint.** An elderly man in hospital had chronic obstructive airways disease, peripheral vascular disease, and had suffered a stroke that left him with right-sided weakness. Previously whilst at home, he had displayed signs of irritability and frustration, and verbal and physical aggression toward his wife. He was admitted to hospital for respite care for social reasons, since he could not cope whilst his wife, his main carer, herself required hospital treatment. He became dis- turbed during the night, after going to the day room to use his nebuliser. Nursing staff restrained him. When his daughter visited she found that he had an injured arm, carpet burns on his face and a cut on his hand.

The health service ombudsman found that the NHS Trust had no policy on control and restraint, and in that respect there was no particular plan for this particular patient. This latter failing was made worse by the fact that there had been a previous incident of restraint a few nights earlier involving the same patient. The ombudsman severely criticised the lack of planning and training which led a disabled, elderly man to be restrained in such a way (*Oldham NHS Trust 1999*).

Legislation governing the provision of care by registered providers of both care homes and domiciliary services states that no service user must be subject to physical restraint of any kind, unless it is the only practicable means of securing the welfare of him or her or of any other service user and there are exceptional circumstances. Any such restraint must be recorded (SI 2001/3965, r.13; SI 2002/3214, r.14).

As far as seclusion goes, the Department of Health guidance on restraint states that if seclusion is required, other than in emergency, for periods of more than a few minutes or more than once a week, then advice should be sought about statutory powers under the Mental Health Act 1983 or Children Act 1989 (DH 2002).

Under the 1983 Act, the Code of Practice contains guidance on seclusion, stating that it should be a last resort, for the shortest possible time and not be used as a punishment, as part of a treatment programme, because of shortage of staff or where there is a risk of suicide or self-harm. It also sets out procedures in terms of length of time, periodic checking and reviewing (DH 1999, paras 19.16–19.23). Adherence to the Code in respect of such procedures was the subject of consideration by the courts:

**Seclusion and the Mental Health Act code of practice.** The courts held that the Code should be followed unless there is good reason not to in the case of an individual patient or individual group of patients. However, it should not be departed from as a matter of policy. Otherwise, this could be in breach of article 8 of the European Convention on Human Rights, because the interference with the right to respect for privacy (including physical and psychological integrity) would then not be in accordance with the law. This would be, in turn, because such interference would not have the necessary degree of predictability and transparency required by article 8. The court also accepted that although seclusion did not necessarily breach article 3 of the Convention, nevertheless it would do so if it resulted in inhuman or degrading treatment. Giving weight and status to the Code of Practice was precisely the sort of step and safeguard required in order to avoid breach of human rights (*Munjaz v Mersey Care NHS Trust*).

Despite the Department of Health's guidance on restraint (DH 2002), the dividing line between what constitutes reasonable and unreasonable restraint might be difficult to discern:

**Use of armchair with fitted table.** During the course of a defamation court case concerning an undercover BBC investigation of practices at a Scottish nursing home, it came to light that a Parker Knoll chair with fitted table was used to restrict the movements of one of the residents. However, the court found that it was acceptable that, for example, at meal times the chair should play a useful part in the care of a resident with dementia. Likewise, because of his disruptiveness and the risk to himself, he was not always in his room at night but installed in his chair in the nurses' sitting room. The judge rejected the allegation that he was in his chair most days for 24 hours (*Baigent v BBC*).

Equally, the findings of the Commission for Health Improvement that patients at an NHS mental health hospital had been tied to commodes while they had breakfast or generally for restraint left no doubt that unacceptable physical restraint had been employed. Such incidents had been part of a culture that allowed unprofessional, counter-therapeutic and degrading – even cruel – practices to take place (CHI 2000, p.10).

## 17.15 FINANCIAL ABUSE

Local authority social services staff sometimes become aware of suspected financial abuse, in situations where a person lacks capacity or undue influence is being exercised. In either case, transactions such as gifts or wills can be set aside in civil law. Alternatively or additionally, the criminal law can sometimes be invoked and a charge such as theft be brought.

### 17.15.1 LACK OF CAPACITY

If it can be shown that a transaction has taken place at a time when a person lacked capacity to take the relevant decision, the transaction will, as a matter of civil law, be void (unless it involved the provision of 'necessaries': see 18.7) and be set aside by a court:

**Gift of farmhouse to carers.** An elderly couple live in a converted farmhouse just outside a village. The husband died and the woman received help and care on a private basis from two carers in the form of mother and daughter from the local village.

In 1996, she was introduced by the mother to a solicitor who had been suspended by the Law Society; he prepared a statement which the woman signed, saying she wished to change solicitors. She never met the new solicitor, although did meet the assistant solicitor twice. Otherwise her 'instructions' were conveyed to the solicitor either by the suspended solicitor or by the mother.

In February 1996, the woman met the assistant solicitor and agreed to transfer her home, a farmhouse, worth nearly £300,000, for £50 and on terms that she would occupy it for the rest of her life and that the carers would provide care for her. She subsequently made a number of lifetime gifts to the mother-carer in order to enable the carer's family to buy three cars; in addition, regular withdrawals of £2000 to £3000 a month were made, with the mother-carer as co-signatory, for some months before the woman's death. The amounts were significantly larger than the woman had previously withdrawn.

The woman was found dead, aged 77 years, in April 1997, with her clothing tangled in the stairlift. Great Ormond Street Hospital was one of the residuary beneficiaries of her will.

The hospital subsequently brought a case to challenge the validity of the transactions that the woman had entered into on grounds of her mental incapacity at the time to enter into them, of undue influence or of unconscionable bargain. In the event, the court decided that the transactions should be set aside, since a wealth of evidence showed that she had been suffering from senile dementia at the time as a consequence of Alzheimer's disease.

Evidence had been taken from many witnesses who had seen the woman in life at the relevant time, and two of whom had examined her brain in death. These included three general practitioners, a hospital senior house officer, a pathologist and another hospital consultant who had examined histological slides of the woman's brain, a chiropodist, friends, neighbours, a social worker, a retired Methodist minister, a solicitors' clerk and a borough council emergency contact service supervisor (*Special Trustees for Great Ormond Street Hospital v Rushin*).

Decision-making capacity is a decision and time specific issue, and the courts will look carefully at both the nature of the transaction and when it was performed (see 18.4.2).

For instance, in the context of adult protection, there is sometimes concern about enduring powers of attorney that are executed one day and then registered by the attorneys the next. Since registration is triggered by loss of capacity or the losing of capacity, the concern would seem well founded, since the implication might be that the donors in such cases probably lacked capacity the day before, when they purportedly executed the powers. This circumstance would invalidate the power. However, this will not necessarily be the outcome; a person might have the mental capacity to execute an enduring power of attorney, whilst lacking the capacity actually to manage the affairs, for the management of which the power is being given (*Re K*).

In the following case, the court had to consider the question of time and whether there had been a lucid interval, in relation to what otherwise were suspicious circumstances:

**Making of will and lucid interval.** An 84-year-old woman lived with her sister. On 8 April she was admitted to hospital, suffering from various matters including uncontrolled diabetes and dehydration. Her medical notes indicated she had been increasingly confused a few days before this admission. A care plan was set up by social services and she was discharged home on 26 April. A friend whom she had known for 20 years then suggested that she make a will, making the friend sole executrix and beneficiary. The will was drawn up by the friend's brother-in-law who was a solicitor and to whom the friend communicated the woman's instructions. The draft will was returned to the friend who made arrangements for its execution when the sister was out of the house, on the afternoon of 13 May. That morning, a GP specialising in geriatric medicine had visited and found the woman confused; towards the end of the day, a neighbour had visited and found the same. However, the friend maintained at the time of the will's execution that the woman had not been confused.

The judge stated that the burden of showing testamentary capacity lay on the friend – since she had procured the execution of the will and was beneficiary. He concluded that the woman's confusion was the product of her diabetes and drug regime – and on all the evidence, it was not credible that she had had a period of lucidity on the day in question in between the earlier and later periods of confusion on that same day (*Richards v Allan*).

A number of other cases on decision-making capacity and potentially relevant to adult protection matters are given in Chapter 18.

## 17.15.2 UNDUE INFLUENCE

Apart from lack of capacity, there is sometimes an alternative ground on which a transaction may be set aside in civil law. This is on the basis of a legal equitable concept known as undue influence. Generally speaking, undue influence can be summarised as follows. First, the exploited person has capacity, otherwise it is arguable that he or she cannot be unduly influenced (e.g. *Tchilingirian v Ouzounian*). Second, he or she is influenced to enter into a transaction not of his or her own free, informed will. Third, the undue influence can be either 'express' or 'presumed'. If it is argued to be express, then evidence is required of how exactly the influence was exercised in terms of overt, improper pressure or coercion (*Royal Bank of Scotland v Etridge (no.2)*).

On the other hand, presumed undue influence relies on a relationship of trust and confidence, and the relationship being abused – resulting in a disadvantageous transaction, or at least a transaction that 'calls for an explanation'. Once these two elements are established, then the 'evidential burden' shifts to the other party to give an innocent explanation for the transaction. If this explanation is not forthcoming, undue influence will be made out; importantly it is thus not necessary to prove that the other party did anything 'wrong'. Relationships of trust and confidence are recognised by the law courts in well-known categories (such as doctor–patient) but also in other relationships (such as carer and cared for person).

This second form of undue influence, presumed, can be relevant in the context of adult protection work and has been broken down in detail by the courts as involving the following:

- **Unfair advantage**. One person takes unfair advantage of another where – as a result of a relationship between them – the first person has gained influence or ascendancy over the second, without any overt acts of persuasion.
- **Advice relationships**. Such a relationship arises where it is the duty of one party to advise another (e.g. solicitor and client, social worker and client).
- **Trust and confidence**. However, such relationships are infinitely various; a key question is whether the one person has posed sufficient trust and confidence in the other.
- **Reliance, dependence, vulnerability**. It is not just a matter of trust and confidence; exploitation of a vulnerable person would be included for example; thus trust and confidence, reliance, dependence, vulnerability – and ascendancy, domination or control – are all relevant terms.
- **Transaction calling for an explanation**. Undue influence must be proved by the person alleging it; however, a relationship of trust and confidence coupled with a transaction that 'calls for explanation' will normally be enough to discharge this burden of proof.
- **Shift of evidential burden**. The evidential burden then shifts to the other person to counter the inference of undue influence, i.e. to rebut the presumption.
- **Trust and confidence assumed**. However, some relationships (e.g. solicitor and client, doctor and patient) will give rise to an irrebuttable presumption that a relationship of trust and confidence existed.
- **Degree of disadvantage**. Even within this special class of special relationships, not every gift or transaction will be assumed to have been down to undue influence unless otherwise proved (otherwise Christmas presents would be caught); it should be only where the transaction calls for an explanation. The greater the disadvantage to the vulnerable person, the greater the explanation called for.

- **Independent advice**. The receipt of independent advice is a relevant consideration but will not necessarily show that a decision was free from undue influence (*Royal Bank of Scotland v Etridge (no.2)*).

In the context of adult protection, when financial abuse takes place, the doctrine of undue influence may give interested parties (e.g. the exploited person or another member of the family) a civil remedy.

Some cases typically concern carers, whether in a person's home (live-in or otherwise) or in a care home. The following court case illustrates how a live-in companion rapidly exercised influence over the elderly man she was purporting to assist, to the point of having him 'at her mercy':

**Depleting an elderly man's estate.** An elderly man's wife died in 1958. Shortly after she died, he employed a woman as secretary-companion. In the last five years before he died in 1964, he made gifts to her of nearly £28,000; his estate had been reduced from £40,000 to £9500. His general practitioner's description of him was that he was elderly, weak, a little vacant, courteous, introspective, depressed at times; a gentle old man. His memory was not worse than that of many people of that age. He was not particularly fit and active; he was happy up to a point.

The companion became increasingly entrusted with handling his financial and business affairs. He agreed to sell his house and to move to another house the companion had always wished to reside in. He made a gift of it to her; he was described on 'some government form' that had to be filled in as the 'lodger'. The judge concluded that at this point he was entirely at the mercy of the companion. The solicitor involved in the transaction was purportedly acting for both the man and the companion; he said nothing to the man about the desirability of independent advice. The man therefore did not receive the independent advice that could have supported the argument that he had exercised 'full, free and informed thought' – which in turn could have removed the influence of the companion.

The judge held that there was a relationship of trust and confidence between the man and the companion; and that there was a presumption of undue influence in the case of the gifts. It was for her to rebut this; she had failed to do this, even though there was no direct evidence of pressure being brought to bear by her. Furthermore the onus on the carer was a heavy one, because of the otherwise seemingly objectionable nature of her behaviour (*Re Craig*).

In the case below, involving a situation where an elderly man was taken under the proverbial wing of a neighbour, the court emphasised the significance of the presumption of undue influence and of the carer having to provide an innocent explanation for what had occurred. In the absence of such an explanation, 'public policy' demanded a finding of undue influence, even were there no direct evidence of a wrongful act. The reference to the 'care authorities' and the 'care coordinator' might suggest (it is unclear) that the local social services authority was unwittingly involved in assisting the woman to exercise the undue influence:

**Taken under the wing of a neighbour.** A 72-year-old retired teacher and bachelor was living alone. He had become physically dependent on others because of limited mobility. His neighbour, whom he had met at a supermarket when he was holding onto railings and was in distress, 'took him under her wing'. Following a fall, hospital admission and then discharge, he became more dependent. She 'volunteered to the care authorities' to be responsible for giving him two meals a day. At the suggestion of the care coordinator, he then signed a third party mandate, authorising her to draw on his current account. After further falls and hospital admission, he said he wanted to make a gift to her of certain investments; these amounted to nearly £300,000, nearly 91 per cent of his liquid assets.

There was a relationship of trust and confidence; the gift was very large. These facts gave rise to a presumption of undue influence. It was for the woman to rebut this. Given that the man had received no advice, independent or otherwise, the presumption was not rebutted, and undue influence was made out. The court also made the point that this would be so even if the woman's conduct had been 'unimpeachable' and there had been nothing 'sinister' in it. This was because the court would inter- fere not on the ground that any wrongful act had in fact been committed by the donee but on the ground of public policy. Such public policy required that it be established affirmatively that the donor's trust and confidence had not been betrayed or abused (*Hammond v Osborne*).

Undue influence might come in different guises, not necessarily in an obvious caring or family situation:

**Undue influence from 'alternative' group.** A woman in her sixties became involved with a group of people sharing an interest in art therapy, alternative medicine and spiritual writing. The group pur- chased a small estate, which they ran partly as a hotel and partly as a cultural centre; they formed a company. The woman first raised a mortgage on her house to loan £34,000 to the group; she subse- quently sold her house, gave the proceeds of some £180,000 to the estate as a loan, repayable when the company/estate was dissolved or was sold.

The judge held that the second larger loan had clearly been procured through undue influence. A relationship of trust and confidence existed; the woman had already allowed her house to be used by the defendants for two years before selling it; she was physically isolated at her house and emotionally reliant and dependent on the defendants. She also believed that one of the defendants had a gift of healing. It was also a transaction that called for explanation, since by the sale she alienated her only re- maining asset for the foreseeable future if not for ever. Furthermore, she did not receive proper, dis- passionate advice from the defendants about the nature of the transaction; and her detachment from her past life and friends meant that the influence of the defendants went unchecked (*Nel v Kean*).

Of course not all transactions are suspicious; indeed it is sometimes the challenge itself that might be dubious:

**Transfer of house to second wife by terminally ill man.** A man transferred his house into the joint names of himself and his second wife as beneficial joint tenants. This followed the death of his first wife, although he had long since known his future second wife. Some months before the transfer, he had been diagnosed with terminal cancer. His children attempted to have the deed of gift set aside on grounds of undue influence. They failed.

The judge took account of various factors. He had been married to his second wife for 14 years; and the judge did not accept the children's view that she did not care for him properly when he was ill. He did not personally lose by the transaction (he continued to own half of, and to live in, the house), and the sons had previously upset the father in relation to family company payments. The judge also took the view that these facts 'did not speak for themselves' so as to raise the question of presumed undue influence. This meant that the burden did not fall on the second wife to explain the transaction; it remained with the children to express undue influence (*Glanville v Glanville*).

Likewise, generous gifts of provisions in wills might be innocent:

**Will in favour of housekeeper.** An elderly woman left her sizeable residuary estate to a live-in housekeeper and her husband. The woman's housekeeper had taken up her role in 1979; she and other members of her family lived in the womans's house until the latter's death in January 2000 at the age of 87. The woman was physically frail but had remained mentally alert. The will was dated May 1999. The woman's next of kin argued that either the woman had not known or approved of the contents of the will; or that there had been undue influence.

The court noted that the housekeeper had been present at two important meetings concerning the will; and that she had sometimes prompted the woman in respect of telephone calls about it. Furthermore, the woman was elderly and vulnerable, substantially dependent on the housekeeper; against this background, there could have been scope for the exercise of subtle undue influence.

Nevertheless, all this was consistent with a 'perfectly innocent' explanation, which the judge preferred, when deciding the case in favour of the housekeeper. The woman had been highly intelligent, had possessed the mental capacity to make the will, and had had the full extent of her estate explained to her only weeks before making it. Although elderly and vulnerable, she had remained intelligent, sensitive and independent minded, capable of making her own decisions. She was genuinely fond of the housekeeper and her family (Re: Ethel Mary Good).

Of course, sometimes the suspicion of undue influence might arise not just in respect of friends or relatives but local authority staff. This occurred in the following case, but the local ombudsman declined to find maladministration, pointing out that genuine kindness could provide an explanation:

**Making of will to benefit local authority care home assistant.** A social services home care assistant was named as beneficiary in the will of a service user for whom she had provided care (£10,000 to her, £10,000 to each of his grandsons, and the rest to his son). When he died she expressed great surprise that she was a beneficiary. The son claimed that she had exercised undue influence; and that the extra jobs she had done for him outside her duties (such as collecting a television and moving a bed downstairs for him) were evidence of her gaining that influence and playing on his father's gullibility.

The council had a policy about refusing gifts or being named as beneficiary in a service user's will. However, the woman and her solicitor pointed out that this provision in the will was unsolicited and that she had been unaware of it – and that to terminate her employment would constitute unfair dismissal. The council's principal solicitor believed that she should not face disciplinary procedures if she kept the bequest. He thought it was common for conscientious workers to be remembered in wills, and there was nothing wrong in this; and refusal to give up the bequest was not evidence of undue influence.

The ombudsman stated that it was for the courts to decide about undue influence; it was his job to decide whether the care assistant's actions equated with maladministration. In his view they did not; the evidence suggested neither coercion nor that she had known the contents of the will; and the television collection and bed moving appeared to be acts of genuine kindness (Bexley LBC 1998).

## 17.15.3 ENDURING POWER OF ATTORNEY

It is recognised that a proportion of enduring powers of attorney (see 18.3.2) is abused, perhaps some 10 to 15 per cent. The extent of abuse ranges from the making of unauthorised gifts at one extreme to criminal fraud on the other. For instance, the largest fraud discovered involved about £2 million, siphoned from a spinster over 90 years old, living in a care home, with no known relatives – and involving an attorney who had not registered the power and was proprietor of the care home (Cretney and Lush 2001, p.133). For instance:

**Abuse of enduring power of attorney.** A spinster in her eighties suffered two strokes and three serious falls. She lost her hearing and ability to write. She entered a nursing home in 1996. Her niece, who was the donee of an enduring power of attorney, operated the power and in March 1997 sold shares worth over £23,000; the next year she sold more shares worth over £72,000. Both sums were placed in her bank account; some of the money was lent to her husband's companies. The courts found that she had abused the power of attorney (*Jennings and Lewis v Cairns*).

## 17.15.4 THEFT

Under s.1 of the Theft Act 1968, a person is guilty of theft if he or she dishonestly appropriates property belonging to somebody else. This must be with the intention of permanently depriving the other person of it. Such an appropriation is not dishonest if the person believes he or she had a right in law to deprive the other person of it. Alternatively it is not dishonest if he or she believed that the other person would consent, if the other person knew of the appropriation and the circumstances.

In the context of adult protection, the question of theft might arise where, for instance, carers financially exploit vulnerable adults. The significance of the following court case is that theft could be made out on the basis of the jury's overall view of whether there had been dishonesty; and that this would not necessarily depend on the man being shown to have lacked the requisite capacity to make a gift of the money involved:

**Financial exploitation of and theft from a vulnerable person.** A man of limited intelligence, 53 years old, was assisted and cared for by a 38-year-old woman on a private basis. Over a period from April to November, he made withdrawals almost every day up to the maximum £300 allowed from the building society – to the amount of £60,000 (his saving inherited from his father).

The money ended up in the carer's bank account. The building society employees stated that the carer did most of the talking and would interrupt the man if he tried to talk. A consultant psychiatrist gave evidence that the man's IQ was between 70 to 80 (as opposed to the average of 90 to 110), that he could lead a normal if undemanding life (he had worked in a dairy as a packer for 30 years) – and that he was naive and trusting and had no idea of the value of his assets or the ability to calculate their value. The consultant however accepted that he would be capable of making a gift and understood the concept of ownership – and so would be able to divest himself of money but could probably not take the decision alone.

The carer was convicted of theft in the Crown Court; the case went on appeal to the House of Lords, which refused to interfere with the conviction. The court placed great weight on leaving the matter to the jury to decide about whether there had been dishonesty in all the circumstances. It was not crucial whether the man had the mental capacity to make a gift of the money. This was because the court was not prepared to read into the s.1 of the Theft Act the words 'without the owner's consent'. In other words, consent was not necessarily fatal to the success of a charge of theft (it had been argued that, as a matter of law, it could not be theft if the man did have the capacity to make a gift; and that the Crown Court judge should have directed the jury to that effect) (*R v Hinks*).

The *Hinks* case effectively overrules a slightly earlier Court of Appeal case, in which a maid, employed by an elderly woman aged 89 years, was prosecuted for allegedly cashing cheques to the value of £37,000 and stealing a brooch and crystal ornament. The appeal against conviction was allowed, on the basis of the failure of the judge's directions to be clear about the relevance of mental capacity. This meant the jury felt able to make a moral judgement about the maid, instead of deciding whether there was theft (*R v Mazo*).

Nevertheless, the *Hinks* case, which takes precedence because it was a House of Lords case, did not follow the *Mazo* approach. Instead it took the approach followed by the Court of Appeal in another earlier case:

**Theft of 99-year-old care home resident's assets.** A 99-year-old woman lived in a care home. She was virtually blind. She went to live there in 1991; her daughter died in 1992; at this point the two owners of the home took control of her affairs. A large number of cheques were drawn on her account; they argued that they were gifts. The owners obtained power of attorney and liquidated the woman's gifts and stocks; the proceeds were paid into a bank account held in their names and the woman's. Only one signature was required. A series of payments was subsequently made from that account for the benefit of the owners of the home. They were prosecuted for theft.

They appealed against their conviction, on the grounds that the judge should have directed the jury that there could be no theft if the woman consented to the 'gifts' (and thus had the capacity to give that consent). Furthermore the judge had failed to indicate the level of mental capacity required in order to make the acts of appropriation dishonest.

The appeal failed. The court held that the relevant term in s.1 of the Theft Act 1968 was 'dishonest appropriation'; this did not necessarily mean 'without the consent of the owner' (*R v Kendrick*).

In the following case, friendly neighbours were convicted of criminal offences following a social worker's visit:

**Friendly neighbours.** When a social worker and police officer visited an elderly woman, they found her to be frail, dirty and unkempt, and the house to be dirty and smelling of urine. She was apparently happy but mentally confused and forgot who her visitors were after five minutes. It became clear subsequently that two friendly neighbours (a married couple) had over a period from 1995 to 2001 obtained sums of money from the woman amounting to £110,000. The couple unsuccessfully challenged the admissibility of evidence relating to the woman's dementia and mental capacity (some of the offences for which they were charged and convicted were under the Forgery and Counterfeiting Act 1981) (*R v Bowles*).

## 17.15.5 DECEPTION

The offence of deception is about the dishonest obtaining of property belonging to another. Deception may be deliberate or reckless, and be by means of words or conduct (Theft Act 1968, s.15).

## 17.16 PROCEDURES AND INVESTIGATIONS

Clearly, effective investigations will be a crucial part of a local authority's adult protection activity. The following local ombudsman cases illustrate failures in policies, procedures and such investigations. One concerned a gift to a carer and the question of whether undue influence had been exercised:

**Bequest to council carer.** In 1984, guidance on the receipt of gifts from service users was issued to its staff by a local authority; in 1990 a further instruction was issued. However, in the case of one particular carer (against whom the complaint of undue influence had been made), it could not be shown that she had received either the guidance or further instruction. She was not asked to sign a record that she had done so. This in itself was maladministration.

The carer was left a significant amount of money in the will of one of the service users for whom she provided care, and had also received £1000 as a lifetime gift. When the service user died, her granddaughter complained to the council that the bequest and gift had been procured by undue influence.

The local ombudsman found maladministration on a number of grounds; one was that the local authority did not investigate the complaint for three years; when it did so, its response was inadequate since it sought no evidence from third parties who might have contributed the relevant evidence (*Suffolk CC 2001*).

A second case involved a failure to investigate the physical injuries received by a severely brain damaged woman at a local authority run centre:

**Failure in investigation and response to abuse.** The parents of a severely brain damaged 30-year-old woman complained that she had been injured on two occasions when receiving respite care at a local authority run facility.

The local ombudsman found maladministration in the council's response. On the first occasion, it did not consider whether to hold an investigation; on the second, it did investigate but did not identify the perpetrator – even though there was no doubt that the injuries were inflicted deliberately (although poor record keeping and failure to communicate and implement the revised care plan were uncovered). The parents understandably withdrew their daughter from the centre. It was then maladministration for the authority not to have considered alternative respite care for the woman at an earlier date; even if this meant spending scarce extra resources; since it still had a statutory duty to meet her needs (*Bedfordshire CC 2003*).

In a third case, even a catalogue of injuries suffered by the service user, and assaults by staff, did not result in either the woman's father or police being informed:

**Failure to report assaults.** A woman had been placed by the local authority in a care home (owned by a housing association but staffed by council employees). She was blind, of partial hearing, had virtually no speech and severe learning difficulties. She weighed six stone. Over a period of 18 months, she suffered a catalogue of injuries including a fractured skull, broken fingers, cuts and bruises. She was assaulted by two members of staff.

The local ombudsman found maladministration; the local authority had provided deficient care, delayed in telling the father about his daughter's fractured skull, failed to tell the woman's father or the police about the assaults on her; and had amended the investigator's report without consulting the investigator (who stated that her integrity had been compromised, and that she could no longer work for the council) (*Southwark LBC 2001a*).

In a fourth case, gathering information (about alleged physical abuse) from council officers but not seeking the views of other people who had known the person concerned, and not gathering medical evidence, was maladministration (*Wakefield MDC 1997*). The consequence of not following adult protection procedures might simply result in people's needs not being met:

**Staff failure to follow adult protection procedures.** A complaint was made to the local ombudsman. A woman with learning disabilities was increasingly at a variance of view with her parents about her life. Despite awareness of this, the local authority had failed to complete a care plan that might have hit on a reasonable compromise between daughter and parents.

She now specifically alleged that her parents, with whom she lived, hit her, locked her in her room, and prevented her from seeing her friends. The local authority had a clear written policy and procedure for dealing with abuse allegations. The procedure required immediate action to determine the risk involved and to assess needs of both disabled person and carers. The policy was not followed; the consequence was that the woman left home in an unplanned and precipitous manner and ended up in unsuitable accommodation with someone who lacked the skill to meet her needs. This was maladministration (*Cumbria CC 2000a*).

Equally, where councils do act decisively in relation to adult protection, they need to be careful to ensure that they keep in focus the overall welfare of the service user. For instance, in the local ombudsman investigation immediately below, adult protection concerns were responded to swiftly but in such a way that arguably placed the woman's welfare at risk, and might or might not have contributed to her death three days later. The case is worth summarising at some length, since it is illustrative of the difficult decisions sometimes facing local authority staff:

**Judging the response to alleged abuse**. A severely physically disabled woman of 26 years lived with her parents. She suffered from spinal muscular atrophy, had severe curvature of the spine and was unable to use her legs. Her mother (and father) had always been her main carer. She had specialist equipment and adaptations including special ripple mattress, customised electric wheelchair, special alarm system, wheelchair accessible bathroom, bath cushion, and adapted toilet seat. She was liable to chest infections, and care had to be taken with her posture both during the day in the wheelchair and during the night; sometimes her mother adjusted her position (but did not turn her over) in bed several times a night.

*Alleged taking of money and slap*. She attended a day centre run by a voluntary body on behalf of social services. This particular day she was upset and explained to the manager of the centre that her mother had taken money from her bank account without her permission; and that when she found out she had an argument with her mother who slapped her legs.

*Emergency placement organised*. The centre manager contacted a social worker who knew the woman. The woman was adamant that she did not want to return home. The mother arrived to collect her daughter but was told that the latter did not want to return home, although not about the allegations. The mother went away and subsequently refused to return to the centre. The social worker talked to his manager and decided to arrange an emergency residential placement. A care home was identified that provided for people with severe physical disabilities.

*Transport arrangements*. The centre arranged transport to the home, though there was not an escort in the van; the social worker drove behind most of the way. On the way, they collected various belongings from the woman's home; the mother said she was not asked about any equipment her daughter might need or about her care needs. The journey lasted much longer than expected (some two hours) because of traffic jams on the M25.

*First night at home, sickness and death three days later*. The woman spent her first night in the care home. She did not have a ripple mattress; a baby alarm was fixed up for her because she could not operate the emergency buzzer system. The notes stated that she needed turning several times a night. In the morning she felt uncomfortable, felt sick, frail and unwell and wanted to go home. Her parents arrived to collect her. She died of bronchial pneumonia three days later.

*Making enquiries before the placement*. The local ombudsman pointed out that the mother had given unstinting care and love to her daughter all her life; that the daughter had been upset and that the local authority staff had been right to take her distress seriously. However, it was maladministration not to make proper enquiries before the placement and before deciding that the woman should travel without an escort. In particular the woman's general practitioner and occupational therapist should have been consulted. This might have resulted in the placement going ahead, an alternative placement, or her going back home. In any event the ombudsman was not satisfied that she might still not have contracted the chest infection; thus he could not blame the council for her death.

Considering a complicated case at a 'deep level'. The ombudsman also agreed with the view expressed by one local authority manager, who had led the investigation into the events, that the staff involved had failed to recognise at a 'deep level' that the woman's case was 'problematic'. They should have realised that only her parents had ever looked after her, and that despite her being articulate and intellectually able, they should have talked to the GP and occupational therapist. Also they had taken the woman's statements as 'absolute' without attempting to verify what had been said; the care home should have been checked for appropriate equipment, and also for its ability to assess the woman's needs, given that the local authority staff involved on the day knew little about her needs. Staff should have sensed that the case was 'more complicated than most'. Furthermore, he felt that the woman should have been accompanied in the vehicle during the trip to the care home (Kent CC 1999).

Likewise, in the next case, the local ombudsman recognised the importance of adult protection policies, but reminded the local authority not to forget the needs and welfare of individual service users – which might call for exceptions to be made to an otherwise sensible policy:

**Blanket policy on visits to staff's homes**. A local authority implemented a new policy, debarring social services staff from taking clients to their homes. The ombudsman recognised the persuasive arguments in favour of such a policy. However, it meant that a woman with learning difficulties could no longer spend seven hours a week with a family aide, employed by social services. Her parents complained that this arrangement had always worked well and was an essential part of meeting their daughter's needs; furthermore the change had now made her unhappy. The ombudsman concluded that the council fettered its discretion by applying the policy so rigidly that it gave no consideration to the individual circumstances of the case. Furthermore, before making the change, the local authority had failed to reassess the woman's needs and to consult with her parents. All this was maladministration (Carmarthenshire CC 1999).

The following local ombudsman case, involving legal action (for defamation), uncovered a situation whereby a relative who had raised adult protection issues, concerning his sister-in-law who had learning disabilities, was in turn made the subject of unsubstantiated allegations that the local authority too readily took at face value:

**Unsubstantiated allegations**. The sister and brother-in-law of a woman with learning disabilities complained that she had suffered abuse at two care homes. In the course of a long and protracted dispute, the owner of one of the care homes made unsubstantiated allegations about the behaviour of the brother-in-law – involving drunkenness, sexual misconduct and racist behaviour. A report by the council's registration and inspection unit repeated the allegations; the report came into the hands of members of another part of the family, which promptly ostracised the brother-in-law. The council wrote to the brother-in-law, repeating the allegations as if they were fact; he regarded the letter as defamatory.

The allegations were finally investigated and found to be without substance; subsequent legal action for defamation was settled by payment of a considerable sum of money, agreement by the council to purge its records and to pay legal costs. In the end, the ombudsman found that abuse had not in fact occurred to the sister, but he was appalled at the 'almost complete lack of planning' behind one placement, and the lack of reasonable social care work that went into it. It was more by luck than judgement that no harm befell her in the resulting placement (Bromley LBC 2003).

Adult protection work is described in Department of Health guidance as being essentially multi-agency in nature; in the following case the health service ombudsman found fault with the NHS for inadequate procedures:

**Rough handling.** An elderly woman was admitted to hospital for repair of a fractured hip. She told her daughter that on Christmas Day a member of the night staff treated her roughly when attending to her because of vomiting and diarrhoea. Now she was frightened. The daughter made an oral complaint. The ward manager investigated and interviewed the staff member, but did not tell the daughter of the result of the investigation. The daughter then made a formal complaint; the Trust apologised for not telling mother and daughter the outcome of the investigation.

The health service ombudsman found that the Trust's complaints procedures and documentation were deficient; and that the Trust had failed to realise that the mother and daughter viewed the incident as an assault. As such, the Trust had not responded sufficiently robustly, and should review its complaints policy in the light of the Department of Health's guidance No Secrets (DH 2000) (Warrington Hospital NHS Trust 2001).

## 17.17 CARE STANDARDS AND ADULT PROTECTION

Under the Care Standards Act 2000, national minimum standards have been published (see 24.4.3). Under the standards for people in care homes, standard 18 relates to abuse, from which the registered person must protect residents. Various aspects are referred to, including policy and practice concerning residents' money and financial affairs. Under the standards for domiciliary care agencies, there is likewise a standard (14) on abuse and a separate one (13) on the safe handling of service users' money and property. This includes reference to matters such as bills, shopping, pension collection, acceptance of gifts, making use of the service user's telephone, borrowing money, etc. These standards in turn derive from the regulations made under the Act for care homes (SI 2001/3965, rr.13, 16) and domiciliary care agencies (SI 2002/3214, r.14), which make explicit reference to the prevention of harm or abuse and to the handling of money. The need for care providers to have effective procedures and safeguards was highlighted in a local ombudsman investigation:

**Lack of financial monitoring.** The local authority arranged for a private care provider to provide care for an elderly man who had suffered a series of strokes. The man's son complained about the standard of care; the council accepted this. However, the ombudsman also found maladministration due to a 'complete breakdown' in financial monitoring; withdrawal of the man's money from the social services department office safe were not always recorded and receipts were frequently unclear. The family, when visiting, noticed that there was little evidence in the house of the shopping that the carer supposedly did; there were also items costed that were never apparent in the flat (Sheffield CC 2001).

The Care Standards Act 2000 does not apply to the NHS in terms of imposing registration and inspection conditions. However, clearly similar standards are required, as the following example concerning loss of jewellery illustrates:

**Loss of jewellery in hospital.** A resident of a care home was admitted to hospital, but the admission document was not fully completed; the section on patient's valuables was left blank. When she was admitted to a particular ward later that day, only her spectacles were recorded as valuables. She lapsed into a coma and died a month later; during this time her close friend realised that she was not wearing her wedding and engagement rings. The evidence was compelling that she had been wearing these on admission to hospital; the health service ombudsman found that the lack of record keeping on admission had contributed to the failure to protect the woman's valuables (*Preston Acute Hospitals NHS Trust 2001*).

CHAPTER 18

# Decision-making capacity

**KEY POINTS**

For the purposes of this chapter, the central question is how health or welfare decisions – and sometimes financial decisions – are to be taken in respect of adults who lack the capacity to take those decisions for themselves. The answer to this question is by no means as straightforward as is sometimes supposed in everyday health and social care practice.

As far as finance, property and business affairs are concerned, decision making for a person lacking capacity is achieved through a number of channels including appointeeship, enduring power of attorney and Court of Protection intervention.

However, in terms of decisions concerning welfare (e.g. where somebody is to live and with whom he or she should have contact) and health care, the position at the time of writing is that legally nobody can consent on an incapable adult's behalf. Certainly interventions without consent are possible under the Mental Health Act 1983 in relation to mental disorder, under s.47 of the National Assistance Act 1948, and under the common law of necessity and best interests. However, none of these are about consenting on a person's behalf.

The Mental Capacity Bill 2004 proposes to change this situation; the advent of lasting powers of attorney and deputies appointed by the Court of Protection will mean that consent will in some circumstances be given on behalf of a person lacking capacity – not only in respect of financial and property affairs, but also welfare, including health care, decisions.

This chapter therefore sets out both the law as it is at the time of writing and, by means of notes at the foot of each section, the law as it is proposed for the future. In particular it considers matters such as the nature of the legal test for decision-making capacity, the presumption of capacity, the 'functional' approach to deciding capacity, the time and decision-specific nature of capacity, advance health care statements, and the role of the courts when they exercise their 'inherent jurisdiction' to intervene.

**Note: Wales, Northern Ireland and Scotland**. The law relating to decision-making capacity is the same in Wales as in England, and similar in Northern Ireland (although there is some different legislation such as the Enduring Powers of Attorney (Northern Ireland) Order 1987 and the Mental Health (Northern Ireland) Order 1986. There is also different terminology; for instance, the equivalent of the Court of Protection appointing receivers in England and Wales under the Mental Health Act 1983 is – in Northern Ireland – the Office of Care and Protection appointing a controller under the Mental Health (Northern Ireland) Order 1986).

In Scotland the position is different, since the law relating to decision-making capacity is governed by the Adults with Incapacity (Scotland) Act 2000. Although there are some broad similarities between the Scottish legislation and the Mental Capacity Bill 2004, there are also significant differences: for a detailed analysis of the Scottish law, see Ward (2003).

## 18.1 BACKGROUND

The law relating to decision-making capacity of adults is currently in a state of flux. During the 1990s, the Law Commission carried out a great deal of work on the topic and produced a number of reports, culminating in a final report entitled *Mental Incapacity Law* (Law Commission 1995). This was then followed by a government consultation paper, *Who Decides?* (Lord Chancellor's Department 1997), and a report, *Making Decisions* (Lord Chancellor 1999). There then followed a pause until in 2003 the government published a draft Mental Incapacity Bill, and followed it up with a Mental Capacity Bill in 2004. In the meantime, the Scottish Parliament had enacted and implemented its own legislation, the Adults with Incapacity (Scotland) Act 2000.

## 18.2 HEALTH OR WELFARE DECISIONS

At the time of writing the principle rule is that nobody can consent to a health or welfare intervention in respect of an adult who is himself or herself unable to take that decision. This includes the law courts. Conversely, if a patient is competent (or has made a valid and relevant advance directive; see 18.9), his or her decision as to his or her best interests is in principle decisive, even when, for example, life-prolonging treatment is in issue. Indeed, the courts have equated this right to decide with article 8 of the European Convention on Human Rights and with a person's physical and psychological integrity. The autonomy and self-determination entailed by article 8 outweigh article 2 (right to life) and article 3 (inhuman and degrading treatment), insofar as neither articles 2 nor 3 'entitle anybody to force life-prolonging treatment on a competent patient who refuses to accept it' (*R(Burke) v General Medical Council*).

Nevertheless, when a person lacks the relevant capacity, interventions are clearly sometimes required in order to safeguard the person's welfare. Apart from the statutory interventions referred to in Chapter 17, such as under the Mental Health Act, the common law of necessity and best interests provides the legal basis for intervention. Sometimes the term proxy or substitute decision making is used; but these terms should perhaps be used with a degree of caution, since they come close to implying 'consent on behalf of', which in principle is not legally possible.

The distinction between all relevant parties reaching a decision about a person's best interests, and consent by one of those parties, is a distinction with a real difference. The following example, albeit involving a person under 18 years old, illustrates this; neither the boy's mother, nor the doctors, had the right simply to exercise consent on his behalf. In case of the significant disagreement that arose, the courts should have been called upon:

**Hospital treatment dispute between family and doctors.** A boy, 12 years old, severely physically and mentally disabled, was admitted to hospital in July. He became critically ill and was put on a ventilator. During treatment, his mother was informed by hospital staff that her son was dying and that further intensive care would be inappropriate. Nevertheless, he improved and returned home on 2 September. He was readmitted six days later. Doctors discussed the possible use of morphine with his mother, to alleviate distress. The mother was opposed to this, wanting instead resuscitation and intubation in case of deterioration. At the time one of the doctors noted that in case of total disagreement a court order might be required.

*Threat to arrest mother.* A few weeks later, on 20 October, his condition deteriorated. The doctors thought he was dying, and recommended diamorphine for distress. The mother did not agree and opposed use of the diamorphine, on the grounds that it would reduce his chances of recovery. A meeting was held between the mother and the doctors, with a police presence. The mother wanted to take her son home; the police officer advised that if she attempted to do so, she would be arrested.

A dispute subsequently broke out involving other family members, who attempted to prevent doctors from entering the hospital room. Hospital security staff were called; they threatened to exclude the family members by force. A 'do not resuscitate' order was put on the patient's notes, without consultation with the mother.

*Physical fight on ward.* The next day the boy's condition had deteriorated; the family demanded cessation of diamorphine. The doctor would only accede to this if the family agreed not to attempt to resuscitate him. The family tried to revive him and a fight broke out between the family members and the doctors. During the fight, the mother successfully resuscitated her son. Police were summoned, several of whom were injured. All but one of the other patients on the ward had to be evacuated. The son's condition improved and he went home on 21 October.

*Breach of human rights.* The European Court of Human Rights held that the boy's article 8 rights had been breached; namely his right to respect for his private life and in particular physical integrity. This was because although the doctors could not have predicted the level of confrontation and hostility that had arisen, nevertheless the NHS Trust should have made a High Court application at an earlier stage since serious disagreement with the mother was clearly foreseeable. Even at a late stage, the court felt that such an application could have been made; if there was time to secure the presence of the police at a meeting, there should have been time to make a court application at short notice. Therefore the decision of the 'authorities' to override the mother's objection was a breach of article 8 of the European Convention (*Glass v UK*).

Equally, it might be all too easy for local authority staff to accede to the wishes of a member of the family without first ensuring that those wishes do indeed equate with the person's best interests:

**Family pressure.** A complaint to the local ombudsman concerned a woman with dementia and a family dispute amongst her three children. Unhappy with the care their mother was receiving at a home within the Doncaster area, the brother and one sister suggested their mother move down to a residential home in the south-west of England. The second sister objected, but the council agreed to fund the placement.

The following year, the second sister contacted the council and alleged that the first sister was not visiting frequently and that her mother was unhappy. The council agreed to arrange for the mother's return to a council-owned home in Doncaster. It was maladministration to take this decision without the reassessment which was 'clearly desirable and mandated by the Council's own policy' – and without at least some attempt at verifying the sister's claims. The second sister collected her mother from the home in the south-west without explaining her intention of removing her permanently, but the council did not inform the brother and first sister. This was maladministration also (*Doncaster MBC 1997*).

**Note. Mental Capacity Bill 2004: 'consent' on welfare and health matters.** The Bill proposes both attorneys with 'lasting power', and Court of Protection appointed deputies, both of whom would have the power to take decisions about personal welfare, including consent or refusal to health care treatment, as well as decisions about finance, property and affairs (cls.9–17). These would then replace the more limited scope (just finance, property and affairs) of the current enduring powers of attorney and of Court of Protection interventions.

## 18.3 APPOINTEES, POWER OF ATTORNEY, COURT OF PROTECTION

As the law stands at the time of writing, neither Court of Protection involvement nor the existence of enduring power of attorney or appointeeship (for social security benefits) directly solves the problem of decision making in respect of health or welfare decisions. However, the Mental Capacity Bill proposes to change this.

## 18.3.1 APPOINTEESHIP FOR SOCIAL SECURITY BENEFITS

Where a person is receiving social security benefits, but is 'for the time being unable to act', then an appointee may be appointed to manage the benefits, assuming that no receiver with the relevant power has been appointed by the Court of Protection (SI 1987/1968). However, appointeeship does not cover health or welfare interventions.

## 18.3.2 ENDURING POWER OF ATTORNEY

At present, a person still retaining capacity can create what is called an 'enduring power of attorney'. If or when the person loses capacity, the power endures and allows the attorney to act on the donor's behalf in respect of the donor's property and affairs (Enduring Powers of Attorney Act 1985). As is the case with intervention by the Court of Protection (see immediately below), this excludes welfare and health care interventions.

This limitation on the extent of enduring powers of attorney is sometimes misunderstood by families and professionals alike, who might believe that the attorney is fully entitled to take welfare or health decisions. Conversely, social workers might not involve attorneys in matters with which really they should be involved, such as the management of personal finances, because they are 'very woolly' about what such an enduring power entails (*Nottinghamshire CC 2002*).

**Note. Mental Capacity Bill 2004: lasting power of attorney.** The Bill proposes that a person, the donor, be able to create a 'lasting power of attorney', whilst he or she retains the capacity to do so. Such a lasting power could give the attorney authorisation to deal with property and affairs, as well as personal welfare matters including health care decisions. There are safeguards, including rules concerning registration of the power with the Court of Protection, and use of the power to restrain the donor (such intervention must be necessary and proportionate, and the person lack capacity or the attorney reasonably believes that the person lacks capacity in relation to the matter).

Also there is a prohibition on use of the personal welfare powers unless the donor lacks capacity or the attorney reasonably believes that he or she lacks capacity. Furthermore, the personal welfare power would be subject to any advance decisions on treatment made previously by the donor – and would not cover decisions about life-sustaining treatment, unless this had been expressly included by the donor in the lasting power of attorney (cls 9–11).

## 18.3.3 COURT OF PROTECTION

Intervention by the Court of Protection under s.93 of the Mental Health Act 1983 is conditional upon the 'patient' being incapable of managing and administering his or her property and affairs by reason of mental disorder. Such intervention may be necessary if, for example, there was no person with an enduring power of attorney to manage the person's affairs.

The Court of Protection may appoint a receiver to deal with the person's affairs (s.99); or it may intervene alternatively, for example by making a 'short order' where a person's assets are limited (up to £16,000) or a direction (SI 2001/824, r.8) where perhaps a one-off matter needs to be dealt with (for instance, winding up a tenancy or a bank account).

The term 'affairs of the patient' has been interpreted by the courts to exclude health or welfare decisions, and to extend only to business matters, legal transactions or other similar dealings (*Re F (Mental patient: sterilisation)*).

There will nevertheless be a grey area, in which a decision concerning property or finance will overlap with welfare matters. For instance, a decision about whether to enter a care home is strictly speaking a welfare decision; but the receiver will be involved with the choice of home in terms of applying the person's assets in his or her best interests – for example, deciding how much money to spend on such a care placement. Nevertheless, the dividing line between 'affairs' and welfare is often inappropriately crossed. Thus, involving receivers in welfare related decisions is one thing, but expecting them to take decisions beyond their authority quite another (e.g. Terrell 2002, para 4.5).

**Note. Mental Capacity Bill 2004: deputies appointed by the Court of Protection**. The Bill proposes that the Court of Protection have the power to appoint a deputy, whose powers may extend to personal welfare, as well as to property and affairs. Personal welfare decisions could include in particular where the incapacitated person is to live, with whom he or she should have contact, consent or refusal to health care treatment. Safeguards are included relating to restraint of the person (such intervention must be necessary and proportionate, and the person lack capacity or the deputy reasonably believes that the person lacks capacity in relation to the matter). In addition, a deputy cannot refuse consent to life-sustaining treatment unless the Court of Protection has expressly conferred that authority on the deputy (cl.17).

## 18.4 ASCERTAINING DECISION-MAKING CAPACITY

Ultimately the question of capacity is a legal one. There is no rule that the evidence about it can only be medical; but in case of doubt, medical doctors are substantially relied upon by the courts:

**Failure to obtain medical evidence**. A woman had a stroke, lacked the ability to communicate, was deteriorating and had suffered a fall. She made a new will under pressure from her family. The will was drafted by one of her sons, the main beneficiary of the new will. He was advised by solicitors that an expert medical opinion be obtained concerning his mother's capacity. He ignored this advice. The judges found the circumstances bristled with suspicion; in which case the son had to prove that his mother had testamentary capacity. He came nowhere near this; the will was set aside because of grave suspicion not only about her knowledge and approval of the contents, but also about her capacity (*Vaughan v Vaughan*).

However, medical evidence is by no means all. For example, in coming to the conclusion in one case that a person did not lack capacity to manage his affairs, the court took particular account of the person's diary entries made over a period of many years (*Masterman-Lister v Brutton*). In another court case, the evidence was from many quarters:

**Evidence about a woman's capacity**. In a case concerning exploitation by carers of an elderly woman (now dead), and whether the transfer of her home to the carers should be set aside, the court heard evidence from a whole range of people including three general practitioners, a hospital senior house officer, a pathologist and another hospital consultant who had examined histological slides of the woman's brain, a chiropodist, friends, neighbours, a social worker, a retired Methodist minister, a solicitors' clerk, and a borough council emergency contact service supervisor (*Special Trustees for Great Ormond Street Hospital v Rushin*).

Likewise the following decision was not based solely on the medical evidence:

**Evidence to establish capacity.** In a dispute about the validity of a will, the court concluded that the woman who made it (the testatrix) lacked testamentary capacity in the light of the medical evidence that cast doubt on such capacity both before and after the signing of the will, a solicitor's assessment that at best she had only lucid intervals at the time, her wandering off, her inability to understand that her husband had died and her failure to recognise close members of her family (*Brown v Mott*).

The decision concerning capacity has to be approached with care. For instance, in practice, aspects to be considered by a medical doctor might include appearance, speech, mood, thinking processes, perceptual disorders, delusional ideas, cognitive functions, orientation, memory, insight and pre-morbid personality. Apparent incapacity may simply be very temporary owing to a chest infection or urinary infection that can rapidly be cleared up. It might well be better to visit a person in his or her own home, choosing the time carefully so that the person is not too tired or otherwise distracted; a couple of visits may be necessary. Even then the doctor may be unable to decide and refer the matter to the courts (Singh 2002). Indeed, in their expert evidence to the court, eminent medical experts might disagree with each other (*Masterman-Lister v Brutton*).

### 18.4.1 FUNCTIONAL APPROACH TO CAPACITY

The courts have advocated what is sometimes called a functional test to deciding a person's decision-making capacity, and rejected what are sometimes referred to as the outcome or status tests (Law Commission 1995, para 3.3). The functional test has roughly boiled down to whether, in respect of the decision in question, a person can recognise a problem; obtain, receive, understand and retain relevant information including advice; and be able to weigh the advice in the balance and to communicate the decision (*Masterman-Lister v Brutton*).

The following example is an illustration of how the courts have in effect rejected both the outcome and status approach, in favour of the functional approach. The outcome of the person's decision was that he might well die; the status issue was that he was a mental health patient in a special hospital. However, neither fact meant that he necessarily lacked the requisite decision making capacity:

**Amputation of gangrenous leg.** A patient detained in a special secure hospital suffered from chronic paranoid schizophrenia. He was found to be suffering from an ulcerated, gangrenous foot and transferred to a general hospital, where the surgeon recommended amputation. The patient refused but agreed to conservative treatment; and sought an injunction to stop amputation unless he consented in writing. The court held that his schizophrenia did not mean that he could not understand the nature, purpose and effects of the treatment. He understood the relevant information, believed it and arrived at a clear choice. The court granted the injunction (*Re C (Adult: refusal of treatment)*).

Similarly:

**Risk of septicaemia.** The courts held that a prisoner had the capacity to refuse medical treatment, which accordingly could not be given. It was required because he was at risk of death from septicaemia, after he had cut open his right leg and kept it open by forcing foreign objects into it (*Re W (Adult: refusal of treatment)*).

However, another court case, also concerning a detained mental health patient, had a different outcome:

**Mental health patient unable to weigh up information on medical treatment.** An elderly woman, detained under s.3 of the Mental Health Act 1983, refused to accept medical treatment because she regarded it as part of a plot against her. The hospital sought the court's declaration that it was in the woman's best interests to have a general anaesthetic and CT scan, in order to investigate a suspected renal carcinoma. They gave the hospital permission to carry out the procedures, since the woman was clearly unable to believe the relevant information and weigh up the benefits; she appeared to have no insight into her condition (*NHS Trust v C*).

Therefore, in line with this functional approach, the fact that a person has learning disabilities and severe behavioural disturbance will not necessarily mean that she lacks capacity:

**Not treating renal failure.** A 25-year-old woman had learning disabilities and severe behavioural problems. Suffering from renal failure, she nevertheless resisted attempts to administer dialysis treatment. The court held that on the evidence she had capacity to make this decision; and that the dialysis could not be provided compulsorily against her will as treatment for mental disorder under the Mental Health Act 1983. Therefore provision of the treatment without her consent would amount to both a criminal assault and a civil wrong (*JT (Adult: refusal of medical treatment)*.

Similarly, age, medication or dementia will not necessarily be legally decisive as to incapacity:

**Cocktail of drugs.** A 79-year-old woman made a will in hospital five days before she died, leaving her entire estate to her brother. Her son contested the will, mainly on the grounds that the cocktail of drugs his mother was receiving must have meant that she lacked testamentary capacity. However, the court accepted that it was not a foregone conclusion that the drugs would have had this effect; and that evidence from medical witnesses suggested that she had had her wits about her (*Barrett v Kasprzyk*).

**Making of will by a woman with mild to moderate dementia.** A woman made a new will in 1994, which changed the terms of her previous will made in 1987; beneficiaries under the 1987 will were displaced as it were by the 1994 will and were aggrieved. At the time she made the second will, the woman suffered at least mild to moderate Alzheimer-type dementia. However, the court found that, on the balance of probabilities, she understood the claims of the former beneficiaries, and was capable of understanding without further explanation, and knew and approved, the contents of the will (*Hoff v Atherton*).

The functional approach to capacity does not equate with 'wisdom'; after all we all make unwise decisions (a point expressly covered by the Mental Capacity Bill 2004). Thus the courts have rejected medical evidence that referred to wisdom as a test of capacity, although at the same time have conceded that outcomes can often 'cast a flood of light on capacity', and are likely to be important, though not conclusive, indicators (*Masterman-Lister v Brutton*).

If a person recognises his or her own limitations in capacity to take certain types of decision concerning property and affairs, and recognises also the need to seek advice, this might indicate overall capacity in respect of this type of decision. The consequence is also that up to a point at least, the risk of – or vulnerability to – making a mistake or being exploited will not in itself indicate a lack of capacity. For instance, in the case immediately below, the judge stated that on the evidence the person was not 'sufficiently vulnerable to the risk of unwise decisions, bad advice or self-interested and manipulative persons to justify the inroads upon his personal freedoms' – were he now to be declared incapable of managing his property and affairs (*Masterman-Lister v Brutton*: High Court stage):

**Dysexecutive syndrome and distinction between lack of capacity and vulnerability.** A challenge was made as to whether or not a person who had suffered a head injury – when a milk float hit his motor cycle – had been capable of managing his property and affairs (for the purpose of Part 7 of the Mental Health Act 1983) when he had previously made a settlement in respect of his personal injury. The court's decision now would affect the validity of that personal injury settlement.

The dysexecutive syndrome that the man suffered from as a consequence of the accident resulted in changes such as obsessionality, immaturity, rigidity of thinking, eccentricity and emotional outbursts. This impaired his ability to organise his life and to plan. However, his pre-accident level of intelligence was largely unchanged. This meant that his relationships with other people and with the problems of life did not always quite 'mesh'. There were conflicting medical views as to his capacity to conduct litigation.

The court made a distinction between wisdom in transactions and understanding; the former was not relevant to capacity. He had perhaps been overly generous to girlfriends, to the Vegan Society or to anti-hunt protestors, caused trouble to some builders, broken a cooker valve and lost the replacement, and overstocked his fridge. But the judge concluded that the evidence of the last 20 years (since the accident) showed that the man was by and large perfectly capable of looking after himself. Indeed there was various evidence of highly responsible actions, such as advising friends on how to maximise social security benefits or avoid sexual harassment at work, alerting the police to the possible exposure of three young girls to sexual abuse at a naturist swimming pool, and writing impressive letters of advice to his nephew who was away at boarding school.

When greater problems arose, he recognised the need to seek assistance. The mental disorders identified in the medical reports were capable of leading to a finding of incapacity, if present to a sufficiently severe degree – but they were not of that degree in this case.

The Court of Appeal agreed, pointing out that the judge rightly distinguished between capacity and outcomes, and between everyday matters and the management of more serious problems. In reaching his decision the judge had considered all the relevant evidence, both medical and lay. He had also considered the man's diaries and letters. Matters such as losing a pressure cooker valve and overstocking the freezer may have been symptomatic of memory loss, but they were mishaps that could occur to those without the claimant's disabilities (*Masterman-Lister v Brutton*).

The following case proceeded on similar lines:

**Ability to manage affairs.** The claimant suffered brain damage in 1976 through leaning out of a train window and hitting his head on a railway bridge. At the time, he was awarded damages of £77,000 plus interest; his father and his solicitor undertook to the court to hold the damages on trust for him. At the time it was undecided whether he had 'capacity' to manage his affairs and whether or not he was a 'patient' for the purpose of Court of Protection intervention.

Twenty-six years later, he was now married, with a young son, and wished to emigrate to India with his family. He wished to gain access to the trust assets to buy a property and live on the remainder. The medical evidence revealed that he suffered a degree of mental disorder as defined in the Mental Health Act 1983. He had lasting brain damage that had reduced his intellectual capacity. However, he recognised his own limitations and that he would need to seek advice from his solicitor in handling so large a sum of money (now £192,000). On the evidence, there was therefore 'no question' of him being a 'patient' under the Mental Health Act 1983 such as to trigger Court of Protection intervention (*Tait v Wedgwood*).

**Note. Mental Capacity Bill 2004: functional test of capacity, not equated with wisdom**. The Bill states that a person should not be treated as unable to take a decision simply because it is an unwise decision (cl.1). It also sets out a functional test: a person lacks capacity in relation to a particular matter if, at the relevant time, he or she cannot make the decision because of an impairment of, or disturbance in functioning of, the mind or brain. A person is unable to take a decision if he or she is unable to (a) understand the relevant information; (b) retain it; (c) use or weigh it as part of the decision-making process; (d) communicate the decision, whether by talking, sign language or any other means. Furthermore, ability to retain the information for a short period only would not necessarily mean that the person is unable to take the decision (cls 2–3).

## 18.4.2 ISSUE AND TIME-SPECIFIC APPROACH TO CAPACITY

Decision-making capacity is not 'all or nothing'. It generally relates to the taking of a particular (type of) decision (*Masterman-Lister v Brutton*). For instance, a person might have the capacity to decide what to eat for breakfast, but not where he or she should live.

In one case the court held that a person could have the capacity to make an enduring power of attorney in respect of the management of her affairs – if she understood the nature and effect of the power – even if at the same time she lacked the capacity to manage those affairs (*Re K*). A similar type of distinction, effectively between making a will and signing it, was drawn in the following court case:

**Validity of a will**. A woman was terminally ill. She made her final will in March, two days before she died. The medical evidence suggested that on that day she lacked the testamentary capacity (i.e. the capacity to make a will). However, the will had been prepared in accordance with instructions she had given in December when she did have undisputed testamentary capacity. In March, she was able to understand that the document she was signing had been in accordance with those instructions. The will was therefore valid (*Clancy v Clancy*).

Tests of capacity for some particular transactions have developed their own rules. For wills, the test relates to an understanding of the nature of the act, the extent of the property, an appreciation of the claims of others, to there being no disorder of mind poisoning the affections, no insane delusions influencing the disposal (*Banks v Goodfellow*). The courts have stated that for the avoidance of doubt, a solicitor who is drawing up a will for an aged or seriously ill person should ensure that it is witnessed by a medical practitioner who in turn should make a record about examination of the person's capacity (*Kenward v Adams*).

In respect of gifts, the degree of understanding required is relative to the transaction; a gift trivial in nature requires less understanding than, for example, at the other extreme, disposal of the person's only valuable asset. This latter would require as high degree of understanding as required for a will (*Re Beaney (deceased)*).

Capacity is also time specific, an issue that might arise in all manner of contexts (for examples in the adult protection context, see 17.15.1). A simple instance of the significance of the time specific nature of capacity is illustrated in the case of a person lacking capacity to take a particular (type of) decision one week only to regain it the next, once a chest infection or urinary infection has cleared up.

**Note. Mental Capacity Bill 2004: time and decision specific nature of capacity**. The Bill states that a person lacks capacity in relation to a particular matter, if at the relevant time he or she cannot make the decision (cl.2): see note to 18.3.1.

## 18.4.3 PRESUMPTION OF CAPACITY

When decisions are made about capacity, the legal presumption is that a person has capacity and that evidence is required to rebut the presumption, rather than the other way around. Once capacity has been shown to have been lost, there is a presumption of continuance of that loss. However, the Court of Appeal rejected this approach in the case of head injury, from which there might be recovery. One reason for taking this approach is because of the drastic consequences of being judged to lack capacity: a person is deprived of important civil rights (*Masterman-Lister v Brutton*).

**Note. Mental Capacity Bill 2004: presumption of capacity**. The Bill states that a person must be assumed to have capacity unless it is established that he or she lacks that capacity (cl.1).

## 18.4.4 COMMUNICATION OF DECISION

Attention must be paid to the question of communication. In other words, all practicable efforts must be made to communicate with a person, before a conclusion is reached that he or she lacks the capacity to decide.

**Slight eyelash movement.** In one court case a man with motor neurone disease had slight eyelash movement as his only means of communication. He could neither initiate communication, nor show emotion. However, he communicated separately to his care coordinator, mother and doctors that he wished artificial ventilation to cease if and when he could no longer communicate at all. The court accepted on the evidence that the communication was reliable and that the man clearly had capacity to take this decision (*Re AK (medical treatment: consent)*).

**Note. Mental Capacity Bill 2004: all practicable steps to help communicate decision**. The Bill states that a person should not be regarded as being unable to take a decision unless all practicable steps have been taken without success to help him or her (cl.1).

## 18.5 BEST INTERESTS

In case of lack of capacity to take a particular health or welfare decision, and in the absence of any relevant statutory intervention, a decision may nevertheless have to be made under common law (i.e. not under legislation) out of necessity and in the person's best interests. The Law Commission defined best interests as comprising (Law Commission 1995, para 3.28):

- ascertainable past and present wishes and factors a person would have considered
- the need to encourage the person to participate as fully as possible in decisions
- the views of other people whom it is appropriate and practical to consult with about best interests
- achieving the purpose of an action or decision by means which least restrict the freedom of action of the person.

The courts have taken a similar approach; they have also confirmed that best interests encompass not just medical but also emotional and all other welfare issues. Furthermore, deciding about a person's best interests is not just about identifying a range of acceptable options but about identifying the 'best' (a superlative term). This does not therefore equate with the common law duty of care (see 23.1) owed by professionals, which is at least to adopt a reasonable course of action, but not necessarily the best (*SL v SL*).

Note. **Mental Capacity Bill 2004**. The Bill states that any act done or decision taken, for or on behalf of a person lacking capacity, must be in that person's best interests. Best interests involve the decision maker (a) considering whether and when the person might regain capacity; (b) allowing and encouraging the person to participate in the decision; (c) considering, if reasonably ascertainable, the person's past and present wishes and feelings, beliefs and values, other factors; (d) taking into account, where consultation is appropriate and practicable, any particular named other person, any other person caring for the person or interested in the person's welfare, any donee of a lasting power of attorney, any Court of Protection appointed deputy (cl.4).

Before an act is done for a person lacking capacity, regard must be had to whether the purpose of the act can be as effectively achieved in a way that is less restrictive of the person's rights and freedom of action (cl.1).

## 18.6 INFORMAL DECISION MAKING

At present, the legal explanation for those (carers or professionals) informally making everyday health and welfare decisions for people without capacity is that they are acting in good faith, from necessity and in the best interests of the person. Otherwise, for instance, those taking such actions could be committing legal civil wrongs, such as trespass to the person or even false imprisonment.

Such informal decisions range, for instance, from deciding what clothes a person will wear or what breakfast cereal they will eat (and assisting them with these matters) – to deciding where they should live (and conveying them there), taking medication, etc.

Thus, when a man with autism was sedated and taken to hospital for mental health treatment, without formal detention under the Mental Health Act 1983, the courts held that this was lawful under common law necessity and best interests. Otherwise there might, for example, have been a claim for false imprisonment (*R v Bournewood Community and Mental Health NHS Trust, ex p L*: but see 17.5.2.8 for the eventual European Court of Human Rights decision on this case).

However, beyond this, at present such carers or decision-makers (whether relatives, friends or professionals) are not explicitly protected in law, and nor is the person with the incapacity (Law Commission 1995, Part 4).

**Note. Mental Capacity Bill 2004: acting informally without express authorisation.** The Bill contains a general defence or protection in respect of informal acts taken in respect of a person lacking capacity to decide. It states that a person is protected from liability if he or she does an act in connection with care or treatment, if (a) he or she took reasonable steps to establish that the person lacked capacity in respect of the matter in question; and (b) reasonably believed that the person lacked that capacity and that it was in his or her own best interests that the act be done (cl.5). If the act involves restraint, the acting person must believe the restraint is necessary to prevent harm to the person lacking capacity; and the restraint must be a proportionate response to the likelihood and seriousness of the harm in respect of the person lacking capacity (cl.6).

The final Act, or the codes of practice that will be published with it, will need to clarify at what point informal decision making should end, and a formal power be created (e.g. appointment of deputy).

## 18.7 NECESSARY GOODS AND SERVICES

If a person lacking capacity to enter into an agreement for necessary goods nevertheless ostensibly does so, then he or she is obliged to pay a reasonable price for them, notwithstanding this lack of mental capacity. Necessary goods are defined as suitable to the person's condition in life and to his or her actual requirements at the time of the sale (Sale of Goods Act 1979, s.8). Common law rules apply in the same way to services, such as medical treatment (Treitel 2003, p.558) or perhaps housing tenancies (see 24.4.5).

**Note. Mental Capacity Bill 2004.** The Bill states that if necessary goods or services are supplied to a person who lacks capacity to contract for their supply, he or she must nevertheless pay a reasonable price for them. Goods and services are necessary if they are suitable to a person's condition in life and to his or her actual requirements at the time (cl.7).

## 18.8 INHERENT JURISDICTION OF THE COURTS

The courts have increasingly identified a gap in the statutory framework, in respect of health and welfare decision making for adults lacking capacity to take those decisions for themselves. That is, outside of the Mental Health Act 1983, there has been effectively no statutory framework for such decision making. Even Mental Health Act interventions do not rely on lack of capacity (they rely instead on certain definitions of mental disorder, which do not necessarily entail lack of mental capacity to take decisions).

In order to fill this gap, and until such time as Parliament does so via legislation, the courts have been called on to exercise what is referred to as their inherent jurisdiction. This involves the court coming to a decision as to where it thinks the best interests of a person lacking capacity lie. It will then make a declaration, or occasionally issue an injunction, to that effect.

Increasingly, the exercise of this jurisdiction has concerned not only health care treatment but also more general welfare issues such as where a person is to live or with whom he or she should have contact. The exercise of the jurisdiction has changed and developed. For instance, in 1994, the court held that it had no legal power to interfere in respect of contact between a woman with learning disabilities and her family (*Cambridgeshire CC v R*). A decade later, declarations in respect of such matters have become an accepted part of the jurisdiction (e.g. *Re F (Adult Patient); Newham LBC v BS*).

Sometimes there is doubt about whether a person has capacity to take the decision in question (*Masterman-Lister v Brutton*), and the court may be asked to declare on this matter first, before considering whether to address the matter of best interests. If a person does have capacity and is refusing an intervention, any application to the court for a declaration concerning best interests would be pointless (*R v Collins, ex p S (no.2)*).

With increased use of the inherent jurisdiction, the courts are called on to make difficult decisions in the field of social care. For example, the following case, which effectively sanctioned the removal of a woman from the care of her father, is illustrative of such difficulty, especially where the evidence of neglect or abuse is not necessarily clear cut:

**Removal of adult daughter from father.** The case concerned a young woman, 33 years old, of Afro-Caribbean background. She had a moderate to severe learning disability, atypical autism and epilepsy. She did not have the capacity to decide where she should live and who should provide care for her. In 1995, her mother died. Since then, her father (now 66 years old) had been her sole carer assisted by support workers, mostly privately arranged.

*Adult protection procedures.* Following an incident in which the father allegedly struck his daughter, the local authority instituted adult protection procedures. A court application was made; exercising the inherent jurisdiction, the court made a number of interim declarations, making it lawful for the authority to place the woman in residential care, to prevent removal by the father and to limit contact.

*Local authority's case.* The local authority then sought confirmation of the interim declaration; the father opposed the local authority. The authority's case was that there was a real risk of further physical abuse; that the father's age and health meant he would find it more difficult to manage as time went on; that his volatile temperament and inability to work cooperatively with social services would probably compromise his ability to care (there was a long history of disputes with the local authority). Also alluded to were his failure in the past to recognise the importance of his daughter's siblings in her life and to put her needs above his own, and his alleged drinking habits.

*The father's case.* The father's case was that many of the local authority's allegations were old and unfounded and many related to the stressful time when his wife died from cancer. At the time the local authority had not acted on any of these concerns. Furthermore, some of his complaints about the local authority's conduct had been upheld. An incident going back to 1991, related by a support worker, when he allegedly threatened to beat his daughter with a belt, the judge discounted for lack of evidence on the file. A 1992 incident, reported by a nurse, that he had hit his daughter four times with his fist about the head and face, the judge also discounted on the evidence. The older allegations of drinking to excess, the judge also discounted, insofar as they came from his two other children, since they were so hostile to their father. A more recent allegation was also found to be unreliable; the judge took account of the fact that the witness, as a Muslim, did not drink alcohol; and a senior local authority community worker pointed out that the father's explanation was that he relieved pain in his neck and shoulder by rubbing them with Bay Rum.

*Appraisal of father's ability to care.* The judge found the father to be a proud man, verging on authoritarian toward his family, a regular member of his local Pentecostal Church. He cared for his daughter and felt it his strong duty to do so. However, he was not an easy person to deal with for the local authority; but the latter had not treated him as sympathetically as it might have. He loved his daughter. He had cared for her with the assistance of carers; he had provided adequately for her needs. He was 66. He had diabetes and arthritis; there was no contingency plan if he should fall ill. He had a fractured relationship with his other two children, which meant they could not come to the house to visit their sister.

*Declaration in favour of the local authority.* When the judge drew up a final balance sheet he recognised the father's sense of duty and love for his daughter. However, he was 66 years old, had diabetes and arthritis and would find it increasingly difficult to cope. Furthermore professional evidence pointed out the advantage of the proposed alternative accommodation in terms of meeting the daughter's needs. The balance sheet therefore pointed to the daughter living in the accommodation proposed by the local authority; this would be in her best interests (*Newham LBC v BS*).

In similar types of case, the courts have likewise ruled in favour of the local authority (see examples in 17.5.2.7). The example above concerned a dispute involving a public body (the local authority). However, the court may be called on to exercise its inherent jurisdiction in relation to private persons as well:

**Removal of man to Norway.** A dispute arose between the family of a man who had become unable to express his preference following a severe stroke, and the woman with whom he had set up home – as to where he was to be cared for and by whom. The court accepted that the issue as to where the patient's best interests lay was a matter it could deal with.

The family had tried to remove the man from a hospital in England and to take him back to Norway; the woman had obtained an interim injunction preventing this. The family claimed that in the absence of a legal relationship between the man and woman, the court had no jurisdiction to grant such relief. The Court of Appeal now found, in the light of the evidence relating to the relationship between the man and woman, that the court anyway did have jurisdiction; but that also, the woman could have demonstrated a legal right had it been necessary for her to do so (which it was not) (*Re S*).

## 18.8.1 EXERCISE OF THE INHERENT JURISDICTION

Generally speaking, the courts are normally called on to make a declaration concerning best interests in the following situations. First, the issue in question needs in all cases to be significant, that is be seriously justiciable; the courts would not wish to make a declaration about breakfast cereal, so to speak.

Second, if the relevant parties involved cannot agree about what a person's best interests are, then resort to the courts might be required – even if the issue is not one that the courts would otherwise have needed to deal with, had all relevant parties agreed as to where a person's best interests lay. Just such a disagreement arose in the following case:

**Hospital treatment of person with severe learning disability.** An 18-year-old had the capacity of a five- to six-year-old child – with severe learning disability, autism and epilepsy. He was admitted to hospital for acute renal failure; haemodialysis was required. A dispute arose between the hospital and mother as to whether or in what circumstances a kidney transplant would ever be suitable for him and whether there was a possibility of a different form of haemodialysis by use of AV fistula.

The court found that the medical and nursing team's approach had been coloured by past experience with the man and the difficulties of verbal communication. However, other evidence in the case showed that steps could be taken to enable him to cope with certain treatment and that the possibility of an AV fistula should not be ruled out and kidney transplantation should not be ruled on non-medical grounds.

The court made the point that it was crucial that he was not given less satisfactory treatment than a person who understood the risks, pain and discomfort of major surgery. 'To act in any other way would be contrary to the rights of a mentally incapacitated patient both under our domestic law and under the European Convention' (*An Hospital NHS Trust v S*).

Where a person lacks capacity and there is uncertainty or disagreement, the courts will wish to be involved in questions of life-prolonging treatment generally. In a case concerned with the withdrawal of artificial hydration and nutrition (ANH), the court stated that it should be involved:

- where there is doubt about the patient's capacity to take a decision
- where there is a lack of unanimity amongst the medical doctors about
  - the patient's condition or prognosis
  - the patient's best interests
  - the likely outcome of ANH being withheld or withdrawn
  - whether ANH should be withheld or withdrawn
- where there is evidence that, if competent, the patient would have wanted ANH to continue
- where there is evidence of the patient (even if a child or lacking capacity) resisting or disputing the proposed withdrawal of ANH
- where people having a reasonable claim to have their views or evidence taken into account assert that withdrawal of ANH is contrary to the patient's wishes or not in the patient's best interests (*Burke v General Medical Council*).

The courts will also wish to be involved as a matter of course for other drastic interventions; for instance, the sterilisation of a woman for non-therapeutic reasons (e.g. *SL v SL*).

Third, as the inherent jurisdiction has been a developing one, there might be uncertainty over whether the matter in question is in principle one that is within the court's inherent jurisdiction (*Re: F (Adult Patient)*: protection of woman with learning disabilities; see 17.5.2.7).

Fourth, there is sometimes uncertainty as to whether the court needs to be resorted to for a decision (even in the absence of disagreement about intervention), in which case it is applied to for clarification:

**Lawfulness of cessation of artificial ventilation.** A man with motor neurone disease had slight eyelash movement as his only means of communication to express his wishes. He indicated that when he lost this last means of communication, he wished the artificial ventilation to cease. The doctors wanted the legal position clarified; in fact the court stated that the law was so clear (since the man had capacity to take this decision) that the doctors need not have applied to the courts and instead simply proceeded in accordance with the man's wishes. In fact, because one of the doctors had received conflicting legal advice, the court held that the court application was a proper one, although would not be necessary in every case (*Re AK (medical treatment: consent)*).

**Note. Mental Capacity Bill 2004: court declarations on capacity and decision taken for a person lacking capacity.** The Bill makes provision for the Court of Protection to make declarations concerning a person's capacity to take a decision, and concerning the lawfulness of any act done or to be done in respect of the person (cl.15). Once this legislation is in force, the extent to which the inherent jurisdiction will in practice be required to be exercised by the courts is unclear.

## 18.8.2 ENFORCEABILITY OF THE INHERENT JURISDICTION

Use of the courts' inherent jurisdiction is largely identified with what is sometimes called 'declaratory relief'. However, the courts themselves have pointed out that a declaration in itself lacks teeth. Furthermore, if it is backed up by an injunction, there is the problem of inflexibility and inability to monitor or vary its contents, as well as the 'appalling vista' of enforcement and of possible contempt proceedings (*Re D-R*). Nevertheless, the courts will be prepared to issue injunctions in some circumstances:

**Injunction restraining publication of report concerning vulnerable adults.** A local authority sought an order from the court, exercising its inherent jurisdiction, authorising it to publish a report – commissioned by the local Area Child Protection Committee. The report concerned a foster mother who adopted most of the children she had previously fostered and created a large family of vulnerable young people who also came to live with her when they were adult. The foster mother, the children and the vulnerable adults resisted publication on grounds of confidentiality and right to respect for private life under article 8 of the European Convention. The children and the vulnerable adults succeeded.

As far as the adults were concerned, the court was exercising its inherent jurisdiction; furthermore it would go beyond a declaration, which would not bind the local authority. It would grant an injunction restraining publication (*A local authority v A Health Authority*).

In a case involving life-prolonging treatment, the court stated that there was no reason why it could not in an appropriate case grant both a declaration and mandatory relief against an NHS Trust to provide that treatment. Such relief would not lie against an individual doctor (who might be professionally unwilling to treat) but against the Trust, which would then have an obligation to find another doctor willing to treat (*R(Burke) v General Medical Council*).

## 18.8.3 INHERENT JURISDICTION AND EFFECT ON COMMUNITY CARE DUTIES

Declarations about best interests are made by the Family Division of the High Court; whereas judicial review (see 4.2) of a local authority's community care decision making takes place in the Administrative Division of the High Court. Different principles are involved in each. The first one concerns private law, involving judicial identification of the best course of action for the person concerned. The other is a public law, supervisory jurisdiction concerned basically with whether a public body has made a decision within a reasonable band of possible decisions that lay open to it within the relevant legislative context (e.g. community care legislation) – but not with whether, irrespective of that context, the 'best' decision has been taken. The question has inevitably arisen in the courts as to how a decision made under one jurisdiction impacts on the other:

**Where a person should live: best interests and community care duties.** A man with learning disabilities, deaf and with no verbal communication lived for many years at a long-stay hospital. He was then resettled in a small care home, funded by the health authority. Following a hip fracture, he was admitted to hospital; he was subsequently removed by his father and taken to the latter's home, where he had since been living. A dispute then arose about where he should live and about contact with his parents (long since divorced). One of the issues considered was the extent to which a declaration by the court as to best interests could bind the local authority or NHS to make particular provision in public law (*A v A health authority*).

The answer in the above case was that a best interests declaration could not in principle bind the local authority or NHS to take a particular decision concerning the service user, in the exercise of their statutory functions (i.e. under community care and NHS legislation). Although such a declaration would be persuasive, the court seemed not to accept that it would be 'coercive', unless a mandatory order were made. The court was at pains to point out the different principles underlying the exercise of the inherent jurisdiction by the Family Division of the High Court, and the exercise of its public law jurisdiction by the Administrative Division of the High Court.

## 18.9 ADVANCE DECISIONS TO REFUSE TREATMENT

The Mental Capacity Bill 2004 covers advance statements relating to the refusal of medical treatment. It sums up what is arguably the current common law position; once it is established that the advance decision is both valid and applicable to the treatment in question, it has binding effect.

For example, the courts gave guidelines in 1998, that treatment and care should normally be subject to an advance directive or statement. However, if there was reason to doubt the reliability of the advance statement (e.g. that it did not apply to the present circumstances), then a court declaration should be sought (where the patient was stating that he or she did not consent to the treatment) (*R v Collins, ex p S (no.2)*).

**Advance statement by means of slight eyelash movement.** A man with motor neurone disease had slight eyelash movement as his only means of communication to express his wishes. By this means, he stated that when he lost this last means of communication, he wished the artificial ventilation to cease. The court stated that such a valid advance indication would be effective and that doctors would not be entitled to act inconsistently with it – so long as he did not subsequently indicate that his wishes had changed (*Re AK (medical treatment: consent)*).

However, for an advance statement to be potentially valid, the person must have the requisite capacity at the time of making the statement. For instance, a person with borderline personality disorder, who self-harmed by cutting herself and blood-letting, made such a statement, refusing blood transfusions. She believed her blood was evil and contaminated the blood being transfused. The evidence showed that she lacked capacity at the time of making the statement; it was therefore not effective (*An NHS Trust v Ms T*).

The difficult issues and decisions involved were illustrated in 2004, when a local authority reportedly agreed (with court involvement) that its carers would respect the advance statement of a woman with multiple sclerosis; namely that if she began to choke, the carers would not attempt to save her (Foggitt 2004).

Also during 2004, the courts stated that, in the context of artificial nutrition and hydration (ANH) as a species of life-prolonging treatment, an advance statement should be treated as applicable also to the requirement to treat and not just to the refusal of treatment (*R (Burke) v General Medical Council*). At the time of writing, the Mental Capacity Bill 2004 does not reflect this judgment, since it covers only refusal.

Note. **Mental Capacity Bill 2004: advance decisions**. The Bill states that a person aged 18 or over may specify the circumstances in which at a future date, if he or she lacks capacity, specified treatment is not to be given.

The advance decision is not valid if the person has withdrawn it; subsequently conferred authority for the making of such a decision through a lasting power of attorney; done anything inconsistent with the advance decision.

The advance decision is not applicable to the particular treatment in issue if that treatment is not specified in the advance decision, the circumstances specified in the advance statement have not arisen – or there are reasonable grounds for believing that circumstances now exist that the person did not anticipate at the time of the advance decision, but which would have affected that decision had they been anticipated.

The advance decision is not applicable to life-sustaining treatment unless this is specified in the decision.

Otherwise an advance decision that is both valid and applicable to the treatment in question has effect as if the person had made it (and had the capacity to do so) at the time when the question arises about whether to carry out the treatment (cll.24–26).

## 18.10 ADVOCACY

The Mental Incapacity Bill 2004 does not impose a general obligation that advocates be appointed for people lacking capacity. However, it does refer to the appointment of independent consultees in relation to decisions in connection with serious medical treatment, provision of hospital or care home accommodation by the NHS, or provision of residential accommodation by a local authority – for a person lacking capacity. In such circumstances, if there is no person to consult about the decision, other than somebody treating or caring for the person professionally or for remuneration, the NHS or local authority must make available an 'independent consultee' – whose advice must be sought (cll. 34–37).

CHAPTER 19

# Information sharing

**KEY POINTS**

It is beyond the scope of this book to cover the subject of information sharing in detail. However, it merits a brief summary in relation to the sharing of personal information both within and between statutory organisations such as local authorities and NHS bodies – and also to the disclosure of personal information to service users. It is also relevant specifically in the context of adult (and child) protection as evidenced by a number of court cases where close scrutiny of the legal basis for information sharing has taken place.

In summary, the law generally affecting the sharing of information consists of the common law of confidentiality, the Data Protection Act 1998 and article 8 of the European Convention on Human Rights. In addition, there are other specific, relevant legislative provisions that affect the balance to be struck between disclosure and non-disclosure of personal information; for instance, the provision of both conviction and 'soft' non-conviction information by the police in the context of enhanced criminal record certificates (see 17.4).

**Note: Wales, Northern Ireland and Scotland**. The principles entailed in the common law of confidentiality, the Data Protection Act 1998 and the European Convention on Human Rights apply across Wales, Northern Ireland and Scotland. (In Scotland, breach of confidence is recognised as a 'delict': Mays 1999, p.371.)

## 19.1 COMMON LAW OF CONFIDENTIALITY AND HUMAN RIGHTS

A common law of confidentiality has in the past existed and in principle remains to the extent that any particular issue is not determined by other legislation.

**Breaching confidentiality to mental health patient.** A consultant psychiatrist prepared a report for a patient prior to a mental review tribunal hearing. The report was unfavourable and the patient withdrew his application. However, the consultant was so concerned about the potential danger that the man represented that he sent the report to both the Home Office and the hospital where the man was detained. The court held that the breach of confidentiality was justified in the public interest (*W v Edgell*).

In one case, the court pointed out that it was not known how, if at all, the relevant information would be recorded and thus whether the Data Protection Act 1998 applied at all. It therefore decided the case with reference to the common law of confidentiality (*R(A) v National Probation Service*; see 17.7).

In the following case, the court found that the Data Protection Act 1998 did apply but was of limited assistance because of its generality. Instead the judge turned to article 8 of the European Convention on Human Rights (right to respect for privacy) and the common law of confidentiality. Both demanded that a balance be struck:

**Disclosure of information to a mother.** A mother was the nearest relative under the Mental Health Act 1983, in relation to her adult son who was under the guardianship of the local authority. He lacked the capacity to take the relevant decisions for himself. She wished to gain access to her son's council files and to his medical records. The council was prepared to let experts appointed by the mother to have access, and for them to communicate information as they thought fit to the mother and her solicitors. The mother challenged this.

The court accepted that the Data Protection Act 1998 helped little; its generality meant that it did not prevent disclosure to the mother, but nor did it require the local authority positively to disclose. The judge turned to the common law of confidentiality and to human rights. Both required a balance to be struck between the 'public and private interests in maintaining the confidentiality of this information and the public and private interests in permitting, indeed requiring, its disclosure for certain purposes'.

The interests to be balanced consisted of the confidentiality of the information, the proper administration of justice and the mother's right of access to legal advice (relating to the guardianship, the mother's exercise of the nearest relative function, and her possible displacement as nearest relative by the local authority); the rights of the mother and son to respect for their family life and adequate involvement in decision-making processes; the son's right to respect for his private life; and the protection of the son's health and welfare.

The court held that the balance came down in favour of disclosure to the mother and her solicitors as well as the experts (*R v Plymouth CC, ex p Stevens*).

In another case, the courts similarly found that disclosure would breach neither confidentiality nor human rights:

**Disclosure by local authority of personal details to university.** A woman was known to social services, because of concerns and difficulties about the bringing up of her child. The woman subsequently wished to study to become a social worker. The local authority had concerns about her fitness for such a job; it disclosed its concerns to the university. The court held that in this instance the local authority's disclosure was lawful, even though it had not maintained confidentiality. The matter was one of public interest. Good practice would have involved the council informing the woman first, so that she could seek an injunction to prevent disclosure; however, breach of good practice did not equate to a breach of the duty of confidence. Likewise the claim failed under article 8 (right to respect for privacy); the means were proportionate and the purpose was to protect others from unsuitable social workers (*Maddock v Devon CC*).

Similarly, in a case concerning allegations surrounding the death of a resident in a nursing home, the courts found disclosure by the police to a regulatory body to be justified. Referring to article 8 of the European Convention on Human Rights, the court accepted the disclosure as necessary in a democratic society for the protection of health or morals or for the protection and rights of freedoms of others:

**Nursing home death and disclosure.** The matron of a nursing home was interviewed following the death of a resident alleged to have followed an overdose of diamorphine. The police concluded there was insufficient evidence to bring charges. The United Kingdom Central Council for Nursing, Midwifery and Health Visiting began an investigation. The police sought the matron's permission to disclose the statements she had made at police interview. The Royal College of Nursing, on behalf of the matron, refused that permission. The court ruled in this case that the police could in such circumstances pass on such confidential information in the interests of public health or safety. Nevertheless, generally, a balance had to be struck between competing public interests in such circumstances; the individual should be notified about the proposed disclosure; and in case of refusal, the court could be applied to (*Woolgar v Chief Constable of Sussex Police*).

In the past, the courts have pointed out that there is generally no presumption of disclosure. For example, even where there were suspicious deaths in the family and care proceedings under the Children Act 1989, the court cautioned against a presumption of disclosure to the policy, but instead insisted that a balancing act be carried out (*Chief Constable v A County Council*). The courts have expected the disclosing organisation to carry out a 'pressing need' test, before any disclosure is made. The disclosure might be justified:

**Disclosure to caravan site owner.** A married couple were released from prison, where they served sentences for serious sexual offences against children. They went to live on a caravan site in the North of England. The local police asked them to move from the site before Easter, when many children would be visiting. The couple refused. The police disclosed their background to the caravan site owner. He asked them to leave. The couple claimed they had been treated unfairly and should have been shown the allegations. The court held that they should have been informed of the gist of the information held by the police, but that this would not have affected the conclusion. The police needed to apply a 'pressing need' test as to whether to disclose, on the basis of as much information as possible. The disclosure was lawful (*R v Chief Constable of North Wales, ex p AB*).

Alternatively, disclosure might be unjustified in the absence of a pressing need test being applied:

**Failure to consider facts of particular case.** An uncorroborated allegation was made that a man had abused a child at a hostel for vulnerable children. A few years later a further allegation that he had abused his daughter was made by the wife during acrimonious divorce proceedings. No action was taken, but the family was placed on the child protection register. He then set up his own bus company with a contract to run school bus services. The police and social services disclosed his background to the education department of the local authority. The latter terminated the contract. The court held that the disclosure by the police and by social services was unlawful because (a) disclosure should be the exception and not the rule and (b) there was no evidence that either had applied the pressing need test in terms of considering the facts of the particular case (*R v A local authority in the Midlands, ex p LM*).

On the other hand, the particular legislative context may alter the balance and even create a presumption of disclosure (see 19.3).

## 19.2 DATA PROTECTION ACT 1998

The Data Protection Act 1998 contains a number of key points that are relevant to the holding, sharing and destruction of information in the context of community care. In particular, reference needs to be made to the data protection principles which include general rules and safeguards concerning the processing of information. There are various basic definitions contained within the Data Protection Act 1998:

- **Personal data**. The Act applies to data controllers in respect of personal data. This means data relating to a living individual who can be identified from those data alone, or from those data together with other information in the possession of, or likely to come into the possession of, the data controller. Personal data include any expression of opinion about the individual, as well as any indication of the intentions toward the individual of the data controller or any other person (s.1).
- **Sensitive personal data**. Sensitive personal data include information, among other things, about the person's racial or ethnic origin, physical or mental health or condition, sexual life, commission of an alleged offence, proceedings for any offence committed or allegedly committed, and court sentence in any such proceedings (s1).
- **Processing**. Processing of information is defined very widely. It means obtaining, recording or holding it or carrying out any operation on it, including (a) its organisation, adaptation or alteration; (b) retrieval, consultation or use; (c) disclosure; (d) alignment, combination, blocking, erasure or destruction (s.1).
- **Relevant filing system: manual information**. In addition to applying to automated, computerised information, the Act also applies to manual information held as part of a relevant filing system. This means a set of information structured so that specific information relating to a particular individual is readily accessible (s.1). The courts have, however, applied a narrow definition of a relevant filing system in respect of manual data, stating that such systems must be comparable to computer systems in terms of sophistication and providing ready accessibility to personal information (*Durant v FSA*).

   The view of the Information Commissioner is that, as a consequence of this judgment, 'most information about individuals held in manual form does not, therefore, fall within the data protection regime'. This would be because a filing system by individual name, with information held in chronological order, would be excluded. Such a file would only be a relevant filing system, if each individual file were subdivided or indexed to allow retrieval of particular types of information about the person without a manual search (Information Commissioner 2004). However, from January 2005, the Freedom of Information Act 2000 (s.68) amends the definition of data in the Data Protection Act 1998 (s.1), so as to include in effect personal information held in unstructured manual filing systems by public authorities. Guidance issued by the Information Commissioner explains that this gives people access, under the 2000 Act, to such information held by public authorities (Information Commissioner 2004a).

- **Accessible record**. This means health record, educational record or accessible public record (s.68).
- **Health record**. This means any record which '(a) consists of information relating to the physical or mental health or condition of an individual, and (b) has been made by or on behalf of a health professional in connection with the care of that individual' (s.68).
- **Accessible public record**. This means record kept by housing and social services authorities for the purpose respectively of any of the authority's tenancies or 'for any purpose of the authority's social services functions' (schedule 12).

## 19.2.1 RIGHTS OF DATA SUBJECT TO INFORMATION

People (data subjects) have a general right to find out about and receive copies of personal data of which they are the subject. There are some provisos to this right of access. One is where complying with a request for information would also mean disclosing information relating to somebody else. In this case, the data controller is not obliged to disclose, unless the other person has consented, or it is nevertheless reasonable in all the circumstances to disclose without that consent. However, the data controller could anyway communicate so much of the information as could be communicated without disclosing the identity of the individual concerned (s.7).

This rule, together with the possibility of independent review by the Information Commissioner or by the courts, is to remedy the problem identified in *Gaskin v United Kingdom*, and which led to a breach of article 8 of the European Convention on Human Rights. Under the earlier Data Protection Act 1984, no process was specified for such disclosure in case of lack of consent of a third party, nor the possibility of independent review. The European Court on Human Rights has accepted that this aspect of the 1998 Act cures the previous defect (*MG v United Kingdom*).

There are specific exemptions relating to disclosure of data concerning information about a person's physical or mental health or condition, or held for social work purposes (s.30). Basically these apply where access by the data subject to the information would be likely to cause serious harm to the physical or mental health of the data subject or any person (SI 2000/413; SI 2000/415).

## 19.2.2 DATA PROTECTION PRINCIPLES

Data controllers must comply with data protection principles. All processing of personal data must comply with principles in Schedule 1 of the Act. These include that, for example:

- **purpose**: the data be obtained for one more specified purposes and should not be processed for another, incompatible purpose
- **relevance**: the data must be adequate, relevant and not excessive for the purpose
- **length of time**: data should be accurate and kept up to date, and not kept for longer than necessary for the purpose for which it had been processed
- **security**: appropriate technical and organisational measures should be taken in relation to the security of the data.

Following the conviction of Ian Huntley for the murder of two children, Jessica Chapman and Holly Wells, concerns were raised that the Act might have been to blame for some of the police and local authority failings to retain and share information. In which case, the principles set out above might have been deficient. However, the subsequent government enquiry concluded that the Act could not be blamed for the failure to retain relevant information (Bichard 2004, para 4.3). It is clear that a large degree of latitude is contained in the Act, so that terms such as adequacy, relevance, excessive and length of time can be interpreted depending on context and circumstances.

All personal data must be processed in accordance with at least one of the principles in Schedule 2 of the Act. These entail either that the data subject has consented or that various principles are satisfied, including that the data processing is necessary; for example:

- **legal obligation**: to comply with a legal obligation
- **vital interests**: to safeguard the vital interests of the data subject
- **justice**: for the administration of justice.
- **legislation**: for the exercise of any functions conferred on any person by or under any enactment (i.e. legislation).
- **Crown functions**: for the exercise of any functions of the Crown, a Minister of the Crown or a government department
- **public interest**: for the exercise of any other functions of a public nature exercised in the public interest by any person.

There is also a 'legitimate interests' principle. In addition, in the case of sensitive personal data (particularly relevant to social care and health care), at least one of the principles in schedule 3 must be complied with. The person must have consented, otherwise the principles include that the processing is necessary, for example:

- **right or obligation**: for the purpose of exercising or performing a right or obligation conferred by law on the data controller in connection with employment
- **inability to consent, protection of others**: to protect the vital interests of the data subject, where either consent cannot be given by or on behalf of the data subject – or to protect the vital interests of someone else, where consent by or on behalf of the data subject has been unreasonably withheld
- **legal proceedings**: for the purpose of legal proceedings, obtaining legal advice, or otherwise in connection with establishing, exercising or defending legal rights
- **justice**: for the administration of justice

- **legislation**: for the exercise of any functions conferred on any person by or under any enactment
- **Crown functions**: for the exercise of any functions of the Crown, a Minister of the Crown or a government department
- **medical purposes**: for medical purposes and is undertaken by a health professional – or by a person who in the circumstances owes a duty of confidentiality which is equivalent to that which would arise if that person were a health professional.

It will be noticed that under schedule 3, in the case of sensitive personal data, the fact that a person refuses consent to disclosure of personal information such that he or she would thereby suffer harm is not in itself sufficient to justify disclosure.

In addition, an order has been passed allowing sensitive personal data to be processed if, amongst other things, the processing is in the substantial public interest; is necessary for the purposes of the prevention or detection of any unlawful act; and must be necessarily carried out without the explicit consent of the data subject being sought, so as not to prejudice those purposes. The schedule to the order refers to the processing being necessary for the exercise of any functions conferred on a constable by any rule of law (SI 2000/417).

**Information passed between police forces and then to education authority.** Non-conviction information was passed from one police force to another; the latter then informed the education authority with whom the person concerned had applied for a job that involved working with children (headship of an infants' school). The job offer was withdrawn.

The court pointed out that the Data Protection Act 1998 was not breached either when the information passed between the police forces, or from one police force to the education authority. This was because the information came under the 2000 Order, which referred to the processing of sensitive personal data by a constable under any rule of law, and to the prevention or detection of unlawful acts (R v Chief Constables of C and D, ex p A).

It can be seen that the data protection principles are so broadly drawn that in case of disclosure matters the courts have sometimes held that the Act only gets one so far. The balancing act has to be performed with reference to principles established in other areas of law such as human rights and the common law of confidentiality (R v Plymouth CC, ex p Stevens).

## 19.3 LEGISLATION SPECIFICALLY REFERRING TO INFORMATION DISCLOSURE

Certain legislation specifically contemplates disclosure and might affect the nature of any balancing test that the courts bring to bear. For example, under s.115 of the Crime and Disorder Act 1998, any person who would not otherwise have the power to disclose information to a relevant authority or to a person acting on behalf of that authority (including the police, local authority, probation committee, health authority) shall have the power to do so in any case where the disclosure is necessary or expedient for the purposes of any provision of that Act.

The Court of Appeal has held that s.115 of the Police Act 1997 tends toward a presumption of disclosure by the police in response to information sought in respect of enhanced criminal record certificates (17.4.2). This decision overrules that of the High Court, which had held that the (common law) presumption of non-disclosure still applied in the context of the Police Act (*R(X) v Chief Constable of West Midlands Police*).

Under the Criminal Justice Act 2003, what are termed Multi-Agency Public Protection Agency arrangements demand cooperation between different bodies, which may involve information sharing (17.7).

## 19.4 CALDICOTT GUARDIANS

The Department of Health has issued guidance to local social services authorities, expecting them to have appointed (by April 2002) a 'Caldicott Guardian'. The function of this person is to safeguard and govern the use made of confidential information, particularly in respect of the requirements of the Data Protection Act 1998 with regard to processing and sharing, and to the security of, confidential information (LAC(2002)2). Caldicott Guardians had already been introduced to the NHS at an earlier date.

## 19.5 LOSS OF INFORMATION

The ability to share information at all or to give people the right of access to their own personal information is severely compromised if that information is lost. This would normally constitute maladministration; for example, in one case involving the loss of a person's adoption files, the local ombudsman recommended compensation of £1000 and £200 in addition for the time and trouble expended in complaining (*Birmingham City Council 1993*). In another case, when one file was lost and access to another delayed, concerning a man's time in care and return home under supervision, the ombudsman recommended £500 compensation (*Tower Hamlets LBC 2004*).

## 19.6 ACCESS TO NON-PERSONAL PUBLIC INFORMATION

In order to explore possible grounds of complaint or challenge to a decision, an individual might need other information beyond the personal – for example, about general council policy, perhaps with a view to finding out how other people have been treated in a similar situation.

The public has a right to attend local authority meetings (with some exceptions) including social services committee meetings. However, access is denied if 'confidential information' is at issue – either information supplied by a government department where disclosure to the public is forbidden, or information disclosure of which is prevented by legislation or a court order. In addition, councils have the power to deny access in relation to 'exempt information', which includes (amongst various items) information about applicants or recipients of services, legal proceedings – or terms relating to proposed contracts or the acquisition or disposal of property. Access to agendas, reports and background documents must be given three days before a meeting, but items can be excluded if they relate to parts of the meeting which will not be open to the public (Local Government Act 1972, s.100A, schedule 12A).

For instance, it was reported that, when consulting about best value and the transfer of care homes to the independent sector, one local authority attempted to keep secret the best value report it had commissioned from a consultancy firm – and to justify this under schedule 12A's reference to disposal of property as an exception to disclosure. In the event a councillor leaked the report to a local voluntary group opposing the transfers (McFadyean and Rowland 2002, p.9).

In addition, the NHS is also subject to a code of practice on openness. Certain categories of information are excluded from disclosure; for example, personal information, unreasonable or excessively general information about internal discussion and advice, management information that would harm the operation of the NHS organisation, information about legal matters where disclosure would be prejudicial to the administration of justice and law, information given in confidence, and information soon to be published (DH 2003i).

In January 2005, the Freedom of Information Act 2000 came into force, applying to public authorities including local authorities and the NHS. Public authorities must have a publication scheme (s.19) and provide information in response to requests (s.1). There are various exempted types of information including the following that are probably the most relevant in the context of social care and health care provision:

- information otherwise reasonably accessible to the applicant
- information intended for future publication
- information held in relation to:
    - security matters
    - public authority investigations and proceedings
    - law enforcement that would otherwise be prejudiced
    - audit functions
    - formulation of government policy
    - conduct of public affairs that would otherwise be prejudiced
    - health and safety
    - personal information
    - information provided in confidence
    - legal professional privilege
    - commercial interests
- information, disclosure of which is prohibited by other legislation, is incompatible with any European Community obligation or would be a contempt of court (ss.21–43).

CHAPTER 20

# Human rights

**KEY POINTS**

In October 2000, the Human Rights Act 1998 embedded the European Convention on Human Rights 1998 into United Kingdom law. The 1998 Act is the vehicle; the main rights themselves lie within the Convention. For the purpose of this book, particularly relevant rights include (but are not confined to):

- article 2 (right to life)
- article 3 (right not to be subjected to torture or to inhuman and degrading treatment)
- article 5 (right not to be arbitrarily deprived of liberty)
- article 8 (right to respect for private and family life, home and correspondence)
- article 14 (right not to be discriminated against).

The decision making (and actions and sometimes omissions) of local authorities, NHS bodies and other public bodies must be consistent not just with all the relevant domestic law, but with the Human Rights Act as well. Thus, community care related cases in which human rights have been considered have involved, for instance, closure of care homes or NHS residential units, provision of suitably adapted accommodation for a disabled woman and her family, disclosure of confidential information, the manual handling of two profoundly disabled women in their own home, renal treatment for a man with learning disabilities, resuscitation in hospital of a man with learning disabilities, etc.

Note: Wales, Northern Ireland and Scotland. The Human Rights Act 1998 applies across the United Kingdom.

## 20.1 HUMAN RIGHTS ACT 1998

The Human Rights Act 1998 (HRA) introduced directly into United Kingdom law the rights contained in the European Convention. Prior to the implementation of the 1998 Act, United Kingdom courts could in principle barely apply those human rights. They sometimes found ways around this; for instance, in respect of asylum seekers they identified a common law of humanity in an old 1803 case (*R v Inhabitants of Eastbourne*); and referred to the Convention when the NHS was closing a disability unit even before the 1998 Act was in force (*R v North and East Devon Health Authority, ex p Coughlan*). But applicants could take their case further to the European Court of Human Rights (e.g. *Z v United Kingdom* concerning child protection) and they can still (e.g. *Pretty v United Kingdom* concerning assisted suicide). However, in theory, resort to the European Court should not be necessary so often in the future. Particular points covered by the Act include the following.

### 20.1.1 COMPATIBILITY OF DOMESTIC LAW

The courts must, as far as possible, interpret domestic legislation as compatible with the Convention (s.3). This gives the court wide scope. However, if the court, try as it might, is unable to find such compatibility, it has the power to make a declaration of incompatibility. This does not mean the legislation in question ceases to have effect (s.4). Instead, central government has the power to make a remedial order, in order to change the legislation in question (s.10).

**Mental disorder and detention.** The courts found that ss.72 and 73 of the Mental Health Act 1983 were incompatible with article 5 of the European Convention, because they effectively placed the burden on the patient – of proving that the criteria justifying detention in hospital no longer existed. The mental health review tribunal had to be satisfied that the person was not suffering from mental disorder in order to direct discharge. This meant that a person could continue to be detained even if the tribunal was not necessarily satisfied that the person was suffering from mental disorder. The courts made a declaration of incompatibility (*R(H) v Mental Health Review Tribunal North and East London Region*); the government subsequently passed the Mental Health Act 1983 (Remedial Order) 2001 (SI 2001/3712) so as to switch the burden of proof to the tribunal. Tribunals now must discharge the patient if they are not satisfied that the person is suffering from mental disorder.

**Incompatibility of automatic appointment of nearest relative.** A woman was detained under the Mental Health Act 1983. She argued that ss.26 and 29 of the Act were incompatible with article 8. This was because 'nearest relatives' were automatically appointed according to the 'pecking order' in s.26. This would mean her adoptive father, against whom she had previously made allegations of sexual abuse, would be the nearest relative. Under the Act, the woman had no legal means to compel his replacement by somebody else, as the Act does not allow the patient to challenge the status of the nearest relative. This meant the Act was incompatible with a.8 of the Convention. The Secretary of State conceded this incompatibility; the European Court had anyway previously identified it in a 'friendly settlement' case (*JT v United Kingdom*).

The Secretary of State nevertheless urged the court not to make a declaration of incompatibility, because the government intended to rectify the situation with new legislation. The judge decided to make such a declaration (under s.4 of the Human Rights Act) because the incompatibility had been identified some time (six years) ago and its anticipated removal had not yet taken place (*R(M) v Secretary of State for Health*).

## 20.1.2 UNLAWFUL ACTS BY PUBLIC AUTHORITIES

It is unlawful for public authorities to act incompatibly with a Convention right, unless an Act of Parliament leaves it with no choice (HRA 1998, s.6).

## 20.1.3 PUBLIC AUTHORITY DEFINITION

The Human Rights Act applies to public authorities only. A public authority is defined to include, in addition to obvious bodies such as local authorities, any person in respect of whom some functions are of a public nature (s.6). This is significant in the context of community care.

**Independent providers of care services: not performing public functions.** The courts have ruled that independent care providers in the context of community care are not public authorities for the purposes of the Human Rights Act. However, there is nothing to stop local authorities placing contractual obligations on such providers to observe human rights (*R(Heather) v Leonard Cheshire Foundation*: closure of care home). Nevertheless, the commercial dealings by a local authority with an independent care provider might well be held by the courts to be public in nature and so subject to human rights considerations (*R(Haggerty) v St Helens Council*: closure of care home).

By contrast, in some contexts other than community care, the courts have held that independent providers will be viewed as public bodies for the purposes of the Human Rights Act. For instance, in a case where a large-scale transfer of council housing had taken place from the local authority to a housing association, the courts ruled that the housing association was carrying out public functions in respect of that housing, and so was subject to the Human Rights Act (*Donoghue v Poplar Housing Association*). Likewise, the following example concerning mental health treatment is in contrast to the community care cases:

**Private psychiatric hospital: public functions.** A patient was detained under the Mental Health Act 1983 in a private psychiatric hospital where she was funded by the health authority. She was on a ward for therapeutic treatment for women patients with personality disorder. The managers of the hospital changed the treatment focus of the ward to medication treatment for women with a mental illness. She claimed that as a result she was not now receiving appropriate care and treatment. She wished to bring a judicial review case, including human rights points, against the hospital as a public body. The court ruled that the change made to the ward was an act of a public nature, given the context of compulsion, and the public concern and interest concerning the care and treatment for mental health patients (*R v Partnerships in Care Ltd, ex p A*).

### 20.1.4 VICTIMS

In order to bring a human rights based case, the person must be classifiable as a victim of the allegedly unlawful act and be a person, any non-governmental organisation or group of persons (HRA 1998, s.7, and a.34 of the Convention).

### 20.1.5 TIME LIMITS

The general rule is that proceedings under the Act must be brought within a year of the act complained of. However, a court or tribunal can waive this requirement if it considers it 'equitable having regard to all the circumstances'. However, the one-year rule is also subject to any rule imposing a stricter time limit in relation to the procedure in question – such as the time limits applying to judicial review (HRA 1998, s.7).

### 20.1.6 REMEDIES

The courts have a discretion to grant a remedy as considered just and appropriate. Damages may be awarded in certain circumstances (s.8). In cases of maladministration, the local government ombudsman's recommendations on compensation for maladministration should be looked to for rough guidance (*R(Anufrijeva) v Southwark LBC*).

**Human rights damages for maladministration.** The local authority failed for nearly two years to meet the assessed community care needs of a seriously disabled woman. This resulted in her and her family living in conditions that breached article 8 of the Convention. The judge identified maladministration basically as the cause. He awarded damages of £10,000 (*R(Bernard) v Enfield LBC*).

In another case damages were awarded by the court where the article 5 rights of a number of patients detained under the Mental Health Act 1983 had been breached; this had been because of delays in hearing their applications to Mental Health Review Tribunals (*R(KB,MK,GM,PD,TB,B) v Mental Health Review Tribunal*).

## 20.2 EUROPEAN CONVENTION ON HUMAN RIGHTS

The Convention itself contains a number of rights. The following is a selection that arguably are the most relevant for the purposes of this book, together with a few selective examples.

### 20.2.1 ARTICLE 2: RIGHT TO LIFE

Article 2 begins by stating: 'Everyone's right to life shall be protected by law.' In the context of community care, it has been argued unsuccessfully in a number of cases concerning the closure of care homes (see 6.15.8).

**Leaving people to perish.** If a local authority were to leave disabled people to drown in the bath or perish in a fire, as a matter of manual handling related policy or protocol, article 2 and the right to life could be engaged (*R(A&B) v East Sussex CC (no.2)*).

**Assisted suicide.** A woman had motor neurone disease. She wanted the Director of Public Prosecutions to assure her that there would be no prosecution of her husband under the Suicide Act 1961, were he to assist her to commit suicide. No such undertaking was given. She challenged this, on the basis that her human rights under articles 2, 3, 8 and 14 would be breached. The House of Lords rejected her claim in respect of all of these, finding they were not engaged let alone breached (*R v Director of Public Prosecutions, ex p Pretty*). The European Court likewise found no breach of article 2 or article 3. It did find that article 8 was 'engaged' insofar as the legal prohibition on assisted suicide interfered with her right to respect for private life; but any such interference was justified as 'necessary' for the protection of the rights of others (such as the weak and vulnerable) who might suffer harm were the law to be otherwise (*Pretty v United Kingdom*).

**Forcible treatment.** The courts have stated that they would treat very seriously the issue of forcible treatment under the Mental Health Act 1983, and were prepared to allow cross-examination of medical specialists even in a judicial review case (not common practice). The court had to reach its own view of whether the man was capable of consenting. Depending on this conclusion, it had to consider whether forcible treatment would threaten the man's life (article 2), be degrading (article 3), and be both necessary and proportionate under article 8.2, given the extent to which the treatment would invade privacy (*R v Responsible Medical Officer Broadmoor Hospital, ex p Wilkinson*).

**Withdrawing artificial hydration and nutrition.** The courts have held that it is in principle lawful and not a breach of article 2 to withdraw artificial hydration and nutrition, as well as treatment, from a person lacking capacity to decide for himself or herself – if this was in his or her best interests. This has arisen in the case of a person in a persistent vegetative state (*NHS Trust A v M*). Where a person with motor neurone disease had capacity to make an advance statement, the court accepted that this could stipulate the discontinuation of not only all life-sustaining treatment but also ventilation, nutrition and hydration (*Re AK (medical treatment: consent)*).

Nevertheless, during 2004, the courts stated that withdrawal of artificial nutrition and hydration (ANH) before a dying patient lapsed into a coma would breach articles 3 and 8 of the Convention, since it would expose him or her to acute mental and physical suffering. This would be unless her or she specifically expressed a wish for such withdrawal (*Burke v General Medical Council*; see 18.8.1).

## 20.2.2 ARTICLE 3: INHUMAN OR DEGRADING TREATMENT
Article 3 states: 'No one shall be subjected to torture or to inhuman or to degrading treatment or punishment.' The courts normally regard article 3 as posing a high threshold; in other words it is not easily breached.

The European Court of Human Rights has stated that inhuman or degrading treatment means that the ill-treatment in question must reach a minimum level of severity, involve actual bodily injury or intense physical or mental suffering. Degrading treatment could occur if it 'humiliates or debases an individual showing a lack of respect for, or diminishing, his or her human dignity or arouses feelings of fear, anguish or inferiority capable of breaking an individual's moral and physical resistance' (*Pretty v United Kingdom*).

The courts have also held in 2004 that treatment is capable of being degrading even if the victim is unconscious or otherwise unaware of the ill-treated; it is enough if it is 'judged by the standard of right-thinking bystanders' as humiliating or debasing, showing a lack of respect for, or diminishing, human dignity. In the same case, it was held that, in general (subject to a few exceptions), and other than when a patient lapses into a final coma or wishes it, the withholding of life-prolonging treatment by the NHS – so as to subject a person 'to acute mental and physical suffering' such that he or she dies in 'avoidably distressing circumstances' – would prima facie constitute a breach of article 3 (*R(Burke) v General Medical Council*).

In one community care case, involving a failure by the local authority to find suitably adapted accommodation for a disabled woman for two years, the judge seriously considered whether article 3 had been breached. However, in the end he found a breach of article 8 only (*R(Bernard) v Enfield LBC*; see 20.2.4.1).

**Leaving people in degrading circumstances.** The court held that if manual handling policies or protocols were to mean that care staff would leave disabled people for hours sitting in their own bodily waste or on the lavatory, article 3 might be engaged – that is, the right not to be subjected to inhuman or degrading treatment. On the other hand, the hoisting of disabled people was not to be regarded as inherently degrading; whether or not it was would depend on the particular circumstances (*R(A&B) v East Sussex CC (no.2)*).

**Death of heroin addict.** The European Court found a breach of article 3 in relation to the distress and hardship caused to a heroin addict in prison who subsequently died there. Amongst the key reasons for this finding were the inability accurately to record her weight loss (through dehydration, vomiting), a gap in monitoring by doctors, failure to admit the person to hospital to ensure medication and fluid intake, and failure to obtain more expert assistance to control the vomiting (*McGlinchey v United Kingdom*).

**Degrading treatment of a disabled prisoner.** A severely physically disabled person was sent to prison for contempt of court, for failing to disclose her assets in a debt case. In the police cell she was unable to use the bed and had to sleep in her wheelchair where she became very cold. When she reached the prison hospital, she could not use the toilet herself, the female duty officer could not manage to move her alone, and male prison officers had to assist. The European Court found that to detain a severely disabled person in conditions where she is dangerously cold, risks developing pressure sores because her bed is too hard or unreachable, and is unable to go to the toilet or keep clean without the greatest difficulty constituted degrading treatment contrary to article 3. Damages of £4500 were awarded (*Price v United Kingdom*).

## 20.2.3 ARTICLE 5: DEPRIVATION OF LIBERTY
Article 5 states:

5.1. Everyone has a right to liberty and security of person. No one shall be deprived of his liberty save in the following cases and in accordance with procedures prescribed by law:

(a) the lawful detention of a person after conviction by a competent court
(b) the lawful arrest or detention of a person for non-compliance with the lawful order of a court or in order to secure the fulfilment of any obligations prescribed by law

(c) the lawful arrest or detention of a person effected for the purpose of bringing him before the competent legal authority on a reasonable suspicion of having committed an offence or when it is reasonably considered necessary to prevent his committing an offence or fleeing after having done so

(d) the detention of a minor by lawful order for the purpose of educational supervision or his lawful detention for the purpose of bringing him before the competent legal authority

(e) the lawful detention of persons for the prevention of the spreading of infectious diseases, of persons of unsound mind, alcoholics or drug addicts or vagrants

(f) the lawful arrest or detention of a person to prevent his effecting an unauthorised entry into the country or of a person against whom action is being taken with a view to deportation or extradition.

5.2. Everyone who is arrested shall be informed promptly, in a language which he understands, of the reasons for his arrest and of any charge against him.

5.3. Everyone arrested or detained in accordance with the provisions of 1(c) of this article shall be brought promptly before a judge or other judicial officer.

5.4. Everyone who is deprived of his liberty by arrest or detention shall be entitled to take proceedings by which the lawfulness of his detention shall be decided speedily by a court and his release ordered if his detention is not lawful.

5.5. Everyone who has been the victim of arrest or detention in contravention of the provisions of this article shall have an enforceable right to compensation.

Article 5 has been applied particularly in the context of criminal law and mental health. It has been held to be breached by the European Court of Human Rights in the case of informal, compliant but incapacitated mental health patients due to the absence of legal safeguards (*HL v United Kingdom*: see 17.5.2.8). A possible question mark also lies against s.47 of the National Assistance Act 1948, concerning removal of people from their homes (see 17.5.1).

**Delay in mental health review tribunal hearings.** Routine delays in convening mental health review tribunal hearings breached article 5(4) in terms of the speed of decisions concerning the lawfulness of detention under the Mental Health Act 1983 (*R v Mental Health Review Tribunal, ex p KB*). Likewise an automatic listing for hearings to take place eight weeks from day of application was a breach of a.5(4), because it did not allow for flexibility according to individual patients' circumstances (*R(C) v London South and West Region Mental Health Review Tribunal*).

## 20.2.4 ARTICLE 8: RIGHT TO RESPECT FOR PRIVATE AND FAMILY LIFE
Article 8 states:

8.1. Everyone has the right to respect for his private and family life, his home and his correspondence.

8.2. There shall be no interference by a public authority with the exercise of this right except such as is in accordance with the law and is necessary in a democratic society in the interests of national security, public safety or the economic well-being of the country, for the prevention of disorder or crime, for the protection of health or morals, or for the protection of the rights and freedom of others.

In a number of cases, the courts have stated that article 8 embraces a person's physical and psychological integrity (the latter in connection with the development of the personality of each individual in his relations with other human beings (*Botta v Italy*)). The following examples are designed to illustrate, step by step, how article 8 tends to be applied in practice.

### 20.2.4.1 Interference with private and family life, home and correspondence

The following examples show how article 8 might be breached in contexts relevant to community care:

**Failing to provide suitably adapted accommodation for a disabled woman.** A 48-year-old woman lived with her husband and six children aged between 3 and 20 years. She had suffered a stroke and was severely disabled. In September 2000, a local authority occupational therapist assessed a pressing need for suitably adapted accommodation for the family.

The housing department of the authority, which currently provided temporary accommodation, would not assist under the Housing Act 1996, because it had previously found the family intentionally homeless on grounds of rent arrears. This finding was upheld in the Court of Appeal, despite the husband's argument that the rent arrears had built up because of all the money he was spending on incontinence pads, carpet cleaner, etc. in dealing with her incontinence – because they were in unsuitable accommodation.

Nearly two years on from the assessment, the family was still in the unsuitable accommodation. The housing department had not yet evicted, in the light of the social services assessment.

The woman could not reach the lavatory and soiled herself several times a day, had no privacy, could not go out of the house, could not go upstairs, and could not go anywhere without her husband's assistance. She had to share a cramped living room with her husband and two youngest children; the other children had to go through that room in order to go upstairs. Her husband's health was at risk; his back problem deteriorated. She felt frustrated and humiliated because she was unable to do anything for her family and was totally dependent on them.

A High Court case was brought by the wife and husband. They argued breach of community care legislation, and breach of human rights.

The court found the local authority, under its social services functions, to be in breach of article 8; its failure to act on the assessment over a period of 20 months showed a singular lack of respect for the claimant's private and family life (*R(Bernard) v Enfield LBC*).

**Breach of promise made by the NHS.** When a health authority breached an explicit promise it had made concerning the continued residence of a group of disabled people in a specialist unit, the court referred to a breach of article 8 (*R v North and East Devon Health Authority, ex p Coughlan*).

**Local authority adult protection intervention.** When the court exercised its inherent jurisdiction to protect an 18-year-old woman from a potentially abusive home situation, it justified its interference with family life on the ground that the right was not to family life, but to a respect for family life. This in turn meant what was benign and positive in family life (*Re F (Adult Patient)*).

**Manual handling, and the physical and psychological integrity of two women with physical and learning disabilities.** Article 8 (right to respect for home, private and family life) has been held to include the physical and psychological integrity of disabled people, both within and without the home. Thus in a manual handling dispute, involving two women with severe physical and learning disabilities, it applied both to matters such as the dignity surrounding hoisting and transfers within the home – and also to their participation in the life of the community, including recreational and cultural activities.

However, the judge pointed out that paid carers, too, had rights relating to integrity and dignity under article 8. He also emphasised that hoisting was not inherently degrading, but that whether it was or not would depend on all the circumstances of the particular situation (*R(A&B) v East Sussex CC (no.2)*).

The courts have accepted that article 8 is not just about not interfering, but that it will sometimes entail positive obligations. This would be where there is a direct and immediate link between the provision sought by the applicant and his or her private life. At the same time, it has been held that article 8 does not apply to interpersonal relations of such 'broad and indeterminate scope' that there is no real link between the provision and the individual's private life.

**Disabled person's access to the beach and sea.** A physically disabled person went on holiday to the seaside. The resort lacked facilities to enable disabled people to gain access to the beach and sea. He complained that the Italian authorities had interfered with his private and personal development. The European Court of Human Rights accepted that article 8 is not just about interfering, but will sometimes entail positive obligations. This would be where there is a direct and immediate link between the provision sought by the applicant and his or her private life. This could involve adopting measures designed to secure respect for private life even in the sphere of relations between individuals. However, access to the beach and sea at a holiday resort distant from his normal place of residence concerned interpersonal relations of such broad and indeterminate scope that there was no real link between the provision and the individual's private life (*Botta v Italy*).

Furthermore, the courts have held that article 8 is not applicable each time an individual's everyday life is disrupted, but only in exceptional cases where the State does not adopt measures – such that this interferes with an individual's right to personal development and to establish and maintain relationships with other human beings and the outside world (*Sentges v Netherlands*).

This means that, generally, article 8 is simply not a broad-brush tool with which to enforce the provision of welfare benefits that a person is aggrieved at not receiving.

**Use of human rights to cure maladministration.** In a case involving the adequacy of accommodation provided by the local authority for asylum seekers, the court held that article 8 could sometimes impose a positive obligation on the state to provide support. However, the court found it hard to conceive of a situation where it would require the provision of welfare support, unless the situation was sufficiently severe to engage article 3 also. However, article 8 could more easily be engaged in family situations and the welfare of children. For example, the court noted that in *R(Bernard) v Enfield LBC*, family life had been seriously inhibited by the 'hideous conditions' prevailing in the home. Thus, generally, if there is culpable delay in administrative processes (i.e. maladministration) necessary to determine an article 8 right, the courts will not intervene unless substantial prejudice is caused to the person ((R)Anufrijeva v Southwark LBC).

Similarly, the Court of Appeal has doubted that refusal to fund medical treatment could constitute an interference in terms of article 8 (*R v North West Lancashire HA, ex p G, A and D*). However, a failure to consider all the relevant factors before deciding to remove a frail, 95-year-old woman from her care home meant that the local authority had not properly weighed up whether it was safeguarding her physical and psychological integrity; it had thus breached article 8 (*R(Goldsmith) v Wandsworth LBC*; see 3.9.1 for details).

### 20.2.4.2 In accordance with the law

If a local authority is to justify under article 8.2 the interference with the right to respect under 8.1, the first ground that must be satisfied is that the interference be in accordance with the law. This means the relevant domestic law.

**Closure of care home.** In one case involving the decision to close a local authority care home, the judge stated that he could not envisage any circumstances in the present case in which the council could act compatibly with the common law and its other statutory obligations and yet be in breach of human rights, whether under articles 2, 3 or 8 (*R(Cowl) v Plymouth CC*: first instance).

In another case, concerning the lawfulness of offering care home places instead of accommodation in the community, the court stated that community care legislation was broad, humane and took account of needs including family and private life. Therefore reference to article 8 of the Convention took the case no further (*R(Khana) v Southwark LBC*: High Court).

On the other hand, when a local social services authority breached article 8 by not arranging suitably adapted accommodation for a disabled woman (*R(Bernard) v Enfield LBC*), any justification in terms of the authority's action being in 'accordance with the law' would have failed. This was because the judge had anyway found the local authority to be in breach of the relevant domestic legislation, namely s.21 of the National Assistance Act 1948.

### 20.2.4.3 Necessary in a democratic society

The interference has to be necessary in the sense of being proportionate. One way of putting this is that a sledgehammer should not be used to crack a nut. For instance, if a supervision order under the Children Act 1989 would suffice to protect a child, a care order should not be granted because it would constitute disproportionate and unjustified interference in family life (*Re O*).

**Closure of NHS premises.** An NHS Trust decided to close a purpose-built complex for people with learning disabilities. The closure was challenged in respect of a 36-year-old resident who was microcephalic, autistic, had spasticity in her lower limbs, limited verbal skills and a mental age of four and a half years. The European Court of Human Rights held that the application was ill-founded and so not admissible to be fully heard before the Court. This was on the grounds that the decision to move the applicant was in accordance with the law (as established in *R(Collins) v Lincolnshire Health Authority*). The evidence showed that the decision to move her into alternative social care was not disproportionate, properly considered her interests and was supported by relevant and sufficient reasons relating to her welfare. The decision was therefore necessary in a democratic society (*Collins v United Kingdom*).

**Necessity, mode of dress and appearance, telephone monitoring.** A decision was made not to allow a woman detained under the Mental Health Act to dress as a woman. Amongst the reasons given were security (access to women's clothing might help other patients to escape) and therapeutic (progress of treatment). The court found that private life was being interfered with under a.8(1) but that it reflected a pressing social need and was proportionate (*R v Ashworth Special Hospital Authority, ex p E*).

The random monitoring of telephone calls in a high security mental health hospital interfered with patients' privacy but was justifiable in relation to security matters (*R v Ashworth Special Hospital Authority, ex p N*).

### 20.2.4.4 Economic well-being of the country

The reference to economic well-being of the country inevitably concerns resources. A number of community care cases concerning the closure of care homes have referred to this part of article 8.2. It cannot be used to undermine clear community care duties to meet people's needs, but can sometimes be used to justify cost-effectiveness in the way in which those needs are being met – for instance, by closing a care home and placing the residents elsewhere (see e.g. *R(Dudley) v East Sussex CC, R(Rowe) v Walsall MBC*).

**Robotic arm.** When a man was unable to obtain a robotic arm to mount on his electric wheelchair, to enable him to carry out many basic daily living tasks, the European Court stated that if article 8 did apply, then the Court would give countries a 'wide margin of appreciation' in deciding how to allocate limited resources. It held the application inadmissible to go to a full hearing (*Sentges v Netherlands*).

### 20.2.4.5 Protection of health

When the NHS wished to close an accommodation lodge for people with mental health problems, the courts stated that any rights under article 8 were inextricably bound up with the trust's obligation to provide medical care. The proposal by the trust was desirable for the benefit of the claimants (*R v Brent, Kensington and Chelsea and Westminster Mental Health NHS Trust, ex p C*).

### 20.2.4.6 Protection of the rights and freedom of others

When an NHS trust wished to close and refurbish an accommodation lodge for people with mental health problems, the court pointed out that the closure would benefit other members of the community to whom the trust owed a duty and who enjoyed the rights and freedoms that trust had to respect (*R v Brent, Kensington and Chelsea and Westminster Mental Health NHS Trust, ex p C*).

## 20.2.5 ARTICLE 14: DISCRIMINATION

Article 14 states:

> The enjoyment of the rights and freedoms set forth in this Convention shall be secured without discrimination on any ground such as sex, race, colour, language, religion, political or other opinion, national or social origin, association with a national minority, property, birth or other status.

The list of grounds contained in the article fail to include explicitly age or disability. However, the grounds are illustrative only; therefore age and disability are implicit. However, a.14 cannot be argued in isolation. It must be argued with one of the other articles in the Convention; although breach of that other article is not necessary in order to establish a breach of a.14.

**Medical treatment for a person lacking capacity to take particular decisions.** An 18-year-old man had kidney failure and was receiving haemodialysis. The question arose as to whether in the future he should receive peritoneal dialysis or a kidney transplant. He had severe learning difficulties, was autistic, epileptic and had the mental capacity of a five- or six-year-old child.

The hospital sought a declaration from the courts that neither the transplant nor the peritoneal dialysis would be in the man's best interests. This would be because he would not be able to understand the purpose of the surgery, be prepared for it, be able to cope with it and be managed by hospital staff without undue distress to him and without undue difficulty. However, the parents disagreed with the hospital's view and there was also conflicting evidence given by the professionals involved.

In deciding what declaration to make, the court noted that it was crucial that the man did not get less satisfactory life-saving treatment simply because he did not understand it. Otherwise there would be a breach of both domestic and human rights legislation (*An Hospital Trust v S*).

Although the court did not refer explicitly to article 14 (linked with article 2, right to life), implicitly it was probably referring here to discrimination and to a.14.

**Mental health, nearest relative and same-sex relationships.** Under s.26 of the Mental Health Act 1983, reference is made to a person 'living with the patient as the patient's husband or wife'. The court held that, to be compliant with a.14 of the Convention, this should be interpreted to include homosexual partners (*R(SSG) v Liverpool City Council*).

**Tenancies and same-sex relationships.** The Rent Act 1977 provided for a surviving spouse or partner to become the statutory tenant after the death of the original tenant. However, this precluded same-sex partners. The court held that in order to comply with a.14, the Act would need to be interpreted by the courts as applying to same-sex relationships (*Mendoza v Ghaidan*).

## 20.2.6 HUMAN RIGHTS ACT NOT RESORTED TO

In some cases, the courts find that existing common law principles adequately protect people's rights, without resort to the Human Rights Act 1998. For instance, irrespective of human rights, closure of a care home could not survive such common law principles applied in judicial review (see 4.2) when it became clear that the local authority had not taken account of all relevant factors (including a promise of a home for life) when taking its decision (*R(Bodimeade) v Camden LBC*).

Likewise, when it was proposed that a man be given treatment against his will under the Mental Health Act 1983, the courts ruled that this was such a fundamental issue that the common law demanded that reasons be given by the 'second opinion appointed doctor' under the Act (*R(Wooder) v Feggetter*). Before the implementation of the Human Rights Act, the courts referred to a common law of humanity when stating that asylum seekers could not be left to starve on the streets. They even referred back to an 1803 case (*R v Inhabitants of Eastbourne*) when the Lord Chief Justice had stated that in relation to maintaining poor foreigners (Napoleonic refugees) 'the law of humanity, which is anterior to all positive laws, obliges us to afford them relief, to save them from starving' (*R v Westminster CC, ex p A*: High Court).

# Disability discrimination

**KEY POINTS**

The Disability Discrimination Act 1995 (DDA) is divided into various sections covering employment, the provision of goods and services, management of premises, education and public transport.

This chapter concerns itself only with goods and services, and briefly with the management and letting of premises and education. It is perhaps unclear what effect these parts of the DDA have had on the provision of community care services; certainly the case law is sparse. Nevertheless, certain parts of the DDA came into force in October 2004; and various amendments have been proposed to the DDA, which would have the effect of placing greater obligations on local authorities (as well as other public bodies). This chapter therefore covers the parts of the Act, and case law examples, that are most relevant to community care.

**Note 1: Disability Discrimination Bill**. At the time of writing, a Disability Discrimination Bill 2004 has proposed various amendments to the DDA. These include extending discrimination to cover use of transport (cl.5); a widening of public body functions that will be covered by the Act (e.g. highway obligations, conduct of elections) (cl.2); private clubs with more than 25 members to be covered by the Act (cl.12); premises: addition of a duty on those letting premises to make reasonable adjustments to policies, practices and procedures and to take reasonable steps to provide an auxiliary aid or service to enable, or make it easier for, a disabled person to rent the property or to facilitate the tenant's enjoyment of the premises (cl.13); duty on public bodies to promote disability equality (cl.3); widening of definition of disability to include progressive conditions even before they experience the effects of the condition (cl.17).

**Note 2: Wales, Scotland and Northern Ireland**. The Disability Discrimination Act 1995 applies to Wales, Northern Ireland and Scotland.

## 21.1 DEFINITION OF DISABILITY

Disability is defined under the DDA 1995 as physical or mental impairment which has a substantial and long-term adverse effect on the person's ability to carry out normal day-to-day activities (s.1).

- **Mental impairment** includes mental illness, which must be clinically recognised (schedule 1), but does not have the same meaning as in the Mental Health Act 1983 (s.68).
- **Long term** means that the disability must have lasted at least 12 months; is likely to last at least 12 months; or likely to last for the rest of the person's life (schedule 1).
- **Recurrence**. If an impairment ceases to have a substantial adverse effect on a person's ability to carry out normal day-to-day activities, it is to be deemed to continue to have that effect if it is likely to recur (schedule 1).
- **Normal day-to-day activities** are defined as mobility; manual dexterity; physical coordination; continence; ability to lift, carry or otherwise move everyday objects; speech, hearing or eyesight; memory or ability to concentrate, learn or understand; or perception of the risk of physical danger (schedule 1).
- **Substantial**. Guidance states that substantial means more than minor or trivial in effect (Secretary of State 1996).
- **Medical treatment, aids/equipment**. An impairment is still deemed to be such even if measures (including medical treatment, prostheses or other aids) treat or correct the impairment (except in the case of spectacles or contact lenses) (schedule 1).
- **Progressive conditions**, for example cancer, MS, muscular dystrophy and HIV, are taken to be having a substantial effect, even if at present there is only an impairment which has an effect (but not a substantial adverse one) on the person's ability to carry out normal day-to-day activities (schedule 1).
- **Future disabilities** are not covered (except where a progressive condition has begun to manifest itself) (schedule 1).
- **Past disabilities**. People who have had a disability in the past are covered (schedule 2).
- **People deemed disabled (in error)** are not covered (schedule 1).
- **Babies and young children**. If a child under six years old has an impairment which does not have an effect on normal day-to-day activities, the impairment will nevertheless be treated as having a substantial and long-term effect if it would normally have that effect on the ability of a child aged over six years (SI 1996/1455).
- **Severe disfigurement** is included (schedule 1), but not tattoos or non-medical body piercing (SI 1996/1455).

- **Addiction** to alcohol, nicotine or any other substance does not amount to an impairment – unless the addiction was originally the consequence of administration of medically prescribed drugs or treatment (SI 1996/1455).
- **Other exclusions**. Hayfever, tendency to start fires, tendency to steal, tendency to physical or sexual abuse, exhibitionism, voyeurism: however, hayfever can be taken into account if it aggravates the effect of another condition (SI 1996/1455).

## 21.2 PROVISION OF GOODS AND SERVICES TO THE PUBLIC

Providers of goods and services to the public must not discriminate against disabled people by refusing to provide or not providing a service that is provided to others, or providing it on worse terms or at a lower standard than it would be provided for others (DDA 1995, s.19). They must also not discriminate by failing to make reasonable adjustments to practices, policies, procedures to or in respect of physical features – or failing to take reasonable steps to provide auxiliary aids or services. The result of this failure to make reasonable adjustments must be to make it impossible or unreasonably difficult for the disabled person to use the service (ss.20–21).

A provider of services discriminates by treating a person less favourably than others – on grounds relating to his or her disability – where that less favourable treatment cannot be justified. What would otherwise be discrimination in terms of less favourable treatment or failure to take reasonable steps is capable of being justified on particular grounds (s.20).

### 21.2.1 LESS FAVOURABLE TREATMENT

Less favourable treatment could be in comparison with non-disabled people, or with people with other disabilities.

**Wheelchair service at airport.** An airline charged for assisting people at the airport to get from the check-in point to the flight at the airport who did not have their own wheelchair, whereas it did not charge people who were more disabled (and who did have their own wheelchair). The judge held that this constituted discrimination on the basis of different classes of disability. The fact that the 'more disabled' were treated more favourably was irrelevant (*Ross v Ryanair*).

Similarly when a blind man was turned away from a restaurant because he had a guide dog, he was treated less favourably for a reason (the dog) relating to his disability (*Purves v Joydisc Ltd*).

However, the alleged discrimination must be disability related. In the following two cases, the courts found that this condition was not made out:

**Charging for community care services.** A local authority imposed a charging policy for non-residential services. This categorised service users into three bands, A, B and C. People in band A received only income support, and no other income or disability benefits (attendance allowance or disability living allowance). They were not charged. People in band B received income support and attendance allowance or disability living allowance; if they received more than 15 hours care per week, they were charged £10.50 per week. People in band C did not receive income support, and may or may not have received attendance allowance or disability living allowance; they were charged £26.25 per week.

The claimant was in band B. She alleged that she was receiving services on worse terms than those in band A, for a reason relating to her disability. The court took the opposite view, stating that the reason she was charged more was because she had the money, wherever it came from.

The court ruled that the DDA simply did not apply at all because the different treatment was not related to disability; it was therefore not necessary even to consider whether the local authority could put forward a justification for less favourable treatment (*R v Powys CC, ex p Hambidge (no.2)*).

In another case, the court ruled also that disability discrimination simply did not arise:

**Rationing of NHS services.** The court held that a policy (including a rationing element) concerning blood product treatment for people with haemophilia was based not on disability, but on age and on previous treatment. This was becasue eligibility for the more recent, potentially more desirable product (recombinant factor as opposed to plasma-derived product) was defined in terms either of the person being under 16 years old, or not having previously had treatment with the plasma derived product. Neither criterion was related to disability (*R(Longstaff) v Newcastle Primary Care Trust*).

## 21.2.2 TAKING REASONABLE STEPS

The duty to make adjustments applies where a provider has a practice, policy or procedure making it impossible or unreasonably difficult for disabled persons to use a service it provides to other members of the public. The provider has a duty to take steps that are reasonable in all the circumstances of the case to change the policy, practice or procedure.

If a physical feature (e.g. in relation to the design or construction of a building or the approach or access to premises) makes it impossible or unreasonably difficult for disabled people to use the service, the provider has a duty to take steps that are reasonable, in all the circumstances of the case, to (a) remove the feature; (b) alter it so it no longer has that effect; (c) provide a reasonable means of avoiding the feature; or (d) provide a reasonable alternative method of accessing the service.

Thus a failure to provide a wheelchair free of charge, for a person to use between an airport check-in desk and departure gate, constituted a failure to provide a reasonable alternative method of making a service available to the person (*Ross v Ryanair*).

**Providing a reasonable alternative to accessing a service.** It was not possible for a disabled person to change platforms at a railway station, and the half-mile route by road was difficult and attended with risk. The railway company stated that he should travel on to another station, change there, and then return to the original station. This would add an hour on to a 36-minute journey. The man argued that the company should instead provide him with a wheelchair-accessible taxi in order to change platforms.

The Court of Appeal agreed with the man, stating that the extra hour required to travel to the other station could not, on any fair view, be considered a reasonable alternative under s.21(2)(c) of the DDA. The court also noted that the policy of the Act was not a minimalist one; it was 'to provide access to a service as close as it is reasonably possible to get to the standard normally offered to the public at large' (*Roads v Central Trains*).

An auxiliary aid or service (e.g. information on audio-tape or a sign language interpreter) might enable disabled people to make use of a service or at least facilitate its use. If so, the provider has a duty to take steps that are in all the circumstances reasonable to provide that auxiliary aid or service (s.21). Failure to provide a wheelchair free of charge at the airport meant that a disabled passenger was prevented from using the airport facilities and services which were useable by other people (either not disabled or with another type of disability). This was a breach of the duty to provide auxiliary aids (*Ross v Ryanair*).

### 21.2.3 JUSTIFYING LESS FAVOURABLE TREATMENT OR NOT TAKING REASONABLE STEPS

Less favourable treatment, or the failure to take reasonable steps, can be justified on grounds of (a) health and safety; (b) the incapacity of the person to enter into a contract; (c) the service provider otherwise being unable to provide the service to the public; (d) enabling the service provider to provide the service to the disabled person or other members of the public; (e) a greater cost being applied to the service, because it reflects a greater cost to the provider (but not the costs incurred by making reasonable adjustments) (DDA 1995, s.20).

Nevertheless, the justification can only be made out if the service provider believed that one of these defences applied, and that it was reasonable for the provider to believe this. However, if the defence is made out, then there is no discrimination under the Act.

**Health and safety justification and inadequate risk assessment.** When a school prevented a diabetic pupil from going on a school trip, on purported health and safety grounds relating to his diabetes, the court nevertheless found discrimination. This was because of a totally inadequate process of risk assessment that failed to involve either the pupil or his parents, the provider of the holiday or even to take account of the views of the pupil's consultant paediatrician (*White v Clitheroe Royal Grammar School*).

## 21.3 MANAGEMENT AND LETTING OF PREMISES

It is unlawful to discriminate against disabled people in the selling, letting or management of residential premises.

### 21.3.1 DISCRIMINATION

In terms of disposal, discrimination could occur in relation to the terms of disposal, to refusal to dispose, or to the way in which a disabled person is treated in respect of a list (e.g. waiting list or register for allocation of housing) of people in need of the premises (DDA 1995, s.22).

In terms of management, discrimination against a disabled person occupying the premises could occur in relation to (a) the way in which the disabled person is permitted to make use of any benefits or facilities; (b) refusing or omitting to allow the disabled person to use such benefits of facilities; (c) evicting the person or subjecting him or her to any other detriment. Discrimination means less favourable treatment of the disabled person for a reason relating to the person's disability – and which the other person cannot show to be justified.

## 21.3.2 JUSTIFYING LESS FAVOURABLE TREATMENT

Less favourable treatment is justifiable if, in the other person's opinion, certain conditions are satisfied. However, it must also be reasonable in all the circumstances of the case for him or her to hold that opinion. The conditions relate to (a) health and safety; (b) incapacity to make an enforceable agreement; (c) that the less favourable treatment is necessary in order for the disabled person or the occupiers of other premises forming part of the building to make use of a benefit or facility; (d) that the refusal to allow the disabled person to make use of a benefit or facility is necessary in order for the occupiers of other premises forming part of the building to make use of the benefit or facility (s.24). There is a small dwellings exemption (DDA 1995, s.23).

**Refusing to let a flat.** A blind person with a guide dog was refused by a landlord the let of a flat for a week during the Edinburgh Festival. This was on the grounds of the absence of a suitable handrail on the steps leading up to the flat. The man brought a case in the Scottish courts under the DDA. The landlord argued a health and safety justification for the less favourable treatment; he succeeded because he brought forward genuine evidence including his attempts to get a suitable rail installed, and also his past letting of premises to disabled people. In particular, the court held that the opinion of the landlord was a reasonable one for him to have reached. He knew that the man was blind and used a guide dog, that the steps without a handrail posed a threat to safety because of the unguarded drop on both sides. This threat to safety was subsequently confirmed by an environmental health officer (*Rose v Bouchet*).

In respect of eviction of tenants, several cases have reached the courts in which possession orders by landlords were disputed with reference to the DDA. These cases centred on whether, in the case of assured or secure tenancies, it was reasonable under the Housing Act 1985 for the court to grant the possession order sought. Even before the DDA, the courts sometimes found that the order would be unreasonable: for example, if the tenant suffered from a mental disorder that might be amenable to treatment (*Croydon LBC v Moody*). However, the judgement of what is reasonable now has to be made in the light of the DDA.

The questions to be asked in such cases are: (a) is the tenant disabled within the meaning of the DDA; (b) if so, is the reason (e.g. aggressive or antisocial behaviour) why the landlord is seeking possession related to the tenant's disability; (c) if so, is there a health and safety justification for the less favourable treatment (which treatment would otherwise inevitably constitute discrimination)? In the first of these cases, the possession order was denied:

**Possession order denied on grounds of discrimination.** A tenant of a housing association was in a chronic state of conflict with her neighbours. She had been diagnosed as suffering a form of paranoid schizophrenia. Following police and social services involvement she was transferred to another property. She continued to be disagreeable and aggressive. She kept the neighbours awake at night by banging and shouting, and used abusive language and rude gestures. The landlord brought possession proceedings. The High Court concluded that there was no doubt that she suffered from a psychotic disorder and that her behaviour stemmed from her illness. Thus the only justification for the eviction would be on grounds of health and safety; but the court found no evidence that the landlord had considered the eviction necessary on such grounds. Nor did the court find that the physical health and safety of neighbours had actually been at risk (*North Devon Homes v Brazier*).

However, in two subsequent Court of Appeal cases, the tenants failed in their objections:

**Possession orders not discriminatory.** A tenant had a depressive mental illness, which meant that she was regarded as disabled under the DDA. The courts held that the conduct complained of, loud hammering and music during the night, could reasonably be held to be endangering the health of a neighbour who was a driving examiner and suffering sleep deprivation as a consequence of the nightly disturbance. In addition, the court anyway doubted whether the music and hammering could be linked to the mental impairment.

A second tenant suffered from a personality disorder, producing violent behaviour, depression and anxiety. The court concluded that by reason of her illness she was unable to learn how to cope with stressful situations and to react appropriately. This resulted in abusive language toward a neighbour and her children; the neighbour was on anti-depressants, felt suicidal and could not leave her house without being called names. The evidence from the neighbour to this effect was sufficient to constitute reasonable justification on health and safety grounds.

The court said that it was enough if a person's health or safety was endangered (not necessarily seriously); it did not have actually to be damaged (*Manchester CC v Romano*).

Nevertheless, in the *Manchester* judgment, the Court of Appeal heavily criticised the way in which the DDA had been drafted and predicted a possible deluge of such cases with possible unfair and absurd consequences. In the meantime it suggested that local authority landlords would need to liaise more closely with social services at an earlier stage, in order to try to deal with problems that could lead to attempted eviction. The court was further concerned that a landlord might perform a discriminatory act even when it did not know that the tenant was disabled.

## 21.4 EDUCATION

From September 2002, the Disability Discrimination Act 1995 was extended to cover the provision of education in schools and further and higher education.

### 21.4.1 FURTHER AND HIGHER EDUCATION

In the case of further and higher education, there are duties on the bodies responsible for educational institutions. These are not to discriminate by treating disabled students less favourably for a reason relating to their disability, or by failing to make reasonable adjustments so as to avoid putting disabled students at a substantial disadvantage (subject to justification).

Matters to which discrimination could apply include admission of students, terms on which admission offers are made, refusal or deliberate omission to accept application for admission or enrolment, provision of services, and exclusions. Discrimination means less favourable treatment for a reason relating to the disabled person's disability that cannot be justified. It also means failing to comply, without justification, with the duty to take reasonable steps under s.28T of the Act (to ensure that disabled people are not placed at a substantial disadvantage in terms of deciding admissions and of student services). Unlike the case of schools, the Act does not explicitly exclude the provision of auxiliary aids and services or physical alterations to premises, in the making of reasonable adjustments.

Justification can be made out if the less favourable treatment (a) is necessary to maintain academic standards or other prescribed standards; (b) is of a prescribed kind. Otherwise less favourable treatment or a failure to comply with s.28T (reasonable steps) can only be justified if it is for a reason that is both material and substantial (DDA 1995, ss.28R–28T).

## 21.5 RELATIONSHIP OF DDA TO OTHER LEGISLATION

Nothing in the DDA makes unlawful any act done in pursuance of another piece of legislation or an instrument made under another piece of legislation (DDA 1995, s.59). This would mean that if the inevitable implication of other legislation were to be discrimination, it would not be unlawful. However, the courts will be slow to find that legislation demands discrimination:

**Requirements not prescribed by legislation, so not immune from discrimination challenge.** The Department of Education and Science imposed certain requirements in relation to granting a Hong Kong Chinese trained teacher teaching status in this country. The requirements imposed however were not prescribed by legislation; they were based on administrative practice and discretion. They were not therefore automatically protected from being discriminatory under the Race Relations Act 1976 (*Hampson v Department of Education and Science*).

PART V

# Health and safety at work, negligence, contract, national regulation of care provision

CHAPTER 22

# Health and safety at work legislation

**KEY POINTS**

A number of duties relevant to community care arise under health and safety at work legislation. They give rise to potential criminal offences; in addition, employees can, under some of the legislation, bring civil personal injury actions for breach of statutory duty. There are duties toward non-employees as well as employees. Furthermore, when local authorities and the NHS contract out service provision to independent providers, potential health and safety at work duties tend to multiply; in such circumstances, local authorities and the NHS should not be taking an 'out of sight, out of mind' approach to health and safety at work matters.

A legal case in 2003 – concerning the manual handling of two women with profound physical and learning disabilities, health and safety at work and human rights – demonstrated in no uncertain terms that local authorities (and the NHS) must pay serious attention to balancing the health and safety at work of staff against people's assessed needs and human rights (*R(A&B) v East Sussex CC (no.2)*).

**Note: Wales, Scotland and Northern Ireland**. Reference is made in this chapter to the Health and Safety at Work Act 1974, Management of Health and Safety at Work Regulations 1999 (SI 1999/3242), and Manual Handling Operations Regulations 1992 (SI 1992/2793). All these apply to England, Wales and Scotland. The equivalent provisions covering Northern Ireland are the Health and Safety at Work Order (Northern Ireland) 1978, Management of Health and Safety at Work Regulations (Northern Ireland) 2000 (SR 2000/388), and Manual Handling Operations Regulations (Northern Ireland) 1992 (SR 1992/535).

## 22.1 REASONABLE PRACTICABILITY IN HEALTH AND SAFETY

The term 'reasonably practicable' recurs frequently in the health and safety at work legislation outlined below, and is of pivotal importance.

### 22.1.1 RISK SET AGAINST COST

The traditional approach by the courts has been to weigh up the level of risk to employees against the cost of doing something about it in terms of resources, staffing, time and effort. If the cost involved would be clearly disproportionate to the risk, then it might not be reasonably practicable to eliminate or reduce the risk.

In an older case, the court stated that the degree of risk should be placed in one scale, and the 'sacrifice' (money, time, trouble) necessary to avert the risk in the other. If there was a gross disproportion, such that the risk was insignificant compared to the sacrifice, then the employer did not have a duty to avert the risk (*Edwards v National Coal Board*).

**Manual handling injury.** A local authority carpenter was carrying doors weighing 72 pounds up the stairs of a block of flats. He sustained an injury. The Court of Appeal accepted that the risk of manual handling injury appeared from the evidence to have been relatively low. However, providing him that day with an assistant would not have been a disproportionate drain on the resources of an employer the size of the local authority. The local authority was therefore found to be in breach of the Manual Handling Operations Regulations 1992 (*Hawkes v Southwark LBC*).

### 22.1.2 UTILITY OR BENEFIT TO THE PUBLIC

In several recent cases the courts have referred to another element that must be taken into account when deciding how far it is reasonably practicable to reduce risk to public service employees. This is the benefit or utility of the activity in question to the relevant member(s) of the public. The courts are in effect pointing out that the test of reasonable practicability can only make sense if one considers the relevant public service context – and the serving of the public by, for instance, local authority personal assistants, NHS care assistants or ambulance staff. Indeed, public authorities and their staff have both statutory duties to provide services and will owe a common law duty of care to the public they serve.

**Manual handling, health and safety and human rights.** A dispute arose about the manual handling of two women with profound physical and learning disabilities. The parents were opposed to the use of hoists within the home and wished their daughters to be manually handled. They also wished their daughters to get out of the house to go swimming, shopping and horse riding. The local authority opposed the parents' wishes because of what it perceived to be the high manual handling risks to staff.

The court held that, when considering reasonable practicability under the Manual Handling Operations Regulations 1992, the local authority had to bring into the equation the assessed community care needs of the women, and most importantly their human rights as well. This would therefore necessitate balanced decision making by the local authority in weighing up competing considerations.

It would not mean that the rights of disabled people should override those of paid carers; nor would it mean that those of paid carers should override those of disabled people. Nevertheless, it might mean that in certain circumstances paid carers might have to work at higher, but not unacceptable, levels of risk – depending on the needs, and threat to the human rights, of a disabled person.

Thus, in considering reasonable practicability, the local authority would have to consider and weigh up the women's wishes, feelings, reluctance, fear, refusal, dignity, integrity and quality of life, as well as the risk to staff (*R(A&B) v East Sussex CC (no.2)*).

**NHS care assistant and risk taking**. A care assistant in an NHS residential home for disabled children sustained an injury through pulling out and making beds which were low and against the wall. The Court of Appeal accepted in principle that certain features of the beds, though potentially increasing the risk to staff, might be justifiable in relation to the needs of the children (*Koonjul v Thameslink NHS Health Care Trust*).

**Urgent ambulance call and risk taking**. The ambulance service received an urgent call to take a man to hospital. The call required a one-hour response. The man lived in a cottage and was upstairs in bed. There was a steep, narrow staircase with a bend. The two ambulance men began to carry the man down the stairs in a carry chair. One of them momentarily lost his grip on the front of the chair. The other ambulance man briefly had to bear the whole weight. He suffered injuries to his thumb, back and knees.

The injured ambulance man brought a personal injury case. He argued that he should have been trained to give serious consideration to the alternative of using the fire brigade to remove the man through a window with a crane; and that the ambulance service wrongly treated use of the fire brigade as an absolute last resort.

The case failed in the Court of Appeal. This was partly on the basis that public service workers sometimes have to work at higher, although not unacceptable, levels of risk. The court also pointed out that in determining whether to call for the fire brigade, in order to achieve quite a drastic form of removal, various relevant factors had to be taken account of. These included distress to the patient and the reaction of the carers (*King v Sussex Ambulance Service*).

These judicial decisions are consistent with Health and Safety Executive guidance. This has always pointed out that reasonable practicability does not entail that all risk be removed. Otherwise there would, for instance, be no adequate fire brigade (HSE 1998, p.8); risk assessment must be performed in context. The Health and Safety Commission also has stated that, within the health service, some situations and activities will call for higher levels of risk taking. One such activity would be rehabilitation (HSC 1998, p.43). This approach is further taken in guidance on manual handling issued by the Chartered Society of Physiotherapy (CSP 2002, p.11).

## 22.1.3 RISK TO STAFF, AND ASSESSED NEEDS AND HUMAN RIGHTS

Legal cases such as the *East Sussex* judgment are particularly helpful in assisting organisations to apply health and safety at work legislation in balanced fashion. This is precisely because some local authorities, NHS bodies and other organisations tend in practice to play the health and safety 'card' inappropriately. Some refuse to provide certain services in order to meet service users' needs, not because of unacceptable levels of risk but because management of that risk would require some effort and resources. That is, staff would have to be reasonably trained and be provided with effective systems of work that placed a premium both on staff safety and meeting the needs of service users.

Yet some care providers appear to believe that if they can avoid risk altogether (even to the considerable detriment of service users), they can 'get away' with employing staff who are unable to identify, assess or manage risk of any sort. Ironically, even this approach does not save staff from injury; since risk cannot be altogether avoided, and a higher risk well managed might anyway pose no more chance of injury than a lower risk unmanaged. If nothing else, the *East Sussex* case militates against such unacceptable shortcuts in services, which result in detriment to service users.

There has been disquiet about the ramifications of such judicial decisions. For instance, some parts of the nursing community seem to be blaming human rights and associated judicial decisions for condemning nurses to much higher rates of personal manual handling injury in the future (e.g. Griffiths and Stevens 2004). However, the courts have in effect stated only that users of public services are part of the health and safety at work equation; their needs and rights must not be forgotten. Sometimes, this might require public service workers accepting 'higher', but not unacceptable, risks; and they, as well as service users, have human rights too (see e.g. *R(A&B) v East Sussex CC (no.2)*). Furthermore, it is worth reiterating that a higher risk well managed might pose no more chance of injury than a lower risk poorly managed. Two legal cases illustrate the point:

**Basic health and safety at work failures causing injury.** Both involved nurses providing care for highly dependent people in hospital. Serious injury was caused to one nurse because of absent or defective hoists; and because of a system of work that sanctioned routine use of an unsafe lifting technique (*Knott v Newham Healthcare NHS Trust*).

In the second case, a lack of adjustable height beds and a flat wheelchair tyre were the main causes of injury (*Commons v Queen's Medical Centre*).

The compensation payments in the above two cases, and therefore direct costs to the NHS, were high; over £400,000 in the first case, and over £200,000 in the second (quite aside from the indirect costs of losing highly trained nurses and having to replace them). But neither had anything to do with nurses taking planned and managed higher risks on the basis of people's assessed needs and human rights – but everything to do with very basic organisational failure to manage risk, and to adhere to the Manual Handling Operations Regulations 1992, despite their having been in force for many years.

## 22.2 DUTIES TO EMPLOYEES
A number of duties are held by employers toward employees.

### 22.2.1 HEALTH AND SAFETY AT WORK ACT 1974
Under s.2 of the Health and Safety at Work Act 1974, employers have a duty to safeguard the health, safety and welfare of their employees at work, so far as is reasonably practica-

ble. This includes the provision and maintenance of safe systems of work together with instruction, information, training and supervision. It also covers safe use, handling, transport and storage of equipment, as well as a safe working environment.

## 22.2.2 MANAGEMENT OF HEALTH AND SAFETY AT WORK REGULATIONS 1999

Under the Management of Health and Safety at Work Regulations 1999, employers have various duties. These include the duty to assess risks to the health and safety of their employees at work, in order to identify what needs to be done to comply with other, relevant health and safety at work legislation.

Employers must also review their risk assessments, and cooperate and coordinate activities in a workplace shared with other employers or self-employed people in order to ensure compliance with relevant health and safety requirements. They are also obliged in a shared workplace to provide health and safety information to other employers or to self-employed people working in the local authority's 'undertaking'.

**Cooperation and coordination of a care package.** A person is receiving a care package in his own home. There is input from NHS district nurses, social services staff and care assistants from an independent care provider. The care package therefore involves three employers in a shared workplace (the person's home).

A failure to communicate and to share information – about a change in the person's abilities, or about who should demonstrate and maintain any equipment being used (e.g. a hoist) – could result in health and safety at work lapses.

## 22.2.3 MANUAL HANDLING OPERATIONS REGULATIONS 1992

Under the Manual Handling Operations Regulations 1992 employers have various duties. As far as is reasonably practicable, they must avoid the need for their employees to undertake manual handling involving a risk of injury. The risk assessment directed to identifying such a risk takes place under the 1999 regulations.

If it is not reasonably practicable for an employer to avoid the risk of injury to its employees, then it must carry out a suitable and sufficient assessment of the manual handling operations in issue, and must take appropriate steps to reduce the risk to the lowest level reasonably practicable. If reasonably practicable it must also provide precise information on the weight, and heaviest side, of the 'load'.

The employer must also have regard to the physical suitability of an employee to carry out the tasks together with clothing, footwear and other personal effects being carried out. It must have regard to any relevant risk assessment under r.3 of the Management of Health and Safety at Work Regulations 1999 and whether an employee has been identified by that assessment as coming within a group of employees particularly at risk. It must also have regard to the results of any health surveillance carried out under r.6 of the 1999 Regulations.

Examples of the taking of higher (albeit managed) risks in the manual handling context have already been given (see 21.1.2).

Risk assessment, aimed at identification of manual handling risk in general, is carried out under the 1999 regulations. If the risk cannot reasonably practicably be avoided, then a specific risk assessment concerning reduction of risk must be carried out under the MHOR 1992. Both 1999 and 1992 sets of regulations impose a duty on employers to review these risk assessments if there is reason to believe that they are no longer valid or if there has been significant change in the situation. The employer must then make any changes required.

**Maintaining risk assessments and care plans.** In one case, the risks posed by a woman who was assisted to walk at a day hospital had increased. This had, correctly, been recorded in her notes. However, the physiotherapist had not taken correspondingly greater precautions, and this had resulted in injury to an occupational therapy assistant. The NHS Trust was held liable for the injury (*Stainton v Chorley and South Ribble NHS Trust*: a negligence case).

Thus, the court was not stating that risks should not have been taken, but that they should have been properly managed on an ongoing basis.

### 22.3 DUTIES OF EMPLOYEES

The Health and Safety at Work Act 1974 (s.7) imposes a duty on an employee to take reasonable care of his or her own health and safety and also that of other people who may be affected by the employee's acts or failure to act. Under the MHOR 1992, an employee must make full and proper use of any system of work provided in relation to the reduction of risk. Under the Management of Health and Safety at Work Regulations 1999, employees must use equipment in accordance with any training provided and with instructions provided by the employer.

### 22.4 DUTY OF SELF-EMPLOYED PEOPLE

Under s.3 of the Health and Safety at Work Act 1974, self-employed people have a duty to conduct their undertaking in such a way as to ensure that, as far as reasonably practicable, other people who may be affected are not exposed to risk to their health and safety. In addition, the duties imposed on employers, as outlined above in both the Management of Health and Safety at Work Regulations 1999 and the MHOR 1992, apply also to self-employed people.

### 22.5 DUTY OF EMPLOYERS TO NON-EMPLOYEES

As already explained, employers such as local authorities and the NHS must take account of service users when deciding what is reasonably practicable in order to safeguard their employees under legislation such as s.2 of the Health and Safety at Work Act 1974 or the Manual Handling Operations Regulations 1992.

However, there are in addition more explicit duties owed toward non-employees. Under s.3 of the 1974 Act, there is a duty on the employer to conduct its undertaking in such a way as to ensure, so far as is reasonably practicable, that non-employees who may be affected are not exposed to risks to their health and safety. In addition, under r.3 of the Management of Health and Safety at Work Regulations 1999, there is a duty to carry out a suitable and sufficient assessment of the risks to the health and safety of non-employees arising from, or connected with, the employer's undertaking.

The term non-employee is wide in scope. Non-employees of a local authority include, for example, community care service users, informal carers, NHS staff, employees of independent care providers and self-employed people providing a service to the local authority. Thus, for instance, a local authority could be prosecuted for risks to the health and safety of an independent care provider's employees, as well as to that of service users, if those risks have arisen through failures in the contracting process:

**Contracting out services: health and safety at work liability.** A local authority contracts out provision of its domiciliary community care services to a local independent care provider. However, the authority is in the throes of what it considers to be a financial crisis. It therefore allocates inadequate funding to the contract. It also fails to check on the safety record of the contractor in question and to monitor the performance of the contract.

Poor practice and unsafe working flourish, leading to two serious accidents to the care provider's staff. The Health and Safety Executive decides to prosecute both the care provider and the local authority under respectively sections 2 and 3 of the Health and Safety at Work Act 1974 (for a comparable case involving a refuse collection service, see *Health and Safety Executive v Barnet LBC*).

## 22.5.1 RISK TAKING BY SERVICE USERS

Health and safety at work legislation (and the law of negligence) are sometimes cited as the reasons for a risk-averse approach taken by local authorities and the NHS in relation to service users. Yet risk elimination is not demanded by the law; rather risk management in terms of weighing up risks and benefits is called for. For instance, the Court of Appeal pointed out that a 'certain degree of risk-taking is often acceptable, rather than compromise independence and break family or home links' (*R(Khana) v Southwark LBC*).

In similar vein, the Health and Safety Executive has issued guidance on 'elective' risk taking in the context of community care, basically telling its inspectors not to look for risk elimination, but to consider how risk has been assessed and managed, given that community care packages might quite properly contain certain elements of risk, in connection with independent living (HSE SIM 7/2000/8).

# Negligence

## KEY POINTS

This chapter is included because of the not infrequent concern of local authority staff, managers and sometimes solicitors about negligence liability in case of accident occurring to service users.

**Note: Wales, Scotland and Northern Ireland**. The law of negligence applies across the United Kingdom; however, in Scotland it forms part of the law of delict, as opposed to part of the law of tort in England, Wales and Northern Ireland.

## 23.1 BASIC RULES OF NEGLIGENCE

The law of negligence is to be found in the 'common law' and not in legislation. This means that the rules are to be found solely in the decisions of the law courts. Negligence cases are about physical (or sometimes psychological and in some circumstances financial) harm allegedly suffered.

The claimant must show that (a) a duty of care was owed by the person who allegedly caused the harm; (b) the duty was breached by a careless action or omission; (c) this breach directly caused the harm complained of. As in the case of reasonable practicability under health and safety at work legislation (see 22.1), a weighing up of risks, costs and benefits (i.e. to the service user) will be relevant.

In many circumstances the duty of care owed by local authority and NHS staff will be straightforward. The large volume of negligence cases brought against the NHS is evidence of this. However, the courts also protect local authorities and the NHS to the extent that the claim concerns a decision, action or omission that is closely related to the carrying out of a statutory function (e.g. community care assessment under legislation), to resources or to policy generally. The protection might occur, even if in reality the local authority or NHS body has been careless. The courts distinguish such policy or statutory type matters from what they sometimes call more straightforward 'operational' matters for which no special protection would be afforded.

## 23.2 PROTECTION OF LOCAL AUTHORITIES FROM NEGLIGENCE

In the past, local services authorities (and sometimes the NHS) have been to some extent protected from negligence liability in respect of service users. The courts have stated that, in some circumstances, there is no duty of care owed by local authorities or their staff to service users. In which case, any carelessness and harm caused are irrelevant, since there can be no breach of a duty of care if that duty does not exist in the first place.

The courts have provided such protection where there are complicated matters of policy, resources or sensitive decision making involved, such as in the context of child protection. They also tend to avoid identifying a duty of care if its existence would interfere with the carrying out of a statutory duty under legislation (e.g. a duty to assess a person and decide about services). The courts tend to contrast this type of decision ('policy'), in connection with which they provide protection from liability, with what they refer to as 'operational' decisions which do not attract this special protection. Nevertheless, it should be noted that such protection appears to have reduced somewhat in the light of the Human Rights Act 1998.

### 23.2.1 PROTECTIVE APPROACH OF THE COURTS

The two cases below illustrate the protective approach, the first concerning child protection and the second mental health aftercare services:

**No duty of care owed to children.** Over a number of years, a local authority failed to protect four children from the severe neglect of their mother. This was despite overwhelming evidence given to the local authority by many different, reliable sources. When a negligence case was brought against the local authority, the courts held there was no duty of care owed (*X v Bedfordshire County Council*). However, a breach of human rights by the local authority in this case was later established in the European Court of Human Rights (*Z v United Kingdom*).

**Aftercare services and negligence.** A man brought a negligence case, arguing that the health authority had failed to provide him with adequate mental health aftercare services under s.117 of the Mental Health Act 1983 – and that as a result he had stabbed a person to death at a London Underground station. The Court of Appeal held that aftercare services were essentially administrative in nature, rather than clinical. The surrounding legal framework meant that it was not fair and reasonable to impose a duty of care on the health authority (*Clunis v Camden and Islington Health Authority*).

However, in a third and more recent case the courts recognised that the law of negligence was in a state of flux, and declined to rule that a registration authority (the local authority at that time: now the registration authority would be the Commission for Social Care Inspection) could owe no duty of care to a care home:

**Duty of care owed to care home proprietors.** A care home argued that a local authority owed it a duty of care in respect of excessive requirements relating to the staffing of the care home – even when there was no maximum occupancy. The council argued that in such a situation, connected with statutory functions (under the Registered Home Act 1984), it owed no duty of care – and the case should be struck out. However, the courts were not prepared to state that there could be no duty of care; the case should therefore proceed to a full hearing. This was particularly because the law of negligence in this field was in a state of flux (*Douce v Staffordshire County Council*). The court came to a like-minded decision in a dispute concerning registration of a care home that resulted in its closure (*Strickland v Woodfield Lodge*).

Likewise, in late 2004 the courts declined to strike out as a matter of course two negligence actions against local authorities, instead holding that the cases could be pleaded. The first concerned the local social services authority's role in assisting a girl to find accommodation in hostel premises, where she was subsequently seriously injured when she jumped from a window to escape an attack by three non-residents (*Bluett v Suffolk CC*). The second involved the killing by a father of his daughter after he had returned home in a disturbed and paranoid state of mind from a business trip to India, which had turned out to be a hoax perpetrated by a rival company. He had a past history of mental health problems; it was alleged that had the local authority acted on the previous concerns, the death of the daughter might have been avoided (*Hall v Monmouthshire CC*).

The NHS, too, will be protected up to a point (although a great deal of the negligence case law brought against the NHS concerns clinical decision making, and thus is of the 'operational' variety). The case below affords an example of where a duty of care was held to exist and to have been breached (because operationally something went wrong), but would probably not have been if lack of resources had been the main issue, therefore taking it into the area of policy:

**NHS duty of care and lack of resources.** A woman suffered a severe attack of asthma and the ambulance was called. Unaccountably it failed to arrive for 40 minutes, despite several reassurances given by the service over the telephone that its much quicker arrival was imminent. The woman suffered respiratory arrest and substantial memory impairment, personality change and a miscarriage as a result. The Court of Appeal found liability in negligence. However, it held that, had the non-arrival of the ambulance stemmed from a lack of resources (i.e. insufficient ambulances or drivers to respond to demand), the outcome of the case could well have been different (*Kent v Griffiths*).

The case below likewise illustrates the courts' distinction between a statutory function (making a decision about services) and a straightforward operational one, such as dropping the service user:

**Dropping a woman or providing a defective bed.** A woman with disseminated sclerosis sought damages for negligence against the local authority. This was in relation to the provision of home help, practical assistance in the home and the provision of an invalid bed. She felt the provision had been inadequate. Because the decision whether to provide such services and to what extent was a statutory one – that is, taken under community care legislation – the court dismissed the negligence claim out of hand.

However, the court noted that a claim in negligence might have been possible if, for instance, the home help had dropped the woman and injured her, or if the bed provided by the local authority had been defective, collapsed and caused injury. This was because such matters would not have been connected to statutory decision making (involving policy, priorities, eligibility criteria, etc.) but would have been straightforward operational matters (*Wyatt v Hillingdon LBC*).

In a child care case, the court felt that a full hearing should proceed, if only to ascertain whether the alleged failures were of the policy or operational type:

**Duty of care to child formerly in care.** A child formerly in care alleged that, as a result of fragmented and inappropriate arrangements over a period of 22 years, he left care with a psychiatric illness, alcoholic problems and a propensity to harm himself. The local authority attempted to get the negligence case struck out as containing no cause of action. The court refused. It held that although the decision to take a child into care was not 'justiciable' (i.e. it could not find a negligence case), nevertheless a local authority could potentially be negligent thereafter in respect to its employees' actions, if they were of an operational rather than a policy nature (*Barrett v Enfield LBC*).

Nevertheless, the hurdles of policy and resources do not mean that local authorities or the NHS will not be penalised for a systemic failure, as opposed to the potential negligence of an individual employee. For instance, when a woman had twins, far too long a time had elapsed following the birth of the first (and vaginal loss of blood) before a doctor attended. The court found that the health authority was negligent in not operating a system that would have allowed reasonably prompt attendance by a responsible doctor (*Bull v Devon AHA*).

## 23.3.2 NO SPECIAL PROTECTION FOR LOCAL AUTHORITIES

The three cases below illustrate, by contrast, more straightforward types of situation where the courts will find a duty of care, on the basis of straightforward, operational-type failure:

**Duty of care owed to injured foster carer?** A woman was the paid foster carer of a disabled teenage boy, who had been placed with her by the council. She claimed that on five occasions between 1991 and 1993 she had suffered back injury when trying to catch, lift, save or restrain him. She now argued she should have been provided with suitable equipment and training in timely fashion and that the local authority had failed to carry out a proper assessment.

The local authority attempted to have the case struck out on grounds of public policy, namely that it was not in the public interest that it should owe a duty of care in such circumstances, even had it acted negligently. The court found that the case should not automatically be struck out. First, it concerned the practical manner in which the local authority was proceeding, not policy; and the judge could not see why the imposition of a duty of care was inconsistent with, or would discourage, the due performance of the authority in carrying out its statutory duties in respect of children. Furthermore, on the public policy question, it would surely be 'poor public policy' to impose a heavy burden on charitable, lowly paid volunteer foster parents, but for those parents to have no recourse if the authority behaved carelessly (*Beasley v Buckinghamshire CC*).

**Duty of care to vicar.** A child with a record of fire raising was in the care of the local authority and set fire to a local church. The court found that in failing to warn his head office, a social worker was not exercising a statutory discretion (e.g. there was no evidence that the decision not to pass on the information had been taken in the interests of the child). Therefore, the scope of the duty of care owed by the local authority was not limited (as it otherwise might have been). The case against the local authority was made out and damages were payable (*Vicar of Writtle v Essex CC*).

**Duty of care to the public owed by ambulance service.** An injured ambulance man brought an unsuccessful personal injury case against an NHS trust in Sussex. The main question was whether the fire brigade should have been called to remove the bedroom window and winch the patient down with a crane – to avoid risk to the ambulance man of using a carry chair down steep and narrow stairs.

As far as negligence was concerned, the Court of Appeal made reference to the weighing up of the risk involved against the social utility of the ambulance service responding to an urgent, if not an emergency, call. It pointed out that whilst the employer had health and safety at work obligations toward its employees, nevertheless it also owed a common law duty of care to the public as well (*King v Sussex Ambulance NHS Trust*).

The extent of any duty of care will vary with the circumstances. For instance, where specific advice is being given, the duty will be all the greater; on the other hand, where general advice is being given, the duty will be less.

**Informal advice.** A negligence case was brought in respect of informal planning advice given over the telephone. In rejecting the claim, the court pointed out that if it were too ready to impose liability, it would be contrary to the public interest, because local authorities would be likely to cease giving any guidance at all (*Tidman v Reading BC*). On the other hand, where a local authority environmental health officer office gave specific advice, in the form of directing a person as to what should be done (altering a hotel kitchen), gave inaccurate information about his own authority, and omitted reference to the person's statutory rights, the court held that a duty of care did exist (*Welton v North Cornwall DC*).

**Child care advice.** The case concerned the failure of a local authority to deregister a childminder who was under suspicion and investigation. Subsequently, an infant was seriously injured while in the childminder's care. Liability was imposed on grounds of a negligent misstatement made to the mother by the local authority's nursery and childminding adviser. He had said to her that he was quite happy that the child be placed with the childminder, even though there was by then a question mark about an injury suffered by another child in the care of that same childminder (*T (A Minor) v Surrey County Council*).

### 23.2.3 DUTY OF CARE TO OWN STAFF
Local authorities will, as employers, owe a normal duty of care to their own staff.

**Injured social worker.** A social worker visited the home of a client who weighed 15 stone. She found him lying half out of bed with a neighbour (who happened to be a nurse) there. Together they moved him; she suffered a serious back injury. She had received neither training nor even information about manual handling. She was awarded over £200,000 compensation (*Colclough v Staffordshire County Council*).

**Social worker and stress.** A social services team leader working on child abuse cases suffered a nervous breakdown. This was not foreseeable. However, when he resumed work, it was foreseeable that he would suffer further illness unless substantial assistance was provided. This did not happen; he suffered a second breakdown, which led to his retiring at the age of 50. The court found the local authority to be in breach of its duty of care and therefore liable to pay damages in negligence (*Walker v Northumberland CC*).

**Social workers, teachers and stress**. A social worker brought a negligence case in relation to stress she had suffered. The court accepted that she was owed a duty of care by her local authority employer. However, on the facts of the case, the authority had taken reasonable steps so as not to breach the duty. It could not reasonably have foreseen the social worker's reaction, on her return from a three-week holiday, to the fact that a promise had not been kept – namely to implement a 'stacking system' where new cases would not be allocated until existing cases had reduced (*Pratley v Surrey CC*).

In contrast, where a local authority was well aware of a teacher's difficulties in terms of stress, but failed to take action, it would be liable. The fact that all the teachers were overworked and stressed did not mean that something could not have been done for this particular teacher (*Barber v Somerset CC*).

## 23.3 WEIGHING UP RISKS AND BENEFITS

As already noted above, part of the determination of liability for negligence will concern whether risks and benefits have been correctly weighed up, and any risk proportionately managed. Community care assessment is not about risk elimination, but about risk management.

A certain degree of risk taking will be acceptable rather than, for instance, compromise independence and break family or home links (*R(Khana) v Southwark LBC*). Likewise, the Health and Safety Executive makes the same point, referring to a level of 'elective' risk taking required in connection with independent living and enabling people to develop the necessary skills associated with 'ordinary living' (HSE SIM 7/2000/8). Department of Health guidance refers to risks that may be acceptable or viewed as a 'natural and healthy part of independent living' (LAC(2002)13, para 41).

**Road-crossing ability of person with learning disabilities**. A person with learning disabilities was knocked down by a car when he was crossing the road to catch a local authority minibus, which would take him to the day centre he attended. He had begun to cross the road, despite being told by an escort to wait. A negligence case was brought on his behalf by the Official Solicitor. Prior to the time of the accident it was not unusual for the man already to be at the pickup point, having crossed the road before the minibus arrived. The evidence indicated that long before the accident he had reached a level of independence and road safety competence so that he was able to cross the road on his own without being exposed to unreasonable risk of foreseeable injury, even in the rush hour. He must have crossed the road in this way, and in safety, many hundreds of times in the five years before the accident. The negligence case failed both in the High Court and Court of Appeal (*Slater v Buckinghamshire CC*).

The fact that not every accident will entail liability is a point put forcibly in a context wider than community care. In one case the House of Lords stressed the importance of taking account of risk, gravity, cost and social value:

**Weighing up risk and social value generally**. When a young man dived from a standing position into the shallow water of a council-owned lake, he broke his neck; this was despite warning signs about the dangers of swimming. In rejecting his claim for damages against the council, the House of Lords stated that they had to weigh up risk, gravity, cost and social value. The social value of giving people access to the edge of the lake was very considerable; the risk of such an accident was minimal; and it was not the role of the courts to protect 'the foolhardy or reckless few' who choose to ignore warning notices and put themselves at risk (*Tomlinson v Congleton BC*).

In cases where there is tension between the risks and benefits to the service user, the solution might not always be easy to find. But the local ombudsman has pointed out that at the very least decisiveness is required, if the service user's needs are not to be neglected. Indeed, while the council argued in the following case the man and his family were perversely at higher risk from manual handling every day:

**Stairlift, health and safety, terminal illness, manual handling.** The complainant was the mother of a man with motor neurone disease; she complained that the council had acted unreasonably in providing home adaptations. The man had three children aged between 11 and 15 years; his wife had recently had heart surgery. Part of the complaint related to a stairlift. The council refused to install it because of a lack of clearance at the top of the stairs (demanded by the council's design brief). However, to remedy this would have involved further adaptation work. This was not acceptable to the family because of the fear of dust and draughts during the works – since colds or respiratory illness could be extremely dangerous for people with motor neurone disease. A stairlift with a swivel chair was considered, but the occupational therapy team leader expressed concern because the chair would block the staircase and constitute a risk for other members of the family.

Differences of opinion persisted on the safety ground between the architects department (which was prepared to proceed) and the building works department, which was not. In the meantime, the man had offered to sign any disclaimer (in case of accident) that the council felt was appropriate. The family felt that the council's preoccupation with safety was somewhat 'hollow', since it appeared to disregard completely the daily risks to the family, when the children and elderly mother carried the man up and down the stairs.

The ombudsman could not 'understand that the importance of the design brief must outweigh' everything else. In the light of the council's policy of enabling people to remain at home, it needed 'to give very careful consideration to those cases where another aspect of their policy contradicts this'. The ombudsman did not believe that the council had thought through adequately the consequences of such a clash; and stated that it should 'put all the facts to Members who will then be in a position to come to a proper reasoned decision' as soon as possible (*Islington LBC 1988*).

# Regulation of care provision

**KEY POINTS**

Under the Care Standards Act 2000, a new system of regulation of care providers replaced the previous system under the Registered Homes Act 1984. The registration and inspection of care providers is governed by the 2000 Act itself, and by various sets of regulations made under it. In addition, the Department of Health has published 'national minimum standards' that must be taken into account when registration and inspection decisions are taken. The registration and inspection bodies covering England comprise the Commission for Social Care Inspection, and the Commission for Healthcare Audit and Inspection (known as the Health Commission). These bodies replaced the National Care Standards Commission in April 2004.

One particular uncertainty concerns the purported transformation of many care homes (that would otherwise be subject to the care home regulatory rules) into 'supported living' situations, where registration as a care home is not required.

**Note: Wales, Scotland and Northern Ireland**. Equivalent statutory provisions exist. In Wales, the Care Standards Inspectorate for Wales is the responsible body under the Care Standards Act 2000 and associated regulations. In Scotland, the Commission for the Regulation of Care is responsible under the Regulation of Care (Scotland) Act 2001 and associated regulations. In Northern Ireland, the Regulation and Improvement Authority will in future be the responsible body under the Health and Personal Social Services (Quality and Improvement and Regulation) (Northern Ireland) Order 2003.

## 24.I REGULATION OF CARE PROVIDERS

The new system covers a wider range of care provision than the previous system under the Registered Homes Act 1984. It embraces children's homes, independent hospitals, independent clinics, care homes, residential family centres, independent medical centres, domiciliary care agencies, fostering agencies, nurse agencies, voluntary adoption agencies and adult placement schemes. Furthermore, local authorities acting as care providers are now covered in the same way as providers in the independent sector. (Previously local autthorities, and as care providers, were not subject to registration and inspection under the 1984 Act.) However, the system does not cover the NHS. It is an offence for care providers, who come within the relevant definitions, not to register (Care Standards Act 2000, s.11).

## 24.2 DEFINITIONS OF CARE HOME AND DOMICILIARY CARE AGENCY

A number of definitions are supplied within the Care Standards Act 2000:

- **Care home**. A care home is an establishment (whether or not for profit) that provides accommodation, together with nursing or personal care for people who are or have been ill (including mental disorder), who are disabled or infirm or who are or have been dependent on alcohol or drugs. However, it is not a care home if it is a hospital, independent clinic or a children's home (Care Standards Act 2000, s.3).
- **Assistance with bodily functions**. An establishment is not a care home for the purposes of the Act unless 'the care which it provides includes assistance with bodily functions where such assistance is required' (s.121).
- **Illness**. Illness includes injury.
- **Disability**. A disabled person is defined as having sight, hearing or speech substantially impaired; having a mental disorder; or being physically substantially disabled by any illness, any impairment present since birth, or otherwise.
- **Mental disorder**. Mental disorder means mental illness, arrested or incomplete development of mind, psychopathic disorder, any other disorder or disability of mind (s.121).
- **Domiciliary care**. A domiciliary care agency is an undertaking (whether or not for profit) which arranges the provision of personal care for people in their own homes who are unable to provide it for themselves because of illness, infirmity or disability (s.4) – excluding a sole self-employed person (S1 2002/3214, r.3).

## 24.3 REGISTRATION AUTHORITIES

In April 2004, the registration authority for England, the National Care Standards Commission, gave way to two new bodies: the Commission for Healthcare Audit and Inspection (CHAI, but commonly referred to as the Healthcare Commission) and the Commission for Social Care Inspection (CSCI) (s.5).

The CHAI has registration responsibilities for independent hospitals, independent clinics and independent medical agencies (s.5A). The CSCI has responsibility for care homes, domiciliary care agencies, children's homes, residential family centres, nurse agencies, fostering agencies, voluntary adoption agencies, adoption support agencies, and adult placement schemes (s.5).

## 24.4 REGULATIONS

Under the Care Standards Act 2000, a number of sets of regulations have been passed to spell out registration requirements for the different types of provider. The following paragraphs outline some of these requirements in relation to care homes and domiciliary care services. However, the original regulations should be referred to for a comprehensive view. Regulations relating to adult placements were reissued in August 2004, so that the regulatory effect and burden would fall on adult placement schemes, rather than individual providers; for example, families (SI 2004/2070).

### 24.4.1 REGULATIONS FOR CARE HOMES

The Care Homes Regulations 2001 (SI 2001/3965) refer to a number of requirements, as set out below:

- **Information**: home's statement of purpose, a service user's guide, information about fees.
- **Fitness**: the fitness of the registered provider (including integrity, good character, physical and mental fitness), fitness of registered manager, fitness of staff (including suitable qualifications, experience, skill).
- **Employment checks**: for people carrying on, managing or working in a care home, certain information is required including proof of identity, birth certificate, current passport, evidence of qualifications, two written references, evidence of mental and physical fitness, and criminal record certificate issued under the Police Act 1997.
- **Staffing and training**: there must be suitably qualified, competent and experienced staff working at the care home as are appropriate for the health and welfare of service users; there must be appropriate training.
- **Health, welfare dignity**: the care home must be conducted so as to promote and properly provide for the health and welfare of service users. As far as practicable service users should be enabled to make decisions about their care. Arrangements must be made to ensure the privacy and dignity of service users, with due regard to sex, religious persuasion, racial origin, cultural and linguistic background, any disability of service users.
- **Access to health care**: arrangements must be made for service users to register with a general practitioner of their choice and to receive where necessary services from any health care professional.
- **Medicines**: arrangements must be made for the recording, handling, safekeeping, safe administration and disposal of medicines.
- **Health and safety**: arrangements must be made for health and safety matters, including a safe system for moving and handling service users.
- **Abuse**: arrangements must be made to prevent service users being harmed or suffering abuse or being placed at risk of harm or abuse.

REGULATION OF CARE PROVISION

- **Restraint**: no service user should be subject to physical restraint, unless it is the only practicable means of securing the welfare of that or any other service user and there are exceptional circumstances; and any such restraint must be recorded.
- **Assessment of service users**: as far as practicable, service users must have been assessed by a suitably qualified or trained person before accommodation is provided for them, the home must have obtained a copy of the assessment, the service user (or his or her representative) have been consulted, and the home have confirmed in writing to the service user that the home is suitable for his or her needs. The assessment of the service user's needs must be kept under review and revised as necessary. A care plan must be prepared, made available to the service user and kept under review.
- **Facilities and services**: the care home must have appropriate facilities and services – for example, in respect of telephones, furniture, laundry, kitchen equipment, food, keeping of valuables, arranging social activities, etc.
- **Premises including adaptations and equipment for disability**: there are many requirements, including suitable adaptations and equipment for old, infirm or physically disabled service users.

For example, in a case concerning the fitness of a manager of a care home, a care standards tribunal (CST) had in effect given the appellant the benefit of the doubt concerning his background (past misconduct involving physical abuse of residents). The CST overturned (what was then) the National Care Standards Commission's decision that he was not fit to be registered. However, in turn the High Court overturned the CST's decision, on the grounds that it had not explicitly addressed the question of whether he was fit to do so in terms of integrity and good character. The Court of Appeal upheld this decision and also confirmed that the burden lay on the applicant to show his or her fitness, rather than on the registration authority to show unfitness (*Jones v National Care Standards Commission*).

### 24.4.2 REGULATIONS FOR DOMICILIARY CARE AGENCIES

The Domiciliary Care Agencies Regulations 2002 (SI 2002/3214) refer to a number of requirements, including those as set out below (but refer to the original regulations for a comprehensive view):

- **Fitness**: fitness of registered provider, manager, staff (similar to fitness requirements for Care Homes Regulations above).
- **Safety, independence**: the agency must ensure the safety of service users, safeguard them against abuse or neglect, promote independence, ensure the safety and security of the property of service users.
- **Dignity, etc.**: respect for privacy, dignity, wishes, confidentiality; also have due regard to sex, religious persuasion, racial origin, cultural and linguistic background and any disability.
- **Care plan**: a care plan must specify the service users' needs, how those needs are to be met. It must be made available to the service user, kept under review and revised as appropriate.

- **Meeting need**: as far as practicable the personal care provided must meet the service user's needs.
- **Wishes and feelings**: as far as practicable, service users' wishes and feelings must be taken account of; they must be provided with comprehensive information and suitable choices and be encouraged to make decisions about their personal care.
- **Abuse**: arrangements must be made to prevent service users being harmed or suffering abuse, and a procedure must be specified for dealing with an allegation of abuse, neglect or harm.
- **Medication**: arrangements must be made for the recording, handling, safe keeping and safe administration of medicines; also circumstances must be specified in which a care worker may administer or assist with medication.
- **Mobility**: arrangements to assist a service user with mobility in the home.
- **Agent/money**: there must be a specified procedure where a worker acts as agent for, or receives money from, a service user.
- **Safe system of work**: suitable arrangements must be made, including training, to ensure a safe system of work, to include the lifting and moving of service users.
- **Physical restraint**: (as for care homes).
- **Staffing**: there must at all times be an appropriate number of suitably skilled and experienced staff; suitable assistance, including appropriate equipment, must be provided at their request in respect of the provision of personal care.

## 24.4.3 CARE STANDARDS

Under the Care Standards Act 2000, a number of sets of care standards have been published in both England and Wales. The registration authority must take them into account when it takes decisions (s.23); therefore, breach of one or more standards does not automatically mean breach of legislation. Various sets of standards have been published, including one set relating to care homes (DH 2003b), and another to domiciliary care agencies (DH 2003c).

## 24.4.4 PERSONAL CARE AND REGISTRATION REQUIREMENTS

The question of whether personal care is being provided is a crucial one, because the answer determines whether the care provider must go through the registration and inspection regime imposed by the Care Standards Act 2000. The Act does not define what is meant by personal care. However, Department of Health guidance states that its ordinary meaning includes:

- assistance with bodily functions such as feeding, bathing and toileting
- care falling just short of assistance with bodily functions, but still involving physical and intimate touching, including activities such as helping a person get out of a bath and helping them to get dressed
- non-physical care, such as advice, encouragement and supervision relating to the foregoing, such as prompting a person to take a bath and supervising them during this

- emotional and psychological support, including the promotion of social functioning, behaviour management, and assistance with cognitive functions (DH 2002b).

Previous case law under other legislation has given the term 'personal care' a wide meaning so as to include the emotional and psychiatric, not just bodily, functions (*Harrison v Cornwall County Council*). In turn, attention in connection with bodily functions has been interpreted widely: for example, including the function of an interpreter for a deaf person, in order that she could communicate during the day with people who were not deaf (*Secretary of State for Social Security v Fairey*).

Under the Care Standards Act 2000, registration as a care home is only required if the care provided includes assistance with bodily functions (s.121(9)). This then is an explicit requirement; however, the *Fairey* case indicates that even assistance with bodily functions has a potentially wide scope.

The Department of Health's interpretation of 'personal care' in respect of domiciliary care providers takes a narrow approach. Guidance states that registration is only required in respect of the first two types of care listed above (assistance with bodily functions, and care falling just short of such assistance). It goes on to suggest that the other two types of personal care do not trigger registration requirements, but could be provided, for example, under the Supporting People scheme (see 15.3).

The guidance supports this approach by arguing that it is s.4 of the Act that restricts registration requirements in this way. Under s.4, a domiciliary care agency is defined as an undertaking that provides personal care that a person is unable to provide for himself or herself without assistance. The guidance maintains that this could not extend to encouragement and emotional support, since it would make no sense to state that a person cannot provide this himself or herself (DH 2002b, para 17). It is not entirely clear whether this interpretation is convincing.

The guidance goes on to state that it would not expect very sheltered housing, extra care housing or group homes (supported housing) to have to register, as a matter of course, as care homes (DH 2002b, para 19). Generally speaking, where personal care is provided, it would be provided by a registered domiciliary care agency. However, it warns that where the circumstances suggest that an establishment (including personal care) is being run by one (or more than one connected) company, then registration as a care home would be still required (DH 2002b, para 33). Indeed, it was the inability to identify a genuine distinction between the provision of the housing and the provision of personal care which led the Care Standards Tribunal to find that a care home was still being operated in the case of *Alternative Futures Ltd v National Care Standards Commission* (see below).

The Department of Health guidance also lays emphasis on whether the personal care is being delivered to a person's own home (occupied, for example, with the right to deny entry to people including care workers without this affecting their right to occupy). It states that shared accommodation could be a characteristic of a person's own home; but that the scale of such accommodation is likely to be relevant (para 40). Beyond family or domestic scale, such accommodation might be more realistically regarded as a care home rather than a person's own home. It also suggests that the distinction between a tenancy and a licence to occupy might be relevant, since the latter would not entail the person having exclusive possession of any part of the premises, and so not be consistent with the accommodation representing the person's own home (para 36).

## 24.4.5 SUPPORTED HOUSING

Since the coming into force of the Care Standards Act 2000, some care homes have decided to 'deregister' themselves as care homes. Apart from avoiding the registration and inspection requirements for care homes, deregistration also results in avoidance of the whole system of local authority placements and charges for residential care. It enables former residents to become tenants and, amongst other things, receive housing benefit. Personal care is then delivered separately by a domiciliary care agency. Where carried out in good faith and with propriety, such changes in status can also accord with policies of encouraging people to live independently. However, in some instances it is suspected that such changes have been driven more by financial considerations than by the welfare of service users.

Such changes to the status of accommodation have a number of possible legal ramifications. These include their very lawfulness and also the consequent duties of local authorities, who in many instances will have originally placed residents in the care home that is now deregistering. One such instance of deregistration was challenged and the dispute reached the care standards tribunal. It ruled against the deregistration in the particular circumstances, stressing the absence of choice for service users to choose a domiciliary care provider, and thus casting doubt on whether there was a genuine separation between the provision of the accommodation and the provision of the personal care:

**Improper deregistration of care home.** The company, called Alternative Futures Ltd, provided residential accommodation until January 2002. At that date, having consulted with residents, it purported to deregister itself as a care home. It split itself into two companies. Alternative Housing covered the housing side of things, Alternative Futures the domiciliary care services required. Tenants were given keys and enjoyed exclusive possession of their rooms. The benefits claimed for the tenants were housing benefit, security of tenure, choice of care provider and extra funding and space that would otherwise have been devoted to registration requirements as a care home.

The care standards tribunal considered various aspects of what had occurred, including whether the residents had the mental capacity to sign the tenancy agreements and whether this would be fatal to the arrangements. Ultimately, however, the tribunal ruled against deregistration, on grounds of choice. This was becasue in practice the domiciliary care services would have to be delivered by Alternative Futures; there were no arrangements in place to allow tenants to express genuine choice to receive such services from another provider (*Alternative Futures Ltd v National Care Standards Commission*).

The tribunal did not answer the question of whether, if mental incapacity had been shown on the part of the tenants, the tenancies would anyway have been invalidated. There appears to be a lack of certainty about this issue. It is argued that if the tenancy were regarded as being a contract for 'necessaries' (see 18.7), it would nevertheless be workable and enforceable in that the rent could be recovered. Department of Health guidance summarises the relevant principles as follows. It reiterates the presumption of a person's capacity until proved otherwise, and the importance of taking the functional approach to deciding capacity (see 18.4). It then goes on to state that a contract is binding if the landlord believed the tenant was capable of making it; that the penalty, if any, for a void contract would fall on the landlord; that the 'necessaries' rule could apply; and that the Official Solicitor is of the view that a tenancy can be granted to a person even if he or she has limited mental capacity (DH 2002b, annex B).

The courts have held that in any case deregistration does not simply happen automatically because there is a change in factual circumstances that appear to take the care home outside of registration requirements; the decision of the registration authority is still required (*Alternative Futures v Sefton MBC*).

### 24.4.5.1 Continuing local authority responsibilities on deregistration

If a local authority has placed a person in a care home that is now proposing deregistration, it would seem the local authority must review and reassess the needs of the service user. This is to ensure that any new arrangements will continue to meet the needs of the service user and, if so, to amend the care plan. If the new arrangements clearly would not meet the needs of a service user, the local authority would need to make alternative arrangements. This was the inference reached in the following court case:

**Change to supported housing and meeting individual needs.** A local authority proposed to sell a residential home to a housing association, which would then redevelop the premises and grant tenancies to the residents. The severely disabled claimant argued that she would not as a consequence benefit from communal dining and would lose the social interaction necessary for her well-being. Other concerns related to arrangements for transport, holidays and in relation to her vomiting in the night.

The court held that the care plan for the woman did not have to be worked out fully in advance of the alterations to the premises; and what was important at present was that neither the care plan nor the structure of the new premises obstructed this. So long as this remained the case, then it would be premature to argue that her needs would not be met in the new set-up (*R(Lloyd) v Barking and Dagenham LBC, CA*).

Thus, if a local authority or NHS trust is considering a change for an individual service user from residential care to supported housing, it needs to be able to justify this:

**Supported living rather than residential care.** The residential panel of a Care Trust providing both NHS and community care services decided that a man with autistic spectrum disorder no longer required residential care and that his needs could be met in a supported housing context (where he would receive housing benefit). The Trust's letter at the time stated that it had to have regard to relative costs; a residential placement would cost £860 per week, whereas supported housing would have no immediate costs to health or social services, because of access to income support, housing benefit, and other benefits. However, the letter also stated that, such issues aside, supported living would be in the man's best interests. A dispute arose about this.

The court refused to intervene on various grounds. These included the fact that, on the evidence, the Trust's belief that the man would benefit from independence in supported housing could not be characterised as legally irrational. The panel had not excluded residential care as a possibility but had preferred the supported housing options, something it was quite entitled to do. Furthermore, article 8 of the European Convention on Human Rights added nothing to the facts of the case (*R(Rodriguez-Bannister) v Somerset Partnership NHS and Social Care Trust*).

# References

## LEGAL CASES

*A v A health authority* [2001] EWHC Fam/Admin 18, High Court.

*A Child 'A' (by his mother and litigation friend 'B') v Ministry of Defence and Guy's and St Thomas Hospital NHS Trust* [2004] EWCA Civ 641, Court of Appeal.

*A local authority v A Health Authority* [2003] EWHC Fam 2746, High Court.

*Alternative Futures Ltd v National Care Standards Commission* [2002] 101–111 NC, Care Standards Tribunal.

*Alternative Futures Ltd v Sefton Metropolitan Borough Council and National Care Standards Commission* [2002] EWHC 3032 (Admin), High Court.

*An Hospital Trust v S* [2003] EWHC Admin 365, High Court.

*An NHS Trust v Ms T* [2004] EWHC Fam 1279, High Court.

*Associated Provincial Picture Houses v Wednesbury Corporation* [1947] 2 All ER 680, Court of Appeal.

*Avon County Council v Hooper* [1997] 1 All ER 532, Court of Appeal.

*Baigent v BBC* (1999) unreported, Court of Session, Outer House.

*Baker v Baker* [1993] 2 FLR 247, Court of Appeal.

*Banks v Goodfellow* (1870) LR 5 QB 549.

*Barber v Somerset County Council* [2004] UKHL 13, House of Lords.

*Barrett v Enfield London Borough Council* [1999] 3 WLR 79, House of Lords.

*Barrett v Kasprzyk* (2000) unreported, High Court (Chancery).

*Beasley v Buckinghamshire County Council* [1997] PIQR P473, High Court (QBD).

*Bell v Todd* [2002] LR Med 12, High Court.

*BetterCare Group v Director General of Fair Trading* [2002] CAT 7, Competition Commission Appeal Tribunal.

*BetterCare Group v North and West Belfast Health and Social Services Trust* (2003) Case no. CA98/09/2003, Office of Fair Trading, 2003.

*Bluett v Suffolk County Council and Others* [2004] EWCA Civ 1707, Court of Appeal.

*Botta v Italy* (1998) Case no. 21439/93, European Court of Human Rights.

*British Oxygen v Board of Trade* [1971] AC 610, House of Lords.

*Brown v Mott* (2002) unreported, High Court (Chancery).

*Bull v Devon Area Health Authority* (1983) 4 Med LR 177.

*Burke v General Medical Council* [2004] EWHC Admin 1879, High Court.

*Cambridgeshire County Council v R* [1994] 2 FCR 973, High Court.

*Campbell v Griffin* [2001] EWCA Civ 990, Court of Appeal.

*CD(A Child) v Anglesey County Council* [2004] EWHC Admin 1635, High Court.

*Cheese v Thomas* [1994] 1 All ER 35, Court of Appeal.

*Chief Adjudication Officer v Palfrey* [1995] SJLB 65, Court of Appeal.

*Chief Adjudication Officer v Quinn* [1996] 1 WLR 1184, House of Lords.

*Chief Constable v A County Council* [2002] EWHC Fam 2198, High Court.

*CIS/3197/2003*. Social Security Commmmissioner decision. Reported in Adviser, July–August 2004.

*Clancy v Clancy* [2003] EWHC 1885, High Court.

*Clunis v Camden and Islington Health Authority* [1998] 3 All ER 180, Court of Appeal.

*Cocks v Thanet District Council* [1983] 2 AC, House of Lords.

*Colclough v Staffordshire County Council* [1994] CL 94/2283, County Court.

*Collins v United Kingdom* (2002), Application 11909/02, European Court of Human Rights.

*Commons v Queen's Medical Centre Nottingham University Hospital NHS Trust* (2001), unreported, County Court.

*Council of Civil Service Unions v Minister of State for the Civil Service* [1985] AC 374, House of Lords.

*Croydon London Borough Council v Moody* (1999) 2 CCLR 93, Court of Appeal.

*Dennis Rye Pension Fund v Sheffield City Council* (1998) 1 WLR 840, Court of Appeal.

*Donoghue v Poplar Housing Association* [2001] EWCA Civ 595, Court of Appeal.

*Douce v Staffordshire County Council* [2002] EWCA Civ 506, Court of Appeal.

*Durant v Financial Services Authority* [2003] EWCA Civ 1746, Court of Appeal.

*Edwards v National Coal Board* [1949] 1 All ER 743, Court of Appeal.

*Faulkner v Talbot* [1981] 3 All ER 468, Court of Appeal.

*Firth v Ackroyd and Bradford Metropolitan District Council* (2000) High Court (QBD).

*Gaskin v UK* (1989) 12 EHRR 36 (Series A, no.160), European Court of Human Rights.

*Glanville v Glanville* [2002] EWHC 1271, High Court (Chancery).

*Glass v United Kingdom* (2004) Application 61827/00, European Court of Human Rights.

*Gogay v Hertfordshire County Council* (2001) 1 FLR 280, Court of Appeal.

*Gwilliam v West Hertfordshire Hospital NHS Trust* [2002] EWCA Civ 1041, Court of Appeal.

*Hall v Monmouthshire County Council, Gwent Healthcare NHS Trust and others* [2004] EWHC QB 2748, High Court.

*Hammond v Osborne* [2002] EWCA Civ 885, Court of Appeal.

*Hampson v Department of Education and Science* [1990] IRLR 302, House of Lords.

*Harris v Harris* (1999) unreported, Court of Appeal.

*Harrison v Cornwall County Council* (1991) 156 Lg Rev R 703, Court of Appeal.

*Hawkes v Southwark London Borough Council* (1998) unreported, Court of Appeal.

*Health and Safety Executive v London Borough of Barnet* (1997) unreported, Crown Court.

*HL v United Kingdom* (2004) Application 45508/99, Times Law Reports, 19th October 2004, European Court of Human Rights.

*HM v Switzerland* (2002) Application 39187/98, European Court of Human Rights.

*Hoff, Beagan, Wiechulla v Atherton* [2004] EWHC 177, High Court (Chancery); [2004] EWCA Civ 1554, Court of Appeal.

*Islington London Borough Council v University College London Hospital NHS Trust* [2004] EWHC 1754, High Court (QBD).

*Jennings and Lewis v Cairns* [2003] EWCA Civ 1935, Court of Appeal.

*Jones v National Care Standards Commission* [2004] EWHC Admin 918, High Court; [2004] EWHC Civ 1713, Court of Appeal.

*JT (Adult: refusal of medical treatment)* [1998] FLR 48, High Court.

*JT v United Kingdom* [2000] 1 FLR 909, European Court of Human Rights.

*Kent v Griffiths* (2000) 3 CCLR 98, Court of Appeal.

*Kenward v Adams* (1975) *The Times,* 29th November 1975, High Court.

*King v Sussex Ambulance Service* [2002] EWCA Civ 953, Court of Appeal.

*Koonjul v Thameslink NHS Health Care Trust* (2000) PIQR 123, Court of Appeal.

*Knott v Newham Healthcare NHS Trust* [2003] EWCA Civ 771, Court of Appeal.

*Lambeth London Borough Council v A* [2002] EWCA Civ 1084, Court of Appeal.

*Law Society v Southall* [2001] EWCA Civ 2001, Court of Appeal.

*Lillie v Newcastle City Council* [2002] EWHC 1600, High Court (QBD).

*M v Bromley London Borough Council* [2002] EWCA Civ 1113, Court of Appeal.

*M v Secretary of State for Health* [2002] 7 PC, Care Standards Tribunal.

*McCarthy v Richmond London Borough Council* [1991] 4 All ER 897, House of Lords.

*McGlinchey v United Kingdom* (2003) Application 50390/99, European Court of Human Rights.

*MacGregor v South Lanarkshire Council* (2001) 4 CCLR 188, Court of Session (Outer House).

*McKellar v Hounslow London Borough Council* [2003] EWHC 3145, High Court (QBD).

*Maddock v Devon County Council* (2003) unreported Case Ex190052, Exeter District Registry, High Court (QBD).

*Manchester City Council v Romano; Manchester City Council v Samari* [2004] EWCA Civ 384, Court of Appeal.

*Masterman-Lister v Brutton* [2002] EWHC 417, High Court (QBD); [2002] EWCA Civ 1889, Court of Appeal.

*Mendoza v Ghaidan* [2004] UKHL 30, House of Lords.

*MG v United Kingdom* (2002) Application 39393/98, European Court of Human Rights.

*Mohammed v Secretary of State for the Home Department* [2003] EWHC Admin 2273.

*Munjaz v Mersey Care NHS Trust* [2003] EWCA Civ 1036, Court of Appeal.

*Nel v Kean* [2003] EWHC 190, High Court (QBD).

*Newham London Borough Council v BS* [2003] EWHC Fam 1909, High Court.

*NHS Trust A v M* (2001) 2 WLR 942, High Court.

*NHS Trust v C* [2004] EWHC Fam 1657, High Court.

*North Devon Homes v Brazier* [2003] EWHC 574, High Court (QBD).

*O'Rourke v Camden London Borough Council* [1997] 3 All ER 23, House of Lords.

*Patchett v Leathem* (1949), TLR, 4 February 1949, High Court, Kings Bench Division.

*Pfizer Corporation v Ministry of Health* [1965] AC 512, House of Lords.

*Pratley v Surrey County Council* [2003] EWCA Civ 1067, Court of Appeal.

*Pretty v United Kingdom* [2002] 2 FCR 97, European Court of Human Rights.

*Price v United Kingdom* (2001) Application 33394/96, European Court of Human Rights.

*Purves v Joydisc Ltd* (2003) SC694/01, Sheriff Court (Scotland), appeal to the Sheriff Principal.

*Purves v Southampton University Hospitals NHS Trust* (2004), Employment Tribunal case no. 3103968/ 2002.

*Qazi v Waltham Forest London Borough Council* (1999) unreported, High Court (QBD).

*R v A local authority in the Midlands, ex p LM* (2000) 1 FLR 612, High Court.

*R v Ali Sed* [2004] EWCA Crim 1295, Court of Appeal.

*R v Ashworth Special Hospital Authority, ex p E* [2001] EWHC Admin 1089, High Court.

*R v Ashworth Special Hospital Authority, ex p N* [2001] EWHC Admin 339, High Court.

*R v Avon County Council, ex p M* [1994] 2 FCR 259, High Court.

*R v Barnet London Borough Council, ex p Shah* (1983), 2 AC 309, House of Lords.

*R v Berkshire County Council, ex p Parker* [1996] 95 LGR 449, High Court.

*R v Bexley London Borough Council, ex p B* [1995] CL 3225, High Court.

*R v Birmingham City Council, ex p A* [1997] 2 FCR 357, High Court.

*R v Birmingham City Council, ex p Birmingham Care Consortium* [2002] EWHC Admin 2118, High Court.

*R v Birmingham City Council, ex p Killigrew* (2000) 3 CCLR 109, High Court.

*R v Birmingham City Council, ex p Mohammed* [2002] EWHC Admin 1511, High Court.

*R v Birmingham City Council, ex p Taj Mohammed* [1998] 1 CCLR 441, High Court.

*R v Bouldstridge* (2000) unreported (but see Kelso, P. (2000). He only wanted to end his wife's pain. He ended up in court, at 84. *The Guardian*, 7 June 2000, p.1).

*R v Bournewood Community and Mental Health NHS Trust, ex p L* [1998] 1 CCLR 390, House of Lords.

*R v Bowles (Lewis) and Bowles (Christine)* [2004] EWCA Crim 1608, Court of Appeal.

*R v Brent, Kensington and Chelsea and Westminster NHS Trust, ex p C* [2002] EWHC 181, High Court.

*R v Brent London Borough Council, ex p D* [1998] 1 CCLR 235, High Court.

*R v Bristol City Council, ex p Bailey* [1995] 27 HLR 307, High Court.

*R v Bristol City Council, ex p Penfold* [1998] 1 CCLR 315, High Court.

*R v Cambridge Health Authority, ex p B* [1995] 6 MLR 250, Court of Appeal.

*R v Central Birmingham Health Authority, ex p Collier* (1998) unreported, Court of Appeal.

*R v Central Birmingham Health Authority, ex p Walker* [1987] 3 BMLR 32, Court of Appeal.

*R v Chief Constable of North Wales, ex p AB* [1998] 3 WLR 57, Court of Appeal.

*R v Chief Constables of C and D, ex p A* [2001] 2 FCR Admin 431, High Court.

*R v Cleveland County Council, ex p Cleveland Care Homes Association* [1993] 158 LGRevR 641, High Court.

*R v Cleveland County Council, ex p Ward* [1994] COD 222, High Court.

*R v Collins, Pathfinder Mental Health Services NHS Trust and St George's Healthcare NHS Trust, ex p S* (1998) 1 CCLR 578, Court of Appeal.

*R v Collins, Pathfinder Mental Health Services NHS Trust and St George's Healthcare NHS Trust, ex p S (no.2)* (1998) 3 WLR 936, Court of Appeal.

*R v Commissioner for Local Administration, ex p PH* (1999) COD 382, High Court; [1999] ELR 314, Court of Appeal.

*R v Cornwall County Council, ex p Goldsack* (1996) unreported, High Court.

*R v Coventry City Council, ex p Coventry Heads of Independent Care Establishments (CHOICE) and Peggs* [1998] 1 CCLR 379, High Court.

*R v D* [2002] EWCA Crim 990, Court of Appeal.

*R v Department of Health and Social Security, ex p Bruce* [1986] TLR 8 February 1986, High Court.

*R v Devon County Council, ex p Baker and Johns; R v Durham County Council, ex p Curtis and Brown* [1992] 158 LGRevR 241, Court of Appeal.

*R v Director of Public Prosecutions, ex p Pretty* [2001] UKHL 61, House of Lords.

*R v Duffy* (1998) 3 WLR 1060, Court of Appeal.

*R v Ealing District Health Authority, ex p Fox* [1993] WLR 373, High Court.

*R v Ealing London Borough Council, ex p C* (2000) 3 CCLR 122, Court of Appeal.

*R v Ealing London Borough Council, ex p Leaman* [1984] TLR, 10 February 1984, High Court.

*R v East Kent Hospital NHS Trust, ex p Smith* [2002] EWHC Admin 2640, High Court.

*R v East Sussex County Council, ex p Tandy* [1997] 3 FCR 525, Court of Appeal; [1998] 2 All ER 769, House of Lords.

*R v East Sussex County Council, ex p Tandy* [1997] 3 FCR 525, Court of Appeal; (1998) 1 CCLR 352, House of Lords.

*R v Essex County Council, ex p Bucke* [1997] COD 66, High Court.

*R v Further Education Funding Council and Bradford Metropolitan District Council, ex p Parkinson* [1997] 2 FCR 67, High Court.

*R v Gloucestershire County Council, ex p Barry* [1995] 160 LGRevR 321, High Court; [1996] 4 All ER 422, Court of Appeal; [1997] 2 All ER 1, House of Lords.

*R v Gloucestershire County Council, ex p Mahfood* [1995] 160 LGRevR 321, High Court.

*R v Gloucestershire County Council, ex p RADAR* [1996] COD 253, High Court.

*R v Hackney London Borough Council, ex p J* (1999) unreported, High Court.

*R v Hammersmith Hospitals NHS Trust, ex p Reffell* (2000) Lloyd's Rep Med 350, Court of Appeal.

*R v Haringey London Borough Council, ex p Norton* [1998] 1 CCLR 168, High Court.

*R v Hereford and Worcester County Council, ex p Chandler* (1992) unreported, noted in *Legal Action* 15, September 2002.

*R v Hillingdon Area Health Authority, ex p Wyatt* (1977) unreported, Court of Appeal.

*R v Hinks* (2001) 2 AC 241, House of Lords.

*R v Inhabitants of Eastbourne* (1803) 4 East 103.

*R v Inner London Education Authority, ex p Ali* [1990] 2 ALR 822, High Court.

*R v Isleworth Crown Court, ex p King* [2001] EWCA Admin 22, Court of Appeal.

*R v Islington London Borough Council, ex p McMillan* [1995] 160 LGRevR 321, High Court.

*R v Islington London Borough Council, ex p Rixon* [1997] 1 ELR 477, High Court.

*R v Kendrick* [1997] 2 Cr App 524, Court of Appeal.

*R v Kensington and Chelsea RB, ex p Kujtim* (1999) 2 CCLR 340, Court of Appeal.

*R v Kent County Council, ex p Marston* (1997) unreported, High Court.

*R v Kent County Council, ex p Salisbury* (2000) 3 CCLR 38, High Court.

*R v Kingston upon Thames Royal Borough, ex p T* [1994] 1 FLR 799, High Court.

*R v Kirklees Metropolitan Borough Council, ex p Daykin* [1996] 3 CL 565, High Court.

*R v Kirklees Metropolitan Borough Council, ex p Good* [1996] 11 CL 288, High Court.

*R v Lambeth London Borough Council, ex p A* [1997] 10 ALR 209, Court of Appeal.

*R v Lambeth London Borough Council, ex p Sarhangi* (1999) 2 CCLR 145, High Court.

*R v Lancashire County Council, ex p RADAR* [1996] 4 All ER 422, Court of Appeal.

*R v Lewisham London Borough Council, ex p Pinzon and Patino* (1999) 2 CCLR 152, High Court.

*R v Manchester City Council, ex p Stennett* (1999) 2 CCLR 402, High Court; [2002] UKHL 34, House of Lords.

*R v Mazo* [1997] 2 Cr App R 518, Court of Appeal.

*R v Mental Health Review Tribunal, Torfaen County Borough Council and Gwent Health Authority, ex p Hall* (1999) 2 CCLR 361, High Court, Administrative Division.

*R v Merton, Sutton and Wandsworth Health Authority, ex p Andrew* (2001) Lloyd's Rep Med 73, High Court.

*R v Newcastle upon Tyne Council, ex p Dixon* [1993] 158 LGRevR 441, High Court.

*R v Newham London Borough Council, ex p Gorenkin* [1997] 30 HLR 278, High Court.

*R v Newham London Borough Council, ex p Medical Foundation for the Care of Victims of Torture* [1998] 1 CCLR 227, High Court.

*R v Newham London Borough Council, ex p Plastin* [1997] 30 HLR 261, High Court.

*R v North Cornwall District Council, ex p Singer* (1994) *The Times*, 12 January 1994, High Court.

*R v North Derbyshire Health Authority, ex p Fisher* [1998] 8 MLR 327, High Court.

*R v North and East Devon Health Authority, ex p Coughlan* (1999) 2 CCLR 285, Court of Appeal.

*R v North West Lancashire Health Authority, ex p G,A,D* (1999) 2 CCLR 419, Court of Appeal.

*R v North Yorkshire County Council, ex p Hargreaves* [1994] 26 BMLR 121, High Court.

*R v North Yorkshire County Council, ex p Hargreaves (no.2)* [1997] 96 LGR 39 High Court.

*R v Northavon District Council, ex p Smith* [1994] 2 FCR 859, House of Lords.

*R v Partnerships in Care Ltd, ex p A* [2002] EWHC Admin 529, High Court.

*R v Plymouth City Council, ex p Stevens* [2002] EWCA Civ 388, Court of Appeal.

*R v Powys County Council, ex p Hambidge* [1998] 1 CCLR 458, Court of Appeal.

*R v Powys County Council, ex p Hambidge (no.2)* [1999] 2 CCLR 460, High Court; (2000) LGR 564, Court of Appeal.

*R v Redbridge London Borough Council ex p East Sussex County Council* [1993] COD 256, High Court.

*R v Responsible Medical Officer Broadmoor Hospital, ex p Wilkinson* [2001] EWCA Civ 1545.

*R v Richmond London Borough Council, ex p H* (2000) unreported High Court.

*R v St Edmundsbury Housing Benefit Review Board, ex p Sandys* (1999) 48 BMLR 24, Court of Appeal.

*R v Savage and Parmenter* [1991] AC 699, House of Lords.

*R v Secretary of State for the Environment, ex p Nottinghamshire County Council* [1986] AC 240, House of Lords.

*R v Secretary of State for Health, ex p Hammersmith and Fulham London Borough Council* (1998) LGR 277, Court of Appeal.

*R v Secretary of State for Health, ex p Manchester Local Committee* [1995] 2 CL 3621, High Court.

*R v Secretary of State for Social Services, ex p Hincks* [1980] 1 BMLR 93, Court of Appeal.

*R v Secretary of State for the Home Department, ex p Doody* [1994] 1 AC 531, House of Lords.

*R v Secretary of State for the Home Department, ex p Joint Council for the Welfare of Immigrants* [1996] 4 All ER 385, Court of Appeal.

*R v Secretary of State for the Home Department, ex p Zakrocki* (1998) 1 CCLR 374, High Court.

*R v Sefton Metropolitan Borough Council, ex p Help the Aged* [1997] 3 FCR 392, High Court; [1997] 3 FCR 573, Court of Appeal.

*R v Servite Houses, ex p Goldsmith* (2000) 3 CCLR 325, High Court.

*R v Sheffield City Council, ex p Low* (2000) unreported, Court of Appeal (renewed application for permission to bring judicial review case).

*R(Grant) v Lambeth London Borough Council* [2004] EWCA Civ 1711, Court of Appeal.

*R(H) v Mental Health Review Tribunal, North and East London Region and the Secretary of State for Health* [2001] EWCA Civ 415, Court of Appeal.

*R(Haggerty) v St Helens Metropolitan Borough Council* [2003] EWHC Admin 803, High Court.

*R(Hands) v Birmingham City Council* [2001] EWHC Admin, High Court.

*R(Heather) v Leonard Cheshire Foundation* [2002] EWCA Civ 366, Court of Appeal.

*R(Heffernan) v Sheffield City Council* [2004] EWCH Admin 1377, High Court.

*R(HP) v Islington London Borough Council* [2004] EWHC Admin 07, High Court.

*R(IH) v Secretary of State* [2003] UKHL 59, House of Lords.

*R(J) v Enfield London Borough Council* [2002] EWHC Admin 432, High Court.

*R(J) v Newham London Borough Council* [2001] EWHC Admin 992, High Court.

*R(K) v Camden and Islington Health Authority* (1999) unreported, High Court.

*R(KB,MK,FR,GM,PD,TB,B) v Mental Health Review Tribunal and Secretary of State for Health* [2003] EWHC 193, High Court.

*R(Kelly) v Hammersmith and Fulham London Borough Council* [2004] EWHC Admin 435, High Court.

*R(Khan) v Oxfordshire County Council* [2004] EWCA Civ 309, Court of Appeal.

*R(Khana) v Southwark London Borough Council* (2000) unreported, High Court; [2001] EWCA Civ 999, Court of Appeal.

*R(Limbuela) v Secretary of State for the Home Department* [2004] EWHC 219, High Court; [2004] EWCA Civ 540, Court of Appeal.

*R(Lloyd) v Barking and Dagenham London Borough Council* (2001) 4 CCLR 196, Court of Appeal.

*R(Longstaff) v Newcastle Primary Care Trust* [2003] EWHC Admin 3252, High Court.

*R(M) v Islington London Borough Council* [2004] EWCA Civ 235, Court of Appeal.

*R(M) v Secretary of State for Health* [2003] EWHC Admin 1094, High Court.

*R(M) v Slough Borough Council* [2004] EWHC Admin 1109, High Court.

*R(Madden) v Bury Metropolitan Borough Council* [2002] EWHC Admin 1882, High Court.

*R(Mani) v Lambeth London Borough Council* [2003] EWCA Civ 836, Court of Appeal.

*R(O) v Haringey London Borough Council* [2004] EWCA Civ 535, Court of Appeal.

*R(P) v Camden London Borough Council* [2004] EWHC 55, High Court.

*R(Panic) v Secretary of State for the Home Department* [2004] EWCA Civ 494, Court of Appeal.

*R(Patrick) v Newham London Borough Council* (2001) 4 CCLR 48, High Court.

*R(Payne) v Surrey Oakland NHS Trust* [2001] EWHC Admin 461, High Court.

*R(Q and Others) v Secretary of State for the Home Department* [2003] EWCA Civ 364, Court of Appeal.

*R(Rodriguez-Bannister) v Somerset Partnership NHS and Social Care Trust* [2003] EWHC Admin 2184, High Court.

*R(Rowe) v Walsall Metropolitan Borough Council* (2001) unreported (leave to apply for judicial review).

*R(S) v Leicester City Council* [2004] EWHC Fam 533, High Court.

*R(SSG) v Liverpool City Council* (2002) 5 CCLR 639, High Court.

*R(Selmour and 42 Others) v West Sussex County Council* [2004] EWHC 2414 (Admin).

*R(Spink) v Wandsworth LBC* [2004] EWHC 2314 (Admin), High Court.

*R(Stephenson) v Stockton-on-Tees Borough Council* [2004] EWHC 2228 (Admin), High Court.

*R(T) v Enfield London Borough Council* [2004] EWHC Admin 2297, High Court.

*R(T) v Secretary of State for the Home Department* [2003] Civ 1285, Court of Appeal.

*R(W) v Doncaster Metropolitan Borough Council* [2004] EWCA Civ 378, Court of Appeal.

*R(Wahid) v Tower Hamlets London Borough Council* [2002] EWCA Civ 287, Court of Appeal.

*R(Watts) v Bedford Primary Care Trust* [2004] EWCA Civ 166, Court of Appeal.

*R(Wooder) v Feggetter* [2002] EWCA Civ 554, Court of Appeal.

*R(X) v Chief Constable of West Midlands Police* [2004] EWHC Admin 61, High Court; [2004] EWCA Civ 1068, Court of Appeal.

*R(Zardasht) v Secretary of State for the Home Department* [2004] EWHC Admin 91, High Court.

*Re AK (medical treatment: consent)* (2001) 1 FLR 129, High Court.

*Re B (Adult: refusal of treatment)* [2002] EWHC 429, High Court.

*Re Beaney (deceased)* [1978] 1 WLR 770, High Court.

*Re C (Adult: refusal of treatment)* [1994] 1 WLR 290, High Court.

*Re Craig* [1970] 2 All ER 390, High Court.

*Re D-R* 1 FLR 1161 (1999), Court of Appeal.

*Re: Ethel Mary Good* [2002] EWHC 640 (Ch), High Court (Chancery).

*Re F (A Child)* (1999) 2 CCLR 445, Court of Appeal.

*Re F (Adult Patient)* (2000) 3 CCLR 210, Court of Appeal.

*Re F (Mental patient: sterilisation)* (1990) 2 AC 1, House of Lords.

*Re K* [1988] 2 FLR 15, High Court.

*Re Margaret Hanna* (2003) unreported, High Court (Northern Ireland).

*Re Margaret Hanna* [2003] NIQB 79, High Court (Northern Ireland).

*Re MB (Adult: medical treatment)* [1997] 2 FCR 541, Court of Appeal.

*Re O (A child)* [2001] EWCA Civ 16, Court of Appeal.

*Re S (Adult patient)* [2002] EWHC Fam 2278, High Court.

*Re S (Hospital Patient: court's jurisdiction)* [1995] 1 FLR 1075, Court of Appeal.

*Re Teresa Judge* [2001] NIQB 14, High Court (Northern Ireland).

*Re W (Adult: refusal of treatment)* [2002] EWHC Fam 901, High Court.

*Re Z* [2004] EWHC Fam 2817, High Court.

*Richards v Allan* (2000) unreported, High Court (Chancery).

*Roads v Central Trains* [2004] EWCA Civ 1541, Court of Appeal.

*Robertson v Fife Council* (2001) 4 CCLR 355, Court of Session (Inner House); [2002] UKHL 35, House of Lords.

*Rose v Bouchet* (1999) IRLR 463, Sheriff's Court, Lothian (appeal to the Sheriff Principal).

*Ross v Ryanair* (2004) Claim CL 209468, Central London County Court; [2004] EWCA Civ 1751, Court of Appeal.

*Rowley v Director of Public Prosecutions* [2003] EWHC Admin 693, High Court.

*Royal Bank of Scotland v Etridge (no.2)* [2001] UKHL 44, House of Lords.

*Ryan and Liverpool City Council v Liverpool Health Authority* (2001), High Court (QBD).

*Secretary of State for Social Security v Fairey* [1995] 26 BMLR 63, Court of Appeal.

*Sentges v Netherlands* (2003) Application 27677/02, European Court of Human Rights.

*SL v SL* (2000) 3 WLR 1288, Court of Appeal.

*Slater v Buckinghamshire County Council* [2004] EWHC, High Court (QBD); [2004] EWHC QB 77, Court of Appeal.

*Smith v South Lanarkshire Council, Employment tribunal case.*

*Sowden v Lodge* [2004] EWCA Civ 1370, Court of Appeal.

*Special Trustees of Great Ormond Street Hospital v Rushin* (1997) unreported, High Court (Chancery).

*Springette v Defoe* (1992) 24 HLR 552, Court of Appeal.

*Stainton v Chorley and South Ribble NHS Trust* (1998) unreported, High Court.

*Steane v Chief Adjudication Officer* [1996] 1 WLR 1195, House of Lords.

*Strickland v Woodfield Lodge* [2003] EWHC 287 (QBD).

*T (A Minor) v Surrey County Council* [1994] 4 All ER 577, High Court.

*Tait v Wedgwood* [2002] EWHC 2594, High Court (Chancery).

*Tchilingirian v Ouzounian* [2003] EWHC 1220 (Chancery).

*Tidman v Reading Borough Council* [1994] 3 PLR 72, High Court.

*Tomlinson v Congleton Borough Council* [2003] UKHL 47, House of Lords.

*Vandyk v Oliver (Valuation Officer)* [1976] AC 659, House of Lords.

*Vaughan v Vaughan* [2002] EWHC 699, High Court (Chancery).

*Vicar of Writtle v Essex County Council* [1979] 77 LGR 656, High Court.

*W v Edgell* [1990] 1 All ER 835, Court of Appeal.

*Walker v Northumberland County Council* (1995) 1 All ER 737.

*Welton v North Cornwall District Council* [1997] 1 WLR 570, Court of Appeal.

*Westminster v NASS (National Asylum Support Service)* [2002] UKHL 38, House of Lords.

*White v Clitheroe Royal Grammar School* (2002) Claim BB 002640, Preston County Court.

*Withnell v Down Lisburn Health and Social Services Trust* (2004), High Court (Northern Ireland).

*Wookey v Wookey* [1991] 3 All ER 365, Court of Appeal.

*Woolgar v Chief Constable of Sussex Police* (2000) 1 WLR 25, Court of Appeal.

*Wyatt v Hillingdon London Borough Council* [1978] 76 LGR 727, Court of Appeal.

*X v Bedfordshire County Council* [1995] 3 All ER 353, House of Lords.

*Yorkshire Care Developments v North Yorkshire County Council* (2004) unreported, Case no. NE 307141, Newcastle upon Tyne County Court.

*Yule v South Lanarkshire Council* (1998) 1 CCLR 571, Court of Session, Outer House.

*Yule v South Lanarkshire Council (no.2)* (2001) 4 CCLR 383, Court of Session (Inner House).

*Z v United Kingdom* [2001] 2 FCR 246, European Court of Human Rights.

## LOCAL GOVERNMENT OMBUDSMAN CASES

*Avon County Council 1997* (95/B/5144).

*Barking and Dagenham London Borough Council 1997* (94/A/4229).

*Barking and Dagenham London Borough Council 1998* (97/A/0337).

*Barking and Dagenham 2000* (98/A/0322).

*Barnet London Borough Council 2000* (98/A/0280).

*Barnsley Metropolitan Borough Council 1998a* (97/C/0433).

*Barnsley Metropolitan Borough Council 1998b* (97/C/1096).

*Bedfordshire County Council 2003* (02/B/16654).

*Bexley London Borough Council 1998* (97/A/2021).

*Bexley London Borough Council 2000* (97/A/4002).

*Birmingham City Council 1993* (91/B/1262).

*Birmingham City Council 2002* (00/C/19154).

*Bolton Metropolitan Borough Council 1992* (92/C/0670).

*Bolton Metropolitan Borough Council 2004* (03/C/02451).

*Bolsover District Council 2003* (02/C/08679, 02/C/08681, 02/C/10389).

*Brent London Borough Council 1994* (93/A/0523).

*Bridgend County Borough Council 2004* (2003/0386/BR/250).

*Bristol City Council 1998* (96/B/4035 and 96/B/4143).

*Bromley London Borough Council 2003* (01/B/17272).

*Buckinghamshire County Council 1992* (90/B/1340).

*Buckinghamshire County Council 1998* (97/B/0876).

*Bury Metropolitan Borough Council 2000* (97/C/3668).

*Bury Metropolitan Borough Council 2004* (02/C/14188).

*Calderdale Metropolitan Borough Council 1998* (96/C/3868).

*Cambridgeshire County Council 2001* (99/B/04621).

*Cambridgeshire County Council 2002* (01/B/00305).

*Cambridgeshire County Council 2004* (02/B/10226).

*Camden London Borough Council 1993* (91/A/1481).

*Cardiff City Council 2004* (2003/0671/CF/490).

*Carmarthenshire County Council 1999* (99/0117/CM/210).
*Castle Morpeth Borough Council 2003* (02/C/04897, 02/C/13783).
*Cleveland County Council 1993* (92/C/1042).
*Clwyd County Council 1997* (97/0177, 97/0755).
*Cornwall County Council 1996* (95/B/0166).
*Croydon London Borough Council 2000* (98/A/2154).
*Cumbria County Council 1992* (90/C/2438).
*Cumbria County Council 2000* (99/C/0619).
*Cumbria County Council 2000a* (98/C/0002).
*Cumbria County Council 2001* (98/C/4738).
*Cyngor Dosbarth Dwyfor 1994* (93/465).
*Derbyshire County Council 2001* (00/C/19118).
*Derbyshire County Council 2004* (02/C/14235 and others).
*Devon County Council 1996* (94/B/2128).
*Dinefwr Borough Council 1995* (94/0772).
*Doncaster Metropolitan Borough Council 1997* (95/C/4390).
*Durham City Council and Durham County Council 1993* (92/C/2753, 92/C/2754).
*Durham County Council 1998* (96/C/4083).
*Durham County Council 2000* (99/C/1983).
*Dyfed County Council 1996* (95/0227).
*Ealing London Borough Council 2004* (03/A/17640).
*Ealing London Borough Council 1993* (91/A/3466).
*Ealing London Borough Council 1999* (97/A/4069).
*East Sussex County Council 1995a* (93/A/3738).
*East Sussex County Council 1995b* (92/A/2085).
*East Sussex County Council 2003* (00/B/18600).
*Essex County Council 1991* (90/A/2675).
*Essex County Council 2001* (99/B/00799).
*Gateshead Metropolitan Borough Council 2001* (99/C/02509, 99/C/02624).
*Gravesham Borough Council 1987 and Kent County Council* (194/A/86).
*Greenwich London Borough Council 1993* (91/A/3782).
*Hackney London Borough Council 1992a* (91/A/0482).
*Hackney London Borough Council 1992b* (90/A/3447).
*Hackney London Borough Council 1995* (93/A3690).
*Hackney London Borough Council 1997a* (96/A/3762).
*Hackney London Borough Council 1997b* (96/A/3072).
*Hackney London Borough Council 1997c* (96/A/0743).
*Hackney London Borough Council 1998* (97/A/2959).
*Hackney London Borough Council 1998a* (97/A/1649).
*Halton Borough Council 2002* (01/C/09625).
*Hampshire County Council 2001* (99/B/03979).
*Haringey London Borough Council 1993* (92/A/3725).
*Haringey London Borough Council 2000* (99/C/2060).
*Harlow District Council 2000* (97/B/4324)
*Harrow London Borough Council 2004* (02/B/03622).
*Hertfordshire County Council 1992* (90/B/1676).
*Hertfordshire County Council 2002* (00/B/09315).
*Hertfordshire County Council 2003* (01/B/09360).
*Hertfordshire County Council 2003a* (00/B/16833).

*Hounslow London Borough Council 1994* (92/A/2493).

*Hounslow London Borough Council 1995* (93/A/3007).

*Hounslow London Borough Council 1999* (96/A/2313).

*Humberside County Council 1992* (91/C/0774).

*Humberside County Council 1996* (and East Yorkshire Borough Council) (94/C/2151).

*Isle of Anglesey County Council 1999a* (98/0374/AN/082).

*Isle of Anglesey County Council 1999b* (98/0092/AN/067).

*Islington London Borough Council 1988* (88/A/303).

*Islington London Borough Council 1994* (92/A/4104).

*Islington London Borough Council 1995* (94/A/2369).

*Kensington and Chelsea Royal Borough 1992* (90/A/2232).

*Kent County Council 1998* (97/A/1305).

*Kent County Council 1999* (98/A/1612).

*Kent County Council 2001* (99/B/3078).

*Kent County Council 2001a* (00/B/00721).

*Kingston upon Hull C 2000* (99/C/1757).

*Kirklees Metropolitan Borough Council 1993* (90/C/1911).

*Kirklees Metropolitan Borough Council 1997* (94/C/3349).

*Kirklees Metropolitan Borough Council 2002* (01/C/02370).

*Kirklees Metropolitan Borough Council 2003* (01/C/00627).

*Knowsley Metropolitan Borough Council 1997* (95/C/4681).

*Leeds City Council 1995* (93/C/2475).

*Leicester City Council 1992a and Leicestershire County Council* (91/B/2154 and 91/B/2155).

*Leicester City Council 1992b and Leicestershire County Council* (91/B/0254 and 91/B/0380).

*Leicester City Council 1995* (94/B/2813).

*Leicester City Council 1998* (97/C/3498).

*Leicestershire County Council 2001* (00/B/08307).

*Lewisham London Borough Council 1993* (92/A/1693).

*Lincolnshire County Council 2004* (03/C/09384).

*Liverpool City Council 1992* (91/C/0121).

*Liverpool City Council 1996/1997* (common points included within the reports involving Liverpool City
    Council: 95/C/0867, 93/C/1485, 92/C/2848, 94/C/0805, 92/C/1165, 93/C/1173, 93/C/4112,
    94/C/1902, 95/C/0859).

*Liverpool City Council 1997a* (96/C/0581).

*Liverpool City Council 1998a* (96/C/4284).

*Liverpool City Council 1998b* (96/C/4315).

*Liverpool City Council 1999* (98/C/2564).

*Maldon District Council 2000 and Essex County Council* (98/B/1691, 98/B/1791).

*Manchester City Council 1993* (90/C/2147).

*Manchester City Council 1994* (92/C/2376).

*Manchester City Council 1996a* (93/C/2330).

*Manchester City Council 1996b* (94/C/1571).

*Manchester City Council 1998* (97/C/1814).

*Merthyr Tydvil 1994* (93/218).

*Merton London Borough Council 1999* (97/A/3218).

*Middlesbrough Borough Council 1996 and Cleveland County Council* (94/C/0964 and 94/C/0965).

*Neath Port Talbot County Borough Council 1999* (99/0149/N/142).

*Neath Port Talbot County Borough Council 2000* (99/0824/N/173).

*Newham London Borough Council 1993a* (91/A/3602).

*Newham London Borough Council 1993b* (91/A/3911).

*Newham London Borough Council 1995* (92/A/4120).

*Newham London Borough Council 1996* (94/A/3185).

*Newham London Borough Council 1997b* (94/A/0503).

*North Somerset County Council 1999* (98/C/4033).

*North Warwickshire District Council 2000a* (99/B/0012).

*North Warwickshire District Council 2000b* (99/B/0012: further report).

*North Yorkshire County Council 1993 and Harrogate Borough Council* (91/C/0565 and 92/C/1400).

*North Yorkshire County Council 2002* (01/C/03521).

*Northumberland County Council 2000* (99/C/1276).

*Nottinghamshire County Council 1998* (97/C/3705).

*Nottinghamshire County Council 1998a* (97/C/2126).

*Nottinghamshire County Council 1999* (98/C/2295).

*Nottinghamshire City Council 2000* (99/C/3355).

*Nottinghamshire County Council 2002 and Nottingham City Council* (00/C/03176, 00/C/05525).

*Oxfordshire County Council 1999* (97/B/3440).

*Redbridge London Borough Council 1993a* (92/A/4108).

*Redbridge London Borough Council 1993b* (92/A/1173).

*Redbridge London Borough Council 1998* (95/C/1472, 95/C/2543).

*Redcar and Cleveland Borough Council 1999* (98/C/2796).

*Rochdale Metropolitan Borough Council 1995* (93/C/3660).

*Rotherham Metropolitan Borough Council 1995* (94/C/2287).

*Salford City Council 1993* (91/C/1972).

*Salford City Council 1996* (94/C/0399).

*Salford City Council 2003* (01/C/17519).

*Sandwell Metropolitan Borough Council 1995* (93/B/3956).

*Sheffield City Council 1989* (88/C/1048).

*Sheffield City Council 1994* (93/C/0005).

*Sheffield City Council 1995* (93/C/1609).

*Sheffield City Council 1996* (95/C/2483).

*Sheffield City Council 1997a* (95/C/3741).

*Sheffield City Council 1997b* (95/C/4413).

*Sheffield City Council 2001* (00/C/10708).

*Sheffield City Council 2002* (00/C/07439).

*Sheffield City Council 2004* (02/C/08690).

*South Tyneside Metropolitan Borough Council 1999* (98/C/1055, 98/C/1802).

*Southwark London Borough Council 2001* (99/A/00988).

*Southwark London Borough Council 2001a* (99/A/4226).

*St Helens Metropolitan Borough Council 1998* (97/C/2492).

*Staffordshire County Council 2000* (99/C/4295).

*Stockport Metropolitan Borough Council 2003* (02/C/03831).

*Stockton-on-Tees Borough Council 1997 and the former Stockton-on-Tees Borough Council and the former Cleveland County Council* (96/C/1523 and others).

*Suffolk County Council 2001* (99/B/1651).

*Sunderland City Council 2002* (00/C/12118, 00/C/12621).

*Tower Hamlets London Borough Council 1992* (91/A/0726).

*Tower Hamlets London Borough Council 1993* (92/A/1374).

*Tower Hamlets London Borough Council 1997* (96/A/1219).

*Tower Hamlets London Borough Council 2004* (03/C/02410).

*Trafford Metropolitan Borough Council 1996* (94/C/3690).
*Wakefield Metropolitan District Council 1992* (90/C/2203).
*Wakefield Metropolitan District Council 1993* (91/C/1246).
*Wakefield Metropolitan District Council 1997* (95/C/3584).
*Wakefield Metropolitan District Council 2000* (98/C/4884).
*Wakefield Metropolitan District Council 2003* (01/C/15652).
*Wakefield Metropolitan District Council 2004* (02/C/14023).
*Walsall Metropolitan Borough Council 1996* (94/B/3584).
*Waltham Forest London Borough Council 1993* (92/A/0543).
*Waltham Forest London Borough Council 1994* (93/A/2536).
*Warwickshire County Council 1997* (96/B/2562).
*Westminster County Council 1996* (93/A/4250).
*Wigan Metropolitan Borough Council 2001* (99/C/05493).
*Wiltshire County Council 1999* (98/B/0341).
*Wirral Metropolitan Borough Council 1992a* (89/C/1114).
*Wirral Metropolitan Borough Council 1992b* (90/C/2413).
*Wirral Metropolitan Borough Council 1992c* (91/C/2038).
*Wirral Metropolitan Borough Council 1992d* (91/C/0729).
*Wirral Metropolitan Borough Council 1993c* (91/C/1852).
*Wirral Metropolitan Borough Council 1993d* (91/C/3108).
*Wirral Metropolitan Borough Council 1993e* (91/C/3811).
*Wirral Metropolitan Borough Council 1993f* (92/C/1254).
*Wirral Metropolitan Borough Council 1994a* (91/C/2376).
*Wirral Metropolitan Borough Council 1994b* (92/C/0298).
*Wirral Metropolitan Borough Council 1994c* (92/C/1403).

## HEALTH SERVICE OMBUDSMAN CASES

*Avon Health Authority 1996* (E.615/94–95 in HSC 1996).
*Barnet Healthcare NHS Trust 2000* (E.33/99–00 in HSO 2000).
*Berkshire Health Authority 2003* (E.814/00–01 in HSO 2003c).
*Bexley and Greenwich Health Authority 1999* (E.1610/97–98 in HSO 1999a).
*Birmingham Health Authority 2003* (E.1626/01–02 in HSO 2003c).
*Bournewood Community and Mental Health NHS Trust 2002* (E.2280/98–99 in HSO 2002a).
*Buckinghamshire Health Authority 1996* (E.118/94–95 in HSC 1996).
*Cambridgeshire Health Authority 2004* (E.22/02–03 in HSO 2004a).
*Central Manchester Primary Care Trust 2003* (E.629/01–02 in HSO 2003).
*Dorset Health Authority 2003* (E.208/99–00 in HSO 2003c).
*East Kent Health Authority 1996* (E.685/94–95 in HSC 1996).
*East Norfolk Health Authority 1996* (E.213/94–95 in HSC 1996a).
*East Sussex, Brighton and Hove Health Authority 1999* (E.1316/98–99 in HSO 1999).
*Epsom and St Helier NHS Trust 2001* (E.559/99–00 in HSO 2001b).
*Gloucestershire Health Authority 2003* (E.112/02–03 in HSO 2003).
*Herefordshire Health Authority 1999* (E.1321/98–99 in HSO 1999).
HSC (1978) Health Service Commissioner. HC 343. *2nd report 1977–1978*. London: HMSO.
HSC (1981) Health Service Commissioner. HC 9. *1st report 1981–1982*. London: HMSO.
HSC (1982) Health Service Commissioner. HC 372. *2nd report 1981–1982*. London: HMSO.
HSC (1984) Health Service Commissioner. HC 418. *2nd report 1984–1985*. London: HSC.

HSC (1985) Health Service Commissioner. HC 33. *1st report 1984–1985.* London: HMSO.

HSC (1985a) Health Service Commissioner. HC 418. *2nd report 1984–1985.* London: HMSO.

HSC (1988) Health Service Commissioner. HC 232. *3rd report 1987–1988.* London: HMSO.

HSC (1988a) Health Service Commissioner. HC 511. *4th report 1987–1988.* London: HMSO.

HSC (1990) Health Service Commissioner. HC 199. *1st report 1989–1990.* London: HMSO.

HSC (1992) Health Service Commissioner. HC 32. *1st report 1991–1992.* London: HMSO.

HSC (1994) Health Service Commissioner. *Failure to provide long term NHS care for brain damaged patient.* London: HMSO.

HSC (1994a) Health Service Commissioner. HC 498. *Selected investigations completed October 1993 to March 1994.* London: HMSO.

HSC (1995) Health Service Commissioner. HC 11. *Selected investigations completed April to September 1995.* London: HMSO.

HSC (1996) Health Service Commissioner. *Investigations of complaints about long term NHS care.* London: HMSO.

HSC (1996a) Health Service Commissioner. HC 464. *Selected investigations completed October 1995 to March 1996.* London: HMSO.

HSC (1996b) Health Service Commissioner. HC 87. *Selected investigations completed April to September 1996.* London: HMSO.

HSC (1996c) Health Service Commissioner. *Guide to the work of the health service ombudsman.* London: HSC.

HSO W.68/77–78 (in HSC 1978).

HSO WW.3/79–80 (in HSC 1981).

HSO W.340/80–81 (in HSC 1982).

HSO W. 420/83–84 (1983: HSC publication unknown).

HSO W.40/84–85 (in HSC 1984).

HSO W.113/84–85 (in HSC 1984).

HSO W.263/83–84 (in HSC 1985).

HSO W.24 and W.56/84–85 (in HSC 1985a).

HSO W.783/85–86 (in HSC 1988).

HSO W.286/86–87 (in HSC 1988a).

HSO SW.82/86–87 (in HSC 1988a).

HSO W.254/88–89 (in HSC 1990).

HSO W.226/91–92 (in HSC 1992).

HSO W.524/92–93 (in HSC 1994a).

HSO (1999) Health Service Ombudsman. HC 19. *Investigations completed April–September 1999.* London: TSO.

HSO (1999a) Health Service Ombudsman. HC 497. *Investigations completed October 1998–March 1999.* London: TSO.

HSO (2000) Health Service Ombudsman. HC 541–I. *Summaries of investigations completed October 1999–March 2000.* London: TSO.

HSO (2001) Health Service Ombudsman. HC 287–I. *Selected investigations completed April–July 2001.* London: TSO.

HSO (2001a) Health Service Ombudsman. HC 4–I. *Selected investigations completed December 2000I–March 2001.* London: TSO.

HSO (2001b) Health Service Ombudsman. HC 278–I. *Selected investigations completed August–November 2000.* London: TSO.

HSO (2002) Health Service Ombudsman. HC 924–I. *Selected investigations completed December 2001– March 2002.* London: TSO.

HSO (2002a) Health Service Ombudsman. HC 679–I. *Selected investigations completed August–November 2001.* London: TSO.

HSO (2003) Health Service Ombudsman. HC 119. *Selected investigations completed April–September 2003.* London: TSO.

HSO (2003a) Health Service Ombudsman. HC 787. *Selected investigations completed December 2002–March 2003.*
    London: TSO.

HSO (2003b) Health Service Ombudsman. HC 532. *Selected investigations completed August–November 2002.*
    London: TSO.

HSO (2003c) Health Service Ombudsman. *NHS funding for long term care.* London: TSO.

HSO (2004) Health Service Ombudsman. *Annual report 2003–4.* London: TSO.

HSO (2004a) Health Service Ombudsman. HC 704. *Selected investigations completed October 2003–March 2004.*
    London: TSO.

HSO (2004b) Health Service Ombudsman. HC 144. *NHS funding for long term care: follow up report.*
    London: HSO.

*Leeds Health Authority 1994* (E.62/93–94 in HSC 1994).

*Newcastle, North Tyneside and Northumberland Mental Health NHS Trust 2001* (E.2495/99–00 in HSO 2001).

*North and Mid-Hampshire Health Authority 1996* (E.639/94–95 in HSC 1996a).

*North Bristol NHS Trust 2000* (E.2041/98–99 in HSO 2000).

*North Cheshire Health Authority 1996* (E.672/94–95 in HSC 1996).

*North Essex Health Authority 2001* (E.1099/00–01 in HSO 2001b).

*North Essex Health Authority 2003* (E.1033/01–02 in HSO 2003a).

*North Worcestershire Health Authority 1995* (E.264/94–95 in HSC 1995).

*North Worcestershire Health Authority 1996* (E.985/94–95 in HSC 1996b).

*Nottinghamshire Healthcare NHS Trust 2003* (E.410/00–01 in HSO 2003b).

*Oldham NHS Trust 1999* (E.1780/97–98 in HSO 1999a).

*Oxfordshire Health Authority 1996* (E.787/94–95 in HSC 1996).

PCA (1982) Parliamentary Commissioner for Local Administration. *5th report for session 1981–1982.*
    London: HMSO.

PCA (1988) Parliamentary Commissioner for Local Administration. HC 672. *6th report for session 1987–1988.*
    London: HMSO.

PCA C.799/81 (in PCA 1982).

PCA C.656/87 (in PCA 1988).

*Plymouth NHS Primary Care Trust 2002.*

*Preston Acute Hospitals NHS Trust 2001* (E.743/99–00 in HSO 2001a).

*St Mary's NHS Trust 2002* (E.231/01–02 in HSO 2002).

*Southampton University Hospitals NHS Trust 2003* (E.2333/01–02 in HSO 2003).

*Southend Hospital NHS Trust 2001* (E.2087/99–00 in HSO 2001b).

*Suffolk Health Authority 2003* (E.2339/01–02 in HSO 2003a).

*Surrey Oaklands NHS Trust 2002* (E.1742/00–01 in HSO 2002).

*Thames Gateway NHS Trust 2001* (E.2380/99–00 in HSO 2001a).

*Warrington Hospital NHS Trust 2001* (E.1846/99–00 in HSO 2001a).

*West Kent Health Authority 2001* (E.1079/99–00 in HSO 2001b).

*West Sussex Health Authority 2002* (E.2080/00–01 in HSO 2002).

*Wigan and Bolton Health Authority 2003* (E.420/00–01 in HSO 2003c).

*Wiltshire and Swindon Health Care NHS Trust 2002* (E.1982/00–01 in HSO 2002).

## ACTS OF PARLIAMENT
## (AND NORTHERN IRELAND ORDERS)

Adults with Incapacity (Scotland) Act 2000

Asylum and Immigration Act 1996

Asylum and Immigration Appeals Act 1993

Asylum and Immigration (Treatment of Claimants) Act 2004
Caravan Sites and Control of Development Act 1960
Care Standards Act 2000
Carers and Direct Payments Act 2000
Carers and Disabled Children Act 2000
Carers (Equal Opportunities) Act 2004
Carers (Recognition and Services) Act 1995
Children Act 1989
Children Act 2004
Children (Northern Ireland) Order 1995
Children (Scotland) Act 1995
Chronically Sick and Disabled Persons Act 1970
Chronically Sick and Disabled Persons (Northern Ireland) Act 1978
Chronically Sick and Disabled Persons (Scotland) Act 1972
Commissioner for Complaints (Northern Ireland) Order 1996
Community Care (Delayed Discharges) Act 2003
Community Care (Direct Payments) Act 1996 (superseded)
Community Care and Health (Scotland) Act 1972
Community Care and Health (Scotland) Act 2002
Contracts (Rights of Third Parties) Act 1999
Crime and Disorder Act 1998
Criminal Justice Act 1988
Criminal Justice Act 2003
Criminal Justice and Court Services Act 2000
Data Protection Act 1998
Disabled Persons (Northern Ireland) Order 1989
Disabled Persons (Services, Consultation and Representation) Act 1986
Disability Discrimination Act 1995
Domestic Violence, Crime and Victims Act 2004
Education Act 1996
Enduring Powers of Attorney Act 1985
Enduring Powers of Attorney (Northern Ireland) Order 1987
Environmental Protection Act 1990
European Convention on Human Rights
Family Law Act 1996
Freedom of Information Act 2000
Gas Act 1995
Health Act 1999
Health and Personal Social Services (Northern Ireland) Order 1972
Health and Personal Social Services (Quality and Improvement and Regulation) (Northern Ireland)
    Order 2003
Health and Safety at Work Act 1974
Health and Safety at Work (Northern Ireland) Order 1978
Health and Social Care Act 2001
Health and Social Care (Community Health and Standards) Act 2003
Health and Social Services and Social Security Adjudications Act 1983
Health Service Commissioners Act 1993
Health Services and Public Health Act 1968
Homelessness Act 2002

Hospital Complaints Procedure Act 1985
Housing Act 1996
Housing Act 2004
Housing Grants, Construction and Regeneration Act 1996
Housing (Northern Ireland) Order 2003
Housing (Northern Ireland) Order 2004
Human Rights Act 1998
Immigration Act 1971
Immigration and Asylum Act 1999
Insolvency Act 1986
Landlord and Tenant Act 1927
Learning and Skills Act 2000
Local Authority Social Services Act 1970
Local Government Act 1972
Local Government Act 1974
Local Government Act 1999
Local Government Act 2000
Local Government Act 2003
Local Government and Housing Act 1989
Local Government Grants (Social Need) Act 1969
Mental Health Act 1983
Mental Health (Care and Treatment) (Scotland) Act 2003
Mental Health (Northern Ireland) Order 1986
National Assistance Act 1948
National Assistance (Amendment) Act 1951
Nationality, Immigration and Asylum Act 2002
NHS Act 1977
NHS and Community Care Act 1990
Ombudsman (Northern Ireland) Order 1996
Police Act 1997
Police and Criminal Evidence Act 1984
Protection from Harassment Act 1997
Protection of Children Act 1999
Public Health Act 1936
Race Relations Act 1976
Registered Home Act 1984
Regulation of Care (Scotland) Act 2001
Rehabilitation of Offenders Act 1974
Rights of Entry (Gas and Electricity Boards) Act 1954
Sale of Goods Act 1979
Scottish Public Services Ombudsman Act 2002
Sexual Offences Act 2003
Social Work (Scotland) Act 1968
Supply of Goods and Services Act 1982
Supreme Court Act 1981
Theft Act 1968
Youth Justice and Criminal Evidence Act 1999

## BILLS

Disability Discrimination Bill 2004
Mental Capacity Bill 2004

## STATUTORY INSTRUMENTS

SI 1974/284. *NHS (Charges for Appliances) Regulations 1974.*

SI 1987/1968. *Social Security (Claims and Payments) Regulations 1987.*

SI 1989/306. *National Health Service (Charges to Overseas Visitors) Regulations 1989.*

SI 1990/2244. *Local Authority Social Services (Complaints Procedure) Order 1990.*

SI 1992/2793. *Manual Handling Operations Regulations 1992.*

SI 1992/2977. *National Assistance (Assessment of Resources) Regulations 1992.*

SI 1996/1455. *Disability Discrimination (Meaning of Disability) Regulations 1996.*

SI 1996/1503. *National Health Service (Wheelchair Charges) Regulations 1996.*

SI 1996/2889. *Housing Renewal Grants (Services and Charges) Order 1996.*

SI 1996/2890. *Housing Renewal Grants Regulations 1996.*

SI 1998/3132. *Civil Procedure Rules 1998.*

SI 1999/3242. *Management of Health and Safety at Work Regulations 1999.*

SI 2000/413. *Data Protection (Subject Access Modification) (Health) Order 2000.*

SI 2000/415. *Data Protection (Subject Access Modification) (Social Work) Order 2000.*

SI 2000/417. *Data Protection (Processing of Sensitive Personal Data) Order 2000.*

SI 2000/617. *NHS Bodies and Local Authorities Partnership Arrangements (Amendment) Regulations 2000.*

SI 2000/620. *NHS (Charges for Drugs and Appliances) Regulations 2000.*

SI 2000/2993. *NHS Bodies and Local Authorities Partnership Arrangements (Wales) Regulations 2000.*

SI 2001/441. *Carers (Services) and Direct Payments (Amendment) (England) Regulations 2001.*

SI 2001/824. *Court of Protection Rules 2001.*

SI 2001/3067. *National Assistance (Residential Accommodation) (Disregarding of Resources) (England) Regulations 2001.*

SI 2001/3069. *National Assistance (Residential Accommodation) (Relevant Contributions) (England) Regulations 2001.*

SI 2001/3441. *National Assistance (Residential Accommodation) (Additional Payments and Assessment of Resources) (Amendment) (England) Regulations 2001.*

SI 2001/3458. *Race Relations Act 1976 (Statutory Duties) Order 2001.*

SI 2001/3712. *Mental Health Act 1983 (Remedial Order) 2001.*

SI 2001/3965. *Care Homes Regulations 2001.*

SI 2002/446. *Police Act 1997 (Enhanced Criminal Record Certificates) (Protection of Vulnerable Adults) Regulations 2002.*

SI 2002/1687. *Magistrates' Courts (Special Measures Directions) Rules 2002.*

SI 2002/1688. *Crown Court (Special Measures Directions and Directions Prohibiting Cross-examination) Rules 2002.*

SI 2002/2375. *NHS (Functions of Strategic Health Authorities and Primary Care Trusts and Administration Arrangements) (England) Regulations 2002.*

SI 2002/3078. *Withholding and Withdrawal of Support (Travel Assistance and Temporary Accommodation) Regulations 2002.*

SI 2002/3048. *Local Authority (Overview and Scrutiny Committees Health Scrutiny Functions) Regulations 2002.*

SI 2002/3214. *Domiciliary Care Agencies Regulations 2002.*

SI 2003/461. *Housing Grants (Assessment of Applicant's Contribution) (Scotland) Regulations 2003.*

SI 2003/628. *National Assistance (Sums for Personal Requirements) (England) Regulations 2003.*

SI 2003/629. *NHS Bodies and Local Authorities Partnership Arrangements (Amendment) Regulations 2000.*

SI 2003/762. *Community Care, Services for Carers and Children's Services (Direct Payments) (England) Regulations 2003.*

SI 2003/907. *Local Authorities (Charges for Specified Welfare Services) Regulations 2003.*

SI 2003/1196. *Community Care (Delayed Discharges) (Qualifying Services) (England) Regulations 2003.*

SI 2003/1216. *Carers and Disabled Children (Vouchers) (England) Regulations 2003.*

SI 2003/2276. *Delayed Discharges (Mental Health Care) (England) Order 2003.*

SI 2003/2277. *Delayed Discharges (England) Regulations 2003.*

SI 2004/291. *NHS (General Medical Services Contracts) Regulations 2004.*

SI 2004/1748. *Community Care, Services for Carers and Children's Services (Direct Payments) Wales Regulations 2004.*

SI 2004/1768. *NHS (Complaints) Regulations 2004.*

SI 2004/2070. *Adult Placement Schemes (England) Regulations 2004.*

SR 1992/535. *Manual Handling Operations (Northern Ireland) Regulations 1992.*

SR 1993/127. *Health and Personal Social Services (Assessment of Resources) Regulations (Northern Ireland) Regulations 1993.*

SR 2000/388. *Management of Health and Safety at Work (Northern Ireland) Regulations 1999.*

SR 2004/8. *Housing Renewal Grants (Reduction of Grant) Regulations (Northern Ireland) 2004.*

## CENTRAL GOVERNMENT GUIDANCE AND DIRECTIONS

Cabinet Office (Regulatory Impact Unit) (2004) *Code of practice on consultation.* London: Cabinet Office.

CCD 2/2003. Scottish Executive. *Community Care and Health (Scotland) Act 2002: new statutory rights for carers: guidance.* Edinburgh: SE.

CCD 4/2003. Scottish Executive. *Social Work (Scotland) Act 1968, sections 12B and 12C direct payments: policy and practice.* Edinburgh: SE.

CCD 5/2003. Scottish Executive. *Free personal and nursing care: consolidated guidance.* Edinburgh: SE.

CCD 8/2001. Scottish Executive. *Single shared assessment of community care needs.* Edinburgh: SE.

CCD 8/2003. Scottish Executive. *Choice of accommodation: discharge from hospital.* Edinburgh: SE.

CHI (2000) Commission for Health Improvement. *Investigation into the North Lakeland NHS Trust: report to the Secretary of State.* London: CHI.

CI(92)34. Social Services Inspectorate. *Implementing care for people: assessment.* London: Department of Health.

CNO(SNC)(77)1. Department of Health and Social Security. *Standards of nursing care: promotion of continence and management of incontinence.* London: DHSS.

CRAG (2004) Department of Health. *Charging for residential accommodation guidance.* London: DH.

CRB (2001) Criminal Records Bureau. *Code of practice and explanatory guide for registered persons and other recipients of disclosure information.* London: CRB.

D(87)45. Department of Health and Social Security. *Provision of incontinence pads.* London: DHSS.

DES (2004) Department for Education and Skills. *Getting the best from complaints: consultation on the changes to the social services complaints procedures for children, young people and other people making a complaint.* London: DES.

DH (1990) Department of Health. *Community care in the next decade and beyond: policy guidance.* London: DH.

DH (1990a) Department of Health. *Complaints procedures directions.* In DH 1990, appendix C.

DH (1995) Department of Health. *Building bridges: a guide to arrangement for inter agency working for the care and protection of severely mentally ill people.* London: DH.

DH (1999) Department of Health; Welsh Office. *Code of practice: Mental Health Act 1983.* London: DH.

DH (1999a) Department of Health. *National Service Framework for Mental Health.* London: DH.

DH (1999b) Department of Health. *Effective care coordination in mental health services: modernising the care programme approach.* London: DH.

DH (2000) Department of Health. *No secrets.* London: DH.

DH (2000a) Department of Health. *Framework for the assessment of children in need and their families.* London: DH.

DH (2000b) Department of Health. *Good practice in continence services.* London: DH.

DH (2001) Department of Health. *Guide to integrating equipment services.* London: DH.

DH (2001a) Department of Health. *Carers and people with parental responsibility for disabled children: policy guidance.* London: DH.

DH (2001b) Department of Health. *Carers and people with parental responsibility for disabled children: practice guidance.* London: DH.

DH (2001c) Department of Health. *National service framework for older people.* London: DH.

DH (2001d) *Valuing people: a new strategy for learning disability for the 21st century.* London: Stationery Office.

DH (2001e) Department of Health. *NHS funded nursing care practice guide and work book.* London: DH.

DH (2002) Department of Health. *Guidance on physically restrictive interventions for people with learning disability and austistic spectrum disorder in health, education and social care settings.* London: DH.

DH (2002a) Department of Health. *Fairer charging policies for home care and other non-residential services: practice guidance.* London: DH.

DH (2002b) Department of Health. *Supported housing and care homes: guidance on regulation.* London: DH.

DH (2003) Department of Health. *Section 54 of the Nationality, Immigration and Asylum Act 2002 and community care and other social services for adults from the European Economic Area living in the UK.* London: DH.

DH (2003a) Department of Health. *Establishing the responsible commissioner.* London: DH.

DH (2003b) Department of Health. *Care homes for older people: national minimum standards.* London: DH.

DH (2003c) Department of Health. *Domiciliary care: national minimum standards.* London: DH.

DH (2003d) Department of Health. *Direct payments guidance: community care, services for carers and children's services (direct payments).* London: DH.

DH (2003e) Department of Health. *Carers and Disabled Children Act 2000: vouchers for short term breaks.* London: DH.

DH (2003f) Department of Health. *Section 54 of the Nationality, Immigration and Asylum Act 2002 and community care and other social services for adults from the European Economic Area living in the UK.* London: DH.

DH (2003g) Department of Health. *Identification, referral and registration of sight loss: action for social services department and optometrists, and explanatory notes.* London: DH.

DH (2003h) Department of Health. *Fair access to care services: practice guidance.* London: DH.

DH (2003i) Department of Health. *Code of practice on openness in the NHS.* London: DH.

DH (2003j) Department of Health. *Fairer charging policies for home and other non-residential social services: guidance for councils with social services responsibilities.* London: DH.

DH (2003k) Department of Health. *Social services performance assessment framework indicators 2002–2003.* London: DH.

DH (2003m) Department of Health. *Discharge from hospital: pathway, process and practice.* London: DH.

DH (2004) Department of Health. *Delayed Discharges (Continuing Care) Directions 2004.* London: DH.

DH (2004a) Department of Health. *Continuing Care (National Health Service Responsibilities) Directions 2004.* London: DH.

DH (2004b) Department of Health. *Implementing the overseas visitors hospital charging regulations: guidance for NHS Trust Hospitals in England.* London: DH.

DH (2004c) Department of Health. *Proposals to exclude overseas visitors from eligibility to free NHS primary medical services: consultation.* London: DH.

DH (2004d) Department of Health. *PSS PAF definitions for 2003–4.* London: DH.

DH (2004e) Department of Health. *Protection of vulnerable adults scheme in England and Wales for care home and domiciliary care agencies: a practical guide.* London: DH.

DH (2004f) Department of Health. *Community care assessment directions.* London: DH.

DH (2004g) Department of Health. *Reforming the adult social services complaints procedure: consultation upon the draft regulations and guidance.* London: DH.

DH (2004h) Department of Health. *Building on the best: end of life care initiative.* London: DH.

DH (2004i) Department of Health. *Achieving timely 'simple' discharge from hospital.* London: DH.

DH (2004j) Department of Health. *Guidance for partnerships(PCTs): commencement of PCTs as responsible authorities from 30 April 2004.* London: DH.

DH (2004k) Department of Health. *Draft Mental Health Bill.* London: DH.

DH (2004m) Department of Health. *Proposed changes to residential care charges from 4 April 2005.* London: DH.

DH (2004n) Department of Health. *Advice on the decision of the European Court of Human Rights in the case of HL v UK (the 'Bournewood' case).* London: DH.

DH/NAFW (2003) Department of Health National Assembly for Wales. *Protocol on cross border issues for NHS-funded nursing care in care homes providing nursing in England and Wales.* London/Cardiff: DH/NAFW.

DHSS 12/70. Department of Health and Social Security. *Chronically Sick and Disabled Persons Act 1970.* London: DHSS.

DHSS 19/71. Department of Health and Social Security. *Welfare of the elderly: implementation of section 45 of the Health Services and Public Health Act 1945.* London: DHSS.

DHSS (1990) Department of Health and Social Services (Northern Ireland). *People first.* Belfast: DHSS.

DHSS (1991) Department of Health and Social Services (Northern Ireland). *Care management: guidance on assessment and the provision of community care.* Belfast: DHSS.

DHSS (1991a) Department of Health and Social Services (Northern Ireland). *People first: guidance on complaints policy and procedures.* Belfast: DHSS.

DHSSPS (1996) Department of Health, Social Services and Public Safety. *Miscellaneous Complaints Procedures (Northern Ireland) 1996.* Belfast: DHSSPS.

DHSSPS (1996a) Department of Health, Social Services and Public Safety. *Social Services Complaints Procedures Directions (Northern Ireland) 1996.* Belfast: DHSSPS.

DHSSPS (2003) Department of Health and Social Services and Public Safety. *Carers and Direct Payments Act (Northern Ireland) 2002: guidance.* Belfast: DHSSPS.

DHSSPS (2004) Department of Health and Social Services and Public Safety. *Asylum seekers and refugees: policy guidance on access to health and social services.* Belfast: DHSSPS.

DHSSPS BP 436/2002. Department of Health, Social Services and Public Safety. *Guidance on implementation of HPSS payments for nursing care in nursing homes.* Belfast: DHSSPS.

DoE 17/96. Department of Environment. *Private sector renewal: a strategic approach.* London: HMSO.

DTLR (2001) Department of Transport, Local Government and the Regions. *Private sector housing renewal: a consultation paper.* London: DTLR.

DTLR (2001a) Department of Transport, Local Government and the Regions. *Regulatory Reform (Housing Assistance) (England and Wales) Order 2002: explanatory document.* London: DTLR.

DTLR 3/2002. Department of Transport, Local Government and the Regions. *Housing Grants, Construction and Regeneration Act 1996, Part 1: amendments to the renovation grant system.* London: DTLR.

DWP (2004) Department of Work and Pensions (Memo DMG Vol. 3 08/04). *Continuing care: NHS responsibilities.* London: DWP.

EL(91)28. NHS Management Executive. *Continence services and the supply of incontinence aids.* London: Department of Health.

EL(91)129. NHS Management Executive. *Charging NHS patients.* London: Department of Health.

EL(92)20. NHS Management Executive. *Provision of equipment by the NHS.* London: Department of Health.

EL(96)8, CI(96)5. NHS Management Executive, Social Services Inspectorate. *NHS responsibilities for meeting continuing health care needs: current progress and future priorities.* London: Department of Health.

HC(89)5. Department of Health. *Discharge of patients from hospital.* London: DH.

HC(90)23. Department of Health. *Care programme approach for people with a mental illness referred to the specialist psychiatric services.* London: DH.

HSC(IS)11. Department of Health and Social Security. *Services for chronic renal failure.* London: DHSS, 1974.

HSC 1998/48. *Transfer of frail older NHS patients to other long stay settings.* London: DH.

HSC 1999/180; LAC(99)30. Department of Health. *Ex parte Coughlan: follow up action.* London: DH.

HSC 2000/3; LAC(2000)3. Department of Health. *After-care under the Mental Health Act 1983.* London: DH.

HSC 2001/001; LAC(2001)11. Department of Health. *Intermediate care.* London: DH.

HSC 2001/008; LAC(2001)13. Department of Health. *Community equipment services.* London: DH.

HSC 2001/15; LAC(2001)18. Department of Health. *Continuing care: NHS and local council's responsibilities.* London: DH.

HSC 2001/17; LAC(2001)26. Department of Health. *Guidance on free nursing care in nursing homes.* London: DH.

HSC 2002/001; LAC(2002)1. Department of Health. *Guidance on the single assessment process for older people.* London: DH.

HSC 2003/006; LAC(2003)7. Department of Health. *Guidance on NHS funded nursing care.* London: DH.

HSC 2003/9; LAC(2003)21. Department of Health. *Community Care (Delayed Discharges) Act 2003.*

HSE (1998) Health and Safety Executive. *Manual handling: Manual Handling Operations Regulations 1992, guidance on regulations.* Sudbury: HSE.

HSE SIM 7/2000/8. Health and Safety Executive. *Social services: social inclusion and elective risk.* Sudbury: HSE.

HSG(92)42. Department of Health. *Health services for people with learning disabilities (mental handicap).* London: DH.

HSG(93)48. Department of Health. *Home dialysis patients: costs of metered water for home dialysis.* London: DH.

HSG(95)8; LAC(95)5. Department of Health. *NHS responsibilities for meeting continuing health care needs.* London: DH.

HSG(96)34. Department of Health. *Powered indoor/outdoor wheelchairs for severely disabled people.* London: DH.

HSG(96)53. Department of Health. *Wheelchair voucher scheme.* London: DH.

HSS(OS5A)4/76. Department of Health and Social Services. *British Wireless for the Blind Fund: batteries supplied by health and social services boards.* Belfast: DHSS.

HSS(OS5A)5/78. Department of Health and Social Services. *Telephones for the handicapped and the elderly.* Belfast: DHSS.

HSS(PH)5/79. Department of Health and Social Services. *Help with television.* Belfast: DHSS.

Home Office (2002a) *Achieving best evidence in criminal proceedings: guidance for vulnerable or intimidated witnesses, including children.* London: Home Office.

Home Office (2002b) *Provision of therapy for vulnerable adults or intimidated witnesses prior to a criminal trial: practice guidance.* London: Home Office.

Home Office (2003) *Police and Criminal Evidence Act 1984: codes of practice A–E revised edition.* London: TSO.

Joint Committee (2004) *Joint Committee on the Draft Disability Discrimination Bill: volume 1, report.* London: Stationery Office.

LAC(92)13. Department of Health. *Further and Higher Education Act 1992: implications of sections 5 and 6 of the Disabled Persons (Services, Consultation and Representation) Act 1986.* London: DH.

LAC(92)15. Department of Health. *Social care for adults with learning disabilities (mental handicap).* London: DH.

LAC(92)27. Department of Health. *National Assistance Act 1948 (Choice of Accommodation) Directions 1992.* London: DH.

LAC(93)2. Department of Health. *Alcohol and drug services within community care.* London: DH.

LAC(93)7. Department of Health. *Ordinary residence.* London: DH.

LAC(93)10. Department of Health. *Approvals and directions for arrangements from 1st April 2003 made under schedule 8 to the NHS Act 1977 and sections 21 and 29 of the National Assistance Act 1948.* London: DH.

LAC(93)12. Department of Health. *Further and Higher Education Act 1992: implications for sections 5 and 6 of the Disabled Persons (Services, Consultation and Representation) Act 1986.* London: DH.

LAC(93)18. *National Assistance Act 1948 (Choice of Accommodation) (Amendment) Directions 1993.* London: DH.

LAC(98)19. Department of Health. *Community Care (Residential Accommodation) Act 1998.* London: DH.

LAC(2001)8. Department of Health. *Social care for deaf-blind children and adults.* London: DH.

LAC(2001)10. Department of Health. *Charges for residential accommodation.* London: DH.

LAC(2001)23; HSC 2001/16. Department of Health. *Valuing people: a new strategy for learning disability for the 21st century: implementation.* London: DH.

LAC(2001)25. Department of Health. *Charges for residential accommodation: CRAG amendment no. 15.* London: DH.

LAC(2001)29. Department of Health. *Charges for residential accommodation: CRAG amendment no 16: National Assistance: (residential accommodation): (additional payments and assessment of resources): (amendment): (England): regulations 2001.* London: DH.

LAC(2001)32. Department of Health. *Fairer charging policies for home and other non-residential social services: guidance for councils with social services responsibilities.* London: DH.

LAC(2002)1. Department of Health. *Guidance on the single assessment process for older people.* London: DH.

LAC(2002)2. Department of Health. *Implementing the Caldicott standard in social care: appointment of 'Caldicott guardians'.* London: DH.

LAC(2002)13. Department of Health. *Fair access to care services: guidance on eligibility criteria for adult social care.*

LAC(2003)13. Department of Health. *Guidance on accommodating children in need and their families.* London: DH.

LAC(2003)14. Department of Health. *Changes to local authorities' charging regime for community equipment and intermediate care services.* London: DH.

LAC(2004)9. Department of Health. *Charges for residential accommodation: CRAG amendment no.21.* London: DH.

LAC(2004)19. Department of Health. *Support grant for social services for people with HIV/AIDS: financial year 2004/2005.* London: DH.

LAC(2004)20. Department of Health. *Guidance on National Assistance Act 1948 (Choice of Accommodation) Directions 1992.* London: DH.

LAC(2004)24. *Community care assessment directions 2004.* London: DH.

LAC(2004)25. Department of Health. *Charges for residential accommodation: CRAG amendment no. 22.* London: DH.

LASSL(2004)3. Department of Health. *Multi-agency public protection arrangements (MAPPA) and the duty to cooperate.* London: DH.

LASSL(2004)20. Department of Health. *National protocol – inter-authority arrangements negotiating support for care leavers resident outside of their responsible authority.* London: DH.

LSC 02/14. Learning and Skills Council. *Specialist college placements.* London: DH.

NAFW (2000) National Assembly for Wales. *In safe hands: implementing adult protection procedures in Wales.* Cardiff: NAFW.

NAFW (2001) National Assembly for Wales. *Carers and Disabled Children Act 2000: guidance.* Cardiff: NAFW.

NAFWC 9/02; WHC(2002)32. National Assembly for Wales. *Health and social care for adults: creating a unified and fair system for assessing and managing care.* Cardiff: NAFW.

NAFWC 10/2004. National Assembly for Wales. *Fairer charging policies for home care and other non- residential social services: update to the guidance to local authorities for post April 2004.* Cardiff: NAFW.

NAFWC 12/2003. National Assembly for Wales. *NHS funded nursing care in care homes providing nursing: supplementary guidance, 2003–4.* Cardiff: NAFW.

NAFWC 20/02. National Assembly for Wales. *Housing renewal guidance.* Cardiff: NAFW.

NAFWC 28/02. National Assembly for Wales. *Fairer charging policies for home care and other non-residential social services: guidance for local authorities.* Cardiff: NAFW.

NAFWC 34/01. National Assembly for Wales. *Paying for NHS funded nursing care in nursing homes.* Cardiff: NAFW.

NHS MEL(1996)22. NHS Management Executive. *NHS responsibility for continuing health care.* Edinburgh: Scottish Office.

NHSE 1996. NHS Executive. *Complaints, listening, acting, improving: guidance on implementation of the NHS complaints procedure.* London: Department of Health.

NPS 54/2004/ National Probation Service. *MAPPA guidance.* London: NPS

ODPM (2002) Office of the Deputy Prime Minister. *Housing renewal guidance: consultative document.* London: ODPM. (These examples were not included in the final document issued (ODPM 5/2003), but as examples are nonetheless valid.) London: ODPM.

ODPM (2003) Office of the Deputy Prime Minister. *General power for best value authorities to charge for discretionary services: guidance on the power in the Local Government Act 2003.* London: ODPM.

ODPM (2003a) Office of the Deputy Prime Minister. *Supporting People guidance.* London: ODPM.

ODPM 5/2003. Office of the Deputy Prime Minister. *Housing renewal.* London: ODPM. London: ODPM.

ODPM (2004) Office of the Deputy Prime Minister; Department for Education and Skills; Department of Health. *Delivering housing adaptations for disabled people: a good practice guide.* London: ODPM.

Prime Minister (1991) *Citizen's Charter.* London: HMSO.

Scottish Executive (2001) *Community Care and Health (Scotland) Bill: policy memorandum.* Edinburgh: Scottish Executive.

Secretaries of State (1989) Secretaries of State for Health, Social Security, Wales and Scotland. *Caring for people: community care in the next decade and beyond.* London: HMSO.

Secretary of State (1996) *Guidance on matters to be taken into account in determining questions relating to the definition of disability.* London: HMSO.

Secretary of State for Health (1998) *Modernising social services: promoting independence, improving protection, raising standards.* London: TSO.

SSI (1991) Social Services Inspectorate. *Right to complain: practice guidance on complaints procedures in social services departments.* London: Department of Health.

SSI/SWSG 1991. Social Services Inspectorate; Social Work Services Group. *Care management and assessment: practitioners' guide.* London/Edinburgh: Department of Health, Scottish Office.

SW7/1972. Social Work Services Group. *Telephones for severely disabled persons living alone.* Edinburgh: Scottish Office.

SWSG 1/96. Social Work Services Group. *Ordinary residence.* Edinburgh: Scottish Office.

SWSG 1/97. Social Work Services Group. *Charging for adult non-residential sector care.* Edinburgh: Scottish Office.

SWSG 5/93. Social Work Services Group. *Social Work (Scotland) Act 1968 (Choice of Accommodation) Directions 1993.* Edinburgh: Scottish Office.

SWSG 5/1996. Social Work Services Group. *Local authority complaints procedures.* Edinburgh: Scottish Office.

SWSG 6/1994. Social Work Services Group. *Choice of accommodation: cross border placements.* Edinburgh: Scottish Office.

SWSG 11/1991. Social Work Services Group. *Community care in Scotland: assessment and care management.* Edinburgh: Scottish Office.

WO (1991) Welsh Office. *Managing care: guidance on assessment and the provision of social and community care.* Cardiff: WO.

WOC 12/93. Welsh Office. *National Assistance Act 1948 (Choice of Accommodation) Directions 1993.* Cardiff: WO.

WOC 35/93. Welsh Office. *Approvals and directions for arrangements from 1 April 1993 made under schedule 8 to the National Health Service Act 1977 and sections 21 and 29 of the National Assistance Act 1948.* Cardiff: WO.

WOC 41/93. Welsh Office. *Ordinary residence.* Cardiff: WO.

WOC 47/95. Welsh Office. *NHS responsibilities for meeting continuing health care needs: arrangements for reviewing decisions on eligibility for NHS continuing inpatient care.* Cardiff: WO.

## OTHER REFERENCES

ACC, AMA 1971. Association of County Councils, Association of Metropolitan Authorities. *Chronically Sick and Disabled Persons Act 1970: provision of telephones as amended by ACC/AMA letter 20/4/72.* London: ACC, AMA.

Audit Commission (2000) *Fully equipped: the provision of equipment to older or disabled people by the NHS and social services in England and Wales.* London: Audit Commission.

Audit Commission (2000a) *Charging with care: how councils charge for home care.* London: Audit Commission.

Audit Commission (2003) *Waiting list accuracy.* London: Audit Commission.

Baldwin, R. (1995) *Rules and government.* Oxford: Clarendon Press.

Bewley, C. (2002) *Pointers to control: consent and control by people with learning difficulties using direct payments.* London: Values into Action.

Bichard, M. (2004) Sir Michael Bichard. *Bichard enquiry report.* London: Stationery Office.

Bilson, A. (2004) Time to buck the system. *Community Care,* 9–15 September 2004, pp.38–39.

Black, D. (1980) *Inequalities in health: the Black Report.* London: Department of Health and Social Security.

Bradley, G. and Manthorpe, J. (1997) *Dilemmas of financial assessment: a practitioner's guide.* Birmingham: Venture Press.

Brazier, M. (1992) *Medicines, patients and the law,* 2nd edn. London: Penguin.

BRTF (2004) Better Regulation Task Force. *Bridging the gap: participation in social care regulation.* London: BRTF.

Calabresi, G. and Bobbit, P. (1978) *Tragic choices.* New York: Norton.

CHI (2000) Commission for Health Improvement. *Investigation into the North Lakeland NHS Trust: report to the Secretary of State.* London: CHI.

CIPFA (2004) Chartered Institute of Public Finance and Accountancy. *Community care direct payments: accounting and financial management guidelines,* 2nd edn. London: CIPFA.

CLAE (1992) Commission for Local Administration in England. *Devising a complaints system.* London: CLAE.

CLAE (1993) Commission for Local Administration in England. *Good administrative practice.* London: CLAE.

CLAE (1994) Commission for Local Administration in England. *The Local Government Ombudsmen 1993/1994.* London: CLAE.

CLAE (2003) Commmission for Local Administration. *Special report: advice and guidance on the funding of aftercare under section 117 of the Mental Health Act 1983.* London: CLAE.

CLAE (2004) Commission for Local Administration in England. *Local Government Ombudsman: annual report 2003/4.* London: CLAE.

Clark, H., Dyer, S. and Horwood, J. (1998) *That bit of help: the high value of low level preventative services for older people.* Bristol: Policy Press.

Clark, H., Gough, H. and Macfarlane, A. (2004) *It pays dividends: direct payments and older people.* Bristol: Policy Press.

Clements, L. (2004) *Community care law,* 3rd edn. London: Legal Action Group.

Coombs, M. (with Sedgwick, A.) (1998) *Right to challenge: the Oxfordshire Community Care Rights Project.* Bristol: Policy Press.

Couldrick, D. (2002) *Protecting the assets of older people.* London: Ark Group.

CPAG (2003) Child Poverty Action Group. *Paying for care handbook,* 4th edn. London: CPAG.

CPAG (2004) Child Poverty Action Group. *Welfare benefits and tax credits handbook 2004–2005.* London: CPAG.

Cretney, S. and Lush, D. (2001) *Cretney and Lush on enduring powers of attorney,* 5th edn. Bristol: Jordan.

CSCI (2004) Commission for Social Care Inspection. *Direct payments: what are the barriers?* London: CSCI.

CSCI (2004a) Commission for Social Care Inspection. *Leaving hospital: the price of delays.* London: CSCI.

CSP (2002) Chartered Society of Physiotherapy. *Guidance on manual handling for chartered physiotherapists.* London: CSP.

Disability Alliance. *Disability rights handbook, April 2004–April 2005,* 29th edn. London: Disability Alliance.

DH (2004o) Department of Health. *New national framework on continuing care: Ladyman.* Department of Health press release. London: DH.

Foggitt, R. (2004) Clash of wills. *Community Care,* 24–30 June.

Ford, A., McLeish, P. and Chester, M. (2002) *Tax on illness? A guide to NHS charges.* London: Association of Community Health Councils for England and Wales.

Ganz, G. (1987) *Quasi-legislation: recent developments in secondary legislation.* London: Sweet and Maxwell.

Glendinning, C., Halliwell, S., Jacobs, S., Rummery, K. and Tyrer, J. (2000) *Buying independence: using direct payments to integrate health and social services.* Bristol: Policy Press.

Gordon, R. and Mackintosh, N. (1996) *Community care assessments: a practical legal framework,* 2nd edn. London: FT Law and Tax.

Griffiths, R. (1998) *Community care: agenda for action, a report to the Secretary of State for Social Services by Sir Roy Griffiths.* London: HMSO.

Griffiths, R. and Stevens, M. (2004) Manual handling and the lawfulness of non-lift policies. *Nursing Standard,* vol 18, no.21, 4th February 2004, pp.39–43.

Grimley Evans, J. (1995) Long term care in later life. *British Medical Journal 311,* p.644.

GSCC (2002) General Social Care Council. *Code of practice for social care workers.* London: GSCC.

GSCC (2002a) General Social Care Council. *Code of practice for employers of social care workers.* London: GSCC.

Henwood, M. (2004) *Continuing health care: review, revision and restitution, summary of an independent research review.* London: Department of Health.

Heywood, F. (2001) *Money well spent: the effectiveness and value of housing adaptations.* Bristol: Policy Press.

House of Commons Health Committee (1996) *Long-term care: future provision and funding.* Volume 1. HC 59–I. London: HMSO.

ILF (2000) Independent Living Fund. *Guidance notes for the 93 Fund and Extension Fund.* Nottingham: ILF.

Information Commissioner (2004a) *Durant case and its impact on the interpretation of the Data Protection Act 1998* (Issued 4/10/04).

Information Commissioner (2004b) *Freedom of Information Act awareness guidance no.1* (see website: www.informationcommissioner.gov.uk).

Ivory, M. (1998) Thinking outside the checklist. *Community Care,* 2–8 July 1998, p.16

Jenkins, S. (2002) Leave running the NHS to the professionals. *The Times,* 19 April.

Jones, R. (2003) *Mental Health Act manual,* 8th edn. London: Sweet and Maxwell.

Jones, R. (2004) *Encyclopaedia of social services and child care law.* London: Sweet and Maxwell.

Jones, R. (2004a) *Mental Health Act manual,* 9th edn. London: Sweet and Maxwell.

Law Commission (1995) *Mental incapacity law.* Law Com no.231. London: HMSO.

Law Society (2000) *Gifts of property: implications for future liability to pay for long-term care.* London: Law Society.

Lee, S. (1988) *Judging judges.* London: Faber and Faber.

Lord Chancellor (1999) *Making decisions: the government's proposals for making decisions on behalf of incapacitated adults.* London: Stationery Office.

Lord Chancellor's Department (1997) *Who decides? Making decisions on behalf of mentally incapacitated adults.* London: Stationery Office.

McFadyean, M. and Rowland, D. (2002) *Selling off the twilight years: the transfer of Birmingham's homes for older people.* London: Menard Press.

Marriott, H. (2003) *Selfish pig's guide to caring.* Clifton-upon-Teme, Polperro: Heritage Press.

Mays, R., Smith, V. and Strachan, V. (1999) *Social work law in Scotland.* Edinburgh: W. Green.

Morris, A. (1997) All the help Parliament prescribed. *The Times,* 26th May 1997.

Morris, J. (2003) *Right support: report of the task force on supporting disabled adults in their parenting role.* York: Joseph Rowntree Foundation.

Morris, J. (2004) *One town for my body, another for my mind: services for people with physical impairments and mental health support needs.* York: York Publishing Services (for the Joseph Rowntree Foundation).

Neilson, W. (2003) *Residential care fees: defend the assets.* Edinburgh: Spinning Acorn Press.

Office of Fair Trading (1998) *Older people as consumers in care homes: a report by the Office of Fair Trading.* London: OFT.

OFT (2004) Office of Fair Trading. *Doorstep selling: a report on the market study.* London: OFT.

Parker, H. (1997) *Money to spend as they wish: the personal expenses allowance in care homes.* London: Age Concern England.

Persaud, R. (2003) *From the edge of the couch.* London: Bantam Press.

Philpot, T. (1999) *Political correctness and social work.* London: IEA Health and Welfare Unit.

Plymouth CC (2002) Plymouth City Council. *Report and findings of the extraordinary complaints panel: closure of Granby Way residential care home for older people, Plymouth.* Plymouth: Plymouth CC.

Revans, L. (2004) Alzheimer's ruling reignites debate on the provision of long-term care. *Community Care*, 12–18 February, pp.16–17.

Richmond, C. (2002) Obituary: Sir Douglas Black: physician who reported social inequalities in British Health. *Independent*, 8 October.

Robinson, J. (2004) *Care services inquiry interim report: concerns about care for older Londoners.* London: King's Fund.

Royal Commission on Long Term Care (1999) *With respect to old age.* London: Stationery Office.

Salvage, A. (1995) *Attitudes and concerns of older people about long-term care funding: evidence for the Joseph Rowntree Foundation Inquiry into meeting the cost of long-term care.* London: Age Concern England.

Sanderson, J. (1991) *An agenda for action on incontinence services.* London: Department of Health.

Secretary of State for Health (2004) Cm 6327. *Government response to House of Commons Health Committee Report on Palliative Care, Fourth Report of Session 2003–04.* London: TSO.

Simons, K. (1995) *I'm not complaining but... Complaints procedures in social services departments.* York: Joseph Rowntree Foundation.

Singh, A. (2002) Capacity for what? Problems in assessing mental capacity. *Elderly Client Adviser,* November/December, pp.14–17.

Smith, N., Middleton, S., Ashton-Brooks, K., Cos, L., Dobson, B. and Reith, L. (2004) *Disabled people's costs of living: more than you would think.* York: Joseph Rowntree Foundation.

SWSI (2004) Social Work Services Inspectorate. *Report of the inspection of Scottish Borders Council social work services for people affected by learning disabilities.* Edinburgh: Scottish Executive.

Terrell, M. (2002) *Practitioner's guide to the Court of Protection.* London: Tolley.

Thompson, P. and Mathew, D. (2004) *Fair enough? Research on the implementation of the Department of Health guidance: fairer charging policies for home care and other non-residential social services.* London: Age Concern England.

Thompson, P. and Wright, F. (2001) *All my worldly goods: a study of the operation of the 'liable relative rules' when a spouse goes into residential or nursing home care.* London: Age Concern England.

Treitel, G.H. (2003) *Law of contract,* 11th edn. London: Sweet and Maxwell.

Ward, A. (2003) *Adult Incapacity.* Edinburgh: W. Green.

# Index